KHRUSHCHEV REMEMBERS

The Last Testament

KHRUSHCHEV REMEMBERS

The Last Testament

Translated and Edited by
Strobe Talbott

With a Foreword by
Edward Crankshaw

and an Introduction by
Jerrold L. Schecter

ANDRE DEUTSCH

First published 1974 by
André Deutsch Limited
105 Great Russell Street London WC1

Printed in Great Britain by
Lowe & Brydone (Printers) Ltd
Thetford Norfolk

ISBN 0 233 96610 2

Unless otherwise indicated, all photographs
are from the *Life* Picture Collection

Foreword

by EDWARD CRANKSHAW

I N my introduction to the first volume of the Khrushchev memoirs I
described how my initial skepticism about their authenticity was
quickly overcome, even though I had nothing to go on but a Russian
typescript. It was clear enough that this typescript must have been
transcribed from a series of tape recordings made by Khrushchev in
retirement at different times and in different moods. Later this sup-
position was confirmed, and I was assured that at some future time
these tapes would be made accessible to Western scholars.

Now this time has arrived, sooner than I expected; and the original
batch of tapes has been augmented by enough new material to make
a second volume. What is more, all the tapes have been subjected to
the ingenious process known as voiceprinting, analagous to finger-
printing, and have passed the test. (Mr. Schecter describes the process in his introduction to this volume.) My own conviction of the
genuineness of these memoirs needed no support from scientific devices, though it is gratifying to have it. The manner is Khrushchev's
manner and the content is perfectly in character.

When the first volume appeared, there was a good deal of controversy but less downright rejection of it as a forgery than I had expected. I was interested and pleased to find in the ensuing weeks
and months that in spite of Khrushchev's own formal disavowal
(which, in the circumstances, was inevitable) the genuineness of the
material was immediately accepted by diplomats and politicians — not just in Western Europe and America but also in Eastern
Europe — who had had direct dealings with Khrushchev and knew

him best. There were a few serious dissenters among professional sovietologists, though some of these later changed their minds. But most of the objections came from those caught up by such strong preconceptions that they rejected the memoirs, as it were, on principle. Apart from one well-known journalist who argued passionately and at length that the whole narrative had been fabricated by a special team of fakers operating within the American CIA, the general line of the objectors was that it had been produced to confuse and mislead by the department of the Soviet KGB responsible for what is known as disinformation. As one who has spent over a quarter of a century surrounded, indeed positively bombarded, by Soviet misinformation of every conceivable kind, I am the last to underrate the talents of the KBG. The trouble is that there is nothing in these memoirs calculated to serve any purpose other than the obvious ones. They offer a reminder of Stalin's crimes (or some of them) at a time when these are being played down by the new leadership; and, above all, they form an apologia for Khrushchev himself.

They are, that is to say, the apologia of a man taken from a very high plane, deposed, placed under house arrest, cut off from the world, consigned to oblivion. For ten years this man had dominated the Soviet Union and held the attention of the world. But so strange, so alien, are the ways of Soviet Russia that from the moment of his fall from power in 1964 he was transformed by his former colleagues (some of whom owed everything to him) into an un-person. He might never have existed.

Very soon after the publication of *Khrushchev Remembers* he died. His death was unpublicized. There was no state funeral. No single member of the government followed his body to its obscure grave in Novodevichy Cemetery. He knew this was going to happen. Is it to be wondered at that he should have sought to salvage his place in history, to put on record his own version of his forgotten career, to save what he could of himself from oblivion?

Those who insisted that the memoirs were forged made much of the inaccuracies and contradictions. I should have been skeptical indeed had these not proliferated. Khrushchev was a compulsive chatterbox. In the days of his supremacy his speech was filled with evasions, distortions, deliberate omissions, contradictions, downright lies. How could he be expected to change in old age? The present volume is also full of the same, as the most casual reader will see for himself. But the serious reader will know by now that to look to Khrushchev for an objective approach to the facts is absurd. The chief value of the memoirs (and they have, it seems to me, a very great historical value) lies not in the facts they offer but in the state of mind they reveal, more often than not unconsciously, and the attitude not only of Khrushchev himself but also of the whole Soviet leadership to the world.

In this respect I found the present volume even more fascinating than the first, though in a different way. The iniquities of Stalin, for example, are taken for granted and referred to only in passing. There is nothing to match the scenes from Khrushchev's own early life. There are still important gaps where inside information is most needed — for example, the smashing of the Anti-Party Group, the fate of the promised inquiry into Kirov's murder, the events leading up to Khrushchev's own fall. Lines of thought suggested in the first volume — for one, the belated half-recognition of the calamitous nature of the collectivization — are developed no further. But with all this, new insights into Soviet life and Soviet government policy abound. Scholars will find a great deal to engage their interest and add to their understanding. They will also find a great deal to argue about. I think especially of Khrushchev's manifest distortions and evasions, such as when he offers absurdly false pictures of the sovietization of Rumania or of the Russian occupation of Poland. To what extent is he consciously concealing the truth and to what extent does he deceive himself?

For me, however, the particular interest of this volume is that it brings home more sharply even than the first (perhaps because there is less action and violence to distract the attention) the primitive nature of the government of the Soviet Union, which wields absolute power over one sixth of all the land in the world and dominates half a dozen other European countries. This seems to me of extreme importance. For one of the most serious mistakes of the West, and perhaps the hardest to overcome in anyone who has not lived in the Soviet Union for any length of time, has been to overrate, often to an absurd degree, the knowledge and understanding of the world enjoyed by the Soviet leadership, to say nothing of the level of intelligence and awareness of those Party functionaries who control every aspect of Soviet life. The mistake is serious because it has led us again and again to attribute great subtlety and exactitude of calculation to manifestations of Soviet government behavior which often arise from ignorance and muddle.

What has been forgotten, or never understood, was the completeness of the destruction, first by Lenin, then by Stalin, of the all-too-thin upper layers of Russian society. Lenin destroyed, or drove out of Russia, not only the whole governing class but also the greater part of the radical and revolutionary intelligentsia who dared to question Bolshevik policies. After Lenin's death in 1924, Stalin proceeded to eliminate the best of the Bolsheviks and those idealists who had decided to accept them. If we remember that in 1917 four-fifths of the population of Russia consisted of the most backward peasantry in Europe and that the celebrated proletariat were urbanized peasants whose fathers or grandfathers had been serfs — slaves, that is — it is no exaggeration to say that by 1928 the Soviet government was a government of peasants ruling over a peasant country brutalized by civil war and revolutionary violence. The men whom Stalin chose to replace the Old Bolshevik intelligentsia were themselves peasants or factory workers who had risen to positions of authority in the bitter school of civil strife. They had nobody to look to for guidance. They were men lacking education and despising culture. Some of them, like Khrushchev himself, were moved by a dream of the future that had its roots in ignorance of Russia's past — of the present too, outside the Soviet Union. Others were possessed simply by a love of power. Their only guide was a sort of kindergarten Marxism. And throughout the whole of Russia, except in books, in monuments, in buildings, in central and local government archives, there were no traces left of the old culture to which the new men could look in the way of learning and self-improvement. Russia had to start being Russia all over again, and its leaders, knowing nothing of the outer world, could only resurrect old institutions and old policies under new names and in the crudest form. Stalin was a special case: he had received a seminarist's education; he was a gangster genius and a great actor. After Litvinov was pushed aside, he had Molotov with a bourgeois background and Mikoyan with an Armenian trader's instincts to send out into the world. He learned how to talk to Western statesmen. But he kept the conduct of foreign affairs entirely to himself. When, after Stalin's death, Khrushchev went abroad for the first time, he was emerging into a world of which he knew nothing. He had to learn, and he learned very quickly.

In the first volume Khrushchev gave us, unconsciously more often than not, telling insight into these truths. In the present volume he gives many more. To get an idea of the backwardness and squalor of Russian peasant life, read what he has to say in Chapter 6 about the sanitary habits of peasants turned revolutionaries. This is not the kind of thing a foreigner can report with credibility or decency; but, having read Khrushchev, please believe me when I say that such conditions applied outside the great cities until very recently indeed — may, for all I know, still apply in many places. Again, when reflecting on Khrushchev's shortcomings as a patron of the arts, it is worth considering his own attitude to culture in his early days as revealed, for example, in his attitude to the ballet: "When we saw postcards of ballerinas, we thought they were simply photographs of women wearing indecent costumes."

The remarkable thing is that this man was able to break out of his past to the extent that he did. And his gradual progress, as revealed in these pages, makes a moving human story. He had everything to learn and everything to prove. What set him above all his colleagues, to say nothing of his successors, was the determination, the aspiration, indeed the vision, with which this very rough and ignorant peasant boy who came to the top as an active and brutal agent of Stalin's terror transformed himself into a world statesman. His failures, his ignorances, his blindnesses, are so abundantly manifest that there is no need to dwell on them. But his positive achievement, less obvious, needs all possible emphasis. For in educating himself he was seeking to educate peasant Russia — and at the same time he was being outstripped by the upsurge of natural talent, above all in the scientific and artistic fields, which left him floundering.

It is this process of self-education, so incomplete, so painfully revealed, which can tell us a great deal about the reality behind his policies. They were the policies of a man possessed by a dogma, who believed that the Soviet way held the key to the future of the world and must ultimately conquer, but who was increasingly conscious of its shortcomings. As he makes abundantly clear, one of the many paradoxes of his position was his feeling of supreme achievement and joy at being received as an equal by the President of the United States — by the symbolic head, that is to say, of the system which this hard-bitten Communist Party chieftain was vowed to overthrow.

Introduction

by JERROLD L. SCHECTER

AFTER his abrupt removal from power in October, 1964, Nikita Khrushchev lived out his forced retirement in a compound of state-owned dachas (country villas) in the village of Petrovo-Dalneye, twenty miles west of Moscow. Although the government kept an eye on him, both the security measures and the surveillance were minimal. His guard did not live inside the family home with Khrushchev and his wife, Nina Petrovna, but was stationed in a small house in the same fenced-in compound.

Khrushchev was free to move alone around the garden and yard of the compound. Sometimes he would slip through an opening in the slats of the fence for a stroll along the paths in the surrounding woods, or along the banks of the nearby Moscow River. On these outings he met fellow pensioners, local villagers, and vacationers staying at a workers' rest and recreation home in the area. Often he stopped to pose for pictures with them. For rare and closely supervised trips to Moscow, such as when he voted in his old neighborhood near the Kremlin, he had the use of a government limousine but was accompanied by his guards. He could also visit relatives and friends in the Moscow area on less closely monitored visits. His family and close friends could come and go freely from the dacha.

For a man who had ruled the Soviet Union for nearly ten years, the role of silent "special pensioner" was bitter. One of the few compensations left to him was the freedom to reminisce about his years in power. This he did at great length and with obvious relish when anyone asked his views on past and present events. His family and friends did more than just listen to the animated narratives that revived his spirits: they prodded him with questions and, in 1967, urged him to begin tape-recording his stories.

Over the next four years, until his death in September, 1971, Khrushchev recorded his recollections. At the outset he worked with a primitive Russian tape recorder, which he had trouble operating. Sometimes he put the microphone on top of the recorder, rendering the tape barely intelligible; often he failed to set the controls properly. Later, when he graduated to superior West German machines, the quality was excellent. When he worked inside the dacha, noise from the kitchen and other rooms was occasionally audible in the background. Often he did his dictating alone in the garden, free from interruptions. In the background dogs were barking, birds singing, children playing, or planes flying in and out of the Moscow airports. When he worked alone he sometimes launched into his reminiscences from written notes (the shuffling of papers can sometimes be heard on the tapes). At other times he simply mused about a topic and tried to remember all he could.

Almost all the tapes from Khrushchev's four years of work are transcribable. On some of the tapes the speed is unsynchronized or his voice is a loud, froggy bass. On others the sound is perfect, his voice alive with laughter and storytelling charm as he mimics the roles and accents of the characters he is describing.

He was seldom disciplined or methodical in his approach. Usually he rambled, compressing years, people, and ideas. News, like the death of Ho Chi Minh or cosmonaut Yuri Gagarin, or an anniversary, such as Red Army Day, would set him off on a series of reminiscences that covered many subjects and years. But his comments were always graphic and sharp on the details of incidents and events in which he participated. As he explains in his prologue: "My technique has been to turn my memory to a certain event, then wait until a photographic plate of the event develops in my mind. That way I can vouch for the basic authenticity of my descriptions, even though certain facts are deeper in shadow than others. If a few mistakes slip in, they won't be of major importance."

Khrushchev and his family would have liked to publish his reminiscences in the Soviet Union in a Russian-language edition. But they realized that publication there was impossible under prevailing political conditions. He and his assistants feared that if the memoirs did not reach the West and appear in print before he died, they might never appear. They would be taken from his home and impounded after his death, a standard practice in the Soviet Union. What he had dictated would molder in the Party archives and never become part of world history.

Khrushchev was too shrewd and too proud to accept this fate. He sensed that as long as he lived he still possessed a special sort of power. He remained a loyal Communist and a loyal Soviet citizen, but he also wanted to preserve his oral memoirs for history and to provide for his heirs. He understood how far the men who succeeded him in the Kremlin would stretch the letter of Soviet law in favor of a former leader. Though publicly powerless, he correctly assessed the degree of personal respect that he still commanded within the Politbureau. He believed he could complete the final work of his life without openly confronting his political successors. He savored the challenge — once again to show the nerve, vitality, and ability that had made him so formidable while in office.

The dictation of his memoirs became a reason for being, a major part of his resistance to the encroachments of old age and failing health. He was determined that future generations of fellow citizens and Party members should treat him better than his former comrades who had deposed him. But how was he to get his work published?

In 1967, shortly after he had begun his project, some of Khrushchev's tape-recorded views reached the United States along with homemade movies of his life at the dacha. These were assembled and shown as a television documentary.

In 1970, three years after the taping began, Khrushchev's associates on the memoir project decided that it was time to act. After careful and necessarily secret negotiation, Little, Brown and *Life* magazine (both of Time Incorporated) acquired the right to publish this first portion of the memoirs throughout the world. It consisted of sample tapes and 820 single-spaced pages (about 400,000 words) of typed transcripts in Russian, together with many photographs from the family albums. Because these were the unsanctioned words of a deposed leader, the transcripts were handled in much the same way as novels, poetry, and other "underground" Soviet texts that reach the West unofficially are handled. Little, Brown and *Life* undertook not to disclose any specifics of how, by whom, and when the material was transcribed or delivered. These restrictions are still in force today. Secrecy was maintained on all details of the process leading to publication.

Little, Brown and *Life* authenticated the sample tapes by voice-printing, and they translated and edited the manuscript. There was no evidence that Khrushchev had any opportunity to go over his dictated reminiscences to correct his mistakes or refine his points. There *was* evidence, from comparison of tapes and transcripts, that some controversial material had been removed before it reached the West. Khrushchev, his family and friends had taken pains not to violate Soviet state secrets or Politbureau security regulations, and not to accuse any living Soviet leaders.

But beyond that, in the opinion of Khrushchev's friends and family, some of the old man's rambling revelations went too far. He had always been earthy and irrepressibly talkative. While traveling abroad, he had sometimes made statements which his interpreters had to tone down or even censor completely. Inside the Soviet Union, his off-the-cuff speeches had had to be edited to remove vulgarities and self-contradictions before the Party press could publish them. His associates on the memoir project thought that if his reminiscences were published intact while he was alive, they might provoke official Soviet action against Khrushchev and his helpers. They reduced this risk by withholding some of the sections. For instance, the transcript contained his account of the Hungarian revolution in 1956, but did not mention the Kremlin's clash with the Polish leadership that same year. It described his official visits to Geneva and London but not his American tour, one of the high points of his career. Many other subjects were omitted. Nevertheless the manuscript was obviously of great historical importance.

Life published four articles from this manuscript in four successive weeks: in the issues of November 27, December 4, 11, and 18, 1970. In late December, Little, Brown published the book, *Khrushchev Remembers*.

Khrushchev himself was never involved directly with Little, Brown or *Life*, nor was he involved in the chain of events whereby his memoirs came out of the Soviet Union. Therefore when Little, Brown and *Life* announced publication, Khrushchev could honestly and accurately tell Arvid Pelshe, Chairman of the Communist Party Control Commission, that he had never "turned over" his memoirs to anyone. He did not, however, deny the existence of his memoirs.

Under pressure from Pelshe, he made a statement issued by TASS, the official Soviet news agency, on November 16, 1970:

"It is seen from reports of the press in the United States and some other capitalist countries that the so-called memoirs or reminiscences of N. S. Khrushchev are now being prepared for publication. This is a fabrication and I am indignant at this. I have never passed on material of a memoir nature either to *Time* or other publishing houses. I did not turn over such materials to the Soviet publishing houses either. Therefore, I declare this a fabrication. The venal bourgeois press has many times been exposed in such lies."

Ironically, that was the first time since his downfall that his name had appeared in public print in the USSR. Per Egil Hegge, a Norwegian expert on the Soviet Union who was then a correspondent in Moscow, noted at the time that Khrushchev's statement "must be one of the most confirming denials the world has ever seen, because it said between the lines that memoir material did exist. What Khrushchev denied was that he, personally, delivered such material to somebody — and nobody claimed that." Hegge reported that Khrushchev was summoned to the Kremlin by Pelshe and handed a prepared statement to sign, and that the meeting was stormy and inconclusive.

According to a private, unpublished account of that same meeting, Khrushchev denied having sent out the memoirs but insisted on his right to work on them. Banging his fist, Khrushchev warned Pelshe that any effort to curb him would put him in the position of Tsar Alexander I, who according to legend, rose from his coffin and trudged across Russia dressed as a peasant, staff in hand, to tell the people his tale.

Later that same month Khrushchev's heart condition worsened and he went to the hospital. It was almost four months before he was able to get back to work on his memoirs. Little, Brown and *Life* were told that when he was given a copy of *Khrushchev Remembers,* he was delighted with the format and had the English text translated back to him in Russian. He expressed pleasure over the way the taped materials had been edited into coherent form and organized into a narrative of his personal life and career. Despite his failing health and the trouble caused by the appearance of the book, he decided to continue to record. He was encouraged to do so not only by his family and friends but by his fellow patients in the Kremlin hospital. On the tapes he recorded after he returned home from the hospital, the sound of his voice is that of a markedly more tired man. It is evident from his comments that the dictation of his memoirs sustained his will to live during his final months. He died in September, 1971, less than a year after the appearance of *Khrushchev Remembers.*

In the months after his death more materials were delivered to Time Incorporated. There were additional tape recordings covering the original transcripts, there were more family pictures, and there was an entirely new set of recordings, in the form of five-inch and seven-inch reels of tape and cassettes. These new tapes, transcribed and translated in the United States, form the basis of this second volume.

Altogether there were 180 hours of tape. All the tapes for both *Khrushchev Remembers* and for the present book were subjected to the voiceprinting test. Every individual's voice, like the whorls on the skin of his fingers, is unique. By spectrographic analysis, the sound of an unknown person's voice is translated into a visual print-out, or spectrogram, which a trained analyst can then compare against a sample of a known voice. If the known and unknown prints of the voice "match" in at least ten different sounds, or points of identification, the known and unknown samples can be identified as spoken by one and the same person. Voiceprints have been held admissible in court as conclusive evidence of identity in twenty-three states and the District of Columbia, where the technique has been used in criminal cases, most commonly in the prosecution of defendants charged with anonymous telephone threats.

An independent firm of recognized voiceprint experts, Voice Identification Services of Somerville, New Jersey, conducted an exhaustive, spectrographic analysis of the Khrushchev tapes. A spectrogram was made every time there was any break or interruption in the tapes, as when the recordings were switched off and then on again. In all, Voice Identification Services made nearly six thousand different spectrograms. This mass of spectrograms was compared on ten points of identification for internal consistency to ascertain whether the same person was speaking throughout the 180 hours of tape. The distinctive features of the person's voice were compared against a sample of a known voice — a tape recording provided by the United Nations of Nikita Khrushchev's address to the General Assembly on September 18, 1959. Voice Identification Services found that the same voice is speaking throughout the 180 hours of tapes, and that the voice is the same as Khrushchev's recorded at the United Nations in 1959. In their final report, the experts wrote:

"The intent of our analysis was to determine how much material could be identified conclusively as the voice of Nikita S. Khrushchev. Identification must be absolute. There is no such thing as partial identification.

"We have positively identified 175.5 of the 180 hours of tape recording or 97.5 percent. We are able to state that those 175.5 hours of tape were recorded by Nikita S. Khrushchev. Further, in no instance throughout the entire 180 hours of tape was there any evidence that there was anyone other than Nikita S. Khrushchev speaking. In those portions of the recordings when we were unable to make an identification, it was not necessarily because it was a different person speaking, but rather because the frequency response of the recordings was inadequate or the recordings were too badly distorted for voice print identification."

After the final report from Voice Identification Services was received, the 4.5 hours that could not be authenticated because of the poor technical quality of the recording were reviewed. The sections in question dealt primarily with World War II, the 1956 trip to England, and agricultural policy. Though these passages were too poorly recorded to be positively identified, there was no electronically detectable evidence that any other voice had been substituted for Khrushchev's, nor was there anything so surprising or controversial in the content of these passages as to raise the suspicion that anyone other than Khrushchev was speaking.

In *Khrushchev Remembers*, the transcript on which the translation is based comes entirely from tape recordings, except for the chapter on the Twentieth Party Congress, where Khrushchev made his famous denunciation of Stalin. This chapter was transcribed from notes of a discussion with Khrushchev. In the current volume, all the material comes from the tapes, which were transcribed by Time Incorporated.

Time Incorporated has given to the Oral History Collection of Columbia University the complete set of tapes and the original Russian-language transcript of those tapes, together with the entire voice-printers' report. These materials will be available to scholars for inspection and research.

No effort was made in either book to challenge Khrushchev's version of events. He has, however, been corrected where he makes glaring mistakes of chronology or where he forgets a name (such as that of Subandrio, the Indonesian Foreign Minister) or confuses John Foster Dulles with Allen Dulles, or André Malraux with Molière. The material from the tapes has been organized by subject and put in chronological sequence, but nowhere has Khrushchev's message or emphasis been altered. Strobe Talbott and I provided the footnotes as basic factual assistance to the general reader. It is left to scholars and specialists on Soviet affairs to quarrel with Khrushchev's interpretation and to check the details of his recollections.

There are still omissions in this volume, sometimes marked by gaps in the tapes, sometimes by Khrushchev's own reluctance to discuss a subject in detail. A typical example of the latter is his account of the Politbureau meeting at which Marshal Zhukov was removed from his post of Defense Minister. "I won't narrate the details here," Khrushchev says. "The discussion can be reconstructed on the basis of the protocols and stenographic minutes of the meetings." Zhukov was still alive, and a Kremlin rule prohibits disclosure of the details of Politbureau meetings. Actual gaps in the tapes are caused by those working with Khrushchev who thought the material might be compromising to them or to Khrushchev himself. There is careful avoidance of certain matters: details about the first Soviet atomic bomb, figures on the cost of a Soviet antiballistic missile system, the names of key personnel in the Soviet defense system, Communist Party secrets, sensitive policy decisions that affect people who are still alive and in power. To have published such details would have subjected Khrushchev and his heirs to charges of disloyalty and violation of the laws governing state secrets. Those closely associated with Khrushchev were loyal to the Soviet Union, as was Khrushchev himself. Accordingly, they screened the tapes to protect both the former leader and themselves.

The most notable omission is the story of Khrushchev's own fall from power. He does not describe this at all, although he provides much internal evidence for its cause: his struggles with the military, his agricultural policy, the way he conducted foreign affairs, the U-2 affair, the Cuban missile crisis. But the fall itself is only referred to, never recounted.

Although Khrushchev tried to escape Stalin's shadow, he could not escape his own Stalinist past. As he describes them in the two books, his pattern and style, strategy and tactics, are all derived from Stalin. The pattern still prevails: his successors are paler copies of Khrushchev, but they are still in the Stalinist mold. Khrushchev's memoirs are thus an insight not only into his own time in power but into the rule of those who have succeeded him.

Yet one great change from Stalin's day has given us these memoirs: fallen leaders are no longer eliminated. Since the execution of Beria and his clique in 1953, removal from office no longer means trial or execution. Khrushchev established the new pattern in July of 1957, when he banished Malenkov and Molotov (both have since returned and live quietly in Moscow). The new pattern permitted him to survive and to record his story.

That story is a full measure of the man. Like Khrushchev in life, his memoirs are filled with contradictions, evasions, and exaggerations, but they are also filled with his passions, his last thoughts about Russian and Communist life. If his tales are often larger than life, they are a reflection of the man who told them.

Translator-Editor's Note

THIS book, like its predecessor published three and a half years ago, is based on the epic dictation of an old man who sought to relive and justify his life by a sheer act of monologue. The result in Russian is sometimes disjointed and fragmentary, but more often rambling and repetitive. It required considerable editing. Therefore the transcripts of the tape recordings have been reorganized and compressed as well as rendered into English, with the intention that Khrushchev's memoirs be both faithful to the original and readable in English.

Nikita Sergeyevich was what Russians call a *boltun* — a windbag and a gossip. While his irrepressibility tried the patience of his colleagues, subordinates, speech writers, and interpreters when he was in power, it also made him more interesting to the outside world than his close-mouthed comrades. In retirement, Khrushchev continued to be a *boltun.* When he sat down in the garden of his dacha to dictate his reminiscences of the past and his testament to posterity, the memories and preachments poured out in fascinating disarray. In the midst of a fire-and-brimstone sermon on the sinister absurdity of Mao Tse-tung's Great Leap Forward, Khrushchev might suddenly launch into a nostalgic hymn of praise to the wonders of Bulgarian agriculture. Or he might end a recording session halfway through an account of his 1960 visit to France, promising to resume the story the next day; but the next day he wants to talk about something else and does not conclude his travelogue about France until weeks later.

In order to make Khrushchev's narrative coherent, I have imposed a structure where there was none. When his effusions became too redundant, wordy, or confused, they were condensed. Of the approximately 800,000 words of Russian which comprise the original of both volumes, only two sections required extensive abridgment. The first was a 150,000-word discourse on World War II, which was reduced to eight chapters under the heading "The Great Patriotic War" in *Khrushchev Remembers*. The second was a 75,000-word dissertation on construction and agriculture in the new material, which in this volume has been shortened to two chapters, "Housing the People" and "Feeding the People." In both cases, an effort was made to draw together what would be of interest to the general reader. No doubt some of the material left out of the translation will be of use to specialists, who will be able to study the complete Russian transcript in the Khrushchev archive of the Columbia Oral History Collection.

Those who peruse the original will find that, despite momentary lapses of memory, Khrushchev's mind remained extraordinarily acute throughout the exhausting and demanding job of composing an autobiography out loud, often off the top of his head. In translating and editing his reminiscences, the guiding principle has been to let him speak for himself. An occasional passage or phrase has been emended only where Khrushchev probably would have altered it himself if he had been able to read over the transcript of his dictation and to check his recollection of the facts against the historical record (he never had an opportunity to do either). When he forgets a name or remembers it incorrectly, the name is provided, where possible, in brackets or in a note. Sometimes, if one of his errors sheds light on how his mind worked, the mistake is not only corrected in the text but also discussed in a note. In general, interpolation has been kept to a minimum. The "imprecisions" Khrushchev admits to in the Prologue — along with the digressions, the bluster, the bombast, and the self-contradictions, self-deceptions, and deliberate deceptions — are just as much a part of his memoirs as are the insights, the revelations, and the occasional but poignant expressions of contrition or compassion. Even when reworking his reminiscences so that they would be easier for the reader to follow, I have tried to preserve what Khrushchev calls "the substance of my viewpoint" — to convey not only the letter of what he said but also the spirit in which he said it.

So that the reader will be able to see what the Russian transcript looks like, thirty-six pages of it are reproduced as an appendix in this book. The appendixes in the first volume are a chronology of Khrushchev's career, an explanatory essay on the structure of the Soviet government and Communist Party, brief biographies of Khrushchev's Kremlin colleagues, and the text of his Secret Speech to the Twentieth Party Congress. The reader may wish to refer to them since many of the same terms and personalities reappear in the new material.

I am grateful to a number of friends and colleagues for their assistance and support. I would especially like to thank Murray J. Gart, chief of correspondents of the Time-Life News Service, who made it possible for me to undertake this project. His help has taken many forms and has come at many times.

— STROBE TALBOTT

Contents

Illustrations

KHRUSHCHEV REMEMBERS

The Last Testament

Prologue

I'M a free cossack. I have nothing to do. A pensioner's lot is simply to exist from one day to the next — and to wait for the end. An idle old age isn't easy for anyone. It's especially difficult for someone who's lived through as tumultuous a career as mine. Now, after a lifetime of weathering countless storms, I've run aground.

But I'm not grumbling. There comes a time when every man, no matter how important, gets old and feeble; his faculties begin to break down. I realize that I'm luckier than many people of my age, some in particular. I haven't seen them, but I hear they just sit around opening and shutting their mouths like fish out of water; their eyes have dimmed; their memories have completely deserted them; they mumble incoherently. I won't point the finger at anyone in particular, but I know who I'm talking about.

I'm grateful that my own memory is still intact. I'm thankful that I have an opportunity to look back and speak out, to express my views openly, to point out our deficiencies, and to suggest how we could organize our society in a more harmonious way. I'm glad that I have a chance to make a few observations which might make it possible for people younger than I to enjoy their lives a bit more than people of my generation have been able to enjoy theirs.

Now that I'm back to dictating my reminiscences I should explain that for a long time I was unable to continue working.[1] I fell ill with a coronary. I spent almost half a year in the hospital. During that

1. Khrushchev was stricken with a heart attack in October, 1970, and admitted to a Moscow hospital a month later; he was bedridden until early spring, 1971. In dictating his memoirs into a tape recorder, he frequently specified the date, said a word or two about the weather and how he was feeling, and introduced the subjects he wished to cover. For example, the day he resumed dictation he began: "I want to continue

time I had a chance to talk with all sorts of people. Many of them asked me if it were true that I was writing my memoirs. When I answered, "No," they would look at me with surprise and disappointment and say, "That's too bad because it would be interesting if you were to leave your memoirs to posterity. They would be of great interest." I agree.[2]

After being sick and lying in the hospital for so long, I'm tired, almost too tired to go on. But nonetheless I'm determined to leave my memoirs for future historians so that they may know my viewpoint, my judgments, and the reasons for my judgments.

One reason I'm determined to leave my own recollections is that there's a lot of trash being written these days. For example, not too long ago I went to the outpatient clinic where I usually go for my checkups, and who should I run into quite by chance but Ivan Khristoforovich Bagramyan. I was pleased to see him. It had been a long time — a number of years — since we'd had a chance to chat.[3]

Bagramyan told me that Marshal Moskalenko has written a filthy book, an utterly despicable book. I didn't even ask Ivan Khristoforovich what was so awful about Moskalenko's memoirs. I know what he's capable of, and I'd believe anything.[4]

Then there's Vasilevsky: he's been writing his memoirs, too.[5] So

---

recording my memoirs. A long time has passed since I've dictated anything. I've been sick. I spent almost half a year in the hospital. . . . Today is the fifteenth of March, 1971. At long last, I feel better; I feel up to continuing my dictation, although I don't know if I have the strength to keep it up. I'll do my best."

2. In November, 1970, the month *Life* magazine began serialization of *Khrushchev Remembers* (the first volume of Khrushchev's memoirs), TASS, the Soviet news agency, carried a statement from Khrushchev disavowing the published memoirs: "I have never passed on any material of a memoir nature either to *Time* or to other publishing houses. . . . I declare that this [the published memoirs] is a fabrication. The venal bourgeois press has many times been exposed in such lies."

In references to the first volume, the title is abbreviated to *KR*, I.

3. I. K. Bagramyan was a much-decorated army officer and a close World War II colleague of Khrushchev's (see *KR*, I, 175–180, 184–186). Marshal Bagramyan's own memoirs, *That Is How the War Began*, were published in 1971. Despite the official policy of not praising Khrushchev in print, Bagramyan saluted Khrushchev as an excellent wartime leader.

4. K. S. Moskalenko served on the Stalingrad, Voronezh, and Ukrainian fronts in World War II and was in frequent contact with Khrushchev. He was instrumental in the overthrow of Stalin's police chief, L. P. Beria, in 1953 (see *KR*, I, 336–338). Marshal Moskalenko's book on the war, *The Southwestern Advance: Memoirs of a Commander*, was published in Moscow in 1969.

5. A. M. Vasilevsky was chief of the Soviet General Staff during the disastrous Kharkov offensive, which was probably Khrushchev's most perilous moment during the war (see *KR*, I, 182–189).

has Zhukov. Comrade Bagramyan remarked on the deviations from the truth which are to be found in Zhukov's book. However, I believe Zhukov's memoirs are a special case. Even though they bear his name, I don't think they contain many of his thoughts. Who the real authors are, God only knows. But the day will come when history will tell us who really wrote Zhukov's memoirs, although I won't be around to find out because I'm too old.[6]

Frankly, I hardly ever read any of these memoirs that are now coming out about World War II. I find them too upsetting. I'm getting along in years, and my nervous system simply can't stand all the self-serving distortions and outright lies. Maybe it's just my subjective viewpoint. Of course, there's nothing unusual about subjectivism: two people are entitled to see the same set of facts somewhat differently. What I can't stand is the spectacle of all these former General Staff officers trying to rewrite and edit history so that they come out looking good. Sometimes they even try to blame innocent people — myself included — for their own mistakes.

But in general what makes me furious is that while these other people who are writing memoirs should be pinning the blame on Stalin, they're more worried about vindicating themselves. They're all too willing to be yes-men and to present events the way someone else would like to have them presented rather than the way they happened.

I firmly believe that the truth will come out in the end. Someday, we'll have another Leo Tolstoy to write a *War and Peace* for our own era. That's in the area of fiction. There will also be historians who won't be afraid to write the truth about the period during which I was active in the leadership of our country. I'm thinking now particularly about the period of the war, but the period of peace as well.

I want to do my share in providing history with information and impressions. I'm no longer in a position to affect the course of events, but I'd like to leave a record of what I saw with my own eyes, what I heard with my own ears. I was active for a long time; I came into contact with the major figures of our country's history and also with the bourgeois leaders of the capitalist world.

If anyone questions the truthfulness of my account, I'd be willing to swear on the Bible as religious people used to do.

6. G. K. Zhukov, whose rise and fall Khrushchev describes in the next chapter, is credited as the author of memoirs published both in Russia and in the West in 1969.

Of course, a certain number of inaccuracies and imprecisions are inevitable. Sometimes I might forget a name or get a name wrong. It's like a photographer working in a darkroom, trying to use all the chemicals and equipment at his disposal to make the image show up on the film. I find it gets harder as the years go by. I can feel my memory slipping away. But that, unfortunately, is all too natural. Despite my occasional slips, I think my memory is pretty good.

Those who read my memoirs should keep in mind that I'm dictating completely from memory. I didn't keep a diary during my political career because there was neither the time nor the necessity. When I made official trips abroad, I was accompanied by journalists who made a record of what happened, and my interpreters kept stenographic transcripts of my talks with other leaders.

However, in the course of dictating my memoirs, I haven't been able to refer to either diplomatic or journalistic archives. Nor have I been able to look over the material I've already dictated myself. I've had to rely exclusively on my own memory. In some cases, Andrei Andreyevich Gromyko might be a better source for reconstructing the details of when and where certain conversations with foreign leaders took place; he's a younger man, and it's his business to keep track of what people said and in what circumstances they said it.[7]

But my powers of recollection aren't too bad for someone of my age, and I've tried to give an objective account of the period when I was the head of the Party and the government. Since I'm not working with notes or written summaries, my technique has been to turn my memory to a certain event, then wait until a photographic plate of the event develops in my mind. That way I can vouch for the basic authenticity of my descriptions, even though certain facts are deeper in shadow than others. If a few mistakes slip in, they won't be of major importance.

When it comes to talking about various technical matters, particularly as regards the development of our defenses after the war, I'd like to make two things clear. First, regardless of whether our newspapers have shied away from certain subjects, I'm not giving away any military secrets by discussing those subjects in my memoirs. The discoveries weren't made yesterday — they were made years ago. I personally participated in the development of our missile system, and I fully intend to talk about it without beating around the bush.

7. A. A. Gromyko has been Foreign Minister since 1957 and a Politbureau member since 1973.

Second, it's possible that I may make a few minor mistakes when discussing highly technical problems. I don't claim to be perfect, nor do I pretend to be entirely up to date in my thinking. After all, I'm making all my observations as a man who hasn't worked for over six years. Those have been eventful years. I'm isolated from the world, and I live by some outdated ideas, especially in the realm of technology. However, since I don't think machines will ever replace man, I believe my thoughts on technological subjects have a solid and correct foundation.

As for confirming my version of events with documents, that I'll have to leave to those people who will study what I say. I'm dictating these memoirs for historians. I'm hoping that this record of mine will fall into the hands of objective scholars who will dig up raw material from other sources and sift out supporting data.

I believe that they will find my memoirs helpful because I was a contemporary and a close associate of Stalin's. I know a lot about him. I was a witness to Stalin's policies of treachery and banditry. With my own ears, I heard Beria say that Stalin had told him at the beginning of the war, "Everything is lost. I give up. Lenin left us a proletarian state, and now we've been caught with our pants down and let the whole thing go to shit."

Our democracy still supplies our people with extremely limited information about our socialist society. To make matters worse, a lot of people now are covering up the true history of our Party; they're misleading readers by whitewashing Stalin's role and playing sycophant to his memory. I know that my recollections won't be of any use to that sort of scholar. My arguments run counter to the line being pushed by our historians at the moment. I don't care. I'm dictating my memoirs for theoreticians, for experts on politics and economics, who will be able to draw the correct conclusions from what I've said. It's not hard to draw the correct conclusions, for they're right on the surface — but it takes courage.

Perhaps the people for whom I'm recording my memoirs aren't even born yet. Then again, maybe they are. Maybe they're the generation that will take over from my own — maybe they're the generation that is just coming into bloom now. I hope so. I'm convinced that if this record of my long life and considerable political experience comes into the hands of objective, courageous scholars, they will find more than a few grains of truth in what I have to say.

ONE

Citizens and Comrades

I

Marshal Zhukov and the Anti-Party Group

I WOULD like to dictate my reminiscences about the measures we undertook after the war, and particularly after Stalin's death, in military policy. Above all else, we had an obligation to ensure the impregnability of our country's defenses. This was no easy task, and Stalin made it even harder for us. Toward the end of his life, he did everything in his own name. He refused to discuss military matters with us; he gave us no training in the management of the army. Defense was his exclusive concern, and he guarded it fiercely. If someone else expressed the slightest interest or curiosity about this or that new weapon, Stalin immediately became jealous and suspicious.

Our people were exhausted by the war, starving for food and in desperate need of clothes, yet Stalin knew that we faced the possibility of still another war — one which would be fought with modern weapons, a war of intellects and of science. He knew that the outcome of the next war would depend on which side could manufacture the latest weaponry faster and better. And he also knew that in this sphere we lagged behind the West.

In a word, Stalin trembled with fear. He ordered that the whole country be put on military alert. Moscow was surrounded by 100 mm. antiaircraft guns, which we purchased from the Skoda works in Czechoslovakia but which we modified and improved in our own factories. We also bought 85 mm. guns, which our engineers converted into 100 mm. guns and mounted on our big tanks for use both as field pieces and as antiaircraft weapons. These guns were set up around Moscow, loaded with shells, and manned around the clock by artillery crews ready to open fire at a moment's notice.

We remained in a state of constant alert right up to the time Stalin died and afterwards as well. It wasn't as though we could afford to concentrate all our attention on military matters. We had a plateful of other problems. We had to increase our economic potential. Above all, we had to find some way of providing more bread, more butter, and other agricultural products for our people. On top of that, we understood that without the restoration and modernization of our industry we were doomed to remain a backward country both economically and militarily. Finally, we had to strengthen the political situation in the country, although in general the political situation wasn't bad: most of the Soviet people supported the Party and the government.

Thus, we had a great responsibility on our shoulders. The Minister of Defense at that time was Bulganin. Frankly, Bulganin didn't inspire much confidence in his ability to look after our defenses. He wasn't a military man by background, and he didn't have a particularly sharp mind in military affairs — or in other areas for that matter. I can't begin to explain Stalin's attitude toward Bulganin. Stalin just kept promoting him and promoting him all the way to the rank of marshal, regardless of Bulganin's lack of training and lack of wartime experience. He'd never commanded any troops in his life. He didn't really know anything about military policy, nor did he show any signs of being able to learn. After Stalin's death, Bulganin became Chairman of the Council of Ministers.[1]

He suggested that since I'd had considerable experience in military affairs I, as First Secretary of the Party Central Committee, take on the job of commander in chief of the armed forces as well. The other comrades in the leadership had no objection, and my appointment as commander in chief was approved. This was a strictly internal decision. We decided not to publicize the decision and made no mention of it in the press. If we had been at war, we would certainly have announced my military appointment to the Soviet people. As for the top officers of our armed forces, they certainly knew who

1. N. A. Bulganin had been a close associate of Khrushchev's since the early thirties. He was Chairman of the Moscow City Soviet, or Mayor, while Khrushchev was head of the City Party Committee (see *KR*, I, 56–70). During World War II, Bulganin was a member of Stalin's war cabinet and later Stalin's successor as Minister of the Armed Forces. He joined the Politbureau in 1948 and became Minister of Defense shortly after Stalin's death. In 1955 he was elevated to the Premiership (or chairmanship of the Council of Ministers), replacing Khrushchev's political rival G. M. Malenkov.

their commander in chief was without having to read an announcement in the newspaper.

At first the Minister of Defense under me was Zhukov. As I've already related, I had been on the best terms with Zhukov during the war. Zhukov had been commander of the Kiev Military District, where I was a member of the Military Council. I was as close to Zhukov as I had been to Timoshenko, and I respected him as much. I knew Zhukov had made a few mistakes during the war, and some of them had cost us dearly, but such mistakes are almost inevitable in a long-drawn-out fight to the death. I had always given Stalin the best reports about Zhukov's performance on the various fronts where I was a member of the Military Council.[2]

I respected Zhukov for his intellect and for his common sense. We spent a lot of time talking business and also duck hunting together. Unlike so many thick-headed types you find wearing uniforms, Zhukov understood the necessity of reducing our military expenditures. We limited the number of commanders and cut the salaries of certain categories in the officers corps. After I retired, some voices of dissatisfaction were heard blaming *me* for this policy. In fact, the cuts were made on Zhukov's initiative, though I unconditionally supported him because I knew we had many abuses and excesses in the military sphere. It was also under Zhukov that we reached an agreement in the leadership to reduce our standing army by half.

I especially liked Zhukov's suggestion that we should set an age limit for our military leaders. Old age, of course, is a fairly broad term and difficult to define. We didn't have a compulsory retirement age then, and we still don't. Zhukov, however, proposed that new commanders of our military districts be no older than fifty or fifty-five. He was thinking about the demands on a commander in wartime. Even if a man was still physically fit, his mind might be getting old, and in time of war we would need the most able cadres [personnel] capable of mental as well as physical exertion. I supported Zhukov's proposal vigorously and did all I could to see that it was implemented.

Furthermore, unlike some others, Zhukov demonstrated a realistic

2. Zhukov is generally acknowledged to have been the USSR's greatest commander in World War II. His biggest "mistake" — at least the one which later caused him the most trouble — was the accumulation of immense prestige and popularity, thus provoking a jealous and paranoid Stalin to relegate him to a series of secondary commands after the war.

approach to the questions of establishing some sort of reciprocal arms control with the United States. In short, Zhukov was exceptionally perceptive and flexible for a military man.[3]

Thanks largely to him, the military took an active stand against the Anti-Party Group of Molotov, Malenkov, Bulganin, and the others who mounted a campaign to remove me from my post as First Secretary of the Central Committee. This Anti-Party Group within the leadership had a majority in the Presidium; they thought they had already achieved their goal of removing me. But the Central Committee decided otherwise. It rectified the decision of the Presidium and removed the Anti-Party Group instead.[4]

After that, Zhukov joined the leadership as a candidate member of the Presidium and for a while played a rather active role. In time, however, he assumed so much power that it began to worry the leadership. One by one the other members of the Presidium started coming up to me and expressing their concern. They asked me whether I could see, as they could, that Zhukov was striving to seize control — that we were heading for a military coup d'etat. We received information that Zhukov was indeed voicing Bonapartist aspirations in his conversations with military commanders. We couldn't let Zhukov stage a South American–style military take-over in our country.

"Yes," I told the other comrades, "I see what Zhukov's up to. I agree with you, and I see what we have to do. His unreasonable activities leave us no choice but to relieve him of his duties." This was the only responsible thing to do, but it was a terribly painful decision for me personally. It was a struggle between my head and my heart. In my heart I was all in favor of Zhukov, but in my head I knew we had to part company with him.

We brought the matter up at a meeting of the leadership. I won't narrate the details here. The discussion can be reconstructed on the basis of the protocols and stenographic minutes of the meetings. Suffice it to say here that our decision to release Zhukov from his post as

3. Khrushchev has earlier, in the first volume, credited Zhukov with favoring such controversial military policies as reducing troop levels and officers' salaries and negotiating reciprocal arms control with the West (*KR*, I, 515).

4. The Anti-Party Group was a loose, *ad hoc* coalition of old Stalinists — principally G. M. Malenkov, V. M. Molotov, and L. M. Kaganovich — who unsuccessfully tried to oust Khrushchev from the post of Party First Secretary in 1957. The Group turned the Presidium against Khrushchev, but with the help of an airlift organized by Zhukov, Khrushchev was able to muster enough Central Committee support to override the Presidium and turn the tables on his opponents.

Minister of Defense was a rather interesting episode in the history of our Party.[5]

We promoted Rodion Yakovlevich Malinovsky to replace Zhukov.[6] I was the one who proposed his candidacy, and I was the one who supported him. This too was a painful decision. I for one believed that Malinovsky was Zhukov's equal in his ability to organize and manage the armed forces. I would even say he was superior to Zhukov in that respect. But his authority and his prestige were lower than Zhukov's, and Zhukov was more energetic, more self-assertive. On the other hand, you could look at it from the standpoint that Malinovsky was calmer and more thoughtful than Zhukov — which I considered to Malinovsky's credit.

I regretted Marshal Zhukov's role in the events which led to his dismissal, but I was downright disgusted by the behavior of Marshal Moskalenko.

I knew from experience that Moskalenko could be both the best and the worst of men. During the war, I'd given a high recommendation of him to Stalin because Moskalenko was devoted to the defense of our country, and he wasn't a bad soldier. He was persistent, energetic, and hard-driving. That was his good side.

On the bad side, he had a violent temper. He was more than just rude — he was mentally unbalanced. He was notorious for abusing his subordinates. His favorite phrases were, "You traitor, scoundrel, enemy of the people! You ought to be court-martialed! You ought to be shot!" His uncontrollable temper made him a deeply moody man who could easily be used by others. He'd do dirt to anyone as long as he felt there was something in it for him.

I was especially struck by Moskalenko's lack of principles when we were discussing in the inner circle of the leadership what to do about the putsch which Zhukov was organizing. Suddenly Moskalenko came out with an impassioned denunciation of Zhukov, spewing out all kinds of accusations against him.

5. In return for his support against the Anti-Party Group, Zhukov became a full member of the Presidium in 1957 (he had been a candidate, or nonvoting, member since the year before). Four months later he was sent to Belgrade on an official visit and returned to find himself dismissed as Defense Minister, divested of his posts in the Party leadership, and disgraced for "violating Leninist principles concerning the administration of the armed forces."

6. R. Ya. Malinovsky was one of Khrushchev's favorites among the military (see *KR*, I, 200–205). He was recalled to Moscow from the Far East to serve as First Deputy Minister of Defense in 1956. A year later he replaced as Defense Minister his old superior from the Battle of Stalingrad, Marshal Zhukov.

[Here there is an interruption in the narrative, but from what follows it appears that Zhukov, on hearing Moskalenko's accusations against him, revealed that Moskalenko himself had criticized the civilian leadership in private conversation with Zhukov — and perhaps that Moskalenko had toyed with the idea of joining the putsch.[7]]

I believe that what Zhukov told us about Moskalenko was true. Why should Zhukov lie? Besides, Zhukov had charged Moskalenko with a serious state offense, yet Moskalenko had nothing to say for himself, not a word in his own defense.

When I told Malinovsky what had happened, he urged that we relieve Moskalenko of his duties then and there.

"Rodion Yakovlevich," I said, "I think that would be a mistake."

[Another interruption occurs here. It would appear, however, that Khrushchev restrained Malinovsky and urged that Moskalenko's behavior be hushed up.[8]]

I'd known Malinovsky during the war when he'd been one of the commanding officers and later the Front commander in the area where I was a member of the Military Council. At the end of the war he'd led our troops against the Japanese in Manchuria and then stayed on as the commander in chief of our Far Eastern Military District, which was headquartered in Khabarovsk. I'd met him on my way home to Moscow from Peking when we inspected the defense installations and observed maneuvers in the Khabarovsk region. I believed then — and I still believe now — that his appointment as Zhukov's successor was in the best interests of the country. I have no regrets.

In terms of both his military and his human qualities, I preferred Malinovsky to Konev, who was Zhukov's choice as his own replacement.[9] When the question was being decided, Zhukov asked me outright — in Konev's presence — who would replace him as Defense Minister. I didn't want to offend Konev because in some respects he was as deserving as Malinovsky, nor did I want to argue the issue

7. For an explanation of the interruptions in the tape recordings on which these memoirs are based, see the Introduction.

8. Khrushchev had just deposed Zhukov, a highly popular and powerful figure; most likely, therefore, he was anxious to avoid another scandal involving the military. Moskalenko kept his post as commander of the Moscow Military District until 1960, when he was put in charge of the Moscow garrison and promoted to the post of commander in chief, USSR Missile Forces.

9. I. S. Konev was then commander in chief of the Warsaw Pact forces and First Deputy Minister of Defense.

with Zhukov. But when Zhukov asked me, "Who are you naming to replace me?" I had to tell him we'd decided on Malinovsky.

"Too bad," snapped Zhukov. "I think you should pick Konev instead." He barked the words like an order. Zhukov could be a real martinet when he wanted.

"The decision's already been made," I replied.

Frankly, Konev made us very uneasy. We were afraid his attitude toward the government and the Party leadership was similar to Zhukov's, and the conversation I've just recounted confirmed to my mind that we'd made the right decision.

Later, we had to retire Konev because he was a sick man; he'd been sick as far back as the war. For the same reason, we had to relieve Sokolovsky of his duties as chief of the General Staff. Like Zhukov, Sokolovsky was a military man of great intelligence and common sense. He was an outstanding theoretician and administrator. I valued him more than any other staff officer. He and I had found a common ground for mutual understanding on many issues, but he fell ill and had to be retired.[10]

After Sokolovsky retired as chief of staff, we had to appoint Zakharov to replace him.[11] Zakharov undoubtedly had the experience, the human qualities, and the honesty required for his new post; but from my own point of view, he belonged to that category of people Zhukov used to call "out of step with the times." Zakharov used to fall asleep during sessions of the Council of Ministers. Malinovsky and I decided we couldn't have a chief of staff who went to sleep during important meetings. We had to find someone with Zakharov's experience and qualifications, but with a fresher head. So we promoted Biryuzov to replace Zakharov. When Biryuzov was killed in an accident, we had to go back to Zakharov again.[12]

In addition to my duties as First Secretary of the Central Committee, I became Chairman of the Council of Ministers as well. I've often criticized Stalin for allowing a single person to have two posts,

10. Konev and Marshal V. D. Sokolovsky, two holdovers from the Zhukov administration, were demoted in a reshuffle of the military command in 1960, reportedly for refusing to support Khrushchev's decision to make further reductions in the armed forces. Konev was replaced as Warsaw Pack commander by A. A. Grechko, the present Defense Minister and a Politbureau member.

11. M. V. Zakharov was promoted from commander in chief of Soviet occupation troops in East Germany to chief of the General Staff, replacing Sokolovsky, in 1960.

12. S. S. Biryuzov succeeded Zakharov in 1963 but died in an airplane crash shortly after Khrushchev was ousted in 1964.

one in the government and one in the Party. Therefore my accep-
tance of [the Premiership] represented a certain weakness on my
part — a bug of some sort which was gnawing away at me and under-
mining my power of resistance. The final judgment on this question
I'll have to leave to the court of history.[13]

---

13. Bulganin was among those whose names were added later to the list of "anti-
Party conspirators." At a Central Committee plenum in 1958, he confessed his guilt
and bowed out of active life. He was given a comfortable pension and retired to his
dacha. Khrushchev then assumed the post of Prime Minister, or Chairman of the
Council of Ministers, in addition to his duties as Party First Secretary.

2

The Navy

The Fall of Admiral Kuznetsov

I'VE seen some memoirs by former military leaders who crawl on their bellies before Stalin's long underwear and vastly overestimate him as a strategist and as a theoretician. Well, I have my own opinion about Stalin's role in the buildup of our armed forces. As I see it, one of his biggest errors was his decision to concentrate our resources on the development of the navy, particularly our surface fleet, rather than on our air force.

Stalin's decision to invest in our navy was probably based on his feeling that since England and the United States — our most likely adversaries in the next war — were sea powers, we should be a sea power, too. Naturally, our top naval officers encouraged him in this direction.

England, of course, is an island and therefore couldn't exist without its navy. Nor could the United States, which relied on its navy to defeat Japan in the Pacific and to transport men and ammunition to Europe in both World Wars. The British and Americans let us have some much-needed transports as part of their Lend-Lease, but they later took them back and sank them before our eyes — before the very eyes of their allies who had suffered such terrible losses in the defeat of the Hitlerite enemy. We were bitterly offended, but what could we do? The transports were their property, to do with as they wished.[1]

1. President Truman's suspension of Lend-Lease in May, 1945, was interpreted in Moscow at the time as a pressure tactic and an act of discrimination against the USSR.

Stalin failed to realize the crucial role which aircraft carriers and submarines had played in World War II — and on top of that he refused to recognize that a surface navy wouldn't be decisive in any future war. Gone were the days when Britannia ruled the waves and therefore ruled the world. Nowadays the country that ruled the air could win the war. Granted, American naval superiority was undeniable. But if Stalin could recognize that fact, he should have seen that we must concentrate on developing our defensive weapons, our means of sinking enemy surface ships, rather than on building up an offensive surface fleet of our own.

I've never really known for sure why Stalin decided as he did. As I've already said, he was the sort of man who kept his opinions to himself. If he talked over some problem with the rest of us, it was only to fish from one of us the information he needed. After one of these fishing expeditions — or so-called "consultations" — he announced we were going to push ahead with the production of cruisers, destroyers, and other auxiliary warships which had been outmoded even in World War I, to say nothing of World War II.

Stalin ordered that the training of cadres begin right away. Students and graduates were sent off to special naval colleges, where they were given all the necessary instruction to man cruisers and destroyers.

Why did Stalin do nothing about aircraft carriers? A navy without aircraft carriers is no navy at all. I think Stalin must have figured we simply couldn't afford the huge cost of building aircraft carriers. Yet the crash program he did order for the construction of cruisers and destroyers was itself terribly expensive. It involved diverting huge sums of money from the development of other more necessary and more reliable forms of warfare, not to mention the funds it diverted from our overwhelming nonmilitary needs.

Stalin became possessed by the stupid idea that the navy was the answer to our problems. One of his favorite movies was the story of Admiral Ushakov — or maybe it was about Tsar Peter I.[2] In any case, a character in the movie says, "Land forces are a sword in one hand; sea forces are a sword in the other." That was Stalin's philosophy in an age when land forces and sea forces alike could be wiped out by nuclear weapons.

2. Admiral F. F. Ushakov was a naval hero of the late eighteenth and early nineteenth centuries. Tsar Peter I is often said to be the founder of the Russian navy.

As a man who was directly involved in the war against Hitler, I had considerable experience with land armies and their commanders, but I didn't know many naval officers. The same was true of many of my comrades in the leadership that was to take over after Stalin's death. Stalin never gave us a chance to get to know military people unless we had specific business with them. We might read about some naval personality in the newspapers, see him at a parade, or meet him at a reception — although there were practically no receptions in the last years of Stalin's life since we had very few foreign visitors.

Our lack of contact with the navy proved a disadvantage after Stalin's death for it meant we didn't know very well the men we put in charge of our fleet. One of these was Admiral Kuznetsov. Back in the thirties he'd been one of those officers promoted to fill the vacuum created by Stalin's butchery of the military command. After the war I knew him only slightly. He seemed to be a good officer and, as far as we could tell, well respected among his fellow naval commanders — although, as I say, we didn't know our navy people well. In short, Kuznetsov impressed us as a real professional. I respected him for the courage and realism he showed at military briefings with Stalin. He was obviously too outspoken and stubborn for Stalin's taste. We knew what kind of man Stalin was — how he could punish people unjustly and arbitrarily — so we weren't surprised when he demoted Kuznetsov. I later insisted we review Stalin's decision about Kuznetsov. We restored him to his rank as a full admiral, and returned him to active service either as commissar or as Bulganin's deputy in charge of the navy.[3]

Once on my way back from China, I stopped off at Khabarovsk to inspect our Far Eastern troops under Marshal Malinovsky's command. I believe this was in 1954. On that same trip Admiral Kuznetsov suggested we see some naval war games near Vladivostok, where our [Pacific] fleet was based.[4]

3. N. G. Kuznetsov had been People's Commissar (Minister) of the navy and commander in chief of the USSR naval forces, during World War II. After the war he was First Deputy Minister of Defense as well as commander in chief of the navy until Stalin demoted him to the command of the Pacific Fleet in 1947. Kuznetsov was reinstated as Minister of the Navy by Stalin in 1951, not by Khrushchev after Stalin's death.
4. Khrushchev stopped off in the Soviet Far East on his way home from his first visit to Peking in 1954.

We went into the open sea aboard a cruiser to watch a mock sea battle. We then got our first look at our coastal defenses in action. It was rather depressing. The "enemy" began its attack. PT boats started spewing smoke and noise and fumes as they launched torpedoes at their target from very close range, but not a single one hit its mark — not a single one! If it had been a real battle, the PT boats would have incurred enormous losses: the cruiser would have been part of a convoy escorted by destroyers which would have sunk every last one of them.

We moved down the coast to a spot where there was a disabled ship. Our forces opened fire and hit it many times. Kuznetsov and his commanders were ecstatic about these maneuvers, but I wasn't very impressed.

Our military wanted to show off their marksmanship, so Kuznetsov arranged for some naval artillery exercises at Port Arthur.[5] I watched through binoculars while our shore batteries fired on special dummy targets. A signal officer pointed out to me each hit and the damage inflicted on the targets. I don't doubt our navy was well qualified when it came to handling such weapons, but the whole spectacle had a rather old-fashioned flavor to it. Why? Because I'd already seen what air-to-surface missiles could do against ships. I think even before Stalin's death we saw a film that showed an airplane making a missile attack against a ship on the Black Sea. The missile was incredibly accurate: the very first one sank the ship. I believe this film can still be found in our military archives.

While I watched our shore batteries in target practice off Port Arthur, I couldn't help thinking about the disadvantages of such outmoded coastal defenses in the age of air-to-surface missiles.

We went on an inspection of the harbor facilities at Golden Horn Bay and Port Arthur. It was at Port Arthur that Japanese destroyers had caught the Russian navy napping and sank the entire fleet during the Russo-Japanese War.[6] The bay had perfect natural defenses; it provided a natural haven against storms for the ships anchored there, and its entrances were easily guarded against enemy submarines and battleships approaching from the sea. However, I called to the atten-

5. Port Arthur, a naval base on the Liotung Peninsula of China, was held by the USSR until 1955 under the terms of the Sino-Soviet Friendship Treaty signed by Stalin and Mao Tse-tung in 1950.
6. In February, 1904. Golden Horn Bay is at Vladivostok.

tion of Comrades Malinovsky, Bulganin, and Kuznetsov — *especially* Kuznetsov, since the navy was his responsibility — that while this bay might have been an ideal harbor back in the days before the airplane, it was a completely unacceptable place in which to keep our Pacific fleet nowadays, even in peacetime. Our ships were defenseless against air attack and would be trapped if war suddenly broke out. Look what happened to the American fleet at Pearl Harbor.

Therefore I ordered our ships withdrawn from the harbor and anchored in the shelter of islands off our Far Eastern coast so that they could escape quickly to open water in the event of a surprise attack.[7]

I remember going to Nikolayevsk, at the mouth of the Amur River. Despite the absence of railroads, Stalin had decided to build a shipyard there, and a lot of construction material had already been transported to the site. We had grave doubts about the wisdom of putting a shipyard in a location which was so isolated and so difficult to defend. We discussed the matter and concluded that it would cost a great deal of money and contribute nothing to our security to have a shipyard so far from the inhabited parts of the country.

From Nikolayevsk, we went to South Sakhalin Island on a destroyer. The sea tossed the ship from side to side. I was told a sailor was washed overboard. I'm not prone to seasickness myself, so the rough voyage had no effect on me. When we got to the town of Sakhalinsk, I found I liked the surrounding countryside very much; it reminded me of the Ukraine with its rich land, wild vegetation, and warm summer sun. The living conditions were no worse than in Georgia or some of our Asian republics. All that was required to make the island inhabitable was organization.

But Sakhalinsk still had a long way to go. The road to the docks was in such awful shape you could hardly drive a car over it. The local fishing industry was woefully underequipped. There were no fish-processing ships, so the catch had to be brought ashore and processed at a fairly primitive factory in the town. As a result, much of the catch was rotten by the time it got to shore and had to be either thrown back into the sea or fed to the pigs. I was told the pigs in the area ate only fish, and hence the pork there had a fishy smell and

7. The islands referred to are South Sakhalin and Kurile. Nikolayevsk is a port on the mainland opposite Sakhalin Island.

taste. In short, the town of Sakhalinsk was terribly poor and badly organized. No one was to blame for this state of affairs. The area used to belong to Japan.[8] Here we were nine years later, and it was up to us to heal the deep wounds inflicted by the war. However, at that time we still didn't have either the strength or the material means to upgrade the conditions in Sakhalinsk.

We inspected the troops on South Sakhalin and stayed for a while with the commander, General Trufanov, whom I'd known and respected since our days together at Stalingrad, where he'd commanded the Fifty-first Army during our encirclement of Paulus and spearheaded our breakthrough of the German lines.[9] I was glad to see Trufanov again on Sakhalin. If I'm not mistaken, his troops staged some maneuvers which impressed us very much.

From Sakhalinsk we traveled to a research station where our people were trying to organize farms to feed the settlers who were coming out to populate the islands. At that time even such basic food supplies as potatoes and vegetables had to be brought over to the islands from the mainland.

At his own suggestion, we left Mikoyan behind to look into the problem of improving the food supply for the islanders while we returned by plane to Vladivostok.[10] He said he'd catch up with us later.

Our tour of the area left us with the impression that the general level of our defenses in the Far East was pretty low. We were particularly unhappy about the coastal defenses around Vladivostok itself. The port was literally impossible to defend. Therefore, even though we knew how expensive it would be to move our Far Eastern base, we ordered Kuznetsov to find us a better, more secure site. Already Kuznetsov was beginning to make an unfavorable impression on us, and our confidence in him was diminishing. In the past, we'd valued and praised him; but now we felt that he, in his military capacity, didn't see the situation as clearly as we civilians did. We had quite a few critical remarks to make to him, and Malinovsky did too.

If Stalin had been alive and had gone out to inspect the naval in-

8. The islands had been annexed from Japan after the USSR's eleventh-hour entry into the Pacific theater in World War II.

9. N. I. Trufanov had been commander of the Fifty-first Army at the Battle of Stalingrad against the Germans under Friedrich von Paulus.

10. A. I. Mikoyan, Khrushchev's Kremlin colleague with the longest record of political survival, was at this time Minister of Trade as well as a Presidium member. Now retired, Mikoyan has been writing his own memoirs, parts of which have been published in the literary monthly *Novy Mir*.

stallations in the Far East at that time, he would probably have concluded that Kuznetsov was a spy or a traitor. Naturally, no such thought occurred to me, but I did begin to regard Kuznetsov as a man who lacked a sharp eye for security and the ability to assess critically the position of our navy. He seemed to be looking at the present through the eyes of the past.

A year or so later we had reason to be even more on our guard against Kuznetsov. I remember it was in the summer. He presented us with a memorandum laying out a series of recommendations for the buildup of our navy. We circulated the memorandum among the members of the Central Committee and scheduled a discussion on the matter [in the Presidium]. We invited various military leaders to attend, including Kuznetsov and Bulganin, who was still our Defense Minister.

The memorandum contained proposals primarily for building cruisers and destroyers — in other words, the surface navy. The projected costs were absolutely staggering. Kuznetsov had obviously worked terribly hard formulating the proposals.

We discussed the matter briefly. Then I moved, "Let's not try to decide this matter today. Let's postpone a decision until our next meeting." (We had meetings [of the Presidium] every week.) I suggested postponing the matter in order to give the other members of the Presidium a chance to study the proposals more carefully. My suggestion was accepted, and the session ended.

After the meeting, I left my Kremlin office in a hurry to get somewhere. There was Kuznetsov waiting for me in the corridor. He started walking along beside me. I could tell he was extremely agitated. Suddenly he turned on me very rudely and belligerently.

"How long do I have to tolerate such an attitude toward my navy?" he shouted.

"What attitude? What are you talking about? I think our attitude toward the navy is perfectly good."

"Then why didn't you make a decision today about my recommendations?" As a specialist in his field, Kuznetsov felt it was up to him to tell us what to do and up to us to approve his recommendations without any deliberation. However, that wouldn't have been a decision by the government — it would have been a dictate by the navy.

"We want some more time to examine your proposals closely," I said.

He made another harsh remark, to which I replied, "Look,

Comrade Kuznetsov, we haven't rejected your memorandum — we've simply put off the decision for a week. Why don't you just be patient? We'll discuss the problem in detail at the next meeting, then we'll make a decision."

Our conversation ended as we came out of the Kremlin. Each of us got into his own car, and we drove off on our separate ways.

I was upset by Kuznetsov's irritable, I'd even say dictatorial, mood. He had no right to expect the Party leadership just to rubberstamp his recommendations, and he certainly had no right to adopt a threatening tone of voice when talking to the head of the Party. I didn't like high-ranking representatives of the armed forces thinking they could dictate their will to the Presidium of the Central Committee.

The following week we met again. By then I'd made up my mind that Kuznetsov's proposals were unsound. I'd decided to oppose his memorandum on grounds of substance — not because he'd offended us. I addressed the following question to him at the meeting:

"Tell us, Comrade Kuznetsov, if we had all the ships you've proposed we build, how would that affect our position vis-à-vis our enemies? Would we be able to withstand the full force of a sea attack by the British and American navies?"

"No," he replied, "we'd still be far inferior to the British and Americans."

"Even if we had all the ships you're asking for?"

"Yes." he said. (At least he was being honest.)

"Then what sense does it make to invest these colossal sums of money? Even if we approved your recommendations, it would take ten years for us to build all the ships you want, and by then the United States would probably be even further ahead of us because the Americans have much greater material capabilities. I don't see how this money you're asking us to spend would contribute to the security of our country."

Everyone around the table exchanged views and came to the same conclusion. I went on to say:

"Let's put off indefinitely the question of building up our navy and concentrate instead on the development of our air force and missiles. Any future war will be won in the air, not on the sea; and our potential adversaries are equipped to attack us from the air. Therefore we should think first about improving our airborne defenses and our means of counterattack."

Defense Minister Bulganin agreed with me. There were no objections, and my proposal carried.

However, I could see Kuznetsov was boiling with hatred. From that day on, he began expressing himself openly not only against the decision we'd made but against our leadership. It was disgraceful: he started speaking out against the post-Stalin leadership and by implication whitewashing Stalin's own incorrect naval policies, which we had now repudiated. Here was Kuznetsov demonstrating with us the same obstinacy and arrogance that had gotten him into trouble with Stalin. Kuznetsov obviously felt that since Stalin was no longer alive, there was nothing to be afraid of and no one he had to respect.

We were indignant. We discussed his behavior in the leadership and decided we had no choice but to relieve him of his duties and demote him — once again — from the highest naval rank to the lower rank he'd held earlier when he'd fallen into disgrace with Stalin.[11]

Malinovsky later told me that other military men were upset about our demotion of Kuznetsov — not because we'd relieved him of his duties but because we'd stripped him of his rank, the rank to which he'd risen in the war against Germany and Japan. Depriving a soldier or naval officer of his rank is always a traumatic punishment — traumatic not only for him but for other military men, too. However, what was done was done. I say very honestly that I was not against Kuznetsov personally; on the contrary, I valued him highly. Yet as I look back on the incident, I'm sure that we were right to dismiss and demote him. We had to put an abrupt halt to any and all manifestations of Bonapartism among the military.

When I say "we," I mean myself and the other members of the Presidium — although, of course, as the Chairman I held a post that gave me a voice which was to a certain extent decisive, as long as I had the support of the others.

I'm told that Kuznetsov has written some good memoirs about the war against Germany and Japan.[12] Someone gave me a copy of his book, and I've got it lying around somewhere. However, I don't read

11. In 1956 Kuznetsov was dismissed as First Deputy Minister of Defense and commander in chief of naval forces and demoted from admiral of the fleet to the rank of vice admiral and became an associate in the central apparatus in the Defense Ministry.

12. Kuznetsov has produced two books: *Memoirs of Participation in the Spanish Civil War* (1966), in which he records his service as a Soviet naval attaché in Spain and as chief naval advisor to the Republican Fleet in the years 1936–37; and *On the Eve* (1969), which Khrushchev refers to here.

that kind of literature. More often than not I disagree sharply with the point of view taken by military men in their memoirs. But that's only natural, for I differed from many representatives of the military after Stalin's death; and now that I've been reduced to the status of a pensioner, it upsets me very much to read what they have to say.

The Rise of Admiral Gorshkov

THE question arose of whom we should appoint to replace Kuznetsov as commander in chief of the navy. We asked Malinovsky, and he recommended Gorshkov. I knew Gorshkov only slightly; I'd met him at the end of the war when he was in charge of our river defenses. Malinovsky's recommendation was good enough for me.

At the time of his appointment, Comrade Gorshkov had the rank of vice admiral; later we promoted him to admiral of the fleet.[13]

Around that time, quite a few members of the Presidium happened to be vacationing in the Crimea. We deliberately took our holidays together so that we could have a meeting to discuss what kind of ships and naval weaponry we should be building. We had become increasingly worried about our navy, which consisted mostly of surface ships armed with outmoded artillery. An incident had recently occurred which vividly illustrated how poorly organized our naval defenses were. One of our cruisers, which we'd seized from the Italians as a trophy during the war, was sitting at anchor in a harbor when suddenly it blew up and sank. At first we suspected sabotage by foreign agents. Then, after an investigation, our specialists reported that apparently the ship's anchor had touched off a stray mine left over from the war. That experience convinced us that the time had come to take serious steps to modernize our navy.

The members of the Presidium who were in the Crimea met in Sevastopol. Our military arranged for us to get acquainted with the naval cadres and to inspect the Black Sea Fleet.

13. S. G. Gorshkov had commanded torpedo boats and cruisers in the Black Sea and river flotillas during World War II. Prior to his promotion to replace Kuznetsov as Deputy Minister of Defense and Commander-in-Chief of the Soviet Navy in 1956, Gorshkov was First Deputy Commander-in-Chief. He is also the author of a series of papers on Soviet naval history and policy appearing in the official periodical *Morskoi Sbornik*. His writings are scheduled for publication in English in late 1974.

I attended some staff maneuvers on board a cruiser. One of our commanders gave a report on how "our" fleet had met and routed "the enemy" in the map exercises. He started rattling off how "our" fleet was sinking "enemy" ships right and left. "We've already approached the Dardanelles," he said. "Now we're entering the Mediterranean and preparing an assault landing on the northwest coast of Africa."

And so forth and so on. He was terribly cocky. It made me sad to listen to him. Finally, I couldn't restrain myself any longer. I interrupted him and said: "Stop! Wait! You keep talking with such certainty about how you've made short work of the enemy, and now you're telling me there's nothing left to do but polish off the enemy. Have you really assessed the situation correctly? If this were a real war and not just a map exercise, your ships would all be lying on the bottom of the sea by now."

He looked at me with complete surprise.

I went on: "You haven't taken into account the missiles which the enemy would certainly be using against you from his shore defenses and from missile-launching planes. We have such a system ourselves, so surely the other side has it, too. It's terribly dangerous to underestimate your enemy's capabilities."

The commander was obviously perplexed. "Comrade Khrushchev," he said, "I've never heard of missile-launching planes before. You're telling me something entirely new."

"Then it's our own fault," I told him. "All this information must be classified." I turned to the other members of the Presidium and suggested, "Comrades, let's interrupt our conference and take our naval officers ashore so that they can familiarize themselves with our missile system. It's important that our commanders know both what we have and what the enemy has. Otherwise, in the event of war, they'll make crude miscalculations and get into big trouble."

After a small number of top-ranking naval officers had learned something about our missile installations, we continued the conference. Either then and there, or later when we returned to Moscow, we decided to stop keeping everything secret from our military commanders.

Among the experts invited to address us during the conference was a fairly young specialist in submarine warfare. He gave an interesting and persuasive report on the advantages of submarines over surface ships. He told us that cruisers and battleships should be seen as nothing more than terribly expensive floating batteries of heavy artillery. Our best naval guns had a maximum range of 40 kilometers, while American Polaris missiles had a range of more than 2,000 kilometers, and I believe that since then the Americans have developed even longer-range missiles which can be launched from submarines. Therefore, in the age of submarine-launched nuclear missiles, a naval artillery shell had become obsolete, except for purposes of softening up shore defenses in preparation for a landing assault. Also, the thick iron plating on surface ships had been rendered helpless against armor-piercing shells, to say nothing of nuclear weapons. The thicker the armor, the heavier the ship, and the faster it will sink. On top of that, carrier-based planes can easily sight and sink surface ships, which usually have to travel in large convoys. Submarines, on the other hand, can operate alone or in small packs, and they can easily escape detection.

Gone were the days when the heavy cruiser and the battleship were the backbone of a navy. It still made a beautiful picture when the crew lined up smartly at attention on the deck of a cruiser to receive an admiral or call on a friendly foreign port. But such ceremonies were now just an elegant luxury.

This was a painful realization, especially for some of our high-ranking naval commanders who were still very much in favor of keeping a strong surface fleet. They couldn't stop thinking of submarines as auxiliary vessels rather than as the most important element in a modern navy. They refused to see that, while cruisers are cumbersome floating artillery batteries, submarines are mobile, underwater missile-launching pads, far easier to conceal from the enemy than stationary silos on land.

We made a decision to convert our navy primarily to submarines. We concentrated on the development of nuclear-powered submarines and soon began turning them out virtually on an assembly line.

Thus we fundamentally changed the strategy and composition of our navy. I take full responsibility on my own shoulders. I have no desire to conceal that I threw my weight to the side of the younger cadres in the navy and helped them overcome the resistance of the older officers who couldn't bring themselves to admit that not only was the submarine much cheaper to build and operate — it was also a much more formidable and effective weapon.

I now recall that when we were considering Gorshkov for commander in chief of the navy, we counted it very much in his favor that he was a former submarine captain. He appreciated the role which German submarines had played in World War II by sinking so much English and American shipping, and he also appreciated the role which submarines could play for us in the event that we might have to go to war against Britain and the United States.

Aircraft carriers, of course, are the second most effective weapon in a modern navy. The Americans had a mighty carrier fleet — no one could deny that. I'll admit I felt a nagging desire to have some in our own navy, but we couldn't afford to build them. They were simply beyond our means. Besides, with a strong submarine force, we felt able to sink the American carriers if it came to war. In other words, submarines represented an effective defensive capability as well as reliable means of launching a missile counterattack.

Some people might have asked, "What about personnel transport ships for landing operations and convoys?" My answer to that was: we are a socialist country; in accordance with Lenin's principle of peaceful coexistence, we are against imperialist wars, and we do not aspire to occupy other countries. Therefore we have no need for those vessels that are used by countries like the United States to pursue aggressive and imperialist goals. We were satisfied to be able to deter the hostile forces in the world by means of our ICBMs. Therefore, we decided against building troop transports. That was just as well because the transportation of soldiers long distances has since been taken over by the air force anyway.

So we relegated our surface fleet to an auxiliary function, primarily for coastal defense. We built PT boats, coast guard cutters, and subchasers armed with depth charges.

The next question was what we should do with the destroyers and cruisers we already had. Some of them had been built as long ago as World War I. They were creaky slowpokes, about as much good to us as a bunch of old shoes. With thousands of crew members, one of these ships cost an enormous amount of money to keep afloat. We used them only for ceremonial occasions in port cities like Leningrad, Sevastopol, and Vladivostok.

We also had at least two or three cruisers already in production which, if we'd outfitted them and put them in action, would have succeeded only in costing us a lot of money. What could we do with them?

We learned either from our intelligence service or from the newspapers that England and the United States, rather than scrapping their outmoded ships, laid them up [in mothballs]. But even that alternative is very expensive. You have to prepare the ships with a special treatment and then keep them in working order in case you ever need to use them again.

We conducted a long and painful deliberation in the leadership about what to do. As Chairman of the Council of Ministers, I didn't want to take the full responsibility on myself. I didn't want to use administrative means to suppress the opinions of the military experts. Marshal Sokolovsky, who was still chief of General Staff, told me that there was a consensus among his colleagues in favor of scrapping the ships, including the ones which were not even finished yet.

Oh, was that hard to swallow! Here we'd spent millions building these ships, and now we had to scrap them. I asked everyone I could think of if there wasn't some way to salvage them. I talked to Malinovsky, I talked to the Minister of the Merchant Marine and to the Minister of Fisheries — hoping to find someone who might be able to put the ships to use.[14] I suggested we convert them into passenger ships but was told that it would be too expensive. I got the same answer when I asked about converting them into fishing boats. I even proposed we turn them into floating hotels, but that too, I was told, wouldn't be economical. Finally, I gave up and accepted the fact that we had no choice but to destroy those "boxes," as we were now calling them.

The Ministry of Defense drew up a formal proposal, which was then approved by the government. We melted down the cruisers in order to extract a valuable alloy which we then used to build other kinds of boats.

There were some men in our navy who couldn't get over being completely deprived of cruisers, so we made a few concessions. A certain number of our surface ships were stripped of conventional artillery and armed with missile launchers. These vessels, however, turned out to be inefficient. Later we started selling off our destroyers, coast guard cutters, and other surface ships. One we sold to Indonesia. As an island state, Indonesia needed a good surface navy.

As another concession, I suggested that perhaps we should have a few high-class modern cruisers for purposes of calling on foreign

14. V. G. Bakayev was the Minister of the Merchant Marine; A. A. Ishkov, the director of fishing industries for the State Planning Commission and Minister of Fisheries.

ports. Comrade Malinovsky, Comrade Gorshkov, and I flew north to inspect the first of these new cruisers on its shakedown cruise in the White Sea. I remember the weather was lovely, and the mood as we stood on the deck was very good — I'd even say merry. The ship was fast, maneuverable, and armed with the very latest weapons. Our naval experts had unanimously decided that since armor impeded cruising speed and maneuverability — and since it provided no protection against modern shells — there was no need for any iron plating on our new cruisers.

I asked Comrade Gorshkov, "What do you think about this new ship our navy has acquired?"

"It's just fine," he said.

"If our enemy had a ship like this, and our navy were to encounter it — what would happen? Would you be able to deal with a cruiser like this with the weapons you already have?"

"Without any problem at all," he answered. "We could sink it to the bottom in no time, either with our air-to-surface missiles or with our submarines. And if it got past our defenses out at sea, we would sink it with our coastal installations or PT boats."

"Well," I said, "in case we ever need them, we can make as many of these cruisers as we want. But it will take time. We can't just pull them out of our pocket like buckwheat."

As I recall, we decided to build four cruisers — one for the Baltic, one for the Black Sea, one for the Far East, and the fourth I forget for where. They were good solely as showpieces, and very expensive showpieces at that. After the first one was finished — and the second one was almost finished — we had second thoughts about whether to build the other two at all. We exchanged opinions in the leadership and decided to go ahead as a concession to the military, which was in favor of these ships. Our naval commanders thought they looked beautiful and liked to show them off to foreigners. An officer likes to hear all the young sailors greet his command with a loud cheer. That always makes a big impression.

A submarine doesn't make much of an impression. There aren't many people on board, and the craft itself looks like a floating metal cigar. But a submarine is still the supreme naval weapon nowadays, and I'm proud of the role I played in reassessing the direction in which our navy was going and introducing submarines as the basis of our sea power.

Now that I'm a pensioner, I follow closely the newspaper reports of military maneuvers. It makes me glad to read about one of our nuclear submarines armed with atomic weapons making a round-the-world undersea cruise.

I know there are now quite a few loudmouths who go around throwing dust in people's eyes, clouding up the issue, trying to extort money from the government to build aircraft carriers. "Look how many carriers the US has!" they say. "Look how many England has! And France! We're a great country, aren't we? Therefore we should have aircraft carriers, too."

Well, my answer to that is: nonsense. Such competition is meaningless and wasteful. Competing with the US can cost us billions.

Once, the United States was demonstrating its aggressiveness against Egypt or Vietnam with its Sixth or Seventh Fleet. After an exchange of opinions in the leadership, I proposed to Malinovsky that we send our own fleets into those areas to counteract the imperialist threat to the underdeveloped world, so that the Americans would know that their fleet might run into resistance from the Soviet Union. The General Staff considered my suggestion, but in the end Malinovsky came out against it on the grounds that it would be ineffective and far too expensive. I now believe Malinovsky and the General Staff were absolutely right to oppose me on that score.

I believe an important part of our military doctrine should be that we *not* try to compete with our adversaries in every area where they are ahead of us; as long as we preserve our nuclear deterrent, we will be defending our country effectively and serving our people well.

3

Bombers and Missiles

Tupolev and Air Power

ONE of the most crucial problems facing us after the war was the superiority — both qualitative and quantitative — of our enemy's air power. We were surrounded by American air bases. Our country was literally a great big target range for American bombers operating from airfields in Norway, Germany, Italy, South Korea, and Japan. For many years after the war, bombers were to represent the major threat in our enemy's arsenal of weapons. It took time and a great deal of work for us to develop a bomber force of our own. We also had to strengthen our defensive air force, our antiaircraft batteries, and our interceptors. I'm proud to say I knew many of the aircraft designers who made possible our rapid technological progress.

Two of our most famous designers were Artem Ivanovich Mikoyan and Gurevich.[1] They worked together, so their planes were called MiGs. They developed the MiG-15, which in its time was acknowledged as the best jet fighter in the world — better than anything the Americans had.

However, our superiority was short-lived. During the Korean War the US started making a jet fighter that was better than the MiG-15, and soon the Americans ruled the air over Korea.[2]

Ilyushin distinguished himself with his fighter-bombers during

1. Artem I. Mikoyan, the brother of Khrushchev's longtime associate Anastas Ivanovich Mikoyan, and M. I. Gurevich began their collaboration on a series of fighter planes with the MiG-1 in 1939. Mikoyan attained the military rank of major general and a corresponding membership in the USSR Academy of Sciences.
2. The US jet fighter in question was the F-86 Sabre.

World War II.[3] These were the best in the world, certainly better than their German counterparts. Ilyushin allowed us to throttle our enemy in the air. However, his planes were weighted down with armor and were quickly outdated after the war.

Ilyushin then developed a twin-engine light jet bomber, the Il-28, which was probably the fastest of its kind — nearly 800 kilometers per hour. But it was a tactical, rather than a strategic, bomber, and therefore didn't represent a decisive means of countering the American threat.

Comrade Ilyushin went on to design a whole series of excellent passenger planes. The most recent is the jet Il-62. I was still in office when it was being tested. True, the introduction of this plane into passenger service was delayed for many years, and I wasn't destined to see it in its final version. But I know from the newspapers that Comrade Ilyushin finally achieved his goal, and now the Il-62 is one of the best passenger planes in the world in terms of range, speed, and capacity.

Another of our mightiest passenger planes was the An-22, designed by Comrade Antonov. He also built some good planes for agricultural aviation.[4]

Our best helicopter designer was the late Mil. He developed a whole family of helicopters capable of carrying large payloads. Thanks to the troop-transport helicopters built by Mil and his colleague, we were able to make our army more mobile.[5] During my discussions with Comrade Mil, I always insisted that new designs should be adequate not only for transporting military personnel but for civilian use as well. I told him to concentrate on building helicopters for peaceful purposes. A helicopter can be used in peacetime to lift pipes and lay pipelines; it can be used as a flying combine harvester or as a flying streetcar. We established helicopter routes in the Crimea and the Caucasus to carry passengers between Simferopol and Yalta and other cities.

During my visit to the United States, President Eisenhower took

3. S. V. Ilyushin started out as a worker in an aircraft hangar, then became an army mechanic. He designed a number of training gliders and long-range planes in the 1930's. His first important military craft was the Il-12 dive bomber, which he developed in 1939.

4. O. K. Antonov was best known for his An-22 turboprop transport. "Agricultural aviation" refers to crop dusting.

5. M. L. Mil and his colleague A. S. Yakovlev specialized in heavy-duty military helicopters, notably the Mi-6, which in the late 1950's was the largest and most powerful in the world.

me from Washington to Camp David aboard an American helicopter that impressed me very much. I asked the President to help me buy two such helicopters for our government. I knew that without Eisenhower's intervention, the Americans would refuse to sell them to me. With some pressure from Eisenhower and after considerable difficulty, the Americans finally agreed; and we managed to purchase two machines. I wanted our scientists and engineers to have a look and see if they could pick up any useful ideas from the American design.[6]

At that time, there was a problem with our own helicopters. They weren't too reliable, and we had quite a few accidents with them. I used to fly in Soviet-made helicopters sometimes, but it wasn't recommended for me to do so.

Now I think our helicopters have been brought up to an excellent technological level in comparison with the Americans'. When India arranged a special exhibition of helicopters from all over the world, including the US, ours must have been among the best, if not the very best, because the Indians themselves bought some.[7]

I don't want to offend others, but I honestly think our greatest aircraft designer is Andrei Nikolayevich Tupolev. I've had many contacts with him over the years. Nowadays, when I see references to him in the newspapers or see planes bearing his name pass overhead, it makes me think of the far distant past when I first knew him.

I met him in 1931, the year I was made Secretary of the Bauman District Party Committee [in Moscow]. At that time I didn't know many people connected with our aircraft industry because their work was top secret, but Tupolev's name was already well known to the Soviet public. He was the head of the design bureau at the Central Aerohydrodynamics Institute, which was the sole organization dealing with aeronautical matters.[8] Even then Tupolev had a well-established reputation as a designer of planes that did not crash — at least, not through any fault of his.

Later, when I was Secretary of the Moscow Party Committee, An-

6. During his trip to the US in September, 1959 (described in detail below), Khrushchev was fascinated by the presidential Sikorsky helicopter.

7. In circumstances Khrushchev describes below in his account of the Sino-Indian War (Chapter 12), the Indians also purchased Soviet MiG-21 jet fighters.

8. A. N. Tupolev was the first Soviet aircraft designer to develop all-metal planes. He is responsible for over one hundred different designs. After the Revolution he helped organize the Central Aerohydrodynamics Institute and for many years afterwards was the director of its design bureau.

drei Nikolayevich developed the *Maxim Gorky*, which was named after our great writer Aleksei Maksimovich Gorky. It had a passenger capacity of over fifty, which made it the largest civilian aircraft in the world. Naturally, it could readily be converted into a bomber or military transport, although at that time military transport planes were still unheard of. The *Maxim Gorky* was really the plane of the future. There was a lot of publicity about it in the press.

Then a terrible catastrophe happened — something completely unforeseen, which was in no way Comrade Tupolev's fault. The *Maxim Gorky* went up for a demonstration flight. It was escorted by a fighter painted red so that the people watching on the ground could compare the size of the two planes. The pilot of the fighter was a famous air ace. I forget his name. He started showing off his skill by executing all kinds of dives, loops, and tricks. In the midst of these daredevil aerobatics, he miscalculated and hit the *Maxim Gorky*. Both planes crashed, and everyone was killed.[9]

I still remember that day vividly. I was at my dacha when I heard the news that the *Maxim Gorky* had crashed, just as I'm at my dacha now recording my reminiscences of the incident. It was a beautiful, sunny summer day — a Sunday — just like today.

So that warm, festive Sunday many years ago ended in tragedy for the people on board the *Maxim Gorky*. If I'm not mistaken, the passengers were award-winning workers. I think so because I was a member of the committee that arranged for the funerals of famous people who perished in accidents.

Stalin was furious about the crash, and his wrath was directed at us, the Moscow city officials. He took his anger out on me, as Secretary of the Party Committee, and on Bulganin, who was then Chairman of the City Soviet. Stalin decided to punish Bulganin and me by making us carry the urns with the ashes of the crash victims from the crematorium to the Hall of Columns. I didn't mind at all. I considered it a special honor to participate in this funeral and to pay my last respects to these courageous people who had died so tragically. I remember the procession of mourners stretched all the way from the crematorium to the Hall of Columns.

9. The crash occurred in 1935, killing 49 people. The giant eight-engine *Maxim Gorky* weighed forty tons and was equipped with a radio station, printing press, photography laboratory, film projectors, loudspeakers and illuminated signs. It was intended to be a flying propaganda studio. The stunt pilot responsible for the crash was N. Blagin.

During Stalin's arbitrary rule, he ordered that Tupolev be arrested and put in jail. I don't know what the reasons were, but I do know that Stalin arranged for a special design bureau to be set up in the prison so that Tupolev could continue to work for the greater good of the Soviet Union. However, Stalin never told us anything about what Tupolev was doing, and we weren't supposed to ask.[10]

Stalin wanted a strategic bomber which could reach the United States and return to the USSR. This was one of the toughest problems facing our designers. Stalin ordered Tupolev to build a plane capable of bombing the territory of the USA. Tupolev refused, explaining that the limits of contemporary technology made such a task simply impossible to fulfill. This incident says something about Tupolev's character. He'd already done time in jail because Stalin had had him arrested, but he understood his responsibility and he understood his profession. He knew such a plane was impossible, and he told Stalin so.

After that, Stalin started to rely on Myasishchev instead of Tupolev.[11] I believe Myasishchev was one of Tupolev's pupils. He may have been a good man, but he was not another Tupolev, either in his character or in his abilities. He agreed to take on the job of building a long-range bomber. He didn't finish the project until after Stalin's death. It was called the Mya-4. This plane failed to satisfy our requirements. It could reach the United States, but it couldn't come back. Myasishchev said the Mya-4 could bomb the United States and then land in Mexico.

We replied to that idea with a joke: "What do you think Mexico is — our mother-in-law? You think we can simply go calling any time we want? The Mexicans would never let us have the plane back."

There were other problems with the Mya-4. We weren't sure it could fly through dense antiaircraft fire. Nor did it perform very well in its flight tests. A number of test pilots were killed. As a result, our fliers didn't have much confidence in it. In the end, we decided to scrap the whole project because it was costing us too much money and contributing nothing to our security.

10. In 1936 Tupolev visited Germany and the US to study the aircraft industries in those countries. In 1938 he was arrested and imprisoned on charges of "divulging aviation secrets." While in prison he designed a twin-engine dive bomber that went into production in 1939. He was released from prison in 1943.

11. V. M. Myasishchev, whose Mya-4 had the NATO code name Bison.

Eventually, Andrei Nikolayevich Tupolev got out of jail and went on with his work diligently. When I became head of the Party and the government, Tupolev came up to me after a meeting and said, "I'd like to ask you a favor, Comrade Khrushchev. I'm still known as an ex-convict. It's a black mark on my career and a stain on my children's lives as well. Don't you think you could assess my role correctly and strike my name from the records of people who have been arrested?"

"All right, Comrade Tupolev," I replied. "We'll discuss the matter. I think we can order the appropriate documents destroyed, so that you'll no longer have to write on questionnaires that you were ever arrested and served a term in prison."

He thanked me, and we parted.[12]

In the decades since the end of World War II, Andrei Nikolayevich has designed a great number of military and, later, civilian aircraft. Some have been more successful than others. One of the less successful was the Tu-4 [a piston-driven heavy bomber], which was a direct copy of the American B-29, the so-called "air fortress" and the best plane in World War II. Naturally, Andrei Nikolayevich couldn't quarrel with the designers of the latest US bomber. The Tu-4 was a perfectly good plane, but it was already outdated by the time it went into production and could hardly compete with the latest models being produced in the United States.

Later Tupolev built the Tu-95 turboprop bomber. It could fly no faster than 800 to 850 kilometers per hour nor any higher than 14,000 meters, or maybe 18,000 meters, which was unimpressive even at that time. Admittedly, the Tu-95 had a range of about 12,000 kilometers, which was excellent, but with such a poor cruising speed and altitude it would be shot down long before it got anywhere near its target. Therefore it couldn't be used as a strategic bomber.

One of the qualities I liked in Tupolev was his practical approach to technical problems. After the Tu-95 was taken out of military service, he came to me and said, "I realize the Tu-95 has failed to meet the air force's specifications, but I believe it can still serve our country. I think we should convert it into a passenger airplane."

I liked this idea and raised the matter in the leadership. After some discussion, Comrade Tupolev's proposal was accepted, and he was instructed to go ahead with his plan. The resulting modified version

12. Tupolev's "rehabilitation," as signaled by his promotion to full membership in the Academy of Sciences, came in 1953, just after Stalin's death.

of the Tu-95 was known as the Tu-114 and became the first passenger plane capable of flying nonstop between Moscow and Washington — an impressive accomplishment for the Soviet State.

I remember once I was vacationing in the Crimea and Comrade Tupolev was staying nearby in Oleandra, a little over five minutes' walk away. He often came over to see me. We'd sit near the beach and talk. More often than not he'd bring a folder and go over his latest ideas with me.

On one such occasion he said, "Comrade Khrushchev, I'd like to tell you my thoughts about the possibility of building a nuclear-powered bomber."

I got very excited and listened to him with great interest. It was one of our dreams to have a plane of unlimited range. We'd even happily settle for one that could go 20,000 kilometers without refueling.

"What about the range, altitude, and speed?" I asked him.

"The range would be virtually unlimited," he said. "The speed and altitude would be about the same as the Tu-95. It would be subsonic and would be able to climb to about 16,000 meters."

"Then how will it be able to get through enemy antiaircraft fire?"

"You have a point," he said. "It wouldn't be able to get through. I'm afraid today's science sets limits on what we can do. We have to sacrifice speed and altitude for range and payload."

"Well, if it will be shot down before it can deliver its payload, what's the point in building it?"

"That's your decision, Comrade Khrushchev. My job is to submit ideas for your consideration. All I can do is tell you that an atomic-powered bomber is within the realm of feasibility."

"You know, Andrei Nikolayevich — as your partner in this conversation, and as someone who holds a post which allows him to decide for or against such an idea — I'm bound to tell you that I don't think the nuclear-powered plane would suit our needs, at least not as a bomber. What about making one for passenger use?"

"No, no — that's out of the question. There would be too great a danger of radiation poisoning. We could insulate the cockpit from contamination, but not the passenger cabin. Besides, it would be too expensive to build special airfields for the plane."

"I'd say that if it can't be used as a passenger plane, we don't need it at all. But let's think it over and talk about it later."

Andrei Nikolayevich was not passionately committed to the project. He was just trying out the idea on me. To put it crudely, you could say he was like a businessman dealing with a good customer. "Here's my product," he was saying. "If you want it and can afford it, I can build it for you."

Comrade Tupolev never tried to force his ideas down my throat, and this particular idea obviously hadn't matured in his mind. He wasn't like most designers and specialists: if you don't accept their proposals, they get mad and stay mad for some time. Andrei Niko-layevich was a diplomat as well as a great scientist and scholar.

I later told the other members of the leadership about Comrade Tupolev's proposal for an atomic-powered bomber. They agreed with me that there was no point in spending the enormous sums which were required just to do the necessary experimental work. But we authorized Tupolev to continue basic research in this field. You never know what tomorrow's scientific breakthroughs will be.[13]

Another of Andrei Nikolayevich's ideas which we *did* accept was his design for a supersonic passenger plane. He brought the blue-prints to me where I was vacationing on the Black Sea coast, and we gave him a go-ahead. We had no doubt that Tupolev would fulfill his task and live up to his reputation as a scientist who could correctly assess the possibilities for the future.

The result of his work is the Tu-144. I see from the newspapers that it's undergoing its final tests.[14] I assume the Franco-British Concorde isn't too bad, either, but I notice the Americans don't have a supersonic transport. Soon ours will be introduced into service. The Tu-144 represents a major contribution to the prestige of our country in the field of aviation, and I don't think that anyone will argue with me when I say that the leader in that field is Comrade Andrei Niko-layevich Tupolev. If not the father of Soviet aviation (that title is sup-posed to belong to Zhukovsky),[15] then he's surely one of a handful of men responsible for the birth and development of our civil and mili-tary aviation. Even though there were other talented designers, An-drei Nikolayevich was head and shoulders above most others.

13. The Soviets publicly predicted in early 1959 that they would begin testing nuclear-powered aircraft engines later that year, but the program apparently petered out in the early 1960's.

14. A Tu-144 supersonic transport crashed at the 1973 Paris Air Show.

15. N. Ye. Zhukovsky, a Russian scientist of the late nineteenth and early twentieth centuries, who was a founder of modern aerodynamics and hydrodynamics.

Korolyov and Rocketry

HAVING nuclear bombs wasn't enough to ensure our security. We needed an effective delivery system as well.

For years we relied on bombers developed by such brilliant designers as Comrade Andrei Nikolayevich Tupolev; but, for both technological and military reasons, the life-span of even the best plane is necessarily short. No matter how good a bomber is, soon another one comes along that is superior. The cost of constantly updating our bomber force was immense.

Furthermore, manned aircraft is limited in speed and therefore vulnerable to antiaircraft fire. On top of that, the range requirements set by our military planners for a strategic bomber were beyond the reach of our technological capability. Whereas the US could easily bomb us from its bases in Europe, we had no way of stationing our planes on the edge of the American border.

I've already related how Comrade Myasishchev, whom I respected very much, failed to come up with a bomber that could reach the United States. We had to abandon his project when the problem of range appeared to be insoluble.

We realized that if we were to deter our adversaries from unleashing war against us, we needed to have some means more reliable than bombers of delivering our bombs to their targets. In short, we needed to develop guided missiles.

Research in this field began while Stalin was still alive. I've already described how Stalin once showed us a movie of planes sinking a ship in the Black Sea with air-to-surface rockets.

The first land-to-sea missile for our coastal defense was developed by Artem Ivanovich Mikoyan. Actually, it wasn't a real missile: it was a modified [remote-control] MiG-15 jet fighter, and it was rather primitive and imperfect. Later we approved a plan presented by Chelomei for a shore-defense missile system and a missile-launching airplane.[16]

It was under Stalin that the decision was made to develop surface-

16. V. N. Chelomei was a full member of the USSR Academy of Sciences and a specialist in aviation propulsion.

to-air missiles. I don't remember the name of the designer who was put in charge of the project, but he was a very talented man. Beria sent his own son Sergei to work on the project.[17] We spent a lot of money to surround Moscow and later Leningrad with missiles. We mistakenly believed they made it impossible for the enemy to slip past our antiaircraft defenses.

Later we realized there were two big drawbacks to stationary surface-to-air missile sites. First, they took a long time to prepare for firing. Second, they were easily spotted by enemy intelligence services. Even though we camouflaged them, you could still pick them out on the ground from a passenger plane as you came in to land at Moscow airport. I myself used to notice them. After Stalin's death we replaced these stationary installations with mobile antiaircraft missile launchers.

One day a designer whose name I forget asked me for an appointment to show me a model of a new missile he'd developed. He explained that it was a tactical missile like the German V-1 flying bomb, but it had some special features: the wings could be folded up, and it could fit into a long barrel. When it was fired, the wings spread so that it looked like an airplane. I thought this comrade had come up with an original and useful idea — a rocket that could be fired from a cannon and used either for surface-to-air or land-to-sea defenses.

At this point, I can easily imagine some know-it-all complaining, "There goes Khrushchev, revealing military secrets." Even a fool can see that what I'm saying about this designer's invention is no longer a secret. His was a first-generation missile, and nowadays we already have the third or fourth generation.

I was impressed by this designer. I told him that what he'd shown me deserved attention and that we'd discuss the matter in the leadership. I asked him if he knew any of the other leaders. He said, yes, he'd met Bulganin, who was then Minister of Defense.

I later told Bulganin about my conversation and asked him what he knew about this designer. "I know him," said Bulganin in a scathing way. Then he made an offensive remark. "Chase him away" — that's what Bulganin always said about people he didn't like. "He showed his project to Stalin once, and Stalin had him fired from the institute where he worked."

17. S. L. Beria, son of Stalin's last police chief, L. P. Beria, was director of a secret scientific institute and stayed on in that job for some time after his father's ouster and execution.

"Listen here, Nikolai Aleksandrovich, the fact that Stalin chased him away proves nothing. Stalin didn't always understand technological problems. Why don't we give the comrade a chance? I suggest we raise the matter at the next session of the Presidium. We'll call him in and have him give us a report. While your attitude toward him may be determined by what Stalin thought, I'm going to suspend judgment until we hear what he has to say."

Bulganin dropped his objection. The rest of the leadership acknowledged my authority where armaments were concerned. In the end we approved the proposal.

"You know," said the designer, "when Stalin fired me from the design bureau where I used to work, he took my research library away from me and gave it to Artem Ivanovich Mikoyan."

I instructed that the library be returned to him. We also set him up with the laboratories, the production facilities, the technicians, the engineers, and everything else he needed to develop his missile. We were not disappointed. His calculations turned out to be correct, and his theory was borne out in practice. His missiles represented a substantial contribution to our coastal and antiaircraft defenses and even to our surface-to-surface capability.

Much as I liked and respected this man, he couldn't hold a candle to Sergei Pavlovich Korolyov, who was probably our most prominent and brilliant missile designer.[18] I got to know him well, though I hadn't known him before Stalin's death, when he'd collaborated with Comrade Lavochkin on the so-called Tempest missile.[19] Lavochkin was one of our most talented aircraft designers; he'd distinguished himself during World War II, and all our military fliers knew and swore by his fighters. The Tempest worked on a rather complicated principle: it had to be carried by an airplane to a certain altitude before it could be fired and fly on its own. But at the time it was all we had. It represented our only hope of reaching the United States.

After Stalin's death, Korolyov began work on a much more sophisticated and promising type of rocket. I keep using Stalin's death as a reference point in time because while Stalin was alive he completely monopolized all decisions about our defenses, including — I'd even

18. S. P. Korolyov, since the early 1930's the head of various rocket propulsion projects. He oversaw the development of ballistic missiles (including the *Semyorka* or T-7), geophysical rockets, and manned spaceships of the Vostok and Voskhod series.

19. S. A. Lavochkin, a major general in the air force as well as a designer, built a series of high-speed fighters with air-cooled engines which proved highly effective against the Luftwaffe.

say *especially* — those involving nuclear weapons and delivery systems. We were sometimes present when such matters were discussed, but we weren't allowed to ask questions. Therefore, when Stalin died, we weren't really prepared to carry the burden which fell on our shoulders. Our experience with Korolyov is a case in point.

Not too long after Stalin's death, Korolyov came to a Politbureau meeting to report on his work. I don't want to exaggerate, but I'd say we gawked at what he showed us as if we were a bunch of sheep seeing a new gate for the first time. When he showed us one of his rockets, we thought it looked like nothing but a huge cigar-shaped tube, and we didn't believe it could fly. Korolyov took us on a tour of a launching pad and tried to explain to us how the rocket worked. We were like peasants in a marketplace. We walked around and around the rocket, touching it, tapping it to see if it was sturdy enough — we did everything but lick it to see how it tasted.

Some people might say we were technological ignoramuses. Well, yes, we were that, but we weren't the only ones. There were some other people who didn't know the first thing about missile technology either.

We had absolute confidence in Comrade Korolyov. We believed him when he told us that his rocket would not only fly, but that it would travel 7,000 kilometers. When he expounded or defended his ideas, you could see passion burning in his eyes, and his reports were always models of clarity. He had unlimited energy and determination, and he was a brilliant organizer.

Finally Korolyov's rocket — which was called a *Semyorka* ["Number 7"] — was ready for testing. The first one exploded, as I recall. In fact, I think we had several unpleasant incidents. They either blew up on the pad or during the liftoff. Fortunately, there were no human victims, but these accidents wasted a lot of money. However, such mistakes and sacrifices are inevitable when technological progress is at issue.

After a while the *Semyorka* was successfully launched. In addition to Comrade Korolyov, much of the credit goes to the engineers who designed the booster for the rocket. I remember once meeting a pilot who told me he would fly in a coffin if it had a good engine. There's something in that. The *Semyorka* certainly had a good engine. The principal designer of the booster was Korolyov's friend and collaborator, whose name I forget. The best booster rocket in the world won't make a broomstick fly. So while Korolyov designed the rocket, his colleague designed the engine. They made an excellent team. Unfortunately, they split up later. I was very upset and did everything I could to patch up their friendship, but all my efforts were in vain.

Thanks to Comrade Korolyov and his associates, we now had a rocket that could carry a nuclear warhead. His invention also had many peacetime uses. With his *Semyorka*, he paved the road into outer space. Eventually, we began to launch our Sputniks, which made our potential enemies cringe in fright but made many other people glow with joy.[20]

I'm only sorry that we didn't manage to send a man to the moon during Comrade Korolyov's iifetime. An untimely death snatched him from our ranks. I heard that he'd gone into the hospital for an operation. The doctors expected the operation to be perfectly routine. Later I was told that the surgeons were finished and washing their hands, thinking the operation had gone well, when suddenly Korolyov went into shock and died.[21]

This tragedy occurred while his creativity was still in full bloom. It was a great loss for our country and for mankind as a whole. However, he left us a legacy, for his superb designs are still used as the basis for even the latest missiles and rockets.

Building a Missile Army

THE late Comrade Korolyov's *Semyorka* rocket represented a major scientific and military breakthrough for our country, although Korolyov himself was aware of its limitations. Launching Sputniks into space didn't solve the problem of how to defend our country. First and foremost we had to develop an electronic guidance system. It always sounded good to say in public speeches that we could hit a fly at any distance with our missiles. Despite the wide radius of destruction caused by our nuclear warheads, pinpoint accuracy was still necessary — and it was difficult to achieve.

20. The first Sputnik was put into orbit in October, 1957.
21. Korolyov died in 1966, at the age of sixty.

I remember that in the first days of our *Semyorka* program, while the missile itself had a range of 7,000 kilometers, we could direct it to a target only by placing guidance systems every 500 kilometers along the way. Therefore the *Semyorka* was reliable neither as a defensive nor as an offensive weapon. Regardless of its range, it represented only a symbolic counterthreat to the United States. That left us only with France, West Germany, and other European countries in striking distance of our medium-range missiles.

My conversations with Comrade Korolyov also made me worry that the enemy might be able to destroy our *Semyorka* before we could get it into the air. The rocket was fired from a launching pad which looked like a huge tabletop and could easily be detected by reconnaissance planes or satellites in orbit around the earth. I've seen high-altitude photographs so accurate that you can actually make out the type of planes sitting at the end of a runway. I've also seen American photographs of our territory, and they were of better quality than our own.

So what could we do to avoid detection? How could we make sure that part of our missile arsenal would survive an enemy attack and enable us to strike a counterblow?

My experience early in life as a coal miner in the Donbass and later as a supervisor during the building of the Moscow Metro came in handy when I began trying to think of ways we could hide our missile sites from enemy reconnaissance. It occurred to me that since missiles are cylindrical, we could put them into sunken, covered shafts. I could see numerous advantages to this idea. To name just two: storing the rocket in a well would allow us to protect it against weather; and second, in order to knock out a site, the enemy would not only have to find it — he'd have to score a direct hit.

I told some engineers about my idea and asked them their views on the feasibility, since they knew better than I the operational characteristics of rockets. One of the specialists assigned to the task of providing launch sites for our rockets and missiles was Engineer Bardin. He's now a member of the USSR Academy of Sciences.[22]

The experts hemmed and hawed and finally told me they thought the idea wouldn't work. Even Bardin, who'd spent many years engaged in useful defense work, refused to go along with my sugges-

22. Academician I. P. Bardin, a metallurgist who presided over the Soviet International Geophysical Year Committee in 1957–58.

tion. I was flabbergasted. I forget what their misgivings were, but —
always mindful of my political status — I realized I had no right to
force the idea down their throats. I assumed these people knew their
own professions, so I let the matter drop.

A year or more passed. My son, who's an engineer himself,[23] had
something to do with missiles and kept me informed on how the testing program was going. He also followed American publications
closely. One day, to my surprise and delight, he told me that he'd
read in some American journal that the US had begun to replace
launching pads with silos.

"Look at this, Father," he said. "The Americans have introduced
the plan which you thought up a year or so ago but which our people
turned down."

This coincidence between my thinking and the Americans' made
me very glad, but it also made me upset and disappointed with our
own engineers. If they'd only picked up my idea when I first suggested it to them, we wouldn't have lost all this time. I'd been careful not to push them around; I'd simply proposed the plan as part of a
free exchange of opinions. But now I felt justified in giving some orders.

I summoned the people responsible and said, "Now look what's
happened! The Americans have begun to dig the ballistic missile
shafts which I proposed a long time ago. Let's get started on this program right away."

I asked our mining engineers to devise a special drill for digging
missile wells. All we had to do was modify the equipment we were
already using to dig shafts for coal elevators. A mine shaft differs
only in diameter and depth from a missile silo. I received regular
reports from Engineer Zasyadko on the work under way in the
region of Mushketov. He was a talented man. Unfortunately, he had
one weakness: he was an alcoholic. Toward the end of his life he lost
all will power and finally drank himself to death.[24]

I don't think it was until after my retirement that we completely
converted our missile system from launching pads to sunken silos,
but I was proud of my role in originating the idea and later seeing
that the conversion was begun.

23. S. N. Khrushchev, an electronics specialist.
24. A. F. Zasyadko, a Donbass miner who rose to become Minister of the Coal Industry and an official of the State Planning Commission. He died in Moscow in 1963.
The Mushketov region is in the Kirghiz Republic in Soviet Central Asia.

However, avoiding detection by enemy reconnaissance wasn't the only problem facing our missile program. There was also the length of time required to prepare a rocket for launching. I remember once asking Comrade Korolyov about this: "Tell me, Sergei Pavlovich, isn't there some way we can put your rocket at constant readiness, so that it can be fired on a moment's notice in the event of a crisis?"

"No," he said.

At that time Korolyov's design bureau was concerned mostly with developing rocketry for the exploration of space. We had another design bureau headed by Comrade Yangel. The burden of developing military missiles fell on his shoulders. His health was poor, but he is still one of our most brilliant designers.[25]

Yangel tackled the problem of perfecting a rocket that could be launched on short notice, and to our great joy he came up with an engine which solved our problem.

I remember that during one of my holidays Comrade Yangel and I met on the Black Sea coast to discuss the implications of his discovery. We agreed that it put us on an equal footing with the United States. I told him about my own idea of launching missiles from metal cylinders sunk in the ground. I'd studied physics in my youth and knew about the ideas of Tsiolkovsky.[26]

I realized we would have to leave some extra space between the outside wall of the rocket and the inside wall of the silo so that the exhaust gases could escape during the launch. I suggested to Comrade Yangel that the buildup of pressure inside the silo might even increase the thrust of the rocket as it was shot into the air. We were sitting at a table drinking coffee, and I demonstrated to him what I was talking about.

"Take two glasses of different diameter and put one inside the other. You see? This space around the edge of the inner glass will prevent the exhaust from crushing the rocket before it can get out of the silo."

He listened to me attentively. He was a good designer and understood my idea. He promised to think it over.

25. Academician M. K. Yangel succeeded Korolyov as head of the Soviet rocketry program and died in October, 1971, shortly after Khrushchev's death.

26. K. E. Tsiolkovsky was a visionary scientist and one of the pioneers of Russian rocketry. In 1929 he proposed a multistage space vehicle, which he called a rocket-train, and he is also credited with first suggesting that the control surface of a rocket should act against the exhaust stream rather than the air stream.

In addition to his work on a quick-firing rocket engine, Yangel also worked on medium-range ballistic missiles that could travel 2,000 to 4,000 kilometers, as well as on ICBMs that could deliver nuclear warheads anywhere on the face of the globe.

Chief Designer Yangel just barely escaped death in a catastrophic accident which occurred during the test of one of our rockets. As the incident was later reported to me, the fuel somehow ignited, and the engine prematurely fired. The rocket reared up and fell, throwing acid and flames all over the place. Just before the accident happened, Yangel happened to step into a specially insulated smoking room to have a cigarette, and thus he miraculously survived.

Dozens of soldiers, specialists, and technical personnel were less lucky. Marshal Nedelin, the commander in chief of our missile forces, was sitting nearby watching the test when the missile malfunctioned, and he was killed. Krylov succeeded him.[27]

Nedelin and later Krylov were instrumental in converting our army into a modern defense structure in which the guided missile played the primary role. We organized the production of rockets on a fully automated assembly line. We started turning them out like sausages at our aircraft plants. After a while, the manufacture of missiles took priority over that of jet bombers and interceptors. Subsequent evidence in Vietnam and the Middle East has shown us that perhaps we overestimated the effectiveness of surface-to-air missiles and underestimated the effectiveness of low-altitude fighter bombers. However, I'm convinced that in the future SAMs will be developed capable of destroying even those planes which can now duck below radar level. In general, I think we made the right decision to convert our military production from aircraft to missiles.

Our industry turned to the task of creating a means of transporting rockets so that our tactical missile forces would have the necessary mobility. Our designers studied the problem of whether these vehicles should have caterpillar treads or wheels. In the end, they decided on a combination of the two.[28]

Once we had devised the means to introduce tactical rocketry to

27. M. I. Nedelin was an artillery commander who was Deputy Defense Minister and commander of Soviet rocket forces until his death in October, 1960. According to the official version, he died in a "plane crash." He was succeeded by Moskalenko, Biryuzov, then N. I. Krylov.
28. That is, a half-track.

our army, we had to overcome the resistance which we encountered among some of our older gunnery officers. I'm thinking particularly of Marshal Varentsov, whom I'd known at the Voronezh and First Ukrainian fronts during World War II.[29] It was Marshal Varentsov who coined the phrase "An artillery barrage is a symphony; a rocket launching is a cacophony." We had to do away with this sort of old-fashioned thinking.

Marshal Varentsov and some of his colleagues argued that a conventional fieldpiece could be camouflaged so that the enemy couldn't locate it, while a missile kicks up a lot of dust when it's fired. This was a ridiculous argument. For one thing, the enemy can locate a fieldpiece by the noise it makes. Besides, who cares how much dust a missile kicks up if it's aimed at a target hundreds or even thousands of kilometers away?

The new cannot live side by side with the old in military policy. We had to hasten the process of replacing the old with the new.

Among our artillery commanders, Marshal Igulin best understood the need for introducing missiles into our armed forces. You wouldn't find *him* making a sour face when he watched a rocket test.

There were incidents when Marshal Grechko insisted that we develop a tactical missile with a small nuclear warhead that could be used by our infantry against an advancing army.[30] I agreed with Grechko that it would be good to arm our troops with tactical nuclear weapons at the platoon and regiment level or even at the division level, but I had to explain to him that the smaller the explosive charge of a warhead, the more raw [fissionable] material you need — and we simply didn't have enough raw material to go around. Therefore we had to concentrate first and foremost on intercontinental — that is, strategic rather than tactical — missiles.

I've noticed over the years that military men have a passion for imitation. For example, I think even before Stalin's death, our artillery experts learned that the United States had come up with a gun which

<hr />

29. S. S. Varentsov was chief marshal of artillery and commander of rocket units from 1961 until 1963, when he was demoted in rank and expelled from the Central Committee in connection with the Oleg Penkovsky spy case, which involved a high-ranking military intelligence officer who was passing information to the West.

30. A. A. Grechko, current Defense Minister and Politbureau member, was commander in chief of Soviet land forces, 1957–60. He was then put in charge of the Warsaw Pact and made Deputy Defense Minister. In that capacity, he planned and executed the 1968 invasion of Czechoslovakia. Khrushchev knew him during the war (see *KR*, I, 215).

fired a shell with an atomic charge. This information wasn't difficult to come by since the Americans announced what they were doing in their newspapers. Our military people were able to get the government to give them the funds to develop a nuclear cannon of our own. We used to haul it out for military parades on Red Square. It had an enormous barrel and always made a powerful impression, but we weren't very enthusiastic about it. The thing was terribly heavy and difficult to transport; it was hard to camouflage; its range was very short; it performed badly on the testing range and required a great expense and huge quantities of raw material to make one small warhead. In short, it was good for nothing.

Finally, our artillery men themselves had to sigh and admit that there was no point in continuing to produce the atomic cannon, especially now that we were developing tactical nuclear weapons for division-level use by our army.

We'd come a long way from the time when Stalin was terrified we would be attacked by our imperialist enemies at any moment. No longer were we contaminated by Stalin's fear; no longer did we look at the world through his eyes. Now it was our enemies who trembled in *their* boots. Thanks to our missiles, we could deliver a nuclear bomb to a target any place in the world. No longer was the industrial heartland of the United States invulnerable to our counterattack.

Of course, we tried to derive maximum political advantage from the fact that we were the first to launch our rockets into space. We wanted to exert pressure on American militarists — and also influence the minds of more reasonable politicians — so that the United States would start treating us better.

However, now that we had nuclear bombs and the means to deliver them, we had no intention of starting a war. We stood firm on Lenin's position of peaceful coexistence. We only wanted to deter the Americans' threats, their aggressiveness, and their attempts to terrorize us.

Exploring the Cosmos

As a former political leader, I'm often asked by chance acquaintances whether it might have been possible to enter into some kind of cooperation with the United States in the exploration of space. While I was in the leadership, we never engaged in direct talks on this issue, but the subject frequently came up in questions from journalists during press conferences. I believe there were even reports printed in official organs of the US that the American government was interested in a joint program to reach the moon, but I don't think there were any concrete proposals — either from their side or ours.

For some time the United States lagged behind us. We were exploring space with our Sputniks. People all over the world recognized our success. Most admired us; the Americans were jealous.

I believe at that time the US might have been willing to cooperate with us, but we weren't willing to cooperate with them. Why? Because while we might have been ahead of the Americans in space exploration, we were still behind them in nuclear weaponry. The US had more warheads, more air bases, and more bombers. At that time airplanes still represented the principal means of delivering atomic weapons to their targets, and all the economic and administrative centers of Russia were within range of American bombers stationed around the periphery of our country. Our missiles were still imperfect in performance and insignificant in number. Taken by themselves, they didn't represent much of a threat to the United States. Essentially, we had only one good missile at the time: it was the *Semyorka*, developed by the late Korolyov. Had we decided to cooperate with the Americans in space research, we would have had to reveal to them the design of the booster for the *Semyorka*.

As I've already mentioned, two major factors had contributed to our success in space exploration: one was Korolyov's rocket, and the other was the booster designed by his friend and colleague. The Americans were terribly curious about our *Semyorka* booster. They were obviously interested in space cooperation merely as a pretext for finding out our secret. We knew that if we let them have a look at our rocket, they'd easily be able to copy it. Then, with their mighty industry and superb technology, they'd be able to start producing replicas of our booster and soon have more than we had. That would have been a threat to our security. In addition to being able to copy our rocket, they would have learned its limitations; and, from a military standpoint, it *did* have serious limitations. In short, by showing the Americans our *Semyorka*, we would have been both giving away our strength and revealing our weakness.

We felt we needed time to test, perfect, produce, and install the booster by ourselves. Once we got our feet planted firmly on the ground and provided for the defense of our country, *then* we could begin space cooperation with the United States. Such cooperation could be to the benefit of both sides. After all, there's enough outer space for everyone.

It's impossible for one country to maintain its leadership in space exploration forever. I remember back in the days when we were still far out in front, bourgeois correspondents used to tell me that the United States was making an all-out effort to catch up. I would answer quietly and calmly that any economically advanced country, the United States included, could build rockets and fly into space, just as we had done.

Reporters used to fire all sorts of stupid questions at me about whether we would be the first to conquer the moon. I thought all this talk about "conquering" the moon was a lot of nonsense. The moon is the moon. It's the common property of all mankind, and no single country is entitled to claim it as private territory.

Of course, once the US had attained the satisfaction of sending first one spaceship to the moon and then another, the whole question of cooperation between the US and the Soviet Union became more difficult. America had clearly demonstrated its ability to reach the moon, while the Soviet Union had not. The impression arose among our people and in other countries that the US had surpassed us. Nevertheless, on the basis of all I've seen and been through, if I could influence policy in this direction, I'd definitely favor an agreement with the US and the establishment of a basis for some sort of international cooperation in the exploration of space. I don't know if the moment for such an agreement has already slipped by. Maybe there never was such a moment. It certainly would have been desirable to reach an agreement back in the days when a moon flight was still only in the planning stages, when the technological means of our country and the US were on a more equal footing. But that never happened. Look at all the noise, conflict, and political uproar created by the United States when it sent its U-2 reconnaissance plane over our territory. We had to refuse to meet with the Americans and demand an apology because our sovereignty had been violated. Well, now our sovereignty is no longer violated, although American satellites are constantly circling the earth, photographing our installations and sending back information.[31]

31. In December, 1962, Adlai Stevenson and P. D. Morozov, the US and Soviet ambassadors to the United Nations, announced that their governments had agreed to co-

Since I retired, I've tried to keep track of developments in space as best I can from the newspapers. I can't say whether our own space program has lost its momentum or not, but one thing is clear: the Americans have fulfilled the program started by Kennedy to land a man on the moon.

Of course, we've been able to land some instruments on the moon, and I'm all in favor of fully automated Soviet space flights. I think some day in the future machines will be able to do a better job than people — just as our satellites can already automatically measure radiation, take photographs, and transmit pictures back to earth. But when it comes actually to exploring another heavenly body, no mechanical gadget can yet replace man. Therefore I think the Soviet Union should send a man to the moon — both for the good of science and for the prestige of our country.

For a man to go to the moon and back is a pinnacle of scientific development. Painful as it is for me to admit, I can't deny that the Americans are now ahead of us in space travel. Their achievements have made a definite impression on our people and on people all over the world.

Acquaintances constantly ask me how it happened that the Americans were first on the moon and why we didn't get there before them. I usually refer them to the transcript of the press conference given by Comrade Keldysh.[32] But in fact that press conference provided little satisfaction to our people. They wanted our country to be the first on the moon, and I don't blame them. I too would have liked our Russian Ivan to get there before the American John, but it just didn't work out that way.

In the years since I've been living in retirement, some very tragic events have occurred. I'm thinking in particular about the death of Yuri Gagarin, our first man in space.[33] I remember how sad it made me when I heard the news over the radio.

operate in space exploration. The announcement culminated negotiations between M. V. Keldysh, president of the USSR Academy of Sciences, and NASA administrator James E. Webb. However, these plans came to nothing, mostly because of the intervening Cuban missile crisis.

32. In October, 1969, three months after the US moon mission of Apollo 11, Keldysh told newsmen in Stockholm that the USSR "no longer has any scheduled plans for lunar flights." A few weeks later, he stated at a press conference in Moscow that the Soviet space program still included plans for an orbiting space station, but he reiterated that there would be no manned moon shots.

33. Colonel Yu. A. Gagarin, who became the first man in space when he circled the earth aboard a Vostok spacecraft in April 1961, died in a plane crash in March, 1968.

Then, more recently, some of our cosmonauts were in the final stages of their reentry: the braking rockets were fired, their contact with ground control was broken, and the spaceship made a soft landing. When the hatch was opened, the crew members were found dead.[34] I heard the whole thing on the radio.

People ask me my opinion. They want me to tell them what happened. How can I tell them anything? I'm isolated from the rest of the world. I don't receive any information. All I can do is guess. Perhaps some malfunction of the equipment on board caused a leak in the hermetically sealed cabin and the oxygen escaped. Or maybe the mishap had something to do with biological factors. Maybe the organisms of the crew reacted violently to the transition from weightlessness to gravity.

I just don't know. At first I thought nobody knew, but now I believe the tragedy must have been investigated and the cause must be known by someone. Yet there still hasn't been any announcement in the press. I believe the cause of the accident should be announced for two reasons: first, so that people who still have no idea what happened may be consoled; second, so that scientists might be able to take the necessary precautions to prevent the same thing from ever happening again. On top of that, I believe the United States should be informed of what went wrong. After all, the Americans, too, are engaged in the exploration of space.

I'm not implying any criticism of the people responsible for the ill-fated flight. It was an experiment, and safety is never guaranteed in such circumstances. Without experiments, science cannot advance. And science inevitably requires sacrifices. It would be unforgivable to impede scientific progress just to avoid sacrifices. I accept that as a reality. But it makes me very sad when for the sake of progress, mankind must pay the dearest price of all — and that is human life.

34. After setting an in-space endurance record of twenty-four days, three cosmonauts were found dead when their Soyuz spacecraft made a soft landing in Kazakhstan in June, 1971. A month later a special commission reported that the deaths were caused by a sudden drop in air pressure inside the ship. Not until October, 1973, did the Soviet authorities elaborate, explaining to visiting US space officials that an exhaust valve was accidentally triggered open by the firing of an explosive bolt when the Soyuz separated from the orbiting capsule.

4

The Scientific Intelligentsia

Academicians Kurchatov, Keldysh, and Lavrentev

THE most urgent military problem facing us after the war was the need to build nuclear weapons. We had to catch up with the Americans, who had been the first to develop atomic bombs and the first to use them in war when they dropped them on Hiroshima and Nagasaki. We knew that the reactionary forces of the world, led by the United States, had decided to place all their bets on nuclear weapons. We also knew that the Western imperialists were not one bit squeamish about the means they used to achieve their goal of liquidating socialism and restoring capitalism.

Our armed forces after the war weren't weak — they were strong in spirit. But unless supported by good equipment and the latest armaments, their spirit would quickly evaporate. We had to assess the situation soberly.

Stalin drew the correct conclusion: he saw that the reactionary forces of the West were mobilizing against us, that they had already accumulated hundreds of atomic bombs, and that the prospect of a military conflict with the United States was all too possible and not at all encouraging for our side.

Stalin was frightened to the point of cowardice. He ordered that all our technological efforts be directed toward developing atomic weapons of our own. I remember that Beria was in full charge of the project.[1] The Americans had their bomb in 1945, and we built ours

1. The day after the US bombed Hiroshima, Stalin put his secret police chief, L. P.

only by 1950, after I'd already left the Ukraine and come to Moscow. That's a gap of five years, not so much when you figure we were mastering the production of atomic weapons, but it gave the US a big head start to build up its stockpile of bombs. We had to keep in mind at first that we had exploded a bomb on the ground but not yet in the air. Then, when we did explode one in the air, it was only a prototype; the US had already used its bombs against Japanese cities.

I would like to recount here my association with various scientists whose efforts made it possible for us to catch up with the Americans and defend our country. Our leading nuclear physicist was Comrade Kurchatov.[2] He was the driving force behind our harnessing of nuclear energy. Thanks to him and atomic scientists like him, we were able to fulfill one of our fondest dreams, which was to have nuclear-powered engines for our submarine fleet. I don't even need to speak about Kurchatov's merits as a scientist because he was recognized the world over. However, I'd like to say a few words about him as a human being.

I had many chances to meet him over the years. He was decent and trustworthy. He kept me abreast of the most recent developments in science. When Eden invited representatives of our leadership to visit England, I suggested that we include Comrade Kurchatov in the delegation. In Stalin's time it would have been unthinkable to send abroad a man who knew everything about our nuclear arsenal and our missile industry.

Naturally, there was still a risk in letting our leading nuclear scientists go abroad. Not that there were grounds for mistrusting them personally — it was the bourgeois world we mistrusted. There had been cases when our people were picked up by a foreign intelligence service while they were abroad. Therefore, for the sake of caution, we usually tried to dissuade our scientists from traveling. In the case of international conferences, we often sent the second- and third-level experts rather than the people in key positions. Thus, any kidnappers would be unable to get their hands on those few scientists who had a concrete, firsthand knowledge of our top-secret projects.

But I believed taking Kurchatov to England with us would serve

---

Beria, in charge of a Soviet version of the Manhattan Project. The Russians' first atomic bomb exploded on the Ust-Urt Desert, between the Caspian and Aral Seas, in July of 1949.
    2. I. V. Kurchatov, a nuclear physicist prominently involved in the development of the Soviet A-bomb.

three purposes that would override the dangers: first, he would elevate the prestige of our delegation; second, he would allow us to establish useful contacts with the Western scientific community; and third, taking him with us would be a welcome demonstration of trust toward our own intelligentsia. Such was our faith in Kurchatov that we let him go around by himself in England, calling on physicists and visiting laboratories.[3]

Kurchatov certainly justified our confidence in him. I don't even like using the word "confidence." It's almost offensive when applied to Academician Kurchatov. It should go without saying that so remarkable a man, so great a scientist, and so devoted a patriot would deserve our complete trust and respect.

Kurchatov was extremely broad-minded and practical. Most specialists — and I don't say this to reproach them — are interested only in their own research projects or in their own branch of science. Kurchatov, on the other hand, understood that government funds must be expended according to a system of priorities. We wanted to advance our cultural, technological, and economic level, but first and foremost we had to think about the defense and security of our country. Kurchatov saw that clearly.

I think other scientists knew how much I liked and trusted Kurchatov. Therefore they tended to regard him as their spokesman.

Once, at the end of a meeting, he came up to me and said, "I have an idea which I'd like you to consider. I think it would be most useful if you appointed me as scientific advisor to you in your capacity as Chairman of the Council of Ministers."

I liked the idea. We needed a man who enjoyed our absolute trust. He could serve as a conduit for information and advice from the scientific world to the government. I told Comrade Kurchatov that in principle I appreciated his offering his services, but that the proposal would have to be considered in the leadership. I told him that the next time we saw each other, I'd let him know what was decided.

But we weren't destined to meet again. Soon after that conversation I learned that Comrade Kurchatov — that great scientist and a wonderful man — had died.[4]

---

3. Khrushchev and Bulganin included Kurchatov on their state visit to England in 1956 (see *KR*, I, 402–403). Earlier he was also allowed abroad to attend the Geneva Conference on Peaceful Uses of Atomic Energy.

4. Kurchatov died in February, 1960, and was buried beside the Kremlin Wall.

I had personal contact with other members of our scientific intelligentsia as well. Take Academician Keldysh, for instance. More often than not, he was the one to give reports. Like Kurchatov, Keldysh was irrevocably committed to our concept of what needed to be done in the development of nuclear missiles, and consequently he was held in especially high regard. No one was surprised when he became president of the Academy of Sciences. Here's how it happened:

Academician Nesmeyanov, the president of the Academy, was invited to a session of the Council of Ministers. Several critical statements were made; I'd say the criticism was pretty restrained in character. But Nesmeyanov, who was a very calm and tactful man, said, "Well, maybe you'd better think about promoting Comrade Keldysh to the post of president of the Academy of Sciences." We said that was an idea worth thinking about and discussing. After the session, we looked into the matter for a few days and came to the conclusion that, yes, it would be better to have Keldysh as president. Nesmeyanov went into retirement, and Keldysh replaced him.[5]

I've heard rumors to the effect that not all the academicians are pleased with Keldysh. As I see it, a certain amount of dissatisfaction is inevitable. The head of an organization like the Academy of Sciences can't possibly please everyone. He has to deal with too many individuals, too many people with different needs and different personalities. The president can't treat everybody on an equal basis. To my mind, if certain individuals are expressing their momentary displeasure with him, it probably means that Comrade Keldysh has run the academy with a firm hand. I believe he was a natural for the post of president, and I still believe he was the right man for the job; it was the right decision to appoint him.

I was always on very good terms with Comrade Lavrentev, the vice-president of the Academy of Sciences. I'd known him since back in the days when he was still head of the Ukrainian academy. I liked him for his straightforwardness, his perseverance, and his brilliance. As a mathematician he contributed a lot to the security of our country. He served as a consultant on many problems facing our defense industry.[6]

5. A. N. Nesmeyanov, an organic chemist, was president of the Academy from 1951 to 1961. M. V. Keldysh was a mathematician and mechanical engineer.
6. Academician M. A. Lavrentev, a mathematician, has been vice-president of the

Lavrentev once invited me to a testing ground where he was studying the phenomenon of cumulative explosions. He demonstrated how he could focus an explosive charge so as to blow right through a sheet of metal. On the basis of his observations, he invented the hollow-charge projectile, which turned out to be a highly effective armor-piercing shell and a major contribution to our war effort.

Comrade Lavrentev was also the one who put forward the courageous proposal to set up a branch of the Academy of Sciences in Siberia. At that time Moscow was still the only major scientific center anywhere in this vast country of ours. Siberia seemed like a particularly unlikely spot to establish a new institute. The very idea of Siberia was still a scarecrow to many people because millions had been imprisoned there (although they'd been allowed to return home after Stalin's death). Therefore, even though I can see now it was irrational and mistaken of me, at first I was most skeptical about Comrade Lavrentev's proposal.

"Do you really think we'll be able to get any of our scientists to go to Siberia?" I asked.

"Yes," he said, "I know some who would be willing." He then listed quite a number of young scientists.

We approved the plan and allocated some money for the foundation of an academy branch in Novosibirsk. I made several visits out there to see how the work was going.

I was pleased and surprised to find that Lavrentev had moved his whole family to Novosibirsk. They lived in a modest dwelling, a typical village house. He willingly gave up all the comforts and conveniences of life in the capital so that he could build a new science center in the heart of Mother Russia, deep in the Siberian taiga. He was a great scientist who walked in crude leather boots. I don't say that walking around in crude leather boots is something all our scientists should do — I bow to the ground before *any* scientist who works for the good of the people, even if he wears an opera hat, which of course isn't the most highly regarded headwear in our society. All I'm saying is this: I particularly liked Lavrentev for the simplicity in which he was willing to live.

Later he suggested we build another research center in the Far

---

USSR Academy of Sciences since 1957. A specialist in applied hydrodynamics and explosions, he developed the theory of cumulative charge, which had military utility for the design of armor-piercing shells.

East. I had to tell him that we simply didn't have the material resources and that we'd have to wait until our country was a bit richer before we could consider opening another one.[7]

Academician Kapitsa: A Confession

KAPITSA was given a chance to work on some problem.[8] I don't know whether it was military or civilian in nature, so I can't go into any detail. Later I was told that he was terribly anxious and upset, but he decided not to go back [to England]; he agreed to stay here.

Stalin offered to build Kapitsa a special institute at the best location in Moscow, which, at that time, was Vorobyov Hills or, as they're now called, Lenin Hills.[9] The land had already been designated as the site for the new American embassy. At first, Mr. Bullitt, the American ambassador, had enjoyed great political confidence; but when it became known what sort of man Bullitt was, Stalin was furious and said, "Let's put Kapitsa's institute — and not the US embassy — on that choice spot in Vorobyov Hills." [10]

And so the institute was built. In the years afterwards, whenever I came to Moscow, I would always go for a walk in Lenin Hills and catch a glimpse of the building. I would think to myself with pleasure, "I wonder what mysteries these miracle workers under Kapitsa's leadership are unfolding? I wonder what wonderful new creations they are working on for the good of our country?"

I never asked this question out loud. Under Stalin there was a

7. The Siberian branch of the Academy of Sciences was organized in 1957, based in Akademgorodok, outside Novosibirsk. Scientists there specialize in mathematics, nuclear physics, hydrodynamics, and geophysics.

8. P. L. Kapitsa, a physicist of the highest international standing, was born in Russia in 1894 and after the Revolution went to England, where he did pioneering work in low-temperature physics at Cambridge. In 1934 he was lured back to the USSR on what he thought was a short visit, with a guarantee that he would be permitted to go back to England; however, once in the USSR, he was not allowed to leave.

9. Vorobyov Hills, a suburb of the capital on the banks of the Moscow River, was renamed Lenin Hills when a new campus of Moscow State University was built there after the war.

10. William C. Bullitt, ambassador to Moscow, 1933–36. In 1919, Bullitt had dealt with Lenin in Moscow during the Paris Peace Conference and, fifteen years later, he found Stalin harder to do business with. According to George Kennan, "Bullitt soon became embittered over the behavior of the Soviet government in a whole series of questions. Increasingly, as the years 1934 and 1935 ran their course, he made himself the advocate of a hard line toward Moscow" (*Memoirs*).

strict rule: if you weren't told, you weren't meant to know and you'd better not ask. However, as time went by, Stalin began expressing his displeasure — I'd even say his indignation — about Kapitsa. He said Kapitsa wasn't doing what he was supposed to; his work wasn't up to our expectations. I had no idea whether these complaints were justified, but at that time I still believed in Stalin; if he said something, I assumed it must be true.

After we exploded our first atomic bomb, the bourgeois press started howling like a pack of mad dogs about how the Russians must have gotten their A-bomb from Kapitsa because he was the only physicist capable of developing the bomb. Stalin was outraged. He said Kapitsa had absolutely nothing to do with the bomb, and I believe that was the truth.

After Stalin's death, we had mixed feelings toward Kapitsa. On the one hand we recognized him as a world-renowned scientist. On the other hand, he hadn't even helped us develop our atomic bomb before the Americans built theirs. In short, I'd say our attitude toward Kapitsa was more than restrained.

Kapitsa used to tell me he'd come up with an earthshaking discovery — a new method of making oxygen. He said, and others confirmed, that this invention would have great significance for the development of our economy.[11] However, we expected more than that from him. We wanted Kapitsa actually to do what the bourgeois press said he had done: we wanted him to work on our nuclear bomb project. I'm no scientist, and I can't say what Kapitsa was capable of doing and what he wasn't. The point is, he refused to touch any military research. He even tried to persuade me that he couldn't undertake military work out of some sort of moral principle.

I remember once he asked for an appointment with me. I received him and listened attentively to what he had to say. He told me about a scientific problem he wanted to work on and asked me for financial support. I asked some other scientists, including Kurchatov, about Kapitsa's works and they told me the problem was not of urgent importance for the Soviet Union. At that time we measured urgency only in terms of military security. As I recall, we turned down Kapitsa's request.

11. In 1939 Kapitsa built an apparatus which could produce liquid oxygen in large quantities. After the invention of the US atomic bomb, he refused to cooperate in the Soviet project. He was accused of "premeditated sabotage of national defense" and fired from the directorship of the Institute of Physical Problems. He was returned to his post after Stalin's death.

Some time later Kapitsa came to see me again. During that conversation, I asked him, "Comrade Kapitsa, why won't you work on something of military significance? We badly need you to work on our defense program."

He gave me a rather long-winded dissertation on the subject of his attitude toward military topics. To the best of my recollection, the gist was as follows: "I'm a scientist, and scientists are like artists. They want other people to talk about their work, to make movies about it, to write articles about it in the newspapers. The trouble with military topics is that they're all secret. If a scientist does research in defense problems, he has to bury himself behind the walls of an institute and never be heard of again. His name disappears from print. I don't want that to happen to me. I want to be famous. I want other people to write and talk about my work."

I must admit that this line of reasoning made a strange impression on me — one not at all favorable to Academician Kapitsa.

"Comrade Kapitsa," I said, "what choice do we have? We're forced to concentrate on military matters. As long as there are antagonistic classes and antagonistic states with armies, we simply must push ahead with defense research. Otherwise we'll be choked to death, smashed to pieces, trampled in the dirt."

"I still refuse to have anything to do with military matters."

How could a Soviet citizen say such a thing? A man who'd lived through World War II and seen what our people had suffered at the hands of Hitler! If he had made the same speech to Stalin, you can be sure Stalin would have drawn a very different conclusion from the one I drew, although I admit I was upset.

Then Kapitsa expressed a desire to go abroad. I could tell he wanted the press to raise a lot of hoopla about his traveling to other countries.

Later I decided to have a talk with Lavrentev. "What's your opinion of Kapitsa?" I asked.

"I think very highly of him. He's a great scientist."

"I know that. He wants to go abroad. What do you think?"

"Let him go."

"Do you think he's an honest man?"

"Yes, I'm absolutely sure he's an honest and decent man."

Then I asked him, "What about Kapitsa's attitude toward military topics?"

"Yes, I know what you mean. In that respect, his thinking is pretty original. But remember: his son is one of our best geographers and a great patriot as well.[12] Therefore I think Kapitsa, too, is an honest and loyal Soviet citizen."

"I'm glad to hear that," I said. Lavrentev had already calmed me down and reassured me that Kapitsa could be trusted. I was beginning to think that maybe we should allow Kapitsa to go abroad and get a bit of fresh air. Perhaps the fact that he didn't touch military topics would make it more, rather than less, advisable to send him on a trip. With this thought in mind, I put another question to Lavrentev: "Do you think Kapitsa knows anything about the military work our other scientists are doing?"

"Yes, of course, he knows everything. After all, academicians are always getting together to consult with each other. Naturally he'd know what his colleagues are doing."

This put me on my guard again. "Then don't you think there's a danger he might talk too much if he goes abroad?"

"I can't speak for him," said Lavrentev, "but I've already told you I think he's a patriot. I don't believe he'll turn traitor."

"Maybe so," I replied, "but it's one thing to be a traitor and it's something else to talk too much."

We deliberated the matter in the leadership and decided to wait a while before sending Kapitsa abroad. We still hadn't accumulated enough atomic weapons. Therefore it was essential that we keep secret from our enemies any and all information which might tip them off about how little we had.

We knew Kapitsa had many friends and colleagues in the West, and we were afraid that if we let him make his trip, he might drop a few words here, a few words there. By his own admission, he was like an actor who loved applause, and he might have not been able to resist saying something just to enhance his own fame. This is a perfectly common human weakness, and I'm not censuring him for it. But as Chairman of the Council of Ministers, I had a duty to be especially cautious.

In the end we refused to give him permission to travel.

A few years ago, after I'd already retired, I read that Academician Kapitsa did make a trip abroad. There was much ado about him in

12. A. P. Kapitsa, a prominent geographer and geomorphologist. He took part in a number of Soviet expeditions to the South Pole, including the first Antarctic mission in 1955.

the press. He received the recognition he deserved and was made an honorary member of the academies of sciences in a number of different countries.[13]

I'm delighted Kapitsa finally got to go abroad. I regret only that he couldn't do so while I was in the leadership. Of course, by the time Kapitsa made his trip, we had already been recognized by President John Kennedy, among others, as a major nuclear power. After that, the danger no longer existed that Kapitsa would give away the secret of how far behind the US we were in our nuclear capability.

However, I have to admit that another reason I refused Kapitsa permission was possibly that Stalin was still belching inside me. Keep in mind, I'd worked under Stalin for years and years, and you don't free yourself from [Stalinist] habits so easily. It takes time to become conscious of your shortcomings and free yourself from them.

But I still maintain that the major consideration in my mind when I turned down Kapitsa's request had nothing to do with Stalin's legacy. No, it was a matter first and foremost of protecting our people, our State, and our national security.

Furthermore, I didn't act alone. As I've already related, I consulted Comrade Lavrentev, who warned me that Kapitsa knew everything about our research in nuclear weapons. I also consulted with the leadership. Not to have done so would have violated the rules of the Party and the State, to say nothing of the moral code of our Party.

So, as you can see, I still have very mixed feelings about Academician Kapitsa and the way I dealt with him. I tried to do my best. I never suspected him of treason, although I did believe he underestimated the importance of creating new weapons to frighten off those who would like to warm their hands at the expense of the Soviet Union.

This is my confession. Now that I've told the story, I feel I've done penance. Some people might criticize me, saying, "Khrushchev was cold-hearted to Academician Kapitsa, a man who contributed so much to Soviet science." Well, I'm only human, and I ask the people

13. After thirty-one years in the Soviet Union, Kapitsa was allowed to leave Soviet soil in May, 1965, when he traveled to Denmark to receive the Bohr Medal from King Frederick IX. A year later he returned to England for the first time since 1934. He was a guest of the Royal Society in London and at his alma mater, Cambridge, where he was presented with an honorary degree and given his old academic robe. He went to the US in 1969. During a press conference in Washington he supported the theory that the Soviet and American systems would someday converge.

to forgive me for the errors I've made. Kapitsa, too, is only human, and he made a mistake by refusing to work on military problems. My mistake was in refusing to let him go abroad. So, as people used to say when I was a child, we can call it quits. I now ask Academician Kapitsa, whom I've always respected as a great scientist, to forgive me.

Academician Sakharov and the H-Bomb

I WOULD like to compare Kapitsa with another of our most brilliant nuclear physicists, Academician Sakharov. He, too, had misgivings about military research. I used to meet frequently with Sakharov, and I considered him an extremely talented and impressive man. He was also a surprisingly young man to be involved in such important and difficult matters. He proposed that we develop a hydrogen bomb. No one else, neither the Americans nor the English, had such a bomb. I was overwhelmed by the idea. We did everything in our power to assure the rapid realization of Sakharov's plans. With the help of engineers, technicians, and workers, our industry was able to develop the bomb in a remarkably short time. The hydrogen bomb represented a great contribution to the Soviet people and a great act of patriotism by Comrade Sakharov.[14]

We later entered into negotiations with the United States and its allies on an agreement to halt the arms race. In the spirit of those negotiations, our side discontinued all nuclear explosions. Our scientists, of course, continued to work on the design of our weapons. They considerably reduced the cost and increased the power of a single explosion. But this was only on paper. Because we had voluntarily and unilaterally suspended our nuclear testing, there was no way our scientific and military experts could see if the new improved designs really worked.

Meanwhile, during the many months that we suspended all tests,

14. Academician A. D. Sakharov, a prodigy of Soviet physics and currently a leader of the dissident intelligentsia. In 1950 he and I. Ye. Tamm devised a method of obtaining a controlled thermonuclear reaction, and he was instrumental in the development of the Russian hydrogen bomb, first exploded in August, 1953, when he was thirty-two years old. His tract *Progress, Coexistence and Intellectual Freedom* was published in the West in 1968.

Nikita Sergeyevich Khrushchev

Khrushchev as a young man in the Ukraine

With his wife, Nina Petrovna, in Yuzovka, 1924

With his daughter Yulia and his son Leonid

Lieutenant General Khrushchev, member of the Military Council, 1943

With General Chistyakov on the Voronezh Front

Decorated by President Kalinin at Stalingrad

With future Defense Minister Malinovsky in a Ukrainian town, 1943

In an inflatable dinghy near Kiev at the end of the war

On an inspection tour of the naval base at Vladivostok, 1954
Above: with local military commanders
Below: saluting with Malinovsky and Bulganin

Leaving the Geneva summit conference with Marshal Zhukov
and Foreign Minister Molotov (hat in hand), 1955

With aircraft designer A. N. Tupolev (*center*) and
physicist I. V. Kurchatov aboard the cruiser *Ordzhonikidze*
en route to England, 1956

On deck with Kurchatov

With aircraft designers Tupolev and Artem Mikoyan
in the Crimea, 1961

the Americans went right on testing, perfecting, and stockpiling their own bombs. We hoped that international public opinion would support us and exert pressure on the United States to stop contaminating the atmosphere, which people all over the world must breathe, but the American government was deaf to all protests. Thus, we were faced with the dilemma of whether we should stick to our position and risk falling far behind — or whether we should resume testing. Naturally, we were under increasing pressure from our military.

We finally decided to announce that if other countries refused to support the nuclear test ban, we would have no choice but to resume testing ourselves. We set a date for our next explosion.[15] Literally a day or two before the resumption of our testing program, I got a telephone call from Academician Sakharov. He addressed me in my capacity as the Chairman of the Council of Ministers, and he said he had a petition to present. The petition called on our government to cancel the scheduled nuclear explosion and not to engage in any further testing, at least not of the hydrogen bomb: "As a scientist and as the designer of the hydrogen bomb, I know what harm these explosions can bring down on the head of mankind."

Sakharov went on in that vein, pleading with me not to allow our military to conduct any further tests. He was obviously guided by moral and humanistic considerations. I knew him and was profoundly impressed by him. Everyone was. He was, as they say, a crystal of morality among our scientists. I'm sure he had none but the best of motives. He was devoted to the idea that science should bring peace and prosperity to the world, that it should help preserve and improve the conditions for human life. He hated the thought that science might be used to destroy life, to contaminate the atmosphere, to kill people slowly by radioactive poisoning. However, he went too far in thinking that he had the right to decide whether the bomb he had developed could ever be used in the future.

"Comrade Sakharov," I said, "you must understand my position. My responsibilities in the post I hold do not allow me to cancel the tests. Our Party and government have already made abundantly clear

15. The Soviets had announced their suspension of testing in March, 1958, just before the US and Britain proceeded with a series of explosions. In October of that year, the US and Britain in turn announced their willingness to stop testing, just as the Soviets prepared for new tests, which took place in November, at the time of the first Berlin Crisis. The USSR later conducted a massive testing program during the second Berlin Crisis in 1961.

that we would like nothing better than to suspend nuclear testing forever. Our leadership has already unilaterally discontinued nuclear testing and called on the United States and other countries to follow our example for the good of all mankind. But we got no answer. The Americans wouldn't listen to our proposals. As a scientist, surely you know that they've gone right on conducting their tests. If we don't test our own bombs, how will we know whether they work or not?"

He wasn't satisfied. He still insisted that we not resume our own testing.

I wanted to be absolutely frank with him: "Comrade Sakharov, believe me, I deeply sympathize with your point of view. But as the man responsible for the security of our country, I have no right to do what you're asking. For me to cancel the tests would be a crime against our state. I'm sure you know what kind of suffering was inflicted on our people during World War II. We can't risk the lives of our people again by giving our adversary a free hand to develop new means of destruction. Can't you understand that? To agree to what you are suggesting would spell doom for our country. Please understand that I simply cannot accept your plea; we must continue our tests."

My arguments didn't change his mind, and his didn't change mine; but that was to be expected. Looking back on the affair, I feel Sakharov had the wrong attitude. Obviously, he was of two minds. On the one hand, he had wanted to help his country defend itself against imperialist aggression. On the other hand, once he'd made it possible for us to develop the bomb, he was afraid of seeing it put to use. I think perhaps he was afraid of having his name associated with the possible implementation of the bomb. In other words, the scientist in him saw his patriotic duty and performed it well, while the pacifist in him made him hesitate. I have nothing against pacifists — or at least I *won't* have anything against them if and when we create conditions which make war impossible. But as long as we live in a world in which we have to keep both eyes open lest the imperialists gobble us up, then pacifism is a dangerous sentiment.

This conflict between Sakharov and me left a lasting imprint on us both. I took it as evidence that he didn't fully understand what was in the best interests of the state, and therefore from that moment on I was somewhat on my guard with him. I hope that the time will come when Comrade Sakharov will see the correctness of my position — if not now, then some time in the future.[16]

We discussed Sakharov's petition in the leadership and decided to go ahead with the test. The bomb made an immensely powerful blast. The world had never seen such an explosion before. Our scientists calculated in advance that the force of the bomb would equal 50 million tons of TNT. That was in theory. In actual fact, the explosion turned out to be equivalent to 57 million tons. It was colossal, just incredible! Our experts later explained to me that if you took into account the shock wave and the radioactive contamination of the air. then the bomb produced as much destruction as 100 million tons of TNT.

I asked our scientists where we could use the bomb in case of war. I wanted to have a concrete idea about what destruction of this magnitude really meant. I was told that we wouldn't be able to bomb West Germany with a 57-megaton bomb because the prevailing westerly winds would blow the fallout over the German Democratic Republic, inflicting damage both on the civilian population and our own armed forces stationed there. However, we would not jeopardize ourselves or our allies if we dropped the bomb on England, Spain, France, or the United States.

It was a terrifying weapon. It gave us an opportunity to exert moral pressure on those who were conducting aggressive policies against the Soviet Union. We developed and tested the hydrogen bomb not in preparation for an attack, but for defense of our country against those who might attack us.

16. In a statement printed on the New York *Times* Op-Ed Page of September 12, 1973, Sakharov wrote, "Beginning in 1958, I have spoken out both in print and in private for ending nuclear tests in the atmosphere." In a collection of writings published in the West in 1974 under the title *Sakharov Speaks*, he recounts in detail his dealings with Khrushchev.

5

The Creative Intelligentsia

I WOULD like to say something about the attitude of our leadership toward the intelligentsia, both during Stalin's time and later when I was head of the government. Of course, the term "intelligentsia" embraces many walks of life in Soviet society. Our intellectuals contribute in various ways to the Party's efforts to consolidate and educate our society, to lead our people towards the attainment of the goals set by Lenin at the time of the October Revolution.

The technological intelligentsia — that is, the sector of society whose intellectual energy is realized in the creation of equipment and other practical objects — is an area where we haven't had too many problems. By the very nature of its activity the technological intelligentsia does not interfere in the more complicated spheres of social life, namely in ideology.

A more difficult and slippery problem is posed by the *creative* intelligentsia. Of course, a member of the technological intelligentsia, indeed every man engaged in useful labor, is creating something for the good of society; but when we say "creative intelligentsia," we mean writers, artists, musicians, sculptors — people who do not directly add to the material wealth of a society, but whose works provide the inspiration without which man cannot live. Yet our creative intelligentsia suffers more than any other category of people in our society. Materially, they're better off than other categories, but spiritually, members of the creative intelligentsia are very troubled.

Creative work, especially by writers, has a tendency to interfere in the political sphere because it is part of the artistic process to analyze relations among people, including relations between those in power on the one hand and common workers on the other. Writers are forever delving into questions of philosophy and ideology — questions on which any ruling party, including the Communist Party, would like to have a monopoly. You can't accomplish much unless you cultivate people's minds and guide them in the right direction. This is the role of the Party, but it is also the role of literature.

Music, too, plays an important role because it uplifts man's spirits. It does so without speaking in man's language, which complicates the business of distinguishing between a good and a bad piece of music. Sometimes you turn on the radio, listen to something, and say to yourself, "Who wrote this junk?" Then you find out it was written by Tchaikovsky or some other famous composer. Then again, sometimes you turn on the radio and hear the same music, only this time you think it's beautiful — all because you're in a different mood. This can even happen with books. For example, I didn't particularly care for Solzhenitsyn's second book, *Matryona's Home*.[1] You can say it's a matter of taste, but I'd say it's more a matter of mood.

However, in general I think it's much easier for an intelligent man — or even a stupid man, for that matter — to understand a work of literature than it is for him to understand a piece of music, a painting, or a piece of sculpture. A writer is like a bricklayer or a lathe operator in that he produces a finished product that can be picked up and looked at from all sides and judged accordingly. In creating interrelations among his characters a writer is forced to enter into all spheres of social life, ranging from that of the Party to that of the people.

Stalin's attitude toward artists had its good points. He was a statesman, a man of lofty intelligence. But many intellectuals suffered during his rule. Some he disliked personally; and the regime did not give these artists the objective treatment, the understanding, and the tolerance they needed in order to survive. If one man or a group of men starts determining what is good and what is bad, this creates serious troubles for the intelligentsia, particularly in certain fields of the arts, like music, where qualitative judgments are so subjective. But even more than composers, painters and writers suffer when they are put in shackles and not allowed to move. Any kind of limitation is like a yoke on the creative process.

Like all despots, Stalin treated writers well only on the condition

1. Nobel Prize–winning novelist A. I. Solzhenitsyn's story *Matryona's Home* was published in 1963. The year before, Khrushchev had personally authorized the publication of *A Day in the Life of Ivan Denisovich*, a novel about a Stalinist labor camp. It appeared in *Novy Mir*, the USSR's outstanding literary journal.

that their works were flattering to him and his reign. In this respect Stalin was like Nicholas I, known as Nicholas the Whip, who persecuted Pushkin. Is there any question that Pushkin was a great writer? Of course not. He wrote beautiful poems which expressed what was in his own soul and the soul of the people. I remember those immortal lines he wrote about himself:

> I have raised to myself a monument not made by hands;
> The grass will not grow on the people's path to this moment.[2]

Yet Pushkin spent most of his life in exile — first in the south, Moldavia, Kishinev, and Odessa, then at his estate near Pskov. To think, all that time he could have been creating.[3] Of course Nicholas I wanted Pushkin to be creative, but he also wanted him to glorify the monarch and bolster the monarchy.

I'm not saying that all writers and artists were oppressed during the time of Stalin. For example, Voroshilov was crazy about the painter Gerasimov.[4] I'm not going to try to judge the artistic quality of Gerasimov's works, but I knew there was one thing Voroshilov particularly liked about him: Gerasimov glorified Voroshilov in his paintings. Voroshilov also had a favorite composer, who was always singing his praises. This was Pokras, who's still very much respected.[5] But look at the way he wrote songs about the cavalry exploits of Budyonny [6] and Voroshilov. There's a special term to describe artists like Gerasimov and Pokras: they're court painters and court musicians. Men in power have always surrounded themselves with such artists, bestowing on them official favor — to say nothing of material rewards.

Some of the intellectuals who enjoyed Stalin's good graces came to tragic ends. Take Fadeyev, for instance. He was a talented writer. His work *The Young Guards* is immortal. I also thought highly of his

---

2. From "The Monument" by A. S. Pushkin (1799–1837).
3. In fact, Pushkin wrote prolifically in exile.
4. Marshal K. Ye. Voroshilov was at various times People's Commissar of Defense, Stalin's "whipping boy" (see *KR*, I, 280–281), Chairman of the Presidium of the Supreme Soviet (titular head of state, 1953–60), and confessed Anti-Party Group conspirator.
A. M. Gerasimov was probably best known for his 1938 painting of Stalin and Voroshilov surveying Moscow from the Kremlin Wall.
5. The reference here is to the two Pokras brothers, Daniil Ya. and Dmitry Ya., who wrote popular martial songs celebrating the exploits of the Red Army in the Russian Civil War.
6. Marshal S. M. Budyonny, a flamboyant cavalry officer. Khrushchev was attached to Budyonny's First Mounted Army in the Civil War.

book about the Civil War in Siberia.[7] However, Fadeyev used to praise Stalin in the Writers' Union and allowed himself to be turned into Stalin's agent, even to the point of giving false evidence against people accused of committing crimes.

Already, at that time, Fadeyev was drinking himself into a stupor. I remember how Stalin would gather us for the deliberations of the Stalin Prize Selection Committee. Stupid as it sounds, such meetings really occurred: Stalin would listen to nominations, then decide who would receive a Stalin Prize. It was really about as low as you could get. Anyway, Fadeyev would report on various candidates for the prize, and later Stalin would say, "Look! He can hardly stand up he's so drunk!" — and it was true. Sometimes Stalin would rouse all the militiamen and Chekists out of bed and send them to look for Fadeyev in one of his grimy hangouts. All these places were on the books, so the police would simply go down the list, poking around from one to the other until they found him. That's the state Fadeyev drank himself into.

Then, a few years later, after Stalin's death, it was revealed that the hundreds of thousands who had been killed, including many writers and members of the creative intelligentsia, were not outlaws or enemies of the people at all. Fadeyev couldn't take it. I believe he realized we were doing the right thing by exposing Stalin's crimes, but Fadeyev couldn't get over the fact that he had so often praised Stalin and, worse, played the role of Stalin's henchman and chief prosecutor against the creative intelligentsia. He realized he had come the full circle, and he committed suicide.[8] Of course, we should bear in mind that by that time Fadeyev had become an alcoholic wreck.

Another writer who was very successful during Stalin's time was Tvardovsky. His name was on the lips of millions of people fighting the Hitlerite hordes during the war. Just as every Red Army soldier during the Civil War was politically and morally fortified by Demyan Bedny's works,[9] so Tvardovsky's books — especially his epic poem about Vasily Tyorkin — were a source of strength to us in World War

7. *The Rout*, which concerns a band of Communist partisans fighting interventionists and White Guards in the Russian Civil War.

8. A. A. Fadeyev committed suicide in May, 1956, three months after the Twentieth Party Congress at which he was, ironically, elected a candidate member of the Central Committee.

9. Demyan Bedny was an officially accepted poet whom Khrushchev had encountered during the purges of the 1930's (see *KR*, I, 79–80).

II. Stalin had a painting of Vasily Tyorkin hung right in front of the entrance to Catherine Hall in the Kremlin, just to the right as you come out of the conference hall of the Supreme Soviet Presidium. I can still remember Stalin staring up at this picture with a look of deep emotion on his face. We were all equally moved by the painting.

Thus, Tvardovsky gave us some great art, but he ended up without recognition, without honor. I think it's impossible not to recognize Tvardovsky. Some may not recognize a man while he's alive, but the people have already recognized him; and tomorrow there will come new people who will evaluate Tvardovsky's role in a different way.[10]

Turning to our attitude toward writers and artists when I came to be head of the Party, I should say a word about Pasternak. I won't try to judge his literary merits, but I trust the opinion of other poets, who value highly Pasternak's works and his translations from foreign languages. After Stalin's death he wrote *Doctor Zhivago* and tried to get it published. There was a terrific commotion about this novel and how to handle it. I was informed and had an opportunity to influence the decision of whether or not to publish it — which boiled down to a question of whether or not to accept the advice of someone who was reporting to us — but I failed to act. I have firm grounds for saying that, if I had influenced the decision [by coming out in favor of publication], I would have been supported. But I did nothing, and now I regret it. When dealing with creative minds, administrative measures are always most destructive and nonprogressive.

Pasternak worked hard on *Doctor Zhivago*. The manuscript found its way abroad, where it was published and caused a stir. It obtained recognition and was awarded the Nobel Prize, though I can't say to what extent this work deserved it. Anyway, Pasternak was chosen to be a Nobel Prize laureate, while here [in the Soviet Union] there were administrative measures. His book was put into cold storage; it

10. A. T. Tvardovsky, poet and longtime editor of *Novy Mir*, created a popular image of the Soviet soldier, both heroic and comic, in Vasily Tyorkin, the protagonist of a long poem published in 1946. The same character reappeared in 1963 in "Tyorkin in the Other World," a parody of Stalinist bureaucracy published in *Izvestia* and introduced by Khrushchev's son-in-law, A. I. Adzhubei, who was editor in chief of the government newspaper until Khrushchev's downfall a year later.

Tvardovsky was an early and steadfast patron of Solzhenitsyn. He published *A Day in the Life of Ivan Denisovich* with Khrushchev's blessing, and then later — when Khrushchev had fallen from power and Solzhenitsyn had fallen from favor — he persisted in trying to print the novelist's works in *Novy Mir*. Largely because of his patronage of Solzhenitsyn, Tvardovsky was abruptly dismissed as editor of *Novy Mir* in 1970. He died in 1971. Solzhenitsyn attended the funeral.

was banned. The decision to use police methods put a whole different coloration on the affair and left a bad aftertaste for a long time to come. People raised a storm of protest against the Soviet Union for not allowing Pasternak to go abroad to receive the prize.

I said, "Let's go ahead and publish the book so that Pasternak will be able to go abroad and pick up his award. We'll give him a passport and some hard currency to make the trip."

Then, quite unexpectedly, Pasternak let it be known through a statement in the newspapers that he had no intention of going abroad and that he wasn't even going to raise the question.

To this day I haven't read his book and therefore can't judge it. People who've spoken to me about it say they don't have any special admiration for the artistic aspect of the work, but that's beside the point. To judge an author and to judge his work are two different matters. If the book was really of low artistic quality, then that judgment should be left up to the reader. If a work fails to touch a responsive chord in a reader — if its ideas or the ways it presents its ideas don't move the reader — then the writer will have to draw the necessary conclusions. Naturally, he'll be morally shaken, but he will have nobody to blame but himself for the failure of his work to embody and communicate some idea worth the reader's attention. The main point is: readers should be given a chance to make their own judgments; and administrative measures, police measures, shouldn't be used. A sentence should not be pronounced over our creative intellectuals as though they were on trial.

In connection with *Doctor Zhivago*, some might say it's too late for me to express regret that the book wasn't published. Yes, maybe it is too late. But better late than never.[11]

I met Ehrenburg more than once over the years. He was a major writer, a great talent. But somehow he managed to reconcile himself to Stalinist methods. Perhaps I'm being too severe toward him, for conditions were such during Stalin's time that one didn't have much choice. Besides, to be fair, I'd have to say Ehrenburg sometimes stood up to Stalin stubbornly.

I remember, for example, at one point Stalin wanted to have a

11. B. L. Pasternak's novel *Doctor Zhivago* was published in Italy, then in the United States, over official Soviet objections, in 1958. In October of that year, Pasternak was awarded the Nobel Prize, which he initially indicated he would accept. He then came under withering attack from the press and the authorities, was expelled from the Writers' Union, and cabled his "voluntary refusal" of the prize to Stockholm.

statement published in the press to the effect that there was no anti-Semitism in the Soviet Union. He ordered Kaganovich [12] and Ehrenburg to join in drafting the statement. He particularly wanted their signatures on it, even though he had no shortage of people to sign it. Kaganovich squirmed around a lot but of course ended up signing, since he did everything Stalin told him. But, to the best of my recollection — and I don't want to make a mistake here — Ehrenburg categorically refused to sign.

By titling his novel *The Thaw*, Ehrenburg coined a term which later became popular to describe the period after Stalin's death. However, we in the leadership couldn't quite agree with his characterization of that period as a "thaw." On the one hand we had allowed a certain degree of relaxation; people started speaking more freely among themselves, as well as in the press and in literature.[13]

There were still certain people who were opposed to the new leniency. I remember one of them once reproached me by saying in my presence about a piece of abstract art, "If Stalin were only alive he would have never permitted this." As I recall, the man who made this remark was a well-known artist who, I was later told, bought a piece of sculpture by Neizvestny and paid big money for it.[14] Neizvestny himself used to say that some of the people who were criticizing him the most were paying a lot to buy his sculpture, though he didn't name any names.

We in the leadership were consciously in favor of the thaw, myself

12. L. M. Kaganovich, Khrushchev's onetime political mentor, later one of his principal rivals. After the war Kaganovich was Khrushchev's replacement as First Secretary of the Ukrainian Communist Party and Deputy Chairman of the Council of Ministers. Khrushchev has accused Kaganovich, a Jew, of being anti-Semitic (see *KR*, I, 243).

13. I. G. Ehrenburg, a Russian-Jewish writer who, because he seemed to enjoy Stalin's tolerance and survived the anti-Semitic purge of 1952, had an ambiguous reputation: some Soviet liberals have considered him one of their own, while others have regarded him as an opportunist. Stalinist critics denounced him for his frank treatment of the Stalin era in his memoirs and other works. *The Thaw* appeared in 1954. Khrushchev publicly expressed the view that the book "gives an inexact, or to be more precise, a wrong and one-sided picture, to say the least, of the events and phenomena associated with [Stalin's] personality cult" (March, 1963).

14. E. I. Neizvestny, a sculptor whose work Khrushchev and his Party associate in charge of ideology and culture, L. F. Ilyichev, denounced as "abstractionist"; Khrushchev and Neizvestny got into a public shouting match at an art exhibition in Moscow.

included, but without naming Ehrenburg by name, we felt we had to criticize his position. We were scared — really scared. We were afraid the thaw might unleash a flood, which we wouldn't be able to control and which could drown us. How could it drown us? It could have overflowed the banks of the Soviet riverbed and formed a tidal wave which would have washed away all the barriers and retaining walls of our society. From the viewpoint of the leadership, this would have been an unfavorable development. We wanted to guide the progress of the thaw so that it would stimulate only those creative forces which would contribute to the strengthening of socialism.

Of course, we too wanted a relaxation of controls over our artists, but we might have been somewhat cowardly on this score. Our people had a good expression for the situation we were in: "You want to scratch where it itches, but your mama won't let you."

We had some talks at the Central Committee with a group of intellectuals and made a point of inviting Ehrenburg.[15] I don't remember for sure whether Comrade Simonov was there, but I do remember Tvardovsky, Yevtushenko, Neizvestny, Galina Serebryakova, and others were all present.[16] Serebryakova delivered a withering speech against Ehrenburg, making him squirm as though he were on a hot griddle. She was a talented writer, though you don't hear much about her today. She was giving Ehrenburg a tongue-lashing for having been a toady to Stalin, almost in so many words. She said that while Stalin was chopping off heads and carting writers off into exile, Ehrenburg had been going around giving speeches in support of Stalin's treatment of the intelligentsia. Ehrenburg got very annoyed and sharply objected to her remarks. I don't remember her concrete

15. Khrushchev held two meetings with intellectuals at the Central Committee headquarters: on December 17, 1962, and on March 7, 1963. The first occasion brought four hundred intellectuals to the Pioneer Palace in Lenin Hills; the second was a gathering of six hundred in Sverdlov Hall of the Kremlin.

16. K. M. Simonov was a poet, prose writer, and playwright who preceded Tvardovsky as editor of *Novy Mir*. He was well known for his patriotic writings during the war.

Ye. A. Yevtushenko had recently published "Stalin's Heirs," a poem warning against the possible resurgence of Stalinism.

Galina Serebryakova, author of a trilogy on the life of Marx and victim of the Stalinist Terror. Two of her husbands died in the purges and she spent almost twenty years in Siberia. At the December, 1962, meeting between Party leaders and intellectuals, she bitterly attacked Ehrenburg as a Stalinist-in-disguise who had betrayed fellow Jews during the postwar anti-Semitic campaign.

accusations or his concrete rebuttals, but I could well understand how she felt. As I say, she's very talented in my opinion. She wrote a trilogy about Marx and Engels. I read it and liked it. She worked hard on that book and collected a lot of interesting material, which she put together very skillfully. Yet now she's disappeared from the horizon. You read about a lot of writers in the press, but you can't find her name anywhere. I don't know what's happened to her. I don't even know whether she's alive. I think if she'd died, there would have been some sort of an announcement. I guess she must be in a position today that doesn't allow her to have any recognition and that doesn't allow her works to see the light of day.

I regret many of the things that were said during those exchanges, including some things I said myself. For instance, I remember criticizing Neizvestny rudely, saying he decided to take his name so he would remain unknown.[17] I wasn't trying to suggest that his name was cause for suspicion, but no matter: it was rude of me to say it, and I'm sorry. There was no excuse for someone who held a high state position, as I did, to say something which could be taken the wrong way against someone. If I met Neizvestny now, I'd apologize for what I said during our discussion at the Central Committee.

Actually, it wasn't so much a discussion as it was a criticism session. It was Yevtushenko who spoke up emotionally in defense of Neizvestny's school of art. Yevtushenko quite rightly pointed out that this wasn't the first time some members of the intelligentsia had attacked the abstractionists. The Futurists, I believe, were abstractionists. In 1917–18 Mayakovsky used to wear a yellow blouse on Nevsky Prospect. He and the Futurists were considered abstractionists in their own time and criticized as such, yet they left works which even now are recognized as a service to the Communist Party in its struggle for a better future. Mayakovsky is a difficult poet to read, but when I listen to people recite his work, I always find it very forceful and ideologically inspiring.[18]

As for Yevtushenko's poems, I haven't read all of them, but I like many of the ones I have read. He wrote an effective poem about the attitude of the Russian people toward war, which was set to music and turned into a song entitled "Do the Russians Want War?" I don't

17. *Neizvestny* in Russian means "unknown."
18. V. V. Mayakovsky was poet laureate of the Revolution and a leader of the Futurists, a group of aesthetically experimental and politically left-wing writers and artists on the eve of the Revolution. His famous "yellow blouse" was a badge of nonconformism.

know why his songs aren't performed more today. Some people criticize his song about war, saying he rejects war and morally disarms our soldiers. I don't agree. I think it's an excellent poem. It says that we Russians don't want war but at the same time warns that if forced to fight we'll not hesitate to deal a deadly counterblow.

In general I consider Yevtushenko a talented poet and a good man. Of course he has a wild, ungovernable, even violent streak in his character, but he's ungovernable only from an administrative point of view. In other words he wouldn't always fit into the framework set by a censor — to put it crudely, the framework set by those who would like him to smooth down his work a little bit around the edges.

What a bore it would be if everybody wrote in exactly the same way, if everybody used the same arguments. There would be no room for creativity, no room for a writer to develop his talent and sharpen his style. It would be like two people speaking into a tube, one saying something from one end and the other repeating the same thing from the other end. If there's too much monotonous cud-chewing in literature, it will make a reader vomit.

In general, I think we should be more tolerant and extend wider opportunities to our creative intelligentsia. While personally I'm against the new schools of painting, sculpture, and music, that doesn't mean I see any need for resorting to administrative and police measures. I remember when defending Neizvestny against our criticisms, Comrade Yevtushenko made the point that in Cuba an abstract artist and a realist artist were comrades and always fought side by side whenever the citizens were called to arms to protect their revolutionary achievements. It was a valid point.

Neizvestny later sent word to me, either through the Minister of Culture, Furtseva, or through Pavlov at the Komsomol,[19] that he would give up abstract art and start doing realist work. Naturally I was pleased. From the press I've seen he has done some excellent things, and I think maybe our criticisms had something to do with putting him on the right track, although I still regret the form our criticism took.[20]

19. Ye. A. Furtseva, who has been Minister of Culture since 1960, was a weaver by training; she has been in the Party and state bureaucracy since 1930.

S. P. Pavlov was First Secretary of the All-Union Communist Youth League, or Komsomol.

20. Khrushchev's family commissioned Neizvestny to sculpt a headstone for Khrushchev's grave in Novodevichy Cemetery in Moscow. However, the authorities denied the family permission for this bust to be placed on the grave.

Speaking of art, I remember a conversation I once had with Mr. Eden when we visited his dacha in England.[21] Eden asked, "Mr. Khrushchev, what do you think of this new kind of art?"

"Frankly, I don't understand it, Mr. Prime Minister. I'm in favor of realism in creative art."

"I don't understand it either. But what about your Picasso?" [22]

"Well, what about him? He's certainly a major artist, and when called upon, he was able to turn his creativity to depicting a dove of peace, which symbolizes the struggle for peace all over the world." I realize it wasn't up to me to play the role of either Picasso's critic or his defender, not that he needs *me* to defend him. I was merely sharing with Eden my observation that the art of a great artist like Picasso is not all abstract.

Moving from painting to music, I should say something about Comrade Shostakovich, for whom I've always had the greatest respect. He was criticized during Stalin's time, but he accepted that criticism, and I wouldn't say he was ever pushed in the background.[23] He wrote a lot, especially during the war. He composed his masterpieces in Leningrad. For years he occupied a prominent position in our creative intelligentsia, particularly in the Union of Composers. Now he's a leading — I'd even say our greatest — composer. However, there were certain ,specific issues on which we couldn't see eye to eye with him. For example, we couldn't understand why he spoke out in favor and support of jazz.

One of the composers attacked for writing jazz was the wonderful composer and musician Utyosov.[24] *Pravda* started lighting into Utyosov and tearing him to pieces. But even when Utyosov was being viciously attacked by *Pravda*, the printers setting the type for those critical articles were humming Utyosov's song "Bublichki" while they worked. I know because I was told by an old friend of mine, a Communist from Odessa, who had friends working on the presses at *Pravda*. I'm an old man, and I'm rather old-fashioned in my taste for music. I've always liked folk songs and dances, as well as classical

21. See *KR*, I, 405.
22. Khrushchev quotes Eden as referring to "your" Picasso because the painter was an early convert to Communism.
23. D. D. Shostakovich was in disfavor during the 1930's, when most of his works were branded as "formalist." *Pravda* attacked his opera *Lady Macbeth of Mtsensk* and his ballet *Bright Brook* for "crude naturalism."
24. L. O. Utyosov, an Odessa-born composer and performer of folk songs.

music. I don't care much for jazz — it sounds to me more like some sort of horrible cacophony than music; I always switch off the radio whenever a jazz program comes on. But I'll confess that I have a few of Utyosov's records, and I take them out and play them sometimes. I like his music very much. I believe that the people themselves should be given a chance to express their taste or distaste for a certain kind of music, and the leadership should not use administrative means in opposing jazz or any other kind of music.

In addition to suffering from the improper means that have sometimes been used against them, some artists and intellectuals have had difficulty getting permission to leave the Soviet Union on trips abroad. I'd like to give a few illustrations of my views on whether it's worthwhile locking up our borders. Everybody knows that after Stalin's death the gates were thrown wide open. We had to recognize that there would be different elements and people of different political convictions, some of them undesirable, and that when we sent abroad a group of performers some might not come back. When that happened it was always upsetting, but sometimes there would be instances of people later coming back to us with tears in their eyes literally begging us to let them return. Of course, some artists were better risks than others.

There was the case of our number one ballerina, Maya Plisetskaya. One day, when a ballet troupe was getting ready to go abroad, I received a long and forthright letter from her saying that she was hurt and insulted because she was excluded from the traveling company of the Bolshoi Theater. I recommended that she be allowed to go on the tour. What if we had continued our "no exit permit" policy? For one thing, it would have appeared to the rest of the world that we had no pride in our most famous ballerina.[25]

I remember when I served in the political department of the Ninth Kuban Army during the Civil War, I was billeted at the house of a petty bourgeois family. There was a woman with a poisonous tongue who spoke out very bravely to me. "Now that you Communists have seized power," she said, "you'll trample our culture into the dirt. You can't possibly appreciate a fragile art like the ballet." She was right — we didn't know the first thing about ballet. When we saw postcards of ballerinas, we thought they were simply photographs of

25. This paragraph is abridged from Khrushchev's account of his handling of the Plisetskaya case in *KR*, I, 522–524.

women wearing indecent costumes. Sometimes we spoke harshly about Lunacharsky because he spent so much on theaters.[26] We thought his support of the arts was a personal weakness and represented a deviation from Communist norms. Of course, we weren't grown up yet. We were straight out of the factories, mines, and fields, and the arts like the ballet were totally alien to us.

Since then, we've come a long way. Soviet performers, notably ballerinas like Plisetskaya, are recognized the world over. I'm an old man, and I watch television quite often. It makes me proud when I see performances by our musicians. It also makes me glad we did not keep Plisetskaya locked in. By refusing her permission to travel, we would have hurt ourselves.

I can think of two other incidents from my own leadership, both involving pianists, which illustrate how we can rid ourselves of this disgraceful heritage of the closed border, which lies like a chain on the consciousness of the Soviet State.

Comrade Richter, one of our concert pianists, appealed for permission to go abroad as part of a cultural exchange.[27] He wanted to represent the Soviet Union as one of its great musicians. Right away the people around me started shaking their heads and saying it would be risky to send Comrade Richter abroad because of his German background. He had a mother living in West Germany, and people warned me that he probably wanted to be reunited with her.

I had to make a decision. I was informed that Comrade Richter's relations with his mother were cool. I told our collective leadership that I was in favor of allowing him to go abroad. They reminded me there was a chance he wouldn't come back. "So what," I replied. "We've got to take certain risks. Naturally it would be a shame to lose such a great musician, but we simply can't mistrust everybody and suspect everybody of being a traitor. He may very well come back after all, and that would be good propaganda for our culture and our regime. We would be showing the world that we are more free and we trust our people."

I was later told that Comrade Richter did make a trip to West Germany and even saw his mother. But he came back. After that he

26. A. V. Lunacharsky, the USSR's first — and by far the most enlightened — People's Commissar of Enlightenment (or Minister of Culture).
27. Svyatoslav T. Richter gave a concert tour in the US in 1960 and in Western Europe in 1962.

made many trips to different countries, and whenever he returned he brought with him greater glory for Soviet musical art. We handled Ashkenazy in a similar way.[28]

28. Khrushchev has also described his decision to let the pianist Vladimir Ashkenazy live abroad (*KR*, I, 520–521).

6

Housing the People

THROUGHOUT my career, I was concerned with the problem of providing housing for our citizens. I would therefore like to record my reminiscences about my activity in the construction industry of the Soviet Union.

When I was growing up, metalworkers tended to treat construction workers with a certain amount of disdain because the building trade was at such a primitive level. In fact, the people who built houses weren't even considered professional tradesmen. They were usually just peasants who knew how to slap bricks and mortar together. The low level of their class consciousness made them frequent objects of mockery by metalworkers. I remember a joke from my childhood about a construction workers' strike:

The workers decide to go on strike, so they tell their boss what they're planning to do.

"Why strike?" asks the boss. "I'd really rather you stay on the job."

"No, we refuse to work."

"What do you want then?"

"We demand either that you increase our number of workdays or that you reduce our salaries."

"No, fellows, I'm sorry. I can't possibly increase your workdays because God has given us only seven days a week. But I'd be happy to reduce your salaries if you want."

"Oh, thanks, boss!" say the peasants.

That story pretty well sums up the state of the construction industry before the Revolution, and it also partly explains why most young people, myself included, chose to be metalworkers rather than housebuilders.

I got married in 1914, when I was twenty years old. Because I had a highly skilled job, I got an apartment right away.[1] The apartment had a sitting room, kitchen, bedroom, and dining room. Years later, after the Revolution, it was painful for me to remember that as a worker under capitalism I'd had much better living conditions than my fellow workers now living under Soviet power. For a long time after the Revolution, we couldn't satisfy even the most elementary needs of our workers, including those who had served in the Red Army. Young couples would come to us before they got married and ask for an apartment to themselves. Not only were we unable to give them a separate apartment — we often couldn't even find a place for them in a dormitory. Isn't that awful?

Here we'd overthrown the monarchy and the bourgeoisie, we'd won our freedom, but people were living worse than before. No wonder some asked, "What kind of freedom is this? You promised us paradise; maybe we'll reach paradise after death, but we'd like to have at least a taste of it here on earth. We're not making any extravagant demands. Just give us a corner to live in." That situation persisted for thirty years after the Revolution. It was scandalous! How could we expect Soviet man, who'd given his all for the future of socialism and the ultimate victory of Communism, to live in a beehive?

Of course, it was understandable that immediately after fighting a world war, a revolution, and a civil war, we were not able to provide for the demands of our people. The consolidation of our defenses and the buildup of our industry necessarily took precedence over the building of houses. However, what was pardonable right after the Civil War was no longer pardonable decades later.

One factor slowing our progress in housing was that many of our people, especially our peasants, came from very primitive backgrounds. Many had never seen hot running water and didn't know what an indoor toilet was. In other words, they had to run outside whenever they felt the urge. I've known people who didn't even know it was possible to satisfy this urge indoors. The very thought struck them as indecent. They were used to going behind a barn.

I remember in 1920, when our Ninth Kuban Army defeated Deni-

1. Khrushchev's first wife died in the devastating famine of 1921, leaving him with a son, Leonid (who perished in World War II), and a daughter, Yulia. Khrushchev remarried in 1924. His second wife, Nina Petrovna, bore him three children: a son, Sergei, and two daughters, Rada and Yelena.

kin and entered Novorossisk, our regiment, the Seventy-fourth, pushed on to Anapa and from there we seized Taman. In May of that year, my friend Pyotr Kabinet and I were sent to Krasnodar to attend a course run by the political department of our army.[2] We were billeted in a house that had been a school for the daughters of the nobility. We were soldiers full of fighting spirit, but we weren't gentlemen in the old-fashioned sense.

We hadn't been in the dormitory two days before it became impossible even to enter the bathroom. Why? Because the people in our group didn't know how to use it properly. Instead of sitting on the toilet seat so that people could use it after them, they perched like eagles on top of the toilet and mucked the place up terribly. And after we'd put the bathroom out of commission, we set to work on the park nearby. After a week or so, the park was so disgusting it was impossible for anyone to walk there.

At the mine where I worked after the Civil War,[3] there was a latrine, but the miners misused it so badly that you had to enter the latrine on stilts if you didn't want to track filth home to your own apartment at the end of the workday. I remember I was once sent somewhere to install some mining equipment and found the miners living in a barracks with double-deck bunks. It wasn't unusual for the men in the upper bunks simply to urinate over the side.

Some people might ask, "Why is Khrushchev telling us about such unpleasant incidents? Those things happened long ago, and they resulted from the low cultural level of the people." Well, my answer is that such conditions persisted for a long time. It took decades for the people to advance from their primitive habits.

I became somewhat more familiar with the housing and construction business when I went to the Industrial Academy in Moscow. The director of the academy was the late Comrade Kaminsky. I liked him very much. As I've related elsewhere, Kaminsky was arrested and executed during Stalin's butchery of the 1930's, and his wife, too, was jailed for a couple years as the wife of an enemy of the people.[4] Just the other day Kaminsky's widow phoned me to congratu-

2. General A. I. Denikin was commander of the White forces which captured the city of Novorossisk during the Civil War in 1918. The Red Army, of which Khrushchev was a part, defeated Denikin in the northern Caucasus and drove him into the Crimea. The Reds liberated Novorossisk in March, 1920. That year Denikin resigned and went into exile in France.

3. As deputy director of the Rutchenkov mines in Yuzovka.

4. Khrushchev has described his transfer to the Stalin Industrial Academy in Moscow (*KR*, I, 34–35) and the fate of G. M. Kaminsky, a onetime People's Commissar of

late me on my birthday. Her call made me think about the time I spent at the Industrial Academy.

I specialized in metallurgy. The year after I entered the academy, construction engineering was added to the curriculum, so I came into contact with the subject in my meetings with students and faculty members. I remember when the decision first came down from the Central Committee to recruit students who wanted to study construction engineering, it was hard to find anyone willing to switch to that field. I admit I was unenthusiastic about the idea myself. At first, the recruiting was done on a voluntary basis, but the response was so poor that people had to be forced into enrolling in the construction department.

After I left the academy and became Second Secretary of the Moscow Party Committee in 1932, I was directly and intimately concerned with the building industry. I've already related how I supervised the excavation of the Moscow Metro, for which I was awarded the Order of Lenin in 1935. The order had been established in 1930. I believe I was the 110th person to be so honored.[5] So in five years only 110 people in all had been awarded the Order of Lenin. That says something about how highly it was regarded. I think that was as it should have been: the more honor and value attached to the award, the better. Later, the Order of Lenin began to be used more widely, and it diminished in significance.

In addition to supervising the Metro, I was also involved in building new bakeries for the city of Moscow. The construction of bread factories was an epic task. We didn't have many to start with, and the old ones were cramped and dirty. More often than not, they occupied the basements of buildings, and they were crawling with filth, cockroaches and other such charming things. The dough was kneaded by hand. As a result, the whole thing was so unsanitary that people would have lost their appetites — or at least quite a bit of their appetites — if they'd been able to see the conditions in which the loaves they were eating were baked. Gorky described all this well; he'd been a baker once, and the conditions I'm describing are shown in the films about his life.

I remember that when we started setting up big industrialized bread factories, we bought quite a bit of modern equipment in En-

---

Health for the Russian Federation who was liquidated after denouncing Beria at a 1939 Party plenum (*KR*, I, 100).

5. See *KR*, I, 64–70.

gland. And then suddenly an engineer who specialized in building bakeries started work in the Red Presnya District [of Moscow] where I was the head of the Party Committee.[6] We built Bread Factory Number 5 according to his plans. Later this factory bore my name — until a decision was made at my instigation to forbid naming enterprises after living Party and public figures. I proposed that rule, and I think it was a good one.

I remember when Aleksei Maksimovich Gorky returned to the USSR from Italy in 1932; he wanted to see how the construction was going in Moscow.[7] As I just said, he'd been a baker himself, so he was particularly interested in the bakeries we'd built. Kaganovich and I took him on a tour to see the highly mechanized plant at Bread Factory Number 5, which had been built according to Engineer Marsakov's system. Gorky saw how the bakers no longer had to work with their hands; they simply supervised the work of huge machines which literally spewed out loaves of bread. Gorky was so impressed that tears of joy came to his eyes.

As time went on, I became increasingly familiar with the terminology and basic principles of the construction industry. Soon the building specialists began to regard me as someone not at all foreign to their profession. Often I made suggestions, and sometimes they were adopted. My knowledge of engineering came in especially handy when we started putting up new bridges over the Moscow River. Nowadays, when I pass those bridges, I proudly remember my own contribution to construction in our capital city.

We solved three pressing problems during the 1930's in Moscow. We built the Metro, supplied the city with drinking water, and made the river fit for navigation. Before work began on the river, it had been a real cesspool into which human waste from all over Moscow was dumped. I remember that Bulganin and I once inspected the river in a police launch.[8] The stench was so terrible that we had to throw away our clothes afterwards. As is well known, human waste doesn't sink; it floats on the surface. Therefore, cleaning up the Moscow River was a task of the utmost importance.

We got our drinking water from a reservoir near the town of Istra.

6. Khrushchev was promoted to First Secretary of the Red Presnya District in Moscow in 1931, while he was still connected with the Industrial Academy.

7. Gorky returned to Russia from Italy in April, 1932, when Khrushchev was Second Secretary under Kaganovich of the Moscow City Party Committee.

8. Bulganin was Chairman of the City Soviet, or Mayor, of Moscow at that time.

Our methods were still quite primitive in those days. The bulk of our labor force consisted of Belorussian peasants who brought their own horses, carts, picks, and shovels to dig out the reservoir.

We built the Moscow-Volga Canal for the most part with convict labor.[9] Back then, convicts were real criminals and were treated accordingly. Actually, I'd say that on the whole our convicts received fairly humane treatment. They were considered to be the products of capitalist society. Therefore, it was felt that our socialist society should reeducate them rather than punish them. (I almost hate to use this word *reeducate*, since the Chinese have bent it all out of shape. When they talk about "reeducation," they mean the repression of those who have protested against Mao Tse-tung's tyranny.)

As a worker in the Moscow City Party organization, I got to know many of the architects who made possible our accomplishments in the area of, first, improving city services and, later, providing housing for Muscovites. Of course, the houses we built were not palaces, but then neither were the dwellings in pre-Revolutionary Moscow.

The chief architect at the time was Comrade Chernyshev. He's a kind and gentle man — maybe a little too kind and gentle. He has a personality like wax; but he's highly intelligent, and I have the greatest respect for him.[10]

Of all the architects I met, my favorite was Aleksei Viktorovich Shchusev.[11] His stature was comparable to Zheltovsky's.[12] Shchusev and Zheltovsky were the giants of Soviet architecture. Some people preferred one, some preferred the other. Personally, I liked and respected Comrade Shchusev.

I remember when we were discussing the interior design for the first line of the Moscow Metro, Shchusev had some very perceptive things to say about the decoration of the Red Gates Station, which had been designed by the famous Leningrad architect Fomin.[13] Fomin was present during the conversation.

9. The eighty-mile Moscow Canal, which links the capital to the Volga at Ivankovo, north of the city, was built between 1932 and 1937.

10. S. Ye. Chernyshev, chief architect for Moscow from 1934 to 1941, collaborated on the design of the Moscow State University complex of which Khrushchev is so critical below.

11. Shchusev was the designer of the Lenin Mausoleum on Red Square and the nearby Moskva Hotel.

12. I. V. Zheltovsky designed the old American embassy building in Moscow on Mokhovaya Ulitsa, facing Red Square and adjoining the National Hotel.

13. I. A. Fomin designed two Moscow Metro stations: Lermontov (formerly Red Gates) and Sverdlov Square.

"What can I say about this station?" said Shchusev. "The project has been designed and executed by the great master, Academician Fomin. But I can't help observing that at first glance, the interior decoration reminds me of nothing so much as red meat."

Fomin looked as though someone had just poured a bucket of boiling water over him. Anyone who's ever been inside Red Gates Station on the Moscow Metro knows that Comrade Shchusev was absolutely right. Like all our Metro stations, Red Gates is a beautifully decorated historical monument, on which we spent enormous sums from our very limited resources. But, as Comrade Shchusev said, the interior has a dirty red color which can best be described as the color of raw meat.

Zheltovsky had a rather sharp tongue, too. I remember when Molotov called a meeting of our most prominent architects to discuss Langman's blueprint for the new State Planning Commission headquarters. I attended this meeting. Langman worked for the Ministry of State Security. He was, you might say, Yagoda's pet architect.[14]

Molotov asked Zheltovsky's opinion about the design of the new building. Zheltovsky always had a slightly sour expression, and his face was very wrinkled. We used to call him The Pope behind his back.

"What can I say about this project?" he said. "I guess I'd have to say that it's acceptable but most undistinguished." He took the display board on which the plan was pasted up and turned it upside down. "Maybe we could just as well build the Planning Commission offices upside down. What do you think? I don't think anyone will know the difference."

Well, you can imagine how Langman felt. He got very angry and defensive. After the meeting broke up, Molotov and I stayed behind.

"What do you think we should do?" asked Molotov.

"I think we should go ahead and accept Langman's plan despite Zheltovsky's criticism. Of course Zheltovsky is right about the design of the building; but given its function, I don't think looks matter much. If we send the project back to the drawing board, the designers might do something like stick a statue of a woman on top of

14. A. Ya. Langman had collaborated with Fomin on a number of projects. Police Chief G. G. Yagoda was both the first supervisor and an eventual victim of the purges in the 1930's. Molotov was then Chairman of the Council of People's Commissars (Prime Minister).

the building or in front of it, but the basic plans will probably stay the same."

When the building was finished, I don't think it bothered anyone aesthetically. It's a perfectly acceptable building.

As I look back on my first years in Moscow, I remember them as exciting but difficult times. As far as material circumstances were concerned, people were still not very well provided for. I won't try to draw any conclusions from the contrast between the way I lived as a worker in the Donbass before the Revolution and as a Party worker in Moscow a dozen years after the Revolution, although I won't deny that I often brooded over the contrast at the time.

I'd earned forty to forty-five rubles a month as a metal fitter before the Revolution; dark bread cost two kopeks a pound, and white bread cost five kopeks a pound. Lard was twenty-two kopeks a pound, eggs one kopek apiece, and the kind of good-quality shoes I have on now cost only six or seven rubles. Suffice it to say that after the Revolution, wages were much lower and prices were much higher.

We didn't let ourselves get discouraged by the physical hardships of life. We used to talk about how we "worked ourselves into a frenzy," even when that frenzy meant giving up our free time and our personal lives — all for the sake of socialism, for the Revolution, for the working class, and for the future. If some people still had to live in conditions of semistarvation, we could still look to the future. Our vision of the future knew no bounds. Our dream was a good dream, a creative and inspiring one. It inspired us to accept a Spartan life and self-sacrifice, and it inspired us to throw ourselves ferociously into the job of improving the material conditions in which our citizens lived. First and foremost, this meant building houses — building, building, building!

However, the construction of residential buildings didn't receive the priority in the 1930's that it did after the war and during the years when I was head of the Party and the government.

During the first years after Stalin sent me to the Ukraine, I had little chance to concern myself with construction. Stalin specifically ordered me to concentrate on agriculture, and I knew better than to disobey Stalin's orders. But after the war, I had no choice but to devote considerable energy and attention to the job of reconstructing

Kiev, which had suffered terrible destruction at the hands of the German occupiers. Shortly after they seized the city, the Hitlerites had
blown up the Kreshchatik, which is the main street in Kiev. It was
one of their Gestapo tricks to make the local populace think the
explosion was an act of sabotage by Ukrainian partisans and thus
sway the citizens of Kiev into cooperating with the Germans. Shevchenko University in Kiev burned down before my very eyes just as
we were liberating the city. The university library was also destroyed. In short, there was a lot of rebuilding to be done.

I invited a number of Moscow architects to come to Kiev for a discussion on how to reconstruct the Kreshchatik and some of the city's
architectural monuments. Among those who came were Aleksei Vik-
terovich Shchusev and Victor Petrovich Mordvinov. The latter was a
marvelous architect and an old Communist who had joined the party
during the Civil War.[15]

I threw myself into the task of reconstructing Kiev. I wanted our
work to be an example to the other cities of the Ukraine. We drew on
volunteers and, later, German prisoners of war to clear the rubble.
There was a desperate need not only for the restoration of municipal
services, but for housing as well.

We were woefully short of building materials, especially bricks,
mortar, and paint; but we didn't let that stop us. With the help of
hard-working, imaginative mechanical engineers like Comrade Ghe-
rard and Comrade Abramovich, we made great progress in a short
time. The main architect on the project was Aleksandr Vasilyevich
Vlasov.

I know there are people who criticize the job we did, saying the
decorations we put up on the Kreshchatik were cheap stuff, but I
don't care. I think the Kreshchatik was beautiful when we finished
with it, and many others agree. I've always loved Kiev, and I'm
proud that I contributed my small share to the rebuilding of its main
street.

My experience in Kiev helped prepare me for the work which was
waiting for me in Moscow.

I think I've already described the circumstances under which I
was recalled to Moscow.[16] It happened in the midst of our struggle

15. Mordvinov was active in the reconstruction of Moscow in the 1930's, especially
in developing rapid techniques for the erection of residential blocks. He was president of the Academy of Architects after the war.

16. Khrushchev described the circumstances of his own recall to Moscow in *KR*, I,
246.

against the Ukrainian nationalists. The Carpathian Mountains were literally out of bounds for us because from behind every bush, from behind every tree, at every turn of the road, a government official was in danger of a terrorist attack.

I had gone into the countryside to address a student rally after the assassination of the writer Galan.[17] While speaking at this rally, I was handed a note which said that Stalin was trying to reach me by phone. I hurried to the temporary quarters which had been set up for me in Lvov and called Moscow.

Stalin told me to drop everything and come to the capital the next day. Our conversation was brief, and I started worrying that I was in for a bad time. I've already described how I'd fallen into disfavor with Stalin after the bad harvest of 1946.[18] I couldn't help feeling anxious about what was in store for me when I got back to Moscow.

I think Malenkov and Beria realized I must have been nervous about being summoned at such short notice and without explanation.[19] Even Beria was capable of sympathy sometimes — although I wouldn't say it was human sympathy because his motives were always strictly selfish. He would often try to butter up a comrade who was in trouble with Stalin in order to lure that comrade into supporting Beria in his intrigues. Beria at that time was already maneuvering to take over [after Stalin] as head of the Party and the government.

Malenkov was a little better. He phoned me up just before I left for Moscow and said, "Don't worry. I can't tell you now why you're being recalled, but I promise, you've got nothing to fear."

I was genuinely touched by Malenkov's call.

When I got to Moscow, I found that I was to take over from Popov as head of the Moscow Party organization.

The major problem facing us at that time was housing. Under Popov and Promyslov, the technological level of the construction industry in the capital was pathetically low.[20] Tools were primitive.

---

17. Ya. A. Galan, a Ukrainian writer who actively supported the incorporation of the Western Ukraine into the USSR, was assassinated by Ukrainian nationalists in Lvov in October, 1949.

18. See *KR*, I, 236–243.

19. Malenkov was Stalin's deputy on the Council of Ministers; Beria was in charge of the security forces.

20. G. M. Popov was Khrushchev's predecessor as postwar Moscow Party chief. V. F. Promyslov, a civil engineer, was an official responsible for construction attached to the Moscow City Executive Committee. In 1963 he became Chairman of the Executive Committee.

Much of the work had to be done by hand. Wood was being used where, in the Ukraine, we would have used concrete or tile. Therefore, even though enormous manpower was being expended on housing construction in Moscow, the results were far from adequate. Most of the residential buildings going up were one- or two-story barracks.

I decided to have Comrade Sadovsky transferred to Moscow. He was one of our best construction experts in the Ukraine. He wasn't much of an administrator, but he was a first-rate engineer; and he had excellent contacts with the scientific community. I liked him very much. Even nowadays he gives me a call from time to time. It always makes me happy to hear his voice and to swap memories about our days together in Kiev and Moscow.

Sadovsky and I dealt closely with the State Building Administration, which was headed by a highly respected construction engineer named Sokolov whom I'd known from work on the Metro in the 1930's. Like myself, he's now retired. I've met his son a couple of times, and once, when this young man and his wife were visiting Sokolov at his dacha nearby on the Moscow River, they came over to see me in a rowboat. Sokolov's son is an architect by training, but he's now working as a painter. He and our cosmonaut Leonov have collaborated on several pictures about outer space.[21] They even organized an exhibition, at which young Sokolov very kindly presented me with an album of his paintings.

Not long after I arrived in Moscow, Comrade Sokolov and I had a number of meetings on the possible application of prefabricated reinforced concrete, an idea of which my old friend Professor Mikhailov had been a strong advocate.[22] I was in favor of using it in our construction campaign, but to my surprise Comrade Sokolov resisted the idea. I think he even took his complaints to Beria, who was then in charge of construction for the Central Committee. Naturally, Beria opposed my idea; he came out against anything new proposed by other members of the Politbureau. More than once he vigorously

21. A. A. Leonov and P. I. Belyayev were launched into orbit aboard the Voskhod 2 in March, 1965, and Leonov made the first space walk.

22. M. I. Mikhailov was a professor of communications engineering and director of technical sciences at the Plekhanov Economic Institute in Moscow. Khrushchev says in the Russian original of these memoirs that he had been an admirer of Mikhailov's since the 1930's and had summoned Mikhailov to Kiev after the war to consult with him on the reconstruction of the Ukrainian capital.

quashed a new idea, then turned around and presented it to Stalin as his own.

On what grounds did Sokolov oppose my suggestion that we use prefabricated reinforced concrete? His argument was that he'd recently been on a trip to the United States and hadn't seen any reinforced concrete in use there. He said that if the Americans weren't using it, it must not be a progressive building technique.

I took up my proposal with Academician Keldysh — not the president [of the Academy of Sciences], but his father — who was our biggest authority on concrete.[23] He too disagreed with me. In fact, only Sadovsky supported me.

I was determined not to give up. I decided to take my proposal directly to Stalin. I knew I'd better be well prepared because Beria would oppose me, and he would enlist Sokolov's opinion on his side. So I instructed Sadovsky to prepare a detailed, cogently argued recommendation. I drafted a covering memorandum of my own in which I mentioned that the State Building Administration opposed prefabricated concrete on the grounds that it hadn't been implemented abroad. Then I sent Sadovsky's report and my memorandum to Stalin.

When I next saw Stalin, I asked him about the dispute over concrete and reminded him of my recommendation.

He looked me straight in the eye and said, "I've read your memorandum."

"And Sadovsky's recommendation, too?"

"Yes, I read it in full."

"And what do you think?"

"I think your conclusions are correct, and I support your proposal."

I was glad. We immediately began to put my proposal into action. On Stalin's instructions, two experimental concrete plants were built. We had so few qualified building engineers for the job that we had to borrow a group of specialists from a Moscow machine-tool factory called Red Proletarian.

It was in the midst of our feverish efforts to make these concrete plants operational that I discovered how badly loused up our cement industry was. I think Kaganovich was largely to blame for that state

---

23. V. M. Keldysh, an architect and specialist in iron-reinforced concrete structures, who was the father of M. V. Keldysh, president of the Academy of Sciences.

of affairs. Kaganovich, of course, wasn't a bad administrator, but his favorite technique for dealing with people was browbeating and highhandedness. He was Minister of Building Materials, and he loved to blab about his achievements to Stalin. He introduced varieties of cement so that when he reported to Stalin he could brag about some "new, improved brand." Frankly, I think the good old-fashioned mortar we inherited from our fathers was much better suited for bricklaying than Kaganovich's newfangled concoctions.

Once we were on our way to solving the problem of building materials, the question of architecture arose. Architects are as much artists as they are craftsmen. They're in favor of maximum flexibility; and they want every building to have a distinctive appearance. I, too, am all for flexibility and distinctiveness — but within certain limits. The looks of a building are important, but I don't think the architecture should bowl you over or look too exotic.

The introduction of prefabricated reinforced concrete into our building industry was not warmly greeted by our architects because the elements of our new buildings began to be mass-produced. This meant that the architects were somewhat more limited in their ability to express their individuality. Inevitably, certain conflicts cropped up from time to time.

However, I don't want to give the impression that I failed to appreciate the architects with whom I dealt. I hope any of them who someday read my memoirs will know that I valued them highly. My dear friends, please forgive me if I was ever harsh with you. I tried to learn as much from you as possible, and I just hope that you understand the position I was in. We desperately needed houses for our populace, and sometimes we had no choice but to meet that need at the expense of architectural initiative.

Stalin, in the last years of his life, played his own role in determining the architectural character of Moscow. He came up with the idea that we must build skyscrapers all around the city. He once said in my presence: "We've won the war and are recognized the world over as the glorious victors. We must be ready for an influx of foreign visitors. What will happen if they walk around Moscow and find no skyscrapers? They will make unfavorable comparisons with capitalist cities."

At Stalin's orders, the skyscrapers were built. When they were finished, our engineers and architects reported that the rent would have to be very high in order to pay for the maintenance of the buildings. The rent was so high that not a single inhabitant of Moscow could possibly afford to live in them, so Stalin decided to reduce the rent somewhat so the apartments could be assigned to certain prominent and well-paid actors, scientists, and writers. The whole thing was pretty stupid, if you ask me. You'd never find capitalists building skyscrapers like ours.

As for the architectural style of the buildings, I don't have a single good word for it. Take Moscow State University for example. Approaching it from a distance, someone who doesn't know better might think it's a church. He sees huge spires and cupolas on the horizon, silhouetted against the sky. From a long way off, the central spire looks just like a cross. When you get closer, the whole complex looks like an ugly, formless mass. I'm not against all skyscrapers — it's just that I think the design of a structure should correspond to its function. I'm proud of having participated in the decision to build the CMEA [Comecon] headquarters, for instance. The trouble with Moscow University is that it doesn't serve the function Stalin assigned to it. He wanted to impress people with the university's grandeur. But it's precisely grandeur that the building lacks.

And what a waste of money! For the same amount it cost to build Moscow University, we could have built ordinary buildings that would have housed three times as many students.

Unfortunately, this waste of money goes on. I think the people responsible should be punished for squandering our limited resources when so much of our population is in desperate need of housing. I understand that in Kiev they've built something as elaborate as the Palace of Congresses in Moscow. I'm told that the new building in Kiev is even more lavishly decorated than the Palace of Congresses. How many millions did it cost? I shudder to think.

I know some people believe I've been too tightfisted about spending money on certain kinds of buildings. Once I met a man from Kiev who told me, "Shelest spoke at a conference recently, and he said, 'Khrushchev wouldn't let us build a beautiful underground restaurant in Kiev.' " [24] I don't doubt that our architects could build a per-

---

24. P. Ye. Shelest was First Secretary of the Ukrainian Party after 1963 and a Politbureau member after 1966 until his abrupt demotion in 1972. One of the hardest of the "hard-liners," he was reported to be the leading Politbureau advocate of the 1968 invasion of Czechoslovakia.

fectly charming underground restaurant, but we've got plenty of space aboveground, so why not build a normal restaurant for one fifth what it costs to build one underground?

I just remembered a story I'd like to tell to all those smart alecks. An archbishop went on a tour of his diocese. According to protocol, the church bells rang out to greet him in each village. Finally he arrived at one town where there was no sound of bells. The archbishop reprimanded the priest who came out to meet him: "Tell me, Father, why haven't you prepared the appropriate ceremony for me?" The priest replied that he had eleven good reasons why there had been no bell-ringing ceremony. He enumerated the first ten reasons and then added, "Besides, Your Grace, we don't have any bells in our church here." I'd like to remind some of those unprincipled politicians that we'd better make sure we have bells in our church towers before we start any fancy celebrations. In other words, we'd better make sure our people have adequate housing before we build underground restaurants.

There's no excuse for us still to be in such desperate straits so many decades after the Revolution.

It wasn't until Stalin's death that the leadership really faced up to the problem of how serious our housing shortage was. Once Stalin was dead, there was a realignment of force in the new leadership, and people began expressing their needs in a more open manner. After Beria's arrest and trial, our people began to feel freer. For the first time, they received an opportunity to exercise their inalienable right to express their desires and their dissatisfactions. It is essential that people enjoy their inalienable rights here in the Soviet Union just as in every other state. It was for these rights that thousands and thousands — even millions, ten million or more — of our citizens paid with their lives in Stalin's jails and camps.

After Stalin's death, Beria demonstrated his "generosity" by letting out a lot of criminals. He wanted to show off his "liberalism." However, in actual fact, this action of his was directed against the people because these criminals who got out of jail went right back to their old trades — thieving and murdering. The people began to express their dissatisfaction, especially over housing conditions. I remember once, not too long after the new leadership had begun to get its feet on the ground, that Molotov addressed a meeting of the Presidium about housing problems. There was panic in his voice as he said,

"There's great dissatisfaction in Moscow over housing conditions!"

You'd have thought he'd been born only yesterday. He acted as though he'd just learned that people were living in overcrowded, vermin-infested, intolerable conditions, often two families to a room. At one of these Presidium meetings, I suggested we centralize our construction administration. Molotov literally exploded with rage: "How can you suggest such a thing? Here we are with an acute shortage of dwellings, and you want to liquidate all the building administrations in the city and put them under one authority. What makes you think that a single organization will do a better job than all these separate ones?"

Obviously, here was someone who didn't know the first thing about construction, nor did he understand the latest theories about division of labor and other progressive management techniques. It was a stormy meeting. The other comrades expressed their views. In the end, they supported me. When Molotov saw he was beaten, he withdrew his objections, and my proposal was approved unanimously.

Slowly but surely we made progress in the struggle for improved housing conditions. We began to subject all aspects of the problem to scrupulous analysis. Take, for example, the question about the best dimensions for an apartment. We had been building apartments with ceilings over three meters high, but we learned from the experience of other countries that it was better to build ceilings only two and a half meters high. I remember once in Finland asking a home owner, who also happened to be a house builder, why they built lower ceilings abroad. He explained that since you only have a limited amount of material, it's better to maximize floor space, rather than the height of the ceiling, so that a family can spread out. Of course, there's nothing luxurious about a two-and-a-half-meter ceiling, and from a medical point of view, a higher ceiling allows better circulation of air; that's why aristocrats used to build palaces with huge halls and high ceilings. But ask any housewife: she'll tell you she'd rather have a little lower ceiling and more floor space. So we changed our building standard from 3.2 meters to either 2.5 or 2.7 meters.

Then there were problems about how many apartments of what size to build and how long people would have to wait for them. I wasn't deaf, so I heard expressions of dissatisfaction. No one likes having to wait ten or fifteen years for an apartment of his own, and everyone prefers an apartment building with a lift, just as everyone prefers an apartment with a bath to one with just a shower. So you have to decide: do you build a thousand adequate apartments or seven hundred very good ones? And would a citizen rather settle for an adequate apartment now, or wait ten or fifteen years for a very good one? The leadership must proceed from the principle of using available material resources to satisfy the needs of the people as soon as possible.

I think ours has been a good record. In its eight hundred years of existence, pre-Revolutionary Moscow had accumulated 11 million square meters of dwelling space. By the end of 1949, when I was transferred from Kiev, another 400,000 square meters had been built. In 1950 we began building up momentum. Despite the fact that the major share of our resources were diverted into defense in the Cold War because of the threat posed by Eisenhower and his shadow Dulles, we were able to build a total of 3.8 million square meters of dwelling space during the time I worked in the collective leadership.

I'm pleased and proud that during my time we made such progress toward satisfying our needs. Of course, there were many difficulties and abuses — bureaucratism, sloppiness, and perversions in the distribution system. For example, we once discovered that some people were receiving new apartments not on the basis of need but on the basis of other considerations.[25] This kind of thing still goes on. I was watching television not long ago and saw a program called "Our Neighbors"; the show was about some people moving into a new apartment and getting hit up for bribes by the builders. I put more blame on people who extort graft than on those who end up having to pay. We punished anyone we caught who allowed this kind of thing to happen, and we made the trade unions and the workers themselves responsible for the distribution of new apartments since there's only so much the administrators can do all by themselves. Despite all the rules and regulations, we failed to liquidate all the evils — but, as I say, we made genuine progress.

We would have made more progress if our citizens had been more demanding in asserting their rights — rights they're entitled to exer-

25. By "other considerations," Khrushchev presumably means influence as well as bribery.

cise in our Soviet state as conceived by Lenin. Our citizens must know the laws and not allow bureaucrats to set up obstacles in the way of improving the conditions in which people live.

We also might have made more progress if the work done by our construction industry had been of higher quality. I used to make inspection tours of houses supposedly ready to be turned over to Muscovites, and I must say the shabby workmanship often made me indignant. The walls would be dirty; there were stains on the wallpapers. Sometimes we'd even find a palm print left by some worker, so our criminal investigators could track down the person responsible.

But what can you do? Sophistication is not acquired overnight. You can't make things work just by going around and delivering speeches and giving orders. A lot depends on the background and training of the workers themselves. I remember Mikoyan and I once went to inspect the interior of an apartment building. We ran into an Armenian who was laying tiles in the bathroom. He'd learned his trade in France and was a real artist. Unfortunately, we had all too few workers like him.

I remember when I was in Moscow I spent a lot of time studying the efforts of some of our builders to put in new plaster panels between apartments in residential buildings so that the walls wouldn't conduct sound from one apartment to another. This was a great event in the cause of housing our citizens. I know people will say, "There goes Khrushchev getting carried away with all sorts of details about housing construction." Well, these things I'm talking about aren't details. They're decisive matters in the building of homes for our people to live in. Only workers actually in the profession can imagine how much time and energy we used up trying to get a proper plastering job done with manual labor — and unskilled manual labor at that. Plastering was left to comrades who had only just arrived on the building sites, more often than not from the villages. So it was no surprise when they messed up the job. It was like what the icon painters used to say when they sold icons which were badly done.

I've always liked that story about the peasant who went to buy himself a Virgin Mary. He hunted and hunted, but all the icons were terrible. Finally he found one he could live with, but when the icon painter quoted him a price, the peasant said, "How can you ask a price like that for a cock-eyed Virgin Mary? Can't you see her eyes are painted crooked?" The icon painter replied, "It's not my fault. Some of the youngsters in my shop were mucking around with the paint one night." It was the same thing with us: our inexperienced construction workers from the villages just mucked around with plaster. And they were supposed to be building houses for people, for people to live in!

Toward the end of my career as a politician and a statesman, we made a decision in the government to build better houses with more modern conveniences. I discussed this plan with Comrade Posokhin, our chief architect for Moscow. He's the one who designed the Palace of Congresses, a building I liked very much. I couldn't understand why the Lenin Prize Committee failed to recognize its merits. I remember the government had to intervene in favor of Comrade Posokhin.[26]

I suggested that he design some high-rise apartments of approximately sixteen stories. He cautioned me that my plan exceeded established norms. I replied that we were past the point when we should be satisfied building just four- or five-story apartment buildings. We'd reached the state where we should be able to equip our apartment buildings not only with elevators, but with quiet elevators — the kind that don't shake the whole building when the doors slam. The Finns could make such elevators. We'd already installed some in the Palace of Congresses.

Thus, when I was the head of the government and the Central Committee, we made a decision to advance to a new stage of housing construction. I'm proud to have participated in this decision. Now that I'm retired, I see these high-rise apartments all over Moscow.

During the last elections for the Moscow Soviet, I turned on my television and watched the broadcast of a preelection meeting at which Promyslov was speaking. He's now the Chairman of the Moscow Soviet. "Comrades," he was saying, "soon we'll be building nothing but high-rise apartments. Up until now, we've been building only five-story houses, but that's because we were acting on orders from above."

It made me bitter to hear this blabbermouth — especially since I

26. M. V. Posokhin, head of the architectural and planning board of the Moscow City Executive Committee until 1963, when he became Chairman of the State Committee for Civic Construction and Architecture. He designed the Kremlin Palace of Congresses in 1961 and won the Lenin Prize in 1962.

used to promote him and respect him. I'd like to have a chance to remind Promyslov about the bedbug-ridden hellholes he was responsible for building when he was in charge of construction for Moscow in 1949, before I even arrived on the scene. What did Promyslov mean, "orders from above"? If he meant Khrushchev, then I gladly accept responsibility for the policies I followed in supervising the construction of houses in Moscow. To use the words of John Reed, we "shook the world" with our massive program to build housing for our people.[27] At first the capitalists made fun of our troubles. But we put an end to their laughter by showing them we were capable of clearing away the jungle of various housing offices, laying down the foundations for centralized housing administration, and setting out to put roofs over all our people's heads and give them comfortable conditions in which to live.

27. John Reed was a leftist American journalist and the author of *Ten Days That Shook the World,* an eyewitness account of the Russian Revolution. He is buried beside the Kremlin wall.

7

Feeding the People

Virgin Lands

PEOPLE often ask me what I do, now that I'm retired. I reply that in the spring and summer, I grow vegetables and flowers to fill the vacuum which surrounds me after a life of stormy political activity. A couple of years ago I even went mushroom hunting. I would have never done such a thing before I became a pensioner, but sometimes I get so bored I could howl like a wolf. So I went mushrooming out of sheer boredom. I did it in order not to turn into a wolf. I work in my garden for the same reason.

Nowadays, when I meet with friends, we often talk about agriculture. The subject also comes up frequently in conversations with chance acquaintances. People know about my deep interest in farming and my dedication to the advancement of Soviet agriculture. It hasn't been easy for me to keep abreast of latest developments since my direct involvement in affairs of state was terminated over six years ago. Nevertheless, even in retirement, I avidly follow press and radio reports on the subject.

The weather today is warm and bright. The date is June 14. According to the old calendar, it is the beginning of summer, while according to the new calendar, thirteen days of summer have already gone down the drain.[1] Personally, I've always preferred spring to summer, and I've never agreed with the many people who like autumn best of all. Autumn may be wonderful because man reaps the

1. The "old" calendar is the Julian, used until the Russian Revolution and replaced by the "new," or Gregorian, calendar, which is ten days ahead of the Julian.

bountiful rewards of nature as a result of his labors, but I still think spring is the most pleasant season.

They've promised good weather today for Muscovites to enjoy. Yesterday it rained, and we even had a hailstorm. Part of my garden was hit by the hail, the other part was spared. Some of the flowers were badly damaged by a handful of hailstones, while other flowers, less than a meter away, weren't even touched. Hail never cuts a wide path of destruction. It does much less damage to crops than drought. A drought can condemn a whole country to famine, such as we suffered in the Ukraine after the war.

That's how it is in nature: you never know what to expect. Therefore agriculture is the most capricious sphere of the economy; harvests can fluctuate dramatically from one year to the next. Agriculture is also the most complex branch of the economy because it means dealing with living organisms rather than just machines.

I'd like to speak now about the development of our agriculture. It's a complicated subject, one in which I was closely and constantly involved during my years first as a member, then as the head, of our country's leadership.

I've been active in agriculture through most of my career. In 1935, when I became First Secretary of the Moscow Regional Party Committee (replacing Kaganovich, who was appointed People's Commissar of Transportation), I took on the responsibility for agriculture in the Moscow Region. Up until then — first as Secretary of the Bauman District Party Committee in Moscow, then as Secretary of the Red Presnya District, and as of 1932, Second Secretary of the Moscow City Party Committee — I'd been primarily concerned with industry and municipal services.

When I say that starting in 1935 I was responsible for agriculture in the Moscow Region, I should make clear that my major concern was supplying Moscow with food products, not actually managing agriculture. The Moscow Region had relatively few cultivated areas. For the most part, these farms produced cabbage, beets and carrots in quantities too small to satisfy the needs of the capital. We had to import much of our food from Belorussia, from the Ukraine, and from other parts of the Russian Federation.

Our difficulties in providing food were a direct result of Stalin's victory over his opponents in the campaign to collectivize agriculture. Stalin forced collectivization on our farmers by police methods.

His policy was an utter perversion of the principles Lenin had bequeathed to us when he died. When Lenin said that only through cooperation could we develop our agriculture, he had something very different in mind from the Stalinist means employed during collectivization. Lenin knew that before you could organize the peasants, you had to provide a material and organizational base; you had to have enough machinery and enough trained cadres. Only then could you proceed.

But Stalin completely forgot what Lenin had said. Even though he called himself a Leninist, Stalin perverted Lenin's principles by imposing collectivization without the proper preparation. (Stalin was very critical of Lenin. Toward the end of his life, when he lost control over what he was saying, he allowed himself to speak badly of Lenin. Of course, this was only in a very narrow circle within the leadership.)

As a result of Stalin's form of collectivization, we experienced severe shortages in Moscow. Other parts of the country suffered terrible famine. Even potatoes and cabbages, which had been the cheapest staples before the Revolution, became scarce because of Stalin's unreasonable agricultural policies. The shelves of state stores were empty. Peasants couldn't bring anything to the peasant markets because private trade was outlawed.

We were back to rationing — just like the period after the Civil War, before the institution of the New Economic Policy.[2] We were back to food requisitioning, only now it was called a tax. Then there was something called "overfulfilling the quota." What did that mean? It meant that a Party secretary would go to a collective farm and determine how much grain the collective farmers would need for their own purposes and how much they had to turn over to the State. Often, not even the local Party committee would determine procurements; the State itself would set a quota for a whole district. As a result, all too frequently the peasants would have to turn everything over they produced — literally everything! Naturally, since they received no compensation whatsoever for their work, they lost interest in the collective farm and concentrated instead on their private plots to feed their families.

If only we'd been able to implement Lenin's plan for the develop-

2. In 1921 Lenin instituted his New Economic Policy, encouraging private enterprise as a device to restore morale and productivity, especially in agriculture. The NEP remained in force until 1926, two years after Lenin's death. See *KR*, I, 20–21.

ment of agriculture, we would have been much better off. Unfortunately, Lenin's ideas were put into practice by a barbarian, by Stalin. Consequently, a lot of damage was done to our country. Many innocent people perished, people who followed the Party line, who went out to work on the collective farms and did the best they could. Hundreds of thousands of lives were lost — maybe even millions. I can't give an exact figure because no one was keeping count. All we knew was that people were dying in enormous numbers.[3]

Certain theoreticians and even literary figures in our country have taken a Stalinist position with regard to collectivization; they have chosen to look at collectivization through Stalin's eyes. These people are now saying that collectivization represented a historically inevitable period of transition from capitalist production in the countryside to a socialist economy; they say that this process inevitably required sacrifices — and that the loss of lives was justified as long as it was on the altar of socialist progress.

What nonsense! What a foolish rationalization of murder and the perversion of Leninist policy. Unfortunately, such rationalizations can be found in our literature, both in works of history and in works of fiction. Some of the authors I'm talking about are still alive and well — and writing from the same point of view.

Nevertheless, I think the time will come when historians will properly analyze the issue of collectivization. I'm sure that when that time comes, historians will be able to find sufficient material to make an objective assessment. In addition to our own experience here in the Soviet Union, they will be able to draw on examples of collectivization in the German Democratic Republic, Czechoslovakia, Bulgaria, Rumania, and elsewhere. In general, collectivization in those countries was based on Leninist principles and therefore achieved great success. There were, of course, cases of revolt and sabotage — I'm thinking particularly of Rumania.[4] But there were nowhere near as many victims as in our country. Even the worst troubles with collectivization in other countries were a far cry from what happened in the Soviet Union under Stalin.

By 1938, when I was transferred to the Ukraine, collectivization

3. With collectivization of agriculture, enforced by massive police terror, Stalin swung the pendulum to the opposite extreme from the relative permissiveness and liberalism of the NEP. See *KR*, I, 71–75.
4. Collectivization in Rumania was a gradual process, carried out in stages. While it elicited local disturbances and resistance, there were no major or widespread riots.

had been completed, and agriculture had been put back on its feet. We were producing our agricultural machinery in large quantities — although not large enough to meet all the needs of the Ukraine.

I arrived there after Academician Williams's grasslands theory had already been adopted. According to Williams, crops should be rotated with clover or some other grass which would enrich the soil with the nitrogen accumulated in its roots, thus serving as a natural fertilizer.

Williams's major opponent was Academician Pryanishnikov, who argued in favor of mineral fertilizer. Pryanishnikov didn't deny that clover and other grasses would improve the soil, but he felt that our farmers should rely first and foremost on mineral fertilizers. He insisted that we should build special machines to process the soil. Accordingly, Pryanishnikov was in favor of shallow tillage.

Williams rejected shallow tillage out of hand. He said that all who advocated it were "wreckers of socialist agriculture." There was one scientist — a Ukrainian agronomist — who designed a special plow for shallow tillage. I think he worked at a Saratov research institute. Well, he was branded an enemy of the people and a wrecker. Later he was arrested, convicted, and shot.

In short, Williams won an unconditional victory over Pryanishnikov and his other opponents. Academician Pryanishnikov himself was not persecuted. At least he survived the terrible Stalinist years and died a natural death after the war. However, his approach to tilling was not recognized or accepted.[5]

Why did Williams prevail over Pryanishnikov? Why did the majority, including Stalin, come out in favor of Williams? The reason had nothing to do with an objective analysis of the relative merits of the two theories; instead, the debate was decided essentially on the basis of capital investments. Pryanishnikov's theory of mineral ferti-

5. Despite his English surname, V. R. Williams (or Vilyams) was a Moscow-born Party member. An agronomist and soil expert, he was an official of the State Planning Commission and Agriculture Ministry. Khrushchev issued a decree repudiating Williams's grasslands plan for the Ukraine in 1962.

D. N. Pryanishnikov was a specialist in agrochemistry and plant physiology; he died in 1948.

The unnamed Ukrainian agronomist referred to in this passage was probably Academician N. I. Vavilov, who quarreled with T. D. Lysenko over agricultural policy and was arrested as a British spy. He was incarcerated in a labor camp near Saratov and died in a Moscow prison.

Note: this section supplements Khrushchev's abbreviated account of the shallow tillage controversy in *KR*, I, 241–242.

lizers would have required enormous capital investments in order to build fertilizer plants and new machinery. We were short of capital at the time and so Williams's theory was more attractive. That's how Williams's grasslands theory came to reign supreme. There were even special government decrees on the subject.

Personally, I had nothing but the greatest respect for Williams. Who knows how many laudatory speeches I made about him? I knew him personally. He was one of our first academicians to join the Party. Not only was he valued as an ideological comrade-in-arms — he was greatly valued as a scientist as well. And he arrived at his theory on the basis of scientific research, so I can't hold him to blame for his grasslands theory.

However, the fact of the matter is that Williams's system didn't work. Even after it had been consistently implemented throughout the Ukraine, there was no improvement in our agricultural production. We were getting the same yields as before. Everything, as the peasants used to say, depended on the Lord God.

It's now clear that in order to get high yields, you have to use mineral fertilizer, to say nothing of soil processing and irrigation.

In short, Pryanishnikov was right and Williams was wrong. Pryanishnikov's theory, which was never recognized during his lifetime, was more sound and more realistic than Williams's. It would have meant a real revolution in our agriculture. Looking back, I saw the great damage that had been inflicted on Ukrainian agriculture because of Williams's grasslands theory. Despite all the times I had spoken in praise of Williams and in support of his system, I had to renounce my own words and admit my mistake. Having belatedly acknowledged that Pryanishnikov was closer to the truth than Williams, we dug Academician Pryanishnikov's notes out of the archives and adopted his theory.

I've already recalled the terrible destruction caused by World War II. I hardly need to remind anyone of it. Our people remember all too well the devastation which the Hitlerite occupiers left in their path. It stretched from the Caucasus, to Volgograd, to Saratov and Moscow, all the way to Leningrad. The whole of Belorussia and enormous regions of the Russian Federation were stripped of their industry and agriculture. The first years after the war were a time of skyrocketing prices and, once again, ration cards.

In the Ukraine, where I was First Secretary of the Communist

Party and Chairman of the Council of People's Commissars, we were in a disastrous situation, especially in 1946 and '47. In addition to being deprived of our best young men and much of our equipment, we suffered a drought and a bad harvest. As a result, there was famine and cannibalism.

The Ukraine was in a terrible way. So was Moldavia. I remember that Kosygin dealt with problems of food rationing, so Stalin sent him to Moldavia.[6] When Kosygin returned to Moscow, he reported to Stalin that there was widespread starvation in Moldavia and that people were suffering from dystrophy, or malnutrition. Stalin blew up and shouted at Kosygin.

For a long time afterwards, when Stalin would see Kosygin, he would laugh and say, "Well, well! If it isn't Brother Dystrophic!" Stalin called him that because Kosygin was so thin. Once Stalin had come up with that nickname for Kosygin, certain others in our circle naturally started copying him. Pretty soon many people were calling Kosygin "Brother Dystrophic."

Even after the Central Committee Plenum of 1947, we continued to experience severe setbacks and shortages.[7] Average annual wheat procurements remained at the level of about two billion pood [36.1 million tons]. Once we couldn't even reach the two billion mark and had to settle for 1.87 billion. That amount satisfied our immediate need for food products, but it left us nothing for the necessary grain reserves.

Why did our agriculture lag so far behind our industry? Why were we so at the mercy of the capriciousness of nature and the fluctuation of harvests that I mentioned above? Stalin deserves much of the blame. He taught us to think of agriculture as a third-rate branch of our economy.

For Stalin, peasants were scum. He had no respect for them or their work. He thought the only way to get farmers to produce was to put pressure on them. Under Stalin, state procurements were forcibly requisitioned from the countryside to feed the cities.

Farmers were paid less for their goods than it cost them to produce. Sometimes just transporting produce from the collective farm to the state collection center cost more than the farmers received for

6. A. N. Kosygin, the present Prime Minister, was then Deputy Prime Minister and a candidate member of the Politbureau.

7. The Central Committee Plenum on agriculture of February, 1947, is described in *KR*, I, 235–239.

their goods. For example, the procurement prices Stalin set for potatoes were literally nothing more than symbolic. The State used to pay three kopeks a kilo.

No wonder peasants weren't interested in working on collective farms. Collective farmers were plunged into the most pathetic conditions. Some were paid about one kopek per workday — others might be paid nothing at all. It sounds strange, doesn't it? [8]

Morale and discipline on the farms hit rock bottom. Potatoes can be a high-yield crop if properly handled, but our peasants had no incentive at all. They were forced to support themselves at subsistence level by raising a few vegetables in their private plots.

On top of the outrageously low prices he set for the peasants' produce, Stalin also proposed that the collective farmers pay a special tax on any fruit trees they planted in private orchards. I remember a conversation I once had with Stalin about this tax. I told him I'd been to see a cousin of mine who lived in Dubovitsa. She told me she was going to have to chop down her apple trees in the fall.

"But why?" I exclaimed. "You have such wonderful apple trees."

"Yes, I know, but with this new tax, it will be too expensive for me to keep them. You see, the neighbors' children often come over and pluck the apples, so I don't get all the fruit myself."

When I told Stalin this story, he asked me what I thought about the tax, and I came up with the idea that we should let collective farmers go ahead and plant fruit trees on their private plots without being penalized. Stalin would hear none of it.[9] The tax on private orchards remained as long as Stalin was alive. Why? Because Stalin considered peasants on collective farms to be like sheep whose wool has to be shorn as soon as it reaches a certain length. Stalin added insult to injury. His low price scales had already deprived the peasants of any material incentive to produce food on the collective farms. Now he

8. A "workday" was a unit of labor on a collective farm. After the harvest the profit would be divided into the total workdays, and each peasant would receive his payment in accordance with the number of workdays he had contributed. Thus, collective farmers, unlike factory workers, did not have fixed incomes. In case of a crop failure, they would not be paid at all.

9. Khrushchev told a more detailed version of this story in public speeches during his career. He said that the exchange with Stalin took place in 1946. Stalin reacted to Khrushchev's suggestion about doing away with the tax by angrily calling him a *narodnik*, a term which designates nineteenth-century populist reformers whom the Bolsheviks disdained as bourgeois liberals.

was depriving them of the motivation to produce a little extra food on the side.

Speaking of incentives — or I should say, the lack of them — I remember during my first year of work in Moscow after the war, I made an inspection tour of the Yegoryevsk Region. I was especially interested in having a look at a wretchedly poor collective farm that was run by a Party man from the city. He was intelligent and well educated, but he was a lawyer by training; he didn't know the first thing about agriculture. He'd simply been sent out into the countryside by the local Party committee.

"Tell me," I asked, "what's your best crop here?"

"Oats."

I couldn't believe my ears. I knew that the soil on this collective farm was so sandy it was barely arable. "Are you trying to tell me you get a high yield of oats around here?"

"No, we get a very low yield."

"Then why do you say oats is your best crop?"

"Because it's the easiest to harvest."

This man's cynicism stemmed from a lack of material incentive. His salary was completely independent of how much his farm produced. You might say, "Here's Khrushchev, playing up an isolated instance in which a single Party member showed himself to be unresponsive to agitation and propaganda."

Well, I can assure you that this collective farm chairman was *not* an exception. He didn't represent the rule either, but all too frequently I encountered men like him, Communists who'd been sent out from the city to help the peasants but who didn't give a damn about doing their job because nothing was done to motivate them.

Unfortunately, material incentive hasn't been used much as an instrument to spur agricultural production. Compensation for collective farmers has only in small part been determined by their productivity.

I realize that by publicly advocating material incentives I'm opening myself up to those know-it-alls who will say our people should be motivated not by money but by ideological considerations. That's nonsense. I'm old enough to know from experience that the majority of collective-farm administrators who are paid a flat salary won't take any chances for the sake of improving production. Stalin refused to acknowledge that fact, and so did some of the people who were in the leadership at the same time I was. The main thing in the struggle for socialism is the productivity of labor. For socialism to be victorious, a country must get the most out of every worker. And when I say "get the most," I don't mean by force.

Another reason for the failure of our agriculture to keep pace with the rest of our economy after the war was too much bureaucracy. Actually, this problem had been with us since before the war. I remember how indignant and annoyed I was when I got to the Ukraine in 1938 and had to deal with an unwieldy and inefficient agricultural administration. The enormous People's Commissariat of Agriculture was primitively organized and wasted staggering amounts of manpower and resources. All decisions had to be cleared through the ministry: what to sow, when to sow, how to sow, when to harvest, and so forth.

I don't for a minute deny the necessity of administration. I haven't forgotten Lenin's words, "socialism is management," but Lenin had in mind that the managers should serve socialism — not the other way around.[10] When I was in the Ukraine both before and after the war, we were forever receiving from the ministry memos and directives that almost invariably ran counter to our understanding of what should be done. Sometimes the ministry's communications were a total waste of our time and energy, such as when the ministry sent us instructions on how to sow our sugar beet crop well after the seeds were already in the ground. That kind of thing happened more than once.

Every bulky administrative apparatus must somehow justify its existence. It does so by grinding out telegrams, dispatching inspectors every which way, quoting cable references back and forth, keeping track of the ministry's own expenses, and issuing proclamations which often came down to platitudes like "one should drink only boiled water."

I remember when Mikoyan was Deputy Chairman of the Council of People's Commissars, he had an excellent agronomist named Starozhuk working for him.[11] Comrade Starozhuk made frequent

10. "Socialism is management": *sotsializm — uchyot*, sometimes translated "socialism is accountancy."

11. Mikoyan became Deputy Prime Minister in 1937 and held the post for two tenures: 1937–55 and 1957–58. Throughout his career he was closely involved in food production. Before becoming Deputy Prime Minister he had been People's Commissar of Supply and People's Commissar of the Food Industry.

Shortly after World War II commissariats and commissars were renamed ministries and ministers, although Khrushchev tends to use the terms interchangeably.

visits to the Ukraine to advise us on the cultivation of sugar beets, a subject on which he was an expert. First, he'd send us a long telegram, signed by Mikoyan, detailing what we should do. Then he'd show up in Kiev, and I'd have to tell him, "Comrade Starozhuk, we've done everything according to your instructions. In fact, we've finished what needed to be done. What's the point in your coming down here to supervise?"

I also asked myself what point there was in the Commissariat's having a sugar beet expert at all, when we were perfectly capable of growing and harvesting the crop on our own? The answer was simply that the Commissariat, like all bureaucratic machines, couldn't stop setting up unnecessary posts and churning out paper work, regardless of how much manpower and money was wasted in the process.

During my work in the Ukraine, and later when I moved to Moscow and assumed responsibility for agriculture, I learned at first hand how poorly organized our research organizations were. I remember in 1950 I went to the Ramensk district to inspect an institute that specialized in potatoes. I had a talk with the woman who ran the place, and she gave me the most pathetic report on the institute's "achievements."

"What yield are you getting from your experimental potato fields here?"

She answered, "Sixty quintals per hectare [2.7 tons per acre]."

"What!? That's horrible! Don't you know there are farms right around here which get 100 to 120 quintals per hectare? How do you expect to be able to advise our farmers if you get half the yield they do?"

Poor thing, she hadn't expected such a reaction. Tears came to her eyes, and she sobbed, "We've been looking forward to your visit with such pleasure, and now you come here and say such unpleasant things to us." I don't think anybody had ever before told her truthfully what a miserable job her institute was doing.

Here were these learned agronomists producing 60 quintals of potatoes per hectare while — according to newspaper accounts at the time — a simple peasant woman named Utkina out in Siberia was reporting a potato harvest of 1,000 quintals per hectare. (Of course, you never know about such stories. There's often a lot of exaggerating and even cheating.) I knew from my own experience in the

Ukraine in 1938 that one woman collective farmer had received the Order of Lenin for getting nearly 700 quintals per hectare.

The point was: I saw with my own eyes that many of our government research institutes were sorely inadequate. The state funded these organizations and paid their researchers the same salary regardless of whether they did their work poorly or well.

The institutes also tended to be overstaffed, which led to an atmosphere of irresponsibility. I'll never forget what my aide Shevchenko told me about a conversation he had with the famous Kharkov agronomist Yuryev, who died not long ago.[12] Comrade Shevchenko came into Yuryev's study and found him deep in thought.

"You must be pondering some important scientific problem," said Shevchenko.

"You could say that, I suppose," replied Yuryev. "I'm trying to figure out how we can get rid of a certain researcher. He has his doctorate in agricultural sciences, but he's a hopeless loafer. Yet there are rules which prevent me from firing him."

Of course, I'm all in favor of rules which protect people from administrative and bureaucratic persecution, but there are certain irresponsible types who exploit these rules and do damage to our socialist system. I'm thinking of the loafers, the charlatans, and the toadies who overcrowd our institutes, bloating the staffs and gobbling up state funds without giving anything in return. They're just so much dead weight. From my own experience both in the Ukraine and in Moscow, I knew we should clear them out and make room for the real scholars who would make a genuine contribution to the cause of getting Soviet agriculture out of the quagmire in which it's been bogged down for so long. I could see that with the proper technological guidance, we might be able to raise the level of advancement — and thereby the productivity and standard of living — of our peasantry.

It used to drive me crazy to see how unsophisticated our farmers were. The fertilizer we produced was of terribly low quality, often of only 10 percent concentration, but it was better than nothing. We delivered it to the collective farms, and what happened? More often than not the peasants let it rot next to the railroad station. For two or

12. A. S. Shevchenko was Khrushchev's longtime principal staff assistant and ghost writer. In 1964 he wrote an introduction to the Soviet edition of *Seven Days in May*. V. Ya. Yuryev, a selectionist and plant physiologist, was director of the Kharkov Selectionism Station.

three years, the stuff would sit there in a huge pile, serving as a perfect slide for the kids in the winter. Why didn't the peasants use the mineral fertilizer we sent them? Because they didn't know anything about it. The only fertilizer they understood and trusted was manure, and insufficient efforts were made to elevate their level of understanding.

Such was the pathetic state of our agriculture in the postwar years.

One possible answer to some of the problems facing us was specialization. The leadership made some tentative steps in this direction during Stalin's last years, but they were the wrong steps. For example, a special ministry was set up to look after the Machine and Tractor Stations.[13]

The first Tractor Stations had been created a long time ago at the suggestion of an agronomist in the Odessa area.[14] They were considered a practical and progressive measure and later spread throughout the Soviet Union. But like many measures which made sense when applied to a specific situation and place, the Machine and Tractor Stations got out of hand. The system was tearing our agriculture apart by depriving our farmers of the machinery they needed to work their farms. In other words, the people directly responsible for agricultural production were cut off from the means of production.

The idea of establishing a separate MTS ministry was Molotov's, and it was approved by Stalin.

After Stalin's death, the new leadership assigned me to supervise agriculture. We quickly discovered that farming lagged even more seriously behind the rest of our economy than we'd realized. At first we set two billion pood [36.1 million tons] of wheat as our target for state procurements. That figure was more or less based on calculations we'd used under Stalin, when wheat procurements were running from 1.2 to 1.8 billion pood annually. However, soon we found that not even three billion was sufficient to meet our needs.

You might ask, "How come two billion was enough under Stalin, while three billion was insufficient only a few years later, after Stalin's death?"

The explanation is simple. Once Stalin was dead, people's mouths were unlocked. They began to state their needs more openly, with-

13. A Machine and Tractor Station, or MTS, was a state-run pool of heavy agricultural equipment which performed sowing and harvesting for nearby farms in exchange for a share of the crop.

14. The first MTS in the Soviet Union was introduced in 1928 at the Taras Shevchenko State Farm near Odessa.

out glancing nervously over their shoulders to see if someone was going to throw them in jail. So it wasn't a matter of the demand for food increasing so much as it was the increase in freedom to speak about the demand.

Not that people could all of a sudden say anything which came into their heads as loudly as they wanted. Unfortunately, some of the old Stalinist threats still hung over people; there were cases of imprisonment and persecution. But the atmosphere was better than it had been under Stalin.

Not long after Stalin's death we arranged a special meeting. Malenkov tried to press me into making a report on agriculture, but I refused. I didn't want to make a speech containing specific proposals about what we should do. I had in mind the proposals I wanted to make, but I couldn't yet substantiate them with concrete arguments. I should mention here that Malenkov then had more influence in the Presidium than the rest of us.[15] However, the other comrades didn't consider him an expert on farming. I, for one, knew how ill equipped he was to deal with agricultural policy. Even Malenkov himself acknowledged his limitations in this regard.

Later the Central Committee met in plenary session to concentrate on the problems of agriculture. For many years afterwards these meetings were referred to as a turning point in the development of our economy. I was assigned the job of delivering the main address.[16] We finally faced up to the peasants' need for material, as well as political, incentives. When I say "material" incentives, I mean real, financial benefits to compensate them for extra labor and reward them for increased production. Members of the Central Committee had an opportunity to express their opinions on this subject freely.

We changed [raised] procurement prices for potatoes and vegeta-

15. After Stalin's death, Malenkov was briefly both Party First Secretary and Prime Minister, although he was relieved of his functions within the Central Committee Secretariat. While Malenkov occupied the limelight as head of the Party and the government, Khrushchev gave up his job as First Secretary of the Moscow Region in order, according to official announcements at the time, to "concentrate on his work in the Secretariat." It was there, in the Secretariat, that Khrushchev built up his power base from which to move against Malenkov.

16. In these paragraphs Khrushchev is referring to a number of different meetings which took place as the dead dictator's would-be successors jockeyed for position. Stalin died in March, 1953. In August there was a budgetary session of the Supreme Soviet at which agriculture was an important item on the agenda. In September the Central Committee held a special plenum devoted to agriculture. At that time Khrushchev succeeded in replacing Malenkov as First Secretary of the Party.

bles. Although the new prices substantially improved the financial condition of the collective farms, they weren't in themselves sufficient to serve as a proper material incentive for the stimulation of production. We also passed a resolution rescinding the tax on private orchards and vegetable patches. I remember that shortly after the Plenum, Malenkov and I were vacationing in the Crimea, so I suggested we go visit a collective farm nearby. One of the peasants we met had nothing but praise for our decision to rescind the tax on private produce. "You were wise to do away with that tax," he said. "Unfortunately, for me it's too late. Right before the Plenum I chopped down all my peach trees."

Later we went on to abolish the system of forced deliveries, whereby peasants had to turn over to the state a certain portion of the meat, eggs, and other goods they produced on their private plots. But by far the most important accomplishment of the Central Committee was our decision to set in motion the Virgin Lands campaign.[17] In our search for ways to increase production, we thought up the idea of bringing under cultivation the enormous expanses of fallow but arable lands in the eastern parts of the USSR. I don't know why we'd never come up with this plan before. Already during Stalin's time we'd had trouble making ends meet, yet for reasons he never explained, Stalin was dead set against the cultivation of new territories. He probably figured that if the peasants were not allowed to farm new lands, they would have to make do with the lands they had — and as a result, out of necessity, they would improve their skills and increase their production.

I'd heard about great opportunities for growing grain in the far reaches of Kazakhstan, so during the Plenum I had a talk with the First Secretary of the Kazakh Communist Party, Comrade Shayakhmetov. I asked him how much land in his Republic was fit for cultivation and what sort of yield the Kazakhs had been getting from their farms. From his answers, I could tell he wasn't being sincere with me. He was deliberately underestimating the possibilities for expansion. In other words, he was clearly trying to convince me that only a small portion of the Virgin Lands in Kazakhstan were arable. He said we might be able to expand cultivation by a little more than three million hectares [7.4 + million acres].

17. At another plenum in February and March, 1954, the Central Committee adopted a proposal made by Khrushchev to cultivate 101,207,000 acres in Soviet Central Asia and Siberia between 1954 and 1960.

Frankly, that sounded encouraging to me. With an average productivity of 10 quintals per hectare [892 pounds per acre], I figured we should get more than three million pood of wheat. That amount was nothing to sniff at then, and it's nothing to sniff at today, either.

After my conversation with Shayakhmetov, I had talks with various regional Party secretaries from Kazakhstan. They knew more than Shayakhmetov about the potential of their lands, and they seemed more sincere in their conversations with me than he had been. These Kazakhs told me that, given high-quality seed, they could get a yield of at least 15 or 16, and perhaps even 20, quintals per hectare.

I was convinced that we could — and should — bring the Virgin Lands of Kazakhstan under cultivation. Our agronomists at the Ministry of Agriculture and the State Planning Commission supplied me with additional information about the Virgin Lands in other parts of the country, particularly in the Altai and Orenburg regions.

The Plenum passed a resolution calling for the expansion of our cultivated lands by 8 to 10 million hectares [20 to 25 million acres]. We arrived at that figure despite the objections of First Secretary Shayakhmetov, who kept arguing for a more modest goal.

After the Plenum, I tried to find out why Shayakhmetov had taken such an [obstructionist] attitude. I formed the opinion that he had political motives for trying to discourage the Virgin Lands campaign. It was my increasingly strong impression — and the other comrades in the leadership agreed with me — that Shayakhmetov was infected by the virus of nationalism. Since Kazakhstan was underpopulated, he was afraid that the expansion of cultivation would necessarily mean an influx of [non-Kazakh farmers] into his Republic. We decided to replace Shayakhmetov with Comrade Ponomarenko, who was an experienced and reliable administrator. He'd received his formal training as a railroad engineer, but he was well qualified in agricultural administration and political work. We also replaced Shayakhmetov's colleague Afonov, the Second Secretary of the Kazakh Central Committee. His post was taken over by Brezhnev, who'd had experience as First Secretary of the Moldavian Communist Party.[18]

Even though we made the correct decision in 1953 to expand our lands under cultivation, there was lingering hesitation and resistance in the leadership. People like Molotov started picking holes in the

18. P. K. Ponomarenko and L. I. Brezhnev, who were both proteges of Khrushchev's, replaced R. O. Shayakhmetov and I. I. Afonov, both Kazakhs, at the head of the Kazakh Party in February, 1954.

idea, asking all sorts of questions, demanding special explanations. Molotov was a schematist and a conservative; he was a total ignoramus about farming, but that didn't stop him from objecting that the Virgin Lands campaign was premature and too expensive.

Molotov and others said we should concentrate instead on raising the productivity of the lands that were already under cultivation. They argued in favor of the "intensification," as opposed to "extensification," of agriculture, but their arguments sounded hollow because the people making them didn't know what they were talking about. They couldn't see that intensification meant developing our agriculture for the future — while we needed bread today, not tomorrow.

In principle, I'm in favor of the intensive development of agriculture, but it requires both a highly advanced farm labor force and enormous material resources. We had neither. The people who advocated intensification rather than extensification were mistaken in thinking that we could bypass or shortcut the process of accumulating sufficient resources and qualified personnel.

In addition to those who stubbornly argued for intensification, we also had to deal with objections on the part of those people who represented the more heavily populated regions of Kazakhstan and other areas from which resources were to be diverted in order to develop the Virgin Lands.

But despite these disagreements, the decisions of the Plenum were put into practice. We had to decide whether to begin drafting people to work the Virgin Lands right away in 1954. There was a lot of work to be done: settlements had to be built and the land had to be opened up and put to plow. But whom should we send?

I presented my comrades with the following proposal: "Let's appeal to our Soviet youth, to our Communist Youth League. I'm sure that hundreds of thousands of young people will respond if it's a matter of providing our country with grain. We'll remind them of the days of hardship and sacrifice during the war. The same spirit of sacrifice will be required, although the development of the Virgin Lands won't be as hard as the war. Our young people will be paid for their labor, and they will have the great moral satisfaction of knowing that they are contributing to the wealth of our country and satisfying our citizens' need for bread, milk, and meat.

"We can get tents from the army reserve for the young people to live in when they get to Kazakhstan, and we'll also provide them with tractors, even if it means diverting newly manufactured tractors which have been designated for other republics. Collective farms in cultivated regions will have to make do with the machinery they already have."

My proposal was accepted. I remember young people who expressed a desire to go to the Virgin Lands gathered for a public rally in the main hall of the Supreme Soviet at the Kremlin. The leadership suggested I make a speech. Some of the youths spoke too. I can't remember what they said, but I can recall vividly the enthusiastic glow on their faces. These were young people ready to make any sacrifice for the sake of their Motherland and for the sake of socialism. Their contribution will never be forgotten.

The youth brigades began arriving in Kazakhstan in the early spring, before the snow had melted. I saw a film showing tractors dragging sleds loaded with building materials and personal belongings through the snow and mud. The young people lived in tents like soldiers on the march.

I asked my comrades in the leadership to let me make a tour of Kazakhstan. I wanted to get a clearer idea of the conditions under which people were living and working out there. My comrades agreed, so I flew there.

That trip gave me my first chance to see what that part of our country was like. I was struck by the wide-open spaces. Sometimes I would have to drive for hours before I would come to a settlement of tents near a plowed field. Sometimes I'd be driving along and see a tractor like a tiny speck on the horizon. The people in Kazakhstan used to say a tractor driver could have breakfast at one end of a field, lunch at the other end, and dinner back where he'd started out in the morning.

It was extremely hard for the young people who went to Kazakhstan to get used to the isolation in the steppes. They had to keep reminding themselves that they were living out in the middle of nowhere for the sake of their country. By and large, they accepted the loneliness and hardship with pride and dignity.

Of course, there were a lot of funny stories and jokes about the shortage of girls. I remember one settlement I visited where there was only one young woman. One of the men — obviously the joker in the group — said, "Comrade Khrushchev, life out here is terribly tedious. Here are all of us guys, but there's only one girl. We all court her, but she'll have nothing to do with any of us. Please, Comrade Khrushchev, send us some more girls!"

We all laughed, and so did the girl. When I got back to Moscow, I spoke to the leadership of the Communist Youth League about the complaint I had heard. "Make a special effort to recruit more girls," I said. "Tell them they won't have any trouble finding either a job or a husband out there."

As I expected, that argument worked. We still had many more women than men in our country because so many men were killed in World War II. As a result, it was hard for young women to find husbands; but there were plenty of prospective husbands in the Virgin Lands.

A few years later, when I went back to Kazakhstan, I saw houses with gardens where there had been only tents before. The farms had begun to look like permanent settlements rather than outposts in the wilderness.

The grain yield in the Virgin Lands averaged about 12 or 14 quintals per hectare [1,000 to 1,300 pounds per acre]. We considered that a good yield for such high-risk territories. Our economists had estimated that as little as 5 quintals per hectare would be sufficient to make the farms there profitable. As it turned out, the Virgin Lands proved to be a real treasure trove for us; they gave us a big return on our investment.

We undertook certain organizational measures in the Virgin Lands, such as setting them aside as a separate region with its capital at Tselinograd.[19] The Virgin Lands region was given administrative autonomy and funded directly by the All-Union government. We didn't want to channel our investments through the Republic [that is, Kazakh] government or planning commission because we were afraid that resources earmarked for the Virgin Lands might end up in other branches of the Kazakh economy. Such a temptation always exists, so we decided to bypass the Republic administration.

As is inevitably the case with a large-scale undertaking, not everything went smoothly with the Virgin Lands. Among the problems that came up, certain regions which had been designated for cultivation turned out to be barren. But often such setbacks could be rec-

19. In March, 1961, the Kazakh regional capital of Akmolinsk was renamed Tselinograd, from the Russian word *tselina*, meaning virgin soil.

tified. There was enough land in Kazakhstan so that when one stretch proved infertile, we would simply mark it off and look for a new stretch. Also, we sent delegations to Canada, where wheat is grown in terrain much like that of Kazakhstan; our delegations learned many lessons from the Canadians about how to cultivate wheat in high-risk areas.

The problem of transportation took time to solve. For a long time the harvested grain was simply piled up in the fields. We didn't even have enough sacks to carry the wheat, and our trucks were inadequate, too. The roads were so bumpy that much of the crop was strewn along the side and lost. But as time went by, we built roads, railroads, and granaries, so that the wheat could be properly stored and moved to the state collection centers as quickly as possible.

During one of my tours of the Virgin Lands, I had a most interesting conversation with an agronomist at a Machine and Tractor Station. He was a Siberian with a typically Ukrainian name.[20] He suggested that we convert collective farms in the Virgin Lands into state farms. He explained that the Machine and Tractor Stations were plowing, sowing, fertilizing, and harvesting the fields on the collective farms and then sharing the crop with the collective farmers as compensation for the work they'd supposedly done.

"If you incorporated the collective farmers into state farms, you could simply pay them in cash as state employees rather than sharing the crop with them. All the wheat would go to the State for distribution. That way the State would receive more wheat at lower cost."

At first, I resisted the idea, but during our conversation this agronomist opened my eyes to the inefficiency of having a Machine and Tractor Station provide the mechanization for a collective farm which concentrates on one grain crop. If tractors and machinery do everything, and there's virtually no manual labor left over for the collective farmers to do themselves, what's the point in having a collective farm at all? Better that the personnel from the MTS and collective farm, along with the farm equipment from the MTS, should be brought together in a single agricultural enterprise — namely a state farm.

When I got back to Moscow, I told my comrades about the agronomist's suggestion. We also held talks with the Kazakh leadership. In the end, we decided that the agronomist was absolutely right. In the

20. The agronomist in question was I. Vinichenko.

case of one-crop farms, we changed our policy from using collective farms with separate Machine and Tractor Stations as the basic organizational unit and started relying on state farms instead.

I suggested we transfer control of the Machine and Tractor Stations directly to the collective farms [in the case of multicrop enterprises]. Molotov blew his stack at that idea. He ranted and raved about how we were resorting to "anti-Marxist measures" and "destroying our socialist achievements." What nonsense. Hadn't we had enough stupid slogans about agriculture? I remember how Zinoviev started promoting the slogan, "a horse for every horseless peasant," back in the twenties. That was stupid because we had millions of horseless peasants and no extra horses to go around. In order to counterbalance Zinoviev, Stalin came up with the idea of switching to a seven-hour workday. Stalin knew as well as anyone else that our economy couldn't stand a seven-hour day, so as soon as he'd established himself as a petty tyrant and dictator without any regard for democratic political norms — and as soon as the Zinoviev opposition had been removed — Stalin went back on his own proposal and again pushed the eight-hour workday.[21]

So you see, fancy-sounding slogans are often motivated by political considerations and have nothing to do with reality. That was certainly the case with Molotov's objection to my proposal on Machine and Tractor Stations as "anti-Marxist." There's not a single word in Marxist-Leninist theory which says that separate Machine and Tractor Stations are a necessary condition for the development of socialism.[22]

It had become completely intolerable to separate the management of agricultural machinery from the collective farms. This separation had inflicted enough damage on our economy already, so we liquidated it. I don't think you can find a single person with common sense about agriculture and economics who would consider our decision incorrect.

21. G. E. Zinoviev was one of the founders of the Soviet state. An early rival and victim of Stalin's, he was executed in 1936 after the first of the great show trials.

22. Except for one-crop enterprises, Khrushchev steadfastly favored collective farms over state farms. Collective farms were virtually the only autonomous units of economic production in the Soviet Union, while state farms were directly responsible to the Ministry of Agriculture. Molotov and Khrushchev's other opponents argued that collective farms must not be allowed to have their own heavy machinery — otherwise they would become too independent of state control. Khrushchev prevailed over this objection. In 1958, after Molotov's removal as a result of the Anti-Party Group affair, Khrushchev was able to pass a measure authorizing that MTS's be dissolved and their heavy agricultural equipment sold to the collective farms.

People who have worked with me know that I was in favor of enlarged collective farms. I felt that small collective farms — that is, enterprises with small amounts of land and small labor forces — had no future because it was impossible for them to introduce highly efficient mechanization. Therefore we had to reorganize the small collective farms in order to allow the utilization of modern technology.

Of course, in the pursuit of this goal, we experienced both success and disappointment. We failed to avoid a certain mania for giantism, and this mania cost us dearly. It wasn't my fault, although probably I should have kept a closer watch to prevent overzealousness on the part of certain people who had unrealistic standards for defining a small, average, or large collective farm. If you want to see where the problem of giantism can lead, look at China: the Chinese drove whole provinces into single, huge communes. Under such conditions, a collective farm becomes an unmanageable, highly inefficient agricultural enterprise. As I say, we made certain errors in the direction of giantism ourselves.

Nevertheless, slowly but surely, we met and solved many of the problems facing us. One year we encountered terrible dust storms, but our scientists devised a way of guarding against that disaster.[23] I'm thinking here of protective planting, which involves a lot of hard work but pays off in the end.

Despite all the difficulties and setbacks, Kazakhstan rapidly evolved from an area of high-risk agriculture to become the breadbasket of our country. I'm proud to have had an opportunity to extend cultivation to lands which had never before been tilled. It was by no means an easy decision to make, but it was certainly the correct one if you considered the alternatives.

Once the Virgin Lands began to yield grain, we found that we had a surplus of both bread and cattle feed, although our reserves were modest: they never reached the desired level, which would have been nearly a full year's supply. However, we were lucky to have any reserves at all when the disastrous harvest of 1963 hit us. It would have been an even worse catastrophe had it not been for the wheat we'd brought in from the Virgin Lands the year before. In the bad year of 1963 the Virgin Lands alone yielded 400 million pood [7.2 million tons] of grain, which was half the annual procurement of Stalin's time.

Nineteen sixty-three may have been a terrible year, but we recov-

23. In June, 1960, the USSR was hit by the worst dust storms in over thirty years.

ered well in 1964. The forecasts for the harvest were promising. We discussed the agricultural situation in the leadership, and I expressed a wish to make another visit to the Virgin Lands. No one objected, so off I flew to Kazakhstan. A special train took me around to see the farms in areas where a plane could not even land. I wanted to see for myself how the farmers were doing. We had good reason to expect an incredibly rich harvest.

At one point I was informed that an English publisher named Thomson wanted to see me.[24] I gladly agreed. He owned 150 newspapers. I thought it might be useful for an objective witness to see with his own eyes what was happening in Kazakhstan. The bourgeois press had been writing quite a bit about the Virgin Lands, and it wasn't always the truth; the bourgeoisie can't help but look at the Soviet Union through dark glasses, which make everything look gloomy. At my invitation, Thomson joined me aboard my special train as we went from village to village.

During my tour of Kazakhstan, I experienced the greatest joy of my life. Perhaps that was appropriate, for 1964 marked my farewell to a long political career as a Party leader and statesman.

Everywhere I went I saw fields of wheat stretching as far as the eye could see. The wheatfields rolled like waves in the wind. And everywhere there was the sweet smell of good, honest sweat. The farmers laughed as they toiled in the fields. They were happy because they knew that they were laboring for the good of their country — and because a rich harvest meant high incomes for them. I saw that villages had sprung up; there were simple but cozy houses with children playing and flowers growing in front of them.

I thought back to the first time I'd ever heard about these lands. It was in my early youth, in 1908, when migrants left for the East from the province where I lived. They didn't go from my own village of Kalinovka, but they went from Shishkino, where my mother's sister lived. I used to visit the village. I knew my aunt and the peasants among whom she lived. At the age of fourteen, I used to work the plow behind a team of bullocks on the Vasilchenkov estate. It was hard work for a boy of my age.

One day when we were out collecting nuts, we noticed there was a

24. Lord (Kenneth Roy) Thomson, publisher of *The Times* (London), joined Khrushchev aboard the Soviet leader's private train for a tour of state farms in Kazakhstan in August, 1964.

fire in Shishkino. We ran into town to help and found that my aunt's house was burning. Later, people said that the fire had been started by peasants who were leaving to migrate to Kazakhstan. In those days it wasn't called Kazakhstan; it was called Siberia. My aunt's husband saw the new lands to the east. We heard that there was as much land as a peasant could possibly want; but it would take great physical strength and material means to develop, and the peasants were terribly poor.

All these memories came back to me as I toured the Virgin Lands in 1964. What had been impossible under the tsars became possible under Soviet power. As I toured the steppes of Kazakhstan, those lines of Nekrasov kept running through my head:

I've seen a miracle, Sasha!
A handful of Russians, condemned as schismatics, has been exiled
  into the God-forsaken wilds.
They've been given the freedom to work the land.
A year has passed unnoticed.
Civil servants come out to supervise.
See? Already there's a village, barns, sheds and granaries, and a
  hammer strikes an anvil in the blacksmith's shop.
Thus, gradually, in half a century a huge settlement grows up.
Man's will and toil work wondrous wonders! [25]

What Nekrasov thought would take half a century took only three or four years in our Soviet era. Not only did we introduce the blacksmith's hammer to the Virgin Lands — we introduced tractors, combine harvesters, trucks, schools, and hospitals. And all this I saw with my own eyes during my tour of the Virgin Lands.

Just talking about what I experienced in Kazakhstan makes me feel the joy and excitement all over again. How I love to immerse myself in those memories! The Virgin Lands campaign showed us how mighty our Party could be if it only had the trust of the people. In fact, the Virgin Lands have been our salvation. Take this year, for example. We've had no precipitation, not even in the Moscow Region. I'm a truck farmer myself, and I can see how my own little garden is suffering. Of course, I'm joking a lot in my memoirs about being a

25. From N. A. Nekrasov's "The Grandfather," published in 1870. Khrushchev quoted from another Nekrasov poem, "Sasha," when describing his feelings toward Svetlana Alliluyeva in *KR*, I, 294.

truck farmer, but it's not funny when our country has to get by without rainfall. The Virgin Lands have given us the ability to get over even the worst periods, and that's no joke.

Naturally, when I got back to Moscow, I kept a close watch on the procurement figures as they started coming in. I was especially interested in how Kazakhstan would do. Because of the Virgin Lands campaign, Kazakhstan had already replaced the Ukraine as the second largest grain producer after the Russian Federation.

Our bureau of statistics compiled the data coming in from local administrators and reported to me. It looked as though we were going to bring in about a billion pood in state procurements from Kazakhstan alone, perhaps even more. At the very least, we could count on 900 to 950 million.

Nineteen sixty-four turned out to be the best year ever for the Virgin Lands. We had special reason to rejoice because 1964 came right after "the hungry year" of 1963. I'm putting "hungry year" in quotation marks because we didn't have a literal famine in 1963, but the situation was undeniably serious.

The total procurement for the whole country in 1964 was probably somewhere around four billion pood. It was certainly no less than 3.5 billion. By our standards, that's a record. Our needs were estimated at from 1.8 to 2 billion pood of high-grade wheat, so the 1964 harvest produced a surplus which would have lasted for almost six months.

I can't speak with absolute certainty about the 1964 harvest because the final figures were never published. A statistical record came out recently, and I asked my friends to buy one for me. I wanted to check if 1964 was, as I suspected, a record year. But guess what? The figures for 1964 are missing. You can find all the data for the five-year periods and for the individual years 1961, 1962, 1963, 1965, 1966, and so on — but not for 1964. [The leadership] obviously has something to hide. I believe that thanks to the Virgin Lands campaign, 1964 was indeed a record year — and subsequent harvests haven't even come close to matching it.

I've been reading in the newspapers about how our agriculture is improving all the time. Well, I should hope so. After all, our country is continually accumulating new material resources and technological expertise, so it would be inexcusable if the situation weren't improving.

Nevertheless, you can't be too sure about what you read in the newspaper or hear on the radio. For instance, I have my doubts about the official report that the 1970 harvest produced an average yield of 15.4 quintals per hectare; that's only slightly under the yield of 16 quintals per hectare that farmers get in the United States.

Having lived under Stalin, I tend to think that the figures for average yield which you read in the press these days reflect wishful thinking rather than reality. I remember how Stalin used to treat Comrade Saveliev, who was head of the committee which determined average yield. If Stalin was unhappy with Comrade Saveliev's report, he'd glower at him like a boa constrictor about to devour a rabbit. Stalin would pat himself on the belly and say, "The rich, black soil of the Ukraine comes up to here; are you trying to tell me you can't get a better yield than such-and-such? You're going too soft on the collective farms! I'm sure the average yield must be at least half again what you say."

In other words, Stalin arbitrarily dictated the average yield. Nowadays it isn't that bad, but I still don't trust our bureau of statistics. I think there remains a tendency among our statisticians to conceal setbacks and tell the leadership what it wants to hear. I know some of these statistical experts. They're the sort who can me't shit into bullets.[26] They're clever at hiding the truth. Sometimes they bury the truth so deep in a report that you can't possibly dig it out.

When I read in the paper that the 1970 harvest had an average yield of 15.4 quintals per hectare, my suspicions are aroused that some sycophant has been buttering up his boss. No matter what they say in the papers, I'm still convinced that our harvest in 1964, with wheat procurements of more than four billion pood and an average yield of 10.5 to 11 quintals per hectare, was far better than any harvest before and better than most if not all since.

In the Virgin Lands, our farmers specialized in growing wheat, a crop in which I took a great personal interest. If I were the chairman of a collective farm, there's no question but that I would cultivate wheat rather than corn because wheat is far less troublesome and more nourishing as a food crop. But corn is terribly important as fodder for our livestock. As the capitalist countries discovered before we did, corn is the best basic ingredient for silage; it is nature's number one cattle feed. I think I was correct in recognizing this fact myself

26. This is a variation of the Russian colloquialism "to make shit into candy," meaning to tell lies.

and introducing corn as the backbone of our dairy and meat industries.

Unfortunately, our climatic and soil conditions differ drastically from those in the United States. At first, this made it difficult to apply capitalist experience to our socialist environment. Soon, however, we discovered that we could grow corn which served as excellent cattle feed in regions where corn wouldn't ripen sufficiently to be a [consumer] product.

I'm not embarrassed to come right out and say that I was the initiator of this development. I was the one who introduced corn as silage in our country; and despite what some people say, I'm still proud of my role in this regard.

People who read my memoirs might be interested that it wasn't until I moved to Moscow after the war that I realized the full potential of corn, even though corn had been highly valued for a long time in the Ukraine. I planted an American variety of corn called Sterling at my dacha outside Moscow and to my delight found that it grew well. I invited Comrades Kozlov and Benediktov out to have a look. Kozlov was then the chief of the agricultural department of the Central Committee; and Benediktov, with whom I often disagreed but whose expertise I respected, was Minister of Agriculture.[27]

The stalks reached above Comrade Benediktov's head. He inspected some of the ears and stalks with great interest and exclaimed, "This would make wonderful silage!" As an expert in animal husbandry, he could calculate what sort of yield we might expect per hectare and how much beef and milk this corn would produce when fed to cattle.

I suggested we plant the corn on an experimental basis at a collective farm right next to my dacha in the village of Ogoryovo. The farm had been doing miserably. It was a miracle that it was still in operation. We set aside a field of about one and a half or two hectares and planted the corn. The results were phenomenal. I took the members of the Presidium to see how well the experiment had turned out. The chairman of the collective farm demonstrated how tall the corn was by riding through the field on horseback — you couldn't even see the top of his head until he came to the road.

27. A. I. Kozlov was in charge of agriculture for the Central Committee from 1948 to 1953, when he became Minister of State Farms. I. A. Benediktov was Commissar, then Minister, of Agriculture from 1947 to 1955; later he was ambassador to India. Khrushchev has accused him of mishandling Svetlana Alliluyeva and provoking her to defect to the West (see *KR,* I, 294–295).

Thanks to my original recommendation and my determination to see the project carried through, this collective farm became one of the country's most advanced and profitable. The administration was able to pay off its debts and raise the pay of the farmers. Agricultural workers who had been drifting away from the farm because conditions were so bad started returning, and there were even cases of industrial workers' leaving the factories to come work on the farm because they could make better money there.

As a result of our first success, I recommended that we introduce corn as a silage crop on a larger scale. Unfortunately, under our Soviet way of life, it sometimes happens that people overreact in implementing the recommendation of a man who holds a high post; and a new measure which starts out as an improvement goes too far. That's exactly what happened with corn in many regions.

When I began a propaganda campaign for corn, I sincerely believed — and I still believe — it was the right thing to do. But certain officials wanted to play up to me. To put it crudely, they acted like a bunch of toadies. They insisted on planting corn on a large scale without properly preparing the peasants first. As a result, the peasants had no idea how to plant and harvest corn correctly. Consequently, corn was discredited as a silage crop — and so was I as the one who had advocated the introduction of corn in the first place.

More than once I went to Comrade Konotop, who was then Secretary of the Moscow Regional Party Committee,[28] and said, "You'd better halt the corn campaign. When I drive down the road, I can see that the farmers are making a mess of the job. I'd rather see our collective farms raising oats than have them growing corn badly. The peasants of the Moscow Region are more familiar with oats."

I remember once Grechko told me he had a brother working on a state farm in the Kharkov Region who complained about being forced to plant too much corn. I thought Grechko's brother had a point. I took the matter up with Comrade Podgorny, who was then in the Ukraine:

"You're overdoing the corn campaign."

"What will we feed our cattle if not corn?" he retorted. He gave me a long song-and-dance about why he had no choice, but I think he was just toadying.[29]

28. V. I. Konotop, a Moscow Regional Party official who was elevated to First Secretary in 1964.
29. N. V. Podgorny was a Ukrainian Party and government official who became

There was a lot of that kind of shameful irresponsibility, and it inflicted serious economic and political damage on our socialist system.

Despite the overzealousness of some officials, I'm still convinced that it was the right decision to introduce corn as silage. While there may have been setbacks in certain areas, there were great triumphs in others. Take, for example, state farm Gorky Number 3, which is right near where I live now. I worked closely with the late Comrade Semyonov, who used to be the chairman there. I once went there to be photographed in his cornfields. Like some other state farms in the Moscow Region, Gorky Number 3 was able to get yields of 700 to 800 quintals per hectare, which is 200 quintals more than necessary to make the crop worthwhile.

However, since my retirement, it looks as though they've given up corn and started planting potatoes instead at Gorky 3. I don't go there any more because the farm's on the other side of the [Moscow] river, and the bridge is a long walk from my house; but I sometimes watch what's going on through my binoculars. I've seen soldiers and schoolchildren and college students being herded into the fields over there to harvest potatoes. I can see that a lot of the soldiers and students stand around leaning on their hoes and talking to each other. That's understandable; these young people aren't farmers.

Frankly, I'm sick and tired of vacationers who've been out in the country coming to me to complain about all this idleness and inefficiency when it comes time to harvest potatoes.

"What's going on?" these vacationers ask me.

"What do you expect me to do?" I answer. "I'm just an observer, like you. Take your complaint to someone who can do something about it. I sympathize with what you're saying. I share your indignation. But there's nothing I can do."

Sometimes people who come to see me ask me if I still grow corn myself. They know I'm a real corn fan. When I answer, "Yes, I grow it, and it does very well, too," they sometimes say a bit skeptically, "Some people say not everyone can make a go of corn in Moscow Region." I reply a little sharply, "Of course not just anyone can make a go of it. Cultivating corn requires intelligence and understanding. Corn won't tolerate stupidity. A fool can't grow it — but, then, a fool can't grow anything, can he?"

Chairman of the Presidium of the Supreme Soviet, titular chief of state, replacing Brezhnev, when Khrushchev fell in 1964.

Speaking of stupidity, it upsets me very much to see farms that have started growing sunflowers for silage in recent years. When I went mushrooming a while back, I noticed fields of sunflowers right next to cornfields. Anyone with a grain of sense knows that sunflower seed is far inferior to corn as cattle feed. So you might ask, "Then why are some people growing it these days?" The answer is: because, unfortunately, our system of controls stresses that farmers meet their deadlines for sowing and harvesting rather than that they get the highest yield possible.

I've always been in favor of strict controls, but they should be meaningful — just as I've always been in favor of demanding administrative measures as long as they're sensible and effective. During the years when I was active at the head of the Party and the State, I was in favor of setting up regional and district-level administrative boards to supervise agriculture and industry. Each agricultural administrative board would have a special advisory council consisting of representatives from the state and collective farms of the area.

The boards would serve both a regulatory and decision-making function. They would do a better job of regulation than our State Control Commission, which is more of a punitive instrument than a mechanism to assure efficient organization and high production.

As for decision-making, I'm convinced that the boards would do a better job than our All-Union Ministry of Agriculture when it comes to deciding what, when, and how to sow and harvest. Local-level representation would assure that the boards would genuinely make decisions by themselves on how best to satisfy the needs of our urban population for food.

The Ministry of Agriculture should concern itself with supplying fertilizers and equipment to our farms; it should also keep tabs on the level of agricultural production at home and abroad, as well as make projections for the future. But for the ministry to try to take a direct hand in the administration of individual farms is as damaging as it is futile. Local agronomists and administrators know the limits and possibilities of their fields far better than any central bureaucracy, and they should be spared interference from the ministry.

Of course, we need central planning in agriculture as in other areas of our economy, but that function should be taken care of by the State Planning Commission, not by a separate ministry.

While I still held a high post, the administrative system I proposed was rejected, unfortunately, and we returned to the old bureaucratic, irresponsible reliance upon the Ministry of Agriculture and its regional branches.

Since then, the division of Party committees into separate industrial and agricultural bodies has been abandoned, and we have returned to the old administrative structure, the same faceless administration which lumps factories and farms together. People may say, "But we still have factory directors and collective farm chairmen, don't we?" Yes, we do, but it has become the rule in our country for Party organizations virtually to dictate orders to farms and factories. And where do those orders originate? All too often they come from on high, from uninformed central authorities who end up doing more harm than good.

Some people might say that the division of regional administrations into industrial and agricultural boards is crude and inefficient. I say it's better than the petty tyranny which comes from [centralized] administration.[30]

Just a few days ago I turned on the radio and picked up a program about an agricultural conference. The main report — I stress the *main* report — was given by Comrade Konotop. He's a perfectly intelligent man, and I knew him well from his days in the Kolomna District Party organization, before he moved up to the Moscow Regional Committee. Although he hasn't had much political experience, he's a good politician and worthy of his current post as First Secretary of the Moscow Region. But he's an engineer by training, not an agronomist.[31] Regardless of his background in engineering, it would be silly for him to give a report on rocket technology, wouldn't it? Well, I think it's even sillier for him to be giving the main report at a conference devoted to agriculture. The fact that he was chosen to make the report indicates that something is wrong with the organizational structure of our agriculture nowadays.

The man in charge of agriculture for a given region should be a specialist — he should be an expert agricultural administrator, and

30. The Central Committee set up territorial administrations for agriculture at a plenum in March, 1962. In November of that year, another plenum voted to divide the regional Party committees, soviets, and executive committees into industrial and agricultural branches. Both measures — the decentralization of agricultural administration and the bifurcation of regional authorities along industrial and agricultural lines — were rescinded at a Central Committee plenum in November, 1964, just after Khrushchev's downfall.

31. Konotop was a designer as well as a Party functionary at the Kolomna Locomotive Works from 1942 to 1952.

he should be respected as such. In every branch of our economy, there are men who stand out and shine like precious gems, and they must be given the proper organizational support. If they don't get that support, their brilliance will be extinguished. No public rally, no newspaper exhortation, no official conference will be able to take their place.

I remember hearing about a graduate of the prestigious Timiryazev Agricultural Academy who took a job as a floor polisher rather than as an agronomist or animal husbandry expert on a collective farm.[32] Why? I was told he could make much more money being a floor polisher than an agronomist. That's shameful. It's the kind of stupidity which will lead to inefficiency and irresponsibility.

We're training sufficient numbers of agricultural experts, but we're not making it attractive for them to work on the collective farms. Perhaps it would help if we recruited more students for our agricultural institutes from the rural, rather than the urban, population.

In my time, we educated a substantial number of agricultural specialists, but we needed to go further than that. We needed to see that our increased specialization was reflected in the management of our agriculture. I wrote a memorandum on specialization, and this memorandum was sent to all regional and district Party committees for discussion. I also made a proposal which was approved at a Central Committee plenum. Now this proposal is considered a mistake, but I'm sure the day will come when it will be readopted. Why am I so sure? Because it is intolerable to let Party administrators manage agriculture when they don't have the proper training, yet that's precisely the situation today: as a rule, the people promoted to the posts of secretaries in the district, regional and territorial Party committees have their training in engineering. In other words, they're experts in urban rather than rural affairs. So they are allowed to administer agriculture while the training of many of our agricultural experts goes to waste.

When I held a prominent position in the Party and the government, I often made trips out into the provinces to inspect our farms. Wherever I went, the first man to report to me was, as a rule, the local Party leader, who overshadowed the local executive committee chairman to say nothing of the agricultural specialists. To a certain extent, that's as it should be.

In our system, the number one man is always the Party leader. But

32. The Timiryazev Agricultural Academy is in Moscow.

the Party should play a strictly *political* role, and technical questions should be left to the experts. In this age of increasingly complicated technology, no political leader can keep abreast of the latest developments. As the Americans have shown us, our administrators must be professionals and specialists if we want to catch up.

We should remember that while the Party plays the leading political role in our system, the function of our socialist institutions is to organize production in the most efficient way. Under private enterprise, profit is the determining factor. Under socialism, we don't have private property, so the determining factors should be sensible controls, sensible administration, and sensible distribution. So far we have failed on all three counts, primarily because we have failed to give more independence to our state and collective farms.

Some people might say that the system of administrative organs that I advocated limited the initiative and authority of collective farm chairmen; some people might say I was proliferating the bureaucracy. Well, I say that all depends on your point of view. Of course, there's always a danger of overbureaucratizing management, but I think the real danger to be avoided is that of setting up too many bureaucratic controls between the collective farms [and the central ministries].

If we want to call ourselves Leninists, we should make more of an effort to follow Lenin's principles in determining what is most expedient for our State. I'm sure that the day will come when my proposals [for decentralized autonomous local agricultural administration] will be readopted in some form. By the way, I'd like to stress that the proposals I originally made weren't implemented just on my say-so. I provided the initiative but the decision was approved by the Central Committee. Perhaps the Central Committee will come up with some modifications and improvements on my plan, but no matter what form the [decentralization] takes, life itself will force us to tear down the bureaucratic obstacles which are impeding our economy. In the meantime, our consumers will suffer.

I can just imagine some people saying, "Khrushchev has let himself get bogged down in details; why is he running on and on about all these petty items?"

Rather than replying, I'll just suggest that anyone who complains about my concern for "details" should shut up and have a taste of soup which consists of water and salt; it's missing "petty items" like potatoes, celery, and meat. Just try to buy them in our stores. They're either unavailable or in short supply.

The Plight of the Consumer

WHEN the State mismanages agriculture, the average Soviet citizen suffers. How do we know when the State is mismanaging agriculture? I believe the food counters more than I believe the statistics I read. For that matter, I think the mood of the average housewife is a better indicator than the bureau of statistics about the health of our economy. As I've already said, our statisticians sometimes deliberately distort reality; the rosy figures they publish in the newspapers can't be sold in the stores and made into soup.

What does the mood of the housewives tell us? What do the food counters in the stores indicate about the current level of our economy? They tell us that all is not well, that the State has failed to satisfy both the quantitative and qualitative demands of our consumers.

Even in Moscow, which has always enjoyed special privileges, shoppers can't be sure of finding the meat they want. There's also a shortage of eggs and poultry. In fact, if you're determined to buy chicken, you'll probably have to settle for poultry imported from Holland and other countries. These birds are usually too fat for our people's taste, and the Dutch chicken has the additional disadvantage of smelling like fish.

The situation with dairy products is apparently better than with beef, pork, and poultry, although I understand butter is in short supply.

Good fish is especially hard to come by. Recently I was in the hospital — and a very aristocratic hospital it was, too.[33] You could order pike perch, which is one of my favorite dishes, but it turned out to be practically inedible. It must have been frozen and refrozen several times. Whatever they did to it, the stuff stuck in my throat like cork.

In general, our people aren't very demanding. If there's frozen pike perch in the stores, they'll buy it up in as great a quantity as they can.

33. After his 1970 heart attack, Khrushchev was in a special Moscow hospital for present and former high Kremlin officials and their families.

The same is true with vegetables. It's spring now and, as always, there's a vegetable shortage. Cucumbers and tomatoes are terribly expensive. So is ordinary lettuce, which is of very poor quality. There's a new, high-quality lettuce which looks like cabbage [iceberg lettuce], but it's available only to special people. You'd never find it in a peasant market or a grocery store.

Nor can you find decent corn. Our consumers love corn — especially the Russians, Ukrainians, and Moldavians, to say nothing of the Georgians, Armenians, and other southern peoples for whom corn used to be a staple. Now they simply can't find it anywhere. Sometimes we've bought corn from speculators in a peasant market, but usually it turns out to be silage corn, fit only for pigs and cows.

There's absolutely no reason at all why high-quality corn shouldn't be available to our consumers. It grows well around Moscow. As I've already mentioned, I have some growing in my own vegetable garden. We often serve it to friends and family, and it's always a special treat for them.

I remember when I was in the hospital, I heard the doctors rushing to the cafeteria because word had spread that some Bulgarian canned summer squash was available to the medical staff. The doctors were buying as many cans as they could. I overheard someone complaining, "Dr. So-and-so bought five cans, and I couldn't get a single one." The doctors were surprised when I told them that summer squash grows well around Moscow and that I have some in my garden.

If it's bad in Moscow, it's worse in the provinces. I sometimes meet people from Kiev, Ryazan, Kalinin, Bryansk, and other regions. I always find it a bit awkward to talk to them because inevitably the subject of food shortages comes up. They tell me loudly and bitterly how eggs and meat are simply unavailable, and how they have to take a couple of days and travel to Moscow by train in order to shop for groceries — and spend hours standing in line when they get there.

Just the other day I met a couple of vacationers near my dacha. They'd been staying at a resort not too far from here. They told me they were going home to Ryazan, and they sighed unhappily when they said it.

"Life is very hard in Ryazan," they explained. "At least in the city we can get meat sometimes, but in the surrounding villages it's absolutely impossible."

Khrushchev and Maxim Gorky, 1933

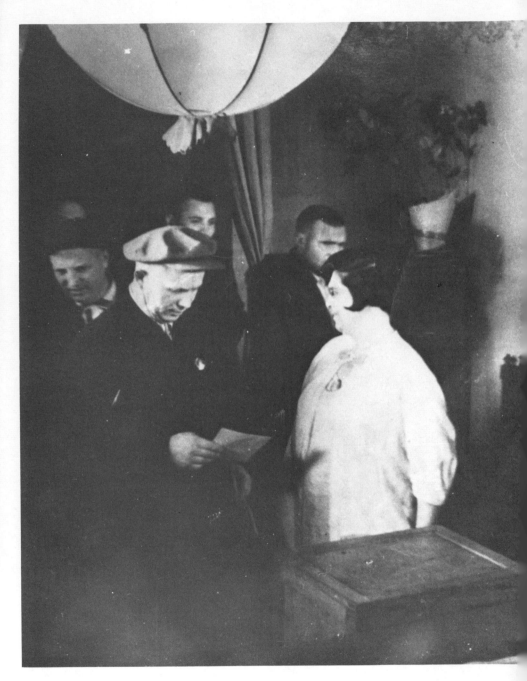

Voting in Moscow in the 1930's

At an award ceremony

Addressing crowds during the May Day celebration
in Kiev, 1947

With Vasily Starchenko, a Ukrainian government official

Fox hunting near Kiev, 1948

Picnicking near Kiev with his wife, Nina Petrovna,
and their daughter Rada

Inspecting orchards in the Ukraine

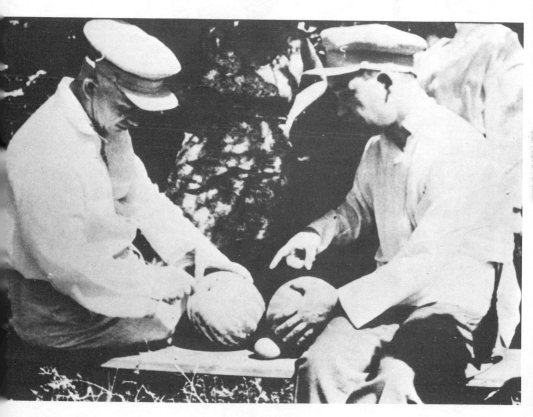

Testing melons

Examining grain at harvest time

Visiting a collective farm

On a tour of the Virgin Lands

Looking over a new Zaporozhets in Kiev

Special Pensioner Khrushchev surrounded by automobile factory
workers who were staying at a rest home near Khrushchev's
retirement dacha, 1969

That conversation reminds me of the story about the gypsy who decides to join the Party:

"May I become a member of the Party?" he asks.

"Yes," he's told, "but first you must fulfill certain requirements. First, work hard. Second, stop stealing, drinking, and chasing after women."

The gypsy throws up his arms in despair and cries, "If I can't do those things, what's the point in living?"

Of course, the person who made up this story somewhat over-simplified the character of gypsies, but the joke still makes a good point: people want to enjoy life. It's not enough to have just the bare essentials. As they say, "man shall not live by bread alone."

In our country, we've reached the stage where people are no longer starving. There's enough grain for bread, but I repeat: "Not by bread alone." We've come to the point now when there should be enough butter to spread on the bread, and there should be meat to put in the soup.

I remember talking once with an American businessman, the president or director of some firm from which we bought a poultry processing plant for one of our state farms in the Crimea.[34] Once the plant was operating, we found that we had to expend five kilograms of feed for every kilo of body weight, while the Americans were fattening up their chickens with only three kilos of feed per kilo of body weight. How could we compete with the US if there was such a vast discrepancy? I was simply ashamed to talk with the president of the American firm, just as it fills me with shame to hear that we're importing chicken from relatively small countries like France, to say nothing of Holland. I asked the American what our problem was.

"Well," he said, "for one thing, you didn't allow our specialists to go to the state farm and install the equipment. We were told that the farm is in a secret district where no foreigners are allowed."

That was ridiculous. Except for our submarine bases, there were no prohibited zones in the Crimea. No, the refusal to let the American specialists onto our state farm was the sort of bureaucratic holdover from Stalin's time that still hasn't been liquidated.

That same American businessman recommended that we set up a bacon factory. He offered to sell us the license for an industrial meat-

34. The businessman in question was George A. Finley, president of the Finley Moody Corporation of Aurora, Illinois, which sold the USSR a poultry plant in the Crimea in 1961 and offered to sell her a bacon factory in April, 1964.

processing plant that would employ 125 people and produce a quarter of a million kilos of pork. He also guaranteed that we'd have to expend only 3.5 kilos of feed per kilo of body weight. How does that compare with the ratio we've been getting? It takes us at least five, and more like seven, kilos of feed per kilo of body weight. In other words, the Americans are getting twice the efficiency we are. Why? Because they have the science, the specialization. For us to match them would have meant setting up special scientific institutes. Yet along came this businessman with a very attractive offer: "We'll give you everything you need — the equipment for mechanized production of feed, all the latest technological elements." The cost of purchasing the license would have been more than repaid in the savings we would have realized from the more efficient production of feed for cattle and poultry. As a result, we would have been able to produce more meat and eggs. Think of the thousands and thousands of people who would have bought all those products if they were available! The purchase of the product would have helped absorb the surplus of paper money which puts such pressure on our economy and leads the state to raise prices, often in secret.

I made a report to the Presidium of the Central Committee, urging that we buy the license for the bacon factory. I think it certainly would have been better from an economic standpoint to buy that license rather than one for a Fiat automobile plant. In the first place, a Fiat is a product that only a limited quantity of people can use. In the second place, we already have pretty good cars of our own — our Zaporozhets, our Moskvich, our Volga, to say nothing of our classier cars. As though it weren't enough to have that Fiat plant on the Volga River, a lot of equipment has been bought from Renault in France, and a truck factory has been built on the Kama River. What's the matter with our own, Soviet-made trucks? [35]

I'm not denying that foreign makes of automobiles are nicer to look at than ours and maybe better in other respects, too. I'm just saying that after fifty years of Soviet power, we're still suffering from shortages in the vital areas of meat and eggs. So before we go around purchasing foreign auto factories, we should concentrate on organizing the production of feed for our livestock, pigs, and poultry on an

35. Fiat of Italy began building a $445 million auto works near the Volga River town of Togliatti in 1967; it had a projected production capacity of 600,000 cars a year. The Renault truck factory deal was announced in 1970.

industrial basis. We still lag seriously behind the capitalist world in food production. It makes good economic and political sense to put the interests of millions who want to be well fed above the interests of thousands who will get pleasure out of buying a Fiat. That's my view. Unfortunately, I'm not in the leadership, and the new leadership either has a different perception of the situation or has lost touch with the true state of affairs.

I met a man recently who asked me, "Say, Comrade Khrushchev, do you think a camel could make it all the way from Moscow to Vladivostok?"

I could tell from the way he was smiling that there was more to the question than met the eye. I answered cautiously, "Well, the camel is a strong animal with lots of stamina, so I think he could probably walk all the way to Vladivostok.

"No, Comrade Khrushchev, you're wrong. The camel would be lucky to make it as far as Sverdlovsk."

"Why?"

"Because, assuming he gets to Sverdlovsk, the people there would eat him."

There's a certain amount of truth in that story: it says something about the shortage of food in the towns and villages across our country. I look forward to the day when a camel would be able to walk from Moscow to Vladivostok without being eaten by hungry peasants or villagers along the way.

Food, of course, is the most essential need of our people, but we must also satisfy their aesthetic demands. Man loves flowers. Without flowers life would be terribly tedious. It's time for our leadership to realize that those goods which add to the beauty of life are not superfluous — they are basic. If our government's allocation of resources were more sensible, we might be able to satisfy both the aesthetic and the nutritional demands of our people.[36]

Economics is a complicated thing. It involves supply, prices, and wages. When I was in the leadership, we tried to improve the intolerable situation in which pensioners and people who had lost their means of livelihood were living. It was unthinkable to leave them on such miserable pensions as they were being paid. So we raised their pensions. The people were very grateful. I remember once when I

36. Khrushchev here launches into a diatribe against Georgian profiteering, a subject he has already covered in KR, I, 305–306.

was walking along the street in Rostov, old men came running up to me and said, "Thank you, Comrade Khrushchev! Thank you for our pensions!"

Despite improvements we made, the wage picture is still fairly gloomy. Not long ago I happened to meet a couple on vacation. They were young, although they already had two children, one thirteen and the other eleven. I asked the man and woman what they did and how much they made. The wife said she was a medical assistant and she made only eighty rubles a month: "It's not much at all, Comrade Khrushchev," she said.

"Yes, it's very little," I replied. "But they're promising to raise wages."

"I know they are, but it's still not much money."

"How about you?" I asked, turning to her husband. He said he was a candidate of technical sciences and earned 130 rubles a month. That strikes me as very low pay, especially considering that there are now categories of workers that make at least that much if not more. In general, I'd say that the wage situation in our country is all messed up, and it doesn't show many signs of getting straightened out. The fair distribution of wealth produced by our people is absolutely essential to the preservation and strengthening of our Soviet society's monolithic quality, its stability. I've never been in favor of reducing everybody and everything to the same level, but at the same time I'm against discrimination. In short, I believe in the rational distribution of wealth, so that there will be neither too much nor too little difference in the incomes of various categories of workers.

So much for wages. What about prices? Not only must we supply our consumers with more and better products, but we must also keep prices down.

People I meet often ask me about our government's price policies when I was in the leadership. I remember someone's saying, "Tell me, please, Comrade Khrushchev, why did you pass a law changing the value of our currency? Didn't the government do that in order to raise prices?"

"The government had no such thing in mind," I say.

"Who exactly proposed the change?"

"What difference does it make? It was a government initiative. It happened to be proposed by Finance Minister Zverev. He reported to me, and he was directly concerned with such matters. Kosygin, as my deputy, had purview over the Finance Ministry and the State Bank.[37] Later he took on other responsibilities as well. In any case, Zverev, Kosygin, and I were proceeding from the fact that costs and revenues had grown many times over, and that it was very complicated to work with such astronomical figures. It complicated bookkeeping. We decided to multiply the ruble by ten, so that something which had cost ten kopeks would now cost one and what had cost a ruble would now cost ten kopeks. This currency reform was simply a matter of convenience; it did nothing to raise the price of products."

The person I was talking to wasn't convinced: "I don't care what you say — the prices went up."

I told him that was ridiculous and worked out the figures with him.

People I meet often ask me why there are so many disguised price increases nowadays. They describe how the brand name of a certain product changes and the price goes up, while the product itself remains the same.

For example, there has recently been a disguised price increase for vodka.[38] This measure has been justified as a way of controlling drunkenness. I, too, once thought that by raising the price of vodka we could bring the level of consumption down. But it didn't work. The only result was that family budgets were hit harder than before, and people had even less money to spend on necessary goods. Besides, it makes people angry when the government arbitrarily raises prices. No one wants to pay more money just for a new brand name.

When people come to me with complaints about price increases nowadays, I always reply, "What are you telling me for? Take your questions to the people who make the decisions and determine the policy. I'm just a pensioner. What do you expect me to do?"

What happens when one of our consumers goes to a state store, buys a low-quality product, and finds he has to pay more money for it than the last time? He starts cursing those who are responsible — that's what happens. Or maybe he can't find what he's looking for at all and has to go to a peasant market where he ends up paying two or three times what he would have paid in a state store if the product

37. A. G. Zverev, longtime Finance Minister (1946–60). Kosygin was First Deputy Chairman of the Council of Ministers, thus Khrushchev's principal deputy in the government, from 1960 until 1964, when he replaced Khrushchev as Prime Minister. It was announced in May, 1960, that old rubles would be exchanged for new rubles at the rate of ten for one, and the currency reform went into effect in January, 1961.

38. The price of vodka was raised in the spring of 1970.

had been available there. To make the situation more complicated, our consumers have developed a marked preference for hard-to-find imported goods, which satisfy their aesthetic demands much better than domestically manufactured products.

As a result of all these factors, it is difficult to be a consumer in our society — and it's all too easy to imagine the foul mood in which our consumers return from their shopping expeditions.

I believe that we can compete successfully with capitalism only if we alter the priorities and organizational structure of our economy so as to supply our citizens with the food and consumer goods they want. A man labors and lives in order to satisfy his material and spiritual needs. If capitalism satisfies these requirements better than socialism, it will become increasingly difficult for us to propagate our point of view and consolidate our way of life. Eventually, we will run the danger of losing everything — of going bankrupt.

The danger is political as well as economic. Just look what happened recently in Danzig and the other Baltic cities in Poland. I have nothing against Comrade Gierek. He's a good Communist. But so was Comrade Gomulka before him; Gomulka was no less devoted to the ideals of Communism than Gierek.[39] Yet by failing to solve the acute economic problems facing his country, especially in the consumer sector, Gomulka lost touch with the masses. His fatal mistake was his decision to raise prices and to deny people the consumer products they were clamoring for. As a result, the bottom fell out of Gomulka's leadership.

What happened in Poland represents a lesson for us. The events on the Baltic coast were a direct result of a food shortage and a consumer revolt against rising prices. That's one of the reasons I'm especially concerned about the shortages and disguised price increases in our own economy.

It's time for us to realize that the teachings of Marx, Engels, and Lenin cannot be hammered into people's heads only in the classroom and newspapers and at political rallies; agitation and propaganda on behalf of Soviet power must also be carried on in our restaurants and cafeterias. Our people must be able to use their wages

39. The leadership of Polish Party Chief Wladyslav Gomulka was toppled by price and wage riots along the Baltic Coast in December, 1970; Gomulka was succeeded by Edward Gierek.
Danzig is the German name for the Polish port of Gdansk.

to buy high-quality products manufactured under socialism if they are ultimately to accept our system and reject capitalism.

Of course, the Chinese would disagree with me on this point. They'd fill our ears with a lot of Mao Tse-tung's gibberish. During the Cultural Revolution, Mao criticized us for trying to satisfy the demands of the Soviet people. The Chinese started hooting and hollering about how we were guilty of "economism." [40] Mao said we should reject material incentives and motivate our people with revolutionary ideas. But you can't make soup out of an idea.

I know some of our own bureaucrats might accuse me of slander simply because I mention all these problems — overbureaucratization of our society, insufficient attention to the needs of the consumer, and so on. But I don't think I'm slandering the Soviet Union at all. I hope that sensible people who read my memoirs will understand that despite all the deficiencies that still exist in our country, I have nothing but the highest respect and gratitude for those who have made a genuine contribution to the improvement of our economy. Moreover, my criticisms are meant to be constructive.

In my old age, I find myself worrying more than ever about the future. I would hate to see the Soviet Union impeded in its progress by its own bureaucracy. If we can keep ourselves from getting bogged down, there's no limit to what we can accomplish. Our greatest strength and hope is hard work. Honest toil is tiring, but it's also rewarding.

I miss work myself. I'm now seventy-seven years old — older than I ever thought I'd live to be when I was a youth. For seven years I've been living in retirement, and often I've been miserable about being deprived of the ability to work for the good of our society. Sometimes the idleness of my life is an unbearable moral anguish.

But I shouldn't complain. I'm fortunate, at least, to have an opportunity to dictate my memoirs about the development of our agriculture and economy. I've been absorbed in this task, and I only hope my efforts will be as useful for others as they've been interesting for me. It's difficult for me to stop, but I'm tired now — and I must rest, at least for a little while.

---

40. "Economism" is a Marxist-Leninist term for an attitude which puts the goal of attaining economic progress and material prosperity apart from and ahead of political and ideological considerations. Trade unions in the West are often accused of "economism," "social democratism," or "right-wing socialism" by Communist ideologists.

8

Poland: The Making of an Ally

Prewar Relations with Poles

I'VE had contact with Poles ever since my childhood. There were
many Poles working in the mines where my father and I worked.
The mines were like an international labor camp. There the peoples
of all nations were equal in that they were equally oppressed by the
yoke of capital. As a result, fraternal feelings built up among us. After
the war one of my friends at Mine Number 31 was a Polish worker.[1]
The times were hard. The railroad wasn't working. So after a while,
when Poland received its independence, my friend bought himself a
horse and loaded his family and belongings into a buggy and moved
to Poland.

I also knew some Polish comrades in the army. Early in 1920, I
was attached to the Ninth Infantry Division, First Brigade. Our division was on the march towards Anapa, which we took at the beginning of April.[2] We were driving the White Army out of the northern
Caucasus. I was assigned as a commissar to the Seventy-fourth Regiment, Second Battalion. The commissar for our brigade was a Pole
named Lukaszewicz, a very respected comrade.[3] The fact that he was
a Pole presented no problem whatsoever. Not a single soldier ques-

1. Khrushchev's father moved the family to Yuzovka (later Stalino, now Donetsk) in
the Donbass region of the Ukraine in 1909. Father and son both worked in the mines
there, Khrushchev as a metal fitter in the generator plants at the French-owned Rutchenkov and Pastukhov mines. He came back to Yuzovka after the Civil War. Mine
Number 31 was part of the Rutchenkov complex.
2. Anapa is a town in Southern Russia on the shore of the Black Sea, where the
White Guards made a stand against the Red Army in the Civil War.
3. Konrad Lukaszewicz, an early Polish revolutionary in the Soviet Union, was in
1917 a member of the Central Council of Delegates for the Ukraine.

tioned his nationality. Later, when Pilsudski attacked the Soviet Union, Lukaszewicz was recalled from the Caucasus and sent to join the Red Army forces that were engaged in operations against Poland.[4] I never met him again.

When working in the Ukrainian Party organization, I knew a number of Poles. For instance, there was Comrade Skarbek, who was in charge of the Polish Section of the Central Committee of the Communist Party in the Ukraine.[5] In other words, he was in charge of propaganda among the Polish population. Later, when I was already working in Kiev,[6] Skarbek was a newspaper editor. He was a good comrade and very well liked. I also knew Krinitsky, who was head of the Agitation and Propaganda Section of the All-Union Party Central Committee and then Secretary of the Saratov Region Party Committee.

I remember my own work with the Poles. As I recall, this was in 1929, when Pilsudski was organizing the All-Polish Congress in Warsaw. Since Poles all over the world were invited to send their representatives to the Congress, the Soviet Union naturally prepared to send representatives of its Polish population. And since for the most part, Soviet Poles lived in the Ukraine, a special committee was created in the Ukraine, under the auspices of the Central Committee. I was put on this Polish committee. It consisted of Krinitsky, who was transferred from Moscow to Kiev to become the chairman of the committee; Comrade Skarbek; and Comrade Baran, who was head of Agitation and Propaganda for the Regional Party Committee. We reviewed many names in order to choose the most worthy representatives of the Polish population in the Ukraine. To be sure, we were looking for people who would represent their constituents from a Marxist-Leninist position. Our work was in vain, however, because Pilsudski never allowed our delegation to enter Poland.

Comrade Krinitsky came to a tragic end. He was arrested and

4. Jozef Pilsudski, the Polish revolutionary-turned-dictator, led an army deep into Russia but was driven back to the outskirts of Warsaw by a Red Army counteroffensive in 1920.

5. Skarbek was the pseudonym for Boleslaw Szacki, who in the late teens and early twenties was a member of the Kharkov Council of Workers' Delegates, the head of the Polish Section of the Military Revolutionary Council of the Western Front, and then head of the Polish Bureau of the Ukrainian Communist Party Central Committee. An early victim of the purges, he was arrested in 1933, liquidated, and posthumously rehabilitated in 1956.

6. In the early and mid-twenties, Khrushchev worked in the Yuzovka regional Party apparatus. In 1928 he was promoted by Kaganovich first to Kharkov, then to Kiev, where he was chief of the Organizational Section of the Kiev Party Committee.

killed as an "enemy of the people" when so many honest Communists were exterminated as a result of the arbitrary rule Stalin imposed on the Party.[7]

Kaganovich was for a long time First Secretary of the Ukrainian
Communist Party. I'd known him since 1917, when we met at a rally
in Yuzovka literally just a few days before the outbreak of the Revolution. He was one of the speakers at the rally. Later that year I ran
into him twice at the Conference of Workers' Deputies in Bakhmut.
At that time he went by the name Kosherovich.[8] Then I lost track of
him until he came to see us in Yuzovka in the twenties in his capacity as First Secretary of the Ukraine. I was First Secretary of the local
Party committee, so we sat together in the presidium.

"Have you ever used the name Kosherovich?" I asked him. He
said yes, and confirmed that we'd met before. I told him he'd find me
in the picture taken of the participants at the Bakhmut conference of
1917. That was about the extent of our conversation.

Kaganovich was later replaced as First Secretary of the Ukrainian
Communist Party by Stanislav Vikentevich Kossior.[9] I'm all but certain that the majority of the Party membership wasn't even aware
that Kossior was a Pole. The question never came up. Nationality
wasn't an issue with us. It didn't prove anything one way or the
other. Kossior didn't conceal the fact that he was a Pole. He didn't
have to; no one cared what nationality he was. What mattered was
whether he was a good Communist or not. He *was* a good Communist, and that's what counted. He enjoyed the full confidence of his
comrades.

I used to work with other Kossiors, too — his brothers. We were
fellow Donbass men. When I was still in the Donbass, I was involved in the amalgamation of a metallurgical organization called
Yugostal, which had its main offices in Kharkov. This was when I
was in charge of the Organizational Committee for the Yuzovka — or

7. A. I. Krinitsky, a veteran Party organizer and troubleshooter who perished in
1938.

8. In 1917 Kaganovich, using the pseudonym Kosherovich, was working in a shoe
factory in Yuzovka and directing the Bolshevik organization in the area. After the February Revolution, he emerged as deputy chairman of the Yuzovka Soviet of Workers'
Deputies. Kosherovich was at least the third alias he had used for underground Party
work: he had also been known as Stomakhin and Goldenberg. Bakhmut, too, has
changed names since those days: the city, near Yuzovka, is now called Artyomovsk.

9. Until his fall, S. V. Kossior was a Politbureau member as well as First Secretary
of the Ukraine. It was with Kossior's support that Khrushchev made his move from the
Ukraine to Moscow in 1929 (*KR*, I, 34–35).

as it was later renamed, Stalino — Region. In that capacity, I met frequently with one of the Kossior brothers — I believe he was called Iosif. He was in charge of the Yugostal amalgamation, and his Polish nationality didn't matter one bit. His life, too, ended tragically. Even though he was a good Communist, he was swept up in the Stalinist extermination of people, which became known from the time of the Twentieth Party Congress on.[10]

As for Stanislav Vikentevich Kossior himself, I'd had nothing but the best relations with him when I was transferred from Moscow to the Ukraine in January, 1938. That summer I learned that Kossior had been arrested. Here's how I found out. The Kiev radio station had borne Kossior's name. It used to identify itself with the announcement, "This is Radio Stanislav Kossior." One day I turned on my set and heard, "This is Radio Kiev." Even though I was a member of the Politbureau, that was the first signal I got that Kossior had been arrested, that he'd disappeared.[11] That's how things were done in those days. One man [Stalin] could do whatever he wanted.

Throughout my career in the Ukrainian Party organization, I had frequent contact with Poles — that is, our Polish agents — who were on their way into Poland to deliver instructions. The situation became much more complicated, of course, when the Communist Party of Poland was dissolved by the Comintern. That happened before I went to the Ukraine, while I was still in Moscow. We received information from the Comintern and from the Central Committee that many of the leaders of the Comintern had been arrested. It was a huge number of people, including representatives of the fraternal Communist Parties as well as our own Party.[12]

Despite the dissolution of the Polish Party by the Comintern, some of the lower Party organizations were never informed — or maybe they simply ignored the Comintern. In any event, they carried on with their work. Gomulka later told me that he never stopped considering himself a Party member while he worked in Drogobych,

10. In fact, I. V. Kossior died of natural causes in 1937, although his death may have been mercifully timed. Both his brothers, S. V. and V. V., fell victim to the Great Terror.

11. Khrushchev succeeded Kossior as First Secretary of the Ukraine in 1938 (*KR*, I, 105–108).

12. An all-out purge of the Comintern began in 1937. Many of the foreign Communist leaders lived in exile in the Hotel Lux in Moscow. When they were arrested there, some resisted and were shot on the spot. The Polish contingent was annihilated almost to a man.

and I think there were many others like him. The late Zawadski is another example. He was sitting in prison in Drogobych. And why was he in jail? Because he was a Communist. After the war he became Chairman of the Presidium of the Polish Supreme Soviet.[13]

Our dealings with Poles in the Ukraine were further complicated during the sovietization of the Western Ukraine.[14] We wound up with many Poles, Ukrainians and Jews on our hands. We received a directive from Moscow not to recognize anyone as a member of the Communist Party, not to transfer any memberships.[15] We were to select only the most deserving people on an individual basis. In fact, this directive meant that none of the people [from the annexed territories] were allowed to join the Party. Only later were we able to start giving memberships to deserving, honest Polish comrades who had been working in the Party underground. We needed their help very much, for they knew the local conditions far better than we did. We started forming Party organizations. Unfortunately, we lost some time in getting started because of those directives from Moscow.

Such were the difficulties we encountered as a result of Stalin's incorrect policies. He acted just as Lenin predicted in his well-known Testament.[16]

Postwar Poland

As the war was coming to an end, Stalin instructed me to turn my attention to the reconstruction of the Ukraine. In that capacity I became familiar with the problems of creating a new Polish army and leadership. Both these matters came under Moscow's jurisdiction; and I used to receive regular orders from Moscow, sometimes from

13. Virtually the only Polish Communist leaders to survive the Comintern purge were those, like Gomulka and Zawadski, lucky enough to be in Polish jails when their comrades in Moscow were being rounded up. After the war, Aleksander Zawadski was Vice Premier and later Chairman of the Council of State, or titular President of Poland.

14. The 1939 Molotov-Ribbentrop Pact made possible Soviet annexation and "sovietization" of the Western Ukraine, or eastern Poland (*KR*, I, 135–149).

15. That is, not to transfer memberships from the pre-partition Polish to the postpartition Soviet or Ukrainian Party.

16. Lenin's Testament was a letter written in 1923 warning that Stalin had concentrated too much power in his hands and had shown a propensity to abuse that power (*KR*, I, 6).

Stalin himself, about how I should assist various Polish Communists who came through Kiev on their way to Poland. Some I met as early as 1944, when the first Polish comrades began crossing the border along our First Ukrainian Front. Comrade Bierut had crossed the front lines even earlier; he was already in place by the time I began having regular contacts with other Poles.[17]

Among those I knew best was Wanda Wasilewska, a leader of the provisional committee set up to help form a postwar Polish government. She was a close friend of mine.[18] I told Stalin many good things about her; later, when he met her himself, she made a positive impression on him. It was said at the time that the provisional committee was formed on the initiative of the Polish population. In fact, however, the composition of the committee was approved by our leadership — namely, by Stalin — because it was formed in our territory, supported at our expense, and would have been impotent without our help. It was in our interests to create a Polish leadership consisting of worthy people, allies who shared our goals and would be faithful to us later on. Wanda Lvovna Wasilewska was a good Communist who satisfied all our requirements.

A Polish army was also formed in our territory. One such army had already been put under the command of a former cavalry general who then turned around and refused to go into battle against the Germans from our territory. He had to be transported by way of Iran to North Africa, where he joined up with the British.[19]

We had far more satisfactory dealings with Rola-Zymierski, an older man who had become a general back in the days of Pilsudski.[20] He'd been jailed because Pilsudski didn't trust him. I don't know exactly what the charge against him was, but in a word he was accused of being a Soviet agent. Whether that was true or not I can't say, but

17. Boleslaw Bierut was a leading Polish Communist trained in the USSR who crossed back into Poland in August, 1943; he was the first Chairman of the National Home Council.

18. Wanda Wasilewska had taken Soviet citizenship and had achieved the rank of colonel in the Soviet army. She was a leader of the wartime Union of Polish Patriots in the USSR and became Khrushchev's friend at the time he headed the Ukrainian Party (KR, I, 145, 248).

19. General Wladyslaw Anders. Khrushchev's account of Anders's exit from Russia with his Polish army is garbled. In fact it was Stalin who changed his mind and refused to allow all three Polish divisions under Anders to fight on the Russian front. Anders's army went on to fight hard in Italy, particularly at Cassino.

20. Marshal Michal Rola-Zymierski, the first commander of the Polish People's Army.

he certainly was our friend. He was an intelligent man, an experienced organizer, and a good soldier. He deserved and received our complete trust. I met him when he came through the Ukraine with some of his men on the way into Poland.

We also raised a few Polish regiments under General Berling, who had previously been in exile in Siberia.[21] I met him several times, first at Stalin's and then in Kiev. His headquarters were attached to the First Belorussian Front, which was commanded by Rokossovsky. It was no accident that Comrade Rokossovsky was put in charge of that particular front.[22] He was a Pole himself, as well as a good Communist and a great military leader; he was respected by Poles and Russians alike and therefore made an ideal commander for General Berling's Polish corps, which was to be the first such unit to cross the border with our troops.

I remember when General Berling was in the final stage of assembling a Polish army in the Ukraine, he complained that the Ukrainians were mistreating his recruits. As the representative of the Ukraine, I asked Berling, "What evidence do you have that there's a bad attitude on the part of the Ukrainian population toward the Polish army?"

"Let's just say they've been expressing their displeasure with us."

"Perhaps with good reason," I retorted. "I think your men have been pillaging from the peasants the way soldiers always do. Perhaps you've been grazing your cattle in fields belonging to Ukrainian farmers. Besides, you've got to remember that the Western Ukraine used to be part of the Polish state, and the Warsaw government conducted a highly unreasonable nationalities policy here: it oppressed and discriminated against Ukrainians. And the problem goes back further than that. Remember your history: the Ukrainians have been fighting against Poland ever since the days of Bogdan Khmelnitsky.[23] So no wonder the Ukrainians still resent you Poles."

21. General Zygmunt Berling, formerly a divisional chief of staff in Anders's army, was given command of the new Soviet-controlled Polish division, which was turned into a corps in 1943 and the First Polish Army in 1944. (In the original, Khrushchev mistakenly calls him "Berlinger," probably because he confuses the name with that of Enrico Berlinguer, the Italian Communist leader.)

22. Marshal K. K. Rokossovsky, a Polish citizen of the USSR, had almost been liquidated during Stalin's 1937 purge of the army. He later distinguished himself at the Battle of Stalingrad.

23. Bogdan Khmelnitsky, a seventeenth-century Ukrainian leader who went to war against the Poles and united the Ukraine with Russia.

Berling found himself in an uncomfortable position. "I didn't look at it that way," he said. "It was thoughtless of me to have complained. Please understand. I make no claims for special treatment. As a soldier I know that such conflicts are bound to occur between an army and a civilian population."

I thought highly of Berling; I even used to send him food parcels full of Ukrainian delicacies, as well as caviar that I received from Moscow. If Berling had simply come to talk over the problem with me, we would have smoothed it over without any fuss. Unfortunately, he had already taken his complaint to the Polish provisional committee and, more seriously, to Stalin himself. Stalin at that time was going out of his way to court Berling's favor. Therefore he raised a stink and sent Malenkov rushing down to Kiev from Moscow to look into the matter for him. As though that weren't enough, Nikolai Aleksandrovich Bulganin flew to Kiev on the same business. Bulganin was Stalin's special representative, his ambassador plenipotentiary, to the Polish provisional committee. Bulganin was more than just an ambassador plenipotentiary. He had special authority, including authority over the army.

Now, you might ask, why did both Malenkov and Bulganin have to get into the act when Berling complained about the treatment of his troops at the hands of the Ukrainian population? The reason is a bit complicated and goes back to the end of 1942 and beginning of 1943, when Bulganin had been a member of the Military Council for the Western Front. At that time our armies under Zhukov had run into trouble in their attempt to follow up on the rout of the Hitlerites outside Moscow. Malenkov told me that Stalin was outraged at the failure of our Western Front to roll back the German advance with a counteroffensive of our own. He appointed a commission to investigate and made Malenkov the chairman. Stalin had to put some soldiers on the committee too, since Malenkov didn't know the first thing about military matters. The commission filed a report blaming the failure on incompetence. As a result Sokolovsky was relieved of his command and Bulganin was relieved of his duties as a member of the Military Council and — I think, though I'm not sure — officially censured.[24] In other words, Malenkov had done dirt to Bulganin.

24. General V. D. Sokolovsky had been Zhukov's chief of staff on the Western Front, and Bulganin was political overseer of the Front. Sokolovsky later moved up to Zhukov's post of commander in chief of the army, only to be dismissed by Stalin for

Stalin was already furious at Bulganin, so all Malenkov had to do was give Stalin the report he wanted to support the conclusions he'd reached beforehand. From a strictly human point of view I felt sorry for Bulganin at the time; I didn't think he deserved the blame. I knew Malenkov had begun to turn against Bulganin, and I didn't trust either his objectivity or his competence as the chairman of the investigation.

That was the background of Malenkov's behavior toward Bulganin when the problem with Berling cropped up. Here was Malenkov trying to play the role of Stalin's special representative from general headquarters and lording it over Bulganin. He arrived in Kiev to meet with Berling and me before Bulganin came, and I could sense immediately that Malenkov was going to use his position for all it was worth.

"We should go out and meet Bulganin when he flies in," I said. "He's never been to Kiev before, and he doesn't know where to come."

Malenkov sneered and said, "There's no reason for us to go pick him up. He'll find his own way, or you can send someone to fetch him."

Malenkov's attitude put me in a very uncomfortable situation. I respected Bulganin and considered him my friend. In fact, as far as I was concerned, all three of us — Bulganin, Malenkov, and I — were friends. I didn't want Bulganin to arrive and find no one there to meet him. On the other hand, I didn't want to put Malenkov in an awkward position by going to the airfield myself if he refused to go. In the end I sent one of my men to pick up Bulganin and bring him back to my apartment.

We convened a meeting of the four of us: I represented the Ukraine, Malenkov represented Stalin, Bulganin represented the Soviet government in its dealings with the Polish provisional committee, and Berling represented the Polish army. We discussed the problem of relations between Ukrainian civilians and Polish soldiers over a very respectable dinner with drinks and so on; it was a meal fit for so important a group. Malenkov still wasn't much of a drinker at that time; but the Ukraine is famous for its hospitality, and I be-

---

failing to break through and drive back the Germans. Sokolovsky went on to become chief of the General Staff of the USSR from 1953 until 1960, when he was sacked for opposing Khrushchev's demobilization policies.

lieve we upheld the tradition. At the end of the meeting Bulganin flew off with Berling and Malenkov left for Moscow. As for the problem we'd been discussing, that took care of itself. There was no more aggravation, and there was certainly no anti-Polish policy as far as the Ukrainian government was concerned.

I had further contact with Berling in 1944, when our army pushed forward into Polish territory. We liberated the town of Lublin, which was then made the seat of the provisional Polish government. Members of the government, including Berling as well as Bierut and Wasilewska, used to make frequent trips to Kiev. I think the governing bodies of the new Polish government were quite right to make their headquarters in Lublin; first, because it was on Polish rather than Soviet territory and second, because it was a former capital.[25]

Using Lublin as a base, the Polish comrades began to explore the surrounding area and set up the governmental organs necessary to administer the lands being liberated by the Soviet army.

A number of non-Communist Poles were also active at that time, among them the two Witos brothers. One was a famous politician who had been a delegate to the Sejm and a leader of the Polish peasantry — which is to say, of course, the kulak class.[26] The other Witos brother actually became a member of the provisional government formed in our territory.[27] He wasn't a politician by background, but a farmer who had made a lot of money off his lands and his mill. Naturally he was against socialism, against collectivization, and against soviets. However, the Soviet government supported his candidacy when he was nominated by certain Polish circles to represent them in the provisional government. For a while at least, he behaved properly toward our system and our State.

One of the first matters the new government in Lublin had to face was an adjustment of Poland's boundaries. Stalin saw an opportunity to heal the wounds which Poland had suffered as a result of the Ribbentrop-Molotov Pact of 1939.[28]

Regaining the good will of the Poles was no easy task. Stalin re-

25. Lublin had been the site of the diet which unified Poland and Lithuania in the sixteenth century as well as the seat of the Polish Socialist government formed in 1918.

26. Andrzej Witos, a leader of the Peasant Party. "Kulak" means rich peasant.

27. Wincenty Witos, an elder statesman of the Peasant Party.

28. The pact partitioned Poland between Nazi Germany and the USSR. Khrushchev has described its genesis and consequences in *KR*, I, 126–143.

viewed the borders which had been established by the Pact and decided to redraw Poland's eastern border along the so-called Curzon Line, which had originated with the Treaty of Versailles and ran to the east of the border established in 1939 by Ribbentrop and Molotov. In the west, the Polish-German border was drawn along the Oder and Neisse rivers in accordance with the Poles' historical claims on lands that had belonged to them in the past. The Oder-Neisse Line was advantageous for both Poland and the Soviet Union. We knew that sooner or later Poland would be a socialist country and our ally. Many of us felt, myself included, that someday Poland would be part of one great country or socialist commonwealth of nations. Therefore we were glad to have the Polish-German border moved as far west as possible.

However, Stalin's decision to set Poland's eastern frontier along the Curzon Line created a problem because he failed to take into account the national interests of both the Ukrainians and the Belorussians. The Ukrainians were particularly unhappy. Only a few years before, in 1939, the eastern and western territories of the Ukraine had been united by the Ribbentrop-Molotov Pact. For the first time in their history the Ukrainian people had found themselves joined in one state, a Soviet state. Triumphant celebrations had taken place in Kiev and Moscow. Our country had attained its maximum territorial gains and simultaneously satisfied the aspirations of the Ukrainian people. Now, after the war, Stalin decided to concede some of the Western Ukraine back to Poland.

Take the town of Kholm for example. Under the terms of the Ribbentrop-Molotov Pact it had become part of the Ukraine. Now, along with other regions, Kholm was to be part of Poland again. The population of these areas was overwhelmingly Ukrainian, and suddenly hundreds of thousands of Ukrainians were to be placed under Polish jurisdiction.

Stalin went about this decision in his typically clumsy and secretive fashion. He didn't ask anyone's advice or give anyone warning. That's the kind of man he was. I didn't even find out about Stalin's decision until after he'd informed the Polish leadership. He put me, the Secretary of the Ukrainian Communist Party and Chairman of the Ukrainian Council of People's Commissars, in a very ticklish situation. Those members of the Ukrainian intelligentsia who supported the Party were angry and upset about the whole state of affairs. What could I tell them? I couldn't sympathize with them because that would have meant disputing Stalin; nor could I explain Stalin's decision to them.

Stalin made major concessions to the Poles, creating great difficulties for our State and for me personally. I'm thinking particularly of the way he played favorites with the new Polish leadership and helped Poland at the expense of the Soviet Union. Bread was sent to Poland from the Ukraine, while Ukrainians were bloated from starvation and in some cases were eating each other.

I wouldn't say there were any hard feelings against the Poles in the Ukraine. After all, only a tiny circle of people even knew about the shipments to Poland. One of those who did was Wanda Wasilewska. She used to make frequent trips to Warsaw, and she'd tell me incredible stories when she came back to Kiev.

"I saw it with my own eyes," she said. "They've got lots of black bread and even some white bread in Warsaw; and they complain about the Soviet government not giving them enough white bread. They say Poles aren't used to eating black bread. Can you imagine?"

So there we were, aiding the Poles economically at great cost to ourselves and restoring to them territories in the Ukraine. Yet, believe it or not, I later met some Polish comrades who were *still* dissatisfied with the borders Stalin had given them in the wake of Hitler's retreat. They thought their border with the Soviet Union should be even farther to the east.

"How can you possibly suggest such a thing?" I asked. "You're talking about annexing lands populated by Ukrainians!"

"That's right," they said, "but it was Lenin's idea, not ours. When war broke out between Poland and the Soviet Union in 1920, Lenin said he would be willing to give Poland the borders it wanted if that would end the war."

It's possible Lenin may have sent a directive to that effect to Dzerzhinsky in the Polish provisional government.[29] But if Lenin made such a proposal, it was only as a way of stopping the war. It did not mean he thought the Ukraine should be transferred from Soviet to Polish rule.

Once Stalin made up his mind to adjust Poland's eastern border back to the Curzon Line, he decided to let any Ukrainians who wished to do so move from the new frontier regions of Poland across

29. In 1920 the Bolsheviks set up what was intended to be an embryo Communist regime in Bialystok, Poland, under Felix Dzerzhinsky, a Pole who from 1918 to 1926 headed the Soviet secret police.

the border into the Soviet Ukraine. Likewise, the Polish population of the Soviet Ukraine was given the option of moving to Poland. The same measures were taken with respect to the Poles and Belorussians living on either side of the frontier around Brest. Stalin ordered me, as the representative of the Ukraine, and Ponomarenko, who was Secretary of the Central Committee of the Belorussian Communist Party, to contact the Polish provisional government and work out a scheme for an exchange of populations. We were not consulted on the decision itself; we were simply told to work out the technicalities and implement it. We appointed Comrade Podgorny, who was the head of the food industry in the Ukraine, to be our representative to the Polish government in ironing out all the provisions of our population-exchange treaty with Poland. I phoned Ponomarenko and arranged for a meeting with him, the Poles, and our ambassador, Bulganin. I flew to Lublin from Kiev, and Ponomarenko came from Minsk.

On the whole we were well received by the Poles. Of course, not all of them had the same idea about their country's postwar development. Some weren't Communists. In fact quite a few wanted to see an independent, bourgeois-democratic Poland rather than a socialist Poland. [Wincenty] Witos was the prime example; the very thought of a collective farm made him act like a crow who's just seen a scarecrow.

I remember there was a huge feast organized for the representatives of the Polish government and peasantry. I asked Bulganin and Bierut, "How about it if I phone Kiev and have them bring us some watermelons to serve the Polish representatives?" As I recall, it was August. We had a lot of watermelons in the Ukraine, and this product wasn't available in Poland. We figured out how many we'd need for all the Polish government and peasant leaders; then we had a couple of planeloads flown to Lublin from Kiev. When we produced the melons at the meeting, Witos objected, saying the government representatives shouldn't get any and the peasants should get them all.

"What's this, Mr. Witos?" I said. "You would deprive us of the pleasure of extending to you our hospitality? And you would deprive yourselves of the pleasure of sampling these wonderful products grown by our Ukrainian collective farmers? At least have a taste of this delicious melon here. It's called a *kolkhoznitsa*." [30]

30. *Kolkhoznitsa* is Russian for a female collective farm worker.

He thought I was joking, but I told him I was telling the truth. "Well then," he said, "if this melon is called a 'collective farm girl,' why isn't it red?"

"It may not be red, Mr. Witos, but you'll find it's very sweet-smelling and delicious. I think you'll learn to like it."

Obviously we were not just talking about melons. We were talking about politics and about Witos's attitude toward the Soviet Union.

During my visit to Lublin, Bulganin suggested we go to a place outside of town where the Germans had built an extermination camp for prisoners from all over Poland and from many Western countries as well.[31] When we arrived there, a commission was excavating the mass graves at the camp. I'd already seen plenty of evidence of the brutality committed by the Germans, but I'd never seen the ovens where they incinerated people. It was a hot summer day. The commission had dug up some of the graves and removed the bodies, but they left alone some corpses which had already begun to decompose. It was hard to come anywhere near where the commission was working. Bulganin couldn't stand the choking stench of rotting human flesh, and he simply ran away. My own will power is pretty strong, so I was able to walk around everywhere and examine everything without showing how revolted I was. I felt we shouldn't behave like a couple of pansies who couldn't stand the smell of dead bodies.

After that, Bulganin and I examined the gas chambers. They looked like makeshift bathhouses. The entrances had peepholes in them, like prison doors, so the warden could see when all the people herded inside were dead. From the gas chambers the corpses were taken to a crematorium and burned in giant ovens. There was a horrible pile of ashes and bones which hadn't burned up completely. We also looked at the prison barracks and a storehouse, where I saw an enormous collection of men's and women's footwear. The guide who was showing us around explained that the Germans sorted all their victims' clothes and took them back to Germany. In another storeroom was a huge quantity of women's hair. In other words the Germans were real professionals. Just as butchers in a slaughterhouse find a use for every part of the animal — hooves, horns, and

31. This was the extermination camp at Maidanek. Bulganin was to refer to his visit there with Khrushchev a decade later, during Konrad Adenauer's trip to Moscow in 1955. "Can we forget the tons of hair taken off the tortured women and stored in the storerooms of Maidanek?" the Soviet Premier asked the West German Chancellor during an argument. "We saw for ourselves all that was found at Maidanek."

fur — so these masterful Germans did the same with human remains. Everything was neatly sorted out — eyeglasses, combs, everything you can imagine. The whole spectacle made a frightening impression. It was absolutely incredible to think that all this had been done by human beings, by supposedly cultured people. We used to hold a high opinion of German culture. Yet look what had happened to this culture under Hitler's leadership.

From the extermination camp Bulganin and I went to see the town of Kholm. It had been a provincial center in tsarist Russia before World War I; then, with the Treaty of Versailles, it was turned over to Poland. As I've already mentioned, Kholm rejoined the Soviet Ukraine after the Ribbentrop-Molotov Pact of 1939, but now it was to revert to Poland once again. While Bulganin and I were looking around the town, we noticed an Orthodox cathedral and decided to go have a closer look. The door was opened by a gray-haired old man, a typical Russian Orthodox priest. He told us how the church had been built as an Orthodox cathedral but that over the years as the town changed hands, the Poles kept converting it into a Catholic church — back and forth, back and forth. He had heard the announcement that the Soviet government was giving Kholm back to Poland, and he spoke with such sadness about how the Catholic priests would now come again and take over the church yet another time. He was pleading with us to do something. We were wearing our military uniforms, and he thought we had some influence on the course of events and the adjustment of the borders. We told him we weren't concerned with church affairs; we didn't care what religion — Catholic or Orthodox — made use of his cathedral. In the Soviet Union church and state are separate, and we weren't going to interfere in the internal church affairs. With that, we got in our car and drove back to Lublin.

After a while it became less necessary for me to travel to Lublin and maintain regular contacts with the Poles. The Polish side appointed officials who came to us in Kiev, and they took care of registering our citizens of Polish nationality who wanted to move to Poland and other administrative matters that went with the process of normalizing our neighborly relations. Even though I no longer made trips to Lublin, I still frequently saw our Polish comrades in Moscow. Stalin was always summoning me to listen to the Poles' requests and complaints because he didn't want to be bothered himself. If a Polish comrade came to ask Stalin to do something and

Stalin didn't want to be the one to refuse, he'd bring me up from Kiev to do his dirty work for him.

"Here's Khrushchev," he'd say. "Let him decide. You two know each other, and I'm sure you can work out an agreement between you." Then he'd just sit there listening, waiting to see how I'd handle the job of turning down whatever request the Polish comrade made. And of course one way or another, I'd have to say no.

For example, Stalin once invited me to sit in on a talk he was having with Bierut, who wondered out loud if we might be willing to return the city of Lvov to Poland: "The Polish people, and especially our intelligentsia, would be gratified if Lvov were once again to be part of our state."

Stalin obviously knew in advance what Bierut had on his mind. He turned to me and said, "Here's Khrushchev. Why don't you find out what he thinks about the idea."

Naturally I wanted Lvov to remain in the Soviet Union; I couldn't imagine the Ukrainian state giving it back to Poland. The Poles had neither ethnological nor historical grounds to claim the city. But why should I have to be the one to tell Bierut that? Stalin forced me to stand up for the interests of the Soviet Union simply because he didn't want to do it himself. Later he told me, "You were absolutely right in the way you handled Bierut. The Poles have let their appetites get out of hand."

Later Bierut came to Moscow with Osobka-Morawski and some other Polish comrades to discuss various issues with Stalin, including another problem concerning Lvov.[32] Stalin summoned me from Kiev to take part in the meeting.

"Comrade Stalin," began Bierut, "there's a historical exhibit in Lvov which is very popular among the Polish people in the area. Would it be possible to move the exhibit to Poland?"

"Clear it with Khrushchev," said Stalin. "I'll go along with whatever you conclude with him."

Bierut looked inquiringly at me, and I said, "You can have the diorama any time you want. We have it in storage. It's been sitting there throughout the occupation and no one's taken care of it. I've been told the damp has gotten to it, and it's badly damaged. It will require a lot of work to restore it."

In fact, it was more complicated than that. After the liberation of

32. Edward Osobka-Morawski was a Socialist leader who cooperated closely with the Communists and later became Premier.

Lvov people had brought the exhibit out of storage and put it on display. It was a panorama of paintings showing scenes from the nineteenth-century Polish revolt against Russian rule. One scene was the aftermath of a battle in which a force of Polish insurgents had defeated some Russian troops, taken the Russian general prisoner, and were leading him off into captivity. There were also other episodes from the history of the Poles' struggle against tsarist Russia. In no time at all the exhibit was literally the object of a pilgrimage by Poles living around Lvov. The exhibit obviously struck a sensitive chord in their hearts. We didn't like the implications of such a pilgrimage, so we took the exhibit down and put it back in storage.

Of course, you could look at the exhibit historically and say the scenes it re-created all belong to the past. But the past is always relevant to the present, and the content of the exhibit could be construed as anti-Russian. Pictures depicting battles between Poles and Russians didn't serve our goal of establishing closer ties among our three fraternal nations: Poland, Russia, and the Ukraine. On the contrary, such an exhibit might serve to induce Poles to repeat that whole episode from their history.

With this in mind, I felt I had to warn Bierut and Osobka-Morawski about the possible consequences of moving the exhibit from Lvov to Warsaw: "Go ahead and take it if you insist, but I'm telling you if you put it on display, it will stir up the opposite of fraternal feelings between our people. It will be like a call to battle, urging your people, 'Fight Russia! Defeat the Russians!'"

Stalin didn't agree. He supported the Polish comrades, saying, "But this is all history, it's over and done with. Look at us: we staged a production of the opera *Ivan Susanin*, which is an anti-Polish work, and it didn't do any harm to our present-day goals."

"That was different," I objected. "*Ivan Susanin* is about our struggle against the Poles when they invaded Moscow — a historical situation which has no parallel today.[33] The exhibit in Lvov concerns the Polish uprising against Russians in Warsaw. Don't you see how Polish viewers might perceive such an exhibit as having to do with more than just ancient history? But I've already said, if the Polish comrades want to take it to Warsaw, let them go ahead and take it."

And they did just that. Sometimes I meet other Polish comrades,

33. The opera *Ivan Susanin* by M. I. Glinka concerns a seventeenth-century Russian peasant hero who tricked a Polish invasion force and paid with his life.

old friends with whom I still maintain good relations, and they remind me of that incident from long ago. These friends once told me that Osobka-Morawski later claimed I had been against letting him take the exhibit back to Warsaw.

"That's not true," I said. "I wasn't against letting him have it. I was only trying to call his attention to a very real danger. Nationalistic elements in Poland might have exploited the exhibit by using it to damage the friendship which was then developing between the Polish and Soviet peoples."

In 1968 my fears were confirmed. A historical drama by Mickiewicz was put on the stage in Warsaw and greeted by anti-Russian catcalls and slogans. The subject of the play was Poland's occupation by Russia [in the nineteenth century]; it included many lines calling for the expulsion of the Russian occupiers. The play had a completely unexpected effect. I'm not saying it didn't reflect artistic and historical truth — just as the exhibit in Lvov may have reflected artistic and historical truth — but under the conditions prevailing at that moment the play caused great difficulties for the leadership of the Polish Communist Party.[34]

We continued to cooperate closely with the Polish comrades as they laid the groundwork for the reconstruction of their country in the territory liberated by the Soviet army. Before the Polish government could move its seat from Lublin to Warsaw, the Hitlerites had to be driven back further. Our troops advanced all the way to the Vistula River, coming literally within a few steps of the German-occupied capital.

Suddenly an uprising broke out in the city. Its leader was General Bor-Komorowski.[35] He was acting on instructions from Mikolajczyk, an outrageous anti-Soviet and anti-Communist who headed the Polish government-in-exile under Churchill's wing in London.[36]

34. The Warsaw production of a nineteenth-century patriotic classic, *Dziady*, by Adam Mickiewicz, was closed in March, 1968, after protests from the Soviet embassy against the nationalistic flavor of the play; the suppression of *Dziady* marked the beginning of a full-scale crackdown on the intelligentsia by the Gomulka regime.

35. Count Tadeusz Bor-Komorowski, commander of the Polish Home Army at the time of the Warsaw uprising in August and September, 1944.

36. Stanislaw Mikolajczyk had succeeded General Wladyslaw Sikorski as Prime Minister of the London-based government-in-exile when the latter died in an airplane crash in 1943; Mikolajczyk visited the USSR twice to negotiate with Stalin and the Polish Communists: first in August, 1944; then two months later, when Winston Churchill was in Moscow. Mikolajczyk resigned as head of the London government in November, 1944. The next year he published a book on his version of events; it ap-

Ever since the Soviet army began its advance into Poland, Bor-Komorowski had been under orders from London not to engage in actions against the Hitlerite occupiers and not to aid the Soviet liberators in any way. It seems Mikolajczyk's anti-Communist government-in-exile wanted to save its armed forces in Poland for the coming struggle against the Soviet army.

The Poles in London wanted postwar Poland to be in the hands of a bourgeois, capitalist, reactionary, anti-socialist, anti-Soviet, pro-Western government headed by Mikolajczyk. The political goals set by Mikolajczyk in cahoots with Churchill required that Warsaw be liberated [by British and American forces] *before* the Soviet army reached the city. That way, a pro-Western government supported by Mikolajczyk would already be in control of the city by the time the Soviets arrived. But it didn't work out that way. Our troops under Rokossovsky got there first. The anti-Communist Poles in London thought the Soviet army would enter the city as soon as we reached the Vistula. That's why they ordered Bor-Komorowski to stage a last-ditch revolt against the Germans.

However, our forces didn't do what the insurgents expected. They didn't enter the city. Instead, Rokossovsky's army waited on the right bank of the Vistula. You might ask why we didn't cross the river immediately and liberate the city. Well, there were a number of factors. First, the river itself posed a major natural obstacle; it would take time to ford and cost us heavily in men and equipment. Second, an advancing force always suffers more casualties than a defending force. Both these considerations meant we had to wait for reinforcements to catch up with our advance units. Furthermore, our commanders figured we would suffer fewer losses if, rather than attacking frontally, we could drive the Germans out of the city by attacking them from the left bank and then closing in on them with a flanking action which our troops were already preparing south of Warsaw where they had established a bridgehead. But all these preparations took time. That's why we had to wait on the far side of the river during the Polish uprising inside the city.

The Germans suppressed the Warsaw revolt and took the insurgents prisoner, including General Bor-Komorowski. Usually when the Hitlerities captured the leader of an insurrection in occupied ter-

---

peared in Britain as *Pattern of Soviet Domination* and in the US as *The Rape of Poland*.

ritory, they would have no mercy; they would shoot him at once. But this Bor-Komorowski was allowed to live and after the war conducted anti-Polish and anti-socialist activities — which makes me wonder what sort of a man he was.

Once the Germans were driven out of the city, the Polish comrades moved from Lublin to Warsaw. I continued to have dealings with them. In January, 1945, while I was still working in the Ukraine, Stalin phoned me and asked, "Can you get to Moscow immediately? We need you here urgently." I flew to Moscow from Kiev. When Stalin met me, he was in the highest spirits. He was strutting around like a peacock with his tail spread — a far cry from four years earlier when he'd been more like a scared rabbit, too paralyzed with fear to lead. Now he was acting as though it had been his brilliant leadership, rather than the courage and sacrifice of our soldiers, which had made possible the success of the Soviet armies.

"The Polish comrades have asked us to help them restore their municipal services, especially their water supply and sewage system. We've liberated Warsaw and our troops have occupied the city, but the Poles are still in a helpless situation. They say Warsaw is in ruins, and they don't know where to begin. You've already had considerable experience with the rapid restoration of essential city services, so we want to send you to Warsaw to oversee the work there."

"Very well," I answered, "I'll go with pleasure. But I'd like to take with me some of our own administrators and electrical engineers. The first thing is to get the Poles' power station working, then their water and sewage works."

I asked Comrade Stramentov to come along. I knew he was a good organizer and an expert manager of electrical facilities. I also included some engineers who specialized in power stations, water supply, and sewage. We all flew to Warsaw.[37]

I arrived in the Polish capital and went on a tour of the city. It was completely devastated, a vast graveyard for many thousands of inhabitants buried under the ruins. The worst part of the city was the famous ghetto into which the Germans had driven the Jewish population, then bombed and shelled it to ruins. I remember seeing a huge heap of rubble where a house had once stood and then noticing that people were still living in the basement. It was impossible to imagine that people could go on living in such conditions, without

37. This paragraph and the three preceding it are in *KR*, I, 357–361.

facilities or services of any kind. Something had to be done — and fast.

Our engineers divided into three groups with their Polish counterparts. One group was detailed to restore electric power as quickly as possible. The second group was to take care of the water supply, and the third was to repair the sewage system. The Poles were to look after the cleaning up of the city themselves. Our services weren't required for that job, although we had to demonstrate our solidarity with the Poles. I remember one of the Polish comrades saying to me, "Come on, Comrade Khrushchev, let's lend a hand. Let's grab some shovels and symbolically join in the reconstruction of Warsaw!" I was glad to oblige.

I put Comrade Stramentov in overall charge of the reconstruction. He had both Polish and Russian specialists under him. It was his job to handle all the specific problems which arose and then report to me on the general situation.

Warsaw got its electricity and water supply back. Where the bridges across the Vistula had been bombed out, we laid pontoon bridges so that trucks and other motorized transport could get into the city. We also temporarily restored the railroad bridges so that trains could bring in supplies for our advancing troops.

I wanted to have a look at the whole of Warsaw from the air. I asked my pilot Nikolai Ivanovich Tsybin, with whom I'd been flying throughout the war, to take me up and circle the city a few times.[38] It was shocking to see what the Hitlerite barbarians had done. The main part of the city on the left bank of the Vistula was in ruins except for a few enclaves in the suburbs where some buildings were left standing. The Praga district on the right bank had been less badly hit, and it was here that the Polish government, or committee as it was still called, had its temporary headquarters.

The Soviet ambassador by then was Comrade Lebedev, whom I'd never met before. He seemed well acquainted with the political situation and filled me in on how the Polish comrades were making out. Later Stalin replaced him because his activities exceeded the proper function of an ambassador; he apparently tried to force his views on the Polish comrades and subjugate them. If these charges were true,

38. N. I. Tsybin also flew Khrushchev to the Adriatic island of Brioni for secret consultations with Yugoslav President Josip Broz Tito during the Hungarian uprising of 1956 (*KR*, I, 420–421).

Stalin was absolutely right to remove him. During my association with him, Comrade Lebedev impressed me as very well informed, although no doubt stubborn and hard-driving. He insisted I stay with him at his residence because our embassy was in such terrible shape.[39]

I also met the mayor of Warsaw, General Spychalski. I liked him from the outset. He was young, energetic, and hard-working.[40]

By that time Osobka-Morawski was Prime Minister. He'd attained that post when his own left-wing Socialists joined forces with the Communist — or, as it was called, Polish Workers' — Party. I got to know him a bit better when, at his request, he accompanied me on a drive down to Lodz, the center of the textile industry. Here fabrics famous all over Russia are manufactured. Lodz was also well known as the center of the class struggle and the revolutionary movement in Poland. During our overnight visit to Lodz, Osobka-Morawski and I had an uproarious dinner with Rola-Zymierski, who was full of good spirits and joking all through the meal. I had the highest respect for Rola-Zymierski, and that's more than I can say for Osobka-Morawski. He impressed me as a mediocre man and a mediocre politician. He specialized in problems of cooperation. The other Polish comrades told me he didn't really figure as an important person in the Party leadership. They gave him the cold shoulder because they felt he wasn't truly committed to the reconstruction of Poland on a socialist basis. That was my feeling, too.

The head of the Polish Workers' Party was Comrade Bierut, who performed the functions of both President of the country and Secretary of the Party Central Committee. I'd already met Bierut a number of times, and I still have the best personal memories of him. His daughter is married to a Georgian architect, and once a year she comes to visit us on her way between Tblisi and Warsaw. Nina Petrovna and I always receive her with great pleasure. Her visits remind us of the good times we had when her father and our friend, Comrade Bierut, was still alive.

During the reconstruction of Warsaw, Bierut was the very soul of leadership. I knew him to be an honest Communist, devoted to the

39. V. Z. Lebedev was ambassador to Poland, 1944–50, a veteran diplomat who had formerly been posted to prewar Yugoslavia and the Allied governments in wartime London.

40. General Marian Spychalski, an army intelligence chief who, in 1945, was shifted from the job of Mayor of Warsaw to become Deputy Minister of Defense.

cause of Marxism-Leninism. However, I must say, even then I sensed in him a certain weakness. He was too soft, too gentle in his handling of people. On the one hand, his human goodness attracted people to him, myself included. But there's such a thing as being overly good-natured and trusting. This quality later led to some complications in Poland when some of his colleagues took advantage of him.

Bierut was delighted with the help we gave him in restoring Warsaw's power and water supplies. He was absolutely radiant. He thanked us profusely and asked us to pass on his thanks to Comrade Stalin. He was obviously speaking very sincerely.

Before we left Warsaw to return to Moscow, Comrade Bierut made a suggestion to me: "We have a very important figure in the Polish Communist Party here, a comrade named Gomulka. I'd like to ask you to pay a call on him at his apartment. He's been quite ill and can't go out."

"All right," I said. "I'd be pleased to."

Someone took me to a gloomy, sooty, one-room apartment. Gomulka's wife was doing the laundry when we arrived. Comrade Gomulka himself was sitting in a chair with some sort of black kerchief wrapped around his cheeks. He didn't speak Russian very well, but with the help of an interpreter we could understand each other. He gave me his appraisal of the general state of affairs in Poland. It was obvious to me he knew where to start in organizing the activities of the Party and the government. In short, he impressed me as being an able political leader and statesman. "I'm sick for the time being," he said, "but I'll be up and around before long."

After returning to Moscow I wrote a memorandum to Stalin describing what we had done and whom we had met. This memorandum is still in the Central Committee archives. Stalin was especially pleased that we had been able to help the Poles; he knew our assistance would make good marks for us with the Polish people. The treaty of 1939 had deeply wounded the Poles, and the wound was still fresh. Stalin wanted to do everything he could to heal that wound as soon as possible. Naturally, he didn't say so to me outright, but I could sense what he was thinking.[41]

In my report to Stalin I mentioned Gomulka very favorably. I don't

41. Khrushchev's account of his first meeting with Gomulka also appears in *KR*, I, 357–361.

know if Stalin had ever heard of him before. None of the rest of us had, and I doubt Stalin had either. "Gomulka holds a commanding position in Poland," I wrote to Stalin. "He's sure to emerge as a leader someday, very likely as the future head of the Polish Workers' Party." It was partly on my recommendation that Stalin singled out Gomulka as one of the men to determine the political direction of the postwar Polish state.

The Communists and left-wing Socialists were united in their commitment to one goal: putting Poland on the road to socialism. But the pursuit of that goal had to be postponed until the Hitlerite enemy was crushed once and for all.

Then, as the war finally came to an end, the Communist Party was able to turn its attention to another struggle, the struggle against the bourgeois political forces led by Mikolajczyk, who returned to Poland from London at the end of the war. Churchill personally put pressure on Stalin to let Mikolajczyk return, saying he was a friend of the Soviet Union and should be the Prime Minister of Poland in a co-alition government. Churchill sent Stalin a message which went something like this: "Mr. Mikolajczyk has the greatest respect for you and your state. He has done an admirable job in his capacity as head of the Polish government-in-exile, and you can count on him to do equally well as the new Polish head-of-state."

Stalin had to take notice of the Allies' wishes and opinions, so Mikolajczyk was allowed to return. I met him at a reception which Stalin gave in his honor. I didn't talk to him myself, but I saw Stalin exchange a few words with him. Mikolajczyk was taller than average and bald-headed. He was a very ordinary-looking man who didn't make much of an impression on people. Of course, my own impression of him was determined by his political convictions, which turned me against him in advance.

Stalin wrote to Churchill that elections were the only way to solve the problem of what political course Poland would follow. A date for the election was set.[42] It was to be basically a referendum to decide

42. The election was set for January 19, 1947. In August, 1946, Stalin had called in Boleslaw Bierut and other Polish Communist and pro-Communist leaders, and had told them, "The election must be won before the election." He instructed them on exactly what percentage of the seats in the Sejm (the Polish Parliament) were to go to each party: "I want to see how influential you actually are." The election was preceded by a campaign of terrorism against non-Communists, and much of the polling was carried out in the open and under the eye of the army. Britain and the US protested that the election contravened the Yalta and Potsdam agreements. US Secretary

whom the Polish people trusted and whom they wanted to have in their leadership. Mikolajczyk had considerable support in the rural areas and, for that matter in the cities as well, for Poland still bore the marks of the Pilsudski regime and the influence of his Socialist Party.[43] On top of that, a great many Poles still had hard feelings toward the Soviet Union because of our treaty with Hitler. The pact signed by Ribbentrop and Molotov had left a bad taste in many mouths. Some Poles believed that the Soviet Union and Hitler had made a deal on when to start the war, which then fell like an avalanche on the Polish people. This lingering resentment against our Soviet State created further complications for the Communist candidates in the Polish elections.

Stalin took an active interest in the elections. I was a witness to many discussions he had with the Polish comrades at that time. I say "witness" because I rarely said anything. All the decisions were made by Stalin himself. He sometimes asked for information but never for advice. In all these consultations with the Polish comrades Stalin's number one confidant was Bierut. Other members of our leadership, myself included, also recognized Bierut as a man who deserved confidence and respect. I think even Gomulka, whose own star was rising at that time, recognized Bierut as his leader.

I'd like to record a few words about some of the other Polish comrades who were active in the election. But first a word about one comrade who did not participate in the election at all. This was Wanda Wasilewska, who was living in Kiev at the time. She rejected nomination for one of the seats in the Sejm. Her decision had nothing to do with political considerations. It was a purely personal matter. She had become deeply involved with Korneichuk.[44] To her, he represented a woman's last hope of finding someone to support her in her old age. She faced a dilemma. She had to choose between Korneichuk and Poland. She chose Korneichuk and refused to return to Poland to run for the Sejm. I remember once speaking to her about her decision.

---

of State George C. Marshall said, "It is clear that the provisional government . . . employed widespread measures of coercion and intimidation against democratic elements which were loyal to Poland although not partisans of the Communist bloc."

43. The Polish Socialist Party, which ruled prewar Poland, had a broad base, including on the one hand nationalistic conservatives, and on the other, leftists sympathetic with the Comintern; the latter had little trouble merging with the Communists in the postwar government.

44. A. Korneichuk, a prominent Ukrainian Communist writer and political figure. See *KR*, I, 248, 330.

"You know, Wanda Lvovna, you'll probably have to go home anyway, now that the war is over."

"I'll never go home as long as Poland has a bourgeois government," she replied. "I won't go back until Poland is a socialist country." She became very worked up and continued, "What are you trying to do, run me out of Kiev? You don't want me here?"

Of course, she wasn't serious. She knew how much I liked and respected her. She was simply dramatizing her unwillingness to return to Poland as a candidate in the elections. She was, however, willing to make short trips home, largely to visit her old mother whom she loved very much. On her return to Kiev, she would always bring with her interesting stories and impressions about the situation unfolding in Poland. I gathered she got on well with Bierut but not with Gomulka.

It was from Wanda Wasilewska that I first heard about Cyrankiewicz, whom she'd known before the war and respected highly.[45] Like Osobka-Morawski, Cyrankiewicz was a left-wing Socialist. He'd been active in youth work for the Socialist Party. "Cyrankiewicz is an energetic and able man," Wanda Lvovna had once told me. "He'll be a prominent politician in the future, mark my words."

She was also on good terms with Comrades Berman and Minc.[46] They were both old Communists, veterans of the Comintern apparatus and dedicated to the Marxist-Leninist cause and doctrine. In the early days after the liberation these men were sent straight to Poland from Moscow and proved themselves to be among the best of our tested cadres who represented the sole support of our people in Poland. They both played a key role in the reconstruction, Berman as a well-trained Party worker and Minc as an outstanding economist. They, too, were active in the Sejm elections.

The elections were a success for us and a failure for Churchill. The essence of his policy had been to promote Mikolajczyk to a position from which he could determine both the internal and foreign policies of the Polish state. When the results were in, however, Mikolajczyk's party had been defeated. The Polish Workers' Party and the parties allied with it received an absolute majority of the votes.

45. Jozef Cyrankiewicz, a Socialist-turned-Communist, was the most durable major figure in postwar Polish politics; he served as Premier from the 1947 elections until 1971.

46. Jakub Berman had entered Poland from the Soviet Union with the Red Army; Hilary Minc, too, was Moscow-trained and Moscow-oriented. They were second in power only to Bierut in the first years after the war.

Wanda Lvovna Wasílewska told me about a rather pointed joke which was popular among the Polish intelligentsia at that time. The Poles are very good at political jokes. They had one about a ballot box: "What sort of box is this? You drop Mikolajczyk in, but take Gomulka out!" [47] The point of this joke — and I think it reflected reality — was that the elections weren't objective. Some people thought the majority had voted for Mikolajczyk and the count had been rigged. The West naturally complained that the Communists had cheated.

After the election Bierut gained the principal post in the new leadership with Stalin's support. Comrade Cyrankiewicz replaced Osobka-Morawski as Chairman of the Council of Ministers. Gomulka, Berman, and Minc were also included in the new government. All these posts were decided in close coordination with Stalin. [48]

The governmental policy took a sharp turn to the left, When Mikolajczyk saw Poland had taken a firm socialist stand, he realized there was nothing more for him to do, and he fled the country. By so doing he acknowledged the failure of his policy. With the help of the West he made it to London.

Thus, despite vacillation on the part of certain elements in the population, the majority — and especially the working class — in the end overwhelmingly decided to engage in the socialist reconstruction of the Polish state. Despite the fact that a vote for Mikolajczyk might have turned into a vote for Gomulka, the Polish people didn't stage any resistance against their newly-elected officials. If they had voted for Mikolajczyk but got Gomulka instead, they didn't do anything about it — which meant, to my mind at least, that they lacked deep, consciously determined political convictions. Before the elections they might have been misled or frightened about what the Communists would do if they came to power, but their fear and mis-

47. Khrushchev quotes half in Russian, half in Polish the following Polish ditty:

Co to za szkatułka?
Wrzucasz Mikołajczyka —
Wyjmujesz Gomułkę.

48. The newly elected Sejm met in February and proclaimed Bierut President of the Republic; a few days later the new government was formed under Prime Minister Cyrankiewicz and included Gomulka and Minc as deputy premiers, with Berman as Under Secretary of State in the Prime Minister's office.

trust were part of a temporary mood which quickly passed. The Party's opponents had tried to scare the voters with the prospect of collectivization, but the Party went out of its way to assure the peasants that their farms would not be collectivized. Perhaps these scare tactics worked to a certain extent; but once the leadership was in power, the peasants quickly changed their minds and willingly followed their new government.

I didn't hear a single report or even a single rumor about armed resistance among the Polish population. If trouble had broken out, I certainly would have known about it. Comrades Bierut and Gomulka would have informed Stalin about it in my presence. Even if they hadn't informed him — even if they'd tried to keep secret an outbreak of some kind — we still would have found out.

Of course, when I say there was no trouble in Poland, I'm speaking about the major urban areas. There were quite a few uprisings in the eastern regions of Poland along the Ukrainian border. However, these flare-ups, which sometimes amounted to war, were instigated by Ukrainian nationalists, not Poles; and the flames were fueled by the Americans, who parachuted arms, machinery, communications equipment, and other supplies to the insurgents. We sympathized with the troubles the new Polish government was having in its eastern territories, for on our own side of the border, in the Western Ukraine, we were engaged in a cruel struggle against the OUN and the followers of Stepan Bandera.[49] We also had to contend with strong resistance to the new system among the kulaks and an armed insurrection in Lithuania.[50]

The Ukrainian nationalist activity within Poland became so serious that the Polish armed forces had to conduct full-scale military operations in the frontier areas of their republic near the Carpathian Mountains. Many good men perished at the hands of the terrorists. Among them was a general who had fought under the name "Walter" against Franco in Spain. He had been a close friend of Marshal Ma-

49. Bandera, the leader of the OUN (Organization of Ukrainian Nationalists) was eventually forced to flee into exile (see *KR*, I, 140). In 1959 he was murdered at the door of his Munich apartment by a KGB (Soviet secret police) agent, who used a gun that fired a poisonous vapor.

50. In the first years of postwar Soviet rule in Lithuania, there were numerous armed clashes between Lithuanian partisans and the Soviet military and secret police forces. Moscow carried out a systematic campaign of mass deportations and forced collectivization of agriculture to subdue the Baltic republic. Lithuania had lost its independence as part of a secret protocol to the Ribbentrop-Molotov Pact.

linovsky. Rodion Yakovlevich once introduced him to me. This Polish general was, as I recall, a Soviet man.[51]

There were a number of Soviet Poles serving in Poland at that time. The most famous, of course, was Marshal Rokossovsky, who was commander in chief of the Polish army. He was a true patriot of the Soviet Union, despite the fact that he'd been arrested and spent his share of time in jail. He escaped execution but wasn't released from prison until after World War II began. He went on to a glorious career in the war and was made a Hero of the Soviet Union. When it came time for the new leadership in Poland to select a military leader, Bierut asked Stalin to give him an experienced soldier. Who could have been a better choice for the post than Rokossovsky? That was Stalin's decision, and Bierut was all for it.[52]

I was present when Stalin summoned Rokossovsky to inform him of his new assignment. Rokossovsky literally fell on his knees and begged Stalin not to send him to Poland. He said all his life he had been intimately connected with the Soviet Union and he couldn't bear to leave. Stalin pressed him and convinced him it was necessary to accept the transfer. Rokossovsky consented, but he asked Stalin one favor: that he be allowed to remain a citizen and a marshal of the Soviet Union, and that he be allowed to keep all the awards and medals he had received for his military conduct. Stalin willingly agreed.

I was pleased and proud for Comrade Rokossovsky, whom I respected very much. It goes without saying that the reactionary forces which had come to the surface correctly understood that Rokossovsky would never raise his hand against the Soviet Union, nor would he lead the Polish army against the Soviet army. In short, he may have been a Polish marshal, but he was also a Soviet marshal — and no one had better forget it.

51. General Karol Swierczewski, also known as "Walter" during the Spanish Civil War, was — like Rokossovsky — a Pole by ethnic background but a "Soviet man" by citizenship. Stalin attached Swierczewski to the postwar Polish army to guarantee its receptivity to directions from Moscow.

52. It was Rokossovsky who, on Stalin's orders, held back the advancing Soviet army on the banks of the Vistula during the Warsaw uprising. Rokossovsky became Defense Minister of Poland in 1949.

Gomulka in Trouble

I FREQUENTLY attended meetings between Stalin and the Polish comrades. There was nothing abstract about the discussion at these meetings; they were devoted to deliberating on the concrete problems facing Poland. When I use the word "deliberating," I should qualify it by repeating what I've said before: Stalin never really consulted others; he made up his own mind for his own reasons, and his reasons for doing what he did were increasingly based on his bestial suspiciousness.

Take, for example, his attitude toward Bierut, a man he clearly liked very much. I remember him saying in the inner circle of our leadership, "About this fellow Bierut: why do you suppose he never got caught by the Germans? What was he doing all that time after we sent him into Poland? And what about his wife? Who is she, anyway? What does it mean that he got to know her in the underground?"

This was typical of Stalin. He was always extracurious about the wives of other leaders. Not that he was attracted to them as women. How could he be? He never even laid eyes on them. But he thought foreign intelligence services always recruited agents among Communists through women. As a result, he was forever asking about the women in other men's lives and how they'd met. And when Stalin started asking that sort of question about someone, disaster might be right around the corner. Fortunately, Bierut managed to avoid such disaster, partly because he knew how to handle Stalin. He treated Stalin with great respect and paid close attention when Stalin spoke, but at the same time Bierut was calm and relaxed in Stalin's presence. He never made Stalin feel nervous or self-conscious; when Stalin was nervous, he got suspicious.

Gomulka was different. He always concentrated intensely when Stalin spoke, staring into his eyes, watching his lips move, and straining to catch every sound Stalin uttered. He even took notes on what Stalin said. On the one hand, Gomulka's attentiveness flattered Stalin. He was a vain man, even though he knew how to disguise the fact by wearing a mask of indifference. He liked to pretend he didn't care what people thought about him because he was leading us on the One True Way; anyone who didn't follow the One True Way was as good as dead, and Stalin had already demonstrated this in 1937 and 1938. So when Gomulka listened to him in rapt attention, Stalin probably concluded that he was like a divine authority for Gomulka, an idea which would appeal to Stalin's vanity. On the other hand, the intensity of Gomulka's concentration made Stalin nervous. This nervousness, too, he concealed under his mask of indifference. Later, however, after the Polish comrades had left, Stalin would confide to us his suspicions: "What kind of fellow is this Gomulka, anyway? He sits there all the time looking into my eyes as though he were searching for something. And why does he bring a notepad and pencil with him? Why does he write down every word I say?"

So we knew Stalin also took Gomulka's behavior as evidence that he might be an imperialist agent and a dangerous enemy, that he was writing down everything in order to inform his bosses what Stalin said.

As time went on, strange rumors began to reach me about the Polish comrades. I say rumors because, despite my membership on the Politbureau, I didn't have any direct knowledge of what was going on in Poland. The same was true of other members of the Politbureau. We were all kept in the dark about a whole range of serious problems facing us both in our country's internal affairs and in our diplomatic relations with other countries. Stalin decided everything completely on his own, like the Lord of Sabaoth.[53] "Investigate and report" — that was all you were supposed to do; and once you gave to Stalin the information he wanted, it was no longer any of your business. Therefore the only way I could keep up with what was going on in Poland was to be present when the Polish comrades reported to Stalin, keep my ears open, and draw my own conclusions. From what I picked up in this way, I realized that pressures were building up inside the Polish leadership — pressures caused by conflicts over personnel policies which could blow the lid off the leadership any time.

You see, Zionism and anti-Semitism are blood brothers. Both are reactionary and inimical to the interests of the working class. It sometimes happens that people of non-Jewish nationality trip up on this slippery ground and slide either toward favoring the Zionists,

53. "The Lord of Sabaoth," literally Lord of Hosts, associated with the Old Testament God in his martial and vengeful aspect.

who are reactionaries, or toward becoming anti-Semites, who are equally reactionary. Let's look at two of the men who contributed to the troubles in the Polish leadership: Berman and Minc, both of whom happened to be Jews.

Berman had great influence on Bierut. Anything he wanted to do he could do through Bierut without stepping forward himself. I doubt that Bierut made a single political move without consulting Berman. However, Berman's attitude toward native Polish cadres was incorrect, and it resulted in certain difficulties for the Polish United Workers' Party.[54] Minc did a fine job as Chairman of the State Planning Commission, and he too was one of Bierut's key advisors and supporters. But, like Berman, Minc demonstrated certain peculiarities for which he later had to be censured by the Party. I would have to say that Bierut may have relied on both these men more than he should have.

Comrade Cyrankiewicz was in an ambiguous, and certainly unenviable, position. He had been a representative of the more numerous Polish Socialist Party before its amalgamation with the Workers' Party.[55] Therefore he continued to be regarded by the other Polish comrades with a certain degree of suspicion.

Keep in mind that the two parties merged not because they held identical political convictions but because they had to make a political deal in order to bring about the socialist reconstruction of Poland. For a long time after the amalgamation, the Communists didn't entirely trust Cyrankiewicz. They used to say such things as, "God knows who that man really is and what he's really thinking. He's a very mysterious type."

There were all sorts of rumors about him, some of which I heard from Gomulka. For instance, I was told Cyrankiewicz liked to drive his own car, without a chauffeur. He really knew how to drive fast, too. His driving habits touched off all sorts of talk. People started saying he was on bad terms with his wife and went off in his car to see other women. It's probably a good thing Stalin was dead by the time we picked up these stories, because if he'd heard them it would have meant a bad end for Comrade Cyrankiewicz.

54. "Native Polish cadres" — as opposed to Jews.
55. The amalgamation of the Polish Socialist Party with the Workers' (Communist) Party took place in December, 1948; the result was the Polish United Workers' Party, headed by Bierut.

However, Stalin was still very much alive when the rumor reached us that Cyrankiewicz was not a Pole at all, but the son of a Jewish merchant, and that Cyrankiewicz was a modified Jewish name. This rumor was meant to show that Cyrankiewicz didn't genuinely belong to the Polish leadership. Comrade Cyrankiewicz is an intelligent man; he knew exactly what was being said about him behind his back and what it meant. All the suspicions and rumors had an impact on his personality. At meetings he kept quiet, speaking only when his opinion was asked, and always addressing himself only to the matter under discussion. It was sometimes hard to know exactly where he stood on the more controversial problems.

Zambrowski was different.[56] Everyone knew where he stood. He was the head of the Personnel Section of the Central Committee, and he was accused of having pro-Zionist sympathies. Because he was a Communist and a veteran of underground Party activity during the Hitlerite occupation, he couldn't be called a Zionist himself. But because he was a Jew and because more Jews than Poles got promoted to key economic and political posts, Zambrowski was accused of showing patronage toward other Jewish comrades.

Of course, promoting *only* Jews would have been a stupid thing to do even if he had been a Zionist in disguise; it would have exposed him to all kinds of charges. Zambrowski was not a stupid man. Personally, I don't think he was a Zionist either. But he did get a reputation for cold-shouldering the Polish cadres in a Polish state and promoting Jewish cadres when there was no objective grounds for choosing them over Poles. Naturally, this irritated the Polish comrades.

I'd be the first to admit that among Poles there were some very strong manifestations of anti-Semitic feeling; we've even had cases here in our own country in which Jews were denounced for Zionism without just cause. But Zambrowski deserved some criticism. The unfair promotion of Jews over Poles represented an absolutely unacceptable case of political myopia on the part of the Polish leadership, and there was more than one example of this myopia.

Gomulka understood how mistaken — indeed, how harmful — it was to let this virus grow unchecked in the Polish leadership.[57] Not

56. Roman Zambrowski, like Berman, had reentered Poland with the Red Army at the end of the war.
57. The "virus" of a Jewish take-over.

only was he a Pole; he was a more mature politician than some of his comrades. He was also more straightforward in expressing himself; I would even say he was abrasive. He started objecting vociferously to Bierut about the personnel policies of Berman, Minc, and most of all, Zambrowski. Bierut, who was deeply under the influence of Berman and Minc, did not accept Gomulka's objections.

The virus spread and, after a while, came to Stalin's attention. You might have thought Stalin would have taken Gomulka's side in the dispute with Berman and Minc, since they were Jews.[58] But there were two factors that led Stalin to oppose Gomulka. First, Bierut supported Berman and Minc, and Stalin had more confidence in Bierut than Gomulka. Second, as far as Stalin was concerned, the conflict in the Polish leadership had nothing to do with the Jewish question. If Gomulka's opponents had accused him of being anti-Semitic, Stalin probably would have taken Gomulka's side. Instead, however, the Polish comrades accused Gomulka of being *pro-Yugoslav*. They didn't make these charges publicly, but they made sure they reached Stalin's ears.

At that time Stalin had broken relations with Yugoslavia and declared Tito an enemy of the people, an enemy of socialism, and a traitor to the cause, bent on returning to capitalism.[59] I'm absolutely sure that if the Soviet Union had a common border with Yugoslavia, Stalin would have intervened militarily. As it was, though, he would have had to go through Bulgaria, and Stalin knew we weren't strong enough to get away with that. He was afraid the American imperialists would have actively supported the Yugoslavs — not out of sympathy with the Yugoslav form of socialism, but in order to split and demoralize the socialist camp.

Now, you might ask, how did Gomulka get mixed up in the Yugoslav problem? How could he be accused of having a pro-Yugoslav position? Gomulka had led a Polish delegation to Yugoslavia before the final break between Stalin and Tito but after a black cat had already crossed the road between them. While in Yugoslavia, Gomulka made some speeches in which, naturally enough, he said some things calculated not to offend his hosts, but rather to praise Tito for

58. Stalin himself was notoriously anti-Semitic (see *KR*, I, 258–269).
59. Stalin expelled Yugoslavia from the Cominform in June, 1948. He had been increasingly impatient with Tito's independent foreign policy and general reluctance to take orders from Moscow.

what he was doing. Later, when conflict arose inside the Polish leadership, Gomulka's opponents used those speeches against him, saying he had sympathized with Titoist positions. This was enough for Stalin. He considered anyone who had close contacts with Tito to be little better than Tito himself. This was typical of Stalin: anyone associated with his enemies was treated as an enemy.

Gomulka was also said to be unwilling to allow collectivization in Poland. Other countries that had been liberated from German occupation and begun building socialism were at this time organizing collective farms — but not Poland, and Gomulka was blamed. Personally I think Gomulka was absolutely right to oppose collectivization. As a result, today Polish agriculture is in good shape. The Poles not only provide for themselves: they export their products. They make wonderful bacon, which for them means hard currency. Even when the United States had an embargo on our crab meat and caviar, it was buying Polish bacon. I can just taste and smell this wonderful product. Talking about it makes my mouth water.

But in the late forties Gomulka's agricultural policies were held against him. Stalin still favored collectivization, and when he heard that Gomulka opposed him on this subject, it was the last straw needed to tip the political scales against Gomulka.

For a while Gomulka was left hanging. Even though he'd already made up his mind, Stalin pretended not to be involved in the conflict dividing the Polish leadership. Stalin always knew how to wait; he knew how to wear a mask of impenetrability. For a certain period, even though I saw Stalin in the presence of the Polish comrades, I didn't realize a cloud had gathered over Gomulka's head.

Then one day, when I was at Stalin's he received a phone call. He listened impassively, hung up, and came back to the table where I was sitting. As was his habit, he didn't sit down but paced aound the room.

"That was Bierut calling," he said. "They've arrested Gomulka. I'm not sure it was the right thing to do. I wonder whether they have sufficient grounds to arrest him."

Stalin knew very well there were absolutely no grounds at all for arresting Gomulka, any more than there were grounds for arresting Spychalski, Kliszko, Loga-Sowinski, or any other comrades who were arrested at the same time.[60]

60. Zenon Kliszko and Ignacy Loga-Sowinski, along with Spychalski, were closely

All had been prominent activists in the underground; all had conducted themselves honorably in the ranks of the Communist Party, and all were loyal, honest men. We didn't know much about the arrests at the time, but we learned quite a bit after Stalin's death and more still after Comrade Bierut's death. Maybe we didn't show enough interest in the arrests at the time they happened. If that's true, it was only because we didn't wish to intervene in the internal affairs of the Polish Republic. Besides, what was done was done. It was already too late for us to do anything about it. The Polish comrades had made their move, and no one was going to stop them from plunging ahead in the direction they wanted.

The arrests were justified as necessary to consolidate the Party. In fact, they had the opposite effect. People in the Polish leadership stopped expressing their own opinions; they stopped debating collectively the best way to further Poland's development. If someone had an opinion of his own, he kept it to himself. Everyone fell silent, and when that happens, anything can happen. Factions develop. Divisive elements spring up. Unity is eroded. The leadership is weakened in the eyes of the people, and as a result the people begin to lose confidence.

That's exactly what began to happen in Poland, and Stalin was largely to blame. Of course Stalin had his aides, but they were just sycophants. Just as Lenin warned us in his Testament, Stalin mistrusted everyone; and he acted cold-bloodedly on his mistrust.

associated with Gomulka. They were all removed from the leadership in late 1949 and arrested in July, 1951.

9

East Europe: The Making of an Alliance

Rumania

I WOULD like to say something about the development of our relations with the other fraternal countries.

During the retreat of the Hitlerite armies from the Soviet Union our troops engaged and destroyed the Germans near Kishinev, then pursued the enemy across the border into Rumania. At the beginning of the war, Hitler had promised Antonescu the annexation of the Crimea in exchange for Rumania's participation in the war against the Soviet Union. Hitler was no miser when it came to making promises, but if he had achieved his goal and won the war, Rumania would have been reduced to being a slave of Germany. With the collapse of the German occupation, the Antonescu government was overthrown by a coup d'etat.[1]

I was later told by Dej that the coup was joined by the young King.[2] By the King's order, Dej himself was released from prison, where he had been sitting throughout the war. Dej was brought to the palace to participate in the formation of a new government. Thus, the King acknowledged that the Communist Party enjoyed wide support among the Rumanian people.

Rumania withdrew from its alliance with Germany. With that the

1. Ion Antonescu, Rumania's wartime fascist Premier, was overthrown by a coup d'etat in August, 1944. Rumania ceased hostilities against Russia, turned around, and joined the war against Germany.

2. Gheorghe Gheorghiu-Dej, the Rumanian Party chief, was later Premier (1952–55), then First Secretary of the Workers' (Communist) Party and President of the State Council from 1955 until his death ten years later. King Michael played a determinative role in Antonescu's overthrow and Rumania's about-face in the war.

Germans began to bomb Bucharest, but for them it was already too late. Our troops had entered Rumania and joined forces with the Rumanian army to drive the Germans out. So Rumania had switched from being a German ally to being a Soviet ally. Of course, we hadn't yet dealt with the question of whether Rumania would become our ideological ally as well — that is, a country dedicated to the building of socialism. Rumania still had a bourgeois system of government and a king as its head of state. The Soviet Union awarded the Order of Victory to the Rumanian King as a token of our gratitude for Rumania's cessation of hostilities against us.

We kept in touch with the developing situation in Rumania through General Zheltov, who was our commissar, or commandant, in Bucharest.[3] He was an old army officer from way back and a highly intelligent man. Not long ago I saw him on television. He made friends with the Rumanian King and frequently went on hunting trips with him.

The King's government was headed by Petru Groza. He was a rich landowner, yet he was also a man of progressive ideas. Even though he wasn't a Communist, he had enough common sense to realize that the day of the big landowners had passed and the time had come to ally himself with "the new order," as they say abroad. He gave up his property, either turning it over to the state or distributing it among the peasants. When he became Prime Minister of the new government, Groza conducted a policy of strengthening ties with the Soviet Union.

After a while he became our friend. I met him in 1951 when he took his vacation with Stalin in Sochi. Stalin literally dragged me along against my will. He was terribly pleased that Petru Groza was going to join us. I remember how all through dinner Stalin kept saying over and over, "Petru Groza is coming, Petru Groza is coming!" He also kept drinking, and pretty soon he was so drunk he didn't even know who this Petru Groza was any more. After Stalin's death, I met Groza at a reception in China. Our meeting was very brief, but he made a good impression on me.[4]

As political developments continued, they were brought under the control of the Communist Party, which gained more and more influ-

3. General A. S. Zheltov, Marshal Konev's deputy at the Allied Control Commission after the war. He did political work in Austria and Hungary.
4. Groza was head of a splinter left-wing party known as the Plowmen's Front. The Soviets directly intervened in Rumania's postwar political scene to install him as Premier. He visited Peking in 1954, as did Khrushchev.

ence over the Rumanian people. Finally the King left Rumania. Dej told me how it happened. The Rumanian comrades went to the King and said, "You can take anything you want with you if you'll leave the country." So he loaded a train and left.[5] Thus the monarchy came to an end, and the red banner of socialism was lifted over Rumania.

Dej, as I recall, was Minister of Transportation in the first government. Another leader was Ana Pauker.[6] I hadn't met her personally, but I'd heard a lot about her from Comrade Manuilsky.[7] She'd been an official of the Comintern. Manuilsky valued her highly as one of the best prepared political workers. Among the new leaders of Rumania, she was considered to have the most thorough grounding in Marxist-Leninist theoretical teaching.

I was personally acquainted with Comrade Luca, another member of the new government. He may have been a Ukrainian originally, though he knew the Rumanian language very well. I'd run across Luca several times when our troops occupied Chernovtsy in 1940. He'd been working in the underground there; and once Chernovtsy was incorporated into the Soviet Union, he was made a Party leader in the area.[8]

Another active politician in the new Rumanian leadership was an excellent comrade whose name I've forgotten, but I remember he was a Jew by nationality.[9] Nevertheless, he'd been well trained and tested as a Communist. He impressed me as a man of knowledge and experience who really knew Party work inside and out. As I recall, he was particularly close to Ana Pauker. I didn't meet him until later, when I came to Rumania for talks with Dej. This was after Ana Pauker and other comrades had already been arrested. The Jewish comrade still held his seat on the Politbureau. However, he must have been living on borrowed time, for not long afterwards he too was arrested. Poor man, they shot him. That was the end of his political career and his life. It was a shame. He'd served more than his

5. King Michael was forced to abdicate in December, 1947.
6. Foreign Minister Ana Pauker was probably the only rabbi's daughter to reach the upper echelons of the postwar Communist leadership. She spent many years working in the Comintern in Moscow before and during the war.
7. D. Z. Manuilsky was one of Stalin's principal agents in the Comintern.
8. Vasile Luca, a Hungarian Jew by background, spent the war years in Moscow. (Chernovtsy, where Luca worked in the Communist underground, was in the pre-partition Polish Ukraine.)
9. In the Soviet Union, Jews are officially considered to comprise a "nationality," just like Russians, Latvians or Georgians.

share of time in prison before the Communists came to power, and I, for one, had never had any reason to doubt his honesty and integrity.[10]

Among the many prominent Rumanian comrades who'd had their schooling in prison were Chivu Stoica and Nicolae Ceausescu, who is now the President of Rumania and the General Secretary of the Rumanian Communist Party.[11] Dej told me Ceausescu had been in jail with him. He'd been a leader of the youth organization, the Rumanian Komsomol, and Dej had the greatest respect for him and trust in him.

Comrade Bodnaras had also spent a long time in prison. He was among the oldest Rumanian Communists. When I met him after Stalin's death, he was either Minister of Internal Affairs or Minister of Defense, and he could speak Russian better than any of the other comrades. It was easy to talk to him without an interpreter. I'd even say he spoke like a native, without a trace of accent.[12]

Bulgaria

THERE are strong brotherly feelings for the Soviet Union among all the peoples of the socialist countries, but I've always found the Bulgarians' friendship for us particularly ardent. Personally, I've always been a great admirer of the Bulgarian people, especially Bulgarian farmers. They are wonderful vegetable growers. I spent my childhood and early manhood in the Donbass, where Bulgarian vegetable farmers ran many of the best agricultural enterprises. They were marvelous organizers. They literally showered the markets with high-quality, low-price produce.

I can still remember how a Bulgarian farmer used to get up early in the morning, load up his two horses, and go to the market in town.

10. Khrushchev is probably referring here to Iosif Chisinevschi, a Bessarabian Jew and hard-line Stalinist who survived the Pauker purge in 1952 but was ousted from all his posts in 1957. Neither Pauker nor Chisinevschi was executed, although it is not surprising for Khrushchev to assume they were.

11. Chivu Stoica took over as Premier in 1955 when Dej assumed the Party leadership. Nicolae Ceausescu, the current President and Party leader, had been active in the Communist youth movement before the war.

12. Emil Bodnaras, of Ukrainian and German parentage, had been an officer in the Royal Rumanian Army until 1933, when he deserted to the USSR. He remained there until 1944, then was sent back behind the lines into Rumania to organize the Communist underground. After the war he was Defense Minister.

He would always wear a wide-brimmed hat. He knew all his clients by name. Most of them were miners' wives. "Ladies, my sweet ladies," he would chant in a singsong voice, "come buy my greens!" You could always get credit from him, too.

Later, when I grew up and went to work, I was able to buy a bicycle. After hours, once I'd changed out of my work clothes, I liked to pedal out into the fields and look at the Bulgarians' farms. I much admired the fruits of their labor — the fat, red tomatoes and purple eggplants, to say nothing of the cabbages and cucumbers. The bright glow of an eggplant field always makes me feel poetic.

Of course, today we still get many vegetables from Bulgaria. I sometimes joke to my relatives, "You know, while the Bulgarians are our brothers, the tomatoes they send us aren't as tasty as the ones they eat themselves." Why? Because they're harvested too early and aren't allowed to ripen on the stem. Therefore they don't taste as though they had just come from the vegetable patch. Sometimes consumers I meet express their dissatisfaction with the tomatoes imported from Bulgaria, but that's another subject.

The point I want to emphasize here is that the Bulgarians truly *are* our brothers. I'd say we have a special relationship with them. Their feelings toward us are understandable. Not so many years have passed since the battlefields of Bulgaria were littered with the bones of Russian warriors who died winning Bulgaria's independence from the Turkish yoke.[13]

The people of Bulgaria also correctly understood that the Soviet Union had spilled its blood to liberate them from the Hitlerite yoke in World War II. So did the people of Czechoslovakia. We had the very best relations with the Czechoslovaks and the Bulgarians after the war. Because our relations with these countries were so good, the capitalists did everything they could to stir up trouble.

I remember once after the war Stalin became terribly concerned that the clouds of war were gathering over Bulgaria. He had received reports alleging that the Americans were getting ready to attack by unleashing the Turks against Bulgaria. The other members of the Politbureau had no idea where Stalin had gotten this report, but we could tell how worried he was when we met with him at the Nearby Dacha.[14]

13. Imperial Russia declared war on Turkey in 1877, the year after Bulgaria rose in revolt against Turkish rule.
14. The Nearby Dacha was Stalin's heavily fortified retreat on the outskirts of Mos-

He gave an order then and there for the Bulgarian leaders to come
to Moscow immediately. They were led by the Chairman of the
Council of Ministers.[15] Lukanov also came. He was an old Communist, a tough warrior, and a veteran of the [Civil] War in Spain.[16]

Stalin instructed the Bulgarian comrades to strengthen their antitank and other land defenses. In other words he gave them a long list
of elementary measures which the Bulgarians were perfectly capable
of taking on their own, without Stalin's instructions. But Stalin had
worked himself into a white heat of worry and, as always, tried to
take direct command of the situation.

He did much the same thing in 1948 at the time of the February
Events in Czechoslovakia. The assumption of power by the working
class there increased tensions with our former allies. I would even
say England, France, and the United States were frightened by what
happened in Czechoslovakia. In any event, they stepped up their
aggressive policies. Hardly a single day went by when American
planes didn't violate Czechoslovak air space. In the Soviet Union
there was considerable alarm that the US might send its troops into
Czechoslovakia and try to restore the capitalist government which
had been overthrown by the working class under the leadership of
the Communist Party.[17]

East Germany

THROUGHOUT my memoirs I've made clear that in our eyes, Germany under Hitler was a scourge and the bitterest of enemies. However, Russia's relations with Germany have not always been so bad.
Before the Revolution — and before Hitler's rise to power — we
used to have close economic ties with Germany. The Germans had a

---

cow where he spent much of his time in his last years and where he died in 1953 (see
KR, I, 296–306, 316).

15. If, as is likely, the Bulgarians were summoned to Moscow after the US broke
diplomatic relations with Bulgaria in February of 1950, the head of this delegation
would have been Vulko Vulev Chervenkov, brother-in-law of Georgi Dimitrov, the
Premier and Party leader who had recently died.

16. Karlo Todorov Lukanov, the Foreign Minister. He also served as Deputy Premier and ambassador to Moscow.

17. In the first volume of *KR*, Khrushchev describes postwar relations with Czechoslovakia, Hungary and Yugoslavia.

ready market for their products in our country. They even had certain concessions here.

When I returned to the Donbass after the Civil War, I remember that a German firm called the Siemens Company operated a concession at Mine Number 30. Our chief miner was upset about the Germans' being given a concession. He went to Abakumov, who was then manager of the mines, and said, "Let me work Mine 17; I promise you, Yegor Trofimovich, we'll do no worse than the Germans in Number 30."[18]

But it wasn't a question of skill — it was a question of equipment. A competition was organized, our workers against the Germans, and we showed that we could work a shaft and come up with new deposits of coal on our own — without any help from the Germans.

Some time later, after I'd studied at the Yuzovka Workers' Faculty and become head of the Organizational Section of the Yuzovka District Party Committee, the Germans finished restoring a coking plant at Mine Number 30. I was invited to attend a rally that was organized to celebrate the opening of the plant. As a veteran miner and metal fitter from the area, I knew everybody and everybody knew me.

Since the Germans had restored the plant, I thought it would be a good idea to bring a German Communist to Yuzovka. It was spring vacation, so I invited a German student to come down from Moscow where he was enrolled at some institute.

The first speaker at the rally was a representative of the German company that had restored the coking plant. He was fat and didn't speak Russian. The workers and peasants in their dirty, tattered clothes stood around gawking at this gross German who couldn't even speak their language. When he finished his speech, no one clapped.

Then I got up and announced that a German comrade from the Comintern in Moscow would speak. He was greeted with cheers. He made a short speech, and the audience burst into stormy applause. I doubt that the workers and peasants understood the substance of the German student's speech any better than they did that of the company man's; but when I introduced the student as being from the Comintern, that was enough for them to welcome him with an outpouring of fraternal warmth.

18. G. T. Abakumov, then manager of the Rutchenkov mines, was later Minister of the Coal Industry and an associate of Khrushchev's in the building of the Moscow Metro (see *KR*, I, 65–68).

I'm telling this story because it illustrates the authority commanded by the Third International.[19] A German representative of the Comintern was a welcome guest to Yuzovka even at a time when German industrialists were milking profits out of us.

There's no need to talk about our relations with Germany after the rise of Hitler and during the Great Patriotic War. We had no "relations." We were at war, the most terrible, bloody war in our people's history. However, even during those awful years, we were on good terms with some German Communists. I've already described Comrade Ulbricht's activities at the Front where I was a member of the Military Council.[20]

After the war, our former allies began restoring capitalist regimes wherever they could — in France, Italy, and Greece. I should add that Greece was a special case because the Communist Party there put up a fierce resistance to the capitalist restoration; but this movement was suppressed, and the reactionary forces triumphed.

Germany was also a special case. Germany was our defeated enemy, yet our former allies were determined to set up the West Germans on their own. This represented a direct threat to our national security, a challenge to the impregnability of our borders and to the conditions necessary for the building of socialism and the ultimate victory of Communism.

To use Lenin's phrase, Stalin responded by prodding the capitalist world with the tip of a bayonet. He imposed a blockade on the city of Berlin.[21] In view of the American imperialists' attempt to restore Germany [to independent status and military potency], I think Stalin's action was justified. You must remember that he was afraid of a new round of destruction, greater, perhaps, than what we had just suffered at the hands of Hitlerite Germany. Stalin imposed the blockade as an act of survival.

Unfortunately, while he might have been right in what he wanted to accomplish, Stalin failed to take account of the realities facing

19. The Third Communist International, founded in 1919, is usually referred to simply as the Comintern.

20. Walter Ulbricht had crossed paths with Khrushchev when he was head of the Moscow-based Political Department of the German Communist Party in exile during the war (see *KR*, I, 205–207).

21. In response to the Western Allies' creation of the nucleus of a future West German state and the introduction of a currency reform in the Western occupation zones, the Soviet authorities imposed a blockade on Allied garrisons in Berlin and the civilian population of West Berlin; the blockade lasted from the summer of 1948 until the summer of 1949 and was broken by the airlift of supplies into the beleaguered city.

him. His plan was badly thought out. I don't know who was advising him at the time. I was a member of the Politbureau, and I know he didn't discuss the matter with any of us — except, perhaps, Molotov. In any event, the capitalists turned out to be too strong for Stalin. He was forced to lift the blockade, and — if I may use such a political expression — he was forced to capitulate. He had to settle for an understanding which was less favorable to us than the Potsdam agreement. Until then, it had looked to the outside world that the German Democratic Republic was firmly in the hands of the Soviet Union and that our mightiest army was stationed on East German soil. Then we were forced to sign a treaty which undercut our position by comparison with the conditions which had been agreed to at Potsdam. This was an agreement which, in the absence of a peace treaty, has regulated our relations with the West right up to the present day.[22]

We considered ourselves to be occupiers of the GDR — and I'm not using the term negatively. We were proud to be occupiers. After all, the GDR had been part of the German Empire, and the Germans had tried to destroy our state and turn our people into slaves. As the victors in the struggle for our independence, we had certain rights. The Germans, naturally, looked at the situation differently, and Stalin made matters worse by overdoing it. Certain antagonistic forces began to develop in the GDR, along with strong Western influences. The Party was still picking up the pieces after the war. The Party was soft; it was in disarray; it was in danger of crumbling apart. Fortunately, the leaders of the Party — our late friend Wilhelm Pieck and his comrade in arms Ulbricht — did what needed to be done. They merged the Communists with the Social Democrats and reworked the Party platform so as to rally the people and set them on a socialist path.[23] But that took time, and meanwhile the people were casting about, not knowing which way to turn. We couldn't count on the sympathies of the East German people in the way we would have liked.

The situation came to a head just a few months after Stalin's death.

22. Stalin, Harry Truman, Winston Churchill, and Clement Attlee met at Potsdam in July and August of 1945 and set up the four-power Allied Control Commission; its breakdown in 1947 led to the Berlin blockade the next year.
23. Under the auspices of the Soviet occupation administration, the Communists merged with the Social Democrats in 1946, forming the Socialist Unity Party. Wilhelm Pieck, one of two joint chairmen of the Socialist Unity Party, became President of the German Democratic Republic in 1949.

There was an uprising — not an armed revolt, but a wave of demonstrations.[24] Thanks to the Party and its leadership, the uprising never got out of hand. As a result of the postwar circumstances which developed in the GDR, we knew we would have to find other ways of establishing East Germany on a solid Marxist-Leninist footing. We knew Stalinism was contrary to Marxism-Leninism, and we knew we would have to strip away the thin coating of Stalinism from our policies and reactivate the ideas of Lenin.

Forming the Warsaw Pact

STALIN'S death came as a great shock to our people. For years the propaganda agencies had been trumpeting, with all the stops pulled, that Stalin was a genius, the friend and father of the people, the safeguard of the very air we breathed: "Stalin gave us our victory over the enemy." Then suddenly, there was no more Stalin. As I say, it was a great shock. Not only for the people, but for us, the others in the leadership, who had worked so many years at Stalin's side. Personally, I took his death hard. I wept for him. I sincerely wept.

When Stalin died, he left us a legacy of anxiety and fear. Beria, more than anyone else, kept that anxiety and fear alive among the rest of us. For a long time I hadn't trusted Beria. More than once I'd confided to Malenkov and Bulganin that I regarded Beria as an adventurist in foreign policy. I knew he was just biding his time, building up his own position and assigning his men to other important posts, waiting for a chance to pervert the development and direction of the international Communist movement. The enemies of socialism and of our Soviet State saw what Beria was up to and would have made good use of it for their own purposes if Beria had not been unmasked and removed.[25]

After Stalin's death, the West continued to stir up trouble and aggravate tensions wherever and however they could, particularly in the form of illegal reconnaissance flights over the German Demo-

---

24. Shortly after Stalin's death in 1953, the East German working population balked at an increase in production quotas, and a wave of strikes swept the country. A general uprising took over whole towns, forcing Soviet troops to intervene in the summer.

25. For a detailed account of Beria's downfall in 1953, see *KR*, I, 321–341.

cratic Republic and Czechoslovakia. What else could we expect? The aims of the West were perfectly obvious: the capitalists wanted to show us that they could still shake a socialist country to its very foundation. They knew we were in a complicated and difficult situation after Stalin's death, that the leadership Stalin had left behind was no good because it was composed of people who had too many differences among them. The capitalists also knew that we were still engaged in the reconstruction of our war-ravaged economy and could ill afford the additional burden of heavy defense costs. They gave us no choice but to think seriously about military preparedness. Imperialism still had its teeth, and its teeth were sharper than ever. We were given no chance to rest on our laurels and forget about defense.

[In the early 1950's] it was decided to unify the armed forces of the socialist countries under a joint command. We had discussions in the leadership over the form and composition of such an organization. There were some differences of opinion on the part of certain members of the leadership.

[At this point in the narrative there is an interruption, but from the context it is clear that during these preliminary discussions inside the Kremlin, Foreign Minister Molotov opposed the inclusion of Albania and other unnamed countries in the alliance — and possibly challenged the idea of the alliance itself on the grounds that the Soviet Union could hardly provide for its own national security, let alone the security of the other socialist countries.]

We later explained to Molotov that what he was advocating was absolutely impossible. On the subject of Albania, for instance: up until then our relations with that country had been good. If we didn't include Albania in the alliance, it would be interpreted in the West as a go-ahead signal for the imperialists to intervene and liquidate the socialist society which the Albanian people had created under the leadership of the Albanian Labor Party.[26] Italy, of course, was still weak at that time and wouldn't have dared invade Albania all by itself, but Italy had the backing of the United States and other powerful capitalist countries.

Of course, Molotov didn't want to see capitalism restored in Albania or any other socialist country. No one could accuse him of *that*. His mistake was that he underestimated our strength and our potential. No doubt, the Soviet Union could continue to exist separately

26. The Albanian Labor Party is the Communist Party.

from the European socialist countries on the one hand and from the Asian Socialist countries — China, North Korea, and the Mongolian People's Republic — on the other; but we felt it was better to take a firm stand and to guard against the ever-present possibility of encroachments.[27] By so doing, we would also be strengthening the internal situation.[28] Finally, we reached an agreement within the leadership that Albania must be included in any pact.

The next step was to convene a meeting of leaders from the other socialist countries to discuss the whole matter. We decided to meet in Warsaw. As I recall, the delegations consisted of representatives of the various foreign ministries, so from our side Molotov went. A document, which became known as the Warsaw Pact, was approved and later published. The alliance established by that Pact has played a positive role in the history of our movement. It has contributed to the strength of our position by consolidating and mobilizing the armed might of the Socialist countries. The Warsaw Pact was — and still is — a force to be reckoned with, and our adversaries have come to recognize it as such.[29]

27. By establishing a collective defense policy uniting the socialist countries.
28. He means the "internal situations" — that is, the stability of Communist rule — within each of the member nations.
29. A twenty-year mutual defense pact was signed in Warsaw in May, 1955, among the USSR, Bulgaria, Czechoslovakia, the GDR, Hungary, Poland, Rumania, and — despite Molotov's evident objections — Albania. The timing was partially in response to the formal induction of West Germany into NATO earlier that same month. The first commander of the Warsaw Pact's six million troops was Marshal Konev.

10

Rough Spots in the Alliance

The Polish October

SOME problems developed in the fraternal countries after Stalin's death. A literal uprising occurred in the German Democratic Republic just a few months after he died, and later the situation became very tense in Poland, too. The difficulties in Poland stemmed from the dissolution of the Polish Communist Party before the War. True, the Party was reconstituted during and after the war, but the recognition which the Party received from the working class and the people was never very deep-rooted or widespread.[1] Hence, there was a certain amount of instability in Poland. Furthermore, the Poles still had fresh memories of the Ribbentrop-Molotov Pact, which had partitioned their country in 1939.

I became acutely aware of the situation developing in Poland when I assumed my duties as First Secretary of the Communist Party of the Soviet Union. On more than one occasion I discussed the situation with the Polish comrades. I was on especially good terms with Comrade Bierut, whom I respected very much.

My relations with Comrade Cyrankiewicz and Comrade Ochab were constantly improving, though I can't say the same for my relations with Zambrowski. He and I kept our distance from each other.

---

1. Stalin virtually annihilated the Polish Communist Party in the years 1937–39, when most of its leadership was living in exile in Moscow. Khrushchev has said, "The only reason Bierut and Gomulka stayed alive was that they were relatively unknown in Party circles" (KR, I, 107). The reconstituted Party was called the Polish Workers' Party.

Unlike the others, he didn't join us for vacations in the south.[2] I really didn't know him very well.

From time to time my colleagues in the leadership and I would raise the question with the Polish comrades of why Gomulka was still in jail. "Tell me, Comrade Bierut," I would ask, "what exactly are the charges against Gomulka? What's he doing still in prison? He always made a good impression on me. I trusted him as a good Communist. I don't see why he's being kept under lock and key."

Bierut would give a slight smile and say, "Well, Comrade Khrushchev, to tell you the truth, I myself don't know what the charges are and why he's in jail."

Of course, during this whole conversation, I knew perfectly well what the charges were against Gomulka, how he'd been accused of following a pro-Yugoslav line and so on — I've already related the story here in my memoirs. Bierut knew the reasons, too. And he knew that *I* knew them. He understood that by asking him what the charges were I was expressing my feelings that the charges didn't seem valid to me — especially since our relations with Yugoslavia had taken a sharp turn for the better, a fact which made it more senseless than ever to keep Gomulka in jail. Finally I realized there was no point in beating around the bush with Bierut, so I said, "If you don't know any good reason to keep him imprisoned, then I think you should let him go." Then I added, "Look here, Comrade Bierut: we've been informed that there are forces in Poland which are highly displeased with the national composition of the present leadership." [3]

Bierut knew I was referring to Berman and Minc, two of the men who had instigated Gomulka's arrest and who had a vested interest in keeping him in jail. As I've already said, Bierut had a soft streak in him, which they were able to take advantage of and exert influence on him. Their influence was so great that as long as he lived, Comrade Bierut never did order Gomulka's release from prison.

Then Bierut died and Ochab succeeded him as head of the Party.[4] He led a delegation to China, by way of the Soviet Union of course,

2. Khrushchev means the south of the USSR, at the Black Sea resorts.
3. "National composition" here means a high proportion of Jews.
4. Edward Ochab succeeded Bierut as Party leader after the latter died in Moscow in March, 1956, just after Khrushchev's secret speech on Stalin's crimes to the Twentieth Party Congress. Khrushchev has said that the text of the speech was leaked to the West through the Polish Party after Bierut's death (*KR*, I, 351).

and I had a chance to talk with him man to man. We didn't even need an interpreter because Comrade Ochab spoke Russian fluently, though of course with a Polish accent. Ochab told me Gomulka had finally been released.[5] I asked how he was after almost five years in prison. Ochab said he was physically weakened and badly in need of rest. That gave me an idea.

"Assuming, of course, Comrade Gomulka agrees, why doesn't he come to the Crimea to recuperate? We would do everything to make him welcome and comfortable."

I could tell immediately from his reaction that Ochab didn't like the idea. I'd even say it shook him up somewhat. In any case, he replied that he didn't think Gomulka should come to the Soviet Union for a rest.

Shortly after Ochab's return to Warsaw we learned from our ambassador that the tensions which had been building up had boiled over.[6] Tumultuous demonstrations and general turmoil had broken out at factories in some cities.[7] These outbreaks had distinctly anti-Soviet overtones. Some Poles were criticizing Soviet policy toward Poland, saying that the treaty signed [after World War II] was unequal and that the Soviet Union was taking unfair advantage of Poland economically. In particular they complained that Poland was being forced to supply the Soviet Union with coal at prices lower than those in the world market.

The demonstrators also demanded the withdrawal of Soviet troops from Polish territory. They said nothing about how much Soviet blood had been shed and how many Soviet lives had been sacrificed for the liberation of Poland; no one mentioned how much bread the Soviet Union had given Poland, bread taken from the mouths of the Soviet people to feed the Poles. All these positive facts were stricken from the record. Some of the criticisms against us were justified, but many were fabricated. The propaganda machinery of our enemies began churning out slander against us and against the international Communist movement.

5. Khrushchev is mistaken here: Gomulka had been released from prison on Bierut's order in 1954, but his release wasn't announced until April, 1956.

6. P. K. Ponomarenko, whom Khrushchev had earlier installed as his man in Kazakhstan (see the section "Virgin Lands" in Chapter 7) was ambassador to Poland during the critical years 1955–57.

7. The riots followed a general strike, which began in the industrial city of Poznan in June. A security police official was lynched. Cyrankiewicz condemned the uprising as part of an imperialist plot, and Rokossovsky ordered the army to crush the insurgency. Scores of people were killed and hundreds wounded and arrested.

It's true, our armed forces were then stationed in Poland, just as they're stationed there today. But what was so terrible about that? According to the terms of the Potsdam agreement, we had every right to keep our troops in certain Socialist countries: Poland, Hungary, Rumania, and the German Democratic Republic (we had none in Bulgaria or Czechoslovakia). It was particularly important to us that we have forces in Poland, for Poland represented the only overland communication and supply route connecting us with our enormous army in the German Democratic Republic. Our navy was still small, so we were all the more dependent on our road and railroad access to Germany through Poland. If Poland were to pull out of the Warsaw Pact, we would have been in a very serious situation.

We had further reason to worry when certain elements began to protest the fact that the commander in chief of the Polish army was Marshal Rokossovsky. Everyone knew he was a Hero of the Soviet Union, a loyal Soviet citizen, and that Stalin had sent him to Poland. The majority of the Poles have always been proud of Rokossovsky and always will be, but some began agitating for his dismissal.

As the opposition gained strength, it began to have an impact on the leadership. In no time at all Ochab became impotent. He could no longer determine policy. People stopped obeying him. About this time a Polish general, who had been thrown in jail for no good reason, was released from prison and put in command of the Internal Security Corps, a body of troops that was supposed to be used for guarding government installations and, if need be, for suppressing rebellions against the government.[8] However, this general was manipulated by the enemies of the Soviet Union, and the security forces under his command were used against the Soviet Union and against the Ochab line. They provided the muscle for those forces which sought to replace the pro-Soviet Ochab leadership with a new leadership headed by Gomulka. Ever since Bierut's death the elements which supported Gomulka had been gaining power. At the same time they had began to smear Bierut's name — which was only natural and to a certain extent justified, because they had been jailed with his consent. Gomulka, of course, was a case in point: he had spent a number of years in prison partly because of Bierut.

In short, it looked to us as though developments in Poland were

---

8. The general was Waclaw Komar, a former head of military intelligence, who had been arrested in 1952 and rehabilitated in 1956, when he was put in command of Poland's internal security troops.

rushing forward on the crest of a giant anti-Soviet wave. Meetings were being held all over the country, and we were afraid Poland might break away from us at any moment.

In Warsaw, an important meeting of the [Polish] Central Committee was under way.[9] We had no time to lose. We expressed our urgent desire to meet with the Polish leadership, to hear their side of the story, and to let them know how we viewed the situation. We called Warsaw and asked permission for our delegation to come right away. We were told not to come then. I think it was Gomulka who recommended we come later. This attempt to put us off only irritated us more and made us all the more determined to go immediately. You have to understand we were terribly high-strung at that point. We were offended at the way the Soviet Union was being abused in Poland. So we made up our minds to disregard Gomulka's advice and go there anyway. Looking back on it now, I think we were too hotheaded. We may have acted rashly. It turned out we should have done as Gomulka suggested. But what's done is done.

We decided the composition of the delegation I was to lead: Mikoyan and Marshal Konev, the commander in chief of the armed forces of the Warsaw Pact.[10] The situation was such that we had to be ready to resort to arms if the threat of an armed struggle in Poland became real and if we were in imminent danger of being cut off from our army.[11]

We flew to Warsaw and were met by the Polish comrades at the airport. We went straight to Belvedere Palace, a huge, picturesque and very old place which history tells us was once the residence of the Russian tsar's viceroy in Poland, Constantine, the brother of Nicholas I. It was where we usually stayed on our visits.[12] The moment we arrived we dropped our suitcases and went straight into a meeting with the Polish Politbureau.

It was a very stormy meeting, conducted in the most venomous, acrimonious atmosphere. Almost immediately it turned into a battle of words. For our part, we made some remarks which weren't intended to be conciliatory: we added oil to the fire. I lit into Ochab

9. The Eighth Plenum of the Polish Central Committee met in October to select a new Politbureau.
10. Molotov and Kaganovich were included in the delegation, too.
11. That is, the Soviet divisions in East Germany.
12. Belvedere Palace, where Grand Duke Constantine had lived in the nineteenth century, was the presidential residence after World War II.

right away, accusing him of being the one responsible for the whole situation by not releasing Gomulka earlier when we told him to.

Of course, while it had been I who had urged Ochab to release Gomulka from prison in the first place, I hadn't said anything to Ochab about the necessity of his stepping down to make way for Gomulka. We could hardly have expected the First Secretary of the Polish Communist Party to release a man from jail if it were prearranged for that man to replace him in the leadership. However, we knew full well that Gomulka's release from prison meant his subsequent appointment to the top post. We anticipated that, and we accepted it. Our only worry was that Gomulka's elevation to First Secretary was partly achieved as a result of political machinations by certain anti-Soviet forces.

As for Ochab himself, he had held a pro-Soviet position in the past, but he seemed to be wavering in his resolve about the importance of strengthening relations between Poland and the Soviet Union. He was a beaten man. He tried to defend himself by saying, "Why are you attacking me? I'm finished. There's nothing more I can do." He was trying to save his own skin.

Our closest and most loyal friend in the leadership at that time was Comrade Zawadski, who was Chairman of the Council of State and therefore President of the Republic. At a time when other comrades were either vacillating or turning their backs on us, Comrade Zawadski spoke out in a loud, clear voice about the necessity, first and foremost, of friendship with the Soviet Union. We could tell Gomulka didn't quite trust Zawadski. Gomulka knew that Zawadski had played no small part in the former Bierut leadership, and he also knew that Bierut hadn't been the only one responsible for his arrest. Gomulka held other members of the Bierut government responsible as well, including Zawadski. Nevertheless Zawadski will always live in our memory as a true friend of the Soviet Union.

Other Polish leaders, notably Zambrowski, could barely conceal their resentment toward us. This was perfectly understandable: we'd told Bierut more than once he should replace Zambrowski with someone of Polish nationality [13] as head of the Personnel Section in the Central Committee, and Bierut had obviously told Zambrowski what we said.

Comrade Cyrankiewicz's position was still rather complicated. Ev-

13. By "someone of Polish nationality" Khrushchev means a non-Jewish Pole.

erybody knew that despite Cyrankiewicz's high position [Prime Minister], he didn't have much influence. His position had been precarious for a number of months. After Bierut's death and Ochab's promotion to First Secretary, the Polish leaders raised the question of whether Cyrankiewicz should be removed from the leadership altogether. I had to step in and persuade them that Cyrankiewicz's removal would be a mistake. "You should keep in mind that your assumption of power [after the war] resulted from the amalgamation of two parties, the Communists and the Socialists," I said. "Comrade Cyrankiewicz represents the Socialists, and if you throw him out you'll destroy your coalition and alienate the larger part of the United Workers' Party. Besides, I personally believe Comrade Cyrankiewicz deserves his post as Chairman of the Council of Ministers."

Some of the Polish comrades objected, arguing that Cyrankiewicz was a bad man, that he had certain weaknesses and so on. But I knew how to deal with that line of argument: "Comrades, you should understand that if he seems indecisive, it's only because he lacks self-confidence; he feels he has no support from the rest of you." Then I added, "One more thing, comrades: if you remove Cyrankiewicz, it'll do a lot of damage to the Communist Parties of other socialist countries."

I had in mind Czechoslovakia, Hungary, and the German Democratic Republic, where the Communists had formed similar coalitions with Social Democratic parties. Socialists in the West kept claiming that Communists merged with Social Democrats out of self-interest, that they couldn't gain a majority without Social Democratic support, and that once the Communists were safely entrenched, they'd throw out their Social Democratic partners. We didn't want to supply the West with evidence to prove this claim. We had to look ahead to the future, when there would be other opportunities in other countries to win votes by creating coalitions between socialists and Communists. So it wasn't just Cyrankiewicz's career at stake; it was a principle, relating not only to Poland but to the political doctrine of the entire international Communist movement.

The Polish comrades agreed, and Comrade Cyrankiewicz remained in the leadership; but he obviously didn't come to feel much more sure of himself. During our meeting with the Polish Politbureau, he was obviously on Gomulka's side, but he didn't go out on a limb. He didn't say much, and when he did speak it was with great caution. You could see he had oriented himself toward Gomulka and was ready to join in the repudiation of the former leadership (of which he'd been a part), but at the same time he spoke out in favor of preserving friendly relations with the Soviet Union.

Marshal Konev and I held separate consultations with Comrade Rokossovsky, who was more obedient to us but had less authority than the other Polish leaders. He told us that anti-Soviet, nationalistic, and reactionary forces were growing in strength, and that if it were necessary to arrest the growth of these counterrevolutionary elements by force of arms, he was at our disposal; we could rely on him to do whatever was necessary to preserve Poland's socialist gains and to assure Poland's continuing fidelity and friendship. That was all very well and good, but as we began to analyze the problem in more detail and calculate which Polish regiments we could count on to obey Rokossovsky, the situation began to look somewhat bleak. Of course, our own armed strength far exceeded that of Poland, but we didn't want to resort to the use of our own troops if at all avoidable. On the other hand we didn't want Poland to become a bourgeois country hostile to the Soviet Union.

Our embassy informed us that a genuine revolt was on the verge of breaking out in Warsaw. For the most part these demonstrations were being organized in support of the new leadership headed by Gomulka, which we too were prepared to support, but the demonstrations also had a dangerously anti-Soviet character. In short, the situation was very complicated.

We had no choice but to order Marshal Konev to move our troops closer to the capital.[14] The situation was further complicated because all the roads were controlled by the general in charge of the Polish Security Corps, who was sitting at Gomulka's side and informing him about our troop movements.[15]

Gomulka, as I've already said, was a very sincere and straightforward man; he always came right out and expressed himself if he was displeased or dissatisfied. He came to me and said, "Comrade Khrushchev, I've just received a report that some of your forces are moving toward Warsaw. I ask — I *demand* — that you order them to

14. The Soviet divisions stationed along the German border in Silesia were marching toward Warsaw, allegedly on maneuvers.
15. General Komar, who was known to be on bad terms with Marshal Rokossovsky.

stop and return to their bases. If you don't, something terrible and irreversible will happen."

I never saw him in such a state, before or since. As he spoke, he kept getting up nervously from his chair, coming over to me, and then going back and sitting down again. He was terribly agitated. There was foam on his lips. His eyes expressed not so much hostility as extraordinary agitation.

Naturally I shied away from giving him a direct reply. "There must be some mistake," I said. "You've received incorrect information."

He went away and came back a few minutes later. "No, Comrade Khrushchev, I've now received confirmation that your troops and tanks are on the move." Again he demanded that I stop them or there would be trouble.

The meeting was declared in recess. As I recall, the Poles wanted us to consult among ourselves and make up our minds about the new leadership and its policy — and also make a decision about our forces. We retired to our own chambers. I argued that we should order our tank troops to halt, not to return to their bases but to stop in place, gathered in groups rather than spread out in march formation. Everyone agreed this was the best plan. Konev was notified of our decision. He relayed the order to our forces and also to Rokossovsky.[16]

The people of Warsaw had been prepared to defend themselves and resist Soviet troops entering the city. Only later we learned that guns had been distributed and workers' regiments formed at the largest automobile factory in Warsaw. A clash would have been good for no one but our enemies. It would have been a fatal conflict, with grave consequences that would have been felt for many years to come. It would have taken a long time to heal the wound that would have been inflicted on Soviet-Polish friendship. Enough such wounds had already been inflicted in the course of history. An armed clash between Soviet solders and Polish workers would have been a fresh one — and the most welcome one of all for the enemies of the Soviet Union, of Communism, and of Poland. But our enemies were disappointed.

After deciding to order our troops to halt in place and approving Gomulka's promotion to First Secretary, we rejoined the Polish

16. In November Rokossovsky was replaced as Defense Minister by General Marian Spychalski, whose fall and rise had closely followed that of Gomulka.

comrades and continued our discussions. Gomulka began to address the meeting. We could tell from the way he acted that he was still physically very weak, but he held a commanding position in the Polish leadership — a position which was most advantageous for us. Here was a man who had come to power on the crest of an anti-Soviet wave, yet who could now speak forcefully about the need to preserve Poland's friendly relations with the Soviet Russia and with the Soviet Communist Party. Perhaps I didn't appreciate this fact right at that moment, but I came to appreciate it afterwards. He was just the man to take charge of the Polish leadership at that tense time. Of course some people criticized him and attacked him, but the overwhelming majority accepted his authority and listened to him attentively.

The Polish comrades presented us with an agenda of matters they wanted to discuss, including various claims, complaints, accusations, and demands. Some people denounced us for having signed a treaty with Hitler which led to the partitioning of Poland, but this charge didn't hold up in light of the blood our Soviet soldiers had shed in the struggle to liberate Poland from Hitlerite Germany.

The Poles also continued to demand the withdrawal of our troops. We reached an agreement about this because we trusted Gomulka; we believed his new leadership would adhere to its policy of strengthening friendly relations with the Soviet Union along both state and Party lines. We believed him when he said he realized we faced a common enemy, Western imperialism. I remember how he almost shrieked with agitation, "Poland needs the friendship of the Soviet Union more than the Soviet Union needs the friendship of Poland!" His voice was almost cracking hysterically. We could tell he was speaking sincerely. We took his word as a promissory note from a man whose good faith we believed in.

We returned to the Soviet Union. The turmoil continued in Poland for some time, but that was to be expected. Political dirt had been collecting for years, and you couldn't simply take a damp cloth or a brush or a broom and wipe everything clean just like that. However, once we acknowledged the past inequality, it was only a matter of time before the process of normalization set in. Slowly but surely we managed to clear away the debris of the past from the path of friendship linking the hearts of our two peoples, and to pave the way toward sharing our economic and military resources, for ours was a common struggle against Western imperialists, against West German revanchists, and against all other enemies of socialism.

As the situation in Poland began to normalize, I developed excellent personal relations with the new Polish leadership. More than once I was invited to visit Poland as a guest of Comrade Gomulka. During one such visit, the Polish comrades suggested we make a tour of the country's western regions. I realized these were populated by Poles who had been forced, very much against their wishes, to leave the lands where they'd lived before the war and resettle here. The land itself in the western regions was excellent, so the Polish resettlers' reluctance must have been due to their fear that these areas would be returned to Germany one day. Szczecin was half-deserted; hardly a single Pole was willing to live there.[17]

I began my tour of the western regions in Szczecin, where, as a representative of the Soviet Union, I was welcomed at a number of festive rallies. I made a speech or two. Then I discovered the Polish comrades were planning to make me an honorary citizen of Szczecin. They'd made no effort to coordinate this plan with me in advance. At first I couldn't figure out why they'd do something like this without clearing it with me. Then I saw the light and said to Comrade Gomulka, "Aha! By making me an honorary citizen of Szczecin, you'll be taking me hostage to guarantee that the city remains Polish! You know that as Chairman of the Council of Ministers of the Soviet Union, I have considerable influence, and to have me formally associated with your claims on this city is as good as having money in the bank. You'll be demonstrating that Poland has its foot firmly planted here. Am I right?"

Gomulka smiled and said only, "Comrade Khrushchev, you must believe that we propose making you an honorary citizen of Szczecin out of our deep respect for you."

So he neither confirmed nor denied my suspicions. In fact, I wasn't against the idea. I was willing to play the role of hostage and be an honorary citizen — not because it fulfilled any secret ambition of mine (though of course it was an honor), but because it would raise morale among the Polish comrades and help guarantee the new western borders.

17. These were the regions annexed from Nazi Germany after the war. The Baltic port of Gdansk, which the Germans had seized at the beginning of the war, reverted to Poland, while the northern part of East Prussia went to the USSR. Poland established its western border along the Oder-Neisse Line in a 1950 treaty with the German Democratic Republic. The Baltic port of Szczecin is just west of Gdansk.

In the eastern frontier area of Poland — that is, the Western Ukraine, which became part of Poland after the war — the Polish comrades decided to remove forcibly to the west all those Ukrainians who didn't behave themselves. In this case, too, many Poles were reluctant to resettle in the eastern areas because they lacked confidence in the permanence of the new borders. But the leadership had no such qualms. Our Polish comrades were sure that the Soviet Union would never go back on its decision and that the former Ukrainian lands would remain Polish forever.

Disputes in Comecon

NOT too long after our emergency trip to Warsaw and Gomulka's elevation to First Secretary, the situation in Poland began to normalize and I developed excellent personal relations with Comrade Gomulka. Similarly, after the restoration of order in Hungary, Comrade Kadar and I came to have a good mutual understanding on many issues which arose between our countries. The development of economic relations with Poland and Hungary was particularly important to the process of normalization. In this regard, we had to right some wrongs which had been committed in the past. The presence of certain inequalities in our economic relations with the fraternal countries since Stalin's time had been partly the cause of the complicated situation which had arisen in 1956. Those mistakes had resulted, as much as anything, from Stalin's prewar and postwar economic policies.[18]

During our visit to Warsaw one of the major accusations brought against us by the Polish comrades concerned the price at which the Poles had to sell us enormous amounts of coal for our factories, mills, and generating plants. (We couldn't produce the coal ourselves because our mines in the Donbass had been destroyed in the war.) We had expected this question to come up and had brought Anastas Ivanovich Mikoyan with us to Warsaw because he dealt with precisely this matter.

18. Khrushchev is referring to the "mistakes" of the Polish and Hungarian leaderships, which defied Moscow in 1956. For Khrushchev's account of the Hungarian uprising and its suppression, and his relations with Party leader Janos Kadar, see *KR*, I, 415–429.

"Is what the Poles say true?" I asked him. "Do we really pay lower than world market prices for their coal?"

"Yes, we do."

"And did anyone from the Polish side sign a contract with us agreeing to these prices?"

"Yes," said Mikoyan, "the agreement was signed by Cyrankiewicz on behalf of the Polish government."

"You see?" I said, turning to the Polish comrades. "Your own Prime Minister signed the agreement! So why are you accusing us?"

"What choice did Cyrankiewicz have?" they shot back at me. "He was just following Stalin's orders."

"Well," I said, "we'll look into the matter when we get home. If you're right and Cyrankiewicz was forced into signing by Stalin — and you probably are right, because Anastas Ivanovich [Mikoyan] doesn't deny it — we'll compensate you. In any event, we promise to inform you of our decision."

I later asked Mikoyan, "How did this happen? How could we pay our Polish comrades such an unfair price for their coal?"

"It was all Stalin's doing," he said.

Stalin had probably felt justified because we had shed our blood for Poland's sake [in World War II], and he felt that Poland should repay us with cheap coal. Furthermore, the Poles mined most of their coal in Silesia, a region which became part of Poland after World War II as a result of a Soviet policy calling for the Polish borders to be moved further west. The Poles, of course, rightly claimed Silesia had belonged to them in the past, but they couldn't have dreamed of retrieving those lands without the defeat of Hitlerite Germany, which was accomplished largely by virtue of huge sacrifices on the part of the Soviet Union. Nevertheless, it was up to us to see the error in Stalin's economic policy toward Poland. It wasn't easy but we did admit the mistake and compensate Poland for the unfair price it had been getting for our coal purchases.

We also told the Poles we would pay them back for their railroad deliveries. These compensations themselves were easy enough for us to make. The Poles owed us a lot of money, so all we had to do was reduce their debt to us. To look at it objectively, to calculate it with a pencil and piece of paper, you could see that the Soviet Union had given Poland much more than Poland had ever given the Soviet Union. I'm talking about strictly material aid, to say nothing of the priceless contribution we had made to them in blood and human lives. However, all such purely mathematical considerations were put aside, forgotten, and Polish national pride was raised on the shield. We had to remember that the unequal commercial treaties forced on Cyrankiewicz by Stalin had helped turn Poland into a resentful neighbor and nearly set off a political explosion.

Similarly, Stalin had created bad feeling in Czechoslovakia, the German Democratic Republic, Rumania, Hungary, China, and Austria as well as Poland by setting up international organizations to exploit our allies' natural resources.[19] We had been meaning to terminate these organizations ever since Stalin's death. But liquidating them wasn't enough. We had to change the whole picture of our economic relations with our allies. We had to give our comrades the benefit of all reasonable doubt. This meant scrupulously analyzing all past treaties and contracts, then rectifying all the mistakes that had been made.

Nevertheless, we had to draw the line somewhere. A number of Poles were making ridiculous charges about our economic relations, accusing us of exploiting them in cases where in fact we had been giving them genuine assistance. For instance, some people said we had forced Poland to build a large steel mill in Nowa Huta near Krakow. Gomulka himself later spoke up heatedly in our defense on this score, saying, "What are you talking about? The Soviet Union helped us build this plant for our own good."

That was true. In addition to being a positive contribution to the Polish economy, the steel mill was originally the Poles' idea, not ours. I remember Bierut once saying to Stalin, "You could help us by giving us credits to build a steel mill near Krakow. The city is our former capital, yet it lacks a well-developed proletarian element. By putting a steel mill there, we could build up working class support for socialism in the Krakow area." [20] Later the Poles named the Nowa Huta steel mill after our great leader, Comrade Lenin: I was glad to hear it announced over the radio not too long ago that, in honor of the hundredth anniversary of Lenin's birth, a new monument to Vladimir Ilyich was unveiled in the Krakow area.

19. "International organizations" were trading concessions favorable to the Russians.

20. A proud, prosperous university town and religious center, Krakow had traditionally been a bastion of Polish cultural and intellectual life, hence "lacks a well-developed proletarian element."

If we hadn't given Poland the necessary credits to build the mill, we would have had to supply them with finished steel. Economically, that might have been advantageous for us, but fraternal relations required that we encourage self-sufficiency and strengthen internal economic forces in Poland. Therefore complaints about our aid in Nowa Huta were ridiculous both from an economic and from a political point of view. I remember there were similar complaints in Hungary about a steel plant we built there.

But we understood even such unreasonable outbursts from our comrades. Sometimes when passions have been aroused, a person will fling a piece of bread back in the face of a friend who gave it to him. That's how it was. Even Gomulka himself was of two minds during our discussions with him in Warsaw. On the one hand he knew what were reasonable complaints and what were not. On the other hand, he was still brooding over the mistreatment he had personally suffered. He knew he had been jailed with Stalin's consent and therefore still nurtured some hard feelings toward the Soviet Union.

As time went on, I had frequent dealings with Comrade Gomulka on various important economic and political matters. With each passing year, Polish-Soviet relations continued to improve. While he and I still differed in our approach to certain specific issues, our personal relations couldn't have been better. Even the few differences of opinion between us were healthy. After all, if there are absolutely no disagreements, that probably means there's no democracy. We'd already had enough of the kind of unanimity and sycophancy which had accompanied the personality cult.[21]

One matter on which Gomulka and I disagreed was the best way to organize a country's agriculture. During my frequent trips to Poland I took a special interest in this subject. By then [late 1950's] most of the collective farms had fallen apart completely. On an earlier trip to Poland just after the war I had visited a collective farm in the Lodz district and gotten to know the chairman. I'd once helped him out by sending one of our agronomists to show him how best to sow feed corn. Now that I was back in Poland as head of a Soviet delegation, I was curious to know whether this collective farm still existed or whether, like so many others, it had failed. I went to Lodz and was pleased to find not only that the collective farm was still going

21. That is, the personality cult of Stalin.

strong, but that the same chairman was there; he greeted my comrades and me in a most fraternal way.

Gomulka, of course, had never favored collective farms in the first place. As I've already recounted, his opposition to collectivization provided the basis for one of the charges brought against him after the war by Bierut and his colleagues. Gomulka preferred "circles," or farmers' cooperatives, which allowed several peasants to pool their resources to buy seed, fertilizers, and machinery; they would till their land collectively, but the land itself would remain divided into patches, each of which was the private property of an individual peasant. The surplus of what was collectively produced could then be sold through the circle. Strictly speaking, this was not a socialist form of production. Nor was it a system of cooperatives in our socialist understanding of the term. The Polish "circles" were closer to what we would call workers' cooperatives or partnerships. They were like small companies in that the land continued to belong to the peasants. Thus the system was a throwback to the old days. However, the organization of farmlands was an internal matter for Poland, and we never took Comrade Gomulka to task for it. If we ever raised questions at all, it was only to inform ourselves about how their system of agriculture worked.

Comrade Gomulka occasionally came to Moscow to discuss economic matters with us. For our part, we invited him largely to demonstrate to the outside world that our relations with Poland had been normalized and that our enemies' hopes for conflict between us had been dashed.

But the Polish comrades had other goals in mind. I sometimes had reason to feel that Gomulka and his colleagues wanted to see our economic and political relations develop in favor of their own interests rather than to our mutual advantage. This [selfishness] on the part of the Poles and others led to certain tensions within the commonwealth of socialist countries, tensions which had been created with the Council for Mutual Economic Assistance.[22]

At one point the Polish comrades wanted us to help them pay back

22. The Council for Mutual Economic Assistance, or Comecon as it is known in the West, was founded in Moscow in January, 1949. The original members were the USSR, Bulgaria, Czechoslovakia, Hungary, Poland, and Rumania. Albania joined a month later, the German Democratic Republic in 1950, and the Mongolian People's Republic in 1962. The People's Republic of China, Cuba, North Korea, North Vietnam have associate memberships, as does Yugoslavia.

certain debts they had incurred in the West. It seemed that during the time of troubles [23] the Poles had thoughtlessly accepted Western credits, which were now falling due and which they didn't have enough money to repay. Now they came to us asking for help. These were very sensitive conversations. Instead of chiding them for their past mistakes, we demonstrated our good will. Both our class and our state interests required that we help Poland out of its awkward situation, and that's exactly what we did.

However, it was more difficult for us to give in to some of the other requests of the Polish comrades. Sometimes they even forced us into regrettable exchanges of harsh words. More than once after an economic plan for CMEA had been decided and approved, we would receive a phone call from the Poles who would say, "Comrade Khrushchev, we have a few questions we'd like to discuss with you. Would you mind if we came to Moscow to see you?" Of course, we wanted to be polite, and they were our comrades, so we'd always consent to receive them.

Our own representatives in CMEA would notify us in advance of what was on the Poles' minds, and it usually followed the same pattern: despite the fact that the delivery and allocation schedule had been decided, the Poles would try to convince us that they were in difficulty and in need of special help from us, usually in the form of increased iron ore deliveries. Since we had to deliver ore to Czechoslovakia, Rumania, Hungary, and the German Democratic Republic as well as Poland — and since the production of our iron ore industry could not be counted on to exceed what we needed for domestic consumption — we couldn't always satisfy the Poles' request for additional deliveries. Naturally, if we had a surplus of iron ore, we'd be only too happy to increase our exports to the fraternal countries. But if, as sometimes happened, we didn't have enough for our own needs, these special requests from the Poles could be unpleasant for both sides.

On other occasions the Poles demanded that we change the quality rather than the quantity of the ore we were sending them; they would tell us they had to have ore with higher iron content for their smelting furnaces. Similar problems often arose with oil: the Poles would ask for more oil than was allotted them in the CMEA plan.

23. The "time of troubles" was the period between Bierut's death and the October crisis in 1956.

Khrushchev meeting near Kharkov with members of the
Ukrainian Central Committee and government, 1943

Khrushchev (*left*); an unidentified girl; Dmitry Manuilsky,
Deputy Chairman of the Ukrainian Council of Ministers;
Wanda Wasilewska; and her husband, the writer
Aleksandr Korneichuk

In the Ukraine after the war

Watching military maneuvers with Anastas Mikoyan (*left*)
and Wladyslaw Gomulka, the leader of the Polish Party

At a shooting competition
in Usovo, outside Moscow

Duck hunting near Kiev

Bear hunting in Rumania,
1964

Speaking in East Berlin before
giant portraits of Marx and
Lenin, 1963

Welcoming Pham Van Dong,
the Premier of North
Vietnam, to Moscow, 1961

On the telephone to cosmonaut Yuri Gagarin,
with Mikoyan looking on, 1961

Speaking to cosmonaut Valentina Tereshkova,
with Brezhnev at his side, 1963

Vacationing with Voroshilov (*left*) and Mikoyan

Taking it easy, 1960

Despite the fact that we sometimes didn't have enough oil for our own uses, we'd try to satisfy the Polish demands. It was usually Comrade Gomulka who presented the demands, and he had a way of turning these matters into a national issue.

The Poles used to come to us with one especially unpleasant request. They always wanted more feed grain than the CMEA plan called for. Every year we'd warn them that we were giving them additional grain for the last time, and the next year they'd come back with the same request. Compared to all the other socialist countries, Poland had the largest per capita agricultural production. Poland could provide feed grain for itself, while the German Democratic Republic, Czechoslovakia, and Bulgaria all needed help from us. (Once, when we had a big surplus, we supplied grain to Rumania, though we did it only on the basis of a loan which they were obliged to repay a few years later.)

Poland's agriculture may have been much less productive than that of Western countries, but it was good compared to the other socialist countries. So why were they always asking us to increase their grain shipments? I'll tell you: they did so for commercial reasons. They needed extra grain from us not to feed livestock for their own market, but to feed hogs which produced bacon *which in turn the Poles exported to the United States as a major source of hard currency.*

While the Poles may have been motivated by commercial considerations, the Americans, I believe, were motivated by political considerations. Despite their embargo on goods manufactured in socialist countries, they imported Polish bacon not just because it was high-quality bacon, but also because they wanted to sow the seeds of discord in the socialist camp. "Divide and conquer," that was their motto. But we wouldn't allow ourselves to be taken in. It didn't make us jealous that the Poles had access to the American market while we were singled out for discrimination. As far as we were concerned, Poland was perfectly justified in taking advantage of a highly favorable opportunity.

However, we were catering to Poland's interests at the expense of our own. I'm sure my countrymen will not object if I say that sometimes for the sake of friendship you must share your last piece of bread with a comrade. But it's not that we were saving Poland from famine — far from it. We were enabling them to trade with the West, and in order to do so we had to tighten our own belt. I'll admit that whenever we heard that Comrade Gomulka was coming to "talk over certain matters," we would grumble among ourselves that the Poles were taking advantage of us.

In 1963 we had one of the worst grain shortages of my experience, and we had to appeal to the good sense of our allies and friends. Yet even then Gomulka came to us asking for increased shipments. I spoke to him very directly, in order to sharpen his perception of the situation: "You know per capita meat consumption in the Soviet Union is lower than in your country. You know we need all the grain we have in order to produce bacon, beef, and eggs for our own people. Yet here you are, asking us to give you extra shipments not so that you can feed your own people — not because you're starving yourselves — but so that you can earn some extra dollars."

"Yes," he admitted, "that's true."

I've noticed that after the recent events in Poland, Comrade Gierek came to the Soviet Union.[24] I have nothing but the greatest admiration for Comrade Gierek; I consider him an honest man, devoted to the cause of Communism. However, he certainly didn't make a special trip to Moscow just to get advice. Shortly after his return home, the newspapers announced that the Soviet Union had given Poland two million tons of wheat. That's a huge amount. It represents about 500,000 kilos of pork. The Poles were able to get this help from us at a time when we weren't able to provide enough meat for our own population. The shops have a limited supply of meat; and the variety of cuts is, to say the least, inadequate. And that's just in Moscow. Outside the capital it's much worse.

So the old tendencies continue among the Polish leaders in their economic dealings with the Soviet Union.

In general, our relations with Poland have been good over the years, but such arguments have come up. Wherever you have trade, you're bound to have conflicts — even within CMEA. I believe history will acknowledge that CMEA has played an absolutely essential role in the regulation of our economic plans, particularly in the way it has allowed us to coordinate the exchange of raw materials for finished products to the mutual benefit of both partners.

In my day we went a long way toward restoring the principle of mutual advantage in our dealings with the other socialist countries.

24. The "recent events" referred to here were the Baltic riots of December, 1970, and the subsequent fall of Gomulka.

Gone were the days when Stalin's international organizations allowed the Soviet Union to exploit, for example, Rumania's uranium ore deposits without just compensation. We started to pay Rumania world prices for its uranium, which we then processed and used to manufacture nuclear weapons. Thus, this trade served the common interests of all the socialist countries — and I'd even say of all progressive peoples who believed in peaceful coexistence and sought to avoid war. Our purchase of uranium also helped promote the development of Rumania's very backward economy.

As is well known, the issue of mutual economic assistance is closely intertwined both with a country's foreign relations and its internal policy. Each country is concerned with trying to develop its own economy in order to improve the people's standard of living. Rumania had further to go in this regard than most countries. Its population was made up primarily of poor peasants. On the other hand, the land is rich in natural resources: in addition to uranium, it has large deposits of oil, natural gas, and timber. Rumania is also geographically well situated, and the soil is fertile. In short, Rumania seemed to have promising conditions for the development of a viable socialist economy and a stable socialist state.

I made a number of visits to Rumania as a member of official delegations. I also went there to rest and to have informal discussions with the Rumanian comrades. I never ceased to be impressed by Rumania's climate, excellent farmlands, abundant harvests, the beautiful Carpathian Mountains, and the plentiful wild game for hunting. The countryside was teeming with deer. The Rumanians organized marvelous bear hunts, and as a result bear hunting was a profitable industry in Rumania.

I also admired the way the Rumanian comrades had rapidly and skillfully undertaken the collectivization of agriculture. Admittedly, there were several uprisings in the villages, but the Rumanian comrades took care of those and got on with the job of setting up very smooth-running collective farms. These enterprises were so successful that the Rumanians often had a surplus of agricultural products, particularly grain and corn, which they could export as a source of hard currency.

For our part, we helped the Rumanians in every way we could. We supplied them with tractors so that they would have the technological basis for mechanizing their collective farms and making them more efficient. We also helped them get started in the manufacture of automobiles and diesel locomotives, as well as the construction of oil refineries and steel plants. Whatever their economy needed and whatever we could afford to give them — whether it was machinery, technology or consultants — was theirs for the asking. All the technical assistance we gave them was free, and the credits we extended to them so that they could purchase our products carried a minimal interest, much lower than the standard world rate. As I recall, we lent Rumania enough to build a number of factories at only 2 or 2½ percent interest. If, rather than giving that money as a loan to the Rumanians, we had invested it in our own economy and then sold Rumania the surplus production, we could have made much more for ourselves. But that would not have been a proper way for one socialist country to behave toward another. We were convinced we had to help the Rumanian people develop their economy, particularly their heavy industry — steel, machine tools, tractors, and automotive products. And I should add: throughout our efforts to assist Rumania economically, we took care not to offend their national feelings, their national pride.

Despite our help and consideration, Rumania was among those socialist countries which sometimes tried to take unfair advantage of us by putting pressure on us through CMEA to enter into unequal contracts. We occasionally found ourselves in the position of having to pay more for a product purchased from another CMEA member than it would have cost us to manufacture ourselves. For example, at one point our farmers had trouble with a weevil blight which was destroying our sugar beet crop in the Ukraine just when we were struggling to increase our sugar beet production. We had to ask the Rumanians for additional shipments of an insecticide they manufactured. The Rumanians agreed to make the extra deliveries on the condition that we pay in gold, hard currency, or in products which could be sold for hard currency on the international market. They justified this request with the same argument we often used when our partners asked us for more of a certain commodity or product than we could supply: the Rumanians said that since their insecticide was marketable for hard currency, we should pay them in hard currency to compensate them for what they could have earned by exporting it to the West. We consented to their demand, but it offended our dignity.

I later brought the insecticide matter up at a meeting with the Rumanian leaders. I told them quite frankly that we were still upset about it. Dej looked sharply at Maurer and asked him something in Rumanian.[25] Maurer nodded his head. Dej turned back to me and said, "Yes, Comrade Khrushchev, we did ask you to pay us in hard currency or the equivalent, but you've made the same demand on us, haven't you?"

Our people — specifically Comrade Kosygin — confirmed that, yes, we had on one occasion demanded payment in hard currency when the Rumanians increased their order for certain additional deliveries.[26] That was the first I'd heard of the incident, and I said so to Comrade Dej. I was unhappy to learn that both countries — Rumania and the Soviet Union — had been using a practice which is alien to Communism and indeed is right out of capitalism's bag of tricks.

I made a proposal which I thought might put an end to such conflicts in the future. "Comrades," I said, "let's agree that from now on we'll set aside in our plans certain hard-currency products which can be traded within CMEA only for other hard-currency products. In other words, when a contract signed by two or more member nations of CMEA is broken or altered, the following arrangement comes into effect: scarce commodities can be exchanged only for other scarce commodities, and orders over and above what the original contract stipulated will be paid for either in hard currency or in goods that can be sold abroad. What do you think about that?"

"An excellent idea!" shouted Comrade Dej. "Let's do it!" His enthusiasm for the idea meant that he must not have seen very clearly what I was driving at. However, his colleague, the chairman of the Rumanian State Planning Commission, saw exactly what I was driving at and objected accordingly.[27]

<hr />

25. Ion Gheorghe Maurer, longtime Prime Minister, had replaced Chivu Stoica in that post.

26. Kosygin was Chairman of Gosplan, or the State Planning Commission, from 1959 to 1960, when he became Khrushchev's chief deputy on the Council of Ministers.

27. The date of this dispute over insecticide is unclear. It can be guessed, however, that the head of the Rumanian Planning Commission was Gheorghe Gaston Marin. At the time of the Soviet drought in 1963, Marin arranged for Rumania to "loan" the USSR 400,000 tons of grain — a gesture which Khrushchev acknowledged as an example of "socialist cooperation."

There is some confusion in the Russian original over who said what to whom in the meeting between the Soviet and Rumanian leaders which Khrushchev recounts here: Khrushchev tells two conflicting versions of the story. In one version, it is the Ruma-

"No, Comrade Khrushchev," he said, "I disagree."

"Why?" I asked. "The agreement I'm proposing would be based on the principle of parity. No transaction would be made at greater expense to one side than the other."

"Maybe so, Comrade Khrushchev, but we purchase many more hard-currency products from the Soviet Union than you purchase from us. According to the arrangement you're suggesting, we'd end up having to pay too much to you."

"That's right," I replied. "We supply you with your copper, correct? Where do we get that copper? We buy it abroad for either gold or hard currency. And what do you give us in return for our copper? You give us a lot of products we could just as well do without. For example, you sell us wooden boxes for packaging. Economically, that makes no sense. We have our own forests in the Carpathians and could manufacture those boxes ourselves. But instead we let you build the boxes which we then use to ship Moldavian fruit and other products. We might as well be giving you our machinery and copper in exchange for firewood. So if you're going to make us pay you hard currency for the insecticide you sell us, then you'll have to pay us hard currency for the copper we sell you. That's only fair. Since the trade between us in hard-currency products seems to cause disagreements, the only thing to do is start conducting that trade on an equivalency basis."

"Please, Comrade Khrushchev, don't insist on such a system. It would cost Rumania dearly."

"All right," I said, "we'll keep doing it the old way."

I've been recounting these incidents of disputes with the Polish and Rumanian comrades because they illustrate an important point: namely, that our economic relations with the fraternal countries have not always been to the advantage of the Soviet Union. People who hear that may make a sour face, but it's true nonetheless.

Conflicts, of course, are inevitable when one country is in the position of a creditor toward another country. In the old days of capitalism, people used to say credit gets in the way of friendship, whether between individuals or between countries. Well, not even the socialist world can do without credit altogether, so disagreements continue to crop up from time to time.

---

nian Gosplan chief who cautions Gheorghiu-Dej against accepting Khrushchev's sly proposal; in the other, it is vice versa. The first version is used here because Khrushchev seems more sure of himself and his memory than in the other version.

During the years that I worked in a high post and had great responsibilities, part of the problem I faced was that compared to other socialist countries we were at an advanced level of scientific and industrial sophistication. Therefore we were able to manufacture better high-technology products than were the other countries — not counting the German Democratic Republic and Czechoslovakia (which in some fields, are even ahead of us). As a result, other countries made continuous — and it sometimes seemed to us, excessive — demands.[28] I'd rather not go into details, but after I became a pensioner, certain charges were made against me in this regard. I don't deny that sometimes I did refuse other countries' requests for additional deliveries. But I did so only in those cases when we were asked for more than we could afford to give — that is, only when we would have been satisfying the needs of another country at the expense of the Soviet consumer.

In general, though, we had good economic relations with other socialist countries. The only exceptions were Albania, China, and Korea, which participated in CMEA either as observers or not at all. (China and Korea pulled out when our relations with China were at the breaking point and our relations with Korea were hanging by a thread; Albania pulled out when it started behaving like the number one troublemaker among socialist countries.) Looking to the future, I believe that as long as the CMEA sticks to the principle of mutual advantage, the organization will continue to play an important and beneficial role in our development. The troublesome moments I have recalled here were nothing more than occasional rough spots on the otherwise smooth surface of our economic relations with the fraternal countries.

Trimming the Warsaw Pact

WHEN I was the head of the government and the Party, I felt it was important to reduce the size of the Soviet army and to begin withdrawing our troops from other countries. We diminished our standing army to almost half what it had reached under Stalin, and we withdrew our forces from Finland, Austria, and Rumania. We also

28. The "other countries" would be Poland, Hungary, Rumania, and Bulgaria.

proposed withdrawing our garrisons from Hungary and Poland. We didn't have any troops in Czechoslovakia or Bulgaria. Only in the German Democratic Republic did we feel it necessary to continue our military presence. It was perfectly clear to everyone that until our former allies, who had organized NATO, agreed to a peace treaty, our troops would have to remain in the GDR.[29] After all, the West had a fairly sizable force stationed in West Germany, and we had to preserve the balance of power.

First, I would like to explain the background for our general decision to reduce our armed forces and, second, to recount how the decision was put into effect with regard to individual countries.

It took us a while before we reached the point that we were ready to make any cutbacks. When Stalin died, we felt terribly vulnerable. The United States was then conducting an arrogant and aggressive policy toward us, never missing a chance to demonstrate its superiority. The Americans had the Soviet Union surrounded with military bases and kept sending reconnaissance planes deep into our territory, sometimes as far as Kiev. We expected an all-out attack any day. Therefore we had no choice but to commit enormous resources to defense in order to avoid another world war. The memory of World War II was still fresh in the minds of our people. Not until we had equipped our armed forces with modern weapons could we contemplate diverting some of the defense money into other areas.

The modernization of our army took years of work and cost billions. However, once we had equipped ourselves with the missiles, airplanes, submarine fleet, and nuclear warheads needed for our defense, we were able to reconsider our military budget.

After we created the Warsaw Pact, I felt the time had come to think about a reduction of our armed forces. I knew that even if the other side refused to sign a disarmament agreement, we would have to find some way of reducing our own army — without, of course, jeopardizing our defense. Why did we have to reduce unilaterally? Because we didn't want to give our adversary an opportunity to exhaust us economically without war by forcing us to compete with them in a never-ending arms race. Even if we couldn't convince them to disarm themselves and to give up the idea of war as a means of political pressure, at least we could demonstrate our own peaceful intentions

29. The peace treaty would have been a treaty clarifying the status of Germany and Berlin and formalizing peace between Germany and the USSR.

and at the same time free some of our resources for the development of our industry, the production of consumer goods, and the improvement of living standards.

The first area of military spending in which we decided to cut back was that of personnel. After all, the strength of a modern army isn't determined by the number of troops but by fire power, particularly missile power. We had stockpiled a great many nuclear weapons, so our fire power had increased many times and we could afford to cut back on our ground troops. Gradually we reduced our standing army from about 5 million to 2 ½ million.

It was also decided to cut salaries in the Soviet army. Later, after I retired from my posts as First Secretary of the Party and Chairman of the Council of Ministers, I heard repercussions of dissatisfaction from people who ascribed this decision to me. I don't deny that officers' salaries were cut under me, but it was actually Marshal Zhukov's idea. I certainly supported him because there were obviously many excesses which had to be curtailed. These matters were worked out when Zhukov was Minister of Defense and then later, after Malinovsky became Minister. I have to give Zhukov his due here. He realized the necessity of reducing expenses in the army, and he took the initiative in trimming expendable personnel from the command staff and ordering salary cuts for some categories of officers.[30]

We had to economize on our army abroad as well as at home. The maintenance of a division abroad — that is, on the territory of another socialist country — costs twice as much as the maintenance of a division on our own territory.

In addition to the economic considerations, there were compelling political reasons for us to pull our troops out of the fraternal countries. We didn't want anyone to think we didn't trust our allies. They were building socialism in their countries because it was in their interest to do so, not because there were Soviet troops stationed in their midst. Marxist-Leninist internationalism has been the main attraction and unifying force for the people of the other socialist countries. You can't herd people into paradise with threats and then post sentries at the gates. People have to choose a better life on their own, and, given the opportunity, they will.

Therefore we wanted to remove a trump card from the hand of

30. This paragraph appears also in *KR*, I, 515.

enemy propaganda. We wanted to give the lie to the enemy's insinuation that the Hungarian, Polish, Rumanian, and other fraternal peoples were being prodded along the path of socialism at bayonet-point by Soviet soldiers.

I'm not denying that these other countries were still, to a certain extent at least, our involuntary allies. It was only natural that there should be some resentment on their part left over from the war and the first years after the war. Some of them — the Rumanians and Hungarians for example — had been dragged into the war against us by Hitler. Therefore our army, as it pursued the retreating Hitlerite invaders back into Germany, had attacked and defeated other countries as well. We didn't make war on them because we wanted to, but because they had been incorporated into Hitler's army.

Then, after the war, Stalin treated these countries very roughly. He dictated his will to them. In his eyes they weren't real friends. He treated them as subjects of the Soviet Union, not as allies. We [the post-Stalin Soviet leadership] were the ones who had to eat this soup that Stalin had cooked for us. Because of the lingering hard feelings and even antagonism on the part of our allies, we found it difficult to achieve the desired degree of monolithism in the socialist camp. We discussed the problem in the leadership and concluded that the time had come to demonstrate our trust in other countries and to earn their good will by reducing our garrisons abroad.

I'd like first to recount how we went about withdrawing our troops from Finland. In accordance with a Soviet-Finnish treaty, we had a military base literally right outside Helsinki, the capital of the country.[31] Trains passing in and out of Helsinki through the property surrounding the base were subject to searches by our soldiers. The curtains on the windows were drawn, and the passengers were prohibited from looking out. It might have seemed to them that the train was passing through occupied territory. The Finns were indignant, and our ambassador kept us informed about their indignation.[32] He used to send messages to the other members of the Politbureau and me, reporting on the latest tension or unpleasantness.

As I saw it, the only solution was to give up our base outside Hel-

31. This was the air and naval base on the Porkkala Peninsula about twelve miles from Helsinki. The USSR had been paying "rent" of about five cents an acre for the 152-square-mile installation, which had been acquired with a fifty-year lease in 1947.
32. The ambassador was V. Z. Lebedev, former ambassador to Poland.

sinki. To do so would not mean sacrificing our security. After all, Finland was a small country with which we had a long common border, so we could easily and quickly reach Helsinki with our artillery and infantry, to say nothing of our bombs and missiles. Therefore there was no good military reason to keep the base, and the political considerations were all against it. Keeping the base could only continue to damage our relations with the Finns. They were afraid the presence of our soldiers on their soil meant we planned to deprive them of their independence and incorporate their country into the Soviet Union. This fear was quite understandable on their part. The Finns knew perfectly well that our troops stationed right outside their capital weren't there to make shashlik or go fishing.

It was high time to demonstrate that we had no territorial claims on Finland and no intention of forcing socialism on the Finns at bayonet point. We had to make clear that our foreign policy was guided by the Leninist principle of peaceful coexistence, which meant leaving other countries to decide their internal political and social problems by themselves, with no outside interference.

There was an additional consideration: at that time we were calling upon other countries to withdraw their troops from foreign territory. As long as we had our base in Finland, other countries could point to us and say, "What about *you?*"

In short, the continued presence of our troops in Finland was an obstacle preventing us from convincing others of our peaceful intentions. I believe I understood this problem better than anyone else in the leadership. I still had to persuade the other comrades.

About that time, Molotov, Bulganin, and Zhukov were all with me in Geneva.[33] I didn't even suggest the idea of giving up our base in Finland to Molotov because I knew he'd disagree. I'd long since learned that he was too rigid in his thinking to assess circumstances realistically and to make a correct decision. However, I did discuss the matter with Bulganin, and he agreed with me that the base should be closed. I decided to broach the subject with Zhukov as well. He and I were on excellent terms. I had the highest respect for his judgment. Depending on the atmosphere, I would address him sometimes just as "Georgi," sometimes as "Georgi Konstantinovich," or, more formally, as "Comrade Zhukov." We were sitting together

33. Molotov, Bulganin, and Zhukov accompanied Khrushchev to the four-power summit meeting in Geneva in the summer of 1955.

alone at a small country house when I asked him, "What would you think about withdrawing our troops from Finland? Our base there is like a splinter sticking in our side. It's poisoning not only our relations with Finland but with other countries as well. Take Sweden and Norway for example: they're right next door to Finland and therefore eyeing us apprehensively to see what we do with the Finns. What do you think?"

"I fully agree with you," Zhukov replied. "From the strategic point of view there's absolutely no point in keeping troops in Finland. On top of that, we spend a lot of money on the construction of fortifications and the upkeep of our soldiers."

"Then that's all there is to it," I said. "Let's go ahead and close the base as soon as we get back to Moscow."

Afterwards we talked the matter over with Molotov. As I expected, he couldn't understand the necessity for withdrawing our troops. He put up an obstinate argument.

When we returned to Moscow, we had a brief discussion in the government leadership as well as in the Central Committee of the Party. Following an agreement among ourselves, we approached the Finns with a proposal for a new treaty which called for the withdrawal of Soviet troops from their territory.[34] Thus, we had liquidated our military base which had been situated right under the nose of the Finnish capital of Helsinki. And what happened as a result? Did our relations with the Finns suffer? On the contrary — our relations improved considerably.

Of course, there will always be reactionary elements in Finland, people who hate the socialist system with a passion and will stop at nothing to drive a wedge between our two countries. But the rank and file of the Finnish people understood that we had no intention of invading their country, nor did we wish to interfere in their affairs in any way. Representatives of the Finnish trade unions and business world alike saw that we meant their country no harm and welcomed our efforts to strengthen economic relations. As for the Communist Party of Finland, we made its job of dealing with the working class and the peasantry much easier; no longer did the Finnish comrades

34. Bulganin announced that the USSR would close its facilities at Porkkala in September, 1955, in return for a twenty-year prolongation of the Soviet-Finnish treaty of mutual assistance. The day after Bulganin's announcement, Zhukov said that the USSR intended eventually to shut down all its military bases on foreign soil.

have the very difficult task of explaining to their countrymen why it was necessary for Soviet troops to be stationed in their midst.

Our decision to give up our base in Finland was also a great victory in our relations with other countries because it showed we were willing to set a good example when we urged the rest of the world to agree on the withdrawal of all troops from foreign territories.

According to the Potsdam agreement, we were completely within our rights to keep troops stationed in Austria, Hungary, the German Democratic Republic, and Rumania until we signed a peace treaty with Germany and the countries which had been its allies in World War II. However, we discussed this question in the leadership and decided to make further reductions in our armed forces abroad. It was I who initiated this policy, and I still think it was correct.

We removed all the troops we had stationed outside Vienna and reduced to about half a million our soldiers in the German Democratic Republic. However, that still left us with a sizable force in Germany.[35] Before we could consider withdrawing troops from Hungary and Poland, we had to be convinced that we wouldn't be cutting ourselves off from our armies in the GDR.

We had come a long way since the end of World War II. The fire power we had concentrated in the GDR, combined with our long- and medium-range ballistic missiles in the Soviet Union, gave us the potential not only of destroying every living thing in West Germany, but of hitting targets anywhere in Europe — and in Africa as well. Therefore we now had a deterrent in the GDR and the USSR alone which was sufficient to restrain any aggressive forces in the United States. We no longer needed to bolster up that deterrent by keeping huge numbers of troops in Poland and Hungary. With motorized infantry, tanks, and airborne transport, we were far more mobile than we had been during World War II. If the need arose, we could move our troops into Hungary and Poland in literally just a few hours.

Some time after the counterrevolutionary mutiny was liquidated in Hungary, I asked Comrade Kadar his reaction to our proposed plan to reduce the size of our garrisons in the Warsaw Pact countries in general and Hungary in particular.

35. Soviet troops were removed from outside Vienna in the summer of 1955. As for East Germany, the Soviet Union still has over twenty divisions stationed there.

Between 1955, the year the Warsaw Pact was formed, and 1960, total Soviet troop strength was reduced from 5,763,000 to 3,623,000. Then, in January, 1960, the Kremlin demobilized 1,200,000 men — a full third of the armed forces.

"Comrade Kadar," I said, "have you given any thought to the presence of our troops in Hungary? We've exchanged opinions in our own leadership and decided we could withdraw our units from Hungary if you felt it was advisable. We rely on your judgment, and we'll do whatever you recommend."

"Comrade Khrushchev, I think you'd best decide this for yourself. There is no resentment in our country against the presence of your troops on our territory. I say this very frankly.[36]

"But let me ask you this: what do the Poles say about your withdrawing your troops from Poland?"

"I haven't talked to the Poles yet. We thought we should speak to you first and then see about them."

As I've already mentioned, it cost twice as much to maintain a division in another Warsaw Pact country as it did to maintain that same division on Soviet territory. It was particularly expensive to keep our armies outside the USSR, and it was profitable for the state on whose territory our troops were stationed. We had to pay the Poles for the barracks they built for us and also compensate them for our bases by giving them the latest weapons and high-technology industrial equipment. All this amounted to a considerable sum. These expenditures put a great strain on our own economy.

After consultations within the [Soviet] leadership, I had a talk with Comrade Gomulka about removing our troops from Poland. I argued that Poland now had a fairly strong army of its own and that the cost of maintaining our own army in Poland no longer seemed politically or strategically justified.

"Remember, Comrade Gomulka," I said, "the West threatens not only Poland; it also threatens us, the Soviet Union. If the imperialists should ever try to unleash war, they would encounter us before they would encounter you because we have a large army stationed in the German Democratic Republic. The West can't invade Poland without coming through the GDR, which means that the imperialists would have to deal with us first. The West knows that, and the West also knows we have nuclear missiles to protect our forces in Germany. Therefore the number of troops we have stationed in Poland ceases to be essential to preserving our deterrent against imperialist aggression. As we understand the situation, it wouldn't endanger either your security or our own if we were to withdraw our troops from

36. Paragraphs similar to this one and the two preceding appear in *KR*, I, 427–428.

Poland." In the face of this reasoning, no one could use the threat of attack from the West as a political argument.[37]

Thus, in both the cases of Hungary and Poland, it was *we* who proposed to *them* either the reduction or complete withdrawal of Soviet troops from their territory. The case of Rumania was the other way around and therefore more complicated. The Rumanians proposed to *us* that we pull our forces out of their country. At first we misunderstood them and tried to convince them the troops should stay, but later, after thinking it over, we changed our minds. Here's what happened:

Not long after Stalin's death I was in Rumania and had a talk with the Minister of Defense, Comrade Bodnaras. As I've already made clear, he was a good friend of the Soviet Union, an Old Bolshevik who had spent some time in prison in Rumania and who enjoyed our absolute confidence and respect. As I recall we had one or two tank divisions and an infantry division in Rumania.

Without warning he brought up the question, "What would you think about pulling your troops out of Rumania?"

I must confess that my initial reaction wasn't very sensible. If you keep in mind that this conversation took place before 1956 — before we exposed Stalin's abuses of power — you'll understand that we were still under the influence of Stalinist policy and still revered everything Stalinist. When Comrade Bodnaras brought up the question of our troops out of the blue, I would even go so far as to say I lost my temper. "What are you saying? How can you suggest such a thing?"

"Well," he explained, "Rumania shares borders only with other socialist countries [Bulgaria, Yugoslavia, Hungary, and the USSR], and there's nobody across the Black Sea from us except the Turks. Therefore what do we need your troops here for?"

"And what about the Turks?" I asked.

"We have you right next door to us. If the Turks attacked, you could always come to our assistance."

"That's easy enough for you to say, but it's not just the Turks I'm thinking about. They control the Bosporus and the Dardanelles, so they could always admit an enemy landing force into the Black Sea to invade your territory."

---

37. That is, an argument for the USSR to maintain its troops in Poland at full strength. There are still two Soviet divisions in Poland and four in Hungary.

The Rumanian comrades exchanged glances. Obviously they had already talked this matter over among themselves. "All right," they said, "if that's how you feel, we'll withdraw the question. We just didn't want you to think that we were standing firmly on a socialist position only because your troops are stationed on our territory. We just want you to know that we sincerely believe in the building of socialism and in following Marxist-Leninist policies, and our people recognize us as their leaders and support us completely. The development of socialism in our country is not determined by pressure from the Soviet Union."

I was more than satisfied with this elucidation of their reason for proposing the removal of Soviet troops from their territory. I believed that the Rumanian comrades were genuinely reaffirming their dedication to the building of socialism. I didn't even begin to construe Comrade Bodnaras's proposal as anti-Soviet in any way. I realized he and the other Rumanian comrades simply wanted to assume complete control of their own leadership.[38]

For the time being, at least, the Rumanian comrades were willing to let drop the question of our troops in view of my objection that they were underestimating the strength of our enemies.

During the next year and a half or so, Comrade Bodnaras's words kept coming back to me, especially after I had a subsequent conversation with Comrade Dej. "We were deeply offended by what you told Bodnaras," he said. "You offended us by suggesting that we don't have the confidence of our own people and that we stay in power solely as a result of your troops' being stationed on our territory." What Dej said worried me very much, particularly because we knew him to be an honest comrade and good friend. I took his words to heart.

During this period I regularly informed our leadership about the discussions I had with the Rumanian comrades. I brought the matter up again when we began considering the possibility of reducing our military expenditures and the size of our army, particularly our units stationed in the other Warsaw Pact countries. No longer were we looking through Stalinist eyeglasses at the danger posed by capitalism. Of course, we were still surrounded by capitalist bases, but now that we had missiles as well as atomic and hydrogen bombs, the socialist camp had one of the mightiest armed forces in the world.

38. This account of the conversation with Bodnaras and the other Rumanians is repeated in *KR*, I, 513–514.

The more I considered the problem, the more sense it seemed to make for us to withdraw the few divisions we had in Rumania and station them nearby in Moldavia and the Ukraine. I felt that if we placed these divisions, say for example, under the command of the Odessa Military District, we would still be able to make our enemies think twice before invading Rumania. Considering the strength of our tactical missile force and our coastal defenses, I was confident that an imperialist invasion of Rumania would be no walk in the woods.

In addition to the strictly strategic and military considerations, there was, as Comrades Bodnaras and Dej suggested, a compelling political reason for us to withdraw our troops from Rumania. We knew that the Rumanian people had indeed chosen the socialist path as the only correct course — not because their leaders were propped up by foreign bayonets, but because socialism was in the interests of the working class, the working peasantry, and the working intelligentsia. The Rumanian comrades would take it as a sign of political trust if we removed our forces.

In short, I decided we should reconsider the proposal Comrade Bodnaras had made. I raised the question in our leadership. We asked our Minister of Defense for his opinion.[39] He agreed fully with my proposal, and we decided to go ahead.

We informed the Rumanian comrades that conditions had changed, and we were now in a position to withdraw our troops from their country without exposing our own country to risk. Naturally the Rumanians were delighted that, despite our initial misunderstanding, their proposal had triumphed. We withdrew the troops, and after that our relations seemed to be improving.[40]

The maintenance of military bases on foreign soil cannot help but accelerate the arms race and intensify the passions of the Cold War. Therefore we hoped that our decision to reduce our forces in the Warsaw Pact countries might prove contagious and that other countries would soon follow suit. Even if our policy wasn't contagious and other countries didn't follow our good example, at least we added a number of strong cards to our hand for purposes of propaganda. Now we could advocate peaceful coexistence with a clear conscience.

39. Malinovsky replaced Zhukov in the fall of 1957.
40. The decision to pull Soviet troops out of Rumania was announced at the May, 1958, meeting of the Warsaw Pact Political Consultative Committee in Moscow.

Some people who read my memoirs may misinterpret the policy of reducing the size of our armed forces. There are those who might say it was wrong for us to cut back our troop levels, given the imperialist dream of destroying the socialist camp. I think the majority of those who might take this view can be found among the military. They opposed our policy even when we were developing it back in Zhukov's and later in Malinovsky's time.

However, I'm convinced we were right to do what we did. I'm still in favor of removing Soviet troops from other countries, and I would fight for implementing that policy if I could. But how can anyone fight for the reduction of armed forces when a certain orator is preaching quite the opposite? How can anyone propagate the doctrine I've been advocating if the troops under the command of this orator are stationed on the territory of other countries? We can't make propaganda [for peaceful coexistence and noninterference] and then turn right around and put troops in other countries. Under such circumstances our propaganda tends to be regarded with suspicion. It accomplishes nothing and earns the confidence of no one.[41]

Conflict with Rumania

As time went on, our relations with Rumania began to deteriorate. Rumors reached us that the Rumanian comrades were saying derogatory things about the Soviet Union at their closed Party meetings. Our embassy in Bucharest informed us that streets which bore the names of famous pre-Revolutionary Russians were being renamed. We were upset to find that our economic policies, which we meant to serve the needs and appeal to the desires of the Rumanians, encountered their ingratitude instead.[42]

We decided to get together with the Rumanian comrades so that we could discuss the situation frankly and give them a chance to explain the reasons for their dissatisfaction. We wanted to erase whatever cause for grievance they had. As far as we were concerned, there should have been nothing standing in the way of fraternal relations between our countries. We wrote the Rumanian comrades an

41. The unnamed "orator" here is clearly Leonid Brezhnev, whom Khrushchev seems to be castigating for the 1968 invasion and occupation of Czechoslovakia.
42. The Rumanians started de-Russifying street names in 1963.

official letter, stating our eagerness to liquidate their reasons for unfriendliness, and went so far as to say we were willing to make concessions to them if that were necessary to restore good relations. "Even if you don't like us," we said in our letter, "the fact remains that history has made us neighbors, and you're stuck with us. Back in the days of the Rumanian monarchy, it was hardly surprising to find your country conducting policies unfriendly toward the Soviet Union; but now that Rumania is a socialist country, there is no reason for us not to have fraternal relations."

I was planning to attend the Rumanian Party Congress, which was coming up in 1960. We proposed a preliminary meeting of the various Parties invited to Bucharest before the opening of the Congress. By that time conflicts had already emerged within the socialist camp — conflicts initiated by China and Albania. These disputes were not confined to the military sphere: they were basically political differences. At the meeting in Bucharest, the majority of the Parties, including the Rumanian, shared our opinion on the development of the international Communist movement. The only exceptions were China and Albania. The Rumanian comrades supported the position which was later worked out at the World Conference of Communist Parties in Moscow.[43]

As far as we could tell, we had no disagreement — I'd even say we had a mutual understanding — with the Rumanians about China. Therefore we couldn't understand why the Rumanian Communist Party engaged in internal propaganda directed against the Communist Party of the Soviet Union. We met with them and asked them to give us a justification for their behavior.

I remember our discussions were held not too far from Bucharest at a nice country house on the edge of a lake and surrounded by forests. The Rumanian countryside is beautiful. But the atmosphere around the long table at which we held our discussions was less pleasant.

"Exactly what complaints do you have?" we asked. "What is it that divides our Parties?"

They seemed to have no reasonable explanation; yet, after the meeting, our relations continued to go downhill. For example, some of our girls had married young Rumanians studying in the Soviet

43. The Third Rumanian Party Congress of June, 1960, was followed five months later by the Moscow Conference of World Communist and Workers' Parties, at which the Sino-Soviet split came into the open for the first time.

Union and had gone back to Rumania with them; now these girls found they were treated with such intolerance in Rumania that they had to divorce their husbands and come home to the Soviet Union. This was very disagreeable for us. And so it continued. At formal meetings the Rumanian comrades acted like our brothers, but their internal propaganda was increasingly directed against us.

Then the problem spread from internal to external policy. I remember that a Rumanian delegation went to China. This was after we'd already stopped going to China ourselves because the Chinese wouldn't invite us any more. On their way back from Peking to Bucharest, the Rumanian delegation passed through Moscow. Anastas Ivanovich Mikoyan and I were then on holiday in Pitsunda, and the Rumanian comrades came to see us there. We had a very friendly and lively discussion.[44]

They described the situation in China and told us the Chinese were displeased with us. Judging from their words alone, we might have concluded that the Rumanian comrades didn't share the Chinese point of view; it might have appeared that they were merely informing us about what they had seen and heard in China. But there was something more to it than that, something that worried us.

"The Chinese said you took Bessarabia away from us," said the Rumanians. "We had no choice but to listen, though of course we don't need Bessarabia any more." So the Rumanians repeated to us what they'd heard from the Chinese — *but they didn't express any disagreement with what the Chinese had said about Bessarabia.* This conversation left a nasty taste in our mouths. We began to suspect that maybe the Rumanians still held a grudge against us for returning Bessarabia to the Soviet Union after the war.

To look at it from the historical standpoint, Moldavia had never been part of the Rumanian state. The Rumanian kingdom had taken it from us after the Revolution when our army was too weak for us to defend ourselves from dismemberment. Therefore, as we saw it, the return of Bessarabia, or Moldavia, after the war represented nothing more than the restoration of our borders which had existed before the Revolution.[45]

44. In March, 1964, a Rumanian delegation headed by Premier Ion Gheorghe Maurer went to Peking to mediate in the Sino-Soviet conflict because Party Boss Dej felt that a complete break between the Soviet Union and China would harm Rumanian interests. Maurer met the Soviet leaders on his way back to Bucharest.

45. The territory in question is the fertile steppe bounded by the Danube, Dniester, and Pruth rivers and by the Black Sea. These lands had been Russian from 1812 until

Perhaps the Rumanians incorrectly understood the historical basis of our claim to Bessarabia. That misunderstanding might have been at the heart of their dissatisfaction with us. I don't know whether that's really what the problem was — it's hard to say. Whatever the reason, the Rumanians kept up the appearance of friendship and courtesy, but the warmth and fraternal feeling which had once characterized our relations were now gone. As for our dealings with the various Rumanian leaders, we suspected that maybe Comrade Maurer might have been pushing Dej in the wrong direction. We had nothing personal against Comrade Maurer. He's a very congenial and tactful man. It was always a pleasure to talk to him and to go hunting with him. He's a good hunter, an excellent marksman. However, he'd joined the Party rather late, after the victory, and this fact led us to suspect that he still had some old nationalist prejudices. I have no concrete evidence with which to prove this contention; it's just an impression.

We were aware that Ceausescu was gaining considerable political influence. He was a highly intelligent young man who'd been through the toughest schooling of the class struggle. I knew he'd spent time in Rumanian prisons, and he certainly couldn't be accused of opportunism.

I still watch the developments in Rumania with great interest. As far as I know — certainly during the period when I was still active — we never had any quarrel with Rumania's internal policies. They collectivized their agriculture in what seemed to us a very reasonable way, and we had no reason to criticize their investment policy either. In fact, we had no *right* to criticize *any* of their internal policies. It's not up to us to oversee our Rumanian comrades. Rumania is an independent country, free to conduct any policies it wants.

However, from the viewpoint of the Communist Party of the Soviet Union, the Rumanian Party — particularly in its foreign policy — has deviated from certain norms which have been established in relations among Communist countries. But there must be something more to it than that. What it is, I just don't know.

From what I read in the newspapers, it appears that Soviet-Rumanian relations continue to be rather cold. I say "continue" because a number of years have passed since I retired — that is, since I

1918, Rumanian under the name Bessarabia from 1918 until 1940, occupied by the Germans and their Rumanian allies during World War II, and formally restored to the Soviet Union as part of the Moldavian Republic in 1947.

was forced to retire. At first, I was blamed for the troubles which arose in our relations with Rùmania. However, since my political career was terminated, not only have those relations failed to improve — they've gotten worse than ever. All I can say is that I was ignorant of the true reasons for the conflict when it first began to develop, and I don't understand the reasons any better now. I just hope — in fact, I'm confident — that the time will come when the true interests of the Rumanian people will prevail and the present state of affairs will change for the better.

II

China

Origins of the Schism

PEOPLE I meet often tell me it would be particularly interesting if I recorded my memoirs about our country's relations with China.[1]

You might say that China is both close to us and far from us. It's close in that it's our next-door neighbor and shares a long border with our country. At the same time, China is far away in that the Chinese have little in common with our people.

When I was growing up, Russia had few contacts with China. Before the Revolution, people like myself knew nothing about it except what we saw in pictures. If we met any Chinese at all, they were the occasional wandering silk merchants.

The Russo-Japanese War brought our nations closer together.[2] Russian soldiers fought the Japanese in Manchuria, which was part of China. Then, after the October Revolution, the leaders of the Soviet Union established contact with the leader of the Chinese people, Sun Yat-sen, who conducted a federalist policy during the war.[3]

I had some indirect contacts with the Chinese during the Civil War. There were no Chinese in the regiments in which I served, but there were some at our Front.[4] I remember that our Red Army sol-

1. This chapter supplements Khrushchev's reminiscences of his dealings with the Chinese leadership as presented in *KR*, I, 461–479.
2. The Russo-Japanese War, 1904–5.
3. Sun Yat-sen, the revolutionary leader and first President of the Chinese Republic. The "war" referred to here was the turmoil which swept over China after the fall of the Manchu dynasty in 1911.
4. Khrushchev took part in the Red offensive to the Black Sea during the Russian Civil War.

diers used to say what fierce fighters the Chinese were. Russian troops used to joke about how the Chinese talked — "Give bread, me eat bread, machine work; no give bread, machine no work" — but indeed the Chinese were absolutely fearless in battle. They were good soldiers and consequently good comrades-in-arms.

After the Civil War, while I was starting my career as a Party organizer in the Donbass and later, when I was attending the [Yuzovka] Workers' Faculty, I remember our newspapers used to carry reports about China. These articles were, by and large, sympathetic to the Chinese people in their struggle for liberation from [foreign] domination and for a progressive system of government.

When Sun Yat-sen died, Chiang Kai-shek seized power and turned against the Communists.[5] Naturally, the sympathies of the Soviet people were on the side of the Communists in their war against Chiang Kai-shek and the other oppressors of the Chinese people.

I recall one interesting incident which happened in '27, when I was still head of the Organizational Section of the Party Committee for the Yuzovka District.[6] An acquaintance of mine came to see me in Yuzovka. His name was Akhtyrsky. He was a man whom people of my generation in the Donbass will remember as a hero of the Civil War. He'd achieved fame during the drive against the Germans early in 1919 and later in the war against the White Guards as the commander of an armored train which bore his name. He was a brave warrior, but I wouldn't say he ever reached a very high level of political maturity. He was half-Communist, half-anarchist, rather like Makhno.[7] Akhtyrsky showed up one day at our District Party Committee headquarters with a Party membership card. As usual, he was drunk.

"Comrade Khrushchev," he said, "give me an official letter so that I can go to China right away. I want to fight against Chiang Kai-shek! I want to take part in the attack on Shanghai!"

5. Sun died in 1925. Two years later the leader of the Nationalist armies, Chiang Kai-shek, who had spent several months in the USSR as Sun's emissary in 1923, turned against the Chinese Communists.

6. By 1927, when this incident occurred, Khrushchev was already a powerful figure in the Ukraine. That year he was a delegate to the Fifteenth All-Union Party Congress in Moscow and promoted from his local district committee to the Regional Party Committee.

7. N. I. Makhno, a Ukrainian anarchist and peasant leader during the Civil War, fought against the White Guards, then turned against the Soviet regime. He escaped abroad and settled in Paris.

I told Akhtyrsky that the Chinese could get along fine without him. They didn't need his help to capture Shanghai when the time was ripe. I'm relating this incident because it illustrates the mood which was whipped up by our Communist press.[8]

The organizers of the armed struggle against Chiang Kai-shek were well known among our people. Perhaps the most popular of all was Colonel Chu Teh, the commander of the [Chinese] Red Army.[9] He was one of the first to raise the banner against the reactionary forces in China. Another well-known hero was Kao Kang.[10] Our people also knew the names of the Communist Party's principal enemies: men like Wu P'ei-fu and Chang Tso-lin, who was considered to be a puppet of Japanese imperialism.[11]

Except for the personalities I've mentioned, I didn't know much about the structure of the Chinese Communist Party and its leaders. Liu Shao-ch'i made a visit to Moscow when I was Secretary of the Moscow Party Committee, but I had nothing to do with him.[12] As for Mao Tse-tung, I'd never even heard of him.[13]

China's representative to the Comintern was Wang Ming. He was extremely popular among the workers of Moscow because he often used to address meetings. We frequently asked him to visit a factory and deliver a speech, and he'd never refuse.[14]

During World War II, we had some contacts with Chiang Kai-shek. Despite his conflict with the Chinese Communist Party, Chiang Kai-shek was fighting against Japanese imperialism. Therefore, Stalin — and consequently the Soviet government — considered Chiang a progressive force. Japan was our number one enemy in the East, so it

8. Chiang launched his campaign to eradicate the Communists with a sudden and bloody purge, or "White Terror," in Shanghai in 1927.

9. Chu Teh, "the father of the Red Army" and a longtime Politbureau member.

10. One of the earliest Party members in Shensi Province, Kao Kang played an important role in securing the Communist redoubt in Shensi, which was the end point of Mao Tse-tung's Long March to escape Chiang's armies.

11. Wu P'ei-fu was a warlord who was supported by the Comintern until he turned anti-Communist. Chang Tso-lin was a Manchurian leader who organized a raid on the Soviet embassy in Peking in 1927.

12. Liu Shao-ch'i, future Vice Chairman of the Chinese Party and President, was a labor leader who in 1921 visited Moscow, where he first joined the Party.

13. Mao Tse-tung during this period (1935–38) set up camp in Shensi and built a "broad national revolutionary united front" against the Japanese, who declared war on China in 1937. Khrushchev's claim not to have heard of Mao before the war says more about Khrushchev than it does about Mao: the Chinese leader had been elected to the Executive Committee of the Comintern at its Seventh Congress in Moscow in 1935.

14. Wang Ming (real name: Ch'en Shao-yu), an active delegate to the 1935 Comintern Congress in Moscow. He spent six years in Moscow during the 1930's.

was in the interests of the Soviet Union to support Chiang. Of course, we supported him only insofar as we didn't want to see him defeated by the Japanese — in much the same way that Churchill, who had been our enemy since the first days of the Soviet Union, was sensible enough to support us in the war against Hitler.

The United States began to threaten Japan proper.[15] The Chinese People's Red Army began winning battles against the Japanese. After the defeat of Hitlerite Germany and its allies, the Soviet Union entered the struggle in the East and did its share to defeat Japan in the concluding stages of the war.

We began to take a greater interest in China than before, and we concentrated our attention on granting the necessary economic and military aid to Mao Tse-tung in his capacity as leader of the Chinese people, the Communist Party, and the Red Army. He needed our help to crush the Japanese imperialists once and for all.

Our advancing army successfully occupied Manchuria. The defeated Japanese laid down their arms, which we then handed over to the Chinese [Communists]. We had certain agreements with our allies [16] concerning the transfer of captured weapons, so we had to avoid giving the impression that we were giving these arms [to the Red Army] directly. As it was explained to me, our method was to collect the weapons and leave them somewhere for the Chinese [Communists] to find. In that manner, we managed to equip the [Red] Army in Manchuria with arms which our own army had captured from the Japanese. This was material aid, for which the Chinese [Communists] had our government to thank. When I say "our government," I mean Stalin. He believed he *was* the government, and he believed he was acting in the interests of the Chinese people. Even though I was a member of the Politbureau, I wasn't let in on all the matters which came up between Stalin and the Chinese. I knew only what I was supposed to know. Stalin made countless decisions with respect to China — usually, I think, in consultation with Molotov.

At the end of World War II, but before the Chinese [Communist] victory in '49, Stalin sent Comrade Mikoyan to Nanking for talks with Chiang Kai-shek; Anastas Ivanovich was supposed to find

15. By "Japan proper," Khrushchev means the home islands, as opposed to the possessions of the Japanese Empire and the territories conquered in the war.
16. That is, agreements with Chiang Kai-shek.

out what Chiang's needs were and offer him aid.[17] I remember that Stalin used to talk over supper with his inner circle about the situation in China. He used to ask over and over, "What kind of a man is this Mao Tse-tung? I don't know anything about him. He's never been to the Soviet Union." Stalin already had his suspicions that Mao held a narrow peasant's position, that he was afraid of [urban] workers, and that he was building his Red Army on an isolated basis, ignoring the working class. The principal evidence for Stalin's doubts was Mao's conduct of the offensive on Shanghai. Chiang Kaishek could no longer defend the city, yet Mao held the Red Army back and refused to capture Shanghai.

It wasn't until Mao came to Moscow late in 1949 that Stalin heard Mao's explanation for the Shanghai offensive — and that explanation completely confirmed Stalin's suspicions.

"Why didn't you seize Shanghai?" asked Stalin.

"Why should we have?" said Mao. "If we'd captured the city we would have had to take on the responsibility for feeding the six million inhabitants."

In his war against the bourgeoisie and the landowners, Mao apparently relied on the peasant masses more than on city dwellers. For some reason he believed that the peasantry was more revolutionary than the working class. Rather than enter Shanghai and enlist the support of the workers there, he'd worried that the job of providing food for the city would detract from his struggle against Chiang.[18]

When Stalin related this conversation to the rest of us, he said, "What kind of a man is Mao, anyway? He calls himself a Marxist, but he doesn't understand the most elementary Marxist truths. Or maybe he doesn't want to understand them." I agreed with Stalin on that score. I think he was justified in his doubts about Mao.

Mao was in Moscow for Stalin's seventieth birthday on December 21, 1949. I came up from Kiev and ran into a secretary of the Moscow District Party.

"Anything new?" I asked him.

"Yeah," he said, "we've got this Matsadoon in town."

"What the hell is a 'Matsadoon'? You must mean Mao Tse-tung, don't you?"

17. Mikoyan was at that time Deputy Chairman of the Council of Ministers with special responsibility for foreign policy.
18. For more on this conversation, see *KR*, I, 462.

"You know," he said, "that Chinaman."

In some respects, Stalin was perfectly hospitable to Mao. He gave dinners in his honor. Stalin loved to show off his hospitality to his esteemed guests, and he knew how to do it very well.

But during Mao's stay, Stalin would sometimes not lay eyes on him for days at a time — and since Stalin neither saw Mao nor ordered anyone else to entertain him, *no* one dared go see him. Rumors began reaching our ears that Mao was not at all happy, that he was under lock and key, and that everyone was ignoring him. Mao let it be known that if the situation continued, he would leave. When Stalin heard about Mao's complaints, I think he had another dinner for him. Stalin was anxious to create the impression that we were on the best of terms with Mao and firmly on the side of the Chinese people. Finally, the Chinese delegation left Moscow and returned to Peking.[19]

About that time, the question of Sinkiang came up. I can't remember whether Stalin discussed the problem directly with Mao while he was in Moscow, or whether the matter was handled through Comrade Mikoyan, who was our first representative sent to China to deal with Mao.

During the war, we had occupied and fortified Sinkiang, sealing it off against Chiang Kai-shek. Our occupation of the province had been in the interests of both the Soviet Union and the Chinese Communists. By the time the Communists defeated Chiang and came to power in China, we were in charge in Sinkiang. We had our own people there, and the whole province was working for us. However, after the Red Army's victory, Stalin acknowledged to Mao that Sinkiang belonged to China.

Then Stalin made a serious mistake: he suggested to Mao that we organize an international society for the exploitation of natural resources in Sinkiang.[20] The Chinese accepted the proposal without objection, but they were undoubtedly not pleased with the idea. They must have felt that the Soviet Union had certain designs on Sinkiang, and that the international society represented an encroach-

19. Mao's nearly ten-week stay in Moscow after Chiang's retreat to Formosa culminated in a treaty negotiated with the participation of Chou En-lai and providing for Soviet military support in exchange for economic concessions and Soviet access to the naval base at Port Arthur. The Sino-Soviet Treaty of Friendship, signed in February, 1950, was supposed to last for thirty years.

20. The "joint stock company" in Sinkiang Province was a commercial concession favorable to the USSR.

ment on China's territory and independence. Thus, Stalin sowed the seeds of hostility and anti-Soviet, anti-Russian feeling in China.[21]

I told Stalin that the Chinese would probably object to our trying to get trading concessions from them in the same way the English, Portuguese, and other foreigners had in the past.

"Why are you sticking your nose in this?" snapped Stalin. "It's none of your business." With that, he dictated a message to Mao, asking for suitable territory on which to set up a rubber plantation.

Some time later we received a cable from Mao containing his reply. There were a number of people present when we read Mao's response to Stalin's proposal: "We agree to establish a rubber plantation for you on the island of Hainan, off the coast of Vietnam — but we do so with certain conditions. Specifically, we propose that you give us the credits, machinery, and technical assistance necessary to build and operate the plantation by ourselves. We will repay you for this help by sending you shipments of rubber."

There was a long silence after Stalin finished reading Mao's message. I avoided Stalin's eyes because I knew he hadn't forgotten my warning against making such a proposal in the first place. Now Mao's reply came as a bitter pill to swallow.

Mao, of course, was absolutely right to have responded as he did. He wasn't trying to be offensive; he was simply emphasizing China's rights and pride.

We agreed to the Chinese counterproposal and gave them the help they asked for to establish the rubber plantation, but nothing came of it in the end. I don't think the Chinese were very enthusiastic about the project. They paid us back for our tractors and loans, but we didn't get any rubber out of the bargain.

The incident must have left its mark on Mao. Like Stalin, Mao wasn't one to forgive, much less to forget. His experience with Stalin, first over Sinkiang and now over the rubber plantation, was sufficient to convince him that Stalin's policy toward China had much in common with the imperialist policies of the capitalist countries. Also like Stalin, Mao was deeply suspicious. Therefore the concrete evidence for distrusting Stalin was magnified many times by his suspiciousness.

However, Mao was careful not to show what he was really think-

21. At this point in the narrative Khrushchev retells, in abbreviated form, the story of the Soviet plan to exploit Chinese diamond deposits and rubber reserves, as already presented in *KR*, I, 463.

ing. He went out of his way to show his respect, even his humility and deference, toward Stalin. For example, Mao appealed to Stalin to recommend a literate Marxist-Leninist theoretician who could help him edit the speeches and articles he had written during the Civil War. Mao was preparing to publish his collected works and wanted someone to check his writings for possible errors.[22]

Stalin, needless to say, was delighted. He took Mao's request as a sign that Mao had no pretensions to any special role in the theory and practice of building socialism in China. Stalin thought Mao was expressing his willingness to look at the world through Stalin's eyes. Of course, that's just what Mao wanted Stalin to think. I believe that, in fact, Mao had other fish to fry — and subsequent events showed that he did indeed.

Stalin replied to Mao's request by sending Yudin to Peking.[23] It was no accident that Stalin chose Yudin for the job of helping Mao prepare his works for publication. Yudin was a philosopher and therefore someone Mao could talk to about philosophy. Mao liked to engage in high-flown discourse, and he used to force all kinds of philosophical subjects upon the mere mortals with whom he came into contact, myself included.

As soon as Yudin got to Peking he began sending back a stream of telegrams gushing with enthusiasm for Mao Tse-tung. Yudin said Mao used to come see him, rather than the other way around, and they'd sit with each other into the small hours of the morning — not so much editing Mao's writings as discussing weighty topics. All this was fine with us. After all, as the peasants used to say, "Give the baby anything to keep it happy — as long as it doesn't cry."

Although he established good relations with Mao and contributed to Sino-Soviet friendship in his capacity as the editor of Mao's works, Yudin didn't become our ambassador to China until after Stalin's death. Instead, Stalin appointed a railroad expert who'd been a people's commissar during the war. I forget his name, but I remember that after the defeat of the Japanese in northern China, Stalin sent this man to supervise the reconstruction of the Manchurian railroads and act as our plenipotentiary representative in Manchuria. We

22. The reference is to ideological errors.
23. Before taking a permanent post in Peking, P. F. Yudin was editor of the Cominform paper, *For Lasting Peace, For People's Democracy!* (1947–50), and political advisor to the Soviet Control Commission in Germany (1950–53).

had confidence in him. Stalin considered him his personal trusty.[24]

This representative of ours [Panyushkin] began showering us with reports that there were many people in the Chinese leadership who were actively dissatisfied with the Soviet Union and with our Party. According to him, our most vocal opponents were Liu Shao-ch'i, Chou En-lai, and others. Mao wasn't among those mentioned — nor was he taking any steps against his colleagues who were spreading anti-Soviet sentiments in the Chinese leadership. Stalin circulated some of these documents from our ambassador, and that's how I was able to familiarize myself with their contents.

Apparently much of this information about the mood in the Chinese Party came to us from Kao Kang, who was then the representative of the Chinese Politbureau and governor in Manchuria, where he'd been on close terms with our own representatives. On one occasion there was a celebration and parade of some kind in Mukden, where Kao Kang had his headquarters.[25] The Chinese officers were complaining about the reconditioned Soviet tanks we'd given Mao for his army. "The Russians have dumped a lot of old, beat-up tanks on us," they grumbled. Whenever there's deep, underlying discontent, every minor detail gets blown out of proportion and becomes grounds for leveling serious charges against the Soviet Union.

Stalin decided he wanted to win Mao's trust and friendship, so he took [Panyushkin's] reports about his conversations with Kao Kang and handed them over to Mao, saying, "Here, you might be interested in these."

God only knows what Stalin thought he was doing. He justified it as a friendly gesture. If you're looking for historical parallels, you could compare the incident to the famous case in which Kochubei informed Peter the Great about Mazepa's treason. Peter, seeking to win Mazepa over to his side, then told Mazepa about Kochubei's denunciation. As a result, Mazepa executed Kochubei and joined forces

24. He was A. S. Panyushkin, an intelligence officer and former envoy both to Washington (1947–52) and to Chiang Kai-shek's wartime government in Chungking (1939–44). Panyushkin was Stalin's second ambassador to the Chinese Communist government, succeeding N. V. Roshchin, who had previously been accredited to Chiang's postwar government until Mao drove the Nationalists from the mainland in 1949.

25. Kao was the Party's strongman in Manchuria after the Communist victory on the mainland. He had his headquarters in Mukden, the provincial capital. Significantly, he served on the Executive Board of the Sino-Soviet Friendship Association. Among the Soviet representatives with whom he was on close terms was Panyushkin, who relayed "information about the mood" to Moscow.

with Charles XII in a campaign against Russia. Pushkin tells the whole story in his poem "Poltava." [26]

What Peter did to Kochubei, Stalin did to Kao Kang — and what Mazepa did to Kochubei, Mao did to Kao Kang.

At first Mao isolated Kao Kang within the leadership. Our representatives in Peking reported that they'd been at a party with a lot of young people who got drunk and began making angry remarks to our diplomats about "your man Kao Kang." At the time, Kao Kang was still in the [Chinese] Politbureau, but we knew he was already on ice. Then we learned that Mao had put him under house arrest. Later we learned he'd poisoned himself.[27] I doubt very much that Kao Kang committed suicide. Most probably Mao had him strangled or poisoned. Mao was capable of such things, just as Stalin was. In that respect, too, Mao and Stalin were kindred spirits.

Because of Stalin's betrayal of Kao Kang, we were deprived of a man who'd proved his friendship and supplied us with valuable information about the true attitude of the Chinese leadership toward the Soviet Union.

Why did Stalin betray Kao Kang? I think he was motivated by his own suspiciousness. As he himself said, Stalin didn't trust anyone — not even himself. He figured that sooner or later Mao would have learned on his own that Kao Kang had been informing on him — and, if that had happened, Mao could accuse Stalin of fomenting opposition to the Chinese government. So Stalin decided it would be better to sacrifice Kao Kang and thereby earn Mao's trust.

However, I don't think Mao ever really trusted Stalin. He saw that Stalin was always trying to prove his superiority. I'm convinced that Mao saw through Stalin's "diplomacy" and was secretly annoyed and alarmed by it.

26. Ivan Mazepa-Koledinsky was a seventeenth-century cossack leader who intrigued with Sweden's King Charles XII against Tsar Peter I for control of the Ukraine. V. L. Kochubei was a wealthy official.

27. Kao was not openly attacked until almost a year after Stalin's death. In 1954 he was purged at a Party plenum, and shortly afterwards he reportedly committed suicide.

First Visit to Peking

IN the first years after Stalin died, Mao Tse-tung treated us with friendship and respect. When I say "us," I mean the leadership formed after Stalin's death.

In 1954 the Central Committee and the Council of Ministers decided I should lead a governmental delegation to Peking. In addition to Bulganin, who was Chairman of the Council of Ministers, the other delegates included Anastas Ivanovich Mikoyan; Shvernik; Minister of Culture Furtseva; Shelepin; the editor of *Pravda;* and Nasriddinova, who represented the Uzbek people.[28]

We were scheduled to arrive in China in time for the celebration of the Chinese people's victory on October 1. The Chinese leaders gave us a warm welcome. We were pleased to be on Chinese soil for the first time and to have a chance for discussions with our Chinese comrades.

Many of us encountered new customs. I remember, for instance, that the Chinese served tea every time we turned around — tea, tea, tea. You couldn't sit down at a meeting without their putting in front of you a cup with a lid. And according to the Chinese tradition, if you didn't drink it up right away, they'd take that cup away and put another one in front of you — over and over again. Finally they'd bring you a steamed towel to wipe off your hands and face. The towel was refreshing, I have to admit.

We weren't accustomed to such ceremonies, but we went along with them out of respect for our hosts. However, enough was enough, and after a while I refused to drink any more tea — first, because it was green tea, which I'm not accustomed to, and second, because I can't take that much liquid.

Bulganin, on the other hand, did what was expected of him by his hosts. As a result, he developed insomnia. The doctor examined him and asked, "Have you been drinking green tea?"

28. N. M. Shvernik, chairman of the Trade Union Council; A. N. Shelepin, then head of the Communist Youth League; D. T. Shepilov, editor in chief of *Pravda;* Ya. S. Nasriddinova, a woman from the Uzbek Party apparatus; and Ye. A. Furtseva, the current Minister of Culture, who was then Secretary of the Moscow City Party Committee.

"Yes."

"How much?"

"A lot."

"If you go on drinking tea in such quantities, you'll lose even more sleep. You'll have either to cut down on your tea-drinking or cut it out altogether. It contains a small dose of a toxic substance which makes you sleep badly."

Bulganin followed the doctor's advice and later told me he was sleeping normally again.

In our talks with the Chinese, our general concern was the protection of the Soviet Union, the other socialist countries, and China. In order to maintain our own defense posture, we had to contribute to the industrial development of the great Chinese people, and therefore we arranged for increased economic aid. We agreed to send military experts, artillery, machine guns, and other weapons in order to strengthen China and thus strengthen the socialist camp. In short, we tried to accommodate the Chinese in as many of their requests as our own material situation would allow. Our efforts were united against a common enemy. One foe, Japan, had been defeated but was still a potential threat. A far greater threat came from the United States, which had already unleashed war in South Korea, right on the edge of China.

We also made an effort to put our relations back on a friendly and equal basis. We conducted official talks on the Port Arthur agreement. On this matter, I fully agreed with our Chinese comrades. They were absolutely right that Port Arthur was on Chinese territory and that we should keep our forces there only as long as it was in the mutual interests of the Soviet Union and the People's Republic of China for us to do so. We'd spent a lot of money renovating the fortifications in Port Arthur, equipping it with the latest weapons, and stationing a sizable garrison there. We also had troops in Dalny.[29]

We said we wanted to remove our troops from Port Arthur and Dalny and hand over to the Chinese all our installations there, with the exception of the very expensive shore batteries we'd just installed. Mao replied that he didn't think it was the right moment for

29. Dalny is the Russian name for Dairen, where the Soviets had obtained free port rights in a 1945 treaty with the Nationalist government. Stalin agreed to evacuate the forces from Port Arthur and Dairen by 1952 at the latest, but the deadline was postponed at the "invitation" of Peking in the face of a perceived American threat to Manchuria during the Korean War.

us to pull out of Port Arthur and Dalny. He was afraid the United States might try to take advantage of such a move and attack China.

"Comrade Mao," I said, "we doubt the US will do anything like that. Of course, we can't give you any guarantees since the United States has just ended its aggressive war in Korea and is still conducting an aggressive policy. But if we withdrew our forces from Port Arthur, they'd be nearby in Vladivostok, so we could come to the rescue in case you were attacked."

After more discussion, Mao agreed, saying, "If you think this is a good time to pull out, we won't stand in your way."

We agreed upon a draft of a new treaty stipulating the withdrawal of our troops.[30]

Some time later Chou En-lai asked us, "What would you think about leaving your heavy artillery behind in Port Arthur?"

We wouldn't have minded obliging if the Chinese had been willing to pay for the guns, but Chou asked us to hand them over free.

"Comrade Chou," I said, "please understand the awkward position in which we find ourselves. We haven't yet recovered from a terribly destructive war. Our economy is in shambles, and our people are poor. We'd be happy to sell you this artillery for a low price, but we simply can't afford to let you have it for nothing. Please try to see our side of the question, and don't insist on your conditions." That's where the matter rested. The Chinese didn't raise the subject again.

We liquidated the international organizations and the equal treaties between our countries. We gave up our rights to the Chinese-Soviet railroad in Manchuria. I don't remember whether we just handed it over to them or whether we sold it to them cheaply; but in any event, the Chinese took over the management of the railroad. I believe this was a correct decision on our part: if you don't want to create conflicts with other socialist countries, you shouldn't have your own installations on their territory.

The Chinese raised another issue. They said the railroad connecting the Soviet Union and China by way of Ulan Bator didn't meet their needs. I couldn't understand why it was no good to them, since it had been most useful to us. Before, we'd always had to transport our cargo through the Far East; the Ulan Bator line considerably shortened the route and connected Moscow directly with Peking.

30. Port Arthur and Dairen were returned to Chinese control in 1955, seven months after Khrushchev's first visit to Peking.

Nevertheless, the Chinese said they wanted a different route, one which would cross our border near Alma Ata and which would cut through the regions of China that had rich deposits of minerals.[31]

We said we'd undertake the construction of the railroad on our side of the border if the Chinese would build it on theirs. Our portion was fairly short, and the conditions were good. Besides, our workmen were better trained and better equipped than the Chinese. It took us no time at all to finish our stretch. The Chinese, however, soon realized they had a tough nut to crack — and they just weren't up to the job. Chou En-lai came to talk the matter over with us. The Chinese always delegated Chou to raise unpleasant matters with us, first, because he was their Prime Minister and, second, because he was a masterful diplomat.

"What would you think," said Chou, "if we asked you to take over the construction of some of the railroad on our side of the border?" — and at our own expense, no less.

That changed everything. We were completely unprepared for such a proposal. We had no idea how much it would cost, but we could be sure it would be a fairly expensive way to pass the time of day. We could see from the map that we'd have to erect bridges and dig tunnels — all of which would cost us dearly.

The unpleasant task of turning down our friends fell to me: "I'm terribly sorry, Comrade Chou, but there's no way we can undertake the construction of the railroad on your territory. We have too many economic problems of our own. We simply can't afford it."

And so the matter was dropped then and there. But our decision to refuse the Chinese request was like another stone on the scales of our relations, and it tipped the balance further against friendship. I knew that financial accounting shouldn't get in the way of friendship — but friendship is one thing, business is another. As long as each government has to serve its own people first and foremost, such disappointments are unavoidable in one country's relations with another. Nevertheless, as I say, the incident added to the strain which was building up between the Soviet Union and China.

31. The Soviets had been transporting cargo to Pacific ports by way of the Trans-Siberian Railroad, which was connected to Peking by a spur through the Mongolian capital of Ulan Bator. The route the Chinese proposed would have crossed the Sino-Soviet border near Alma Ata, capital of the Kazakh Republic in Soviet Central Asia. (This account of the altercation is more detailed and more accurate than the version in *KR*, I, 466.)

For our part, we had a proposal to make to the Chinese. We wanted to help them with their severe unemployment problem. At the time, our ministers were of the opinion that we had a labor shortage in Siberia. (This was before we realized that we were simply utilizing our own labor force inefficiently and that in order to tap the riches of Siberia we had to attract workers from the European part of Russia.) We proposed that a million or more Chinese workers be sent to Siberia to help us take advantage of the vast timber resources there.

Mao's response to our proposal was typical of him — and indicative of what was to come. He really knew how to put us down. First, you have to imagine what Mao was like in person. He moved as calmly and slowly as a bear, swaying from side to side. He would look at you for a long time, then lower his eyes and begin talking in a relaxed, quiet voice: "You know, Comrade Khrushchev, for years it's been a widely held view that because China is an underdeveloped and overpopulated country, with widespread unemployment, it represents a good source of cheap labor. But you know, we Chinese find this attitude very offensive. Coming from you, it's rather embarrassing. If we were to accept your proposal, others might get the wrong idea about the relationship between the Soviet Union and China. They might think that the Soviet Union has the same image of China that the capitalist West has."

Obviously, Mao wanted to make us sorry we'd raised the question. It was most disagreeable for us to hear him talk this way, especially to hear him compare us to the capitalists. After all, we hadn't beaten around the bush: we had come right out and presented a proposal that we sincerely believed was in the interests of the Chinese because it would have helped them get rid of some extra mouths to feed.

By agreement with my comrades, I was conducting these talks on behalf of our delegation, so at our next meeting I said, "Comrade Mao, we certainly had no intention of creating difficulties for you. We certainly don't insist on our proposition. If you feel it would damage China's national pride, then by all means forget we mentioned it. We'll make do with our own workers."

When we came back to Peking after a tour of the country and a visit to Harbin and Mukden, the Chinese representatives dragged up the matter of using Chinese labor in Siberia. Our [Soviet] comrades replied that Mao was against the idea. The Chinese then came back with an official message to the effect that Mao was now willing to help us by accepting our original proposal.

We were sorry we'd ever suggested the idea, but since we'd been the first to propose the plan, we couldn't very well back down now that the Chinese had agreed. Otherwise, we would have had to explain to the Chinese why we'd changed our minds, and that would have added insult to injury.

So, reluctantly, we agreed to go through with a treaty and let the first batch of about two hundred thousand Chinese laborers come to work in Siberia. As soon as their time was up, we deliberately avoided initiating negotiations for any further treaties. However, the Chinese themselves began pressing us to import more workers into Siberia, despite what Mao had said about resenting China being used as a cheap labor pool.

"Why don't you let us send some more?" they said. "Don't be bashful. We're glad to help you."

At a later meeting with Mao, I apologized for having overestimated our need to import labor. We made sure that once the contracts for the Chinese in Siberia had expired, they weren't renewed; and the workers went home.

What had the Chinese been up to? I'll tell you: they wanted to occupy Siberia without war. They wanted to penetrate and take over the Siberian economy. They wanted to make sure that Chinese settlers in Siberia outnumbered Russians and people of other nationalities who lived there. In short, they wanted to make Siberia Chinese rather than Russian. It was a clever maneuver, but it didn't work.

Mao in Moscow

AT the Twentieth Congress of the Communist Party of the Soviet Union we exposed Stalin for his excesses, for his arbitrary punishment of millions of honest people, and for his one-man rule, which violated the principle of collective leadership.[32] At first, Mao Tsetung took the position that we were right to censure Stalin for his

32. See *KR*, I, 341–353.

abuses of power. He said that the decisions taken at the Twentieth Party Congress showed great "wisdom."

In a way, Mao was right not to underestimate the role of certain people in the leadership who insisted on facing the crimes of the Stalin era head on.[33] To have remained silent about Stalin's abuses — as Voroshilov, Molotov, and Kaganovich urged — would have been wrong. However, any wisdom we showed at the Twentieth Party Congress wasn't our own — it was Lenin's wisdom, which we belatedly rediscovered. By giving all the credit to us, Mao was simply trying to win us over with flattery.

Mao started registering his own complaints about Stalin. For example, he reproached Stalin for having supported Chiang Kai-shek. He produced concrete evidence to prove that Stalin had harmed the interests of the Chinese Communist Party. I can't remember the exact contents, but I recall that Mao referred to certain letters which Stalin had written to Chiang.

Mao [also] accused Stalin of misunderstanding the nature of the Chinese revolution. More specifically, Mao said Stalin had underrated — and had therefore impeded — the revolutionary potential of the Chinese working class.

Mao was particularly critical of how the Comintern had dealt with China. Stalin, of course, had had overall responsibility for the Comintern, but China's special representative had been Wang Ming, who had worked out most of the Comintern directives for the Chinese Party. As I've already mentioned, Wang Ming was a good Communist who understood the necessity of preserving unity and friendship between the Soviet Union and China.

After the [Chinese] revolution prevailed, Mao got rid of Wang Ming in a clever way. He didn't want to stain his hands with Wang Ming's blood. Instead of killing him, Mao arranged for Wang Ming to be elected to the Chinese Central Committee and then immediately banned him from living in China. Wang Ming wasn't allowed to go home to China after the Communist victory. He had to stay in Moscow. It's a good thing he did because later on, if Mao had been able to get his hands on him, Wang Ming probably would have lost his head.

Subsequently we were informed about various attempts on Wang Ming's life. He received packages of food [from China]. Before eat-

33. "Those who insisted . . ." — Khrushchev has himself in mind.

ing it himself, he tested the food on his cat and the cat died. Who would have wanted to poison Wang Ming? The only answer is Mao Tse-tung. Just as Stalin had Beria, so Mao had *his* own butcher — K'ang Sheng.[34] Fortunately, Wang Ming was cautious. He must have known what sort of "friends" would be sending him packages of food. I'm convinced these items were sent by K'ang Sheng.

Comrade Wang Ming still lives in Moscow, and he continues to maintain friendly relations with our Party and our people.[35] I always had the impression that Mao's criticisms of Stalin's Comintern policies were meant, as much as anything, to justify Mao's shabby treatment of Wang Ming.

After having congratulated us for the decisions of the Twentieth Party Congress and after delivering a whole raft of his own criticisms against Stalin, Mao later turned around 180 degrees and started praising Stalin. He realized flattery wouldn't work with us. I think that, secretly, he disapproved all along of our censuring Stalin for his crimes. Why do I think so? Because I believe Mao suffered from the same megalomania Stalin had all his life. He had the same diseased outlook on other people.

Like Stalin, Mao never recognized his comrades as his equals. He treated the people around him like pieces of furniture, useful for the time being but expendable. When, in his opinion, a piece of furniture — or a comrade — became worn out and lost its usefulness, he would just throw it away and replace it.

I remember my conversations with Mao around the time of the conference of Communist Parties.[36] I was struck by how much he sounded like Stalin. These discussions were perfectly cordial, but I was put on my guard by the way Mao talked about the other members of the Chinese Politbureau. He painted everything black. He had nothing good to say about anyone.

I can't remember exactly what he said about Liu Shao-ch'i and

34. K'ang Sheng, the Chinese Politbureau's top intelligence and security official, who was also in charge of liaison with foreign Communist Parties. K'ang had been with Wang Ming in Moscow for the 1935 Comintern Congress.

35. Wang Ming has been openly castigated in China since 1956 for "errors" dating back to the 1930's; nevertheless, he remained on the membership list of the Chinese Central Committee until 1969, despite his virtual exile in Moscow. In the spring and summer of 1969 he made propaganda broadcasts for the Soviet Union during the border dispute with China.

36. The meeting was held in Moscow in November, 1957, on the occasion of the fortieth anniversary of the Russian Revolution.

Chou En-lai, but it wasn't favorable to either of them. In criticizing these people, he gave me names, dates, and specific incidents to back up his negative reports. Then he started in on Chu Teh, who wasn't even a politician — he was a soldier. Everyone knows Chu Teh was a great general and a good Communist, but that didn't stop Mao from smearing him. As for Kao Kang, who was already dead by then — you couldn't even mention his name in Mao's presence.

The only one of his comrades whom Mao seemed to approve of was Teng Hsiao-p'ing.[37] I remember Mao pointing out Teng to me and saying, "See that little man there? He's highly intelligent and has a great future ahead of him." I knew nothing about this Teng Hsiao-p'ing. I'd heard his name mentioned a few times since the victory of the Chinese people, but never before that.

The more I listened to Mao, the more I had to compare him to Stalin. But even though I was spotting similarities between Stalin and Mao, I was still a long way from drawing any final conclusions. I couldn't yet foresee the form in which Mao's character would reveal itself and the tragedies into which he would plunge the Chinese Communist Party.

Mao asked me about how our Party was coming along. I answered that everything was fine and that we were proceeding with our work in an atmosphere of friendship. I said, though, that some comrades were dissatisfied with the job Bulganin was doing [as Chairman of the Council of Ministers], and that the question came up from time to time of moving him to another post. I decided to share this information with Mao because I didn't want him to find out about changes in our leadership after his departure from Moscow. If I hadn't said something to him about the situation inside our leadership, he might have regretted having told me about Chinese intra-Party matters.

Mao asked me whom we were going to appoint as Bulganin's replacement. I replied that the question hadn't been decided yet for sure, but that I thought our comrades were leaning in the direction of Kosygin.

"Kosygin?" said Mao. "Who's this Kosygin?"

37. Teng Hsiao-p'ing, who had been trained in France and the USSR during the 1920's, led the attack against Kao Kang in 1954 and 1955. By the time he came to Moscow with Mao in 1957, Teng was Deputy Premier and head of the Central Committee Secretariat. He was disgraced during the Cultural Revolution but reemerged as Deputy Premier in early 1974.

I told him, and he asked me to introduce him to Kosygin. I was glad that Mao wanted to get acquainted with the man who might head the government of the Soviet Union. I took it as an indication of his desire to strengthen relations between our Parties and governments.[38] Mao took Kosygin into a corner and had a talk with him.

I think during the Moscow conference, but I'm not sure, we suggested that the task of the international Communist movement would be more readily accomplished if we adopted some kind of division of labor. Since the Chinese Communist Party had won a great revolutionary victory in Asia, we thought it would be a good idea for the Chinese to concentrate on establishing closer contacts with the other Asian countries and Africa. We were primarily concerned about India, Pakistan, and Indonesia — three nations with economic conditions similar to China's. As for our own Party, it seemed to make sense for us to be responsible for keeping in touch with the revolutionary movements in Western Europe and the Americas.

When we presented this idea to the Chinese comrades, Mao Tsetung said, "No, it's out of the question. The leading role in Africa and Asia should belong to the Soviet Union. The Communist Party of the Soviet Union is the Party of Lenin; its cadres understand Marxism-Leninism more profoundly than anyone else. We of the Chinese Communist Party look to the Soviet Union for guidance. Therefore I think the CPSU should be the one and only center of the international Communist movement, and the rest of us should be united around that center."[39]

As we listened to Mao pay recognition to the Soviet Union and the CPSU, we couldn't help suspecting that his thoughts were probably very different from his words. We had the unsettling feeling that sooner or later, friction was bound to develop between our countries and our Parties.

During the course of the conference, there were some telltale indications of what form that friction might take. When the more than

38. In 1957 Kosygin was Deputy Chairman of the Council of Ministers. Despite what Khrushchev may have told Mao, Kosygin at that time still had seven years to wait before becoming Chairman of the Council of Ministers. It was Khrushchev himself who succeeded Bulganin as Premier in 1958, four months after the conversation with Mao related here.

39. On the eve of the 1957 conference, Mao gave a speech at Moscow State University declaring, "The socialist camp must have one head, and that head can only be the USSR." It was the most unqualified endorsement of Soviet hegemony over the bloc voice by any conference delegate.

eighty delegations present turned to the possibility of thermonuclear war, Mao gave a speech, the gist of which was as follows: "We shouldn't fear war. We shouldn't be afraid of atomic bombs and missiles. No matter what kind of war breaks out — conventional or thermonuclear — we'll win. As for China, if the imperialists unleash war on us, we may lose more than three hundred million people. So what? War is war. The years will pass, and we'll get to work producing more babies than ever before."

This last statement he put more crudely than I've related here. He allowed himself to use an indecent expression, though I don't remember exactly what it was. I was sitting next to Sun Yat-sen's widow.[40] She burst out laughing at Mao's racy language. Mao laughed, too, so we all joined in with laughter. But there was nothing funny about what he'd said. First of all, Mao should have had more consideration for the people around him. He should have watched his language. More seriously, the content of his speech was deeply disturbing. Except for the one outburst led by [Madame] Sun Yat-sen, the audience was dead silent. No one was prepared for such a speech.

During one of the recesses, Comrade Gomulka expressed his indignation in no uncertain terms. Comrade Novotny said, "Mao Tse-tung says he's prepared to lose three hundred million people out of a population of six hundred million. What about us? We have only twelve million people in Czechoslovakia. We'd lose every last soul in a war. There wouldn't be anyone left to start over again."[41]

Everybody except Mao was thinking about how to avoid war. Our principal slogan was "On with the Struggle for Peace and Peaceful Coexistence." Yet suddenly here came Mao Tse-tung, saying we shouldn't be afraid of war.

During his stay in Moscow there was other evidence that Mao was intent on striking a warlike posture. I remember when I told him about our desire to dissolve the NATO and Warsaw Pact military alliances, he expressed his doubts: "I don't think you should make such

40. Madame Sun Yat-sen (also known by her maiden name, Sung Ch'ing-ling) was the widow of modern China's founding father. Her brother, T. V. Soong, was one of Chiang Kai-shek's right-hand men, while her sister is Chiang's wife; yet Madame Sun herself cast her lot with the Peking regime. She was a member of Mao's delegation to Moscow in 1957. She now lives in Shanghai.

41. Anton Novotny was the strongman of Czechoslovakia, whom Khrushchev says he admired (*KR*, I, 364).

a proposal at this time. Suppose the West accepts; you'll have to withdraw your troops from the German Democratic Republic. As a result, the GDR won't be able to maintain its independence. It will fall apart. Then where will we be? We'll have lost the GDR."

This was still in the days when Mao said "we," meaning the socialist camp. He might have had a point about the GDR, but I explained to him that we were publicly proposing to dissolve the two alliances for propaganda purposes. We were sure the United States wouldn't accept right away, and by the time conditions for an agreement on NATO and the Warsaw Pact were ripe, the GDR would have evolved into a more stable country, able to maintain a socialist system on its own.

I remember one conversation I had with Mao in Moscow which illustrates his attitude as it was developing at that time. Not long before our meeting, Defense Minister Zhukov made a public statement, based on a policy line worked out in the government. The statement warned that the Soviet Union would strike a counterblow against any aggressive force which attacked a socialist country — that is, an ally of the Soviet Union. I'd made a similar statement, but Mao diplomatically chose to comment only on what Zhukov had said.

"I think Zhukov was wrong in that statement of his," said Mao.

"What do you mean? If we don't take the position he stated, the aggressive forces will destroy us bit by bit — first one country, then another, and another, until they finish us off. That's what the imperialists are bent on doing. They want to divide and conquer. Dulles has said it in so many words.[42] Besides, Comrade Mao, what Zhukov said didn't represent just his point of view. He was reflecting the view of our government and of the Central Committee. We believe we have no choice but to take the line Zhukov expressed."

"Not so," replied Mao. "If the Soviet Union is attacked from the West, you shouldn't engage the enemy in battle; you shouldn't counterattack — you should fall back."

"What do you mean, 'fall back'?"

"I mean retreat and hold out for a year, two years, even three years."

42. Throughout Khrushchev's oral memoirs, he tends to use interchangeably the names of John Foster Dulles, the late Secretary of State, and his brother Allen W. Dulles, the former director of the Central Intelligence Agency. He often says Allen Dulles when he clearly means John Foster, as he does here. The confusion has been corrected in the text.

"Where exactly do you suggest we retreat *to*? And *why* should we retreat? To do so would mean inviting defeat."

"Not necessarily," said Mao. "Look at World War II: didn't you retreat all the way to Stalingrad, then mobilize your forces into a counteroffensive and advance all the way to Berlin?"

"Of course we did, but our retreat wasn't motivated by either tactical or strategic considerations. The enemy drove us back. The enemy *forced* us to retreat. You, Comrade Mao, seem to be one of those who believes that Stalin lured Hitler deep into Russian territory and then crushed him — or that Kutuzov deliberately let Napoleon get all the way to Moscow before beating him. Neither was true. Stalin simply wasn't able to turn the tide of the German invasion until Stalingrad, just as Kutuzov couldn't defeat the French until they reached Borodino. If you want to go into this subject in more detail, I suggest you read *War and Peace* by Leo Tolstoy.[43] In point of fact, we were simply unprepared for our war against Hitler — and our unpreparedness almost turned out to be fatal. There's no way we could count on being able to retreat for three years and withstand an invasion."

"I don't agree," said Mao. "If you fell back to the Urals, then we Chinese could enter the war."

I looked at him closely, but I couldn't tell from his face whether he was joking or not.

"Comrade Mao, the next war wouldn't be anything like World War II. Today the Americans have so many atomic bombs they don't know what to do with them all. We, too, have nuclear weapons and are rushing ahead to equip our armed forces with them. The next war won't begin with the enemy launching an invasion across our border. It will begin with a missile or bomb attack on our major administrative and industrial centers. Therefore, it's our policy to arm ourselves with enough weapons to inflict the same damage on our enemy as he can inflict on us."

Mao wasn't convinced. Later on he would begin to torpedo our policy of peaceful coexistence, claiming outright that it was un-Leninist and bound to give way to pacifism. But for the time being, he simply expressed his doubts.

---

43. M. I. Kutuzov was the Russian commander who battled Napoleon at Borodino outside Moscow in 1812. This is another in a series of references to *War and Peace* in these memoirs. Their inclusion suggests that in his retirement Khrushchev read, or reread, Tolstoy's novel, along with the poetry of Pushkin and Nekrasov.

Second Visit to Peking

ONCE we began to produce diesel and nuclear-powered submarines, our navy suggested that we request of the Chinese government permission to build a radio station in China so that we could maintain communications with our submarine fleet operating in the Pacific. We discussed the matter in the leadership and decided to make a formal proposal to the Chinese. We considered the idea to be as much in China's interests as it was in our own. After all, we shared with the Chinese the common goal of protecting the socialist countries against the imperialists.

Besides, we'd willingly complied with Mao's request that we help him build submarines. As far as I remember, we let the Chinese have our designs and sent our experts to help them choose a place in which to build the submarines. Therefore we fully expected the Chinese to cooperate with us when we asked for a radio station on their territory.

As it turned out, though, the Chinese were anything but cooperative. Their reaction was stormy and irate. When our ambassador in Peking, Yudin, presented the proposal to the Chinese leadership, Mao shouted, "How dare you suggest such a thing! This proposal is an insult to our national pride and our sovereignty!" Yudin sent an alarming telegram to the Central Committee, describing Mao's angry reaction.[44]

We had a discussion in the leadership and decided that I should fly to China at the behest of the Presidium of the Central Committee.

44. This is the same telegram referred to in *KR*, I, 465: "Then, out of the blue, we received from Yudin a long, coded dispatch in which he described all sorts of incredible things which he had heard from Mao Tse-tung about the Soviet Union, our Communist Party, and about Yudin himself. There was no longer any need to worry that Mao was fawning over Yudin. Now it was obvious that Mao had no respect for Yudin at all. We decided we'd better get Yudin out of China. As an ambassador, Yudin had been a weak administrator and poor diplomat, but he had been useful as long as his personal relations with Mao remained friendly. To hell with his strictly ambassadorial work; we could always let our embassy officials in Peking take care of that. But when he clashed with Mao on philosophical grounds, he was no good to us either as an ambassador or as a contact with Mao. So we recalled him."

Yudin finally left Peking in early 1959, shortly after Khrushchev's visit described in this section.

Because we were going to be discussing military affairs, I was accompanied by Malinovsky and also by Kuznetsov.[45] Ours was to be a secret visit. We traveled *incognito*. We asked the Chinese comrades to receive us, and they agreed.

We were met at the airport by Mao, Ch'en Yi, and someone else.[46] They set us up in a residence somewhere in Peking, but most of the time we spent beside a swimming pool with some shade next to it. Of course, I couldn't compete with Mao in the pool — as everyone knows, he's since set a world record for both speed and distance. I'm a poor swimmer and was perfectly willing to take my hat off to Mao when it comes to swimming. However, the subject at hand had nothing to do with swimming. We lay there sunning ourselves on our towels like seals on the warm sand. We had informal discussions on political matters.

On the subject of the radio station we'd requested, I apologized to Mao, saying we had in no way intended to violate China's sovereignty, interfere in its internal affairs, impose upon its economy, or damage its national pride.

Mao replied by making a counterproposal: "Give us the necessary credits, and we'll build the radio station ourselves."

"Fine," I said, "that's a good solution. We'll send you the blueprints, the equipment, the technical advisors, and we'll loan you the money you need."

"All right," said Mao, "we agree."

So much for that problem, but there was something else. Our navy wanted to refuel our submarines and to give our crews shore leave at the ports along the Chinese coast. When I put this idea to Mao, once again he became adamant. He rejected the suggestion out of hand.

"Comrade Mao," I said, "we can't understand you at all. It would serve your interests as well as ours for us to be able to use your ports."

"I won't hear of it," he replied. "We're building a submarine fleet of our own, and it would constitute an encroachment upon our sovereignty if Soviet submarines had access to our ports."

"Well, maybe you'd agree to a reciprocal arrangement by which you could have submarine bases in the Arctic Ocean along the Soviet coast in exchange for our rights to your Pacific ports?"

45. V. V. Kuznetsov, ambassador to China in the years 1953–55, became Deputy Minister of Foreign Affairs and then First Deputy Foreign Minister.
46. Ch'en Yi was the Chinese Foreign Minister.

"No," said Mao, "we won't agree to that either. Every country should keep its armed forces on its own territory and on no one else's."

"All right, we won't insist. We'll make do with the facilities we already have at our disposal. We'll base our Pacific submarine fleet in our own Far Eastern ports."

I couldn't object too strenuously to Mao's reaction. Perhaps we'd been a bit hasty in suggesting that he give us a submarine base in China. He'd obviously suspected us of trying to get a foothold for further encroachments.

In general, I'm against asking a country to relinquish its sovereignty over any of its territory unless there is a concrete danger of war — and even then, I think countries should yield their sovereignty only on a reciprocal basis.

As for the radio station, nothing ever came of that in the end either. The Chinese reneged on their agreement and didn't build the station. Later, we started launching satellites, which are better for maintaining radio contact with submarines anyway.

Despite Mao's occasionally abrasive outbursts, our conversations in general were conducted in a calm, friendly tone. However, he expressed some perplexing views on the possibility of another war. From what he'd said in Moscow a year earlier,[47] I was already familiar with some of his ideas; but during our talks around the swimming pool in Peking, he went further than I'd ever heard him go before.

"Let's try to imagine a future war," he began. He sounded just like Stalin, who also loved to raise hypothetical questions of that sort. "How many divisions does the United States have? We know the population of the United States, so we can figure out how many divisions the Americans could raise if they conscripted their able-bodied men." Then he went down the list of the other capitalist countries: England, France, and so on. "Now," he continued, "how many divisions can we raise? Consider the population of China, of the Soviet Union, and the other socialist countries, and you'll see what I mean."

He was smiling at me as though to say, "See how the balance of power is in our favor?"

I was too appalled and embarrassed by his line of thinking even to argue with him. To me, his words sounded like baby talk. How was it possible for a man like this to think such things? For that matter,

47. At the Moscow World Conference of Communist and Workers' Parties in 1957.

how was it possible for him to have risen to such an important post?

"Comrade Mao," I said, "you're making a fundamental error in your calculations. You realize things have changed since the time of Suvarov.[48] Modern soldiers no longer live by the motto 'A bullet is a fool, but a bayonet is a sure friend.' Battles are no longer won with bayonets, or bullets either for that matter. Even Suvarov used to say that a better-trained and better-armed force can defeat an enemy that outnumbers it. In his day, arms meant swords and cannon. With the invention of the machine gun, the nature of warfare changed. A few machine gunners could mow down huge numbers of infantrymen like a farmer with a scythe. Now, in the age of missiles and nuclear bombs, the number of divisions on one side or the other has practically no effect on the outcome of a battle. A hydrogen bomb can turn whole divisions into so much cooked meat. One bomb has an enormous radius of destruction."

Mao's only reply was that he'd grown up as a guerrilla warrior; he was used to battles in which rifles and bayonets — more than machine guns, to say nothing of bombs — played the key role. He was the leader of such a great country as China, but he expressed opinions and made grandiose claims that were hopelessly outdated.

Later, when I informed our leadership about my conversation with Mao, everyone was perplexed; no one supported Mao's point of view. We couldn't understand how our ally, a man who we already sensed had aspirations to be the leader of the world Communist movement, could have such a childish outlook on the problem of war.

Mao had given us a lot of food for thought.

The Formosa Strait Crisis

DESPITE their reluctance to let us use their ports for our submarines, the Chinese in 1958 requested considerable military aid from us. They said they wanted it in order to stage a military operation against Chiang Kai-shek. They asked for aircraft, long-range artillery, and air force advisors.

48. A. V. Suvarov, an eighteenth-century Russian field marshal who fought in the Russo-Turkish wars and suppressed the Pugachev and Kosciusko rebellions.

We gave them what they asked for in the belief that they were planning a decisive action to liquidate Chiang Kai-shek. We made no move to try to restrain our Chinese comrades because we thought they were absolutely right in trying to unify all the territories of China.

However, when we offered to station our interceptor squadrons on their territory, they reacted in an extremely odd way. They made it clear that our offer had offended them. I couldn't understand why. We weren't trying to force ourselves on them. We weren't pursuing any goals except those of fraternal solidarity in the cause of strengthening the borders of China, incorporating Taiwan into the Chinese People's Republic, destroying the regime of Chiang Kai-shek, and uniting all Chinese people in one republic.

The Chinese operation against Chiang Kai-shek took the form of shelling two small offshore islands.[49] We were all in favor of Mao Tse-tung's liquidating these two islands as potential jumping-off points for a landing assault on the mainland by the forces of Chiang Kai-shek. At that time, Chiang dreamed of retaking the mainland, and we were informed that the Americans were egging him on. We considered it possible that the People's Republic of China might be attacked any day.

At first it looked as though the [Communist] Chinese had bitten off more than they could chew. The Americans began actively supporting Chiang, and Mao's forces were bogged down in a lengthy artillery duel. You can imagine our surprise when the balance tipped in favor of Mao Tse-tung and the People's Republic of China. Mao's forces devastated both islands and liberated one of them, forcing Chiang Kai-shek to evacuate his soldiers. However, just when the [Communist] Chinese were in a position to cross the strait and occupy the islands, they suddenly halted their offensive. As a result, the whole operation came to nothing.

We were very perplexed, and when Chou En-lai came to see us, we asked him about what had happened. Later, we also brought the subject up with Mao himself: "Comrade Mao, why did you stop just as you were within reach of victory?"

"We knew what we were doing."

"What do you mean, you knew what you were doing? You started

49. Quemoy and Matsu in Formosa Strait, between the Communist mainland and the Nationalist stronghold on Formosa.

the operation in the first place in order to seize the islands, and you stopped just short of your objective. What did that prove? Are you now trying to tell me you never intended to go through with your plan?"

"All we wanted to do was show our potential. We don't want Chiang to be too far away from us. We want to keep him within our reach. Having him [on Quemoy and Matsu] means we can get at him with our shore batteries as well as our air force. If we'd occupied the islands, we would have lost the ability to cause him discomfort any time we want."

That seemed like a strange explanation. By allowing Chiang to keep his forces [on Quemoy and Matsu], Mao was keeping himself open to an enemy invasion any day.[50]

Third Visit to Peking

LATER, when I give my account of the Sino-Indian War, I will relate how Mao tried to dictate to the Soviet Union a foreign policy which contradicted the correct Marxist-Leninist position we held at the time. He started the war out of some sick fantasy — and out of a desire to draw us and the other socialist countries into the conflict so that he could exert his will on us.[51]

I have to admit I wasn't at all enthusiastic about flying to Peking when hostilities broke out between China and India in 1959. I knew my official welcome would be laid on according to form, but I didn't expect to be greeted with the same fraternal good will I'd encountered in 1954, on my first trip to Peking. The warmth had gone out of our relations with China, and it had been replaced by a chill that I could sense as soon as I arrived.

I was prepared for the change in atmosphere because I'd been following what the Chinese press was saying about us. I also knew how

50. Khrushchev claims here that the Soviets were exasperated with the Chinese for not going through with their assault on the islands in August and September, 1958; however, the more recent official Soviet line criticizes Mao for picking a fight in the first place — for "recklessly and deliberately provoking American and Chiang Kai-shek troops in the region of the islands."
51. See the section "The Sino-Indian War," in Chapter 12.

the Chinese were treating the Soviet specialists, scientists, doctors, engineers, and advisors we'd sent to help build the new plants and other enterprises our loans made possible. The Chinese did everything to discredit our people there. Rather than thanking us for our help, they resented the presence of our experts in China and complained about the machinery we'd given them. In other words, they smeared everything Soviet.

Meanwhile, Chinese students in the USSR started spreading anti-Soviet leaflets in our schools. Later, they organized anti-Soviet demonstrations in our streets and squares. They even staged demonstrations in our trains while traveling from our country to China.

I remember one incident in particular. It took place at a railroad station near Mongolia. There are no decent words to describe what the Chinese students did. They took down their pants and made a mess on the platform — right there in the railroad station. They were supposed to be cultured people, yet they were nothing but swine. They couldn't use the excuse that they didn't know better. They knew perfectly well what they were doing — although the devil alone knows what they thought they were proving.

There was no way to look the other way and ignore such incidents. After a while, relations became so heated that we had to send home Chinese students who were misbehaving.

Back in China, the conditions in which our advisors were living became simply intolerable. Gangs of drunken Chinese started abusing them. They called us "limiters." We knew this term only too well. It had been a common insult during a certain stage of our own development, but there was no excuse for the Chinese to be repeating our own stupid mistakes.

Our engineers in China began informing us about incredible events. They would go back to their apartments or hotels at the end of the day and find their suitcases turned upside down and their rooms ransacked. These were not isolated incidents, either; they were frequent occurrences. Who knows what the Chinese thought they would find by searching our workers' rooms. Anti-Chinese literature perhaps? The idea of printing such stuff never occurred to us. There was no such thing as "anti-Chinese literature" in the Soviet Union.

So that was the thanks we got for building whole plants for the Chinese and for giving them credits at 2 to 2½ percent interest, which is about a third the interest rate in the capitalist world. That was the thanks we got for sending our top specialists to help them develop their industry.

Finally, we were confronted with the question: what was to be done? We couldn't simply stand by, allowing some of our best-qualified specialists — people who'd been trained in our own agriculture and industry — to receive nothing but harassment in exchange for their help. Finally, we had no choice but to recall our advisors from China.[52]

Once we'd brought them home, the Chinese started smearing us behind our backs in their conversations with Communists from other countries, saying we'd withdrawn our assistance for no reason. They played this game of slander with the skill which only the Chinese are capable of.

I hope people who read my memoirs will understand that when I say "the Chinese" here, I don't mean the Chinese people, who are on the whole friendly and hard-working, nor do I mean the rank and file of the Chinese Communist Party. Instead, I'm talking about Mao Tse-tung and his colleagues, who are engaged in a broad campaign to throw mud on the Soviet leadership, the Soviet state, and the whole Soviet system.

In addition to discrediting us, the Chinese also started mistreating our comrades [from other countries]. I'm thinking in particular about the conflicts between China and North Vietnam, which led the Chinese to recall their experts and workers from Vietnam.

On a wider front, Mao's conduct during the Sino-Indian conflict was just one example of his systematic campaign to torpedo and subvert our efforts at promoting peaceful coexistence. At Party conferences, the Chinese did everything to undermine our position and succeeded in stirring up trouble for the representatives of those countries which supported the fight for peace. For every proposal of ours, Mao and the people around him came up with a counterproposal. They argued that working for peace through international organizations violated true Leninist principles, that it led to pacifism, that it weakened and disarmed the revolutionary instinct in people. They believed that in order to replace capitalism with socialism, the peoples of the world must engage in a more active revolutionary struggle.

52. Soviet advisors were recalled from China in the summer of 1960. This dramatic and sudden move virtually ended Soviet aid to China, and trade between the two countries fell off sharply.

Fortunately, the movement for peaceful coexistence went on, despite China's attempt to turn world public opinion against it.

The Albanians and the Moscow Conference

AT one point an Albanian delegation went to China. We didn't think anything about it. We thought their visit was in the natural order of things. This was still in the days when we were willing to make trips to China ourselves, just as we were happy to visit any fraternal country. We didn't know it at the time, but the Albanians already had other goals in mind.

The delegation returned to Albania from Peking by way of the Soviet Union. Mehmet Shehu asked to see a doctor and was hospitalized in Moscow.[53] The other members of the delegation decided to stay and wait for his recovery.

Among the Albanian comrades was a very interesting woman.[54] She'd gone through the most grueling struggle during the Italian occupation of Albania [in World War II]. The Fascists had captured her and put out one of her eyes. She was a good person, a thoroughly trustworthy Communist. Like so many other true Albanian Communists, she was wholeheartedly in favor of preserving her country's friendship with the Soviet Union. She knew the USSR had unselfishly granted Albania economic aid, much of it free, and provided the Albanian army with food, clothing, and weapons. She wasn't guilty of the double-dealing we later encountered in some of her colleagues.

This woman told us about the talks Mehmet Shehu had held with either Chou En-lai or Liu Shao-ch'i. We were flabbergasted by what she said. What black ingratitude! We couldn't understand why the Chinese would say such things. She said that the Chinese were the initiators of all the vicious talk against us and that the Albanians had simply followed their lead.

Then we did something which shows how naive we were. We thought that Mehmet Shehu and Enver Hoxha[55] were our friends

53. Here Khrushchev is probably confusing Prime Minister Mehmet Shehu with Chief of State Hadji Lehi, for it was Lehi who led the Albanian delegation to several Asian countries, including China, in the summer of 1960.

54. Lira Belishova, an Albanian war hero and Politbureau member.

55. Enver Hoxha, First Secretary of the Albanian Labor (Communist) Party.

and that they would be as shocked as we were by what the Chinese said to them. We didn't think for a moment that they might have actually agreed with the Chinese. Unfortunately, we couldn't have been more mistaken.

[There is an interruption in the narrative, but from what follows it is clear that the Soviets sent someone to the hospital to ask about Belishova's report on the Albanians' conversations in Peking.]

As soon as our representative left, Mehmet Shehu jumped out of bed, threw off his hospital gown, put on his own clothes, and flew straight back to Albania.

Shortly afterward, the Albanian government began literally hunting down people who were friendly toward the Soviet Union. All of a sudden these people were declared enemies of the Albanian Labor [Communist] Party. The woman who had informed us about what happened in Peking was thrown out of the leadership and later expelled from the Party. It was only a matter of time before she was arrested. I think in the end she was eliminated. [If so], I wouldn't be surprised, because the Albanians are worse than beasts — they're monsters. Only later did we learn how the Albanian Communist leaders punished members of their own Party. They had a sort of troika: Enver Hoxha and Mehmet Shehu would sentence the accused to death, and Balluku would personally carry out the execution.[56]

Then, at the Rumanian Party Congress in 1960, the Albanians took a pro-Chinese position and spoke against us. I remember having a talk with one of the Albanian Party representatives. I don't remember his name now, but he was a good, honest man and a friend of the Soviet Union.[57]

I told him I was hard put to understand why his comrades had

56. Bequir Balluku, Defense Minister and a Politbureau member. In *KR*, I, 476, Khrushchev tells a somewhat abbreviated version of this story, but adds the detail that Belishova was strangled. Khrushchev was probably not present when Belishova informed the Soviets that Liu Shao-ch'i had made "outrageous statements" about them in Peking. Khrushchev was in Austria on an official visit when Brezhnev and F. R. Kozlov received their Albanian guests at a Kremlin luncheon. The Peking press noted four years later that Belishova had been "used as a tool to organize subversion against a fraternal Party. . . . The Albanian comrades treated the Belishova case as it deserved."

57. Russia's friends in Tirana included Belishova; her husband, Maqo Como, who was Minister of Agriculture; and Koco Tashko, the chief of the Control Commission. But none of these three is known to have attended the Bucharest meeting in June, 1960. The Albanian Party was represented there by Hysni Kapo, a political ally of Enver Hoxha who fully supported the Chinese.

chosen to accept help from China rather than from the Soviet Union and asked him why his delegation was coming out against us at the conference.

He looked at me for a moment, then said, "Comrade Khrushchev, all I can tell you is that I've received my orders, and I must follow them."

Obviously, he was being as candid as possible, but I wasn't satisfied by his answer then, and I'm still not now. I'd like to hear a full explanation of why the Albanian Labor Party followed China's lead. I don't think even the Albanians themselves could really tell me.

Later in 1960, the Albanians joined the Chinese in opposing the decisions passed by the more than seventy delegations at the World Conference of Communist Parties. The most rude and vicious attacks on the Soviet position were delivered by Enver Hoxha, who emerged as one of the chief spokesmen and agents for Mao's ideas. He even attacked me personally.

I remember Dolores Ibarruri's impassioned speech in which she likened Enver Hoxha to a dog which bites the hand that feeds it.[58] She was a Communist who'd been through the revolutionary struggle in Spain; and she couldn't stand to hear the likes of Enver Hoxha attack the Soviet Union, a country which had been doing everything in its power to consolidate the world Communist movement and help other socialist countries — not least of all Albania itself.

And so a fight broke out between those who supported the policy of the Soviet Union on the one hand and the Pro-Chinese wing on the other. Thus, the conflict was publicly revealed for the first time.

Military Technology

BEFORE the rupture in our relations, we'd given the Chinese almost everything they asked for. We kept no secrets from them. Our nuclear experts cooperated with their engineers and designers who were busy building an atomic bomb. We trained their scientists in our own laboratories.

58. Dolores Ibarruri, "La Pasionaria," was a Spanish Communist living in exile in Moscow. The Moscow Conference of eighty-one World Parties took place in November, 1960, with Liu Shao-ch'i representing the Peking regime.

Our specialists suggested we give the Chinese a prototype of the atomic bomb. They put the thing together and packed it up, so it was ready to send to China. At that point our minister in charge of nuclear weapons reported to me. He knew our relations with China had deteriorated hopelessly.

"We've been given instructions to ship an A-bomb prototype to China," he said. "It's ready to go. What shall we do? We await your instructions."

We convened a meeting and tried to decide what to do. We knew that if we failed to send the bomb to China, the Chinese would accuse us of reneging on an agreement, breaking a treaty, and so forth. On the other hand, they had already begun their smear campaign against us and were beginning to make all sorts of incredible territorial claims as well. We didn't want them to get the idea that we were their obedient slaves who would give them whatever they wanted, no matter how much they insulted us. In the end we decided to postpone sending them the prototype.[59]

As we expected, the Chinese began exploiting our decision for all it was worth. I think they were glad to have another argument to use against us. They stepped up their anti-Soviet propaganda among other fraternal socialist Parties. They said we refused to share our military accomplishments with them because we were no longer interested in helping China.

What a lie! All the modern weaponry in China's arsenal at the time was Soviet-made or copied from samples and blueprints provided by our engineers, our research institutes. We'd given them tanks, artillery, rockets, aircraft, naval and infantry weapons. Virtually our entire defense industry had been at their disposal.

But we had to draw the line somewhere.

Evidence kept building up that we would be fools to trust the Chinese any longer. For example, some of our rocketry experts were training the Chinese in missile technology, with emphasis on the operation of surface-to-air missiles. One day our people were demonstrating how to put a SAM together and take it apart again. When they came back the next morning, they found that the Chinese had been fooling around with the missile during the night. It was our rocket, and the Chinese had no business working on it without our advisors there to supervise.

59. In June, 1959, Moscow rescinded the Sino-Soviet agreement on atomic cooperation which had been in effect since 1957.

Then something else happened. I received a call one day from our [rocketry] research institute and was invited to come have a look at a most interesting American missile we'd gotten from the Chinese. I decided to go because in those days I spent quite a bit of time on military matters, especially where our missiles and air force were concerned — two areas where we worried about lagging behind our enemy, the USA.

The institute was just outside of Moscow. Our designers showed me how quickly they could take the missile apart and put it back together again. All it required was a single key. Soldiers could assemble it under battle conditions. It was lightweight and easy to operate.

Our own missiles were no worse than this one in performance, but they were much heavier and more complicated. Everyone agreed that the American missile was better designed than ours — at least that was the gist of the report our engineers wrote. They were highly objective people. Our designers spent a lot of time studying the American rocket. Then we copied it and put it into production.

There was one problem: when the missile was sent to us from China, certain parts were missing. They were little buttons which had something to do with the magnetic field, I think. These were essential for the rocket to operate properly. We asked the Chinese why they hadn't given us these parts along with the rest of the missile, and they answered that they'd sent us everything. That left our researchers to work out the problem themselves. It took them a long time. They had to come up with a new alloy and miniaturize some chemical batteries. In the end the problem was solved, but at considerable expense. Either the Chinese had lost the parts, or they'd kept them from us on purpose. Whatever the truth, the incident further contaminated our thoughts and feelings about the Chinese.

It was getting harder and harder to view China through the eager and innocent eyes of a child. No longer could we rejoice about the solidarity of our socialist camp. China was China, and the Chinese were acting in increasingly strange ways.

I've already dictated my thoughts on the treacherous policies Mao followed with respect to other countries, including other socialist countries. Now I'd like to say something about the dictatorial policies he inflicted on his own people. I'm thinking about the so-called Hundred Flowers campaign, the Great Leap Forward, and the Cultural Revolution.

The Hundred Flowers

THE Chinese press started trumpeting, "Let a hundred flowers bloom." [60]

Our own propagandists asked how we should respond. "Our people are reading in the newspapers about this new campaign in China," they said. "This Hundred Flowers talk is already creeping into Soviet society." We instructed our newspaper editors and propagandists to drop the subject of the Chinese campaign and not to touch it again. Our position was that the Hundred Flowers was a Chinese slogan for internal consumption only, and that it did not apply in the USSR. We avoided any direct criticism of the campaign but we also refrained from supporting it.

Our refusal to propagate the Hundred Flowers campaign in the USSR didn't escape the notice of the Chinese. I don't remember when or where it was, but Mao Tse-tung prodded me about this matter: [61] "What do you think about our new slogan, 'Let a hundred flowers bloom,' Comrade Khrushchev?"

"Frankly, Comrade Mao, the exact meaning of the slogan isn't quite clear to us. Therefore we've found it difficult to implement under the conditions which prevail in our own country. We're afraid that people might misunderstand it and that it might not serve our purposes."

"I see what you mean," said Mao. "In our country this proverb has been around for a long time." He gave me some examples from the long-forgotten past and from ancient Chinese literature.

Mao knew perfectly well that we didn't approve of his new policy — that we were against the blooming of all those different flowers. Any peasant knows that certain flowers ought to be cultivated but others should be cut down. Some plants bear fruit which is bitter to the taste or damaging to the health — while others grow uncontrollably and choke the roots of the crops around them. Be-

60. Under the slogan "Let a hundred flowers bloom, let a hundred schools of thought contend," Mao introduced in 1957 a brief policy allowing open discussion. He then reversed himself and crushed criticism with a "rectification campaign."

61. This was most likely during Mao's visit to Moscow in the fall of 1957.

sides, I think the slogan "Let a hundred flowers bloom" was a provocation. Mao pretended to be opening wide the floodgates of democracy and free expression. He wanted to goad people into expressing their innermost thoughts, both in speech and in print, so that he could destroy those whose thinking he considered harmful.

I'm glad I had a chance to remind Mao that we wouldn't automatically adopt any new line he came up with. However, my reminder unquestionably didn't contribute to the strengthening of our relations. Mao thought of himself as a man sent by God to do God's bidding. In fact, Mao probably thought God did Mao's *own* bidding. He could do no wrong.

He was intelligent and tactful enough to pretend that I was completely within my rights as head of the Soviet Party not to accept a Chinese slogan, but I knew our relations had slipped a few notches.

The Great Leap Forward

I'M the first to admit that the Chinese had huge obstacles to overcome in developing their economy and that for a while they seemed to be making impressive progress.

Lenin used to say that the collectivization of agriculture should be conducted on the basis of mechanization, and that if you give the peasants enough tractors, they'll willingly submit to collectivization. Well, the Chinese not only didn't have enough tractors, they didn't have enough wooden plows. As a result, they pooled their meager means of production so as to consolidate their labor. We were pleased to observe their success.

I remember when we toured China, we used to laugh at their primitive forms of organization. At an earthworks, for instance, some manual laborers would stand in single file and pass baskets of dirt from one man to the next. Others carried baskets on their shoulders. They looked like a human conveyor belt. Some wit in our delegation said that for the first time in his life he'd seen a Chinese walking steam shovel. Our Chinese comrades liked a good joke, so we told them this one at the dinner table; they roared with laughter. If they were offended, they didn't let on. The Chinese know how to wear a mask which conceals their true feelings.

For a while it had looked as though Mao might succeed in showing the world a Chinese economic miracle. If, for example, you compared China to India, you'd see that while India had a broader industrial base, China's standard of living was inproving faster. We were full of pride and wonder at what our Chinese comrades were accomplishing. However, just as China seemed about to perfect an exemplary socialist system, Mao began abusing his power. He ruined the economy, all in the name of the so-called Great Leap Forward.[62]

The Chinese are good at inventing catchy phrases. The Great Leap Forward came after the Hundred Flowers campaign. Part and parcel of the Great Leap Forward was another slogan: "Catch up with England in five years — America in a little bit longer!" When we read that, we couldn't believe our eyes. Of course, it doesn't hurt for a leadership to spur its people on toward technological and economic progress, but the idea of overtaking the most advanced capitalist countries in such a short time was ridiculous. We, too, wanted to catch up with the United States, but we weren't yet at a stage where we could afford to set a definite deadline — though we were sometimes tempted.

It was obvious what Mao was up to: he thought that if he could match England and then catch the US by the tail in five years, he would be able to outdistance the Party of Lenin and surpass the strides the Soviet people had made since the October Revolution.

What happened? Well, when China made its Great Leap Forward, it landed in a lot of trouble. The economy actually fell backward in a number of different ways at once.

Mao broke up China's collective farms and created communes in their place. He communized the peasants together with all their personal belongings. This was absurd. Collectivization of the means of production is one thing, but communization of personal belongings is quite another — and it's sure to lead to undesirable consequences. After a while, the communes were converted into military settlements. As a result, Chinese agriculture — which had been coming along so promisingly — suddenly suffered a severe setback, and famine broke out in the countryside.

Industry, too, was wrecked. The Chinese began experiencing raw-material shortages, and their factory equipment was badly dam-

62. The Great Leap Forward, begun in 1958, was a massive crash program to modernize China and catch up with the West in one paroxysm of mobilization and industrialization.

aged — largely because they started saying that rated capacity for machinery was a "bourgeois notion." They bragged, for example, that they could get more production out of a machine purchased from the Soviet Union than the manufacturer's manual recommended. As a result, the life span of their machinery was seriously impaired. Engineers who had technical expertise were denounced as "bourgeois sycophants" or "subversives" and reassigned to menial jobs. Chinese industry became disorganized. In fact, their whole economy was degenerating into anarchy.

We began to read about how the Chinese were building a "backyard steel industry," with [miniature] blast furnaces behind people's houses. We couldn't help wondering about the quality and cost of pig iron produced in this manner. The technology of these backyard furnaces was extremely primitive; the Chinese were reverting to a method which hadn't been used for hundreds of years. It was like an epidemic. Collectives and even individual families were supposed to erect their own blast furnaces. I was even told by someone just back from China that Sun Yat-sen's widow had one. I don't know whether she ever produced any pig iron from her furnace, but she showed it off and bragged about it to visitors.

Chou En-lai had been keeping us posted about the latest developments in Chinese industry and agriculture. We always eagerly awaited his trips to Moscow and received him with pleasure. After the beginning of the Great Leap Forward, our embassy [in Peking] relayed to us word from Comrade Chou that he was coming to Moscow and wanted to see us. We answered straightaway that we'd be glad to hear what he had to say.

Comrade Chou flew in and came for talks with us. He said that the Chinese steel industry was in a bad way and asked us to send our experts to help sort things out.

"We need more qualified specialists than your advisors presently in China," he explained. "We need someone who can tell us what we're doing wrong and what we ought to be doing instead."

After discussing the problem in our leadership, we decided to send Comrade Zasyadko, who was then a deputy prime minister and Deputy Chairman of the State Planning Commission. I knew him well, from the time when he'd been the head of the largest coal mine in the Stalino Region.[63] Comrade Zasyadko had only one draw-

63. Zasyadko appears in the section "Building a Missile Army" in Chapter 3.

The delegation for the first visit to Peking, 1954
Front row: Mikoyan (*left*), Furtseva, Khrushchev, Bulganin, and
Molotov. At the far right in the back row are Nasriddinova and Yudin

Seeing the sights
in China, 1954

Inspecting naval facilities at Port Arthur with Malinovsky,
Bulganin, and Mikoyan

With Nina Petrovna and their personal pilot, N. I. Tsybin

In parade whites

Vacationing with Mikoyan

At ease

back — and it was to be his undoing: he couldn't control his drinking. Nevertheless, we sent him to China. Undoubtedly, he took a supply of vodka with him on the train. After a few weeks, he returned and reported to me.

"What's the situation there, Comrade Zasyadko?" I asked. "What advice did you have to offer our Chinese brothers?"

He never minced words; he came straight to the point: "All I can tell you, Comrade Khrushchev, is that they've got no one but themselves to blame for their troubles. I inspected one of their steel plants. They've let the whole thing go to pot. Their open-hearth furnaces, blast furnaces, rolling mills — everything's in a shambles. When I asked to meet the manager of the plant, he turned out to be a veterinarian. I asked Chou En-lai, 'Comrade Chou, where are all the steel engineers whom we trained in the USSR and who graduated from our schools?' He told me they're working in the countryside, 'forging their proletarian consciousness,' while people like this veterinarian, who don't know the first thing about metallurgy, are trying to run the steel mills. I could tell that Chou himself thought the whole thing was pretty stupid, but there isn't anything he can do about it — the Great Leap Forward wasn't *his* idea."

No, the Great Leap Forward was the invention of Mao Tse-tung and no one else. He wanted to show that there could be a special Chinese method for building socialism. He wanted to impress the world — especially the socialist world — with his genius and his leadership. For anyone who's interested in learning more about the Great Leap Forward after reading my memoirs, I recommend the report I gave at the Twenty-first Congress of the CPSU. That document contains a fairly hard-hitting, and I believe accurate, analysis of what was going on in China at that time, although I didn't refer to China by name. We made it clear that our attitude toward the Great Leap Forward was negative.

The Bulgarian Leap Forward

As I've already said, the Chinese are good at coming up with catchy phrases. They know how to introduce the right slogan at the right time. They started showering the other socialist countries with propaganda about how everyone should follow China's lead, organize communes, and copy the Great Leap Forward. This kind of propaganda was all over the Chinese press, and after a while it began cropping up in newspapers published by our own people in the frontier regions near China. To be honest, I'd have to say we were frightened by the Chinese attempts to get us to adopt their slogans and their policies. It got so bad we could no longer be silent. We had to speak up — not against China and the Great Leap Forward itself (that was an internal matter and therefore none of our business), but against the implementation of their mottoes under our own Soviet conditions.

We became concerned when we learned that Chinese propaganda was beginning to have an effect in Bulgaria. The Secretary of the Bulgarian Central Committee was a good comrade, but he didn't quite understand what was going on in China. A Bulgarian Party delegation made an official visit there, and as soon as it got home, the Bulgarian press started gushing with praise for Chinese communes and the Great Leap Forward. The next thing we knew, the Bulgarians began putting the Chinese slogans into practice in their own country.[64] They started enlarging their collective farms to ridiculous sizes, and they overinvested in heavy industry. We received warnings about where this could lead from some of our Bulgarian comrades. That was the last straw. We felt compelled to talk things over with the Bulgarian comrades and give them an opportunity to hear our point of view.[65] We invited our Bulgarian friends to Moscow for talks.

I should say here that you couldn't dream of better relations than those which existed between the Soviet Union and Bulgaria. I don't know a single representative of the Bulgarian Communist Party who doesn't have the best interests of his country at heart. Therefore, our talks with them were sincere and constructive.

"Comrades," we said, "you know how we value our fraternal relations with you, and you know that we want to develop these relations further. We feel that Chinese experience is not applicable to European conditions, and that if you persist in your efforts to imitate

64. Todor Zhivkov was the Bulgarian Party leader. The Bulgarians sent a delegation to China in September–October, 1959, and at their Party plenum in December of that year launched a campaign to speed up economic development, a campaign which required them to place large orders for industrial equipment with the West.

65. F. R. Kozlov — a Presidium member and Khrushchev's deputy, then regarded as a likely successor to Khrushchev — led a Soviet delegation to Sofia in August, 1960.

China's Great Leap Forward, it may result in serious complications.

"As far as heavy industry is concerned, you've embarked upon a policy that could put your entire economy in jeopardy. We've received information that you've been forced to place large orders [for industrial equipment] with the capitalist world. You're incurring debts which you might not be able to repay. We're afraid you'll have to ask us for money, and we won't be able to help you. Remember, we both have limited gold reserves, and you may be overextending yourselves."

That argument seemed to hit home.

We also expressed to the Bulgarians our opinion that Chinese methods of organization were ill suited to their predominantly vegetable and fruit agriculture, that in their efforts to imitate communes, they'd expanded their collective farms to an unworkable size. We told them that we weren't trying to force them to agree with us, but that we just wanted to call their attention to the dangers.

Later we learned that the Bulgarians had taken certain measures. For one thing, they somewhat reduced the size of their collective farms. As for their investments in the industrial sector of the economy, that problem was more complicated. A year and a half after the beginning of the Bulgarian experiment, they came to us with a request for more money. They'd exhausted all their loans — even their short-term ones, which, of course, are the most expensive. A long-term loan usually carries 5 to 7 percent interest, while a short-term one can go as high as 10 to 15 percent. Banks can literally skin you alive on short-term loans.

Despite our own economic difficulties, including a shortage of gold, we had to give some of our gold to our Bulgarian friends so that they could pay their debts [to the West]. Otherwise, they would have been faced with bankruptcy. That's where too much enthusiasm for imitating the Chinese can lead.[66]

You might ask, "How did the Chinese themselves avoid the troubles from which the Bulgarians suffered?" The answer is simple: the Chinese had no controls whatsoever in their economy. Under Mao, the Chinese interpret Marxism-Leninism any way they please. Instead of adhering to the scientific laws of economics, they operate on slogans — nothing but slogans.

66. The Soviets granted Bulgaria $65 million in long-term credits on December 31, 1960.

We felt we owed an explanation of the problem to our own Party. We felt we should point out the dangers and inconsistencies in the Great Leap Forward, especially when a number of regional and territorial Party committees in Siberia took up the Chinese slogans. We decided to air the issue at the Twenty-first Party Congress, which was meant to firm up the basis of our Seven-Year Plan. In my main report to the Congress, I tried to build up the resistance of our Party leaders against the temptation to imitate Chinese economic measures blindly. After all, politics depends largely on economics.

The Cultural Revolution

SINCE I retired, Mao has thought up another slogan: the Cultural Revolution.[67]
What exactly is the Cultural Revolution? It's hard for me to say. I don't know what sort of explanation is being given to the [Soviet] Party. Obviously, Mao had wanted for a long time to be recognized by his people not only as a leader but as a god. To an extent, he's succeeded in foisting just such a [personality cult] on his country.

Of course, we've seen the same thing in our own country. When Stalin was alive, people would have to jump up and sit down again every time Stalin's name was mentioned at public meetings and Party conferences. It was a sort of physical culture we all engaged in.

Well, Mao has made it easier [to glorify his personality]. He's published excerpts from his speeches and proclaimed them as commandments which everybody is supposed to learn by heart. I've seen on television a film made by the Chinese themselves; it shows people acting like a bunch of idiots, chanting the quotations of Mao Tsetung over and over. It makes me sick to see such degradation of human dignity.

Sometimes I listen to their radio,[68] but I get so disgusted I have to switch it off. They repeat the same thing over and over again, and it's always the same announcer, a girl who speaks lousy Russian. There's

67. The Great Leap Forward was abandoned in 1961. The Great Proletarian Cultural Revolution was officially launched in 1966, almost two years after Khrushchev's downfall.

68. Khrushchev is referring to the Russian-language propaganda broadcasts of Radio Peking.

also some guy who acts as an announcer, too, Even their voices are familiar. They may have been interpreters when I went to China.

I've heard on the radio how a surgeon was forced to deliver some stupid Mao quotation before he performed an operation. How is it possible that in the twentieth century, when a human foot has stepped on the surface of the moon, for a country to believe in witch doctors and magic mumbo jumbo? Do the Chinese really think Mao has supernatural powers, and that a surgeon will be able to cure his patient if he knows Mao's sayings by heart? There's nothing supernatural about Mao as far as *I'm* concerned. He's acting like a lunatic on a throne and is turning his country upside down.

I've already explained how the Hundred Flowers campaign was the most vicious and treacherous provocation. Well, so is the Cultural Revolution. Once again Mao is pretending to open wide the floodgates of democracy and free expression, only to destroy those people whose thinking and activity he considers harmful or useless. And who is "harmful" or "useless"? Anyone who disagrees with Mao, naturally.

In China they may call it a Cultural Revolution, but in our country, we called it "the struggle against the enemies of the people." [69] It's six of one, half dozen of the other.

Both Stalin and Mao strengthened their personal dictatorships — not the dictatorship of the proletariat, but the dictatorship of an individual personality *over* the proletariat, over the Party, over the leader's own colleagues. Either you bow down before the authority of the leader, or you share the fate of all the other "enemies." Of course, there are different ways for the leader to punish his prey. Stalin used to do it by arrest, execution, and denunciation of "enemies of the people." Back in the days of the tsar, the court would stage so-called "civil punishments" of writers like Chernyshevsky and Dostoevsky. [70]

Mao's approach is similar to the tsars': he puts his opponent on display in a public square with a fool's hood on his head and a sign

69. "The struggle against the enemies of the people" was Stalin's slogan for the Great Terror of the 1930's.

70. "Civil punishment" or "civil execution" (*grazhdanskaya kazn'*) in Imperial Russia consisted of a public ceremony at which a sword was broken over a convicted criminal's head to signify that he was being deprived of all rights, ranks, and privileges. Both N. G. Chernyshevsky, a nineteenth-century radical writer, and the novelist F. M. Dostoevsky were sentenced to "civil punishment" and hard labor in Siberia for their political views.

around his neck; the townspeople do a barbaric dance around the prisoner. I'm not saying the Chinese are savages in a literal sense, but they've been driven into a state of savagery by Mao Tse-tung.

I'm thinking particularly about the Chinese students and youth in general, the so-called Red Guards, who are no better than Chinese equivalents of Ivan the Terrible's Oprichniki.[71]

In addition to the Red Guards, Mao has also resorted to military force in order to get his way. And to think — all this is being done under the aegis of the struggle for the interests of the working class and the peasantry. Some of the best representatives of the Chinese people have been exiled, imprisoned, or executed in the name of the people — and supposedly for the sake of the people.

I would like to say something here about the various Chinese leaders who have either fallen victim or played roles as Mao's henchmen during the Cultural Revolution.

I've always liked Liu Shao-ch'i. When we met and talked, I found we immediately understood each other and had similar ways of thinking — although, of course, we had to communicate through an interpreter. I particularly admired Liu's report to the Eighth [Chinese] Party Congress, in which he laid out the tasks confronting the Chinese people and Party. He seemed to agree with the point of view held by the leaders of our own Party as reflected in the decisions of the Twentieth, Twenty-first, and Twenty-second [Soviet] Party Congresses.

Of course, Liu did come out against us in his talks with the Albanians, but I think he did so under pressure. I don't think it was his own idea. We suspected that at the time, and subsequent events have proved us right: Liu Shao-ch'i has become the number one casualty of the Cultural Revolution.[72]

It's no wonder Liu has fallen and, like so many other prominent Chinese comrades, has been put in isolation. He was second only to Mao in power and influence, and he was the most reasonable leader of the Chinese Communist Party.

After Liu, our favorite Chinese leader was Chou En-lai. Despite his present opposition to the Soviet Union and his support for Mao's

71. Khrushchev uses the Chinese phrase *hung-wei-ping* for Red Guards to distinguish them from the Red Guards of the Russian Civil War. The Oprichina was a personal army in the service of Tsar Ivan IV.

72. Liu was one of the earliest and most prominent victims of the Cultural Revolution. Among the epithets hurled at him was "the Chinese Khrushchev."

bloody policies, Chou has always impressed us as a charming man with a good grasp on the industrial and agricultural problems facing his country. Chu Teh also made a good impression on me. I think he has much in common with Mikhail Ivanovich Kalinin.[73]

I didn't know Ch'en Yi well, but I was told he's a most able man. As far as I know, he's now in limbo and has been subjected to attacks by those crazy Red Guards.[74]

I always liked the former head of the Peking City Party Committee, although his name escapes me now. He came from a worker's background and was highly intelligent. I always respected him despite the heated arguments we had over whether or not to convene an international conference of Communist Parties. I could see a certain anxiety, a certain pensiveness in his face even as he followed Mao's orders and took Mao's side in the dispute. I'm not sure what it was exactly, but something about him made me feel sorry for him. I could tell he was undergoing some kind of inner turmoil. I think he saw where Mao was leading the Party, but he couldn't bring himself to take decisive countermeasures. I don't know what became of him in the end. I don't even know whether he's still alive, although politically, of course, he's long since dead.[75]

I also liked P'eng Te-huai. He was a good Marxist. What's happened to him only confirms my impression of him.[76]

Now a word about Teng Hsiao-p'ing. As I've already related, Mao regarded him as the most up-and-coming member of the leadership. Teng showed up later at the Bucharest Conference just before the Rumanian Party Congress. He held an incorrect position at that conference, but he had no choice. Mao Tse-tung had already begun to usurp the power of the Central Committee, and even the Politbureau itself was losing its say in the affairs of the Chinese Communist Party.

K'ang Sheng was at that same conference in Bucharest. He's

73. M. I. Kalinin, figurehead President of the USSR, 1938–46. Chu was eighty years old when the Cultural Revolution began and had already assumed a mostly ceremonial position.

74. Ch'en Yi, the Foreign Minister and Khrushchev's principal antagonist during the latter's third trip to Peking in 1959 during the Sino-Indian confrontation (see the section "The Sino-Indian War" in Chapter 12).

75. Khrushchev is referring here to P'eng Chen, the Mayor of Peking and a Politbureau member who was purged at the outset of the Cultural Revolution.

76. P'eng Te-huai, the commander of the Chinese "volunteers" in the Korean War and Defense Minister (see *KR*, I, 372). P'eng fell from political grace in 1959, six years before the Cultural Revolution. He was accused of collusion with the Soviets.

always been Mao's hatchet man. If you want to compare K'ang to historical figures from the time of Ivan the Terrible, I'd say he's just like Malyuta Skuratov.[77] I remember I once got into an agitated discussion with K'ang Sheng and accidentally addressed him as Chiang Kai-shek. It was a simple mistake, and naturally I apologized. However, basically he's no better than Chiang Kai-shek if not worse. They're both cutthroats.

If anyone doubts that Mao is promoting his own personal power, just look at Lin Piao, whom Mao has selected as his deputy. As a military commander, Lin Piao may be perfectly able; but as Mao's right-hand man, he's been just like our Yezhov.[78]

During the Cultural Revolution, Mao's sole support has been the army, but Lin is experienced enough to know that the army can't be relied upon 100 percent. He's probably the one who formed these regiments of thugs who have been taking over educational institutions, annihilating Party members, destroying the intelligentsia, and wreaking havoc on the political life of the country.

Mao has been perpetrating unheard-of perversities. To think that he would appoint his wife to be in charge of the Cultural Revolution! [79] Some people say she was once a talented actress, while others say her only talent was in serving as a nice mattress for Mao to sleep on. Regardless of her merits as an actress, she's carried out the most vicious campaign against writers, composers, scientists, teachers, critics, and intellectuals of all sorts — all in the name of Chinese culture.

As far as I'm concerned, the Cultural Revolution is no revolution at all — it's a *counter*revolution, directed against the Chinese people and Party.

77. Malyuta Skuratov was one of Ivan IV's closest courtiers; he served as the Tsar's chief investigator, interrogator, and executioner.

78. N. I. Yezhov, Stalin's police chief at the height of the purges.
Lin Piao replaced P'eng as Defense Minister and Liu as Mao's heir apparent, only to fall suddenly in 1971, when he allegedly plotted against Mao's life. He is believed to have died in a plane crash while fleeing China.

79. Chiang Ch'ing was politically not very active until 1966, when she emerged as a stand-in for her husband and a power in her own right. She assumed a major role in supervising the ideological campaign of the Cultural Revolution.

The Border

FOR years Mao Tse-tung has been spoiling for a fight. He has been looking for an opportunity to take control of the international Communist movement, and he knows that in order to do so he must challenge the Soviet Union. It doesn't matter [what Soviet leader] he picks a fight with — Khrushchev or Petrov or Ivanov or Sidorov.[80]

Since I retired, Mao has intensified his struggle, aggravating tensions to the point where they might explode into military conflict any day. I've seen reports recently that the Chinese are taking certain defensive measures, such as digging trenches and building bomb shelters. The Chinese leadership has dragged the split out into the open by appealing to the masses to prepare for war. For some time now, the work going on in Chinese defense research institutes and design bureaus has seemed to be directed against us.

During the years when I held a high post in the government and the Party, I saw the buildup of the tendencies that are now coming to a head. I was put on my guard against Mao's chauvinism as early as 1954, when I first went to Peking. Despite his exceptionally cordial manner, I could sense an undercurrent of nationalism in his praise of the Chinese nation. His words reflected his belief in the superiority of the Chinese race — an idea which is completely contrary to the correct Marxist notion about nationalities. According to our Communist view of the world, all nations are equal; individuals should be distinguished not by their nationality but by their class affiliation.

We had to sit through Mao's long-winded lectures on the history of China, in which he told us about all the conquerors, Genghis Khan and the rest, who tried to impose their rule on China and ended up being absorbed by the Chinese instead. Mao kept stressing the claim that "the Chinese people are immune to assimilation by other peoples." He loved to tell us how the Chinese are the greatest people in the world, how they have had a superior culture since prehistoric times, and how they have a unique role to play in history.

When we returned to Moscow after our trip, we exchanged opinions and impressions within the leadership — at closed meetings, naturally. In my capacity as the head of our delegation, I pointed out

80. The last three are common Russian surnames, like Jones, Brown, and Smith.

to my comrades that Mao's tendency to equate himself with the Chinese people as a whole and his air of superiority toward other nationalities boded ill for the future. As I had predicted, it later became apparent that Mao's egotism got the better of him, and he refused to accept an equal partnership in the collective leadership of the international Communist movement. He wanted others to acknowledge his hegemony.

Mao's chauvinism and arrogance are especially manifest in the territorial claims which the Chinese have made against the Soviet Union. After Stalin's death we not only liquidated the joint companies formed for the exploitation of the natural resources in Sinkiang, we gave up all our interests there. We liquidated all unequal treaties and arranged for the return of Port Arthur to China and the evacuation of our troops. Any delays in those negotiations were caused by the Chinese side, not ours.

Later we were informed that certain bourgeois newspapers in China were complaining that "the Chinese people" weren't satisfied with the Sino-Soviet border, especially around Vladivostok. According to this line of argument, the Russian tsars had "imposed" the Far Eastern frontier on the Chinese.[81]

As far as we were concerned, we weren't responsible for what our tsars had done, but the lands gained from those tsarist treaties were now Soviet territory. We weren't the only socialist country which had to administer and defend the territory inherited from a pre-Revolutionary regime.

We were afraid that if we started remapping our frontiers according to historical considerations, the situation could get out of hand and lead to conflict. Besides, a true Communist and internationalist wouldn't assign any particular importance to the question of borders, especially borders between fellow socialist states. National borders

81. By "bourgeois newspapers," Khrushchev is referring to the Communist press in Hong Kong, which frequently came out with propaganda positions reflecting the publicly unexpressed views of the Peking regime. Moscow and Peking began trading insults in the open in the early 1960's. The Chinese chided Khrushchev for backing down in the face of an "imperialist" threat in the Caribbean during the Cuban missile crisis. A few months later, at the end of 1962, Khrushchev scolded Peking for tolerating a Portuguese colony at Macao on the Chinese mainland. China then escalated the quarrel by attacking the Kremlin for holding territories which the tsars had acquired by imperialist means. In March, 1963, the *People's Daily* took up a theme which the Communist papers in Hong Kong had been developing for some time. It reopened the smoldering dispute over the borders established by "unequal and temporary treaties" in the nineteenth century, when the tsarist government was able to bully the declining Manchu court into ceding what is now the Soviet Maritime Province and other territories to the Russian Empire.

should pale into insignificance in the light of Marxist-Leninist philosophy, which holds that the international revolutionary movement, a force that transcends national boundaries, will triumph everywhere in the end.

We communicated these reactions to the Chinese and let them know we were concerned about the unfriendly articles which had been appearing in the [Hong Kong] press. They replied that we shouldn't pay attention to what bourgeois newspapers wrote. They said those newspapers were simply reflecting the sentiments of the hostile classes, and not the sentiments of the leadership. We contented ourselves with this explanation, although we asked the Chinese comrades to issue a statement publicly clarifying their views on the border issue. They refused, and we didn't insist. We decided to take their word.

Then the question of Mongolia came up. I think it was when we were in China for a joint conference of our two Parties.[82] The Chinese delegation was headed by Mao Tse-tung, but the matter of the Mongolian-Chinese border was raised by Chou En-lai — though of course we knew that Chou's words reflected Mao's thoughts

Chou handled the question very diplomatically. "What would you think if Mongolia became part of the Chinese state?" he began.

"You're raising a matter which is difficult for us to comment on," I replied. "This is an issue which concerns Mongolia and China. We have nothing to do with it. We're a third party. Don't you think you should address yourselves to the Mongolians?"

I believe the Chinese had expected me to answer that way. Chou was ready with his next question: "Fair enough, but we'd like to know in advance what your reaction would be if Mongolia did become part of China."

"Our attitude would depend on the attitude of the Mongolian comrades, but I can give you my personal opinion: I very much doubt that the Mongolians will welcome your suggestion. Besides, Mongolia is about to become a member of the United Nations and has recently established diplomatic relations with a number of states. The Mongolians would lose that recognition if they were absorbed into China. However, I certainly don't want to speak for the Mongolian leaders." [83]

82. This was during Khrushchev's first visit to Peking in 1954.
83. Mongolia was denied membership at that time, though it was finally admitted in 1961. Chou En-lai had visited Ulan Bator in July, 1954; Mao Tse-tung had long been

That's all we heard or said on the subject, but I know the Mongolians were anxious to define their border with China more clearly. It's a complicated problem because Mongolia is divided into two parts: the People's Republic of Mongolia, which is independent, and so-called Inner Mongolia, which is inside China. It's almost impossible to use ethnological or historical criteria to divide the two since no matter how you slice Mongolia, you can't help — so to speak — cutting into the body of the Mongolian people.

Therefore the Mongolians began reviewing the problem themselves. They told us they were exchanging maps with the Chinese and conducting negotiations. Finally, they arrived at a mutually expedient agreement and established a border satisfactory to both sides.

We would have liked to have done the same thing with the Chinese. But our relations deteriorated, the Chinese began to pursue two lines of attack in their propaganda about our borders. First, they dragged out the old question about how the Soviet Union had seized the Baltic states and then annexed certain territories from Rumania and Poland — territories which, by the way, had belonged to Russia before World War I. In the words of their treacherous radio station, the Chinese accused us of following a "tsarist policy of conquest."

I won't even bother to reply to such charges. I think the Soviet government has issued enough statements through TASS and the press. If we were to renounce the lands we inherited from the bourgeois government of the tsars, we'd find ourselves in a hopeless tangle of historical confusion and political quarrels. For example, what should we do with those nationality groups who migrated from their countries of origin in the not-too-distant past and who now have their own lands? Should we drive them out and make them go live on the moon? [84]

To my way of thinking, the whole theory of historical borders is nonsense. It's a dead issue, one which our enemies try to revive when they want to stir up trouble or conduct an aggressive policy against the Soviet Union and other socialist countries. I think it's shameful for China to be using such tactics, as they were when I was in the leadership and still are today.

expressing the hope that Mongolia would eventually become part of a Chinese federation.

84. Khrushchev must be thinking here of ethnic enclaves like the Abkhazians, a Moslem minority that has an "autonomous state" in Georgia.

In addition to making accusations about how we'd incorporated certain lands in Europe, the Chinese started up again with hostile statements about how we'd seized territory from them in the Far East. We wanted to put a stop to such talk once and for all. To do so, we had to reach an agreement with China and redraw our boundaries. One complication here was that since the time of the tsarist treaty with China, the riverbeds of the [Amur] and Ussuri rivers had shifted somewhat, forming new islands. According to the old treaty, the border followed the riverbank on the Chinese side, so the islands technically belonged to the USSR. Nevertheless, we were willing to recognize the interests of the Chinese population living along the border, and we allowed the local herders to graze their sheep and cattle and collect firewood on territory which was not, strictly speaking, part of China. In short, we adopted a friendly and considerate attitude towards the needs of the Chinese state. Our border guards served a primarily symbolic function and were lenient about border violations committed by the other side. In certain designated areas we made no demands on the Chinese and no protests against them. But soon the Chinese began firing at our patrol boats on the river. When I say "the Chinese," I don't mean soldiers in uniform, but our border guards reported that they'd seen Chinese troops disguised as peasants. A number of fistfights broke out between Chinese and Soviet guards, but our own men were under strict orders not to let themselves be provoked into armed conflict. Usually, the scuffles went no further than pushing and shoving, with the guards tearing off each other's buttons.

Rather than let these clashes get worse until they led to a skirmish which would do neither side any good, we put together a governmental committee and appealed to the Chinese for talks. After a long back-and-forth of messages, the Chinese finally agreed to a meeting. We offered to let them choose the site. They said they wanted to talk on their territory, and we agreed.

At the beginning of the negotiations, both sides presented their claims orally. The Chinese stated that they had a right to Vladivostok and a substantial area in [Soviet] Central Asia. There was no way we could entertain such claims. After all, the [Soviet] Far East wasn't even populated by Chinese; nor was Central Asia. The population in the Far East consisted mostly of Russians, while in Central Asia it was made up of Kazakhs, Tadzhiks, Uighurs, and Kirghizes. An especially troublesome point was the status of the Pamir Mountains, which weren't included in any treaty between the Soviet and Chinese governments. We instructed our delegation to explain to the Chinese that the Pamirs were populated by Tadzhiks and that therefore the mountains were quite reasonably part of the Tadzhik Republic.[85]

In the second stage of our talks, both sides presented maps outlining their claims. When the Chinese handed us their map, we saw that they no longer claimed Vladivostok or Central Asia, but they did claim those islands in the border rivers that were closer to the Chinese than the Soviet side. They proposed that we redraw the boundary: instead of running along the Chinese bank, it would run down the middle of the river. This proposal was in keeping with international practice, so we agreed, even though it meant relinquishing control of most of the islands.

Thus we resolved the disputes between us — at least in principle. However, one issue remained unresolved. The Chinese demanded navigation rights along the Amur River that would have allowed them to come literally right up to the walls of Khabarovsk. We insisted that they stick to an old treaty signed between Russia and China which restricted Chinese shipping to the so-called Kazakevich Channel. On that matter, we reached an impasse.

When it finally came time to sign a limited agreement setting new borders, we were willing to give a little as well as take a little. Plus some territory here, minus some there — that's what we proposed. As for the disputed areas, just divide them in half. In other words, we were ready to take a ruler and draw a line through the middle. That was a wise decision. It would have meant concessions on both sides. We simply wanted to find a mutually acceptable solution which would damage neither the prestige nor the material well-being either of China or of the Soviet Union. "Don't tease the geese," as we Russians like to say. Why make trouble? The rectification and redrawing of the borders was just a matter of common sense. After all, borders don't exist for the good of birds, who can fly anywhere they want: borders must be accessible to frontier guards who are responsible for protecting the security of the country.

But what seemed conciliatory and sensible to us wasn't good enough for the Chinese. When our representatives returned to China

85. Tadzhikitstan, one of the fifteen Soviet Socialists Republics in the USSR.

for the final round of negotiations, the Chinese wouldn't accept our position. Even though they had given up their claims to Vladivostok and more than half of Central Asia, they wanted us to acknowledge that the existing borders were based on illegal and unequal treaties which the tsars had forced upon a weak Chinese government. They wanted our new treaty to include a clause specifying that the new borders perpetuated an injustice foisted on China over a hundred years ago.

How could any sovereign state sign such a document? If we'd signed it, we would have been tacitly acknowledging that the injustice must be rectified — in other words, that we would have to renounce our claim to the territories in question. We were back to square one. The talks were broken off, and our delegation came home. To this day, the "inequality" clause has stuck in our throats.

The next round of negotiations was to take place in the USSR. We discussed the matter in the government and issued the appropriate instructions to our delegation, which was headed by Gheneralov. He was a calm, sensible, highly competent man, who was well suited to dealing with the Chinese.[86] However, the Chinese never replied to our last initiatives, and the talks were never resumed while I was in the leadership.

Since the end of my political career, I've followed the Sino-Soviet border dispute in the newspapers, and I gather our government's position hasn't changed. In fact, I think today the Soviet Union is pursuing the same policies which were conducted when I was head of the government and the Party.

Is There a Yellow Peril?

DURING the years that I was in the leadership, neither we nor the Chinese ever allowed ourselves to wash our dirty linen in public. We never let our scandals and conflicts come out in the press. Furthermore, even during the most heated moments of our disputes,

---

86. N. I. Gheneralov, a veteran diplomat with experience in the Far East as a prewar political advisor to the Soviet embassy in Japan, and after the war, attached to the Allied Control Commission in Japan.

both sides were careful not to attack individual leaders. However, since I've been retired, I've read in the newspapers and heard on the radio statements the Chinese have made about me personally and about the leadership which was formed after my retirement. This upsets me very much.

I've also heard since I retired that [former ambassador to Peking] Yudin gave a speech at a meeting in which he accused me of damaging our relations with China by treating Mao with disrespect. How can Yudin — a man who is supposedly an expert on philosophy and agitation and propaganda — make such shameful allegations? If he wants to find the true origins of our conflict with China, he has only to look at himself. The cable he sent us, before we had any real conflicts with the Chinese, was like a thunderbolt out of a clear blue sky — he was the first swallow bringing us tidings of the coming deterioration in our relations with China. I'm sure someday, when the archives are opened, historians will see for themselves what Yudin said about Mao.

Before ending my recollections on China, I would like to tell one last anecdote.

During my visit to France, I attended a reception given in my honor by the French government. I had an opportunity to meet a shade out of the past — the prewar French Premier, Mr. Daladier. He'd been one of the men responsible for France's failure to unite with the Soviet Union against Hitlerite Germany.[87]

Later Daladier went to China. I believe he made the trip as a tourist. On his way home, he passed through Moscow and asked the Ministry of Foreign Affairs for an appointment with me. I discussed his request with my comrades (I never received foreign visitors without consulting the leadership first). We decided I should meet him, and I did so in the Kremlin.

I was curious to have another look at the man who, along with Chamberlain, had led us into that terrible, bloody war. However, I never would have agreed to see him in order to argue about the policies he'd conducted when he was Premier. I was simply interested in hearing what he had to say. He brought up the subject of China.

"Here I am, just back from China," he began. "I've toured the country and seen all the wonderful things you've been doing for the

87. Edouard Daladier, whom Khrushchev met during his 1960 tour of France, which is described in detail in Chapter 17.

Chinese. Has it occurred to you that by building up their economy, you might be creating dangers for yourselves?"

"No," I replied, "we see no such danger. On the contrary, we're convinced we're doing the right thing. The Chinese are our friends and our brothers."

"Aren't you worried about the Yellow Peril? All over Europe — in fact, all over the world — people are talking about the Yellow Peril. Don't you feel threatened by it, too?"

Frankly, I was taken aback by his question, and I rebuked him sharply: "I should tell you, Mr. Daladier, that we look at things differently. We don't discriminate among people according to the color of their skin. We don't care if they're yellow, white, black, or brown. The only distinction that matters to us is the class distinction. China is a socialist country. Therefore the Chinese are our class brothers. We have a direct interest in helping them — because it is expedient for us and because our class solidarity obliges us to maintain friendly and fraternal relations."

He didn't argue with me. We talked for a while longer, and then he left.

Not too long ago, I heard that Daladier died.[88] I've thought about our conversation many times since. Of course, I was quite right to have rejected his talk about the "Yellow Peril," but I can't help thinking that old Mr. Daladier would have laughed if he'd lived long enough to see what's happened in our relations with China — and to hear some of the things I myself have said since my meeting with him. He would have claimed that he, a bourgeois leader, was right about what was happening between two Communist leaders, Mao Tse-tung and myself.

But it's not a "Yellow Peril" which threatens the Soviet Union — it's the policies being conducted by Mao. Furthermore, Daladier hasn't had the last laugh, because he's dead and I'm alive and Mao is alive. However, as the preachers used to say, no one under the sun is immortal, and the hour will come when Mao Tse-tung will also have to depart from the political arena. Therefore I believe that the seeds of friendship sown by the Soviet Union will someday be given a chance to grow and bear fruit. The assistance we have given China over the years has left a deep mark on the Chinese people. Despite what some say, I'm sure our money, our credit, our technical aid have not been wasted.

88. Daladier died in October, 1970.

A ray of sunshine will break through the clouds and show the Chinese people the way back to the path set for us by the great Karl Marx and Vladimir Ilyich Lenin. Mao is too old to see that ray of sunshine himself, but no one lives forever. Mao Tse-tungs can come and go but the Chinese people will remain. In the end, the time will come — though I don't know how soon — when China will return to a correct policy toward the USSR and the other socialist countries.

As a man who supported the Chinese people in their struggle for liberation, who rejoiced in their victory, and who wishes nothing but the best for them in the future, I hope that the Chinese Communist Party will soon find the strength to overcome the sickness which has befallen it.

TWO

Foreign Policy and Travels

12

Neighbors

Turkey

As I've said many times, from the moment our State came into being, Lenin promoted the principle of establishing normal relations with all countries, regardless of their social and political systems. It was he who made a famous statement to the effect that if we didn't want to recognize the capitalist countries on this planet, we'd simply have to fly to the moon. Particularly important were those countries with which we shared a common border.

Lenin conceded to Turkey some vast territories that Russian troops had occupied after World War I. In fact, of course, we couldn't have held those territories anyway after the October Revolution, but our claims to them were valid because the Turkish lands in question around Mount Ararat were populated by Armenians. Even today Mount Ararat is depicted on the Armenian coat of arms. The Armenians have a joke about this inconsistency: "When the Turks start complaining that we have no right to display Mount Ararat on our coat of arms since Mount Ararat doesn't belong to Armenia, we can always reply that the Turks have no right to display a crescent on *their* coat of arms because the moon doesn't belong to Turkey."

As I've already mentioned, Stalin jealously guarded foreign policy as his own special province. The one person able to advise Stalin on foreign policy was Beria, who used his influence for all it was worth. At one of those interminable "suppers" at Stalin's, Beria started harping on how certain territories, now part of Turkey, used to belong to Georgia and how the Soviet Union ought to demand their return.[1] Beria was probably right, but you had to go pretty far back in history to the time when the Turks seized those lands from Georgia. Beria kept bringing this subject up, teasing Stalin with it, goading him into doing something.[2] He convinced Stalin that now was the time to get those territories back. He argued that Turkey was weakened by World War II and wouldn't be able to resist.

Stalin gave in and sent an official memorandum to the Turkish government pressing our territorial claims. Well, the whole thing backfired. Beria didn't foresee that Turkey would respond to our demand by accepting American support. So Beria and Stalin succeeded only in frightening the Turks right into the open arms of the Americans. Because of Stalin's note to the Turkish government, the Americans were able to penetrate Turkey and set up bases right next to our borders.[3]

At about that time newspapers in the West announced that the US was organizing a so-called "scientific expedition," supposedly to explore Mount Ararat in search of Noah's Ark. That didn't fool anyone. We knew perfectly well what sort of expedition it really was. It was a border action directed against Soviet Armenia and our oil fields in Azerbaidzhan, which were then our sole source of petroleum in the USSR.[4]

Thus, thanks to his inflexibility and the psychic disturbance which came over him at the end of his life, Stalin ruined our relations with the Turks. Turkey has allowed the US to have military bases on its territory ever since.

Iran

PERSIA — or Iran as it's now called — was certainly no less afraid of us than Turkey, and probably more so. The Persians had known us as

1. For a description of the "suppers" at Stalin's, see *KR*, I, 296–306.
2. Beria and Stalin were both Georgians.
3. Molotov first made Soviet claims on the Turkish provinces of Kars, Ardelian, and Artvin in eastern Anatolia in June, 1945, then reiterated them at the Potsdam Conference in August. The USSR offered to drop its claims in June, 1953, shortly after Stalin's death and Beria's liquidation.
4. A US expedition headed by a scientist from North Carolina spent twelve days in a futile search for Noah's Ark in 1949; the venture was attacked by Moscow at the time as espionage in disguise.

occupiers ever since tsarist troops were stationed in Persia in the last century.

Because of Persia's historical legacy of resentment against our country, the Shah — that is, the father of the present Shah — conducted a pro-German policy during World War II. As a result, the Soviet Union conducted an agreement with England toward the end of the war whereby half of Persia would be occupied by Soviet troops, the other half by the English. So once again, the Persians knew us as occupiers.[5]

We, of course, had only one goal: to guarantee the security of our southern borders. But whenever one country occupies another, the occupation is always justified on the grounds of maintaining peace and security. More often than not, the occupying troops stay — or at least try to stay — permanently.

Stalin did indeed delay the withdrawal of our troops. While he was stalling, a civil war broke out in Iran. The Shah suppressed the revolt, and some of the people who were fighting on the side of the insurgents fled across the border into the Soviet Union.[6] The Shah knew perfectly well not only that we had sympathized with the rebellion, but that we had armed the rebels. This caused the Iranians to distrust us more than ever.

The United States did everything it could to exploit Iran's distrust of the Soviet Union. We received intelligence reports that the Americans had set up a missile site, an air base, and several other military installations. We thought these bases were meant to threaten our [oil fields around] Baku, just across the border. The Shah repeatedly denied there were any American bases in Iran, but we didn't believe him. Later we found out that, in fact, there were no US bases there, but that doesn't mean the Americans couldn't have set up bases in a hurry if they'd wanted. It would have taken nothing for the United States to move in and occupy Iran. Or the Americans could simply have gotten some sheik to let them use his airfields for operations against the Soviet Union.

5. British and Soviet troops occupied Iran in 1941 and forced the elder Shah, Reza Shah Pahlevi, to abdicate in favor of his son, the present ruler, Mohammed Reza Shah Pahlevi.
6. At the instigation of Soviet agents left behind after the delayed evacuation of Russian occupation troops from Iran, "a war of national liberation" broke out in late 1945 in the northern provinces adjacent to Soviet Azerbaidzhan. The Iranian government suppressed the secessionist movement in 1946.

On top of all these tensions, we had a border dispute with Iran which dragged on for many years.

This whole situation had to be put right. We invited the Shah to negotiate with us. We made considerable concessions to Iran on the disputed border. Some of their claims we compromised on, and others we satisfied completely. We signed a protocol establishing a mutually acceptable line of demarcation on the map. We were pleased to have liquidated one of the major obstacles which had stood in the way of good Soviet-Iranian relations. We also made the Shah an offer to build a hydroelectric plant on the river [the Araxes] that forms the border between the Soviet Union and Iran. The Shah didn't accept our offer at first, but now I see from the press that construction of the dam is under way. Soon the dam will be irrigating crops and generating power to the benefit of both the Soviet and Iranian peoples.

Afghanistan

THE Americans also put pressure on another neighbor to the south. They started pouring material and technological assistance into Afghanistan, giving credits, building roads, and undertaking all kinds of projects at their own expense.

In its desire to encircle us with military bases, America threw itself all over a country like Afghanistan — one moment courting the Afghans, the next moment trying to scare them. We knew that the Americans were attempting to frighten the King into having nothing to do with the Soviet Union by spreading the story that we had military intentions in Afghanistan.[7] But history had already proved that we wished nothing but the best for Afghanistan. Lenin had been quick to recognize the Afghan kingdom as an independent state after the October Revolution.[8] Then, for many years, our relations were frozen. It wasn't until after Stalin's death, when a new leadership came to power in our country, that we managed to reestablish friendship with Afghanistan.

7. Mohammed Zahir Shah was King of Afghanistan from 1933 until his overthrow by a coup d'etat in 1973.

8. In fact, Afghanistan's independence had already been guaranteed by an Anglo-Russian agreement in 1907.

The Afghans didn't even wait for us to make the first move. They took the initiative and came to us for help. The King invited Bulganin and me to stop over in Kabul on our way back from India. As a result of our discussions with the King and his ministers, we had a fairly clear idea of what an economically backward country Afghanistan was. We could sense that the Afghans were looking for a way our of their problems. And we could also tell we weren't the only ones available to help: at the time of our visit to Kabul, it was clear that the Americans were penetrating Afghanistan with the obvious intent of setting up a military base there.

The Afghans asked us to help them build several hundred kilometers of road near the Iranian border. It cost us a hefty sum since we had to tunnel through the mountains. However, because Afghanistan didn't have railroads, such a highway would be a main artery, carrying the economic lifeblood of the country. The road also had great strategic significance because it would have allowed us to transport troops and supplies in the event of war with either Pakistan or Iran.

It was up to us to persuade the King and his government that we wouldn't misuse the road — that it would serve the cause of peaceful economic development. It took some time for the ice to melt entirely and for the Afghan leaders to understand that we weren't pursuing mercenary or military goals in their country.[9]

For a long time we tried to get the King to take his vacation in the Soviet Union. Time and again we'd invite him, but invariably he'd politely decline and go off to France or some other country. Finally he agreed to come for a holiday to one of our hunting lodges in the Crimea.[10] It wasn't hunting season, so we didn't shoot anything. We simply entertained our guest and showed him the beautiful sights and the wild game — the deer and the mountain sheep.

During our talks I told him we'd been exploring for natural re-

9. This paragraph and the two preceding it are an abridgement of *KR*, I, 507–508. Khrushchev and Bulganin visited Kabul for four days during a month's tour of Asia in 1955. They concluded an agreement granting $100 million in aid to Afghanistan. Khrushchev went to Kabul again in 1960. The highway and tunnel through the Hindu Kush Mountains, linking the Afghan capital with the Oxus Valley, was built in 1964.

10. Zahir paid a state visit to the USSR in 1957. He went to the Crimea and Baku as well as to Moscow, Leningrad, and Minsk. At the end of the tour Zahir's Foreign Minister, Sardar Mohammed Naim, and Gromyko released a joint communiqué announcing that the Soviet Union had "decided to render Afghanistan disinterested technical and material assistance, which is not contingent on any political or other similar conditions." Zahir visisted Russia again in the summer of 1964.

sources near the Soviet-Afghan border and had found huge deposits
of oil and gas there. I suggested we agree on joint exploitation of
these resources. He and his ministers listened to us attentively and
watched us closely, but they didn't say anything. Obviously they
were still somewhat cautious. However, since I retired, I've read in
the newspapers that the Afghans have agreed to share their reserves
with us; they're laying a pipeline so they can supply us with natural
gas in exchange for our machinery and industrial goods.[11]

Some people of limited vision may say there's no point in getting
gas and oil from Afghanistan since we have these same resources in
our own country. My reply to that is: if we don't assist our neighbors,
they'll remain in a state of abject poverty and, sooner or later, turn
against us. Besides, American capitalists would be only too glad to
take our place if we didn't assist the Afghans.

It's my strong feeling that the capital we've invested in Afghanistan hasn't been wasted. We've earned the Afghans' trust and friendship, and their country hasn't fallen into the trap the Americans set
for it; Afghanistan hasn't been caught on the hook baited with American money. There's no doubt in my mind that if the Afghans hadn't
become our friends, the Americans would have managed to ingra-
tiate themselves with their "humanitarian aid," as they call it.

The amount of money we spent in gratuitous assistance to Afghanistan is a drop in the ocean compared to the price we would have had
to pay in order to counter the threat of an American military base on
Afghan territory. Think of the capital we would have had to lay out to
finance the deployment of our own military might along our side of
the border, and it would have been an expense that would have
sucked the blood of our people without augmenting our means of
production one whit.

We must be statesmen, not misers, in our approach to neighboring
countries. We must be willing to make advance payments which
promise in the future to bring us enormous returns in the form of
peace and friendship. I'm proud to have been part of the leadership
when our relations with Afghanistan took a dramatic turn for the better.

11. The Soviets began building a gas pipeline in Afghanistan in 1969.

Nehru and the Bhilai Steel Mill

OF the two countries that won their independence from Great Britain after the war, Pakistan joined SEATO, but India — thanks to Nehru's progressive leadership — refused. India has stood firm as a country independent of all military blocs.

Nehru had once visited the Soviet Union, but it wasn't until after Stalin's death, when Bulganin and I went to India, that the foundations for Soviet-Indian relations were securely laid.[12]

I remember that when Nehru and I were conducting our negotiations, we were served mango. I'd never seen this wonderful fruit before. Nehru smiled and watched closely to see how we would deal with the mango. Peeling one is a complicated operation, requiring time and skill. Besides, mango juice is very sweet and sticky. After a while he said, "Look at how I do it. I'll show you how to eat one according to our tradition."

Indira Gandhi, who was sitting with us, joked, "You know, Mr. Khrushchev, our people say the best place to eat mango is in the bathtub because that way you can peel the fruit and wash your hands at the same time." [13]

We offered India economic and technological assistance. Some people might ask, "But what could the Indians give us in return?" Of course, there wasn't anything they could do for us except express their gratitude. We're not like the Americans, who spend billions of dollars in foreign aid but — capitalists that they are — always look for some way of getting concessions on raw materials or setting up joint ventures so that they can squeeze a profit out of the "presents" they've given to other countries. We simply wanted to create the basis of friendship and mutual confidence on which to build our relations with India.

To his credit, Nehru graciously accepted. I've already told about

12. Prime Minister Jawaharlal Nehru had been to Russia in 1927; he came again for a two-week state visit in June, 1955. Khrushchev, Bulganin, and Gromyko (then First Deputy Foreign Minister under Molotov) flew to New Delhi in November of that year.

13. Indira Gandhi, Nehru's daughter and the current Prime Minister, was then her father's official hostess.

how the Afghan leaders were at first reluctant and suspicious when we tried to loan them hard currency to develop their wretchedly poor country — how they tried to figure out whether we had some hidden motives. Well, we encountered no such mistrust on the part of the Indian leaders.

They inquired whether we would like to build a steel plant for them in Bhilai. We knew they'd made similar approaches to England and West Germany. When we said we were willing to extend the necessary credits and the services of our technical personnel, the Indians signed a formal agreement with us.

Our engineers prepared a blueprint for the project and submitted it to the Indians, who asked if we'd mind if they let some English engineers review the plan. That seemed like a fairly original way of doing business, but we had no obligation. We were confident that the Indians didn't suspect us of anything; the problem was simply that they didn't have competent engineers of their own to check our plan for mistakes. However, in exchange it was agreed that our engineers would look over the plans which the English engineers had drawn up for the plant they were going to construct.

I knew from my childhood that the English were first-rate steelmen. Yuzovka, the town where I grew up, was named after the owner of the local steel factory, Hughes.[14] The British, in general, have always been marvelous with technology. They've invented many machines to help our Russian *muzhik* [peasant] do his work. I remember our laborers singing a variation on the old working song "Dubina." It went like this:

> *The years have passed, and, thank God, by now*
> *A change has come over our native scene;*
> *The cudgel is laid to rest with the plow*
> *And our work is done by an iron machine.*

We turned our blueprints for the steel mill over to the English engineers. The Indian government later informed us that the Englishmen's report on their findings was most flattering to us. They didn't recommend any changes at all. In reviewing the *English* blueprints, however, *our* engineers pointed out certain improvements and corrections which needed to be made in accordance with modern science and technology.

14. The Welshman John Hughes founded the Yuzovka Metal Factory near the coal mine where Khrushchev's father worked (see *KR*, I, 403).

As for the Germans, we had no diplomatic relations with them and therefore no direct contact with them in India. However, they had a head start on us, and it looked for a while as if they might finish their plant ahead of ours.[15]

At one point, when our construction was falling behind schedule, I summoned Comrade Dymshits and sent him to India to help with the project.[16] I'd known Dymshits from our postwar reconstruction in the south. He'd demonstrated his great administrative talents in Dnepropetrovsk and Zaporozhie. He'd developed a new method of restoring bombed-out blast furnaces by putting them back together in sections, then lifting them onto the old foundation by crane and riveting them together. This process had saved us six months or even a year in some cases. Comrade Dymshits went to India, where he reported directly to Nehru.

There was one tragedy which marred our experience in India. One of our best engineers went hunting with his young son in the swamps near Bhilai. He shot a duck and went to retrieve it. He was sucked into a bog and drowned. We were terribly upset.

Our workers in India kept to themselves. Originally, the Indians had wanted to build the steel mill on a mutual basis, but we refused.[17] We didn't openly explain our reason, but it was this: we didn't want our supervisors and planners to be in the position of employers standing over native laborers. If we had allowed ourselves to be put in that role, conflicts would inevitably have arisen, and — worse — we would have dirtied our policy in the eyes of workers all over the world.[18]

In the end, to our great satisfaction, we finished our plant before the Germans finished theirs. We were the first to smelt pig iron and to produce steel in India.[19] The Germans were plagued by construction delays and faulty equipment. The Indians told us they considered our work superior to the Germans'. Naturally, we were in a competition with the German and English engineers, and I don't think there's any question that we won.

Let me say here that I don't want to be like some of our people

15. In fact, the Soviet project was accepted and begun before the German one.

16. V. E. Dymshits, chief engineer at the Bhilai Steel Plant from 1957 to 1959, went on to become Deputy Premier of the USSR in 1962.

17. "Mutual basis" would have meant using Indian labor.

18. The policy referred to here is that of solidarity with the proletariat of other countries.

19. The Soviet-built plant blew in its first blast furnace in February, 1959, shortly before the West German plant at Rourkela began operation.

who go around talking as though we've grabbed God by the beard. I'm not saying that our technicians are the best in the world. I realize full well that we lag behind other countries in a number of areas, and it pains me very much that despite the passage of more than fifty years since the Revolution, we haven't been able to catch up yet.

However, we should acknowledge our achievements and call these things by their own names. Our engineers deserve nothing but praise for the fine job they did in India. They had mastered to the point of perfection the metallurgical problems facing them.

Initially, our steel mill's capacity was nearly one million tons a year, but the Indian government immediately began talks on the possibility of expanding it to about 2.5 million tons. We accepted their proposal and began work.

I remember going to Bhilai with Nehru to inspect the finished plant.[20] Much had changed since my first visit to India. Then I had looked at the exotic sights through the eyes of a tourist, a foreigner from the north seeing the miraculous lands to the south for the first time. But now we looked at the Indian leaders and worked as old friends with whom we had just completed a common undertaking.

My relations with Nehru couldn't have been more friendly. He took me around to many factories and farms so that I could acquaint myself firsthand with India's problems and possibilities. I remember he took me into a lunchroom at some plant. It was just like the ones I had seen in the United States. I think it must have been copied after an American lunchroom. "Mr. Khrushchev," Nehru explained, "no one is going to serve us here. We'll have to take our silverware and go to the counter over there for the food." We then had a good, big lunch. As I could see with my own eyes, though, India still had a long way to go before it would rid itself of the colonial legacy of poverty and backwardness. I remember being struck especially by how poor the people of Calcutta seemed.

I went there once to address a rally. There are more workers in Calcutta than any other Indian state, and they vote heavily for the leftist parties. Therefore our delegation was received with extra warmth and enthusiasm. An enormous quantity of doves was re-

20. This was on Khrushchev's second trip to India, in 1960, when he was making another grand tour of Asia. Khrushchev was accompanied this time by Foreign Minister Gromyko and G. A. (Yuri) Zhukov of the State Committee on Cultural Relations, as well as by various members of the Khrushchev family.

leased. The dove is a symbol of peace — thanks partly to Picasso, whose drawing of a dove can now be found on the banners of all countries that are fighting to maintain peaceful coexistence. I still recall that rally in Calcutta vividly. Night was falling. One of the doves landed on my arm. People started laughing and making jokes, and the photographers naturally couldn't resist taking pictures. I'd been speaking out in favor of peace in all the countries I'd visited, so people remarked that here was a dove who knew where to perch.

We told Nehru we would build more plants on credit. We also gave him free the tractors, combine harvesters, sowing and irrigation equipment he needed to set up an agricultural enterprise similar to one of our state farms. We sent him some of our best agronomists and agricultural engineers. Nehru took me to inspect this farm after it was in operation. I was pleased to see grain being harvested by modern equipment.

I know there are some people who grumble that our government gave away too many presents like that farm. I don't know whether these people were simply never briefed or whether they were briefed in such a way as to make our gifts look extravagant. As far as I'm concerned, the best way to propagandize for socialism is to set concrete examples. By giving the Indians the farm, we showed them how well our socialist method of agriculture works and strengthened our friendly relations with them.

India has been a leader among those countries freeing themselves from colonialism, and Nehru conducted a policy of peaceful coexistence. Therefore he was a valuable friend. I think we have been rewarded for our aid to India by the trust, gratitude, and understanding that Nehru expressed many times to us.

Of course, the internal political situation in India has been complicated from our standpoint. I mentioned a moment ago my visit to the city of Calcutta, where the population is poorer and therefore more sympathetic to the Communist cause. The leftists poll more votes and win more seats [in the parliament] in Calcutta than in other parts of the country. But nowadays the Communist Party of India is split. There's one party which calls itself Marxist and another which calls itself the CP. Well, this is already a direct result of those senseless policies which Mao Tse-tung has been following. He caused the split in the Indian Party, and the split widened after China's armed attack against India. Fortunately, the effect of Mao's policies has not reached deep into the masses. The forces of the left rallied together and demonstrated more support for the Soviet Union than for China.

The Sino-Indian War

OVER the years our relations with Nehru grew stronger and stronger. While he wasn't a Communist, he was more than just another bourgeois liberal politician — he was a true people's democrat. Even though he didn't espouse Marxism, he did begin to make references and gestures in the direction of socialism.[21] Of course, we had no way of knowing for sure exactly what kind of socialism he had in mind; the word "socialism" has been bandied about by all sorts of different people, including Hitler.

However, we were eager to give Nehru a chance. We thought that if we were patient, Nehru would, of his own accord, choose the correct course for India. Naturally, we did everything we could to help him make the right choice. Meanwhile, we cultivated very close ties with the Communist Party of India.

Because of our special interest in India, we were deeply concerned about the deterioration of relations between India and the People's Republic of China. We had welcomed the Bandung Conference, at which Chou En-lai and Nehru laid the foundations for peaceful coexistence between their countries,[22] but since then there had been upsetting signs of trouble along the Sino-Indian border.

First, a revolt broke out in Tibet. The Tibetans almost seized power.[23] The Indians took a pro-Tibetan position. They didn't intervene directly, but they sympathized with the insurgents. For our part, we publicly took the Chinese side, although we understood the

21. Nehru's Avadi Resolution of 1955 proclaimed a "socialist pattern of society" as the objective of Indian state planning.
22. This meeting of twenty-nine Afro-Asian countries in Indonesia in 1955 marked the political emergence of the Third World and the policy of nonalignment based on five principles: mutual respect for sovereignty and territorial integrity, nonaggression, noninterference in each other's internal affairs, equality and mutual benefit, and peaceful coexistence.
23. Tibet had been a province of China since 1950, when Chinese troops occupied the country. An insurrection broke out in 1956, initially among the northeastern tribesmen, then spreading by 1959 throughout the whole country. The anti-Chinese Tibetan rebels, under the Dalai Lama, tried to establish independence from China. The attempt was defeated, and the Dalai Lama was driven into exile.

position in which Nehru found himself. He regarded a Chinese Tibet as an eyesore on the border of India.

Then suddenly, in 1959, China began aggressive military actions against India, and an armed conflict broke out.[24] The Chinese, who've always been good at name-calling, started abusing Nehru as the number one enemy of socialism.

About this time I returned from my visit to the United States.[25] We had no choice but to make a public statement, expressing our attitude toward the Sino-Indian border conflict. Even though we suspected Mao was to blame, we couldn't accuse him of starting the war. After all, China was ideologically closer to us than India. At the same time, we knew Nehru to be a reasonable and peace-loving man. Even if he'd been a militarist, he was realistic enough to know that India was too weak to attack China. Such an attack would have been doomed to failure.

In short, we didn't want to call either side the aggressor. In our statement released through TASS, we took the position that a misunderstanding had led to accidental hostilities between our Indian friends and our Chinese brothers. We expressed our regret and called upon both sides to negotiate a cease-fire and resume friendly relations. We knew in advance our statement wouldn't be well received in Peking.

Even though I'd just returned home from Washington, my comrades in the leadership told me I'd have to muster my strength and fly straight to Peking to represent the Communist Party of the Soviet Union in talks with the Chinese leadership. Everyone agreed I was the only one who could lead our delegation. Why? Because at just that time the Chinese were celebrating their national holiday,[26] and unless I, as the head of our Party, attended, the Chinese might think we were deliberately downgrading their role in the international revolutionary movement.

I flew to Peking and was met at the airport by Mao Tse-tung, Chou

24. Khrushchev refers here to the Longju Incident of August, 1959, in which the Indians unilaterally adjusted northward the disputed McMahon Line demarcating India from Tibet. There were skirmishes between Indian and Chinese border patrols.

25. This last visit to Peking came immediately after the conclusion of Khrushchev's first trip to the US in the fall of 1959. For more on this acrimonious encounter with the Chinese and its consequences, see the section "Third Visit to Peking" in Chapter 11.

26. The tenth anniversary of the October 1, 1949, Communist victory on the mainland.

En-lai, Liu Shao-ch'i, Chu Teh, and Ch'en Yi. On the surface every-one was extremely polite, but I could sense that they were seething with resentment against the Soviet Union and against me personally.

I believe it was Mao himself who stirred up the trouble with India. I think he did so because of some sick fantasy. He had started the war with India, and now he wanted to drag the Soviet Union into the conflict. Here was Mao trying to dictate policy to other socialist countries — just as Stalin had done before him. Here, once again, was the dictatorship of one individual masquerading as the dicta-torship of the proletariat.

Mao didn't come right out and say what I suspected. As a rule, he himself would never discuss unpleasant subjects with me. He would always designate someone else to speak for him when we got down to business. In this case, the Chinese side decided to unleash Ch'en Yi on me. The talks immediately became agitated and tense. Ch'en Yi was downright rude. I don't know whether his rudeness was a calculated political move or whether it was a character trait.

The Chinese started interrogating me about why the Soviet Union had released such a statement on the Sino-Indian border clash. Mao said one or two things against our policy, but for the most part every-one was silent except Ch'en Yi. Obviously they'd rehearsed their roles in advance. Ch'en Yi stopped just short of directly criticizing our leadership, but he heaped all sorts of abuse on our good friend Nehru.

"How could you make such a statement?" he blurted out. "Don't you know Nehru is nothing but an agent of American imperialism? Don't you know Nehru must be destroyed if the progressive forces in India are to prevail?" I forget exactly what names Ch'en Yi called Nehru, but who cares? Why revive the Chinese lexicon of abuse? Anyone who's really interested can just take a look at the Chinese press of that period.

We told Ch'en Yi, "We have a rather different assessment of Mr. Nehru. He may be a bourgeois politician, but he's the most progres-sive leader in India outside the Communist Party. His policies have been steadfastly neutralist and anti-imperialist, and, unlike the Pak-istanis, he's signed no treaties with the Americans. If Nehru should be overthrown, you can be sure more reactionary forces would take power. Therefore what's the point of alienating Nehru or in weaken-ing his position in his own country?"

The Chinese then took the position that since both of our countries were socialist, the Soviet Union had an obligation to take China's side in any conflict with a nonsocialist country like India.

I replied that it wasn't worth starting a war over a territorial disagreement. I gave them some examples of how we'd peacefully resolved our own border disputes with Turkey and Iran.

"The way to solve the problem is by diplomacy, not war," I said. "Besides, the territories you're fighting over are high up in the sparsely populated mountains of Tibet. Are these patches of desolate highlands really worth bloodshed? You've gone all this time without fighting a war. The border was established decades ago.[27] Why wait until now to kick up a fuss about it?"

"You have it all wrong," said Ch'en Yi. "We need that territory, and it's rightfully ours. The English seized it from us when India was their colony."

"Maybe so," I replied, "but since then India has liberated itself from British colonial oppression, just as China has liberated itself from foreign domination. China and India have both joined the ranks of those countries pitted against the landlords and capitalist exploiters of this world. Therefore why should you resort to war to resolve the disputes between you?"

I told the Chinese they should be more tolerant and understanding of Nehru's position. "Look here," I said. "Tibet is right on India's border. Can't you see that the Indians consider it of vital importance to have an independent neighbor? Tibet is a weak country and can't pose any threat to India on its own. A *Chinese* Tibet, however, *does* pose a threat to India. Can't you see that?"

The Chinese stubbornly insisted they would fight to the end — that they wouldn't relent until India was defeated. We left Peking filled with apprehension about what might happen.

The Indians could now see better than before how committed we were to justice. They saw that we weren't afraid to tell the truth as we saw it to our Chinese brothers — even though justice and truth favored the Indian, rather than the Chinese, side in the conflict between them.

Soon the Indian government began negotiating with us for the purchase of some MiG-21 fighters and for a license to manufacture those planes in their own country. We knew that there were oppos-

27. The Tibetan-Indian border had been established in 1914 by the British with the so-called McMahon Line.

ing forces in India which vigorously advocated buying American planes instead, and that the United States had already agreed to turn over the blueprints for its jet fighter to India. Thus, we had a choice: we could sell our planes to the Indians, or sit by and watch them be tied to the American aircraft industry.

The design of the MiG-21 was no longer a military secret. I believe we'd already sold it to several countries, including Egypt and Yugoslavia. In other words, our enemies knew all about the MiG-21. It was a difficult question, but in the end we let the Indians have a few of the fighters.[28]

Naturally, China blew the whole affair wildly out of proportion and made all sorts of crazy propaganda against the Soviet Union among the other fraternal Communist Parties. We explained the reasons for our decision to the other Parties, and the absolute majority accepted our position — although you can still find people who claim that we made a mistake, that we should have disregarded our relations with India and should have thought instead about Soviet relations with our Chinese fellow socialists. In any event, the MiG-21s we gave India didn't play a significant role during the Sino-Indian conflict.

Soon a full-scale war was raging on the border.[29] Sizable forces were thrown in on both sides, and large losses were incurred. The Indians suffered far heavier casualties than the Chinese. The Chinese had spent years fighting Chiang Kai-shek and the Japanese. India had less military experience and inferior weapons. The Indian army withstood one defeat after another. The Chinese seized Indian territory.

The war created great difficulties for the Indian people and put the Communist Party of India into a most awkward position. The war even caused a split in the Party. The majority of the Indian Communists supported Nehru's policy of defending the country against Chinese aggression, while the other faction — including some good Communists, members of the Indian Central Committee whom I knew personally — took the Chinese side.[30]

28. Negotiations for the MiGs began in 1960, but — largely because of British and American protests — the deal was not sealed until the summer of 1962.
29. Full-scale fighting broke out in October, 1962, and continued until November, when the Chinese unilaterally declared a cease-fire.
30. Many Indian Communists, pro-Moscow as well as pro-Peking, were rounded up and imprisoned.

The Chinese then started a vigorous propaganda campaign against the Indian Communist Party and also against the Soviet Union. Our position throughout remained in support of a cessation of hostilities with neither defeat nor victory for either side. That, in fact, was how the war ended. China and India found some way of stopping the war. As I recall, China failed to achieve its original objectives.[31]

Many years have passed since the Sino-Indian conflict, and I believe time has proved our position correct, as expressed in the TASS statement. Had we acted or publicly stated otherwise, we would have succeeded only in making a gift of India to the American imperialists. It's true, of course, that we didn't do our relations with China any good; but, nevertheless, we didn't think that our relations with China would be hopelessly damaged.

I think Mao created the Sino-Indian conflict precisely in order to draw the Soviet Union into it. He wanted to put us in the position of having no choice but to support him. He wanted to be the one who decided what we should do. But Mao made a mistake in thinking we would agree to sacrifice our independence in foreign policy. We knew perfectly well that foreign and domestic policies are closely intertwined — and are based on the same ideological principles. Had we taken a pro-Chinese position on India, just as surely as night follows day we would have had to support the Chinese on their Hundred Flowers campaign, on their Great Leap Forward, and on their Cultural Revolution — and that would have been impossible.

However, I don't want to talk about all that now. I'm too tired. Let's just leave it, when all is said and done, that I have no regrets about the policy we conducted toward both sides of the Sino-Indian conflict when I was the head of the leadership. At this point I'm going to announce an intermission for myself.[32]

31. China probably never intended to annex Indian territory. The "aggression" Khrushchev charges the Chinese with here was more of a punitive expedition in retaliation for what China saw as numerous Indian provocations and incursions into Tibet. Some scholars believe China was also seeking to challenge India's increasingly powerful and prestigious position in the Third World.

32. In the tape recordings on which these memoirs are based, Khrushchev more than once ends a recording session with a sometimes formal, sometimes playful, concluding remark such as this one.

13

Indonesia and Burma

Sukarno

INDONESIA is an important country which attracted our attention when I was in the leadership, and it still deserves our attention now. The land is rich and beautiful. It has a population of nearly 100 million. The Indonesians are a wonderful people who will prevail in the end, despite the defeat they suffered in 1965.[1]

It took decades for the Soviet Union to realize the importance of Indonesia. In the first years after the October Revolution we were too concerned with internal politics and relations with our immediate neighbors to give a single thought to Indonesia. As far as I can recall, Stalin never so much as mentioned Indonesia. I don't think he knew anything about the country except what he'd read in geography books. He probably knew there were some islands called Sumatra and Borneo, but that's all.

After Stalin's death, our leadership became aware of Indonesia at the time of the Bandung Conference. A joint declaration was drawn up and signed by a number of leaders present, including Nehru and Chou En-lai. Later Mao and the other Chinese leaders proudly claimed that Chou was the one who drafted the document. Of course, that was before everything turned upside down in China. In any event, the Bandung Declaration was a good document. It was signed by Sukarno on behalf of the Indonesian delegation to the conference.[2]

1. In 1965 a leftist coup misfired and touched off a frenzied slaughter of Communists and others.
2. Opening the Bandung Conference of 1955, President Sukarno denounced colon-

Thus Sukarno emerged as a major political figure in our eyes. Soon his name began to pop up frequently in the press and on the radio. We members of the Presidium followed his activities through information supplied to us by TASS, which compiled excerpts of articles in newspapers from all over the world. TASS put together a huge amount of material that we couldn't possibly digest ourselves. Each of us had aides who selected items of interest for us.

In this manner we learned that, much to his credit, Sukarno was conducting a neutralist policy. We read that he had established good relations with Yugoslavia, which at that time was implementing Marxism-Leninism in a somewhat more flexible manner. As a result of our Stalinist legacy, there were still certain unnecessary and incorrect aspects of the way in which Marxist-Leninist doctrine was being implemented in our country — certain holdovers from the Stalinist perversions, which were later exposed and repudiated at the Twentieth and Twenty-second Party Congresses. Therefore, Sukarno had first been attracted to Yugoslavia as a more liberal country than the Soviet Union.

However, as the years went by, Indonesia drew closer to the Soviet Union. We established economic contacts and helped the Indonesians mine their natural resources. We got to know Sukarno quite well. He impressed us as a good man, well educated and intelligent. Intelligence and education don't always go together. I've known plenty of highly educated people who had no brains, and I've known people without a formal education but with good heads on their shoulders. Sukarno had both schooling and brains. Of course, he had his weaknesses. We didn't always agree with the tactics he used to get what he wanted, and some of his actions were simply inexplicable; but that's to be expected from a bourgeois leader. I'd like to recount here in some detail my encounters with Sukarno and Indonesia.

We were hoping to receive an invitation to visit Indonesia, and it came. I was named to lead our delegation. As a rule, Comrade Gromyko accompanied me on all my state visits. We flew to Indonesia aboard one of our Il-18s. We stopped off in India and Burma on the way and finally landed on the island of Sumatra.[3]

We were greeted by huge crowds and with much pomp, in a man-

ialism and warned that the Afro-Asian countries "are no longer the playthings of forces they cannot influence."

3. Khrushchev spent twelve days in Indonesia in 1960.

ner appropriate to our rank. President Sukarno welcomed us to Indonesia. He obviously loved big ceremonies and celebrations. He had a theatrical streak in him. This was one of the weaknesses I spoke of a moment ago. For example, when the Indonesian government began making requests to us for economic aid, Sukarno seemed particularly anxious for us to help him build an enormous stadium. I was rather surprised. A fancy stadium seemed like a waste of money for a country as backward as Indonesia.

"Why do you want a stadium?" I asked Sukarno.

"As a place to hold public rallies," he said.

We gave him the technical personnel and credits he asked for, and when I arrived in Indonesia, Sukarno took me to see how the construction was coming along. He wanted the public to know that he, too, participated in the work, so he got the two of us to fool around with a pneumatic hammer for the photographers. Sukarno had a theatrical streak in him, and, frankly, it lowered him somewhat in my eyes. Of course, Nehru, too, gave speeches and appeared at public meetings, but you'd never find Nehru building a stadium at great expense just so he could have a bigger audience.

I recall another example of Sukarno's love for pompous displays and grand processions. After we arrived in Jakarta, he suggested, "Why don't we take an excursion and see how our peasants live? We'll organize a reception in a village and put on a show of Indonesian folk art for you."

I agreed. Soon it was time to leave, but Sukarno was late to pick me up. I waited and waited. Finally, Sukarno came for me, and we drove out of the city. Only then did I realize what had caused the delay. Sukarno had arranged for the road from Jakarta to the village to be lined with peasants cheering and waving as we went past. I didn't like that at all. I admit that when I was in the leadership, we also used to lay on such welcomes for our guests, and sometimes the people who took part did so against their will. Nevertheless, I don't approve of that method of greeting official visitors.

As Sukarno and I drove along, he didn't offer me a chance to get out of the car until we reached a tiny village. I was shocked by the wretchedness of the houses and the villagers. People lived in bamboo shacks and slept on rags instead of beds. The women standing around were dressed only in tattered skirts. They had no blouses. They covered themselves only from the waist down. Their breasts were completely exposed. Some of them were holding babies in their arms. I remember one woman was nursing her baby at her breast. She wasn't young or beautiful like the women described by the poets. I remember a passage from *War and Peace* in which Tolstoy talks about how all the young men couldn't take their eyes off Hélène Kuragina's lovely figure and voluptuous breasts. There were no such women in the Indonesian village I visited. On the contrary, it was an ugly and unpleasant scene. I felt sorry for these pathetic people.

We drove on farther to a town where a pageant was performed for us. It was a procession representing the ages of man. First came a group with a newborn baby, then a wedding party, and finally a funeral. The pageant reminded me of a print by Sytin called "Man's Life from Birth to Death," which I used to see on the walls of peasant houses in my childhood.[4] The people in the procession were dressed up in picturesque costumes, and they all looked fairly prosperous. Perhaps only wealthy people were allowed to participate in the pageant. In general, though, the Indonesians struck me as being terribly poor. Fortunately, they live in a warm climate and need only a roof over their heads to shelter them from the sun and rain.

Personally, I found the climate almost unbearably hot, damp, and sticky. There were fans everywhere — in the bedrooms, the dining rooms, the halls where meetings were held — but the heat was still stifling. I felt like I was in a sauna bath the whole time. My underwear stuck to my body, and it was almost impossible to breathe. On top of that, there were mosquitoes everywhere; the only way to keep them away was to wear netting. In short, I found Indonesia hard for a European to get used to, especially for someone from Russia, which of course is in the northern part of Europe.

In this regard, I was fascinated to watch Sukarno. He didn't perspire at all when I was dripping. One day we had to fly somewhere. As soon as the airplane took off and climbed to its cruising altitude, the air became cooler, and I felt as though I were back in my native element. I could breathe freely again. I looked over at Sukarno and saw he was bundled up in every piece of clothing he could lay his hands on, and he was shivering.

"What's the matter with you?" I asked.

4. I. D. Sytin was a publisher and lithographer of the late nineteenth and early twentieth centuries.

"I'm freezing," he said. "How can you stand this cold?"

It just goes to show you: everything's a matter of habit.

While I found the heat oppressive and the air stuffy, I thought the scenery and wildlife in Indonesia were beautiful. I particularly remember the area around Bogor, where President Sukarno had a palace.[5] The building itself had been the residence of a Dutchman, the former governor of Indonesia. It was spacious and luxurious, much more so even than Livadia Palace in the Crimea; and it was surrounded by a vast lawn trimmed in the English manner.[6] The grass was so green it reminded me of the peasant celebrations I'd seen in my childhood around Easter, when nature would be bursting out all over and man would be full of joy at the passing of winter.

I felt there was a certain rhythm in nature around Bogor. At three o'clock in the afternoon there would be a tropical downpour for about an hour. Then the sun would come out and make the drops of water glitter on the grass. Sometimes a few dozen deer would come out from the forest and graze on the lawn. There were other, more unusual animals, too. I noticed some black objects hanging from the trees. When I asked what they were, I was told, "Wait and see. Around five o'clock they'll fly away."

They were flying foxes — something like our bats. They were nocturnal animals, and when they flew through the evening air, they looked as black as rooks, only bigger. I asked what they ate and was told that the peasants considered them a pest because they attacked fruit trees and picked them clean.

Walking through the woods near the palace, I saw two huge apes — orangutans, I believe — chained to a tree. I went closer to have a look. They just sat there with sad expressions on their faces. They seemed resigned to their misery. I felt sorry for them. Later I said to Sukarno, "Why do you keep those apes chained up out there? It makes a very bad impression." I forget how he answered but he didn't do anything about them.

Not far from the palace was a natural history museum. I was of-

5. Bogor, where Sukarno frequently spent his weekends, is forty miles south of the capital, Jakarta.

6. Indonesia's independence from Holland was proclaimed in 1945, but the Dutch did not accept the new country's sovereignty until December, 1949. Livadia Palace was a tsarist seaside retreat in Yalta and the site of the 1945 talks among Churchill, Roosevelt, and Stalin. Khrushchev says he lived at Livadia for a while in 1948, when Stalin summoned him to spend his vacation in the Crimea.

fered a chance to go there for a tour, and I accepted with pleasure. I was told that the founder of the museum had been a German and that he'd spent dozens of years in Indonesia building up his collection of reptiles, insects and other animals. All kinds of butterflies were there — butterflies of every imaginable color. My son Seryozha collects butterflies and had asked me to bring him back some from the various countries I visited.[7] I often asked my bodyguards to catch some for me, and they in turn would ask the Indonesian security men. So these guards would be running around at night with nets, and they came up with some interesting specimens. When President Sukarno learned that my son collected butterflies, he too began running around trying to catch them. I saw him do it with my own eyes. He was a good-natured man and didn't mind us joking about how the President of Indonesia went butterfly-hunting for Khrushchev's son.

Sukarno arranged for us to fly to an island where he wanted to show us the mightiest lizards on earth.[8] They looked like mythical dragons or prehistoric dinosaurs. We stood by and watched while they stalked around in a pit and devoured the carcass of an animal. Maybe some people like that sort of thing, but I didn't care much for it. Since then I've seen an excellent French documentary film showing these extraordinary animals in their natural habitat.

My tour of Indonesia also included numerous meetings, rallies, and speeches. Sukarno was a good orator, and he obviously relished speaking publicly. I, too, gave a number of talks. I remember one in particular. It was on an island ruled by a hereditary king where the government had build an educational institution of some kind, either a technical college or a university.

We had worked out a plan for our political activity and decided the topics of all my speeches in advance. I used my speech to the Indonesian students as an occasion to announce the founding of a new university in Moscow to give an education to people who had liberated themselves from colonialist oppression. The university cost us a hefty sum, but it was worth it. Later it was named after Lumumba, who was brutally murdered by the colonialists and who, by giving

7. Khrushchev's son Sergei was with him on his 1960 Asian tour, as were his daughters Yulia and Rada, and Rada's husband A. I. Adzhubei, editor of *Izvestia*. This family contingent was a steady part of Khrushchev's entourage during his trips abroad in his last years of power.
8. The island of Komodo is the home of the so-called Komodo Dragon.

his life in the struggle for independence, became a symbol in the eyes of his people.[9]

Our major consideration in setting up the university was that the United States, England, and France were all educating their own cadres in their colonies so that they would have a reservoir of young people they could rely on for the future conduct of their colonialist policies. We thought there was a need for a school to educate anticolonialist cadres, cadres who would be familiar with Soviet culture and the Communist world view. As a country which had recently liberated itself from colonial rule, Indonesia seemed like a logical place to unveil our plan.

I attended many banquets in Jakarta, and I was introduced to wonderful dishes which I'd never had before. I was particularly interested in a certain fruit called a *durian*. Like a walnut, it had a thick, meaty skin covered with a prickly rind, although it was much bigger than a walnut — about ten centimeters long. Inside, the fruit was a pale yellow. The first time I was served a durian, I noticed that the Indonesians sitting around me were smiling and whispering to each other, as though something funny were about to happen. Sukarno took a bite out of a durian and then offered it to me. I lifted it to my mouth and was suddenly overcome by the foulest, most repulsive smell — an odor like rotten meat. However, Sukarno had eaten it, and it would have been impolite for me not to taste it at least. I wouldn't say the taste was delicious, but it was tolerable — as long as you held your nose to block out the smell. I was told that the smell of the one I'd been given was nothing compared to the stench a freshly peeled durian exudes. The Indonesians usually peel the fruit in the kitchen and then set it aside until the worst of the odor evaporates.

I decided to treat my friends back in Moscow to this exotic delicacy. We'd just established regular flights between Moscow and Jakarta, so I told my security guards to send cartons of durian to all the members and candidate members of the Presidium. Since our plane flew to Moscow by way of Delhi and Kabul, I gave instructions for cartons to be delivered to Nehru and the King of Afghanistan as well.

Later Nehru and the King thanked me, but said they'd had to

9. Patrice Lumumba, leader of the Congolese National Movement and first Premier of the Congo was killed in January, 1961.

On a visit to the city of Jogjakarta, Khrushchev addressed the students at Gadjah Mada University.

throw out the fruit I'd sent them because it was rotten. My comrades on the Presidium told me the same thing. I laughed and replied that the fruit wasn't rotten at all — that it was supposed to stink.

At one point during my stay in Indonesia, Sukarno took me for a few days to Bandung, the site of the Bandung Conference. The place is a resort for Indonesian political figures of governmental rank. I don't know whether mere mortals are even allowed to visit there. Bandung is high up in the mountains. Because of the elevation, the air is fairly cool.

When our plane landed, Sukarno said, "Mr. Khrushchev, I know you're an atheist, and I don't believe in God either; but we're just going to have to be patient because, according to Indonesian tradition, the local priests are going to greet us here. The island population is divided between two religions, so there'll be two priests. They'll read prayers and conduct rituals, but they won't touch us. If you don't mind, I'd appreciate your going through with this since it will make a good impression on the people — it will help your image and mine, too."

I said I didn't mind. I was a bit curious to see what was going to happen. At first, one of the priests started murmuring something in Indonesian. He sounded exactly like one of our Orthodox priests. Then he was joined by others, and the whole ritual began to sound like the mating calls of a flock of lyrebirds. The asphalt under my feet was so hot I felt as though I were on a frying pan. I tried standing first on one foot, then on the other. Meanwhile the priests droned on and on. I looked over at Sukarno. He was standing there patiently. As I've already said, he was accustomed to the heat, and maybe his shoes were better insulated than mine. I whispered to Sukarno's interpreter, "Wouldn't it be possible to shorten this ceremony?" and he passed my request on to Sukarno. Sukarno made a sign with his hand, and within minutes the priests wound up the service, blessed us, and left.

During our stay in Bandung, there were a number of parties with orchestras playing native music. Sukarno was a very sociable man. He loved to dance. He loved to dance so much that he made everyone else dance, too. I wouldn't say that I never dance — it's just that I don't know how. When I was a young man, I was too shy to dance, though I liked to watch other people dancing and, even if I stood on the side, I always secretly wanted to participate. The only dance I knew was one that was popular in the Donbass when I was young. Everybody joined hands and danced around in a circle. We also used to have dances in which couples paired up, but I didn't care for those. I thought they were monotonous.

The first night in Bandung Sukarno stayed up dancing until he was about to collapse. The second night I warned him in advance, "Mr. President, I'm not going to take part this evening; I'm tired, and I just don't feel like it."

"You must! If you don't join in, others will be offended." But he had a smile on his face, and I could tell he thought I must have been joking.

Later, while the tables and chairs were being removed to make room for a dance floor, I said, "Mr. President, I don't want there to be any misunderstanding. I was being serious when I warned you earlier: I really am too tired to dance. I want to go and rest now."

He looked at me with an expression of surprise, said good night, and walked off. I went to bed, but the rest of our delegation stayed. I believe Gromyko was the number one dancer on our side.

We also had two doctors with us. One was Comrade Markov, the chief of the Fourth Medical Department — that is, the Kremlin Department. He was a good comrade and a good doctor. I think he was an ear, nose, and throat specialist. We'd anticipated that members of our delegation might develop respiratory problems in the tropical climate, and it turned out to be prudent of us to have included a doctor.[10] Our other doctor was a woman. While we stayed in Bandung, she accompanied part of our delegation to the seacoast, about fifty kilometers away.

The next morning over breakfast I noticed that Sukarno, who'd finished dancing about the time I'd awakened, looked as though he were suffering from a head cold himself. "Mr. President," I said jokingly, "you obviously need medical assistance. You've already met Comrade Markov, but we have another doctor, too — a beautiful woman. She's not here. She's gone to the coast with the rest of our delegation."

"Really?" He perked up his ears.

Around lunchtime I learned that Comrade Markov, even though he

10. Professor A. M. Markov, senior official of the Soviet Health Ministry and Khrushchev's principal physician on his travels abroad.

was the senior medical officer accompanying our delegation, had been sent to the coast, and the woman doctor had been brought to Bandung. Sukarno couldn't have cared who outranked whom, and Markov chivalrously gave up his place to his woman colleague. That night, there she was, dancing with President Sukarno. Later, I joked with her about what it was like to dance with the President of Indonesia. She smiled and said, "He's a lot of fun." I could hear a note of conceit in her voice. She obviously felt as though she were coming up in the world.

However, Sukarno never danced with just one woman. He danced with literally every woman in sight. Even if a girl first refused, he'd press her onto the dance floor — although he always did so very politely and tactfully. I couldn't help feeling that Sukarno had a weakness for dancing. On the one hand, he was just being a good host. On the other hand, he seemed to me to be a bit too passionate about this kind of entertainment. And it wasn't just dancing with women that he had a weakness for. He loved women. He couldn't have enough of them. His reputation was scandalous. He simply couldn't control his passion for them. I'd read about his weakness in the special reports that TASS compiled for the Party and government leadership. Some people explained to me that Sukarno's behavior with women was typical of Moslems. Others said it was his particular idiosyncrasy. Whatever the truth, his enemies mocked him for it.

We had difficulty understanding how a man with such habits could be allowed to hold a lofty and responsible post. His affairs with women certainly discredited him in international circles, and I think they were used against him in his own country, although I'm told that Moslems look through their fingers at such matters.

In any case, I myself saw plenty of evidence of this peculiarity of Sukarno's. I remember that one time when we were watching a musical performance, a group of lovely girls appeared and started to dance. Sukarno turned to me and asked, "Which one do you like best?"

"I like them all. They're exceptionally beautiful young women." Then I added, "I think they're dressed nicely, too."

"Well, I like that one there."

"Yes, she's very attractive, but so are the others." I was trying to let him know in a polite way that I didn't want to continue this line of conversation, but Sukarno couldn't get enough of such talk.

Another time he and I went for a walk near some ponds. He spotted a woman washing herself and her child nearby. I could see she didn't have on a bathing suit. Sukarno immediately started walking toward her. I didn't know what to do. I tried to protest, but Sukarno said, "Oh, don't give it a thought. Here in Indonesia it's perfectly all right."

While I walked off and watched from some distance, he went up to the woman. He took her child from her and talked with her for a moment. Then he rejoined me.

"What kind of a business was that?" I asked him. "In our country we consider it indecent for a man to go near a naked woman with a baby. Don't you know there are women in our delegation who would be terribly offended?"

"I just wanted to hold the baby in my arms," he said. He was just saying that. I knew perfectly well he really wanted to have a closeup look at the woman without any clothes on. He also tried to persuade me that Indonesian women didn't mind men seeing them undressed, but I think the whole incident revealed more about Sukarno's personal traits than it did about Indonesian social customs.

However, I don't want to give the wrong impression. I want people who read my memoirs to draw the correct conclusions. Like all of us, Sukarno had certain human weaknesses, but in general, I liked him very much and greatly respected him for the courageous and praiseworthy role he played in Indonesia's political development. Later, after the massacre, Sukarno's situation became very tragic. His own life was threatened, and he was deprived of his ability to influence policy. Nevertheless, he continued to make public statements in favor of the Party's continuing participation in the government. Now that he's been removed from the political scene altogether and put in isolation, I still retain my admiration for the useful contribution he made.[11]

11. The failure of the October, 1965, coup drastically tipped the balance of power against Sukarno; in March of 1966 he was forced to turn over the reins to General Suharto. Sukarno was kept under house arrest until his death in 1970.

Aidit

SUKARNO launched a campaign to incorporate West Irian into Indonesia.[12] Our [moral] support for him was no secret. We issued public statements endorsing Indonesia's struggle to liberate her territory from colonial rule. But as tensions rose, we realized that Sukarno might need material aid as well.

Sukarno threatened to seize West Irian by force if the Dutch refused to negotiate. I familiarized myself with the military preparations Sukarno was undertaking and decided to make our position known. We did so through certain progressive Indonesian generals who had close ties with Sukarno. Unbeknownst to him, some of these generals were even Communist Party members. They reported both to Sukarno as President of the country and to Comrade Aidit, who was General Secretary of the Indonesian Central Committee.[13]

I should say a few words here about the role of the Communist Party in Indonesian life. I forget what Sukarno's own affiliation was, but it doesn't matter because he stood outside and above all political parties. However, throughout his career — to the bitter end, in fact — Sukarno maintained a correct attitude toward the Communist Party. Under him, the Party had its representatives in parliament, and Sukarno even included Aidit in his government. The Indonesian Politbureau impressed me as being made up of sturdy, courageous people devoted to Marxist-Leninist ideals.

The imperialist camp and the wealthy elite of the Indonesian population did everything they could to discredit the Communist Party. However, Sukarno — even if he didn't adopt the socialist program of the Party himself — realized that the Communist Party had won wide support among the working people and peasantry. Therefore he didn't give in to pressure from reactionary, antidemocratic forces.

As I've already indicated, a considerable number of commanding

12. In 1962 Sukarno began pressing his claim to Dutch West New Guinea, or West Irian, the status of which had been unresolved ever since Indonesia won recognition of its independence from Holland in 1949.

13. Dipa Nusantara Aidit, General Secretary of the Central Committee of the Indonesian Communist Party.

officers in the Indonesian armed forces were either Party members or Communist sympathizers. This fact further enhanced the authority enjoyed by the Party.

There was a certain amount of tension between Sukarno and the army. I sensed this tension myself during my visit to Indonesia. I remember one banquet at which I was told it would be a good idea if I gave a toast in honor of the air force chief, so I got up and gave a toast.[14] Everyone applauded, but as soon as I sat down Sukarno jumped up and proposed a toast to General Nasution.[15] I felt that Sukarno hadn't been too pleased about my toast [to General Dhani]. I'd even noticed a look of alarm on his face when I mentioned the name of the air force chief. He'd obviously decided, so to speak, to neutralize my toast by making one of his own to General Nasution.

That incident gave me an idea of the special position General Nasution held. He was more than just chief of staff. He was also an influential political figure, one whom Sukarno treated with great caution and deference. I remember Nasution as a relatively young man — about forty years old — well groomed, handsome, and intelligent. In my conversations with him he never openly showed any disrespect, either to me or to the Indonesian Communist Party. But he was not a Communist, nor was he sympathetic to the Communist cause. Behind his mask, he was an enemy of the Party.

What's more, we had reason to suspect that General Nasution was secretly assisting certain pro-American forces that were trying to orient Indonesia toward capitalism. For example, our intelligence service knew that the United States was supplying arms to right-wing rebels who were seeking to overthrow Sukarno. Government forces captured an insurgent leader who was also an American agent. Later we learned from our intelligence service that the prisoner had been released on Nasution's orders while Sukarno was out of the country — in Japan, I believe.[16] Sukarno was always on the move; he

14. The air force chief of staff, Air Marshal Omar Dhani, was among those officers whom Khrushchev categorizes as "Communist sympathizers." In 1965 he worked closely with the Indonesian Communist Party to provide weapons from Communist China for the abortive leftist uprising.

15. General Abdul Haris Nasution, army chief of staff with ministerial rank.

16. Khrushchev is apparently referring here to the case of Allen Lawrence Pope, an American pilot whose B-26 bomber was shot down in 1958 while he was providing air cover for a rebellion against President Sukarno. Pope was captured and sentenced to death. He had been paid by the CIA, but Howard P. Jones, the US ambassador to Indonesia, said that Pope was "a private American citizen involved as a paid soldier of

spent more time abroad than in his own country. He flew from Tokyo to Moscow for private talks with us. At that time, we were receiving information that General Nasution was preparing to stage a coup d'etat and overthrow Sukarno.

"Mr. President," I said, "are you aware that your troops captured one of the rebel leaders, but that he's been let go, apparently under pressure from American intelligence? And are you aware that General Nasution played a decisive role in this affair?"

Sukarno paused for a moment before answering. "Yes," he finally said, "I know all about it. In fact, Nasution was acting on my instructions. We had our own reasons for releasing the man."

"Well, I simply wanted to share with you the information we've received."

What else could I say. I knew Sukarno wasn't telling me the truth, and I think I understood why: he thought it would be better to tell me a lie than to confirm that one of his own officers had done something without authorization. In other words, Sukarno was protecting his prestige and his presidential dignity. He thanked me for my concern and asked me to keep him informed about any developments I thought would be useful for him to know.

Nasution turned out to be instrumental when I felt the time had come to offer Sukarno material aid in his struggle to free West Irian from Dutch colonial rule and unite it with Indonesia. On one of his many trips to Moscow, Nasution signed an agreement with us for military aid.[17] We sold Indonesia on credit a cruiser, a few destroyers, submarines, PT boats, missiles, torpedoes, antiaircraft guns, fighter planes, and Tu-16 bombers. We also agreed to send some of our best naval experts and military advisors to Indonesia, since Sukarno had told us he didn't have enough trained personnel of his own.

Throughout our dealings with him, Nasution skillfully masked his pro-Americanism. Our own military men held him in high regard. But we kept receiving information on him that only confirmed my

---

fortune." Only three days before Pope was shot down, President Eisenhower had denied that the US was supporting the rebellion. In 1962, six months after Robert Kennedy visited Indonesia and appealed to Sukarno for Pope's release, Pope was freed, his death sentence still under appeal.

17. General Nasution, then Defense Minister and chief of staff, headed an arms-procuring mission to Moscow and conducted talks with Mikoyan and Malinovsky in January, 1961.

suspicions. I know Comrade Aidit and the Indonesian Communists didn't trust him, and I don't think Sukarno did either.

Nasution wasn't the only Indonesian political figure about whom we had our doubts and worries. We also had reason to suspect that Sukarno's Foreign Minister, whose name I can't remember, was playing a double game — that while working for the government, he was secretly in cahoots with Sukarno's enemies.[18]

[Subandrio] was one of Sukarno's right-hand men. He'd been ambassador to Moscow for a number of years. I think he replaced Malik, who, according to our information, sided with the reactionary, capitalist forces pitted against the strengthening of Soviet-Indonesian relations.[19]

[Subandrio], on the other hand, was our friend. He wasn't a Communist, but, again according to our information, he was a Communist sympathizer. He had a lovely wife, a singer or an actress, who made a great hit in ladies' circles in Moscow because she could sing Russian songs. After he'd returned to Jakarta to head the foreign ministry, he made a number of visits to the Soviet Union in his capacity as Sukarno's principal foreign policy advisor.

He came to see me just as the dispute between Indonesia and Holland over West Irian was heating up. He said he had a message from President Sukarno. He spoke Russian, so I could talk to him without an interpreter. We met each other man to man and had a free — I thought confidential — exchange of views. He told me that the Dutch were concentrating their military forces in the region of West Irian and that Holland was probably going to fight for control of the island.

I said, "Well, if you don't succeed . . ."

[At this point there is an interruption in Khrushchev's narrative. To judge from what follows, it appears that Subandrio informed Khrushchev that the Dutch had a good chance of winning the war unless the Soviet Union intervened on the Indonesian side. Subandrio probably then obtained from Khrushchev a pledge that the USSR would send Soviet military personnel to Indonesia to man Sukarno's

---

18. This was Foreign Minister Subandrio, who had taken part in the talks between Khrushchev and Sukarno in Bogor in 1960.

19. Subandrio became Indonesia's first ambassador to Moscow in 1954. He returned to Indonesia in 1956 and became Foreign Minister in 1957. Adam Malik was ambassador to the USSR from 1959 to 1962.

Soviet-supplied ships, planes, and other weapons in the war against the Dutch navy. Later, as Khrushchev goes on to say, the Kremlin received information that Subandrio — presumably on Sukarno's instructions — had told the United States about Khrushchev's pledge, thus violating the confidentiality of the Subandrio-Khrushchev talks.]

I have the strong impression that [Subandrio leaked word of the Soviet pledge to the Americans] on Sukarno's orders. Why did Sukarno do it? I think he did it because he wanted the US to know that Indonesia had adequate means to deal with the Dutch navy — thanks to the Russian pilots who were flying Indonesian planes and the Russian officers who were commanding Indonesian submarines. I assume that by making this information available [to the US], Sukarno was hoping the United States would use its influence with Holland to negotiate a settlement rather than fight. That's the game Sukarno was playing.

Why should the United States exert pressure on Holland? First, because the United States, as Holland's NATO ally, would be in a very ticklish situation if the Dutch navy were destroyed by Indonesian planes and submarines under the command of Soviet officers. Also, the United States didn't want to dirty its hands by appearing to support the Dutch colonialists in their oppression of a small, developing people.[20]

Thus, Sukarno cleverly utilized both the Soviet Union and the United States to achieve his goal of getting Holland to back down. In other words, he played off one power against the other. I must say, though, that we felt it was wrong of him not to inform us of his intentions in advance. In any event, while continuing to support the Dutch publicly, the Americans obviously put pressure on them behind the scenes. As a result, Holland submitted to negotiations and agreed to hand over West Irian to Indonesia after some kind of a referendum. Sukarno had achieved his goal without firing a shot. Since armed conflict had been avoided, our advisors who had been training the Indonesians were no longer needed, so they came home.

Thus, with our diplomatic and military assistance, West Irian and Indonesia were united. Later we received information that the peo-

20. That is, the people of West Irian. A treaty between the Netherlands and Indonesia, giving Indonesia administrative control of West Irian (New Guinea), had been signed under UN auspices in August, 1962.

ple of West Irian turned out to be pretty backward and that things weren't going smoothly there. The Indonesian government began experiencing difficulties, probably at the instigation of Dutch and American agents. Later Sukarno launched another campaign for the incorporation into Indonesia of Borneo, an island which the Indonesians called Kalimantan. He never accomplished that goal because there was a military coup in Indonesia and Sukarno fell from power.

I'd already retired by that time, but I followed the developments in the newspapers. The Foreign Minister [Subandrio] fell from his post. He was arrested and sentenced to death. I was disgusted when I read how he behaved at his trial. He implored the judges to spare his life. He claimed that when Sukarno had been making short work of the reactionary Moslem party, he [Subandrio] had been an antigovernment informer. So we'd been right about his playing a double game.[21]

I was much sorrier to hear about the fate of Comrade Aidit. In the first days of the tragic and tumultuous events of 1965, Aidit went into hiding and for a long time managed to stay underground. Then the Polish press reported that Indonesian soldiers had caught him in the jungle and summarily executed him.[22]

What were the real reasons for the coup? The bourgeois press claims that it started when the Communist Party tried to stage a putsch and seize power on behalf of the dictatorship of the proletariat. I can neither confirm nor deny that version of the events because I was already in retirement by then, and our Soviet press carried no definitive statements about what happened. However, on the basis of what I know and from what I've heard on the radio, I personally believe that the Indonesian Communist Party came to a sad end because its leaders followed poor advice from Mao Tse-tung. Aidit was a good Communist, but he lacked will power and common sense. He and his comrades believed in all the right Communist slogans, but their Party was still immature and unprepared. Therefore they easily fell under Chinese influence.

21. Subandrio was sentenced to death for treason in 1967, although the death sentence was later commuted to life imprisonment. Malik replaced him as Foreign Minister.

22. Although previously rumored to have escaped to China, Aidit was captured and executed by an army posse in November, 1965. The "tumultuous events" Khrushchev refers to here were the rightist countercoup and the massacre of tens of thousands of leftists.

I remember that at the World Conference of Communist Parties in Moscow in 1960,[23] Aidit seemed somewhat too flexible at the expense of his principles. He gave a wishy-washy speech that was neither for nor against the policy then being conducted by China, and he abstained from signing the conference resolution.

Soon China began exerting a powerful influence in Singapore and Malaysia, as well as in Indonesia — all countries with sizable Chinese populations and with powerful companies run by Chinese businessmen. I was informed that one or two members of the Indonesian Politbureau were of Chinese origin and held pro-Chinese views.

I remember vividly my last meeting with Aidit. It was in 1964, the year I retired. I argued with him that the Chinese were detracting from the strength of the international Communist movement, that they weren't following a true class policy, and that their thinking was riddled with Trotskyite elements. (Ponomarev sat in on these talks.) [24] While I told him our point of view and tried to make him understand the reasoning behind the resolution of the 1960 Moscow Conference, Aidit just sat there looking at me and nodding in agreement. His agreement took a noticeably passive form. He didn't tell us what *he* was thinking, but I could see perfectly clearly that he was leaning heavily toward the Chinese position. We parted, and he left. From Moscow he flew home by way of Peking. I'd been afraid he wouldn't be able to stand up to Mao — that's why I made a point of talking to him — and I was right. The Chinese welcomed him with open arms. They really gave him the works, as only the Chinese can do, and Mao proceeded to wrap Aidit around his little finger. We were helpless. All we could do was stand by and watch as the Chinese made a big display of how Aidit stood firmly for the Chinese position.

I have to give Aidit his due: he was led astray and, along with his comrades, ended up paying dearly for being deluded by the Chinese — but I believe Aidit was sincere when he chose a pro-Chinese position. After they caught him and put him on trial, he held his head up high when they sentenced him to be shot. He may have lacked a strong will and a sober mind when he allowed himself to fall under

23. This was the 1960 World Conference of Communist and Workers' Parties, at which the Sino-Soviet schism first came into the open.

24. B. N. Ponomarev, a Central Committee official in charge of relations with other Parties. Aidit made a tour of Communist countries, including the USSR and China, in 1963. He left Moscow in July of that year, saying he would like to see a world congress of Communist Parties to help solve the Sino-Soviet ideological rift.

the spell of the Chinese, but he died a worthy death, as a true Communist, without betraying his ideals, his Party, or his class.

Thus, because of the Chinese influence which worked its way into the leadership of the Indonesian Party, many members of the Indonesian Politbureau and hundreds of thousands of other progressive people were murdered. It was a great tragedy and a great shame. If the leadership of the Indonesian Party had acted wisely, showing more resistance to Mao Tse-tung, Indonesia might have chosen the correct course and become a socialist country. It would have been one of the most powerful socialist countries in the world, occupying a strategic place in the struggle against imperialism.

Stopover in Rangoon

AT the time of our visit to Indonesia, we also took advantage of an invitation from General Ne Win to visit Burma. I should say something about the circumstances under which Ne Win had come to power.

Previously, the head of the government [Prime Minister] had been U Nu, but he had been plagued by difficulties. There were strong separatist tendencies among Burma's various nationality groups. Finally, U Nu realized that he could no longer govern, and he asked Ne Win to form a government until new elections could be held. Naturally, U Nu hoped he would be able to return to power after the elections.

Ne Win was head of the armed forces, and we had an unfavorable opinion of the Burmese army. Why? Because the army was fighting against Communist-led guerrillas. However, despite our dislike for the Burmese army, we decided to accept Ne Win's invitation, and we flew to Rangoon.[25]

He arranged a banquet for us at his house, and afterwards we held a discussion on various matters. Ne Win impressed me as an intelligent man and a good politician. He regaled us with stories about the Burmese resistance to the Japanese during World War II. He had nothing but good words for the Communists who had commanded

25. Khrushchev's stopover in Rangoon lasted a day and a half. His hosts were Premier Ne Win and President Win Maung. Khrushchev had visited Burma earlier, in December, 1955, and had met with U Nu at that time.

partisan units in the war. Of course, after the war, the Communists had been the subject of terrorist attacks by reactionary forces; even though the Communists had come out on top in the postwar elections and had been invited to join the government at one point, they had gone underground and prepared to seize power on their own terms later on.

General Ne Win claimed sympathy for the Communist Party and respect for the Communist partisan leaders with whom he had fought side by side against the Japanese, but he criticized them for their refusal to participate in a [coalition] government.

"The Burmese Communists are on the wrong track," he told us. "They've isolated themselves from the people by fighting against our army in the jungle. They have no opportunity to broaden their propaganda among the masses. They should have accepted a legal and open role in the political life of our country when they had a chance."

Ne Win also gave us his evaluation of U Nu. It was negative, and it was correct. He argued persuasively that socialism was the best course for Burma. In general, his statements were close to my own convictions; and I concluded that if he remained in power, Burma would become a socialist country. I should say, though, that I couldn't help thinking that perhaps he didn't really believe what he was saying and that his real goals were very different from what he told me.

Nevertheless, compared to U Nu, whom I'd met and talked with in the past, Ne Win was a breath of fresh air. I was also very impressed by his wife. She was witty, well educated, and altogether a worthy companion for him. She contrasted favorably with U Nu's wife, who was nothing but a peddler, the proprietor of some commercial enterprise. Ne Win's wife told me a lot about Burma. She said she dearly wanted to visit the USSR because she was especially fond of the ballet.

"I've read and heard about the Russian ballet all my life," she said, "and I'd like to visit Moscow at least once."

"You're always welcome to come and visit our theaters," I replied.

"When's the best time to go?"

I explained that our theatrical season is in the autumn and winter, but I warned her that our cold Russian winters were hard on people from warm climates: "I'm afraid you'll have to suffer a little if you want to enjoy our theater." We kidded around with each other. In short, I thoroughly enjoyed Ne Win and his family.

When I got back to the Soviet Union, I told my comrades about General Ne Win. I proposed we suspend judgment about him, despite his campaign against the Communist guerrillas. I said we should find out more about his political views and goals in case it should prove worthwhile to establish contacts with him. We still had a lingering distrust of him. It occurred to us that perhaps his hospitality and soothing words had been meant merely to neutralize our support for the Communist underground movement and to camouflage the reactionary political goals he was actually pursuing.

The elections took place shortly after our visit, and U Nu's party won an overwhelming victory.[26] The new government headed by U Nu continued Burma's old policy of maneuvering between the socialist and imperialist camps. The leaders tried to pretend they were leftists while conducting reactionary policies. They allowed Burma's rich natural resources of oil, gold, and rare minerals to be exploited by foreign forces. The antigovernment and secessionist elements in Burma again gathered strength, creating more difficulties than ever for U Nu. Armed uprisings became increasingly frequent and serious. Finally, there was a coup d'etat. Ne Win seized control, arrested U Nu and the other members of his government, and transferred power from the civilian authorities to the army both in the center and in the provinces.[27] Once again Ne Win became head of the government and the armed forces.

Our attitude toward the coup was restrained. Regardless of the good impression Ne Win had made on us — regardless of his stated convictions about the necessity of socializing the Burmese economy — we continued to regard him with mistrust. We delayed recognizing his government for some time. We wanted to make sure we had correctly assessed what he was up to.

China, however, recognized Ne Win's government right away. Chou En-lai flew there very soon after the coup.[28] We were somewhat perplexed. We couldn't figure out why the Chinese were in

26. The election was held in February, 1960, just after Khrushchev's stopover.
27. The coup took place in 1962. By "center," Khrushchev means the capital, Rangoon.
28. Chou stopped off in Rangoon for talks with U Nu in April, 1960. U Nu and Ne Win visited Peking in the fall. Then Chou was back in Rangoon in January, 1961, to see U Nu, and again in February, 1964, for a meeting with Ne Win.

such a hurry to recognize a military regime that had seized power in a coup.

Later, though, our embassy let us know that Ne Win had proved himself to be sincere in the views he had expressed to us about the direction he would take. We changed our attitude toward him and recognized his government. Our relations with Burma have been improving ever since, and now they're far better than our relations used to be with U Nu.

After I went into retirement, I read in the papers that Ne Win had released U Nu from jail.[29] Since then, U Nu has been pestering the American imperialists to mobilize against the progressive government of Burma. U Nu has shown himself to be a reactionary through and through. He's now completely on the leash of the American intelligence service.

For our part, we've been giving all-out diplomatic and economic support to Burma. If General Ne Win continues to rely on Marxist-Leninist teaching, I'm sure his influence and popular support will grow, and U Nu will fail in his efforts to discredit and undermine Ne Win's enlightened government.

29. U Nu was released by Ne Win in November, 1966, having spent four and a half years in custody.

14

Africa and the Middle East

African Leaders

PEOPLE who come to see me often ask about the development of our country's relations with various African states during the period when I occupied a high position in the Party and the government. It's with great pleasure that I set down here my recollections on that subject.

Our attitude toward all liberation movements stems from the teaching of our great leader, Vladimir Ilyich Lenin, whose theories and tactics opened the way for workers everywhere. The October Revolution lifted the banner not only of our own proletariat in its fight against the capitalist system, but also of all oppressed peoples in their struggle against the crumbling colonialist system.

The first country in Africa to gain its independence from Britain was Ghana. I had several meetings with President Kwame Nkrumah. He was a most interesting, intelligent, and highly educated man, but he didn't have a sufficiently clear perspective on political and social issues. For one thing, he'd been brought up on English culture and had received his higher education in Britain. Even after his country gained its independence, all the officers in the Ghanaian army were still Englishmen. What kind of independence is that? How can a former colony choose its own course of development if the commanding officers in its army are all colonialists?

In a very cautious way, we warned Nkrumah that he ought to do something about his officer corps, otherwise the existing situation could lead to significant difficulties. He seemed to accept our point, but he didn't follow our advice. I can't say what kept him from doing so. I think there were internal restraining forces of some kind — forces which were later his undoing.

Judging from personal conversations I had with him, I'd say that, given more favorable conditions, he might have publicly declared a socialist course for Ghana. But he never made such a declaration, although as time went on he became increasingly confident in the government of the Soviet Union.

I remember his visit to the USSR. At that time Anastas Ivanovich [Mikoyan] and I were vacationing in the Crimea. Nkrumah joined us there and brought his wife. She was a white Arab woman, originally from Cairo, I believe. Once again I warned Nkrumah that unless he rid himself of the commanding officers in his army, he would face a threat from Western capitalists and from internal antidemocratic forces which were gathering strength. He must have taken my words to heart because shortly afterwards he asked us to send him a few officers to serve as consultants for his private security force. We sent the people he asked for, but what could a few men do? Nkrumah's bodyguards couldn't guarantee the stability of the state, especially when the army was in the hands of Englishmen.

Soon we learned that these bourgeois capitalist elements had staged a coup d'etat. They overthrew the Nkrumah government and changed the political system of the country. The new military regime liquidated all the democratic institutions that Nkrumah had created.

At the time of the coup our friend Nkrumah himself was on his way home from China aboard one of our airplanes. He was prohibited from returning to his own country and forced into emigration, so he flew back to the Soviet Union.

Unfortunately, if I can trust the information which has been made available to me, Ghana has been following an antisocialist, pro-Western policy ever since.[1]

Another African country which has experienced a coup d'etat is Somalia, with which we've had good relations ever since it won its independence.[2] I remember that a government delegation from So-

1. Kwame Nkrumah visited Moscow for two weeks in 1961. Shortly afterwards he promoted Ghanians to replace Englishmen as army, navy and air force chiefs. He was overthrown in February, 1966, and died in 1972 in Bucharest, where he was undergoing treatment for cancer.

2. Somalia won internal autonomy in 1956 and independence in 1960.

malia visited the Soviet Union and asked us for arms, which we agreed to supply on very easy terms.

At that time Somalia was involved in a border dispute with Ethiopia, and Emperor Haile Selassie, with whom we had excellent relations, expressed his concern about our sale of arms to Somalia. Thus we were in a rather delicate situation and had to exercise a certain amount of diplomatic flexibility.[3]

Since my retirement, I've learned from the press that there has been a take-over by progressive forces in Somalia. The new leadership has announced that it will maintain friendly relations with the Soviet Union and build its policies on the basis of scientific socialism.[4]

I must say, I don't really understand the mechanics of these African coups. Sometimes, as in the case of Somalia, one progressive regime replaces another. But in other cases, such as I've described in Ghana, a progressive regime is overthrown by a reactionary one. The same thing has happened in Mali. I've read that an antisocialist, therefore necessarily anti-Soviet, military government has ousted our good friend Modibo Keita.

When he was President of Mali, Modibo Keita led a delegation to the Soviet Union. I received him at the Presidium. He was an enormous man, both in height and weight — a real giant. I later saw a photograph of him embracing me during our meeting, and it looks like I'm being hugged by a huge bear.[5]

Compared to the leaders of the other Negro republics that won their independence from France and Britain, Modibo Keita was an interesting and intelligent man. We didn't have to woo him or pressure him into making public statements about where he stood. He chose on his own accord to declare that Mali would follow the path of scientific socialism. I'm only sorry he didn't have the strength to incapacitate the antisocialist forces that eventually brought him down.

As a Communist, I'm confident that despite the setbacks which the

3. The Kremlin sent Deputy Foreign Minister Ya. A. Malik to Addis Ababa in March, 1964, to reassure the Ethiopians on the subject of the USSR's $30 million military-aid program to Somalia.

4. An independent brand of socialism originally propounded by Arab nationalists like Nasser (see *KR*, I, 443–444).

5. Modibo Keita, the President of Mali, visited Moscow in May, 1962; he was deposed in 1968.

With Bulganin in India

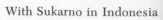

Reviewing plans with Mikoyan in the Crimea

After his fall from power: Khrushchev leaves a school building
in Moscow where he has just cast his ballot
in a municipal election

Khrushchev, in retirement, visits an art exhibition at the
Manège Hall in Moscow with Nina Petrovna and is approached
by the American journalist Robert Korengold,
who asks him a question

With his daughter Rada near Riga, 1947

Sightseeing in the Kremlin with his daughter-in-law
and two grandsons

With his youngest daughter, Yelena

Posing with vacationing workers in the woods
near his dacha, 1970

With his grandchildren

Khrushchev in retirement

cause of progressivism has suffered in both Ghana and Mali, the truth will eventually prevail. Leaders like Kwame Nkrumah and Modibo Keita will rise again and choose the correct path to the future, the path of scientific socialism; and they will serve the interests of the broad masses, the proletariat, the peasantry, and the working intelligentsia.

Before leaving the subject of Ghana for good, I must do justice to Sekou Toure, the President of Guinea. After Nkrumah was overthrown by pro-capitalist forces in his own country, Comrade Sekou Toure gave him a fraternal welcome and created a high position for him in Guinea.[6]

Guinea was the only French colony to vote for withdrawal from the so-called French Community and to win independence without armed struggle.[7] It goes without saying that the referendum by which the people of Guinea determined their destiny did not turn out the way President de Gaulle would have liked. His reaction to Guinean independence is well known from the press. He recalled all his officials, specialists, and civil servants. By depriving Guinea of its entire government apparatus, de Gaulle wanted to force the new country into bankruptcy. The banks were closed, and the economy was paralyzed. The French thought the Guineans wouldn't be able to manage on their own and would have no choice but to return to the French Community.

At this point the Soviet Union, impelled by the ideas of our Great Lenin, gave a helping hand to Guinea. Sekou Toure asked us for aid, and we gave it to him unconditionally. We remembered our own first days of independence and felt it our duty to assist others.[8] We sent both specialists and material assistance.

Comrade Thorez had given us the most glowing report on Sekou Toure.[9] Apparently Thorez had previously had contacts with Sekou Toure in the trade-union movement. Sekou Toure was the head of the Guinean trade unions as well as head of the major political party and the leader of his people. Thorez also told us that Sekou Toure

6. After his overthrow in 1966, Nkrumah sought refuge in Guinea, where President Sekou Toure made him honorary head of state.
7. In September, 1958.
8. By "independence," Khrushchev here means Russia's freedom from tsarist rule.
9. Maurice Thorez was the French Communist leader for over three decades, until his death in 1964 aboard a Soviet ship en route to Yalta. Khrushchev offers more recollections of Thorez in Chapter 17, "The Tour of France."

was associated with the Communist movement. Therefore, when we later met President Sekou Toure on his first visit to the Soviet Union, we called him "Comrade." He made a good impression on us. We could see that here was an educated man with an understanding of the class struggle as well as the struggle for national independence. But something about him put us on our guard. What was it? For one thing, he showed a certain disrespect toward the French Communist Party and toward Comrade Thorez in particular. I was especially offended by his attitude because the French Party was doing everything it could to help the people of Guinea establish their independence. As for Comrade Thorez, he was not only the French Party leader of many years' standing: he was also a fine, upstanding example of the French worker — and, what's more, my colleague in the coal industry. He was a former miner, and that meant a lot to me. To this very day I have a lot of respect for Comrade Thorez, and I was upset by Sekou Toure's attitude toward him in our negotiations.

Later there were other upsetting incidents. The Guineans asked us to build them an airfield capable of handling the heaviest planes. We willingly obliged and sent our specialists down there to build the airfield. Then along came the so-called Caribbean crisis, when military conflict threatened any moment to flare up between the USSR and the United States.[10] Our communications with Cuba took on vital importance. Our planes needed at least one stopover on their way to Havana, but the countries where our planes usually stopped suddenly refused us landing rights.

The airfield we'd built in Guinea would have been a perfect refueling point, but the Guinean government wouldn't let us use it. They tried to justify their refusal on the grounds that "technical conditions" weren't right. We might well have asked, who knew more about the technical conditions — the government of Guinea or the Soviet engineers who built the field? Guinea's action seemed clearly in favor of the United States and contrary to the interests not only of the Soviet Union, but of all peoples struggling for independence. After that incident we no longer trusted Guinea's motives.

During my second round of talks with Sekou Toure in the Soviet Union, he continued to demonstrate a very odd attitude toward the Communist Party of France — an attitude which was later to pop up in the form of attacks on the Soviet Union. I'm thinking here of the

10. In October, 1962.

acute struggle waged by the forces of truth against the forces of false-hood, by socialism against imperialism — in other words, the class struggle.[11]

There were other upsetting incidents. For example, we received information from our embassy that some Guinean leaders were ac-quiring property and amassing vast personal fortunes. I'm not talking about Sekou Toure himself so much as his brother. Even though this was an internal matter in which we had no right to interfere, it disap-pointed us greatly because we'd hoped the Guinean regime would reflect the will and the interests of the Guinean people by es-tablishing a truly socialist system.

Some silly problems also came up, and some of them were our fault. I'm thinking now of what happened when a Soviet teacher whom we'd sent to Guinea refused to come home to the USSR. I don't know what made her stay, but I think it had something to do with sex. Unfortunately, our organization that deals with such prob-lems displayed a certain bureaucratic overzealousness and tried to deliver the teacher back to the Soviet Union. That was a bad move. It was downright stupid. It touched off a full-scale diplomatic skirmish. Sekou Toure and the other Guinean leaders were terribly offended, and I could well understand their annoyance. The incident sug-gested that we were upset because our teacher, a white woman, wanted to live in an African country with a black man.

As far as I was concerned, that was her own business. We've always been free from prejudice on such issues. For us, it makes no difference whether a man is white or black or yellow. What matters is his class affiliation. When I learned what had happened, I was furious. "So what if this woman wants to remain in Guinea?" I said. "So she's found a friend. Maybe he's a worthy man. Let her alone. Let her stay where she is." [12]

Despite such incidents — I'd even say ruptures — in our relations with Guinea, we tried to smooth over our conflicts. We felt that

11. Khrushchev is probably referring here to the USSR's displeasure with Guinea's increasingly close political and economic ties to the US.

12. In the early months of 1963, relations between the USSR and Guinea were so strained that some Guinea politicians were calling for the expulsion of the Soviet am-bassador. One cause of the trouble was the affair of Svetlana Ushakova, a fair-haired Russian teacher who violated embassy rules against forming close friendships with local citizens. Twice Guinean police rescued her from her would-be Soviet kidnap-pers, who tried to smuggle her aboard an Aeroflot flight disguised as a stewardess.

sooner or later Sekou Toure would realize *his* mistakes and see the light. We held on to our hope that we could find with him a common ground for our struggle against capitalist and colonialist oppression.

Relations with the Arab World

OUR relations with the Arab world improved dramatically after 1956, when we intervened to put an end to the English, French, and Israeli aggression against Egypt.[13]

Then we counteracted the US landing in Lebanon, not by military means but by mobilizing world public opinion. The invasion met with outbursts of public protest from all over the world. We also began demonstrative military preparations to show that we would be ready and willing to extend military aid in the Near East if it were needed. We then raised the matter in the United Nations and forced the Americans to withdraw their troops from Lebanon.[14]

At the same time, the Syrian government was conducting an independent policy, which we wholeheartedly supported. Representatives of Syria often came to the Soviet Union, and we sent our delegations there.

Iraq had the most reactionary government of all the Arab states. The government was headed by Nuri Said, a puppet of British imperialism and a faithful dog of the colonialists. Our support of the Iraqi revolution, under the leadership of Kassem further enhanced our prestige in the Arab world.[15]

I'd like to say a few words about Yemen. Even before our visit to England in 1955, Crown Prince al-Badr asked us to give his country military aid and we agreed. As I've already mentioned, the British Minister of War told me in London that a little birdie had whispered in his ear that we were selling arms to Yemen.[16] The little birdie was right. As a result, al-Badr became confident in us, and we continued to help him over the years.

13. For Khrushchev's reminiscences of the 1956 Suez crisis, as well as a detailed account of his relations with Gamal Abdel Nasser, see *KR*, I, 430–451.
14. In July, 1958, President Eisenhower ordered five thousand US Marines to help the Lebanese government quell a rebellion.
15. The regime of Prime Minister Nuri Said fell in 1958, when Abdul Karim Kassem led a leftist coup (see *KR*, I, 438).
16. The conversation with Selwyn Lloyd is reported in *KR*, I, 404.

I had two or three personal meetings with the Prince. I remember the impression he made on me the first time I met him. An enormously tall, well-built, broad-shouldered, handsome man walked into my study. He seemed to be reasonable and intelligent. For the most part, we dwelt on the subject of how much military aid would be necessary for the Yemenites to chase out the British and make their kingdom fully independent.

He asked us to give him economic assistance so that Yemen could build a port. The British wouldn't let them use the harbor in Aden any more. Al-Badr said, "Can you imagine that since ships have to anchor a great distance offshore, all the cargo and passengers have to be carried ashore on the dockers' backs?" We agreed to build a seaport for them.

Yemen was a feudal society. Al-Badr told me how a group of princes had banded together and staged a rebellion against his father, the King, while al-Badr was out of the country. Al-Badr returned home, organized some other princes who supported the King, suppressed the rebellion, and restored order. I didn't know quite what to make of this story. As our people say, horseradish is no sweeter than turnip. I couldn't have cared less who was the king of Yemen.

As far as we could tell, al-Badr's father was conducting the most reactionary policies. Judging from my conversation with him, I expected that al-Badr himself would be more liberal in governing his country.

After his father died, al-Badr ascended the throne. As often happens, a liberal prince became a reactionary king. He turned out to be an extremely cruel leader, a literal slave driver. After a while, the chief of the royal security guard led a palace revolt and overthrew him.

For a long time there were rumors that al-Badr had been killed and buried under the rubble of the palace, but it turned out that by some miracle he had survived. He'd put on woman's clothing and snuck away. I believe they've used that method of escape more than once in the Arab world. For that matter, for whatever it's worth, it's been written that Kerensky borrowed that trick when he changed into a woman's dress and fled at the time of the October uprising.[17] In any

17. At the time of the October Revolution in 1917, Alexander Kerensky, the leader of the Provisional Government, avoided capture at the hands of the Bolsheviks by disguising himself as a sailor (not as a woman).

event, al-Badr organized resistance to the new regime. He had the help of some imperialist countries. I think the struggle is still going on inside Yemen.[18]

We had good relations with the Arab state headed by Bourguiba [19] and also with Morocco. I'll describe later how I met the present King of Morocco, Hassan II, at the United Nations General Assembly, when he was still the Crown Prince. Our short conversation there resulted in favorable developments.[20]

I remember the Moroccan government invited a Soviet delegation to pay a visit. As our representative we sent Brezhnev, who was then Chairman of the Presidium of the Supreme Soviet. He was received by the King. That visit contributed to the strengthening of our relations.

Hassan II is now the King. I read recently that he's going to make a trip to the Soviet Union. While we invite rulers like him and stick to a policy of noninterference in the internal affairs of other countries, we should keep in mind that Hassan won't live forever. History will show what sort of system will ultimately triumph in Morocco. Naturally, we hope it will be a socialist system, because socialism provides the best conditions for the working people.[21]

We have had our disagreements with Morocco. I remember that after the Algerian people won their independence, Morocco began to claim certain border territories. At one point, it looked as though armed conflict was about to flare up between Algeria and Morocco. Our sympathies were with the Algerians.

I had the greatest respect for Ben Bella. He was a highly intelligent man, a great son of the Algerian people. I met him more than once in the Soviet Union; my last meeting with him was when I was President Nasser's guest in Egypt.

18. The Yemen uprising referred to above took place in 1955, when Crown Prince al-Badr rallied loyal tribesmen, defeated an army revolt, and restored his father, Saif al-Islam Ahmad. Al-Badr visited the USSR in 1956.

Yemen lost the port of Aden when southern Yemen split off from the realm in 1958. The Soviets built a deep-water port for Yemen at Ahmedi; it was completed in 1961.

When the King, or Imam, died in 1962, al-Badr ascended to the throne — he lasted for one week — and was then toppled by another army revolt. He escaped into the hills and waged a protracted struggle against the new regime.

19. Habib Bourguiba, President of Tunisia.

20. See Chapter 19, "The United Nations."

21. Brezhnev, in his capacity as chief of state (Chairman of the Presidium of the Supreme Soviet), visited Morocco in February, 1961. He was received by King Mohammed V, who died later that month and was succeeded by his son Hassan II. Hassan visited Moscow in October, 1966.

Unfortunately, the chief of the General Staff of the Algerian army, Boumedienne, later enlisted the aid of several members of the government and carried out a coup d'etat. I don't know for sure what Ben Bella's fate was, but I've read in the press that his mother was allowed to see him and that he's alive and well. It's a shame that he's now doomed to a life of idleness; he's a young man and could have accomplished a lot.[22]

I know from the press that Boumedienne has continued Ben Bella's policies, including the development of friendly relations with the Soviet Union and the other socialist countries. I'm sure Boumedienne is worthy of his post. It's no accident that he's risen so high. He participated from the beginning in the struggle against the French colonialists' occupation of his country.

I don't know Boumedienne personally because whenever he came to the Soviet Union, there was no point in my meeting him. He was interested in military matters and therefore always dealt with Comrade Malinovsky, our Minister of Defense. However, even though Boumedienne has followed sound policies, it's my impression that Ben Bella was more of a politician and had a clearer vision of the path which Algeria should follow toward a better future.

The Six-Day War

I'VE already related how brilliantly we dealt with Egypt, France, and Israel in 1956 at the time of their aggression against Egypt. We took several diplomatic and political steps which made it clear that we were committed to Egypt. We announced publicly in the press that we were recruiting volunteers and advisors to help the Egyptian army. That had an immediate effect on the boss of the imperialists — that is, on the United States — with the result that the Americans put pressure on the British, French, and Israelis, forcing them to withdraw their troops.

Yet eleven years later, in 1967, despite the fact that our military might had increased many times over, we badly mishandled the situ-

22. Algeria won its independence in 1962. Mohammed Ben Bella, Premier and later President of Algeria until 1965, was overthrown by Houari Boumedienne. Khrushchev has described meeting Ben Bella in Egypt in *KR*, I, 443–445.

ation in the Near East and allowed our Egyptian friends to get into a miserable situation. I'd like to give my thoughts on the background of the Arab-Israeli war and explain where we went wrong.

When I was in the leadership, I set both internal and foreign policy to a considerable extent. My record speaks for itself as far as Egypt was concerned. I was categorically against the war which Israel, Britain, and France launched against Egypt in 1956; and we used all our influence and might, all the means at our disposal, to cut short that war in Egypt's favor. But I was also categorically against Nasser's going to war against Israel. And when I was his guest in Egypt for the opening of the Aswan Dam in 1964, I strongly urged him not to try to take on the Israelis again.[23]

"I advise you to stay out of war," I told him. "You don't really want war, do you? You don't really want to destroy Israel? If you do, you're wrong. It's too tough a nut to crack. Israel may be smaller than Egypt, but the Israelis are more advanced. Their army is better trained; they've got more modern weapons. Furthermore, you've placed yourself in such a position that if you do start a war, other countries won't understand and won't sympathize with you. You'd also be placing the Soviet Union in a most awkward position, since, as you know, our country voted for the creation of Israel in the United Nations. I hasten to add that we did so only under pressure and with grave reservations and with many conditions. I don't have to tell you that our Party has never sympathized with Zionism. We fought the Zionists in our country both before and after the Revolution. We've always regarded the Zionists as a bourgeois reactionary party. But that's beside the point. The state of Israel exists, and we must both accept that fact."

Nasser agreed with me. "I don't want war," he said. "I know what my responsibility is. If I make certain [warlike] speeches sometimes, it's just because I'm paying my debt and my tribute to the mood of the people."

That made sense to me. Israel was conducting a reactionary, imperialist policy toward Egypt, and the Egyptians had to arm themselves in case of attack. However, under no circumstances should Egypt start a war. The United Nations sent troops to the Near East, and for a while peaceful coexistence was maintained even though both sides

23. This material supplements Khrushchev's earlier observations of the 1967 Arab-Israeli War in *KR*, I, 450–451.

were armed to the teeth. Then, in 1967, after my retirement, the situation changed.

The Egyptians demanded that U Thant remove the UN troops. I have the highest respect for U Thant; he was more deserving of his post than anyone else.[24] But he had to yield to the Egyptians' demand. Then Egypt closed the Gulf of Aqaba to Israeli shipping. Once that happened, war was inevitable.

I have no doubt whatsoever that Israel started the war. Israel launched the first strike. But it was preventive attack. The Israeli army was equipped with American arms and aircraft, which were technologically superior to the planes we'd given Egypt. Israel also had superior military cadres. The General Staff had served with the Americans, the French, and especially the British in World War II. Some of them, I think, were even former officers of the Soviet army. Moshe Dayan turned out to be a fine organizer and an excellent strategist. He put his advantage to good use.

The Egyptians didn't know what they were up against, and they had to learn the hard way, poor things. They were used to fighting on camels, and they couldn't handle any arms more sophisticated than rifles. As a result, the Egyptian army was routed, and an enormous portion of Egypt was occupied. Fortunately, nuclear weapons weren't used. Israel won the war easily by conventional means.

I think the Soviet Union has to bear a large share of responsibility for what happened. Given our influence with Nasser, given our ability to exert pressure on Egypt, we should have restrained the Egyptians from demonstrating their belligerence. You don't have to be very clever to realize that if someone insists on the removal of a neutral [UN] buffer force between himself and his enemy, he has fairly definite intentions with regard to that enemy. We shouldn't have let Nasser aggravate the tensions that were building up, nor should we have let him provoke the Israelis into striking first. Rather than trying to destroy Israel — a wholly unreasonable goal — Nasser should have used other means to protect the rights of the Arabs living in Israel.

I think our military men, more than our diplomats, are to blame. They should never have let the Egyptians force Israel into betting everything it had on a preventive attack. I have nothing personal

24. Khrushchev offers a more detailed assessment of U Thant below, at the end of Chapter 19.

against Zakharov, but he's an old man who keeps falling asleep in meetings.[25] He and our military had an influential voice in the decision-making which preceded the Six-Day War. They made a mistake by allowing the war to happen in the first place, and they didn't use our might to liquidate the consequences of the war after it was over.

25. For more on M. V. Zakharov, chief of the Soviet General Staff, see the last paragraphs of Chapter 1.

15

Contacts with the West

De Gaulle's Wartime Visit to Moscow

TOWARD the end of the war, de Gaulle came to the Soviet Union. I remembered his name from the press back in the days before the war when he was still a colonel. He'd been an originator of the concept of the tank corps and the mobile armored army.[1] While he may have been a military innovator, our press treated him as a political reactionary.

However, when the war started, de Gaulle emerged as a hero, a worthy patriot, and an irreconcilable enemy of Nazism who refused to lay down his arms until the Wehrmacht was crushed. While the French Communist Party was the principal organizer of the struggle against the Hitlerite occupation, de Gaulle was in overall charge of the resistance from his government-in-exile in England.

It was to de Gaulle's credit that French fliers, piloting Soviet airplanes, fought side by side with our air force against the common enemy. I'm sure de Gaulle had something to do with arranging for a special group of French pilots to make its way to the Soviet Union under wartime conditions. They were organized into the so-called Normandy-Neman Squadron.

I was in Moscow when de Gaulle came to visit. It goes without saying that Stalin summoned me to Moscow, since I never came to the capital [from the Ukraine] of my own accord.

1. In the early 1930's, de Gaulle urged a defense strategy based on a mobile army and air force rather than on fixed fortifications. In his capacity as head of the newly formed French Provisional Government, de Gaulle visited Moscow at Stalin's invitation in December, 1944.

What was Stalin's attitude toward de Gaulle? In general Stalin didn't hold a very high opinion of the military. He was especially scornful of soldiers' ability to understand, much less engage in, politics. He'd implanted in the rest of us the idea that generals in other countries were narrow-minded martinets and dunderheads — pick any epithet you want. As for de Gaulle in particular, Stalin had no special respect for him.

Nevertheless, I could hear the note of pride in Stalin's voice when he told us, "De Gaulle has come." He was proud that this anti-Communist general, this representative of the reactionary forces in France, had taken it upon himself to visit Moscow and pay his respects to the Soviet government. It showed that de Gaulle had a better understanding than the other Western Allies of what had really happened in the war: the West had waited to launch its own landing and open its own beachhead against the Germans until Hitler was barely able to stand on his feet and until his army was already bled white by the Soviet army. The West had been waiting for a chance to sit down at a table and accept Germany's capitulation, which had been won at the cost of vast amounts of blood shed by our soldiers. De Gaulle saw that more clearly than Churchill or the Americans.

I met de Gaulle at a dinner which Stalin gave in his honor. I think it must have been held in Stalin's [Kremlin] apartment, because I remember there were only a few people there. Stalin said that de Gaulle had proposed to sign a treaty with us restoring Franco-Russian relations as they had existed before World War I. I forget the details of the treaty. No doubt Stalin had already worked them out with Molotov.

After dinner, Stalin invited de Gaulle to the movies. He invited all his guests to the movies. Why? Because he liked watching them himself. De Gaulle thanked Stalin but didn't go. He said he wanted to think over certain questions before we signed the treaty.

However, de Gaulle's Foreign Minister consented to watch some movies with us.[2] When we got to the theater, we were served fruit as usual — and, as a special treat, champagne. It was Stalin who ordered the champagne. He also invited the French fliers of the Normandy-Neman Squadron.

Stalin chatted courteously with the pilots, but we could all see that he was slightly drunk. In fact, he was more than just slightly drunk.

2. Georges Bidault. He and Molotov worked out a pact of alliance and mutual assistance.

He was swaying from side to side as he refilled the Frenchmen's glasses with champagne. Beria, Malenkov, Molotov, and I were all present. We kept looking at each other nervously.

Molotov and de Gaulle's Foreign Minister continued their negotiations over the terms of the treaty while we were all gathered in the movie theater. They ironed out any remaining disagreements.

Soon afterwards, de Gaulle and Stalin signed the treaty. Throughout the signing ceremony, de Gaulle behaved with great pride and dignity. You could see he wasn't bowing his head to anybody. He walked straight and tall, like a man who had swallowed a stick. He struck me as being rather aloof and austere.

De Gaulle had already earned our respect as an intelligent military leader. He soon impressed us as a subtle politician. At first, he included Comrade Thorez and the French Communist Party in his government. Then, when he'd gathered enough strength so that he could do without the Communists, he dumped them.

The Soviet representative who had the most contact with France during that period was our ambassador, Bogomolov.[3] After Stalin's death, we appointed Vinogradov to the embassy in Paris.[4] He turned out to be a most flexible diplomat and developed good contacts with de Gaulle even before he became President. The President used to invite Comrade Vinogradov to his estate for political discussions. De Gaulle never refused a request from Vinogradov for an appointment, and they even used to go hunting together.

Harriman and MacDuffie

I NEVER met President Roosevelt myself, but I heard about him from an American businessman named Johnston who told us he had been close to Roosevelt.[5] Administrations come and go, but this man kept his ties with ruling circles in the US. I think he was sometimes entrusted with unofficial diplomatic assignments. He visited the Soviet

3. A. Ye. Bogomolov, the USSR's envoy to the Free French in Algeria, then ambassador in Paris.
4. S. A. Vinogradov headed the Paris embassy from 1953 until 1965. Khrushchev offers more recollections of Vinogradov below, in the account of his 1960 tour of France (Chapter 17).
5. Eric Allen Johnston, president of the US Chamber of Commerce, was in Moscow for eight weeks in 1944; he had three hours of talks with Stalin.

Union at least twice. In American terms, he was a liberal; that is, he believed in peaceful coexistence.

Johnston told me about the origins of what I was later to know as Camp David. "During the war, I went to see Roosevelt and found him looking exhausted," Johnston told me. "I said to him, 'Mr. President, you need a rest.'

" 'What can I do?' the President replied. 'There's a war going on. I can't leave Washington.'

"I suggested he build a place right outside Washington where he could breathe a bit of fresh air and get away from it all."

On the subject of the President's need for a place to rest, this businessman told us a joke which he'd heard from Roosevelt. The joke went more or less like this:

"A farmer gave a farmhand a shovel and told him to go dig a ditch. After a while, the farmhand came back and said he'd finished. So the farmer gave him an ax and told him to go chop some firewood. The farmhand went off and came back with an armful of logs. Then the farmer told him to go sort a pile of potatoes into two smaller piles, one of small potatoes and one of big. Hours passed, but there was no sign of the farmhand. Finally, the farmer went searching for him. He found him out cold in the barn. The farmer poured a bucket of water on him. When the farmhand came to, he explained, 'I don't mind digging ditches or chopping wood, but I can't handle this job of sorting out the big potatoes from the little potatoes. I can't stand all those decisions, decisions, decisions! Give me a job that doesn't require any thinking.'

"After Roosevelt told me this joke, he added, 'Each to his own taste. I can't handle any job which does *not* require thinking and decision-making. That's why I look so drained. But what can I do? There's a war going on.' "

That's the sort of joke Americans like to tell. I don't know whether Roosevelt ever told such a story or whether Johnston just made it up.

Another of Roosevelt's close associates was Averell Harriman. Our information was that Harriman had been one of the President's confidants even before the war. During the war, he was US ambassador to the Soviet Union. He conducted policies that were very much to our liking. He considered it necessary to strengthen our military alliance in order to deal a decisive blow to Hitler, and he did everything in his power as ambassador to support the USSR.

The Hitlerite occupation of our country deprived us of many regions that yielded steel, aluminum, and petroleum. Thanks largely to Harriman, the United States gave us considerable material aid, which allowed us to keep up our production of the arms necessary for victory.

It was common knowledge — I think I even read about it in our press — that Harriman's family used to own some manganese mines in Georgia before the Revolution. I heard confirmation of this from Stalin's own mouth after the war. Harriman had also held an interest in a Canadian company which owned some nickel mines in the Far North, near Petsamo. The Finns seized that area from Russia after the October Revolution, but we subsequently reoccupied it. After the war, Petsamo became part of the Soviet Union because, as Stalin explained, we needed to have a common border with Norway. The region was strategically important because of its proximity to the year-round port of Murmansk, and it was economically important in view of the nickel mines. Besides, the lands up there were historically Russian.[6]

Stalin mentioned in passing that it might be a good idea to compensate Harriman in some way for the loss of his mines. I don't know if anything ever came of the suggestion. I know it wasn't discussed in the leadership. Nothing was discussed in the leadership. Stalin could not stand to have his ideas questioned or deliberated. He might let you talk to him if you agreed with him. Sometimes he just told you to shut up no matter what you were saying.

Despite our excellent relations with Harriman, we had a bitter experience with the Americans over the question of Lend-Lease. They wanted us to pay them a certain percentage of the cost of the aid they'd given us during the war. Stalin quite rightly refused to pay unless we received $3 billion in credits.

I can't be too specific here because I found out only what I happened to hear from Stalin. There were no official documents or reports or memoranda or consultations either in the Politbureau or in the Council of Ministers. As a matter of fact, the Council of Ministers had ceased to exist except as a list of names. If a plan was raised in the Council of Ministers, it was only for rubber-stamp approval.

The situation reminded me of a joke I used to hear from miners in my youth. A priest gets up at the pulpit and shows a huge book to the

6. Harriman and some associates had a nickel concession in Georgia, which was sold to the state in the mid-1920's, but he had no financial interests in the Far North.

congregation. "Have you read this book?" he asks. Everyone is silent. "Good," he says. "Then I don't have to read it either."

That's more or less what a Council of Ministers meeting under Stalin was like. We spent as much time discussing government documents as the congregation in that church spent talking about the book.

Returning to the subject of Lend-Lease, I remember that the United States insisted we return the cargo ships they'd given us during the war. What did the Americans do with those ships after we gave them back? They didn't even bother to take them back to the US to scrap them — they just took them out to sea and sank them then and there. That's how much our former allies cared for the blood we'd shed in the fight against our common enemy.

I'm sure that the Americans' stubbornness and unreasonableness over Lend-Lease had nothing to do with money. Just look how much the United States had made from the war. While all of Europe was being impoverished and laid to waste, the big American monopolies were doubling and tripling their capital, making profits off the blood of Russian soldiers, off the tears of our women and old men.

When the war was over, the Americans saw that we had not only survived and defeated the strongest army, but that we were going right ahead and reconstructing our industry. They felt threatened and decided to do everything they could to impede our progress. If possible, they wanted to drive us into bankruptcy, thus wiping socialism off the face of the earth.[7]

The United Nations set up an organization to aid the countries which had suffered from Hitlerite occupation. The overall head of the organization was La Guardia, the mayor of New York.[8] He'd been a friend of Roosevelt's. He made a trip to the Soviet Union, and I arranged a reception for him in Kiev. He was of Italian nationality.

La Guardia seemed to like our country and did all he could for us. However, his help often didn't square with our needs. I'm referring to the kinds of supplies the West kept trying to give us. The Americans sent us leftover consumer goods from the war, particularly canned beef. What we really needed, though, was machinery.

After a while, we got them to sell us machines for laying and

7. For more of Khrushchev's views on Lend-Lease and Stalin's relations with the Allies, see *KR*, I, 220–226.

8. Fiorello La Guardia, director-general of the United Nations Relief and Rehabilitation Agency, met Stalin in Moscow in August, 1946.

insulating gas pipelines. Our own specialists had never seen such equipment. We took the machines we'd purchased from the West and used them as technological samples for manufacture in our own factories.

Not long after the war, La Guardia died, and the UN relief agency was disbanded.[9] However, I continued to see something of the American who'd come to the Ukraine. He came back to the Soviet Union, and I received him. His name was MacDuffie.[10] I remember well what Mr. MacDuffie said to me on his second visit to the Soviet Union: "Mr. Khrushchev, if you could only come to the United States and let the American people have a look at you — let them see that you're a human being. They think Soviets are practically subhuman. Our people are already beginning to forget that you fought side by side with us to defeat Hitler."

Unfortunately, MacDuffie was right. The honeymoon was over. We were already in the thick of the Cold War — the ideological war in which Churchill fired the first shot with his notorious speech at Fulton.

The Origins of the Cold War

I HAVE already dictated in my memoirs some thoughts and recollections on the measures we took after World War II in the field of defense: the strengthening of our army, navy, air force, missile system and nuclear arsenal. However, preserving the impregnability of our defenses required more than just building up the Soviet Union's own armed forces; it also required certain concrete steps in our relations with the fraternal countries. After the war we could rightfully say that we had broken the ring of capitalist encirclement around our country. No longer was the Soviet Union the only socialist country. Now there were many socialist countries in Europe and Asia, altogether accounting for one third of the world's economic output. This was a consoling and inspiring thought for all Communists who had been fighting with such dedication for socialism and justice.

9. Both events occurred in 1947.
10. Marshall MacDuffie, head of the UNRRA mission to the Ukraine in 1946; he resigned in protest against US legislation barring UNRRA funds from countries which censored American correspondents.

We'd come a long way from the early period of Soviet power when the United States waited thirteen years before President Roosevelt finally decided to recognize the existence of our State and establish diplomatic relations with us. I remember I used to remind foreign journalists of how stupid the United States had been — and I also remember how the journalists replied: "Mr. Khrushchev," they said, "you shouldn't be so upset about the United States waiting thirteen years to recognize the USSR. Don't forget tsarist Russia waited for *twenty-six* years before it recognized the United States after it gained independence from England." [11] They had a point, of course, but it didn't refute mine. It was only natural that the reactionary government of the tsars should treat any state called a republic as dangerous and seditious. Therefore, the Tsar could not bring himself to recognize the United States. But why should the United States have the same attitude to the Soviet Union?

Even after Roosevelt granted us diplomatic recognition, the United States continued to blockade and isolate us. This policy was not only unfair to us: it was harmful to the US as well, for the Americans could have benefited culturally, economically, and scientifically from more normal relations with the Soviet Union. But American politicians were deaf to all reasonable arguments. Reactionary forces remained antagonistic to us after the war, and if anything, they were stronger than before. While our industry had been demolished by the Germans, the United States had grown richer than ever. Representatives of big monopolistic capital had made money off of war production and, to put it crudely, stuffed their bellies full of stolen goods. Assembly lines in the United States were operating in high gear, producing all kinds of top-quality products — including powerful military equipment. Our country, on the other hand, was stricken by famine; food was still rationed. True, our army had gained formidably in quantity of troops and in quality of command. But our industrial capacity was too devastated and our material resources too depleted for us to withstand another war.

The thought of another war was far from the minds of the English, French, and other European peoples who had just emerged from the war against Hitler — and who recognized the Soviet Union's con-

11. Tsarist Russia recognized the US in 1809, twenty-six years after Francis Dana of Massachusetts and his secretary, the young John Quincy Adams, tried and failed to win recognition from Empress Catherine II. The US recognized the Soviet Union in 1933.

tribution to Hitler's defeat. But certain statesmen in the West had short memories. They began to conduct policies which put a strain on the friendship we tried to preserve with our former allies. Some politicians, particularly in England and the United States, were already preparing for the possibility of a new war.

Our postwar relations with the capitalist countries were damaged severely by that arsonist and militarist Churchill. His famous speech urging the imperialist forces of the world to mobilize against the Soviet Union served as a signal for the start of the Cold War. Churchill gave his speech in a small town called Fulton.[12] It hardly matters where in the United States the town is; but it was extremely significant that, of all the times and places he could have given that speech, he chose to give it during a visit *to America*. We knew that if there were to be another war, we would find ourselves confronted with a coalition of Western countries led by the United States. Furthermore, the Cold War was sure to profit big American monopolistic capital. Therefore Churchill's choice of an American platform made his speech all the more threatening to us.

It was largely because of Churchill's speech that Stalin exaggerated our enemies' strength and their intention to unleash war on us. As a result he became obsessed with shoring up our defenses against the West. Stalin remembered that it was Churchill who, before World War II, called the Soviet Union a "colossus on feet of clay" and thus encouraged Hitler to hurl his troops against our country, promising him an easy victory. Of course, that same phrase had been used by many people in many languages before Churchill.[13] Now here was Churchill at Fulton, making the same noises again. As far as Stalin was concerned, Churchill's speech marked a return to prewar attitudes.

Our relations with England, France, the USA, and the other countries who had cooperated with us in crushing Hitlerite Germany were, for all intents and purposes, ruined. We dropped all pretense of friendship. We stopped rejoicing with our allies over our common

12. In March of 1946, President Harry S. Truman introduced Winston Churchill to an audience at Westminster College in Fulton, Missouri, saying, "I know he will have something constructive to say." Churchill then proclaimed that an "Iron Curtain" had "descended across the Continent" and urged an Anglo-American "fraternal association," or military alliance, against the USSR.

13. In fact, the originator of this particular term of derision for Russia was Emperor Joseph II of Austria (1741–90), who called Russia "a colossus of brass on a pedestal of clay."

victory and began to regard them with anxiety and suspicion. Stalin was convinced the West was deliberately creating tensions, and he assumed that another war was not only possible, but inevitable.

By then Roosevelt — who had always treated us with such understanding — was dead, and the United States was headed by Truman, an aggressive man and a fool. His policies reflected his stupidity and his class hatred. He was vicious and spiteful toward the Soviet Union. He had neither an ounce of statesmanship nor an iota of common sense. I can't imagine how anyone ever considered him worthy of the Vice-Presidency, much less the Presidency. The whole world knows from the newspapers how he once slapped a journalist for criticizing his daughter's singing. That incident alone told us something about Truman's statesmanship, to say nothing of his suitability for so important a post as the Presidency of the United States.[14]

All this might sound rude, but under Truman and his equally obstinate and aggressive Secretary of State, that political half-wit Mr. Acheson, American foreign policy was calculated to provoke and bully us from a position of strength.[15] The Americans had the atomic bomb, and they knew we didn't. They did everything they could to demonstrate their superiority over us. Their air force was the best in the world both in quality and the quantity of its planes. American Flying Fortresses and Superfortresses had played a big part in winning the war against Germany and Japan, and they were still unmatched by any other planes in the world. I would even say the Americans were invincible at that time, and they flaunted this fact by sending their planes all over Europe, violating borders from one end of the continent to the other. Not only did they overfly the territories of the German Democratic Republic, Czechoslovakia, Bulgaria, and the other socialist countries — they violated the air space of the Soviet Union itself, mostly along the Baltic coast and in the north near Murmansk.

Since we had troops stationed in Poland and Hungary at the end of the war, Stalin took an active personal interest in the affairs of that part of Europe. His interest became obsessive when the United States began its repeated overflights of the socialist countries. The rest of us in the leadership were careful not to poke our noses into these matters unless Stalin himself pushed our noses in that direc-

14. This paragraph also appears in *KR*, I, 361–362.
15. Dean Acheson was Secretary of State from 1949 to 1953.

tion. He jealously guarded foreign policy in general and our policy toward other socialist countries in particular as his own special province. He had never gone out of his way to take other people's advice into account, and this was especially true after the war. The rest of us were just errand boys. Stalin would snarl threateningly at anyone who overstepped the mark.

Adenauer's Visit to Moscow

AFTER Stalin's death, Adenauer and his colleagues thought at last they would be able to achieve their principal goal — the incorporation of the German Democratic Republic into the Federal Republic of Germany and the creation of a single capitalist German state. Adenauer was encouraged in this plan by his allies. He was hoping to use economic leverage against us. [West] Germany had already gained considerable economic might and was in a position to extend credits to the Soviet Union — money we badly needed in order to buy modern industrial equipment that was available neither in our own country nor from any other socialist state.

So we knew what to expect when Adenauer came to Moscow. We knew that the tycoons in Germany would be trying to use Adenauer's visit as a means of cutting a window for access into Russia, since trade with Russia would be profitable for German capitalism.[16]

For our part, we welcomed Adenauer's visit as an opportunity to rectify the abnormal situation which existed between our countries.[17] The meeting was arranged by mutual initiative, and we hoped it would prove to our mutual benefit.

Adenauer was accompanied by Kiesinger, who was Chancellor until the last Bundestag elections, and by Arnold, Schmid, and Hallstein. Hallstein had worked out a well-known doctrine.[18] Here's how

16. At Soviet invitation, Chancellor Konrad Adenauer visited Moscow in September, 1955. Khrushchev's remark about Adenauer's "cutting a window for access into Russia" is a turn of a familiar phrase often applied to Tsar Peter the Great, who is described as having "cut a window into Europe" by establishing broad commercial contacts with the West.

17. The "abnormal situation" was the absence of a peace treaty.

18. Kurt-Georg Kiesinger, Karl Arnold, Carlo Schmid (the Social Democratic leader referred to later in this section), and Walter Hallstein, State Secretary for the West German Foreign Office. The so-called Hallstein doctrine held that the Federal Republic would be entitled to sever relations with any country recognizing the East German state.

it worked: The Yugoslavs had signed a treaty with West Germany when their relations with the other socialist countries were very bad; but as soon as the situation normalized,[19] the Yugoslavs recognized the German Democratic Republic, and the Federal Republic of Germany automatically broke its ties with Yugoslavia. Comrade Tito deserves credit for resisting West German pressure and for dealing a blow to the Hallstein Doctrine. Later, West Germany reestablished relations with Yugoslavia, so the Hallstein Doctrine failed to accomplish anything.

The major issue dividing the Soviet Union and the FRG was the matter of a peace treaty. Both the [East] Germans and Adenauer were in favor of liquidating the technical state of war that still existed between Germany and the Soviet Union. A treaty would allow us to establish diplomatic relations with Bonn, then develop economic and cultural ties.

As we expected, Adenauer told us that the German government was ready to extend credits to us and also to pay us the reparations, or compensations as they may have been called, they owed us according to the Potsdam Agreement. He was talking in terms of something like 500 million West German marks. The mark was a highly valued currency at that time.

And what did Adenauer want in exchange? He wanted the German Democratic Republic. We had to set him straight by making clear, first, that we were not going to interfere in the internal affairs of the GDR, and, second, that it was in our ideological interests not to liquidate, but to strengthen, the GDR.

The GDR was our ally. We had a strategic, economic, and political — as well as an ideological — stake in its independence. To allow [West] Germany to create a single capitalist German state allied with the West would have meant for us to retreat to the borders of Poland. That would have been a major political and military setback. It would have been the beginning of a chain reaction, and it would have encouraged aggressive forces in the West to put more and more pressure on us. Once you start retreating, it's difficult to stop. In short, Adenauer's initial bargaining terms were wholly unacceptable to us.

We still wanted some sort of agreement to come out of the meet-

19. The "normalization" between Moscow and Belgrade came about in 1955 on Khrushchev's initiative. See "Burying the Hatchet with Tito," *KR*, I, 374–391.

ing. Both sides pressed hard for their goals. As I recall, both at the conference table and in private talks, Arnold, who was a trade unionist for Adenauer's party, and Schmid, who was a Social Democrat, demonstrated a sincere interest in normalizing our relations. But Adenauer was in full command of the German delegations and Kiesinger was his right-hand man. For our part, we demonstrated great firmness and told the Germans they could expect no concessions from us.

At one point, we rejected a specific proposal made by Adenauer, and he announced that his delegation would break off negotiations and go home the next day.[20]

I said, "Well, I deeply regret that we can't reach an agreement. It will harm both sides if we fail to come up with a treaty. Certainly, it would damage the Federal Republic if our negotiations fail. However, that's your business. You may leave whenever you wish."

We were fully prepared for the Germans to leave the following day without the usual treaty-signing ceremony. However, at the last minute, Adenauer and his delegation sent word that they weren't leaving and that they wanted another meeting with us. So their threat of leaving had been a bluff. It had been meant to test us, to see how firmly we held our position. They thought perhaps we were too frightened to let a technical state of war continue between our countries. But they were wrong.

In the end, it was Adenauer, not we, who felt forced to continue the negotiations. The talks resumed, and we agreed on the draft of a mutually acceptable document.

At one point, the German delegation hinted that Charles Bohlen, the American ambassador, was trying to get Adenauer not to agree to the treaty.[21] We'd known and liked Bohlen back in the days when he was a close associate of Roosevelt's; he'd been Roosevelt's personal

20. The deadlock arose over the question of the USSR's continued detention of German prisoners of war.

21. Charles Bohlen, US ambassador to Moscow from 1953 to 1957. In his own memoirs, *Witness to History,* Bohlen accuses Adenauer of "arrogance" in his dealings with him and "buckling" under Soviet pressure: "I had told Adenauer and members of his entourage my feelings [that the West Germans should not accept the Soviet conditions for recognition] both before and after the Soviet offer, while emphasizing, on instructions from Washington, that the decision was up to the Chancellor. I also felt that it was a mistake for a leader of a country to go to Moscow to make a deal on diplomatic recognition, and I said so. Adenauer was trapped into accepting a less than satisfactory agreement. Someone on his staff, which was deeply divided, told him about the reservations I was expressing to Washington, and Adenauer denounced me before American newsmen for 'poisoning' the atmosphere."

interpreter at Teheran and in the Crimea [Yalta]. However, later, when he became ambassador to the Soviet Union, he turned out to be a shameless reactionary who supported all the most hateful policies then being conducted by antagonistic forces in the United States. He pulled every dirty trick he thought he could get away with. Rather than improving US relations with us, Bohlen succeeded in freezing them.

Now here was Bohlen again, trying to knock the spokes out of our wheels. He did everything he could to stall and sidetrack our negotiations with Adenauer. I can't say for sure whether Bohlen was following instructions from Washington, but it seems plausible to me that he might have been acting on his own to block any improvement in our relations with West Germany. He knew that such an improvement would diminish American — and therefore his own — influence on the Bonn government.

Perhaps Adenauer, too, suspected that Bohlen was acting on his own, so he urged us to hurry up and sign the revised draft of the treaty before Bohlen had a chance to see it and before Bohlen's superiors started applying pressure directly from Washington. Adenauer may have been a faithful servant of West German capitalism, but he resisted the meddling by Bohlen.

Adenauer seemed gleeful about resuming the talks and reaching an agreement in spite of Bohlen's attempted interference. Later I was informed that Bohlen was furious with Adenauer. But by then it was already too late — the agreement had already been signed.

Of course, Adenauer's motives had nothing to do with any noble sentiments about peace or friendship. Our treaty was strictly business. The expanding German economy was looking for new markets. The desire for profits on the part of German capitalists therefore overrode the United States' opposing desire to keep the Soviet Union in a state of isolation. We were able to break the American blockade because the prospect of our commercial contracts appealed to German business interests. Later I received representatives from Krupp and other big German firms.

What more can I say about Adenauer? For one thing, he was capable of the most oily flattery. I remember he once said to me — I forget in what connection — "Oh, Herr Khrushchev, this could happen only as a result of your benevolent influence and great wisdom." He was forever saying that kind of thing in front of other people.

Also, he liked to lean over to me and whisper extravagant courtesies in my ear during banquets. I found such behavior disagreeable and undignified coming from a statesman of his standing. Either he was petty-minded himself, or he assumed other people were petty-minded.

Nevertheless, I have to give our departed enemy credit for his intelligence and his common sense. Whenever journalists attacked him and accused West Germany of being an aggressor bent upon unleashing another world war, Adenauer always pretended to be a perfect little Christ. "I don't know what you're talking about," he would say. "If World War III were to break out, West Germany would be the first country to perish." Adenauer was absolutely right, and I was pleased to hear him say it. For him to be making public statements like that represented a great achievement on our part. Not only were we keeping our number one enemy in line, but Adenauer was helping us to keep our other enemies in line, too.[22]

Adenauer was also a worthy representative of German capital. He had to be in order to maintain his political support and keep winning elections for all those years. I remember his asking me, "Herr Khrushchev, do you think the German workers vote for the Social Democrats? No. The majority of them vote for me." Unfortunately that was true. To give him his due, he laid the foundations of the Christian Democratic Party, which still has great influence in Germany.

Once Adenauer overheard Schmid address me with the German word for "Comrade." Adenauer smiled sarcastically. After that, he, too, started calling me *"Genosse* Khrushchev." So I called him *"Genosse* Adenauer" back.

During his visit to the Soviet Union, Adenauer presented me with a wonderful souvenir — a pair of Zeiss binoculars. They're light and powerful. I often take them with me when I go for walks. When I meet people, I sometimes show them the binoculars and mention that they were a gift from Adenauer. That always makes people do a double-take. I wouldn't say that they're any better than the ones we produce in the Soviet Union or in the German Democratic Republic, but I have to admit that I find them handier than any of the other binoculars I have. Thanks to them, I can see more of the fields, forests, and meadows that make the landscape around Moscow so

22. This paragraph also appears in *KR*, I, 517.

beautiful. Thus, with a little help from Adenauer, I've been able to broaden my horizons. You could say that I have two mementos from my meeting with Adenauer — my binoculars and my memories.

John Foster Dulles

CHURCHILL took the initiative in suggesting a summit meeting before we were really ready. He later explained that he'd wanted to convene a conference with the new Soviet leadership immediately after Stalin's death — before the corpse was cold, so to speak. He thought the West could wring some concessions out of Stalin's successors before we had our feet firmly on the ground.

We went to Geneva hoping to reach an agreement that would not only be mutually beneficial to those countries represented at the meeting, but to all countries in the world. We wished to defend international peace. Churchill, however, had other fish to fry. He wanted the summit to benefit only himself — that is, the West: Great Britain, the United States, and France. Even though he was already retired, his unrealistic ideas dominated the meeting. Certainly his influence on the proceedings was greater than Eisenhower's.

Eisenhower was very much under the influence of [John Foster] Dulles, an aggressive man who had a physical revulsion against the Soviet Union and an ideological hatred for everything new, everything Communist, everything socialist. This hatred stayed with him to the end of his days. He was famous for coming up with formulations on how to oppose us. His best-known formula for foreign policy was to approach the brink of war but never overstep it. Of course, that attitude is outdated now.

I should say we were of two minds about Dulles. On the one hand, we considered him to be our number one ideological enemy. On the other hand, he proved more than once that he didn't really want war. For example, American foreign policy was in his hands when we intervened to put an end to the English, French, and Israeli aggression against Egypt in 1956. Despite his obsession with politically and economically isolating the Soviet Union, Dulles showed great caution and helped avoid a real catastrophe in the Near East. Even when the United States sent its paratroops and marines into Lebanon, Dulles was intelligent enough not to allow the conflict to develop into war. He also showed restraint when we came into a near-conflict with the United States over Syria.[23]

On those occasions and others, Dulles was a worthy and interesting adversary who forced us either to lay down our arms or marshal some good reasons to continue the struggle. It always kept us on our toes to match wits with him.

I think I've already mentioned my conversation with Nehru about Dulles when I led the Soviet delegation to the United Nations General Assembly.[24]

"Did you actually shake hands with Dulles?" Nehru asked.

"Yes," I said. "Just imagine! We not only greeted each other, but I was seated next to him at a dinner which Eisenhower gave in our honor."

Nehru smiled at me in that special warm, calm way of his and said, "I can't get over the idea of Khrushchev sitting next to Dulles. And did you talk to each other?"

"Yes, but our conversation wasn't very deep. It consisted mostly of short questions and short answers. We were just trying to be polite. I think we spent more time talking about the food than anything else. 'Do you like this dish?' Or, 'Delicious, don't you think?' — that kind of thing."

Even though I sometimes called Dulles a chained cur of imperialism or a faithful dog of capitalism, I knew the day would come when we would find a good word to say for him.

When he died, Gromyko was at a meeting in Geneva. The other participants all went to Dulles's funeral. We recommended that Gromyko go, too. After all, what's wrong with having our representative attend the funeral of our number one ideological enemy? Under the surface of my argument, I was making a more weighty and serious historical point. But Gromyko resisted. I tried to persuade him he was making a mistake — that his attendance at such a ceremony wouldn't be unpleasant. But he wanted to stay behind in Geneva.[25]

After Dulles's death, I often commented to friends that we should miss him, that the day would come when we would have a good

23. This was at the time of the tension between Syria and Turkey in 1957 and Syrian initiative for the formation of the United Arab Republic in 1958.

24. See *KR*, I, 397–398.

25. Dulles died in May, 1959, while the four-power Foreign Ministers' Conference on Berlin was under way in Geneva. Despite his apparent reluctance, Soviet Foreign Minister Gromyko joined Christian Herter, Selwyn Lloyd, and Maurice Couve de Murville and flew to Washington for the funeral. The four met with Eisenhower, and Gromyko was their spokesman at a news conference afterwards.

word to say about him. I was only half-joking. He may have been an enemy, but he had the common sense never to overstep that "brink" he was always talking about.

Nixon and the Kitchen Debate

NOT long before President Eisenhower invited me to visit the United States, the Americans organized an exhibition in Sokolniky Park. Mr. Nixon, the Vice-President of the US, came to Moscow for the opening.[26] The exhibition wasn't very successful. The organizers were obviously not serious about displaying American life and culture; they were more interested in drumming up a lot of propaganda. Our official representatives who attended the opening informed me about what the Americans had come up with, but I decided to go have a look for myself. For one thing, I was curious about new artistic styles that were catching on in the US. My curiosity had been touched off before the exhibition even opened, when I went around to watch the Americans putting up their pavilion: they assembled the whole thing from prefabricated sections that had been manufactured in America. This seemed like a novel and sensible way of constructing buildings.

No formal decision was required for me to visit the exhibition; anyone from the leadership who wanted to go was free to do so. So I simply showed up. All sorts of diagrams and photographs were on display. Everything was laid out attractively to impress the public. But it was all too showy and promotional. The objects being exhibited didn't really have anything to offer to our people, particularly our technological personnel, our Party members, and our leadership. One should realize that we were quite demanding in our attitude here: for us, the major consideration was the usefulness of a product or an item. In this regard, the American exhibition was a failure. The things on display might be aesthetically pleasing but they were of no earthly use. And, I might add, some of them weren't even aesthetically pleasing. For instance, there were a lot of paintings and pieces

26. In July, 1959, Vice-President Richard Nixon arrived in Moscow   open the American National Exhibition. He and Mrs. Nixon were on an official ·   ıt to Poland and the USSR.

of sculpture in a style which the Americans consider modernism. Most of these didn't impress me much. In fact, I found them revolting. Some of them were downright perverted. I was especially upset by one statue of a woman. I'm simply not eloquent enough to express in words how disgusting it was. It was a monster-woman, all out of proportion, with a huge behind and grotesque in every other way.

As I walked through the arts section the American journalists kept pumping me with questions. They knew perfectly well how I felt about this kind of art, and they were baiting me. I told them, "How would this sculptor's mother feel to see how he depicts a woman? He must be abnormal in some way, a pervert or a pederast. No man who loves life and nature, who loves women, could depict a female this way!"

Maybe some people like this sort of art. Every society passes through a stage in its development when all sorts of strange ideas are born: some are progressive, others are regressive, but some are just plain perverse.

With Nixon accompanying me, I moved on to a display supposedly showing a typical American kitchen. I began to inspect some of the appliances. There were some interesting things, but there were also a number of things which seemed purely for show and of no use. Once I commented on this I had swallowed the hook and was caught in a lengthy conversation with Nixon which newsmen would refer to for years to come as characterizing Soviet-American relations. The conversation began like this: I picked up an automatic device for squeezing lemon juice for tea and said, "What a silly thing for your people to exhibit in the Soviet Union, Mr. Nixon! All you need for tea is a couple of drops of lemon juice. I think it would take a housewife longer to use this gadget than it would for her to do what our housewives do: slice a piece of lemon, drop it into a glass of tea, then squeeze a few drops out with a spoon. That's the way we always did it when I was a child, and I don't think this appliance of yours is an improvement in any way. It's not really a time-saver or a labor-saver at all. In fact, you can squeeze a lemon faster by hand. This kind of nonsense is an insult to our intelligence."

Well, Nixon disagreed, and he tried to bring me around to his way of thinking, arguing in that very exuberant way of his. I responded in kind. I have my own way of being exuberant in a political dispute. The debate began to flare up and went on and on. The newsmen

pressed around us with their tape recorders going and their microphones shoved into our faces. After a while I put a direct question to
him: "Mr. Nixon, you've brought all this wonderful equipment here
to show us, but have you really put it into widespread, practical use?
Do American housewives have it in their kitchens?" To be fair to
him, Nixon answered honestly that what they were showing us
hadn't yet come onto the market. At that point people burst out
laughing. I said, "Hah! So you're showing off to us a lot of stuff
which you haven't even introduced in your own country! You didn't
think we'd figure that out; you thought you'd get us to ooh and ah
over all this junk you've brought here!"

Of course, what we were really debating was not a question of
kitchen appliances but a question of two opposing systems: capitalism and socialism. The Americans wanted to impress Russians with a
lot of fancy gadgets. They were sure that Russians wouldn't know the
difference if the exhibit included some things which most American
housewives have never laid eyes on. To a certain extent the organizers of the exhibit may have been right about this. They wanted
the Russians to think, "So, this is the sort of equipment they have in
capitalist countries! Why don't we have such things under socialism?" That was the idea, anyway, unrealistic as it may have been. As
for Nixon, he was behaving as a representative of the world's largest
capitalist country. I'm not saying that America doesn't have great
riches, as well as technological skills and inventiveness. Of course it
does: what's true is true. I'm just talking about the exhibit, which
consisted mostly of a bunch of photographs, some household products you won't find in any household, and some pieces of sculpture
which were good for nothing but laughing and spitting at.

One day Nixon decided to visit our produce market. There he met
one of our workers and for some reason offered him a sum of money.
The worker made a big point of refusing; he really told Nixon off.
Our own press did a good job of informing us about Nixon's meeting
with the worker; our papers had already influenced the thinking of
the Soviet people in the right direction so that they knew what to expect from Nixon and the US exhibition in Sokolniky Park. As for the
bourgeois press abroad, it had fun with the "Khrushchev-Nixon
Kitchen debate" for many years afterwards.

So much for my first personal introduction to Richard Nixon. Naturally I'd known of him from the press since long before because he'd

occupied a special position among American political leaders. We considered him a man of reactionary views, a man hostile to the Soviet Union. In a word, he was a McCarthyite.

However, I'd like to add a final word about Nixon. When I was already in retirement, Nixon and his wife came to the Soviet Union. He was touring around the country, traveling on a tourist visa. He passed through Moscow before returning to the United States.[27] After he'd already flown away, I learned that he and his wife had found out where my apartment was and had tried to come see me. He thought I was living in the city and wanted to call on me. He was told I wasn't there. To be honest, I very much regretted missing him. I was touched that he would take the trouble. I was especially touched in view of the fact that our relations had always been tense. On the occasions we met we rarely exchanged kind words. More often than not we bickered. But he showed genuine human courtesy when he tried to see me after my retirement. I'm very sorry I didn't have an opportunity to thank him for his consideration, to shake hands with him and his wife.

27. While on a tour of Europe with a group of industrialists, Nixon made a brief, unplanned trip to Moscow in April, 1965, and sought out Khrushchev at the retired Soviet leader's apartment. But Khrushchev was at his dacha in Petrovo-Dalneye at the time. Khrushchev is mistaken in one respect: Mrs. Nixon was not with her husband on his private visit to Moscow in 1965.

16

Eisenhower and the American Tour

IN 1959 an invitation to visit the United States came out of the blue. Here's how it happened.

A delegation of influential American industrialists, some of whom probably had close ties with the Eisenhower government, came to the USSR to look into certain branches of Soviet industry, particularly shipbuilding. We let them see the atomic-powered icebreaker we were building at the time. After they finished their tour, they invited us to send our own delegation to see shipyards in America. We accepted the invitation with pleasure. Contacts like this helped relieve tensions between the United States and the Soviet Union and were in the interests of both sides. We included Comrade Kozlov in the delegation.[1] He was a metallurgist by training, but for many years he had been Secretary of the Leningrad Regional Party Committee and therefore was familiar with shipbuilding.

As Kozlov later told me, he and our engineers were given a look at a nuclear-powered ship the Americans were building. He managed to crawl around inside it and examine it thoroughly. Naturally, the Americans showed us only what they wanted us to see, but Kozlov told me our engineers nonetheless noticed a number of interesting things. As our delegation's visit was drawing to an end, a courier from the President got in touch with Kozlov, gave him an envelope, and said, "Give this to Khrushchev." Our delegation flew home. When he arrived in Moscow — I think it was on a Sunday — Kozlov

1. First Deputy Premier F. R. Kozlov visited the US in June, 1959. He was given a tour of the Camden, New Jersey, shipyard, where the first nuclear-powered freighter, the *Savannah*, was being built. A month later, during his visit to the USSR, Nixon insisted that Admiral Hyman G. Rickover, who was traveling with the vice-presidential party, be allowed to inspect the Soviet nuclear-powered icebreaker *Lenin* as closely as Kozlov had inspected the *Savannah*.

called me at my dacha outside of town and said, "I have a special message for you from President Eisenhower."

The contents were brief. The President invited me to pay a friendly visit to the United States. I must say, I couldn't believe my eyes. We had no reason to expect such an invitation — not then, or ever for that matter. Our relations had been extremely strained. Yet here was Eisenhower, President of the United States, inviting Khrushchev, the Chairman of the Council of Ministers of the Soviet Union and the Secretary of the Central Committee, to head a government delegation on a friendly visit. (Eisenhower addressed me only by my title of Chairman of the Council of Ministers, though of course he knew I was head of the Party as well.)

America had been boycotting us completely, even to the point of issuing a special ban on the purchase of crab meat from the Soviet Union. They said our goods were manufactured by slave labor. It sounds crazy, but there really was such a law. They also refused to buy our caviar and vodka, even though connoisseurs in the US think ours is the best in the world. In the past we had sold anthracite coal to the Americans, but they put a ban on that, too.

And now, suddenly, this invitation. What did it mean? A shift of some kind? It was hard to believe. It occurred to us that part of the reason may have been that public opinion in the United States had begun more and more to favor an improvement in relations with the Soviet Union. Eisenhower was being forced to listen to voices in democratic circles and in the business community which advocated concrete measures to reduce tensions.

I'll admit I was curious to have a look at America, although it wouldn't be my first trip abroad. After all, I'd been to England, Switzerland, France, India, Indonesia, Burma, and so on. These were all foreign countries, but they weren't America. America occupied a special position in our thinking and our view of the world. And why shouldn't it? It was our strongest opponent among the capitalist countries, the leader that called the tune of anti-Sovietism for the rest. Take the economic blockade of the USSR: whose idea was that? While some of America's partners were already willing to enter into certain economic contacts for the purchase of our raw materials, the United States was still holding out. No wonder we were interested in a firsthand look at our number one capitalist enemy.

A decision had to be made on how to respond to Eisenhower's invitation. The Presidium of the Central Committee met in the Kremlin to consider the matter. We decided in principle to accept it with thanks. But that left us with a problem. We had previously received an invitation from the Scandinavian countries to make an official visit there. Where should we go first? According to etiquette we ought to visit first the countries which had invited us first, but of course we were more eager to visit the United States.

We had a ready excuse for postponing our visit to Scandinavia. The bourgeois newspapers there were raising a storm of protest against their governments for having invited me. As I recall, they were abusing me by name. So we decided to inform those countries we would put off our visit because their press was creating an atmosphere unfavorable to our presence.

We instructed our ambassador to Washington, Comrade Menshikov, to make all the necessary arrangements for our trip.[2] As preparations got under way, some questions came up which began to worry us. First, how would we be received? Was I to be officially welcomed as our head of state or head of government? (My position was head of government — the head of state would be the Chairman of the Supreme Soviet.) The Americans reassured our ambassador that they would treat me with maximum honors.[3] Still, there was some concern on our part that we might encounter discrimination, that our reception might not correspond to the requirements of protocol in keeping with our rank. Some of our worries turned out to be justified.

We made a series of demands about how we expected my arrival in Washington to be arranged. On some points we may have gone a little overboard; but nonetheless we wanted to emphasize from the outset that we knew there would be a temptation to discriminate against us, and we wanted to guard against any such discrimination.

The Americans agreed to our conditions. The date of my arrival in Washington was set, and my schedule was arranged.[4] The time came to determine the composition of our delegation. Naturally Comrade Gromyko, the Minister of Foreign Affairs, was included. I remem-

2. M. A. Menshikov, ambassador to Washington from 1958 to 1961.

3. Strictly speaking, Khrushchev, as Chairman of the Council of Ministers, was head of government but not head of state; the Soviet head of state is technically the Chairman of the Presidium of the Supreme Soviet — at that time, K. Ye. Voroshilov. After some haggling between the Soviet Foreign Ministry and the US State Department, it was agreed that for purposes of protocol Khrushchev was coming "in the capacity of head of state."

4. The trip lasted thirteen days in September, 1959. Khrushchev visited seven cities.

bered that when Bulganin and I visited England, we took Kurchatov with us, so this time I suggested we include a writer who could establish contacts with American literary circles. Of course Comrade Sholokhov's name came up. He was an obvious choice, although we knew he had a weakness for drink. I'd talked to him about it in the past. Once he came to me and said, "I've been invited to Norway, but the authorities won't let me go." I explained it wasn't because he was politically untrustworthy; rather, we were afraid he'd lose his wits and stumble about, perhaps inflicting physical injury on himself and moral injury on our country. He promised to restrain himself, so we let him go. He visited a number of countries — England, Sweden, Norway, and Finland — and we didn't receive a single report against him from our ambassadors there. In such a case they would certainly have reported his making a fool of himself. Since Sholokhov had a resounding reputation as a novelist both in the Soviet Union and abroad, we decided to include him in our delegation to the US.

The question came up of whether or not to take our wives. When Bulganin and I went to Geneva and London, we left our wives at home. Leaving them behind was one of our legacies from Stalin's time. Stalin was very suspicious of anyone who took his wife on a trip with him. I can remember only once when he made Mikoyan go somewhere with his wife. In general, we had always considered it unbusinesslike — and a petty-bourgeois luxury — to travel with our wives. I was planning to go to America alone. It was Mikoyan who first suggested that it might make a better impression on the general public abroad if I took Nina Petrovna and some members of my family.[5] I had my doubts, but all the rest of the leadership supported Anastas Ivanovich [Mikoyan], and finally I gave in. We suggested that Andrei Andreyevich [Gromyko] bring his wife as well.

Since we in the leadership had been up to our ears in internal problems, we had a lot to learn about the United States. For example, when informed by our embassy in Washington that a certain number of days in our schedule had been set aside for meetings with the President at Camp David, I couldn't for the life of me find out what this Camp David was. I began to make inquiries from our Ministry [of Foreign Affairs]. They said they didn't know what it was ei-

5. The family members in his entourage was his wife, his son Sergei, his daughters Yulia Gontar and Rada Adzhubei, and his son-in-law A. I. Adzhubei, the editor of *Izvestia*.

ther. Then we turned to our embassy in Washington and asked them what it was. One reason I was suspicious was that I remembered in the early years after the Revolution, when contacts were first being established with the bourgeois world, a Soviet delegation was invited to a meeting held someplace called the Prince's Islands. It came out in the newspapers that it was to these islands that stray dogs were sent to die. In other words, the Soviet delegation was being discriminated against by being invited there. In those days the capitalists never missed a chance to embarrass or offend the Soviet Union. I was afraid maybe this Camp David was the same sort of place, where people who were mistrusted could be kept in quarantine.

Not even our embassy in Washington could tell us for certain what Camp David was. We had to make special inquiries and get someone to research the problem. Finally we were informed that Camp David was what we would call a dacha, a country retreat built by Roosevelt during the war as a place for him to get away for a rest. Far from being an insult or an act of discrimination, I learned it was a great honor for me to be invited to spend a few days at Camp David with Eisenhower.

We never told anyone at the time about not knowing what Camp David was. I can laugh about it now, but I'm a little bit ashamed. It shows how ignorant we were in some respects.

The day of our departure was drawing near. We had to decide how we were going to make the trip. By boat it would take too long. If we flew in an Il-18 we'd have to make a number of stops along the way. We could always fly in a foreign plane, but we knew it would make a better impression if we took one of our own planes. The only one we had which could reach Washington nonstop was the Tu-114. It had already attracted a lot of attention in the world of technology. It had a larger passenger capacity, longer range, greater thrust, and faster cruising speed than any other. However, Tupolev had been testing it and found some problems. Cracks or something were appearing from time to time and causing some concern. I decided to have a talk with Tupolev.

"I'm absolutely certain you won't have any trouble," he said. "The plane's performance is quite reliable, but let me send a couple of my technicians with you just in case. I'd like to show you how much confidence I have in this plane, so, if you'll allow me, I'll send my own son, Alyosha, with you."

"I couldn't ask for more than that," I replied. "I'll take your word for it. I don't need any guarantees. I certainly don't need to take your son as a hostage on the flight. If something catastrophic happens, it won't matter to me who else dies. I'm going to fly in this plane because I trust you."

However, in the end we did take Alyosha with us because he knew the plane inside out and would have been useful to have on board if anything unexpected had happened. Besides, both Andrei Nicolayevich and Alyosha himself wanted the boy to have a look at the United States. We didn't publicize the fact that Tupolev's son was with us; to do so would have meant giving explanations, and these might have been damaging to our image.[6]

We carefully calculated how long the flight from Moscow to Washington would take. A special ceremony was planned for us on our arrival, and we couldn't afford to be late, nor did we want to land too early. We could always circle a few times over Washington in order not to arrive before the scheduled time, but if we were late it would be a blow to our prestige.

As you can see, I had a lot on my mind when we took off from Moscow and headed West. We flew over Scandinavia and out over the ocean. The flight was smooth and relatively quiet, although the hum of the engines made it difficult to sleep. We weren't used to the noise, but after a while I was able to force myself to relax and finally dropped off. It was important that we be rested when we arrived in Washington the next day.

When I woke up the sun had come up. All sorts of thoughts went through my head as I looked out the window at the ocean below. It made me proud to think that we were on our way to the United States in our new passenger plane. Not that we worshipped America. On the contrary, we'd read Gorky's description of capitalist America in *The Yellow Devil*, as well as Ilf and Petrov's *One-storied America*, and we knew about all its perversities.[7] Besides, I'd met some Americans during the first years after the Civil War, when I came home

---

6. As it turned out, A. A. Tupolev, the designer's son, did not travel incognito; his presence in the Khrushchev entourage was acknowledged. Nor was Khrushchev the first Soviet official to fly to the US aboard the Tu-114; Kozlov had done so three months earlier, bringing the senior Tupolev with him.

7. I. A. Ilf and Ye. P. Petrov collaborated on numerous satirical stories, novels, and plays, including humorous travel notes on their 1935 trip to the US, which provided many Soviets with their image of America and Americans.

Maxim Gorky wrote *The City of the Yellow Devil* after a trip to New York in 1906.

from serving in the Red Army and went to work in the Rutchenkov mines as a deputy director. Some miners came from the US to help us. That was my first contact with the working man's America. I'd heard from American workers themselves about the US, and I knew it was no paradise.

No, the reason we were proud was that we had finally forced the United States to recognize the necessity of establishing closer contacts with us. If the President of the United States himself invites the Chairman of the Council of Ministers of the USSR, then you know conditions have changed. We'd come a long way from the time when the United States wouldn't even grant us diplomatic recognition. We felt pride in our country, our Party, our people, and the victories they had achieved. We had transformed Russia into a highly developed country. The main factors forcing the President to seek improved relations were our economic might, the might of our armed forces, and that of the whole socialist camp.

I won't try to conceal that subconsciously we had some other thoughts and feelings as well. I was pondering my coming meeting with Eisenhower. I'd met him twice before — on May 9, 1945, when Stalin introduced me to him at our victory celebration after the defeat of Germany, and in Geneva.[8] But this would be different. I would be meeting with him man to man. Of course, I wouldn't be completely on my own: Andrei Andreyevich Gromyko would be with me. I respected Gromyko then, and I respect him now, as a fine Foreign Minister. But I wouldn't be able to start whispering questions back and forth with him in the middle of my talks with Eisenhower. I'd been very disdainful of the way Eisenhower had let Dulles shove notes in front of him all through our negotiations in Geneva, and I didn't want to do the same sort of thing myself. It's not that I was frightened, but I'll admit that I was worried. I felt as though I were about to undergo an important test.

We'd already passed the test in India, in Indonesia, and in England. But this was different — this was America. Not that we considered American culture to be on a higher plane than English culture, but American power was of decisive significance. Therefore our task would be both to represent our country with dignity, yet treat our

8. For a description of his two previous meetings with Eisenhower, see *KR*, I, 222, 395–399.

negotiating partner with respect. You shouldn't forget that all during Stalin's life, right up to the day he died, he kept telling us we'd never be able to stand up to the forces of imperialism, that the first time we came into contact with the outside world our enemies would smash us to pieces; we would get confused and be unable to defend our land. In his words, we would become "agents" of some kind.

As all these thoughts rushed through my mind, I didn't let myself get depressed — in fact, the opposite was true: the challenge of the situation helped me mobilize all my forces to prepare for the meeting. I was about to meet with the leader of the country which represented the biggest military threat in the world and to discuss with him the major issues of our times: peaceful coexistence, an agreement on the ban of nuclear weapons, the reduction of armed forces, the withdrawal of troops, and the liquidation of bases on foreign territories. I was also looking forward to establishing contacts with the American business world. Even Stalin had been interested in obtaining American credits. We wanted the Americans [9] to call off the trade embargo against the Soviet Union and other socialist countries. With so many matters to be negotiated, problems were bound to arise. Naturally, we also expected to meet with representatives of the Communist Party of the United States, though we didn't anticipate any difficulties or disagreements there.

In the midst of these thoughts I was informed that we were approaching the United States. We had begun to circle and were about to land. In a few minutes we would be face to face with America, the America which I'd read about in Ilf and Petrov and Gorky — now I'd be able to see it with my own eyes, to touch it with my own fingers. All this put me on my guard, and my nerves were strained with excitement.

The weather in Washington gave us a wonderful welcome. The sky was sunny and the air warm. Looking out the window as our plane came in for a landing, I could spot throngs of people, all dressed in colorful summer clothes. From the air the crowd looked like a

9. Khrushchev here uses the word *amerikeny*, rather than the correct Russian noun, *amerikantsy*, explaining, "I just used the word *amerikeny* because it comes from the play *Armored Train 1469*. The partisans are interrogating an American, and one of them says, 'We've captured an *amerikeny.*' "

V. V. Ivanov wrote the Civil War drama *Armored Train 1469* as a novella in 1922 and as a play in 1927.

flowerbed of different colors. I could see a podium and an honor guard and a red carpet.

We landed and taxied to the place where we were supposed to disembark. Here we encountered some difficulty. It turned out that our plane was too high for American standards, so when the motorized stairs were brought up, they didn't reach up to the door. Our pilot said we'd have to use the emergency ladder on board. Therefore we had to leave the plane not in the formal, dignified way called for by protocol, but practically climbing down using our hands and legs!

We didn't let ourselves be embarrassed by this problem. Far from it. It was an embarrassment for the Americans. They hadn't known our plane was such a giant. We could see the wonder in their eyes as they looked at it. They'd never seen anything like it, and they certainly didn't have anything like it themselves, nor would they have one for a long time. (Later when we negotiated an agreement to open an air route between our two countries, the United States asked us to postpone the ratification of the agreement because they didn't have a plane which could fly nonstop from Washington to Moscow.)

After we climbed down from our Tu-114, I was met by the President. He was in civilian dress rather than a military uniform. He introduced me to other members of the government. Then I greeted our ambassador and the other embassy officials and their wives. Some little children presented me with flowers. The official reception went perfectly, though as I recall the public was noticeably restrained in its greeting. In our country greetings are usually loud and enthusiastic, but not in the US. I think these people were looking at us as if we were some kind of oddity. They were thinking to themselves, "So these are Bolsheviks; I wonder what we can expect from them." I even got the impression there were some people in the crowd who disapproved of our being there.

Eisenhower invited us to the podium. It was decorated with a red carpet and equipped with microphones so that our speech could be heard not just all over the airfield but perhaps broadcast outside the country as well. I was terribly impressed. Everything was shining and glittering. We didn't do such things in our country; we always did things in a proletarian way, which sometimes, I'm afraid, meant they were done a bit carelessly. Those Americans really know how to lay on a reception.

Eisenhower, as the host, gave a traditional speech of welcome, and I responded with a few words of my own. Then a band played the anthems of our two countries, followed by a twenty-one-gun salute. It was a very solemn moment, and it made me immensely proud; it even shook me up a bit. We took off our hats and stood at attention.

So far, the United States was treating us strictly according to what protocol required for the arrival of a head of government. Here was the United States of America, the greatest capitalist power in the world, bestowing honor on the representative of our socialist homeland — a country which, in the eyes of capitalist America, had always been unworthy or, worse, infected with some sort of plague.

After inspecting the honor guard, Eisenhower and I got into one car, while Nina Petrovna and the President's wife got in another. We set off very slowly, with Eisenhower's bodyguard running along beside us on either side. We'd already witnessed the same procedure in Geneva. It was for security. We were unaccustomed to this way of protecting a leader, but maybe it's justified in the United States. I'm thinking now about the subsequent assassinations within such a short period of President Kennedy, his brother who was a candidate for the Presidency, and the Negro leader who fought for equal rights.[10]

Of course, some of the protection may have been for my benefit. I had a lot of enemies. Not me personally, but the Soviet Union. However, while riding along with President Eisenhower, I didn't give a thought to the possibility of terrorism, and I didn't show the slightest sign of anxiety. There were too many other things to think about.

I noticed that along the road there weren't any protesters carrying placards with slogans against us. Some people might say, well, the police took care of that. I don't think so. I think it was explained by the Americans' attitude toward my visit. "Let's have a look at this fellow," they were saying. "Let's see what kind of man this head of the Russian government is." I'm not saying that the American public has ever suffered from a shortage of anti-Soviet forces in its midst — that would be stupid and naive. But I do think that, out of respect for their own President riding in the limousine with me, the Americans were restraining themselves.

10. Robert F. Kennedy and Martin Luther King, both assassinated in 1968.

During my visit to Washington I had a series of conversations with Eisenhower on various burning issues. Andrei Andreyevich Gromyko and I represented our side, while Eisenhower had his Secretary of State. Dulles was already dead by then, and the Secretary of State was Herter. He wasn't much better than Acheson. Dillon, a representative of big monopolistic capital, was also there.[11] The President received us in his White House study. The atmosphere was informal; there was no conference table — just a group of chairs.

Eisenhower raised the matter of our Lend-Lease debt, and Dillon quoted the sum of money we owed the United States for the wartime economic assistance we had received in the form of goods on credit. Dillon was very hostile. He was the other side of the Dulles coin. He held in his hands the keys to Soviet-American trade, and he was clearly going to use that fact to dictate terms to us. He had plenty of support from other members of the Eisenhower government who were equally aggressive and antagonistic. It was obvious Dillon couldn't stand us. You didn't even have to touch him — all you had to do was come near him, and he would start fuming and sputtering as though he were about to explode, as though something inside him had short-circuited (I've seen such explosions in laboratories).

I heard Dillon out and then turned to Eisenhower: "Mr. President, as far as we're concerned, we owe you nothing. Nevertheless, we agree to repay our debt on one condition: that you give us three billion dollars in credit." Had not Eisenhower been blinded by his class hatred for the Soviet Union, he could have seen that our position was based on simple arithmetic: we had already paid back the US in the blood shed during our struggle against Hitlerite Germany. But of course we weren't talking arithmetic; we were talking politics, and — politically — there was no room for agreement.

Lend-Lease was part of the larger issue of peaceful coexistence, and, here too, Dillon exuded hostility toward us. He tried to restrain himself because we were guests of the President, but we could still sense his attitude. At one point, when I mentioned peaceful coexistence, his eyes flashed and he snapped at me with an incredible question, "What's this peaceful coexistence you're talking about?"

That irritated me, but I hope I didn't show it. "Mr. Dillon, if you

11. Secretary of State Christian Herter and Under Secretary of State Douglas Dillon. In the original, Khrushchev refers to Dillon as "Finance Minister," perhaps because he recalls that Dillon later served as Secretary of the Treasury.

don't understand what peaceful coexistence between two systems is, then I'm sorry. The time will come when you'll have to learn. It's pointless for me to try to explain it to you now."

Eisenhower didn't take a particularly active part in the discussion. He would simply throw in remarks from time to time. Our chief adversaries were Dillon and Herter. When it became clear that we weren't going to solve these problems then and there, we agreed not to upset ourselves and to postpone our exchange of views until the concluding stage of my visit to the US.

When not tied up in working sessions with Eisenhower, I took some time to drive around Washington in order to familiarize myself with the city. I even went for walks, though of course never straying far from the embassy. Washington is a clean city, green and very pleasant. It's also quiet. Nothing like New York. Washington is a rich place, but it looks like a provincial town. I liked very much both the planning and the architecture. It has good, solid buildings rather than skyscrapers. Once when I was looking around — as always, with an army of journalists following me — I went to the monument in memory of President Lincoln. I walked into the building, took off my hat and made a bow of respect to the former President who had started the war against the slave owners. I thought it would be a good idea if journalists wrote that the Prime Minister of the Soviet Union, who had once been a miner, paid homage to a former American President, who had once been a woodcutter.

The President suggested that I make a tour of the United States and kindly offered me the use of his private plane, a Boeing 707. It was a good plane, very powerful and with excellent on-board services. The interior was beautiful. It had two passenger compartments as well as private quarters for the President or, in this case, myself. However, I don't think the Boeing was any faster than our Tu-104, though it had four engines while our Tu-104 had two; and I don't think it was any more comfortable on the inside than our Tu-114 — except, perhaps, it wasn't quite as noisy. You see, the Boeing was a turbojet, while our Tu-114 was a turboprop.

Eisenhower told me I would be accompanied on my cross-country tour by Mr. Cabot Lodge. We were introduced. Lodge was a middle-aged man — tall and strapping. He told me he'd been an officer in the war. According to our system his rank would have been major general. Lodge and I got to know each other well because we spent a lot of time with each other one-to-one. He was a clever man — I guess he still is — but I can't say the same for the policies he's always stood for. I'd say he is an intelligent official of a not-so-intelligent government. He's served two terms as ambassador to Vietnam and once as head of the United States delegation to the talks in Paris.[12] As for my own experience with him, when it came to politics, there was never any doubt that he belonged to the Republican party. He treated me well and joked with me often.

"Mr. Lodge," I once said, "you're a former military man and therefore you know the rules of rank. You're a major general, and I'm a lieutenant general. Therefore you're my subordinate, and I'll expect you to behave as befits a junior officer."

He started laughing. "Yes, sir. I understand, General." Sometimes when we'd meet, he'd salute and snap, "Major General Lodge, reporting for duty, sir!"

In short, he had a good sense of humor; he was a pleasant companion to pass the time with during the many hours we spent on planes and trains. We tried to avoid talking business if possible. There was no need to get ourselves all worked up debating politics if we didn't have to. After all, he wasn't in a position to make decisions, and besides, why damage the friendly relations that were developing between us? But you know how it is: sometimes politicians can't help talking politics, even if they don't really want to, and Lodge and I would occasionally find ourselves discussing politics just out of boredom.

Someone from the State Department also accompanied me. I was told he was very rich and was in the foreign service, not to earn a living but just to gain a position of status in the government. His attitude toward us was rather cool if not downright unfriendly, though he always saw to my needs and looked after my schedule.[13] The other members of our party on the American side were Mr. Thompson, the US ambassador, and his wife.[14] On our side we had Nina Petrovna, Gromyko, Gromyko's wife, and Menshikov, our ambassador to the United States. Menshikov knew America very well. Of course, he was supposed to, for he had a whole apparatus to draw from and it

12. Henry Cabot Lodge, then ambassador to the UN, later (in 1969), US representative to the Vietnam peace talks in Paris.
  In the original, Khrushchev says he thinks Lodge told him he had been a naval officer, but Khrushchev admits he is uncertain. In fact, Lodge served in the US Army. He was a major general in the Reserves when Khrushchev knew him.
13. Wiley T. Buchanan, Jr., chief of protocol.
14. Llewellyn Thompson, US ambassador to Moscow, and his wife Jane.

wasn't his first year in the US. He gave me good information and advice. At his request, I met with the comrades at our embassy. It was a simple meeting which gave them a chance to welcome me and gave me a chance to bring them greetings from the homeland. In general, I'd say that Ambassador Menshikov was a man who did his duty. As for Comrade Sholokhov, as I recall, he didn't accompany me throughout the cross-country tour; he visited several cities with me but then expressed his wish to remain in Washington in order to meet with writers.

The first stop on our tour was New York City. We traveled by train from Washington and were met by Wagner, who at that time was head of what we might call the New York City Soviet — in other words, he was mayor. He was a Democrat, while the governor of New York State, Rockefeller, was a Republican who had recently replaced Harriman, another Democrat — not that it matters much, politically speaking.[15] Republican, Democrat — there's not that much difference.

Our welcome was all very proper and bourgeois in tone and style, complete with official courtesies, flowers, and all the rest of it. During my stay I was given a sightseeing tour of the city. An official in my capacity is very limited in what he can see of a big city in a foreign country. Therefore my only impression was of a huge, noisy city with an enormous number of neon signs and automobiles, hence vast quantities of exhaust fumes that were choking people. Basically, New York was like any other capitalist city: it had great wealth and luxury, and it had terrible poverty and slums. I was taken to see the highest building of all, the one all the tourists go to. The manager showed me around.[16] Of course, as I've mentioned, I'd already read about such buildings in Ilf and Petrov's *One-storied America,* where they're accurately described. I wasn't very impressed. If you've seen one skyscraper, you've seen them all. One thing I'll say for climbing to the top of the highest skyscraper in New York: at least the air is fresh up there. On the whole New York has a humid, unpleasant climate, and the air is filthy.

15. Mayor Robert F. Wagner, Governor Nelson Rockefeller, and former Governor W. Averell Harriman, whose tour of duty as US ambassador to Moscow Khrushchev has described in Chapter 15 above (see the section "Harriman and MacDuffie").

16. Khrushchev was taken on a tour of the Empire State Building by Colonel Henry Crown, chairman of the company that owned the building.

Wagner gave a luncheon in our honor. I gave a standard speech about the need for peaceful coexistence, friendship, economic cooperation, and so on. I also received an invitation from Mr. Harriman, asking me to visit him at his own home for a reception. He told me that if it were all right with me, he would invite some friends, all big capitalists — or, as they say in America, "businessmen of the highest caliber" — who would like to meet me and exchange opinions with me over a glass of wine. I thought this was an excellent suggestion. It promised to be a real business meeting. I knew Harriman to be a highly realistic man, an experienced specialist who understood us, who stood for peaceful coexistence, and who wanted to see a widening of scientific and cultural ties between our countries.

I arrived on schedule and found myself in a fairly big room filled with people, about fifteen or twenty, of all different ages, sizes, and appearances. Some looked like typical capitalists, right out of the posters painted during our Civil War — only they didn't have the pigs' snouts our artists always gave them. Others were dressed rather modestly. To look at them you wouldn't know they were the biggest capitalists in America. Harriman took me around, introducing me to all the guests, explaining what products their firms manufactured and so on. Then he called for wine — and champagne, as I recall. The reception was organized in quite an unusual and useful way: instead of making us sit at a table in an assigned place, Harriman had us moving around freely, talking to the people we were interested in.

I must confess that one reason I eagerly accepted Harriman's invitation was that I hoped we might be able to establish certain useful contacts with influential people who owned factories and who might be talked into economic cooperation with us. But after a few conversations I realized that conditions for the establishment of economic contacts weren't yet ripe and my expectations were premature. But never mind. These things take time. Moscow wasn't built over night. I was just breaking the ice.

I was introduced to an obese man of fifty or sixty who spoke Russian well. I think he was a Jew by nationality. I remember to this day what he said to me: "Why should we trade with you? What do you have to sell us?" [17] And he wasn't the only capitalist we heard this

17. In the Russian original of the memoirs, Khrushchev remembers the Jewish businessman with whom he argued in Russian as "the owner of some chemical plants," but it was David Sarnoff, chairman of RCA, who had emigrated from Belorussia at an early age. Sarnoff was one of twenty-seven industrialists and civil leaders, including former Senator Herbert H. Lehman and the economist John Kenneth Galbraith, who

from. I was to hear the same thing over and over again during my meetings with American businessmen.

One thing I couldn't help noticing about Harriman's guests was that they smoked a lot. Tobacco smoke hung in the room like a cloud, and through this cloud people kept coming up to me to exchange a few words, obviously trying to sound me out and see what kind of man I was. After a while it became clear that they had an exaggerated idea of how much we needed to trade with the United States and therefore they were trying to form a united front in pressuring us into accepting the terms they would dictate. It also became clear that these terms would be political as well as economic — terms we would never, *ever* accept, not even if it meant fighting down to our last drop of blood.

I wouldn't say Harriman's reception had been disappointing, but I wouldn't say it produced any results either. I'll admit I'd come with some hope that these people might express a willingness to mobilize their government and public opinion into developing our trade relations. But they demonstrated no such willingness. It was when this became clear that I felt the time had come for me to end the discussion. I thanked Harriman and said good-bye to him and to the other guests.

I went back to the hotel we were staying at, where a businessmen's organization was giving a dinner in my honor.[18] The dinner was held in a large hall with hundreds of people at long tables arranged in the way they always are at banquets in capitalist countries. In our country, guests are always seated at two or three tables according to their rank, while in capitalist countries it's much more disorganized — as in a restaurant. The table where I was seated, however, was higher than the rest, like the Presidium's podium at one of our Party meetings.

I gave a speech emphasizing that improved trade would be good for both our countries — and that it would be profitable for business circles in the US. I noticed that off to one side, on my left, a number of young men otherwise undistinguished from the rest, were making unfriendly remarks while I was delivering my address. I assumed

attended the reception. One prominent figure invited, former President Truman, pointedly sent his regrets.

18. The dinner was given by the Economic Club of New York at the Waldorf-Astoria Hotel.

they were either businessmen or the sons of businessmen. Their behavior made me indignant. They were acting like a bunch of tomcats
on a fence, and they obviously wanted to stage a demonstration
against the Soviet Union and against me personally as its representative. I decided to counteract at once. I interrupted my speech and
turned to them. I wasn't going to say "please." No, I had made up
my mind to go onto the attack: "It's clear to me you are against the
Soviet Union, against socialism, against our system. Well, I want you
to know I didn't come here to beg. I didn't come here with an outstretched hand asking for alms. I represent the great Soviet Union, a
revolutionary state, and I represent the working class. We have
achieved stupendous progress. Now we offer you a chance to trade
with us, and we offer you peace." I went on in that vein, and they
calmed down right away. Other guests expressed their displeasure
with these young men by hissing at them. Then everyone listened attentively while I finished my speech.

While I was in New York, Mr. Rockefeller, the governor of the
state, sent word that he would like to pay a call on me. I answered
that I'd be happy to receive him. I'd known him from our meeting in
Geneva.[19] He was a tall, lively man, very energetic and dignified-
looking. He certainly wasn't dressed in cheap clothes, but I wouldn't
say he was dressed elegantly either. He was dressed more or less
like other Americans. I say this only because here was Rockefeller
himself — not just a plain capitalist, but the biggest capitalist in the
world!

His visit was brief. He greeted me, and we exchanged a couple of
sentences about our previous meeting. There was no real discussion.
He simply said, "As the governor of New York, I am honored to welcome you to our state" — everything according to etiquette. And
then he dropped an interesting remark: "I don't exclude the possibility that this meeting won't be the last. I hope we might be able to
have certain business contacts with you." I replied I would be delighted to meet him again, especially on business matters. I took his
remark as a hint that he hoped to occupy a certain position in the

19. Khrushchev has described his meeting with Rockefeller in Geneva in *KR*, I,
399. After their reunion described here, Rockefeller told the press that Khrushchev
had made "an oblique allusion" to the possibility that Rockefeller might become a
candidate for President and, said Rockefeller, "I made an oblique reply. We dropped
the subject as quickly as we could."

White House, namely the position of President. In that case, of course, he would be meeting me in a different capacity, and we would have an opportunity to build new relations between our countries.

During my visit to New York, I went to the United Nations, where I was treated according to the procedure for the most important guests. I was led into the General Assembly hall and seated at a special chair facing the delegates near the main podium. It was a memorable day.

The next day we flew to Los Angeles, where I was met by a city official who spoke Russian, but poorly — with a thick Jewish accent.[20]

"How do you know Russian so well?" I asked him.

"I used to live in Rostov."

There was only one way a Jew could have lived in Rostov. That city was the seat of the Don Army, the homeland of the Cossacks, and Jews were forbidden by law to live there before the Revolution. He explained what I'd already guessed: "Yes, I'm a Jew, but my father was a big factory owner in Rostov, a member of the highest merchants' guild and therefore, according to tsarist laws, entitled to live anywhere in Russia." Naturally I found it curious that I was to be accompanied around Los Angeles by an emigrant from Russia.

We were supposed to visit a place near Los Angeles called Disneyland, a sort of fairy-tale park. They say it's very beautiful, but in the end we didn't get to go. Lodge and the other official tried to talk me out of going because some people had decided to stage an organized demonstration against me. There were even threats of violence. I was faced with the decision of whether to insist on going there anyway. It occurred to me that if I did go and if there were disorders against me, this man whose father had lost his factories in Rostov might be pleased for me to get just such a reception. I don't think a hostile demonstration would have made him one bit unhappy, to say nothing of worse things that might have happened. Therefore I decided not to insist. Instead, we went sightseeing around the city — in an open car, as I recall. I remember being struck by how warm and humid it was and how many flowers there were.

We were invited to visit a film studio in Hollywood, where the

20. Victor Carter, head of the City of Hope, a California Hospital.

film industry has its headquarters. Hollywood is like a special republic within the larger republic of the USA. They make all sorts of movies there, although when I was there they were no longer making progressive movies by progressive directors like Chaplin.

We were taken onto the set where a movie about can-can dancing was being shot. I don't think they were doing it especially because of my visit; they were simply filming a movie and letting us see how it was done. We arrived just as all these girls in short dresses began to dance. This particular dance, the can-can, has certain aspects which not everyone accepts as entirely decent. In fact, it's downright *indecent*. Well, after they finished, the girls gathered around Nina Petrovna and myself, and the photographers starting snapping away with their cameras. I heard one of the newsmen say something to one of the girls, but I didn't pay any attention. Afterwards our interpreter told me the man had told the girl, "Raise your dress higher, higher!" And she was only too glad to oblige. What kind of man was this who would ask a girl to do something like that!? He just wanted to get a juicy picture of a girl in that sort of outfit next to Khrushchev. I still have these pictures somewhere.[21]

What can I tell you about this can-can business? Later, when I went to Denmark, the Prime Minister and his wife took me to a can-can show during which the girls danced toward the audience and then, in a peculiar theatrical gesture, just bared their behinds at us — well, not literally, because they were wearing drawers. There were letters on their behinds, one letter for each girl. At dinner I asked the Prime Minister's wife (she was an actress herself, a good one and a very nice lady) what had been spelled out by the girls. She looked at me and said three words: "Happy . . . New . . . Year!"[22]

So much for the can-can. You can see why for our public, for the Soviet people, the movie *Can-Can* was fairly provocative. We weren't accustomed to such things. We considered it indecent or, at best, barely decent. In other words, it was a movie for adults only.

The management of Hollywood gave a luncheon in our honor.[23]

21. *Can-Can*, starring Shirley MacLaine and Frank Sinatra, was in production at the Twentieth Century–Fox studios.

22. Khrushchev describes in detail his trip to Scandinavia in 1964 and his visit with Prime Minister Jens Otto Krag of Denmark and his wife Helle Virkner in Chapter 21 below.

23. The luncheon at the Beverly Hills studios of Twentieth Century–Fox was given for Khrushchev by Spyros P. Skouras, president of the studios, and Eric Johnston,

The flower of Hollywood society was there, all the movie actors and actresses. The lunch was lively and informal, with nothing anti-Soviet in the atmosphere. That's more than I can say for a dinner attended by the Mayor, a Republican who I was told ahead of time held an extremely anti-Soviet position. We anticipated that there might be some sort of provocation. We were very sensitive and had no intention of tolerating even a hint of anti-Sovietism.

The dining hall was packed with four or five hundred people, all sitting at tables which were beautifully decorated and gently lit, as though by candlelight. The meal was delicious and lavishly served. No sour cabbage soup for these people. The middle-aged woman sitting on my right explained how such banquets are organized. She must have been very rich; she had to possess huge amounts of capital — otherwise she wouldn't have been there.

"You have no idea how many people wanted to come to this dinner," she said to me. "I came alone and left my husband at home. He's terribly envious of me. We paid a large sum of money just for me to be invited. Of course, we could have paid even more and my husband might have come too, but there were so many people clamoring to come that the dinner was limited to one person per family, either the husband or the wife but not both. So I'm the lucky one while my husband sits at home, bored and jealous."

She treated me civilly, though that didn't mean she approved of our system. She obviously considered us exotic. I could imagine her thinking to herself: "How exciting! Here's a real Russian bear! In Russia, bears actually roam the streets. This one has come to our country and is sitting right here beside me. How interesting! And the bear isn't even growling!"

She had paid money to buy a ticket for the dinner, just as though she were going to the theater. It reminded me of something from my childhood. When I was a boy working in a factory, we had a fair every year on September 14. Peasants would bring agricultural products to sell so they could buy tools and other goods. And gypsies would bring their horses for sale. There would always be a circus with all sorts of animals. It cost fifty kopecks just to have a look at the elephant. I remember one factory worker saying, "Guess what? I

president of the Motion Picture Association of America. Johnston had been the source of Khrushchev's favorite anecdote about Franklin D. Roosevelt (see the section "Harriman and MacDuffie" in the previous chapter).

paid my fifty kopecks to look at the elephant and on top of seeing him I got to pull his tail!" Well, maybe it's a crude comparison, but the banquet in Los Angeles was much the same. The people came more out of curiosity than friendship. They had paid their fifty ko-pecks to have a look at this Russian bear. What does he look like? Does he know how to sit at a table in polite society and properly hold a knife and fork, or will he lap up his food off his plate? Some of the people there also wanted to hear what the Russian bear would have to say, especially on the question of war and peace which oc-cupied everybody's mind.

Everything was going fine until the Mayor got up to make a speech. His remarks were brief but very offensive to us. He stuck all kinds of pins in the Soviet Union and our system, mostly in the form of comparisons with the United States. He didn't come right out in the open with his anti-Sovietism; it was somewhat camouflaged. Many people there may have missed what he was saying, but not I. Of course, I could have let it pass, but I was furious. I couldn't pre-tend I didn't know what he was really saying, so I decided to deal him a counterblow then and there, publicly.

"Mr. Mayor," I said, "I'm here as a guest of the President. I didn't come to your city to be insulted or to listen to you denigrate our great country and our great people. If my presence is unwelcome, then my plane is always ready to take me straight back to the Soviet Union." In my indignation I may have been a bit rude, but I made quite an impression.[24] The woman sitting next to me tried to calm me down. She said I was absolutely right and began reproaching the Mayor. I was later told that the wife of the American ambassador to the USSR, Mrs. Thompson, even burst into tears and got terribly angry at the Mayor for causing a scene. She was afraid there would be a war or something.

As for the Mayor himself, he decided not to start a fight. Instead he said something to play down the whole thing. I didn't regret having rebuffed him then, and I don't regret it to this very day. Sometimes

24. During a dinner given in Khrushchev's honor by the Los Angeles World Affairs Council, Mayor Norris Poulson chided Khrushchev for his famous "we will bury you" remark. Khrushchev replied that he had explained the benign intention of that state-ment before and added, "In Russia, a provincial mayor would not be reelected if he failed to keep up with the news." In dictating his memoirs, Khrushchev probably remembered Poulson's post correctly but was confused about his title: he continually refers to Poulson as "the governor" in the Russian original.

these anti-Soviet types need a good kick in the teeth, and that's exactly what he got. When the dinner was over I naturally said goodbye to the Mayor and thanked him, explaining that we had to be up early in the morning to take the train to San Francisco.

When we got back to our hotel, we all gathered in one of the suites. I was still upset about the way we had been treated and seriously considered canceling the rest of our tour. "How dare this man attack the guest of the President like that!" I shouted. Gromyko's wife, a lovely woman, ran off to get me a tranquilizer. I threw a look in her direction and made a sign so she would stop worrying and realize I was in full control of my nerves: I was giving vent to my indignation for the ears of the American accompanying us. I was sure that there were eavesdropping devices in our room and that Mr. Lodge, who was staying in the same hotel, was sitting in front of a speaker with an interpreter and listening to our whole conversation. So, for his benefit, I ranted on about how I wouldn't tolerate being treated like this, and so on. Finally I told Comrade Gromyko, in his capacity as Foreign Minister, to deliver my protest to Mr. Lodge, as the President's representative: "Tell Mr. Lodge I refuse to go to San Francisco tomorrow!"

Comrade Gromyko did as I said and came back with Lodge's apologies for the Mayor's behavior and his assurances that nothing of the same sort would happen in San Francisco. He implored me not to cancel the rest of our tour. Well, I accepted his assurances and told him I would go to San Francisco and see what happened. But if anything more happened, that would be the end of our visit and we'd go straight back to the Soviet Union.

The next morning Lodge accompanied me from the hotel to the railroad station in a car, and we had a talk along the way. He brought up the previous evening's unpleasantness. "Mr. Khrushchev," he said, "I had a look at the Mayor's speech before he gave it. I told him he simply couldn't give such a speech. You should have seen all the things I crossed out and told him he couldn't possibly say. He went ahead and said it all anyway. But forget about it. He's a fool, a nincompoop." I don't know if it really happened quite the way Lodge told me, but I was willing to let the matter drop there.

The train ride from Los Angeles to San Francisco was pleasant enough. The railroad carriages had good suspension and gave us a comfortable ride. Along the way we stopped at a small station and a crowd gathered. Farmers had come out from nearby villages to try to catch a glimpse of the Soviet delegation.

"Let's go out onto the platform," I said to Mr. Lodge.

"Oh, no! There are too many people around. I don't think you should."

All these people had come to see us. How could we stay in the train and not go out to greet them? There might be a misunderstanding. They might think we were either ignoring them or showing disrespect to them. Or they might think I was frightened.

"No, Mr. Lodge, I want to do it. Let's go." With that, I went to the exit and hopped off the car onto the platform. The crowd surrounded me. Some asked questions, but most were busy elbowing their way closer to get a good look at us. The whistle blew, and we climbed back on board. I still felt I should say a few words, so I made some remarks from the car, speaking into a megaphone which Lodge held for me. Just before the train pulled out of the station, I noticed Lodge disappear into a group of officials. Then, as the train started moving, he came into the car and handed me my medal.

"I believe this is your Order of Lenin, isn't it?"

I looked at my jacket lapel and realized it must have fallen off; the pin had probably broken when everyone was pressing around me. "Yes, it's mine, all right." It was in fact the Order of Lenin, with Lenin's portrait on it, which I had received at the nomination of the Society for Peaceful Coexistence. "How did you find it?"

"Someone found it and brought it to me, saying, 'Here's something probably lost by Mr. Khrushchev. Please give it back to him.' "

The incident pleased me very much. I would have been upset to lose that medal, and there are plenty of types who might have been tempted to keep it as a souvenir. The fact that the person returned it to me made me respect these people.[25]

We arrived in San Francisco and were greeted with speeches and flowers. The Mayor [26] introduced me to his wife, who went right

25. On its way to San Francisco, Khrushchev's train stopped at Santa Barbara and other towns along the way. Khrushchev insisted on getting out and mixing with the crowds. His son-in-law, A. I. Adzhubei, explained in a dispatch printed by *Izvestia* (of which he was editor) that Khrushchev had been feeling isolated and suspected there was an official campaign to prevent him from rubbing shoulders with ordinary citizens. Adzhubei wrote that his father-in-law was particularly upset about missing a chance to see Disneyland. During one of his whistle-stop plunges into the crowds en route to San Francisco, Khrushchev reportedly remarked, "For the first time in six days of house arrest, I've breathed fresh American air."

26. George W. Christopher.

over to Nina Petrovna and began talking to her. The Mayor's wife was obviously assigned to entertain the women in our delegation, while the Mayor himself took care of the men. In general, our reception was warm and friendly. "You see," said Lodge, "I promised you it would be better here than in Los Angeles."

"Yes, I see, and I very much appreciate it."

I would say that our visit to San Francisco had a direct impact on the political affairs of the city. The Mayor explained to me he had already served two terms and was running for a third. The reception and dinner he gave in our honor tipped the scale in favor of his reelection. Of course, if he'd treated us the way the Mayor of Los Angeles did, he might have picked up a few extra votes among anti-Soviet elements, but San Francisco was a different sort of city. Here a candidate for mayor could win votes by treating a visiting Soviet delegation hospitably.

I invited him to let us return his hospitality by coming to the Soviet Union. Later, after he was reelected, he and his wife came to Moscow as guests of the Moscow City Soviet, and I received them at the Council of Ministers or the Central Committee.

When the Mayor explained to me that he and his wife were both Greeks, I joked with him: "Then we're brothers, aren't we? When the people of Russia were converted to Christianity, they chose the Greek Orthodox Church. I'm not a religious man myself; I hope you won't be offended if I tell you I'm an atheist. But never mind. Historically we've always had good relations with the Greeks, and our people have always been ready to come to the aid of the Greeks in their struggle for liberation against the Turks." [27]

I remember the Mayor had an interest in a dairy farm. He let me taste one of his products. I was impressed both by the quality and by the packaging, and I told him so. Later, I made a point of praising his wares in public: "I wholeheartedly endorse San Francisco dairy products!" I was kidding, but my joke was sure to help him increase his sales and profits.

The Mayor also took me out to the edge of the city to visit a build-

27. Apparently Khrushchev had very similar conversations with Christopher in San Francisco, and with Skouras in Los Angeles a few days earlier. At the Twentieth Century–Fox luncheon in Los Angeles, Khrushchev opened his formal remarks by calling Skouras "my dear brother Greek," and went on to say, "Yes, ladies and gentlemen, the Russians did call the Greeks brothers because the Russians took part in the war to liberate Greece. And in the old days the Russians took the Greek religion, so we are also friends."

ing site where workers were assembling family cottages from prefabricated panels. I wanted to take a look at one of these panels and asked a worker, "What do you put in these for insulation? Just wood shavings and sawdust, eh?"

"That's right. It's pretty cheap stuff."

I asked how much the finished house would cost and was told a figure that was low by American standards. The cottages looked a lot like the ones we built as temporary shelters in the Soviet Union after the war. Those had had both their good and their bad sides. On the one hand people were glad to have a roof over their heads, but on the other hand they complained about the fleas: "The fleas are killing us!" they'd say. Evidently fleas like sawdust and made life miserable for people living in houses with sawdust insulation. Of course, whether you have fleas or not depends on the cultural level of the people and the upkeep of the buildings. For example, the Finns sometimes insulate their houses with sawdust, yet they manage to avoid being eaten alive by fleas. I suppose it was the same with the houses I saw going up outside San Francisco.

The cottages were all brightly painted, so the buyer could select a color according to his taste — yellow, green, anything you want. I asked the workmen how long one of these houses would last.

"We guarantee them for twenty years."

"And what then?"

"Why should we build a house that will stand for a hundred years? Twenty years from now the owner will buy another house from us."

This attitude was expedient from a commercial point of view. That was fine if your people could afford to buy a new house every twenty years. I know our peasants in Kursk Province, where I grew up, used to build their cabins out of aspen, which they bought from the local landlord. Oak, which didn't rot as fast as aspen, was too expensive, and there was no pine in our forests. A house made of aspen logs would last for thirty years. And here this American firm was building houses that would last for only twenty years, saying, "Come back to us in twenty years and we'll build you a new one!"

One morning during my stay in San Francisco I woke up very early and left the hotel to walk around a bit. I hadn't given any prior notice; nevertheless, as soon as I stepped out on the street my American security guard started to follow me. They weren't wearing uniforms, but I knew perfectly well who they were. As it turned out, even though I sometimes received angry or even insulting letters, I didn't encounter any hostile demonstrations or incidents, not counting, of course, what I've described in Los Angeles. It was always the representatives of certain political circles, and not the American people themselves, who expressed the hostility that existed between our two systems.

For another example, take my meeting in San Francisco with Mr. Walter Reuther, the head of the auto workers' union. I was told that Reuther and some other trade-union bosses wanted to have a discussion with me at the hotel where I was staying. I was interested to meet Reuther, whom I had read quite a bit about in the press. I knew, for instance, that he'd once been a leftist and a member of an international organization in which the Soviet Union participated, but that later he'd left the organization and switched to anti-Soviet political activity. So I didn't expect anything good to come of my meeting with him, but I was willing to have a talk with him nonetheless.[28]

He showed up with his brother and an older man who represented the brewer's union for the whole United States, as well as some others.[29] I was the host, so I arranged for us to be served snacks and drinks — just refreshments, no hard liquor. We sat at a long table, with Reuther and his brother on one side and our group on the other. Reuther's brother had photographic gear, a movie camera, and, we later learned, a tape recorder with him and made a recording of the whole conversation. I had nothing against that: "Go right ahead, Mr. Reuther, record our talk!" Our side consisted of Gromyko and a number of our journalists, among them Yuri Zhukov, who in my opinion is one of the best Soviet newspapermen.[30]

I studied Reuther closely. He was obviously an intelligent man. He came from a worker's family, had worked in Ford factories most

28. Despite Khrushchev's characterization of Reuther as hostile and blindly anti-Soviet, it should be recalled that the president of the United Auto Workers was conciliatory compared to George Meany, president of the AFL-CIO. Meany refused to attend the meeting with Khrushchev. On the eve of Khrushchev's arrival, the AFL-CIO executive committee had voted to oppose any US labor contacts with the Soviet leader. Reuther was one of three AFL-CIO vice presidents who had dissented from that resolution.

29. Over dinner with Walter and Victor Reuther of the UAW, Khrushchev met Karl F. Feller of the United Brewery Workers, and four other labor leaders. All seven were vice-presidents of the AFL-CIO.

30. G. A. (Yuri) Zhukov, then chairman of the State Committee on Cultural Relations, now a political commentator for *Pravda*.

of his life, and been sent to the Soviet Union as an instructor to teach our workers when we built an auto plant in Gorky. As he told me, he had spent two or three years in Gorky and knew a lot about the conditions in which our workers live. He said he had many memories of those years and began to recall contacts he'd had. When I say "contacts," I'm deliberately avoiding the word "friendships," although it could be that he had made some friends. He told me how he used to go out with girls in Gorky, and he made some rather obvious and playful hints to let us know that he'd really been around, been to parties given by young people, and so on and so forth.[31]

Yet here was a man who had betrayed the class struggle. As the head of a big trade union, he organized strikes — but always within certain permissible limits so as not to endanger or weaken the capitalist regime. His was the struggle for an extra nickel or dime, not the struggle for the victory of the working class. It was an economic, rather than a political, struggle. Politically, he was allied to government parties. He might have been a Democrat rather than a Republican, but, as I've said, it's six of one, half dozen of the other. There's no substantive difference between the two parties: they're both capitalist, and they both suppress the workers' movement.

Sometimes I hear on the radio or read in the newspapers about a strike in America, and it always brings to mind my meeting with Reuther. Our talk left an unpleasant taste in my mouth. I was later told how much salary he received. He made as much money as the directors of the biggest American corporations, like Ford. In other words, the capitalists had bought him off; they'd paid him enough to make him represent their interests rather than those of the workers, and to make him support the policies of the United States government rather than the class struggle. I have always favored peaceful coexistence among countries, but Reuther favored peaceful coexistence among classes, which is in fundamental contradiction to our Marxist-Leninist teaching. Worse, it is treason to the cause of his fellow workers. I'm afraid such treason is all too common among American trade-union leaders.[32]

31. After Khrushchev returned to Moscow, the Soviet trade union newspaper ran a story headlined, "Get Acquainted with Mr. Reuther, Lackey of the Monopolists." The article alleged that while in Gorky during the 1930's, Reuther had married a nineteen-year-old Russian girl whom he had known only for a week and whom he then never legally divorced. The story was dismissed as outrageous slander.

32. Two years later, during his Vienna summit meeting with John F. Kennedy, Khrushchev reportedly remarked, "We hanged the likes of Reuther in Russia in 1917."

As for the other men he brought with him, the less said the better. Reuther's brother barely entered into the discussion at all. He was there just as an observer, or more exactly as Reuther's secretary, who took everything down on tape. Another union leader, who was in his mid-fifties, seemed like a reasonable enough man; he made certain remarks which appeared to reflect an understanding of our position, but he did so very timidly. I don't know whether he was genuinely opposed to Reuther's arrogance and intolerance toward the Soviet Union, or whether he was just playing the American game of democracy, showing off how he could disagree with his boss on some specific issues while toeing the general line.

The old man who headed the brewers' union had completely lost his wits, and I don't think his craziness had anything to do with his age. I think he'd probably been a piece of crap as a young man, too. I didn't hear a single sensible word from him. There was no point in taking him seriously. He just sat there through the whole meeting drinking beer and eating everything within reach. When he reached for another glass of beer or piece of food, I noticed he had gold wrist watches on both his left and right arms. Well, I can understand one gold watch, but why did he need two? What did he think they were, decorations? Bracelets? The fact that such a stupid idiot, such an old fool, could be elected head of a trade union demonstrated the incredibly low political level of the workers he represented.

I had a much more satisfactory meeting on another occasion in San Francisco with the head of the Longshoremen's Union.[33] Unlike Reuther and his kind, he was a true progressive, and he supported the policy of the Soviet Union, although he wasn't a Communist. He invited me to attend and address one of the longshoremen's meetings. I accepted with pleasure. We were a bit disappointed to find that not too many people showed up. Perhaps we were already a bit spoiled, since we were accustomed to big crowds. But the longshoremen made up for it by receiving me warmly and sincerely. A few gave speeches expressing friendship toward the Soviet Union.

When my turn to speak came, my interpreter translated each sentence one by one, and almost every sentence brought applause. After the meeting when I came down off the podium, a young longshore-

---

33. Harry Bridges, president of the International Longshoremen's and Warehousemen's Union.

man, a trade-union activist, came running up to me, took my hat and put it on his head, then gave me his own cap. Then we embraced in the display of friendship and proletarian solidarity. Everyone else burst into applause. Naturally the newsmen took pictures and wrote about it in the press. For once there was no way they could follow their natural inclination to distort the facts. Such was my fraternal encounter with the true representatives of the American working class. Moments like that one give a man cause to rejoice.

After San Francisco the next stop on our journey was the state of Iowa. The most important event on our schedule was a visit to the farm of Mr. Garst. I'd first met him years before, in the mid-1950's, when he and his wife, a lovely woman, had come to the Soviet Union. Once they came to see me when I was vacationing in Sochi. We spent a few relaxed hours on the balcony of our state dacha on the shore of the blue waters of the Black Sea.[34]

He may have been a capitalist and we may have been Communists, but that didn't stop him from giving us the benefit of his experience and knowledge about agriculture. When taken on a tour of our farms in the Soviet Union, he would literally jump up and down with anger if he saw someone doing something stupid. I was told that one day he dropped in at a state farm during corn planting. He saw that the farmers were sowing the corn without simultaneously fertilizing the soil. He pounced on somebody, saying "What do you think you're doing? Don't you know you need fertilizer here?" The chairman of the collective farm explained that mineral fertilizer had already been put in the soil. Garst brought himself up short, his eyes flashing under his thick brows. Who knows what he would have done if he'd been in charge?

I'm telling this story to show that Garst was the sort of man who couldn't tolerate mistakes. His determination to see things done correctly did not distinguish between socialism and capitalism. During our talks in the Soviet Union, Garst had taught me a lot. He was the sort of man you could profitably listen to and memorize everything he said, so that his experience might be transplanted into Soviet soil. To tell the truth, he usually did all the talking while I just listened. He knew agriculture backwards and forwards. He wasn't a lecturer,

34. Khrushchev toured Des Moines, then visited Roswell Garst, a wealthy hybrid-corn grower who had met the Soviet leader on several visits to the USSR.

and he wasn't a reporter: I would call him a real *activist* in the field of agriculture. He'd told me about the very profitable farm he managed in Iowa, and I was anxious to see it with my own eyes.

My assistant, Andrei Stepanovich Shevchenko, was a respected agronomist. He accompanied me to Iowa. But before we went, he established confidential contacts with Garst and asked what would be the best way to arrange for me to visit the farm. Here's what Garst said: "I'm a farmer. I get up with the sun. From our conversations in the past, I know Mr. Khrushchev remembers what it's like to live in the country; he knows what a peasant's life is like, that it means rising early and working hard. I suggest, Mr. Shevchenko, it would be nice if Mr. Khrushchev agreed to get up early and drive out to my farm — just the three of us: yourself, Mr. Khrushchev, and me. As for the rest of the people with Mr. Khrushchev, well, they're city folks. They don't even know what a sunrise is. We'll let them sleep and they can join us later."

When Shevchenko passed Garst's suggestion on to me, I thought to myself: "Here's a good farmer who knows a lot about agriculture but who doesn't have the slightest idea how important the guest is that he wants to invite to his farm. He doesn't seem to understand that I can't just sneak out of the hotel early one morning without even notifying my hosts where I'm going. He's being absolutely unrealistic." I was going to be accompanied to Iowa by Lodge and was going to have all sorts of police guarding me, never letting me out of their sight. If I tried to run off secretly with Garst when he came to fetch me, it might appear that I'd been kidnapped, like a bride in the Caucasus or in Central Asia.

As it was, we all went out to Garst's farm together — Lodge, Gromyko, all the policemen and journalists, everybody. Among the other guests was Mr. Stevenson. I liked him. He seemed to have a clear understanding of the need for strengthening friendly relations between our two countries.[35]

We began our walking tour of the farm. There were hordes of people following us, a whole army of journalists — journalists in all directions as far as the eye could see. It reminded me of what Prokop, the gamekeeper on our shooting preserve in the Ukraine, used to say when I asked him how the hunting looked.

35. Adlai Stevenson was then seeking the 1960 Democratic presidential nomination.

"Well, Comrade Prokop, any ducks today?"

"Ducks everywhere, Comrade Khrushchev," he'd answer in Ukrainian. "Ducks as far as the eye can see — more ducks than shit." Well, that's how many journalists there were tramping around after us on Garst's farm. Now, I realize Prokop's figure of speech might rub some people the wrong way; I just hope those who someday read my memoirs won't take the expression too literally. Comrade Prokop spoke very expressively, and he just couldn't help throwing in an impolite word for "dung."

Anyway, Garst led us to the part of his farm where he raised steers; he showed us the silos where feed was stored, and then he took us to see his cornfields. I know a thing or two myself when it comes to planting corn in order to get the highest yield. I saw that Garst had planted his corn with two or three stems in one spot. I pointed this out to him, saying, "Look, the best way of planting corn is to keep the stems separate. You should have them twenty to thirty centimeters apart in rows at least sixty, or better yet eighty, centimeters apart. That way you give each root system maximum room to spread out and take advantage of the fertilizer in the soil. Besides, corn needs good exposure to the sun. If you plant it close together, the long stems will cast too much shade and prevent the sun from warming the roots and the soil. If you don't mind my saying so, you've got your corn planted too densely here."

"You're being a bit nit-picking," he said, "but you're right. The problem is: our sowing combine can't plant the corn any further apart, and we can't afford to plant by hand."

As we were walking across his cornfield, the newsmen kept running on the right of us, on the left, behind us and in front of us, snapping away with their cameras, shouting questions and making remarks. At one point Mr. Salisbury, a well-known American correspondent, came up alongside of us. At different times he has written about life in the Soviet Union in various ways. There have been times when he seemed to have a correct understanding of the need to build the relationship between our countries on a firm basis.[36] At any rate, some photographers wanted to take a picture of Garst, Salisbury, and me together. Garst got so annoyed he kicked

36. Harrison E. Salisbury, assistant managing editor of the New York *Times* until his retirement at the end of 1973, is the author and editor of a number of books on the Soviet Union and Communist affairs.

the photographer and left a footprint on his behind. Someone else took a picture of this whole scene, and we had some good laughs over it later.

Of course, we should look at it from Garst's point of view. He probably thought to himself, "This is my farm, my land. I invited Khrushchev to inspect the place, but I didn't invite these other people. They keep getting in the way and preventing me from showing my guest around the way I want." So he exercised his rights and gave the photographer a good swift kick in the ass. Later he grabbed an ear of corn and threw it at another newsman to make him get out of our way. He was absolutely outraged. He'd never seen anything like this invasion before. He must have felt as though the Golden Horde had overrun his farm, trampling all his fields and causing severe damage to his crops.

When lunchtime came, we went back to his house. Nina Petrovna and I took a look around. It was a nice little house. I say "little" because I don't want people to get the impression it was a palace. It was a pleasant, ordinary house, the sort you'd expect of a businessman who knows how to live well but who also knows how to spend money wisely. Garst had enough capital that he could have lived in luxury and made a big show of it, but he was the sort of man who felt that money spent on anything other than business was money down the drain. I'm not saying he was a miser — just that he was frugal.

One should spend as much money as necessary on something which is worthwhile; anything over and above that is a senseless expenditure which should be eliminated. That's a good capitalist principle which those who administer our social enterprises would do well to learn. Sometimes I read absolutely incredible stories in the newspaper about how careless administrators have wasted the people's money. Well, there is a lesson to be learned from Mr. Garst here.

Some people might say: "How can Khrushchev, a Communist, a former proletarian, a man who worked so many years in the Party and in the leadership of our country — how can he have such an opinion of a *capitalist*, an exploiter of the working class?" That's beside the point. The point is, the capitalists have accumulated a great deal of experience, especially when it comes to spending their money in efficient ways. Now, of course, this money is the result of the workers' toil, which the capitalists exploit to make themselves rich. But if we took all the positive features of the capitalist economy and transplanted them into socialist soil, we would get socialist results. That's what Lenin meant when he said we should learn from the capitalists. Unfortunately, we keep repeating this advice of Lenin's like parrots, but we don't really put his advice into practice. Naturally, we can't learn anything from the capitalists about how to pay for work performed, how to distribute the work load, and how to serve the working people; but there are many, many things we could learn from our class enemies. I came to appreciate this all the more acutely through my association with Mr. Garst, particularly when I had a chance to see him in his native environment, in action on his own farm.

After we had finished inspecting the farm, he and his wife served us a meal. He didn't let the others in. All my bodyguards, the policemen, the journalists, and so on had to go into town to eat. The meal was good, rich and meaty. Americans really know how to eat. They have delicious canned foods, not to mention all sorts of fresh dishes. As I recall, the Garsts served turkey. The turkey is very much respected in the United States, not just as a bird but as meat, too. The Americans have a poultry research institute outside Washington, and they even have a special "turkey day" when every American absolutely has to eat roast turkey.

The weather was sunny and warm. We went into the garden and sat in the shade of some fruit trees. As Garst and I came out of the house, Stevenson joined us. He was in a good mood. He and Garst suggested that the three of us have our picture taken together. We put our arms around each other's shoulders and struck a relaxed pose for the photographer. I took Stevenson's willingness to be in a picture with me as a sign of tolerance toward the Soviet Union. As for Garst, he was laughing with his mouth wide open — as wide as possible. He really knew how to laugh. I recognized Garst for what he was: a capitalist and therefore one of my class enemies, but also a human being whom I respected for his energy, his knowledge, his willingness to share his experience and, so to speak, his trade secrets with others, even with us to put to use in our socialist enterprises. Such capitalists are hard to find. They're a great rarity. I'd say maybe there are two or three like him, but no more.

The next stop on my itinerary was Pittsburgh. But here a problem arose. A strike was under way in the American steel industry, which is based in Pittsburgh. When the press carried an announcement of my scheduled visit to Pittsburgh, the trade unions published a statement in the newspapers warning that I shouldn't count on meeting any of their leaders. In short, they didn't want to meet me. Once again, I found myself faced with hostility on the part of American union leaders, who didn't want to stain their clothes by coming into contact with the representatives of the Soviet Union. They were demonstrating their doglike loyalty to capitalism and their unfriendliness toward socialism. Even today you find this attitude not only in the United States, but in other capitalist countries as well.

Despite the public antagonism of Pittsburgh's union leaders, we decided not to change our plans and to go through with our visit to the city. After all, steel isn't the only industry there. As we drove from the airport to the hotel, we could see whole families alongside the road.[37] They seemed to be waving their greetings, and there were no angry shouts — at least my interpreters didn't tell me about any. I was struck by the colorful print dresses and cotton pants the ladies were wearing. Our own women, back at that time, used to wear rather dark, austere dresses which covered most of their bodies. I liked the dresses Americans wore; they looked pretty and seemed practical, too.

While I didn't meet with any trade union leaders or any striking workers in Pittsburgh, I did get to see some industrial enterprises. We visited a machine-tool factory owned by some woman who was a friend of President Eisenhower's.[38] There I noticed a number of interesting differences from the practices used in plants in our own country. For instance, in our factories, work stops if an official delegation comes for an inspection. But in the US, or at least in the factory I visited in Pittsburgh, everyone sticks to his job, without breaking the rhythm of production. Working hours are working hours, and that's all there is to it. The workers are very disciplined.

I went up to a drill press and said to one of the plant engineers or foremen, "This machine must be at least as old as I am because I

37. Khrushchev arrived in Pittsburgh at night and was greeted by the acting mayor of the city, Thomas J. Gallagher. He stayed at the Carlton House.

38. This was the factory of the Mesta Machine Company in Homestead, Pennsylvania. As a nonunion shop, it was one of the few large steel fabricating plants not closed by the steel strike. It was owned by the in-laws of Perle Mesta, the Washington hostess.

remember we had the same sort of drill press in the machine-tool factory where I worked in my youth."

"Yes, Mr. Khrushchev, ours is a fairly old plant. We have equipment ranging from the most advanced to the practically prehistoric."

I laughed. "Yes, indeed! This one here must be even older than prehistoric." I couldn't figure out how the owners of such an ancient plant could compete with more modern factories. The answer, of course, is capitalist skillfulness. The very fact that the plant was in business meant it was productive and profitable. It had to be, or it would close down. For capitalists, there's no alternative. We could learn something from them in that respect. In our country if someone gets the bright idea of collecting medieval equipment of some kind, he can start a museum and be comfortably supported at the expense of the state. But in capitalist countries anything which is not expedient — which doesn't have practical, productive use — simply doesn't survive. Equipment which no longer produces profits is bound to be junked.

As we were walking along among the machines, I noticed fresh patches of asphalt on the floor. The asphalt was literally still warm. I pointed these out to the plant manager who was showing us around and said, "You know, in our country when the leadership goes to inspect a factory, the plant managers always order all the cracks and holes in the floor to be patched up. I see you do the same here."

He smiled. "Yes, we took care of that just before your arrival, Mr. Khrushchev."

We passed a machine, and the man operating it turned it off and came over to me. He offered me a cigar and patted me on the shoulder in a friendly way. All the others standing around obviously shared his sentiments. Perhaps he had been delegated to make a gesture on behalf of the collective. I gave him a friendly slap on the shoulder, took off my wristwatch and presented it to him. It was a sturdy, steel watch made by our Kuibyshev factory. He smiled, obviously very pleased, and then went back to work.

Afterward an American journalist asked me, "Mr. Khrushchev, what should we make of your giving that watch to a machine-tool operator? When Mr. Nixon was in Moscow he offered a sum of money to a worker, and your press reproached him, accusing him of trying to bribe the man."

I answered, "The worker I met had demonstrated his warm feelings toward me by giving me a cigar, and I was just repaying his kindness. There's a difference between mutual expressions of good will and bribery. My gesture had nothing in common with what Nixon was trying to accomplish by offering our worker money."

I'm recounting this incident here because it illustrates how carefully the American press was watching my every move, my every step. They kept their eyes glued on me, waiting for me to do something rash so they could use it against the Soviet Union — and against me as the head of the Soviet Union.

In addition to the machine-tool works, somewhere along the way we also visited a sausage factory.[39] As I recall, the workers there, too, were on strike, so we had been warned by the trade unions not to go to the factory. It was all part of their open demonstration of opposition to our Soviet State. But the trade unions hadn't invited us to visit the sausage factory — the owner had; he wanted us to see his machinery, not his workers, and we agreed to go. This capitalist knew what publicity was all about. There were movie and television cameras all over the place, and everything was set for the big wiener-tasting. We ate some wieners, and I must say they were delicious. They were served with mustard of superior quality — not at all bitter, and with a nice smell. We stood around joking and stuffing ourselves with wieners in front of the television cameras. Lodge, too, was stuffing himself and smiling. He knew what was going on. I said to him afterwards, as we were leaving, "Mr. Lodge, that was all just a big promotion, wasn't it?"

He looked at me, smiled, and nodded.

"Will he make money off of it?"

"Undoubtedly. You just made a lot of money for him."

"Well," I said with a laugh (Lodge had a good sense of humor), "you should get a share of the commission since you brought me here."

The owner of the factory had obviously decided to make a bit of money by having me promote his product and thereby increase his sales. Now he could say: "Khrushchev and his delegation, along with the President's representative, Mr. Lodge, visited our factory, tasted

39. During his stopover in Des Moines, before coming to Pittsburgh, Khrushchev was a guest of Harry Bookey, an owner of the Des Moines Packing Company. Khrushchev donned a butcher's hat and sampled a hot dog, with mustard, from one of the company's vending machines. "We have beaten you to the moon," he proclaimed, "but you have beaten us in sausage-making."

our product, and praised our wieners highly! Buy our wieners — they're the best!" In other words, his invitation wasn't an expression of friendship; it was strictly business.

One other visit to a factory sticks in my mind. According to our itinerary, we were supposed to see the plants of an agricultural machinery firm called John Deere. It's a well-known company because the Soviet Union had bought farm equipment from two firms, McCormick and John Deere. I'm sure there were commercial motives for inviting me to the factory; the directors hoped my visit would lead to more purchases by our country. But I didn't mind. John Deere and McCormick make world-famous products that are highly regarded by our workers and engineers on our collective and state farms. The director of the company took us to lunch in a common mess hall. He said he always had lunch there, along with the plant managers and the workers. Everyone would go to a special table and pick up silverware, then go to a counter where they were served food. After you finished one helping you could go back and get another. It was all very democratic. I confess I was impressed. Later, when I got home, I mentioned this system in my speeches, trying to promote the same form of service at our factories. We could cover the tables with a plastic sheet and simply wipe them off with a towel after each meal. In those days we used to have a large number of waitresses who served the workers in one hall and the administration in special, separate rooms. If we borrowed the American system, we could also eliminate the long lines of people waiting for tables in our lunchrooms, which the workers used to complain about.

From Pittsburgh we flew back to Washington, where our embassy informed me that a group of American capitalists wanted to organize a banquet in my honor.[40]

I wasn't very enthusiastic about attending another meeting with businessmen. I'd already had two such meetings in New York, and nothing much had come of either of them. But I was advised to go ahead and attend the dinner in Washington, because the guests would be a select circle of top representatives of the American business community, and it would be useful for me to talk with them. So I gave my consent.

40. The Washington businessmen's dinner was given by Eric Ridder, publisher of the *Journal of Commerce*.

The dinner was held not too far from our embassy. The whole thing was arranged in an English manner, with dim lighting and candles on the tables. First we were served *zakusky* [hors d'oeuvres] and drinks, though of course in moderate amounts. As I recall, nobody got drunk. In general, businessmen abroad know how to drink a lot and not get drunk. They know how to conduct themselves in polite society.

During the discussion, the guests began to ask all sorts of questions, although some of the questions were rather long-winded, more like anecdotes than questions. I remember one feeble old man who tried to find out how much gold we were mining and why we didn't conduct our trade with America in gold.[41] The capitalist world has always had a weak spot for gold. Of course we were mining it, but we preferred to stash it away for a rainy day, so to speak. Who knows when our country might need all the gold it has? Anyway, even if we wanted to buy foreign goods for gold, we weren't mining it in sufficient quantity to pay for all our needs. No, we wanted mutually profitable foreign trade, the sort which would increase our national wealth rather than diminish it. We used to sell our manganese and other raw materials to the US, but now they were buying it from other countries, like Turkey.

Here's how I answered the old man's question: "Perhaps you're familiar with a statement made by our leader, Vladimir Ilyich Lenin, about gold. He said it should be stored away so that at a certain stage of mankind's development, gold will lose its exchange value and society will use it to decorate public toilets. That's why we're hoarding our gold. We're waiting for the time when Communism is achieved and we can follow Lenin's dictum."

The capitalists reacted with a storm of laughter. They thought my answer was terribly witty. The old man himself, however, wasn't satisfied. He started firing all sorts of questions at me about our country and our political system. I gave each question the answer it deserved, and if he said something very unreasonable, I would reply ironically. The other guests seemed to like the way I handled him. Later one of the capitalists came up to me and whispered in my ear that he and his friends were embarrassed by the stupid questions the old man had been asking. I was pleased that my ironic rebuffs had

41. Philip Cortney, president of the Coty Company, questioned Khrushchev along these lines.

been correctly understood by the people who invited me to the banquet. It was still premature to expect concrete business contacts, but I felt that some useful personal contacts had been established with these businessmen. Naturally, my handling of the questions that evening was reported in our press.

The last important event on my visit to the United States was a round of talks with President Eisenhower at Camp David. I've already related how ignorant we had been about Camp David when our embassy first notified us that we were scheduled to go there, how we had thought the President didn't want to receive us in the White House and was discriminating against the Soviet Union by meeting us at some place called Camp David instead. We had been afraid it was like a leper colony. Well, by the time we got to the United States we realized what an honor it was to be invited to Camp David.

Nowadays I sometimes read in the newspaper or hear on the radio that President Nixon has received some foreign guest at the presidential dacha where I met with Eisenhower. For Nixon, Camp David has special significance. It was named after Eisenhower's grandson, who has now grown up and become Nixon's son-in-law by marrying his daughter.[42]

Eisenhower asked me if I would mind flying to Camp David by helicopter since the roads were clogged with traffic. "We'll take off near the White House, and we'll be there in ten minutes," he said. "Besides, you'll get a bird's-eye view of Washington."

Of course I agreed. I was curious to see what Washington looked like from the air. The President's helicopter was a good machine. I think it was made by Sikorsky, a former Russian who ended up in America and made a great contribution to the development of American aviation. As we flew over Washington, the city looked like a table-sized model. Eisenhower pointed out various neighborhoods. At one point we flew over a big green field where he told me he played golf. He asked whether I liked this game. I didn't have the slightest idea what it was all about. He told me it was a very healthy sport.

42. The presidential retreat was built in the late 1930's on a six-thousand-acre preserve in the Catoctin Mountains of Maryland. Franklin Roosevelt named the hideaway Shangri-La. Eisenhower renamed it Camp David after his grandson. After the Khrushchev-Eisenhower meeting there, the phrase "spirit of Camp David" was coined to describe Soviet-American detente.

With Bulganin bound for England, 1956

Khrushchev and his family

With Paul Robeson, the American singer and actor

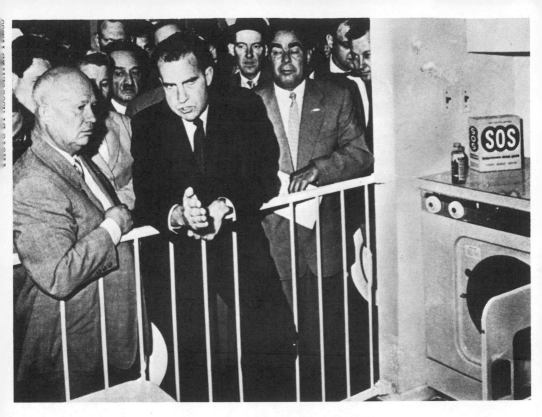

The "Kitchen Debate" with Richard Nixon. Brezhnev is at the right

Surveying the fields with US Ambassador Llewellyn Thompson

On the porch at Blair House in Washington at the beginning of his American tour

Waving to reporters with Averell Harriman and Henry Cabot Lodge

Receiving Harriman in Moscow for preliminary talks on the
nuclear test ban treaty, 1963; Foreign Minister Andrei Gromyko
is at the right

Addressing a luncheon in his honor in New York;
Mayor Robert F. Wagner is at the left

On the set of *Can-Can*. Nina Petrovna is flanked by Shirley MacLaine
and Frank Sinatra. Louis Jourdan is at the left

On Roswell Garst's farm in Iowa

Khrushchev receiving American senators and statesmen in Moscow
before the signing of the nuclear test ban treaty, 1963:
Senator J. William Fulbright (*left*), Foreign Minister Gromyko,
Secretary of State Dean Rusk, Khrushchev, Ambassador Anatoly
Dobrynin, Adlai E. Stevenson, and Senator Hubert Humphrey

With President Eisenhower at Camp David

In the garden of the Soviet embassy in Washington
with foreign-policy advisor Shuisky

Back in Moscow from the United States aboard the Tu-114

Leaving the city behind, we began to descend over a forest. There were cars waiting for us when we landed. We drove past some structures resembling the plywood barracks we used to put up for construction workers at building sites; our workers were eaten alive by the bedbugs in those shacks, so we burned them down and built proper dormitories for them.

Eisenhower showed me into the main house. On the outside it looked just like a barracks; but on the inside it was luxuriously decorated, yet at the same time very businesslike — typically American. Everything was sturdily built, clean, and comfortable. I was shown to my private quarters, and the other members of our delegation — Comrade Gromyko and the rest [43] — were also settled in nicely.

Eisenhower asked if I like watching movies. I said of course I did, as long as they were good movies.

"What kind of movies do you prefer?" he asked with a smile. Eisenhower's face was always very pleasant when he smiled. "Personally, I like Westerns," he added. "I know they don't have any substance to them and don't require any thought to appreciate, but they always have a lot of fancy tricks. Also, I like the horses."

"You know," I told him, "when Stalin was still alive, we used to watch Westerns all the time.[44] When the movie ended, Stalin always denounced it for its ideological content. But the very next day we'd be back in the movie theater watching another Western. I too have a weakness for this sort of film."

"Good. We'll have some Westerns and other movies. I've also invited our navy band to play. Do you mind?"

"Oh, that will be very pleasant. I enjoy music, and I like to look at young faces."

"Fine. They'll play for us at dinnertime."

Wheareas we had to dress up for official dinners in Washington, at Camp David we just wore our usual clothes to meals.

During my stay at Camp David President Eisenhower proposed, "What do you think about flying over to my farm? It's not far from here." [45]

---

43. Also on the Russian side were Ambassador Menshikov and A. A. Soldatov, chief of the American department of the Soviet Foreign Ministry.

44. Khrushchev has described Stalin's taste in movies in *KR*, I, 297–298.

45. At Gettysburg, Pennsylvania.

"I'd be delighted," I said.

When we got there, we were met by the manager of the farm, whom Eisenhower introduced to me as a general: "He fought with me during the war, and after the war I suggested he look after my farm." [46] The manager took me on a tour of the farm. Then we went back to the house and Eisenhower introduced me to some of his family. As I recall his son and daughter-in-law lived at the farm: "I decided not to take all my family with me to the White House because the President's term of residence there is temporary, and I didn't want my family to get too accustomed to all the conveniences of the White House." [47]

I saw his point. Eisenhower was a reasonable and modest man. Not that his own house at the farm was a poor man's home. Of course not. It was a rich man's house, but not a millionaire's.

Later the manager led us on an inspection of Eisenhower's cattle farm. It was smaller than our collective and state farms and didn't impress me by its size. But the beef cattle were a good, dark-brown color, with short legs and sturdy bodies. They were obviously well fed. I was informed this breed of cattle yielded as much as 65 percent beef — literally like a hog! If I recall correctly from our reference books, a good porker yields about 70 percent meat when it's slaughtered. I expressed my admiration for these cattle. Eisenhower gave a big smile and, right then and there, asked me to accept one of his herd as a present.[48] I thanked him and in exchange offered him some of our birch trees to plant on his farm — "as an expression of gratitude and a token of our meeting." He seemed very pleased. I kept my word. I asked our specialists to select some of our best birch trees, and we sent a whole planeload to him.

After seeing the cattle, we went out into the fields and Eisenhower pointed out to me the boundaries of his property. He took me to a field where a plant was growing which looked like wheat, only smaller. He explained, "We don't harvest this crop. I just have it mowed before winter. This field attracts birds. Partridge, quail, and other game come here when the other fields have been harvested. As a result, we have excellent hunting here."

46. Brigadier General Arthur S. Nevins, who had served with Eisenhower overseas.
47. Khrushchev was introduced to the President's daughter-in-law, Mrs. John Eisenhower, and his grandchildren, including David Eisenhower, then eleven years old.
48. Eisenhower raised Black Angus cattle and sent one to Russia.

In other words he had set aside this whole field just as a hunting preserve. This was too much. I'd say he even outdid our landowners in pre-Revolutionary Russia. At least they did their hunting on horseback. A number of times I've read Lev Nikolayevich Tolstoy's description of those hunts, and every time it makes my temperature rise with excitement. Tolstoy's passages about hunting would do the same to any man who has a weakness for the sport. But President Eisenhower's sort of hunting was different. For a really passionate hunter, like myself, I'd say his idea óf hunting is downright dull. If you know for certain that you're going to kick up a bird every few feet, you might as well be shooting clay pigeons at a target range.

When we finished walking around the property, Eisenhower took us back to the house for tea. Then we flew back to Camp David. The whole trip had taken only a few hours.

In the morning Andrei Andreyevich and I would get up early and go out for a walk along a secluded path in order to talk things over. We were completely alone — except, of course, for our bodyguards, but they were well trained and kept out of sight. Now, people might ask, "What's this about Khrushchev and Gromyko going out for walks to exchange opinions? Why couldn't they just talk in their rooms?" The answer is perfectly obvious to any statesman. We knew that American intelligence was well equipped with scientific listening devices, and we were simply taking precautions to avoid being overheard. Eisenhower and I were discussing a number of highly sensitive matters of mutual concern, and we knew that the Americans would like to eavesdrop on my confidential deliberations with Gromyko before the working session and get some advance notice of what positions our side would take.

Among the issues still to be discussed were cultural, scientific, and economic cooperation. When I say "economic cooperation," I'm not talking about the Lend-Lease problem any more. We had exhausted, although not solved, that issue during our earlier talks at the White House at the beginning of my visit. The Americans wanted a much broader exchange of tourists, scientists, and students. They even suggested we send our plant managers for retraining in the US. This proposal appealed to us because it would have allowed us to take advantage of their experience and expertise in industrial organization and management. Many of their suggestions were clearly intended to make us open our borders, to increase the flow of people back and forth. They were also trying to pressure me into permitting stores to be opened in the Soviet Union where our citizens could buy American literature; in exchange they would allow us to open outlets in America where we could sell our books.

But all these issues were of secondary importance. The primary problem before us during our talks at Camp David was disarmament. I could tell just from looking at Eisenhower how anxious he was to reach an agreement which would create conditions eliminating the possibility of war.

"Mr. Khrushchev," he said, "I'm a military man; I've been a soldier all my life. I've fought in more than one war in the past, but I'm not embarrassed to tell you that now I fear war very much. I'd like to do anything I can to help us avoid war. First and foremost I want to come to some sort of agreement with you."

"Mr. President, nobody would be happier than I if we could reach an agreement. But the question is, how?"

We spent the greater part of our talks together trying to answer that question.

It was our side who raised the matter of withdrawing troops from other countries — in other words, eliminating our military bases on foreign territory. This would have meant dismantling both the NATO and Warsaw Pact alliances. The Americans weren't prepared to go this far. They rejected our proposal. Actually, we knew that the conditions for such an agreement were not yet ripe and that our proposal was premature. In fact, our proposal was intended to serve a propagandistic, rather than a realistic, purpose.

The Americans, for their part, were willing to accept a ban on the production and testing of nuclear weapons, but only on the condition that international controls were established. Specifically, they insisted on an agreement which would allow both sides to conduct reconnaissance flights over each other's territories. This condition was unacceptable to us at that time. I stress, *at that time*. First, America was in a much stronger position than we were as regards both the number of nuclear weapons it had and also its delivery system. Second, the Americans had us surrounded on all sides with their military bases, including air bases, while our own airplanes couldn't even reach the United States. Third, certain instruments can be mounted on foreign territory to detect atomic testing at a great distance, but, here again, the Americans had an advantage because they had their military installations all around our borders. In short, their suggestion for a system of international supervision wasn't fair or equal. Therefore we couldn't accept it.

What you have to remember is that when I faced the problem of disarmament, we lagged significantly behind the US in both warheads and missiles, and the US was out of range for our bombers. We could blast into dust America's allies in Europe and Asia, but America itself — with its huge economic and military potential — was beyond our reach. As long as they had such superiority over us, it was easier for them to determine the most expedient moment to start a war. Remember: we had enemies who believed conflict was inevitable and were in a hurry to finish us off before it was too late. That's why I was convinced that as long as the US held a big advantage over us, we couldn't submit to international disarmament controls. That was my point of view, and I think, at the time, it was correct. Now that I'm in retirement, I still give this whole question serious thought, and I've come to the conclusion that today international controls are possible because they would be truly mutual. An internationally supervised arms ban wouldn't harm our defense capacity now, as it would have then. The situation has changed since I was in the leadership and discussed the problem with Eisenhower.

There was one point on which Eisenhower and I agreed in our private talks at Camp David: that was the problem of military spending. I've said how I always admired Eisenhower for his modesty, his common sense, and his many years of experience. Gromyko must have been present, and no doubt so was somebody from the American side, but in this case Eisenhower and I did all the talking, man to man. He brought up the subject:

"Tell me, Mr. Khrushchev, how do you decide on funds for military expenditures?" Then, before I had a chance to say anything, he continued, "Perhaps first I should tell you how it is with us."

"Well, how is it with you?"

He smiled, and I smiled back at him. I had a feeling what he was going to say. "It's like this. My military leaders come to me and say, 'Mr. President, we need such and such a sum for such and such a program. If we don't get the funds we need, we'll fall behind the Soviet Union.' So I invariably give in. That's how they wring money out of me. They keep grabbing for more, and I keep giving it to them. Now tell me, how is it with you?"

"It's just the same. Some people from our military department come and say, 'Comrade Khrushchev, look at this! The Americans are developing such and such a system. We could develop the same system, but it would cost such and such.' I tell them there's no money; it's all been allotted already. So they say, 'If we don't get the money we need and if there's a war, then the enemy will have superiority over us.' So we talk about it some more; I mull over their request and finally come to the conclusion that the military should be supported with whatever funds they say they need. Then I put the matter to the government and we take the steps which our military people have recommended."

"Yes," he said, "that's what I thought. You know, we really should come to some sort of an agreement in order to stop this fruitless, really wasteful rivalry."

"That's one of our dreams. We've been devoting all our efforts to reaching some kind of agreement with you on the limitation of the arms race. Part of my reason for coming to the US was to see if some sort of understanding might not come out of our meetings and conversations. But how can we agree? On what basis?"

That was the problem: we couldn't agree then, and we can't agree now.[49]

To sum up: our conversations weren't too productive. In fact, they had failed. We had failed to remove the major obstacles between us; we'd examined those obstacles, but we hadn't removed them. I could tell Eisenhower was deflated. He looked like a man who had fallen through a hole in the ice and been dragged from the river with freezing water still dripping off of him. Perhaps Eisenhower had promised the ruling circles in his government that he would reach an agreement with us, and now his hopes were dashed. Maybe that's why he looked so bitterly disappointed.

As for myself, naturally I was upset, too, though not as much as he was. I hadn't come to the US with any illusions, and I had known all along that it was premature to expect an agreement. Of course, we would have liked to have come to an agreement, but not at the expense of making any unilateral concessions.

Our negotiations were coming to an end. We had lost all hope of finding a realistic exit from the impasse our talks had led to. Except for agreeing that Eisenhower would pay a return visit to the USSR,

49. This conversation with Eisenhower about dealing with the military is also in *KR*, I, 519–520.

we didn't even know how to formulate a final communiqué. This upset Eisenhower all the more.

Lunchtime came. It was more like a funeral than a wedding feast. Well, maybe that's going too far: it wasn't so much like a funeral as it was like a meal served at the bedside of a critically ill patient. Afterwards Eisenhower suggested we go back into Washington by car. That was fine with me. I'd read about all the roads in America, and I was curious to see for myself what they looked like. If we'd both been more satisfied with the outcome of our talks, it might have been a pleasant drive. But we weren't, and it wasn't. I asked some questions just to be polite, and he answered with a few words. It wasn't really a conversation at all. Every sentence was a strain to get out. I could see how depressed and worried Eisenhower was; and I knew how he felt, but there wasn't anything I could do to help him.

When we got back to Washington, Eisenhower dropped me off where I was staying.[50] He then went back to the White House. The day of our departure had come. At the airport that evening we went through more or less the same ceremony which we had experienced on our arrival: speeches, an honor guard, the podium decked out in glittering decorations, a red carpet, and all the pomp which is part of the standard high-level protocol in all countries. At the end of the ceremony we had to use a ladder to climb into our plane, just as we had when we arrived. They still hadn't found a set of proper stairs high enough for our Tu-114.

Once everyone was on board and waiting to take off, our security chief informed us that we had received an anonymous telephone call warning that there was a bomb on board Khrushchev's plane. The caller had just phoned in that message and hung up. Our security chief assured me that it was just a provocation. The plane had been under guard round the clock, and all the luggage had been carefully checked before it was loaded. I figured our security chief must be right; the call must have been from some American who wanted to test our nerves and see if we would panic. But who was this provocateur? Was he just one individual, acting on his own, or was he part of some supposedly respectable organization? In any case, he didn't have any success; we gave no satisfaction to the people who had staged this last-minute provocation against us.

I gave the order: "All right, let's take off." As is well known we crossed the ocean and landed in Moscow without mishap.

50. Khrushchev was staying at Blair House, near the White House.

After my return home some of our journalists published a collective work on my tour of the United States. I think it's a fairly objective and useful book.[51] Even now I sometimes run into people who tell me they have read this book and still cherish it as a token of those times.

A short time later, I went to Peking to celebrate the October 1 anniversary of the Chinese people's victory and the Communists' rise to power. On my way back to Moscow, I stopped in the Far East to inspect our naval installations at Golden Horn Bay.[52] A spontaneous meeting was held at which I was asked to speak about my visit to the United States. I described how I had walked along a red carpet and reviewed an honor guard, then stood at attention while a twenty-one-gun salute was fired in our honor.

"As I looked down from the podium at the people receiving me," I said in my speech at Golden Horn Bay, "I knew full well that they did not belong to the proletarian class. I knew that even as they welcomed me to the United States, they still regarded the Soviet Union with hostility. I knew that they were not so much honoring me as they were honoring their own President. Nevertheless, I knew that the occasion represented a great triumph not only for our delegation, but for Soviet power, for the working class, for Lenin, for Lenin's ideas and teaching — and for the Soviet armed forces."

My words evoked a tumultuous reaction from the people listening to me. There were shouts of "Hurrah!" and outbursts of literally thunderous applause. They were not cheering for me personally. After all, each of us can only do his job according to the trust vested in him when he represents his country in this or that post for a certain period. The audience was applauding an achievement of our policy, of our Marxist-Leninist teaching, and of our people, who by their sweat and blood had raised our poverty-stricken country to such heights that others now had no choice but to recognize our greatness. Even a country like the United States, which had conducted reactionary policies against the Soviet Union as far back as the Civil War, when it landed interventionist forces against us in the Far East — even a country which had arrogantly refused to recognize us for thir-

51. Published in Moscow in 1960 as *Face to Face with America*.
52. Golden Horn Bay, in the Pacific port city of Vladivostok, is the site of a major naval base.

teen years after the Revolution — such a country had at last been forced to invite our representatives to its capital and to receive us with honor!

Some people might say nothing came of our visit to the US. My answer to that is: yes and no. Something did come of it, though not at once. We were plowing virgin soil, so to speak; we broke the ice which had held our relations in a paralyzing grip. Now it remained for our diplomats to remove the stubborn chunks of ice from our path and to clear the way for further improvement in relations. This process continues even today.

Still, there are people who insist on asking, "Don't you think it was a mistake to accept Eisenhower's invitation in the first place?" I tell them, "No. That would have been unreasonable." By going we gave the Americans a chance to learn more about the Soviet Union. To those fair-minded representatives of the bourgeois press who were willing to open their eyes, we gave a chance to see that relations between our two countries had changed, regardless of whether we signed any concrete agreements.

Then there are those who argue that the trip was just camouflage and window dressing, particularly the pomp and ceremony with which we were received in America. Maybe so, but window dressing has its own significance in the bourgeois world. It meant that the Americans recognized the failure of their past efforts to discredit us, to humiliate us, and to eliminate us.

Even if we didn't reap material benefits right away, my talks with Eisenhower represented a colossal moral victory. I still remember how delighted I was the first time my interpreter told me that Eisenhower had called me, in English, "my friend."

Some will say, "Well, those are just words." Of course they're just words! What do you expect? Do you think when two representatives holding diametrically opposing views get together and shake hands, the contradictions between our systems will simply melt away? What kind of day dream is that?!

Most important: the Americans took the initiative of inviting us to their country after a long ideological war. They had no hope — and they certainly didn't succeed — in forcing us to compromise our basic principles and dignity. On the contrary, we emerged from the visit and the talks with our position in the world strengthened, firm as a rock, and ready to defend our positions in the future.

Unfortunately, not long after my visit to the US, our relations suffered a sudden setback, all because of the treacherous policies of the American government and Dulles in particular.[53] This setback came as a great disappointment to us, since up until then the US seemed to be showing its good will. We had greatly appreciated the enlightenment American political leaders, especially President Eisenhower, had shown in inviting me to the US. I had thought the President sincerely wanted to change his policies and improve relations. Then, all of a sudden, came an outrageous violation of our sovereignty. And it came as a bitter, shameful disappointment.[54]

53. Here he is referring to Allen Dulles, director of the CIA.
54. Khrushchev is referring to the U-2 affair, which he describes in detail in Chapter 18 below, after his account of his intervening trip to France.

17

The Tour of France

EARLY in 1960 I received an invitation from President de Gaulle to visit France. I must admit we were caught by surprise. It came at a time when France had been deeply involved in the aggressive activities of the NATO alliance and had been pursuing anti-Soviet policies to such a degree that we felt forced to threaten cancellation of the friendship treaty which had been signed by our two countries after the war. We had hoped the threat would make French politicians take a sober look at what would be in store for them if the Soviet Union withdrew its friendship at a time when Germany was becoming economically strong once again. Our position had been that the Soviet-French Friendship Treaty created in the eyes of the French people an illusion of good relations that was in fact contradicted by the French government's participation in NATO and its anti-Soviet policies. We wanted to confront the French with a dilemma. We knew they hadn't forgotten how many times their country had been occupied by German armies, and we knew they feared that a strong Germany might turn against them once again.[1]

When we said we would no longer consider ourselves bound by the treaty, it had an immediate effect on some French people. The left-wing parties were thunderstruck. So was the French Communist Party, which of course correctly understood our position. But the men who actually determined French policy didn't give a damn. They'd long since decided to sacrifice the treaty. Therefore we had

1. After 1955, the year in which West Germany formally entered NATO, the USSR claimed that France was in violation of the spirit of the 1944 Franco-Soviet pact worked out by de Gaulle during his wartime visit to Moscow (see Chapter 15 above). This dispute was still very much alive when Khrushchev made his eleven-day state visit to France in March and April, 1960.

no reason to expect that these same ruling circles in France would suddenly turn around and extend their hospitality to the head of the Soviet Union. Nonetheless, there it was — an invitation from the French President, General de Gaulle.

No sooner did we decide to accept the invitation than a serious problem came up. We agreed to spend ten days and visit several cities in France, but that apparently wasn't enough to satisfy the French leaders. They insisted I also make a trip to Algeria, where they wanted me to see the oil wells in the Sahara Desert. Right up until we left Moscow and even after we arrived in Paris, they kept pressing us, promising that President de Gaulle would accompany us to Algeria. We steadfastly refused. It was clear to us that the trip they wanted us to make to Algeria would be of strictly political significance; it would have amounted to a gesture of recognition on our part of France's claim that Algeria belonged to the French state. The French knew perfectly well that we were in total sympathy with the Arab movement. I had already said as much when I told the French governmental delegation headed by Prime Minister Guy Mollet that France had no choice but to grant independence to the Algerian people. Guy Mollet may have been a onetime member of the leftist Socialists, but at heart he was a colonialist.[2]

De Gaulle, of course, was different. He showed common sense and firmness of character in his handling of extremists seeking to preserve colonial rule in Algeria; more than once I told journalists that except for de Gaulle, there was only one other political force in France capable of ending the war in Algeria, and that was the French Communist Party. Despite de Gaulle's basically reactionary political outlook, in this instance he acted soberly, courageously, and correctly in recognizing that France was doomed to defeat in its bloody, costly struggle against the Algerian people. But my high respect for de Gaulle didn't change the fact that it would have been inappropriate for me to go to Algeria as part of an official visit to France; and although we accepted the invitation to come to France, we had to reject repeatedly our hosts' efforts to get us to include Algeria on our itinerary.

We convened the leadership and decided on the composition of the delegation I would lead. Gromyko was included in his capacity as Foreign Minister. So was Kosygin. Why Kosygin? Because we

2. Mollet had visited Russia in May, 1956.

knew we would be meeting with French industrialists, and Kosygin had a useful background in this regard. I think he'd been the director of some factory in Leningrad. When he was transferred to Moscow, he was put in charge of light industry — or maybe it was the shoe industry, which is an even narrower responsibility. I know he had something to do with shoe production because I used to have dealings with him over the production of leather. I was in the Ukraine at the time, and we supplied leather to the shoe industry. I won't go into details about my dealings with Kosygin; suffice it to say, there was plenty of friction.[3] Anyway, because of his concern with light industry, we decided he should go to Paris with us.

When the day came to leave Moscow, the French ambassador, Monsieur Dejean, joined our party and flew with us in our plane.[4] I had great respect for him and his wife.

It was important that we arrive in Paris according to schedule, since a full-dress reception ceremony had been carefully prepared, and President de Gaulle himself would be waiting for us. We landed right on time. I remember being impressed by how well constructed the concrete runway was and how well equipped the airport was.[5] We should give the West credit: there are some things they can do better than we can, and this runway was an example. It didn't have a single defect. It looked as though it had been finished literally just before I arrived. Much as I've tried over the years and much as I've criticized our construction engineers, our runways still look worn out and potholed a year after they're built. I don't think there's any secret about why everything is always so neat in the West: it's a matter of good production discipline, strict standards, and well-designed processes, especially when it comes to manufacturing and laying concrete. It's just a higher level of culture in the West. This isn't the first time I've mentioned the problem. I used to speak of it whenever I came home from a trip abroad; unfortunately, the comparisons I made were rarely in our favor.

As our plane taxied to a prearranged spot, I looked out the window

3. As Deputy Prime Minister and Chairman of the State Planning Commission, Kosygin was more powerful than Khrushchev suggests here. As for his earlier career, Kosygin had been the director of a spinning mill in Leningrad in the late 1930's until he was promoted to the Leningrad Regional Party leadership, then transferred to Moscow as People's Commissar of the Textile Industry in 1939.
4. Maurice Dejean, ambassador to the USSR, 1955–1964.
5. Orly Field.

and saw a red carpet, an honor guard, and a group of officials. It was easy to pick out President de Gaulle from the rest. As I recall, his wife was standing next to him. She was there because Nina Petrovna was traveling with me.[6] The President and I greeted each other. He took me to review the honor guard, which then marched smartly past us. After exchanging brief remarks, the President and I got in his car and drove into Paris under special escort.

Paris impressed me greatly. Naturally I'd read about the city, but, as they say, it's better to see something with your own eyes than to hear about it. Crowds of people lined the streets to watch us as we went past. They cheered and shouted greetings to us. Obviously they approved of their President's decision to invite the representatives of the Soviet Union to France and to improve relations between our countries. I'm sure the French Communist Party wasn't standing idle at that time; I'm sure it had something to do with the demonstrations organized for us. The Party had great influence. Therefore there was no shortage of people with the right political attitudes who sympathized with the socialist movement and who hadn't forgotten the Soviet Union's role in the defeat of our mutual enemy, Hitlerite Germany.

We were taken to the Elysée Palace, where the presidential guard met us. I was surprised that they actually came out on horseback and rode alongside our car. Maybe it was some sort of tradition passed down from Napoleonic times. They were all dressed up and looked very elegant and handsome. I'm sure they were specially selected for this duty. I know the palace guard of our tsars used to be selected by height and by hair color, a practice copied from the French and Austrian royal courts, and I think de Gaulle's guard was a holdover from those times.

When we arrived at the palace, an iron gate was thrown open, and we were led into a richly decorated courtyard. The crowds and the guards remained outside. The President showed us to our quarters and left us to get settled.

During my stay in Paris the French government arranged an enormous reception in my honor. De Gaulle himself was there, towering over everyone else, and seemed full of energy. He made a point of introducing me to representatives of African states belonging to the so-called French Community — in other words, the colonies. He kept leading some Negro over to me and saying, "This is Monsieur

6. Also included were Khrushchev's daughters, son, and son-in-law.

So-and-so; he represents such-and-such a province of France." Naturally these people always smiled and acted very courteous with the President, and as soon as they'd been introduced to me, he'd run off to find some more. I remember particularly one dark-skinned woman from Algiers. De Gaulle introduced us, then left us alone to chat. She started talking very fast, heaping praise on France, on de Gaulle, on the existing political system, trying to convince me it was good for the Algerian Arabs to live in the French Community. I didn't like listening to her one bit, but I couldn't start arguing with her, not in such surroundings anyway. It would have caused a scene. I decided to ask her just one simple question:

"Madame, perhaps not everyone feels the way you do. I wouldn't necessarily hear the same thing from all your compatriots, would I?"

"Yes," she said, "ask anyone. Of course, maybe you'd find some who would disagree, but certainly the majority feels the way I do."

"Then who are these people fighting against French rule? There's been a war going on for years in Algeria. The facts, madame, seem to contradict what you say. You seem to like the situation the way it is, but I doubt your words reflect the true feelings of the Algerian people."

The conversation ended there because de Gaulle brought over two more Africans for me to meet. One was a Senegalese, a tall, handsome man, so black that there was almost a purplish tint to his skin. He, too, was in favor of the Community and said he wanted Senegal to remain part of the French Republic.

It was quite natural for de Gaulle to want me to meet this select group of well-fed, well-groomed, well-educated, and probably wealthy colonial representatives who would tell me how France treats her colonies so well. These were colonials who liked the colonialists, and de Gaulle presented each of them to me as if he or she were a voice of the masses. It reminds me once again of what the great Ukrainian poet and thinker Taras Grigoryevich Shevchenko once said: "From the land of the Moldavians to the land of the Finns, all tongues are silent because the times are good." [7] Shevchenko meant those lines to be ironic, and I could have quoted them to de Gaulle now. But I was his guest, and knew I had better keep my own tongue silent.

At one of these receptions someone mentioned Sekou Toure, the

7. Taras Shevchenko, a nineteenth-century Ukrainian poet. These same lines are quoted in *KR*, I, 235.

President of Guinea. I said that I knew him, that he'd been to the Soviet Union more than once, and that I thought very highly of him. De Gaulle's voice turned noticeably sad and regretful: "Yes, I used to know him too. France gave Sekou Toure his education, and now he has pulled Guinea out of the French Community." De Gaulle didn't permit himself to say anything which would downgrade or denounce Sekou Toure, but I could still hear a note of grief in his voice. For a long time we had mistrusted France, wondering if the French would really keep their promise to withdraw their troops from Guinea; but here again, as in the case of Algeria, de Gaulle did the honest and correct thing.

While de Gaulle busied himself mostly with introducing Africans to me, I met some other guests who were from France proper, including my old friend from the Geneva conference, the former Prime Minister, Faure. I used to call him Edgar Fyodorovich. I liked him very much. He was an extremely sociable and pleasant man. He introduced me to his wife, who I think was an editor of some woman's magazine.[8]

Many Frenchmen came up to me on their own, among them quite a few big capitalists. They would exchange a couple of sentences with me, then wander off while someone else came over to meet me. It was just like in a railroad station: you could talk to anyone you wanted for as long as you wanted, then he could go his way and you could go yours. Receptions create much better conditions for communication than sit-down dinners. When you have to sit according to prearranged order at a table, it's as though you'd drawn a lottery ticket for your dinner partner, whom you're then stuck with, like it or not, for the rest of the evening. That's why I much prefer receptions.

A particularly memorable one was given for us at our embassy by our ambassador, Comrade Vinogradov and his wife. I remember standing in line with Comrade Vinogradov receiving guests. Many prominent people showed up. We could tell they were prominent because they had names beginning with "de," which I believe means a person who belongs to the nobility. Of course, the French Revolution settled accounts with a lot of people whose names began with "de," and we all know who came out on top — Monsieur Capital! In France now, it still helps to have a "de" in front of your name, but what *really* counts is how much money you have.

8. Edgar Faure, whom Khrushchev knew from Geneva (*KR*, I, 399). His wife, Lucie Faure, a journalist, was founder and director of *La Nef*.

While I was standing in the receiving line, along came a good-looking young man with a black mustache and his hair groomed in a fancy way. His face looked just like one of those that used to be drawn on the signs outside a barbershop. Our ambassador whispered to me that I would now meet the biggest capitalist in all of France, Rothschild.[9] Of course it's a terribly famous name. I'd known about the Rothschilds from the newspapers back in the days when I was a worker because their own workers were always going on strike.

When he was introduced to me, I said, "I'm very pleased to meet you, Mr. Rothschild. I've heard a lot about you. I'm glad to have the honor of shaking hands with you. I welcome you as a guest of our embassy." He murmured something in reply.

The reason I'm relating this incident is that we attached some significance to Rothschild's attendance at our reception. Of course, he wouldn't have come if we hadn't invited him. As Comrade Vinogradov said, "If Rothschild does come, it means he isn't boycotting our invitation, and therefore he's expressing his recognition of us." That wasn't to say Rothschild was showing his *respect* for us. After all, what kind of respect could a Rothschild have for the representatives of the Soviet State, especially for the Chairman of the Council of Ministers and Secretary of the Central Committee?

Another of France's biggest capitalists also showed up. This was Mr. Boussac, who owned I don't know how many textile mills and garment factories with thousands of people working for him and an enormous amount of capital under his control.[10] He was also the publisher of the newspaper *L'Aurore*, which was considered to be the most reactionary paper in France; it treated us mercilessly. Yet for some reason this man Boussac seemed to harbor good feelings toward our State and toward me personally.

Not long before, he had come to the Soviet Union. He cabled ahead, asking for an appointment with me. We discussed this request in the leadership and decided to tell the Ministry of Foreign Affairs to inform Boussac that I would see him. He came, I received him, we talked for a long time, then he thanked me and left. I was somewhat perplexed because he didn't seem to have any concrete matters on his mind. He just wanted to talk about general problems of peace,

9. Baron Elie de Rothschild, who maintained contact with the Soviet and East European governments on behalf of his family's business interests.

10. Marcel Boussac, textile entrepreneur and the founder and owner of Christian Dior. His trip to the USSR, described in succeeding paragraphs, was in September, 1959.

things he could have found out simply by reading our speeches and articles in the press. Why had he come? For a long time I couldn't figure it out.

Maybe it was just that he admired the way we were trying to maintain peace all over the world and wanted to establish contact with me as the political leader whom he considered the number one man in the Soviet government and Communist Party. A capitalist is a capitalist, so obviously he had no use for our internal policies; but apparently he approved of our foreign policy and wished to hear about it from us personally rather than read about it in the newspaper. Who knows why, but there are such cases among capitalists: men who believe that states and individuals on opposite sides of the class struggle should work together towards peaceful coexistence.

Mr. Boussac was an example. I was told he was a Czech by nationality but had lived in France for a long time. He was well along in years, obese and already getting a bit feeble. He organized an exhibition in our honor at one of his factories. The products he showed us were wonderful: fabrics, ties, women's wear, all kinds of clothing. Everything was beautifully made. I think he had more than one fish to fry. In other words, he was hoping to sell some of his products to the Soviet Union.

The exhibition included a display of pictures depicting the life of his workers, with emphasis on all the social benefits he provided for them: rest homes, hospitals, child-care centers, and so on. The children in the photographs looked no worse off than our children — maybe even a little better. No doubt he really did create such conditions for his workers, but the important question was: does capitalism really take care of *all* its workers this well? I kept this question to myself rather than argue it with him. After all, it's essentially a debate between Communism and capitalism, not between two men, and I've always known who will win that debate in the long run. Arguing with Boussac wasn't going to accomplish anything. It certainly wasn't going to convert him to socialism.

Besides, he was being a very gracious host, and there was no denying that we had a lot to learn from him. Many of the things he showed us could have been usefully implemented in our own factories. I had it in mind to try to transplant some of Boussac's methods into our industry, and he was willing to cooperate fully.

"You're welcome to have a look at anything which interests you in the manufacturing process at my factory," he said. "You're free to come any time you want. I'll show you not only how we produce our current line of goods, but also how we adapt our production to a new line when fashions change." I was later told by our officials at the embassy that Boussac had a special research center where practically no one except his own staff was ever allowed. He made an exception for us, so I asked Comrade Kosygin — who, as I've already mentioned, accompanied me to Paris — to inspect Mr. Boussac's operation in more detail.

Incidentally, I kept in contact with Boussac long afterwards. For years he would always send me something for my birthday. I remember on my seventieth he sent me a case of brandy almost eighty years old and several bottles of a very strong alcoholic French drink called calvados, which is made from apple juice. The brandy was from his own cellar. Every time I had a glass of it I would think of Mr. Boussac with gratitude. As I think about him now, it occurs to me that Boussac was something like our Morozov, who had contacts with Gorky even though he knew full well that Gorky was connected with the Bolsheviks.[11] Boussac was the same sort of eccentric. He dealt with me as the head of the Soviet government but had nothing to do with the French Communist Party. In fact, all the while he was behaving so civilly to me, his newspaper *L'Aurore* was engaged in the most vicious attacks against the Communist Party. Maybe by maintaining good relations with the head of the Soviet government he simply hoped to do business and trade with us, thereby making more money. Well, in a way we had the same attitude toward him. So I believe we understood each other correctly and based our evaluations of each other on correct assumptions. When all was said and done, I believe our contacts with Mr. Boussac were undoubtedly helpful.

So far I've only talked about the big capitalists who attended the reception given for us at our embassy. Naturally, there were French Communists there, too. Comrades Thorez and Duclos came. So did Thorez's wife, Vermeersch, who was a leader of the French working class and Communist Party in her own right. She was a former worker, distinguished by a long career of political activity.[12] With our French comrades we would embrace, shake hands, and exchange

11. Sava Morozov, a Moscow millionaire textile manufacturer who contributed heavily to radical causes.

12. Jacques Duclos had been a member of the French Party Central Committee since 1925. Maurice Thorez's wife, Julie-Marie, was known in Party circles as Jeannette Vermeersch.

greetings, but we didn't spend much time on serious talk. That left us more time to meet other, nonproletarian guests at the reception. We knew that our French comrades would be coming around to our embassy later for private discussions on issues of mutual interest to us as politicians, as friends, and as brothers sharing a common political worldview.

I remember once Comrade Thorez came to see us and told us he wholeheartedly approved of our courageous speeches, in which we didn't try to smooth over the differences between the two systems. He said our willingness to speak forthrightly about our class sympathies represented a great contribution to his own efforts at propagandizing on behalf of socialism. Thorez expressed these sentiments to us not just with his words, but with his face and his whole manner. He always smiled when he talked to us; you could see his teeth, and his eyes sparkled. I never suspected him of camouflaging his true feelings; I never regarded him as an actor sitting in front of me and putting on a show. No, I knew he wasn't capable of falsehood. He was a great political leader who was irreconcilable in his determination to defend and fight for what he felt was right. I knew him best of all the French comrades. We used to take our vacations together in the Caucasus, and we also met frequently in Moscow.

We also had great respect for Comrade Duclos and Waldeck Rochet. We had no disagreements with either of them on any matters relating to foreign policy or the international Communist movement. I still have the greatest respect for Comrade Rochet. I remember when he celebrated his sixty-fifth birthday.[13] For well-known reasons, I couldn't express my best wishes to him publicly, but now that I'm dictating my reminiscences about my visit to France, I'd like to send him my greetings: I wish him and his comrades well in achieving the goals which the French Communist Party has set before itself; I wish them every success in their struggle for freedom and for the victory of socialism in France.

When Comrade Thorez congratulated me on the directness of my speeches, he might have been referring to an address I gave at a meeting of the Soviet-French Friendship Society. The hall was packed, and later I was told by the comrades that an enormous crowd outside listened to my speech carried over loudspeakers to the square. The atmosphere was exceptionally warm. Here was yet an-

13. Rochet, a French Politbureau member, turned sixty-five in April, 1970.

other reminder that the French people had a special sympathy for the Soviet Union. Why? Because they owed us a large debt for their liberation from the Hitlerite occupation; also, they knew that their country had been occupied by the Germans in the first place as a direct result of their government's irreconcilable hostility toward the Soviet Union. The French government had partly sealed its own doom when it refused to ally itself with us in the fight against Germany. I think that fact was understood by every Frenchman — not just by French Communists, but also by people who did not share our view of a better life.

We spoke out strongly at press conferences, too. We told gatherings of journalists that the capitalist system must give way to the more progressive socialist society, although we emphasized that it was up to the people of each country to find their own solutions for their own problems. We said we sympathized with the forces of change but did not want to interfere in anyone else's internal affairs: neither revolution nor counterrevolution is for export.

Of course, some disagreed with my public statements. That's to be expected in a bourgeois society where there are organizations specifically designed to reflect the views of the government. We knew that de Gaulle's government was diametrically opposed to our political views and locked in struggle with the Communist Party. Therefore, as de Gaulle's guests, we had to be careful to avoid getting embroiled in debates and passing judgment publicly on the French social system. We limited ourselves to expressing general ideas implied by the teachings of Marx, Engels, and Lenin.

Lenin, by the way, had once stayed in Paris, and during my visit there the Central Committee of the French Communist Party suggested we go see the apartment where he used to live.[14] It had been turned into a museum, and I must say, going there made a deep impression on us. Such good care had been taken of the memory of our Great Lenin! I call him "our" Lenin, though of course he now belongs to the working class of all progressive mankind throughout the world. Nevertheless, he was *our* compatriot, *our* leader, and the first to cry out that conditions were ripe for a socialist revolution in Russia. So we still considered him our own Vladimir Ilyich. After

14. Lenin lived in exile in Paris from 1909 to 1912. The Lenin apartment on the Left Bank was the only Communist shrine which the French government allowed Khrushchev to visit during his tour of the country.

inspecting the rooms where our leader had once lived, Comrade Thorez and I came out onto a balcony and addressed the crowds of workers and their families who had gathered on the street below. They greeted our delegation with an outpouring of sympathy because we represented the great Soviet people.

We also met with members of the French working class at the Renault automobile plant near Paris. As I recall, there were many Communists among the workers there. The plant director was very obliging toward our delegation. He even presented me with a small car.[15] He expressed the wish that Renault might establish cooperation with our own automobile industry. I couldn't have agreed with him more and told him so. Unfortunately, nothing ever came of it. It's difficult to establish economic cooperation between two countries with such different political systems.

As you can see, my schedule allowed me quite a bit of time to meet people and familiarize myself with all sides of French life. I was especially eager to see some of the famous historical and cultural sites.

France is one great, rich museum of history and architecture. Everywhere you go there's something to astonish you, something for you to admire and enjoy. However, in the words of Kozma Prutkov, you can't embrace the unembraceable, so naturally I managed to see only a fraction of the interesting places, buildings, paintings, sculptures, and so on.[16]

While still in Paris at the beginning of my visit, I went to the Louvre. It reminded me of my youth when I once toured the Winter Palace in Leningrad; after a whole day of moving as quickly as I could from room to room, I was so exhausted that I couldn't walk; I just collapsed on a park bench to rest — and that was when I was young and strong! Well, the Louvre is even bigger and richer in its collection of beautiful things. You can't possibly see everything in one visit. I was also shown the Champs Elysées and taken out to Versailles by our guide, the Minister of Culture, a famous writer named

15. At the Renault works in Flins, Khrushchev was presented with a blue Floride sports car. In this, as in other chapters, Khrushchev is sometimes mistaken about the chronology of episodes and the itinerary of his travels. For example, the incident at the Renault factory described here actually occurred at the end of his swing through the provinces.

16. Kozma Prutkov was the pseudonym of four nineteenth-century poets — A. K. Tolstoy and the three brothers Zhemchuzhnikov — who collaborated on a collection of satirical aphorisms and humorous verses.

[Malraux].[17] I was told he had had an interesting life. He'd started off as an active Communist, then later become an equally active Gaullist. I found him warm and sincere. He wanted me to get a good impression of France and of all its cultural treasures.

According to the schedule of our visit, we were supposed to make a tour of the provinces, or departments as they're called. I was told that in each city along the way we would be met by a presidential representative, or prefect — in other words, an appointed, rather than elected official, who among other duties had administrative jurisdiction over the police. At first I was somewhat offended by this aspect of the protocol for our visit. I didn't like the idea of traveling under the wing of the French police. I thought our delegation was being discriminated against in some way. However, we consulted Comrade Thorez, and he explained that President de Gaulle ordered his representatives to receive only the most honored guests.

We were accompanied on the trip by a number of close associates of the President, and during our stopovers in some cities we were met by an official from the French Foreign Ministry, who had preceded Dejean as ambassador to Moscow and who knew Russian. He would join us for dinner in each city along the way, and over brandy or liqueurs he'd reach a point in the conversation where he would feel an urge to sing Russian songs. The rest of us would accompany him as best we could. We're not the sort who overestimate our singing abilities, but it was pleasant to find a Frenchman who enjoyed sharing our company this way. Because Nina Petrovna was with me, we were also accompanied by Ambassador Dejean's wife, an old acquaintance from Moscow and an extremely nice woman.[18]

Everywhere we went we were delighted with the attitude of the Frenchmen we met. I saw no signs of hostility anywhere. Sometimes our visit to a city would coincide with a holiday. For example, in one town the citizens were electing a beauty queen, and they invited us to watch. Everyone was all dressed up in national costume. Nina Petrovna and I were introduced to their beauty queen. She was indeed

17. André Malraux was de Gaulle's Minister of Culture. In the original Russian, Khrushchev says, "The Minister of Culture was a well-known writer. I think he had the same last name as that other famous French writer, Molière."
18. Khrushchev's main guide was Louis Joxe, Minister of Education, who had been envoy to Moscow from 1952 to 1955. The entourage also included Minister of State Louis Jacquinot, Jean-Marcel Jeanneney, and the Dejeans.

a very beautiful girl. I think if I had a picture of her and showed it to people, they'd agree she could have been a Russian beauty queen. She looked just like a Russian girl: plump, red-cheeked, and healthy. At the end of the celebration the townspeople presented Nina Petrovna with a doll. I'm recounting this incident because it illustrates how well received we were everywhere.

From my visit to Bordeaux I remember best the mayor, an energetic and — compared to me — young man named Chaban-Delmas.[19] He took me on a driving tour of the city and told me with great enthusiasm about his plans for the reconstruction of Bordeaux. He kept pointing out whole blocks of apartment buildings which he said were going to be demolished. I listened to him carefully but didn't press him with too many questions since he was talking about a local matter that was none of my business. However, I have to admit I couldn't really understand — not to mention sympathize with — his eagerness to demolish all these apartments. Maybe it was simply because in the Soviet Union we felt a greater need for dwellings and therefore cherished even the oldest house, as long as it could still serve its function and satisfy the most basic requirement of our urban population. I was particularly aware of the housing problem in Moscow, but the situation in other cities was no better. In cities all over our country, people suffered from overcrowding and poor facilities, living like bedbugs in every crack in the wall. Often one room would be shared by two families. It's incredible! I don't know how a family can live in such conditions. It was because thoughts like this were going through my mind that I was surprised to hear Chaban-Delmas putting so much stress on the demolition of old buildings.

I thought to myself, "Well, I've got to remember these men are capitalists, and they have their own considerations. We Communists are different. For us tearing down an apartment building and moving the people out is a difficult social problem."

Nevertheless, Chaban-Delmas made a good impression on me. I'd been told he was a Gaullist, and he certainly didn't conceal it from me. Throughout our conversation he kept proudly referring to his close contacts with President de Gaulle.

I liked Marseilles very much. The surrounding countryside reminded me of our own Black Sea coast with its dry soil and scrubby

19. Jacques Chaban-Delmas, Mayor of Bordeaux and President of the National Assembly.

vegetation, and the city itself looked a lot like Odessa. In fact Marseilles and Odessa later became sister cities. I knew that the two cities had maintained close economic ties for a very long time. Back when I was much younger and living in the Ukraine, I remember we had something called Marseilles tile. It was explained to me that the French coming to Odessa for Russian wheat would load their ships in Marseilles with a special sort of tile for ballast; then, when they reached Odessa, they'd sell the tile and fill their holds with wheat. And now, as a Russian who'd seen Odessa many times, I was finally seeing Marseilles myself.

I stayed in a palace or manor house reserved for special guests. The presidential representative who welcomed me to Marseilles said to me jokingly, "Mr. Khrushchev, this whole house is at your disposal. You might be interested to know that the bed you'll be sleeping in was where Napoleon III used to sleep."

I could take a joke, so I replied in the same spirit, "That doesn't make it any easier for me to stay here."

He meant by his remark that the house was a historical monument, where French kings used to live when they came to Marseilles and therefore was for only the most honored guests. He chose to make light of it because he knew I wouldn't be greatly impressed — and he was right. We continued the joke at dinner.

His wife turned out to be a very nice English woman. She told us she loved Russian vodka. We'd brought some presents with us, including a few bottles of vodka, so we broke it out and drank it. After we finished it off, I felt there was a definite need for more; I asked our security guards who were traveling with us if they had any. They produced some immediately. At about this point the English lady was smiling happily, and we polished off our guards' vodka without any trouble. I'd like to be correctly understood here. I don't want anyone to think I'm saying that the presidential representative's wife had a weakness for alcohol. Nothing of the sort. She conducted herself with dignity and didn't get even the slightest bit drunk. She was considerably younger than her husband and obviously in excellent health. She just knew how to hold her liquor. But she knew her limit, too. I don't want to create a bad impression about the wife of the man who received us so hospitably in Marseilles. She was a good woman, a good wife, and a good mother. She was also very gay. I don't know: maybe gaiety is a national characteristic of the English. In the unrestrained atmosphere of our meal together, both she and her husband treated us with warmth, courtesy, and good will.[20]

Now, I know maybe some people are going to say, "How can Khrushchev, a Communist, have such a benevolent attitude toward the French administration in Marseilles, especially toward a man who was in charge of the local police?" My answer to that is: can I help it if even under a police uniform sometimes beats a human heart? Of course, maybe his heart had nothing to do with it, and he was just discharging the task assigned to him by the President. I wouldn't try to guess. All I know is, I was treated very well.

I remember at the same meal the Foreign Ministry official who had formerly been ambassador to Moscow [Louis Joxe] got slightly drunk and started singing songs. Pretty soon we all began singing the *Marseillaise*. I mean, after all, how could you be in Marseilles and *not* sing the *Marseillaise?* We began to remember the history of the great French Revolution. The mood was all very pleasant. I enjoyed singing the *Marseillaise* because I had been brought up on it; it was the song of my youth. Each of us, of course, felt about the song in a different way. The Frenchmen sang it as the French national anthem, while we were singing it as the revolutionary battle hymn of the working class.

I said to the former ambassador, "Do you know how we used to sing this song? I'm not sure what our host will think about the lyrics in our version." I told him the lyrics. They went like this:

General Trepov summoned all his gendarmes;
"Oh, you bluecoats, search all the apartments!"
"We have searched three hundred, sir, and found not a single socialist,
But in the three hundred and first we found a student and under his coat
We found a bottle of water!"

It must have been just a folk song, because no poet would compose lyrics like that. The song had been popular in my youth, but only among Donbass miners because even an old revolutionary like Voroshilov, who was older than I, hadn't heard it.

After I'd told him the lyrics, the former ambassador said, "Oh, sure, let's sing it!" So we began to sing, and he joined in. It made me

20. The prefect in Marseilles was Raymond Haas-Picard. His wife, the former Phyllis Spacey, was English.

think of my distant youth, but it also made me a bit uncomfortable. I kept looking over my shoulder to see if there were any policemen around. The gendarme who was our host didn't understand the lyrics, but the former ambassador understood every word — and was roaring with laughter. After a while I decided we should stop before we offended our host, who was a gendarme himself.

"Let's sing something else instead," I said. "It would be too bad if our singing this song were misinterpreted." The former ambassador just laughed all the harder. I liked him very much; he really knew how to put people at ease.

The next city on our itinerary was Dijon. The former ambassador showed up there, too, and joined us at a huge feast the local officials gave in my honor. In the middle of the meal, a Frenchman dressed up as a peasant shepherd suddenly appeared and presented me with a white lamb. Cameras were clicking and whirring as the photographers recorded the presentation of this gift. Everyone started making jokes. We had to decide whether the lamb should live or die — whether we would grant it life or sentence it to death. In the end we granted it life. It would have been appropriate to roast and eat it but we decided a live lamb would better symbolize friendly relations and peaceful coexistence since a lamb, like a dove, is a nonaggressive beast. That was the theme of our joking. The atmosphere was relaxed and full of fun. We felt completely at home.

There were more serious, I would even say unfortunate, moments during our stay in Dijon. We had been told before we got there about Canon Kir, who was the mayor of the city and had been active in organizing the anti-Nazi resistance during the war. If my memory doesn't betray me, I think I was told he was sentenced to death twice by the Germans. He also held an especially friendly position towards the Soviet Union because of our role in the defeat of the Germans. He was a man who hated Fascism and who was sympathetically disposed to the Soviet State. He was even considered by some to be pro-Soviet. In a word, he was a unique man, and I looked forward to meeting him.

Well, we were given a reception fit for a king in Dijon, and we were welcomed by all kinds of people — but not by Canon Kir. I learned that the hierarchy of the French Catholic Church didn't want him to meet me since I was an atheist and a Communist, so they ordered him to go somewhere else. I think they confined him temporarily in a monastery. It was even rumored he had been arrested and taken away for good.[21]

After we settled into the quarters assigned to us, a huge crowd gathered near our residence and started shouting something at us. I asked my interpreter to translate, and he said they were chanting: "Khrushchev! Free Kir!" They wanted me to interfere and force someone to let Kir come home, but no one knew where Kir was. Even if I had known, I wouldn't have been able to do anything, no matter how much our sympathies were with him. Some officials later explained that he was a hothead and a bit unbalanced. I took that to mean they were afraid he might have gone too far in welcoming us. Obviously the French authorities wanted our reception to be warm — but not *too* warm. I regretted the whole incident very much, because I would have liked to have met Kir.

I have happier memories of my visit to a French province near the Spanish border where President de Gaulle suggested I might be interested in inspecting an experimental irrigation system.[22] For the first time in my life I saw fields irrigated not by channels or ditches but by an ingenious, modern method utilizing a network of cement-lined trays and troughs, so that there wouldn't be any loss of water through leakage. I was extremely impressed. It was all organized on the highest technological level. The system required industrial as well as agricultural innovation, since you'd have to build a plant for manufacturing the concrete-lined trays. Still, I was absolutely determined to introduce such a system in the Soviet Union. When I got back to Moscow, I described the whole thing to my own irrigation experts and sent some of them to France to study the method. Later we put it into wide use in Tadzhikistan, Uzbekistan, Kirghizia, and Turkmenistan.

I was also interested to note how the French plant fruit trees, especially pears, in trellised orchards. As a result the branches of the trees are outstretched in a way that makes it easier to pick the fruit. The pickers can select only the ripe fruit, rather than having to shake the fruit out of the tree. You can also plant more trees in a given area.

21. The Catholic Church actively boycotted Khrushchev's provincial tour. The Mayor of Dijon, Canon Félix Kir, a Resistance hero, was forbidden by church superiors from attending the welcome ceremonies for Khrushchev. It was later reported that Kir had been removed from Dijon by the police for the duration of Khrushchev's stay.

22. Khrushchev visited a number of irrigation projects in southern France. He has described his enthusiasm for one near the Spanish border, in which he later tried to interest Nasser (*KR*, I, 449).

Of course, with this method the trees don't live quite as long as they would otherwise, but you still come out ahead economically. Our own agronomic literature favors this method of planting fruit trees, but I haven't seen it used in our country except in a few small orchards belonging to amateur agronomists.

I was grateful to de Gaulle for recommending stops of such a practical nature.

Before rejoining de Gaulle for a long round of talks, I was taken to Verdun, where I visited the graves of soldiers who perished in World War I. Of course, we and the French had been allies; our troops fought on French soil and were buried side by side with the Frenchmen killed in the struggle against the Kaiser of Germany. My visit to the cemetery was a solemn and memorable moment. We came to a whole field of crosses — I don't know how many thousands of crosses. We paid our respects and bared our heads while the Soviet and French anthems were played.

A crowd of workers had come out to the cemetery by bus from the city; they unfurled a red banner as a fraternal demonstration by proletarians greeting a former proletarian now the head of the Soviet State and the head of the Soviet Party. The presidential representative who was accompanying me said, "I greatly appreciate the tact of the Communist Party, which sent these workers out to greet you. They've avoided doing anything which might detract from the ceremony. They aren't shouting any slogans or opposition to the President, and they're not trying to turn this occasion into a rally of some kind. Obviously they remember that in the war all Frenchmen, proletarian and otherwise, fought together as a single nation. The Communist leadership of the workers gathered here has decided to show respect for our national flag, even though they brought their own red banner here." [23]

I remember also being driven to one memorial service by de Gaulle's Minister of Internal Affairs, a young man who could speak to me in Russian without an interpreter.[24] Much to my surprise, he began singing a Russian song in the car. I asked him how he had learned it.

"Oh," he replied, "I know many Russian songs. I like them, and

23. Khrushchev was taken to the World War I memorial at Verdun by Minister of State Louis Jacquinot.
24. The Minister of Internal Affairs at that time was Pierre Chatanet, but Chatanet did not fit the description offered here: he was never a prisoner of war. Khrushchev is apparently confusing him with some other French official.

that's why I'm singing one for you now. I was in a German prisoner-of-war camp with quite a few Russians, and they taught me their language and their songs." He spoke warmly about his Russian fellow prisoners.

Here was a man who sincerely wanted to improve our relations. I think he had probably become convinced of the need to avoid the tragedy of another war in the future while still a prisoner with the Russians in the Hitlerite camp during World War II. He came to realize then that the only sure way to prevent another German attack on France would be an alliance with the Soviet Union. It was an unexpected pleasure to find someone like this among the members of de Gaulle's cabinet.

Throughout our tour of France we didn't have much chance for direct political exchanges. Since we couldn't allow ourselves to engage in any activity that might meet with the President's disapproval and since we knew only too well what *his* political convictions were, there wasn't much way we could have contacts with either Communist Party or workers' organizations in the provinces. Nor did I have any specially organized meetings with the peasants, though of course there were plenty of chance meetings along the way. I remember once as we were driving past a vineyard I saw some peasants picking grapes; one of them caught sight of our car; he waved his arms over his head and started running toward us holding up a wine bottle and a glass. We took this to mean that the French peasants wanted their country to improve relations with the Soviet Union so they could have a more certain future and not have to be afraid of war.

By and large the French people seemed to understand that the foreign policy of the Soviet Union was directed toward the strengthening of peace. Regardless of their social and political convictions, all Frenchmen could see the expedience and reasonableness of Lenin's policy of friendship. As I've already indicated, even certain capitalists understood the need for further improving our relations. Unfortunately, however, as they've demonstrated more than once at the polls during their elections, the majority of the French people did not agree with us on the way for them to achieve a better life. The Communist way, of course, is through the revolutionary transformation of a capitalist system into a socialist system.

As for de Gaulle himself, he was committed to the defeat of the

Communist movement, and we had to keep this in mind when in the company of his representatives during our tour of the country. There's an old saying: If you tell me who your friends are, I can tell you what sort of person you are. Well, these men who received us in various French cities were friends of de Gaulle, therefore we knew well enough to stick to abstract subjects and avoid politics in our talks. To conduct political discussions in the presence of people who perform functions of a police nature is sheer stupidity.

Of course, there was no way to avoid politics in my talks with de Gaulle himself. On the contrary, my number one reason for coming to France was to discuss with him in depth a number of important and troublesome issues. These discussions became possible at the end of our tour of France when we returned to Paris. The President suggested we go to his country residence, a palace where we would be able to get away from the distractions of the city; no one would be able to bother us, and we would be able to have complete freedom to exchange views over breakfast, lunch, and supper.[25] I thanked him for his kind offer, understanding that such an invitation was an expression of special respect and esteem for our country. It was comparable to my stay at Camp David with President Eisenhower.

Nina Petrovna came with me to de Gaulle's palace, and, naturally, his wife was there, too. I don't know whether it's true or not, but people who claimed to know the political views of de Gaulle's wife warned us that she was a convinced Catholic and therefore an equally convinced anti-Communist; it would be a great effort for her to be a good hostess to Communists at her palace, even to sit at the same table with them. Be that as it may, we didn't sense any unfriendliness on her part. She was warm and courteous; and when de Gaulle and I were having our talks, she made sure that Nina Petrovna was always entertained. I could tell she was a cultured woman, and even if deep down, because of her religious feelings, she couldn't stand Communists, she knew how to restrain her dislike for us as atheists and representatives of the Soviet State.

Once, when I was at the table with de Gaulle, his wife, Nina Petrovna, and our interpreter, the President addressed a question to me with the words, *"mon ami."* I asked my interpreter what it meant. He explained that it meant "my friend" in French. I looked at de Gaulle and noticed he wasn't smiling. He smiled rarely. I took that to

25. Rambouillet, a former royal château thirty-five miles southwest of Paris.

mean he seriously considered me his friend and a friend of France. This was a good omen; it indicated de Gaulle wanted to underscore that even though we held diametrically opposing political convictions, we were joined in a common effort to maintain peace. I responded in the appropriate manner: I started calling him "my friend."

Before saying something about the substance of our talks, I'd like to give some idea of our general assessment of de Gaulle as a man and as a political leader. Talleyrand once said that a diplomat is given a tongue in order to hide his true thoughts. The same goes for a politician. De Gaulle is a case in point. Was he smart or stupid? For a while he was considered an idiot and a fascist. But in fact he was a very smart fellow.

I'd first met de Gaulle at the end of the war when he came to Moscow at Stalin's invitation. We were afraid de Gaulle would start throwing all the French Communists in jail. Comrade Thorez, who had been in Moscow during the war, was about to return to France, and Stalin asked de Gaulle if Thorez would be arrested as soon as Thorez set foot in Paris. As it turned out, not only was Thorez not arrested — he was included in the government as a representative of the French Communist Party and even became one of de Gaulle's deputies in the leadership.

Then, when de Gaulle came back to lead the country for the second time, he strengthened the power of the Presidency (in other words, his own power); he established a reactionary election law opening the floodgates for rightist forces; but he did *not* create conditions for the suppression of the French Communist Party. He correctly understood that the Communist Party has deep roots in the French working class and peasantry, and something curbed his intolerance towards the ideals of Communism. Perhaps he was afraid an outright suppression of the Party might cause unrest or even civil war. Whatever his motivation, he demonstrated common sense by allowing the Communist Party to provide representation for the French peasantry and proletariat in the parliament. Of course, he left only a narrow opening, the slightest crack, yet it was enough for the Communist Party and its press to survive.

It was a good thing, too, because someone had to lead the attack on de Gaulle's immense personal power. He himself said, "I am France." The government formed by him was supposed to do nothing but stand at his side while he made all the decisions. The government passively accepted its status; it didn't claim any rights to sharing in some sort of collective leadership. It was left to the Communist Party and press to declare war on the concentration of all that power in the hands of one man — one man who let himself become the faithful servant and ideologue of his own class, the capitalists and landowners. Even today, now that de Gaulle is no longer there, the power in France is still concentrated in the hands of a few outspoken Gaullists who pursue the same reactionary internal policies.

However, when it came to foreign policy, we considered de Gaulle one of the most intelligent statesmen in the world, at least among the bourgeois leaders. I've already mentioned how we approved of his common sense in his treatment of the French colonies, Algeria and Guinea. Furthermore he had a correct and sober-minded evaluation of the Soviet Union's importance in the world. In much the same words Macmillan had used, de Gaulle admitted to me that he knew France didn't have the stature and influence she once had possessed; he recognized that the United States and the Soviet Union were now *the* two great powers, and — while he didn't necessarily approve of our foreign policy — his own foreign policy did not represent an aggressive force directed against us.

Before I settled down with de Gaulle for our talks, our ambassador, Vinogradov, stressed to me the positive aspects of the President's foreign policy. Vinogradov was completely won over by the General. Jokingly, we used to refer to Vinogradov among ourselves as a Gaullist. I should add, however, that as a result of my own experience with de Gaulle, I shared Vinogradov's high estimation of him.

One thing I liked about de Gaulle was his self-confidence and air of authority. He didn't need anyone else to tell him what was and was not in France's best interests. He spoke for himself throughout our discussions. His Foreign Minister and Prime Minister were present during the talks, but their presence was only a formality; Gromyko was present on our side during some of the sessions, and de Gaulle wanted to have equal representation on the French side.[26] But the point is, he rarely if ever consulted his ministers, and I don't know whether they dared express their own opinions in his presence — at least not during our discussions. If they said anything at

26. Maurice Couve de Murville was the Foreign Minister and Michel Debré the Prime Minister. On the Soviet side were Kosygin and Gromyko.

all, you could be sure it would follow exactly the line set by de Gaulle.

He and I agreed to stick to matters of foreign policy. In other words, questions relating to the internal systems of France and the Soviet Union were absolutely excluded and not touched on in any way. De Gaulle understood that matters of internal policy can be decided only by the country involved, and he didn't so much as hint at any disagreement he might have had with our political system, though of course I knew perfectly well he was against it. Nor did I make any hints about the French system of government.

The most important problem before us was the German question — and that, in turn, meant agreeing upon a peace treaty we could both sign. A peace treaty was of life-or-death urgency. With it, tensions would relax, and men could breathe more easily. Without it, we couldn't hope to solve a whole range of other problems: disarmament, trade, cultural and scientific contacts, to mention only a few. The German question was the crux of relations between our two countries. It was by far the toughest nut to crack, and until we cracked it there would be no basis on which to normalize our relations.

De Gaulle was incredibly calm and unhurried in conducting his side of the discussions. I might even say his slow pace bothered us somewhat. "What's the hurry, Mr. Khrushchev?" he said. "Why do you want to sign this peace treaty right now? The time isn't ripe yet. Our views on the ultimate solution to the German problem are still too far apart."

And what were his views? For one thing, I could tell he still mistrusted Germany deeply. He even gave me his solemn assurance that he would never let France get sucked into a war against the Soviet Union on the side of West Germany and NATO: "Mr. Khrushchev, I can promise you with absolute certainty that France will never fight against the Soviet Union as an ally of Germany." Perhaps the most important thing about de Gaulle's position on Germany was that he differed from other [NATO] countries on the question of German reunification. Other countries supported those forces which strived to liquidate the German Democratic Republic and reunite Germany on a capitalist basis.

De Gaulle, too, was against the political system of the GDR, but his position was unique in that he did *not* want to see Germany reunited at all. On the contrary, he reminded us that ever since the war he had wanted to see Germany dismembered as much as possible. (I think Churchill had once expressed the same point of view.) I won't take the time and effort to try to describe de Gaulle's position in detail, and I can't exactly show you how he wanted to redraw the boundaries on the map, but he said outright: "Two Germanies is not enough; our preference has always been for a larger number of independent Germanies." In the meantime de Gaulle was content to let Germany remain divided between NATO and the Warsaw Pact. He said so, in so many words, several times: "Let's leave everything the way it is now. East Germany belongs to the Warsaw Alliance — in other words, it belongs to you; and West Germany belongs to NATO. Let's keep it that way." I took this to mean that de Gaulle genuinely appreciated the German danger, but it also meant — as he himself said — that there was no room for agreement between us on a peace treaty, since we wanted the German Democratic Republic to be truly independent — and not "belong" to anybody.

He seemed not to want to weaken NATO, but at the same time he said he didn't want to weaken our Warsaw Alliance. He wanted to preserve both the borders and the military alliances established after the war. In other words, he wanted to preserve the *status quo*. That wouldn't rule out the possibility of accidents which might lead to military conflict, but his position represented the best of a bad lot of solutions proposed by bourgeois leaders, so we were satisfied with it.

De Gaulle also tried to promote his idea that Europe should be united into one entity from the Atlantic to the Urals. I couldn't understand the idea then, and I can't understand it now. Europe consists of many states with different social and political systems, participating in different political and military alliances. So how can it be united "from the Atlantic to the Urals"? Besides, in addition to being impractical, the idea also had an unpleasant historical association for us. Hitler, too, had wanted to get to the Urals. I couldn't help thinking to myself, "How surprising! We already defeated one of them, and now here's another one toying with the same idea." I'm sure de Gaulle wasn't the only capitalist leader who wanted to unite Europe. For that matter, we wanted to unite it, too. There was only one difference between us: they wanted to establish capitalism throughout the continent, while we wanted to eliminate capitalism and establish socialism.

While favoring some sort of increased unity among the nations of Europe, de Gaulle also told us that France's position in the NATO alliance was increasingly uncomfortable, and he told us flatly that it was the guardianship of Europe by the United States which caused this discomfort. He repeatedly expressed his belief that Europe should free itself from US guardianship and even suggested that we might help France and other European countries rid themselves of excess American influence. I had to give de Gaulle credit for one thing: he had a clear understanding of where France's interests lay, and he was not subject to outside influences; it was impossible for anyone — including the Americans — to force upon him any position which was not in France's best interests as he saw them. Therefore he favored those conditions which would lead to the noninterference of the United States in the internal affairs of Europe. He did not want France to be simply a pawn on the board of America's global policy to isolate the Soviet Union, nor did he want France to be a blind weapon in the hands of the United States.

Naturally this position of his was expedient and reasonable from our point of view, although I must say it perplexed me somewhat. Given de Gaulle's class affiliation, I felt then — and I still feel — France would fight on the side of the United States in the event that war broke out with the Soviet Union. Therefore I couldn't figure out exactly what he had in mind. He dropped some hints, but I couldn't tell exactly where they were leading. He made clear only that he was uncomfortable about France's participation in NATO, but at the time it was hard to conceive that he would actually pull out of the alliance. You can imagine my interest when, much later, de Gaulle did indeed withdraw his troops from under the command of NATO, thereby undoubtedly weakening the aggressive forces directed against the socialist countries.[27] Thus he remained true to his ideal of uniting Europe from the Atlantic to the Urals; not that he expected political and social unity, but he took a step in the right direction, toward allowing Europeans to decide for themselves the questions of war and peace on the continent without American interference.

Later, after I'd already gone into retirement and assumed the status of a pensioner, de Gaulle paid a return visit to the Soviet Union.[28] Our contacts and cooperation with France have been increasing ever since.

27. In February of 1966, de Gaulle announced that France would assume control of all NATO installations on its territory.
28. De Gaulle visited the USSR in June, 1966.

18

The U-2 Affair

A Plane Is Downed

AFTER my trip to the United States, the governments of four nations — the US, England, France, and the Soviet Union — arranged to meet in Paris to discuss the possibility of an agreement on disarmament and peaceful coexistence. We didn't have much hope that the negotiations would produce a meaningful agreement among countries with different political systems, but, regardless, we began preparing in a serious way for the meeting, which was scheduled for May.[1]

Then, suddenly, something happened which dashed any hopes we might have had. At five o'clock on the morning of May 1 my telephone rang. I picked up the receiver, and the voice on the other end said, "Minister of Defense Marshal Malinovsky reporting." He went on to tell me that an American U-2 reconnaissance plane had crossed the border of Afghanistan into Soviet airspace and was flying toward Sverdlovsk. I replied that it was up to him to shoot down the plane by whatever means he could. Malinovsky said he'd already given the order, adding, "If our antiaircraft units can just keep their eyes open and stop yawning long enough, I'm sure we'll knock the plane down." He was referring to the fact that already in April we'd had an opportunity to shoot down a U-2, but our antiaircraft batteries were caught napping and didn't open fire soon enough.

We'd been acquainted with the U-2 for some time. On several oc-

1. Eisenhower, Macmillan, de Gaulle, and Khrushchev were to meet in mid-May, 1960, in Paris to discuss the German question and disarmament.

casions we'd protested its violations of our airspace, but each time the US brushed our protest aside, saying none of their planes were overflying our territory. We were more infuriated and disgusted every time a violation occurred. We did everything we could to intercept the U-2 and shoot it down with our fighters, but they couldn't reach the altitude the U-2 was flying at. As I recall, our fighters could climb only to 18,000 or 20,000 meters, while the U-2 operated at 21,000 meters. Fortunately, by that time our surface-to-air missiles had already started rolling off the production line. It looked like they were going to be the answer to our problem.

Comrade Gromyko had other ideas. He was a good civil servant who always went by the book. When word reached him that another U-2 was flying over our country, he prepared a draft of a protest to be issued either as a diplomatic note or as a TASS statement. He submitted this document to me, but I proposed to the comrades in the leadership that we not accept it. I said official protests were no longer enough. A public protest could be registered in our press, but we weren't going to resort to public protests and diplomatic channels any more. What good did it do? The Americans knew perfectly well that they were in the wrong. They knew they were causing us terrible headaches whenever one of these planes took off on a mission.

This latest flight, towards Sverdlovsk, was an especially deep penetration into our territory and therefore an especially arrogant violation of our sovereignty. We were sick and tired of these unpleasant surprises, sick and tired of being subjected to these indignities. They were making these flights to show up our impotence. Well, we weren't impotent any longer.

Later on in the day, after Comrade Malinovsky notified me about the U-2 flight, the annual May Day military parade took place on Red Square. The sky was sunny and beautiful. The celebration was jubilant; the mood of the working people was joyous. In the midst of the proceedings Marshal Biryuzov, commander in chief of our antiaircraft defenses, mounted the reviewing stand on top of the Mausoleum and whispered in my ear. He informed me the U-2 had been shot down; the pilot had been taken prisoner and was already under interrogation. According to Marshal Biryuzov's report, several of our antiaircraft installations had been arranged in a chessboard pattern, so that the U-2 was bound to run into one or another. When the plane came within range of one battery, two missiles were launched. As I recall, the plane was hit by the first missile; the second was fired for good measure, to make sure it couldn't escape. I congratulated Marshal Biryuzov on this wonderful news; I shook his hand and he left. The fact that Biryuzov had appeared on the Mausoleum during the parade did not go unnoticed. Afterwards, diplomats said they knew right away something important was happening because Marshal Biryuzov was wearing an ordinary tunic and uniform rather than his parade outfit and was whispering in my ear.

The U-2 pilot, Powers, ejected from his plane when it was hit and parachuted to earth.[2] He was seized immediately by workers on a collective farm, who turned him over to our military. When they searched him, they confiscated an ampoule of fast-acting poison. If anything happened to his plane, he was supposed to kill himself by pricking his finger with the poison. However well trained Powers may have been, he didn't do as he was told. His will power wasn't strong enough to overcome his desire to go on living; he just couldn't bring himself to commit suicide. So we captured him alive, and the pin and ampoule became our trophy. We instructed that the wreckage of the plane be brought to Moscow and displayed publicly in Gorky Recreational Park. People came pouring in from all over to view and touch the remains of the plane which the United States had used to spy against us.

Powers didn't resist when our people interrogated him. This was logical since he'd already decided not to use the means he'd been equipped with to keep silent. He told us how long he'd been in espionage work, how much he was paid, who his wife was — in other words, everything. I think we also captured a map with his flight plan, from which we learned that he had originally been stationed at an air base in Turkey, but that he later flew to Pakistan and from there via Afghanistan into the Soviet Union. His flight plan was to have taken him over Chelyabinsk and Sverdlovsk into Norway, where he would have landed.

We were all the more indignant because these flights had been going on for years. The United States was using against other countries intelligence-gathering methods which were inadmissible in

2. A U-2 high-altitude jet reconnaissance plane piloted by Francis Gary Powers, a former air force lieutenant working for the CIA, was shot down on May 1 near Sverdlovsk. He was on a photographic mission that would have taken him from Peshawar in Pakistan to Bodo in Norway.

peacetime. Napoleon once said, even if the cannon are silent, the war of diplomacy goes on. Well, as far as we were concerned, this sort of espionage was war — war waged by other means.

The next day the American press published the story that a US plane based in Turkey had disappeared while flying over the Caucasus Mountains — but on the Turkish side of the border. We smiled with pleasure as we anticipated the discomfort which the spies who cooked up this false statement would feel when confronted with the evidence we already had in our pocket.

Our intelligence organs continued with their interrogation of Powers, going over his testimony and sending reports to the government. During a session of the Supreme Soviet we discussed the matter in the leadership. I proposed the following plan: I would make a speech at the session and inform the Supreme Soviet that the Americans had violated the sovereignty of our State; I would announce that the plane had been shot down, but — and this was important — I would *not* reveal that the pilot had been captured alive and was in our hands. Our intention here was to confuse the government circles of the United States. As long as the Americans thought the pilot was dead, they would keep putting out the story that perhaps the plane had accidentally strayed off course and had been shot down in the mountains on the Soviet side of the border.

Two or three days later, after they talked themselves out and got thoroughly wound up in this unbelievable story, we decided to tell the world what had really happened. The time had come to pin down the Americans and expose their lies. I was authorized to make the statement. We laid out everything just as it had occurred: the plane's point of origin, its route, its destination, and its mission. But the biggest blow for the Americans was the announcement that the pilot was in custody and that he was giving us evidence that we would reveal to the world. The Supreme Soviet heard my report with great wrath and jubilation. The wrath was aimed against the policies of the United States, while the jubilation was addressed to our armed forces. We were especially grateful to the technicians and engineers who had equipped our army with weapons which enabled us to shoot down a plane the Americans considered invincible. We have an old folk proverb: no matter how many times you fetch water from the well in the same pitcher, sooner or later the day comes when the pitcher breaks. Well, no matter how many times this American spy plane had flown over us with impunity, its time had finally come.

America had been pursuing a two-faced policy. On the one hand, the US had been approaching us with outstretched arms and all sorts of assurances about their peaceful and friendly intentions. On the other hand they were stabbing us in the back. As I've often said, the U-2 incident was war waged by other means. Napoleon used to say that if the cannon were silent, then war was waged by diplomatic means. Well, when the Americans committed its hostile act against us, they may have been waging diplomatic warfare, but they were using military means. And they couldn't hide behind their technology forever. Fortunately, we caught them in the act and made the most of it.

Once we had exposed them outright in their lie, the American press started saying that Eisenhower didn't know about these flights: they were the responsibility of Allen Dulles, the brother of the late Secretary of State, and Eisenhower would never have approved such tricks had Dulles ever reported them to him. This, of course, was the most reasonable explanation for an unreasonable action. It gave the President a chance to vindicate himself and to save face in light of the meeting which was to take place in Paris.

I went out of my way not to accuse the President in my own statements. For example, when Marshal Biryuzov and I went out to Gorky Park to look at the wreckage of the U-2 (I was curious to see the plane too), I talked to the foreign newsmen and other people gathered in the pavilion. Naturally there were a lot of questions which I was glad to have a chance to answer. In my remarks, I followed the same line which had appeared in the American press — in other words, that Dulles and the US military establishment were to blame for the U-2. I said nothing about the President. After all, it was in our interests to say that undisciplined people in the American intelligence organization, rather than the President, were responsible. As long as President Eisenhower was dissociated from the U-2 affair, we could continue our policy of strengthening Soviet-US relations which had begun with my trip to America and my talks with Eisenhower.

But the Americans wouldn't let the matter rest there.

One day in May we got a report that President Eisenhower had made a statement saying he had known about the U-2 flight in advance, and he had approved it. He argued that he was forced to resort to such means because the Soviet Union was, as they used to say, a "closed society" that doesn't allow correspondents or other

Americans on its territory. He claimed he had an obligation to protect the security of the United States, which left him no choice but to conduct intelligence-gathering by means of such flights. Speaking as commander in chief, he said he felt the US had a right to guarantee its own security, regardless of other countries' interests, and that the US would continue to conduct such flights in the future.

This was a highly unreasonable statement, not to say a foolish one. It was as though Eisenhower were boasting arrogantly about what the United States could do and would do. Eisenhower's stand canceled any opportunity for us to get him out of the ticklish situation he was in. Here was the President of the United States, the man whom we were supposed to negotiate with at the meeting in Paris, defending outrageous, inadmissible actions! We had no choice but to come out with the strongest denunciation of the way the President justified the U-2 flights. It was no longer possible for us to spare the President. He had, so to speak, offered us his back end, and we obliged him by kicking it as hard as we could. Our resolute response had an immediate effect.

It used to be common for American and even British planes operating out of West Germany to violate the borders of Czechoslovakia and the German Democratic Republic, but we decided to put a stop to that, too. We forced a few of these planes to land and even shot one down. What effect did our countermeasures have? Well, the commander of the American forces issued an order that American planes were to keep at least fifty kilometers from the borders of the GDR. Then, some US reconnaissance planes were flying over our northern territorial waters, collecting intelligence on our radar installations along the Arctic Circle. We shot one of them down. The American practice in such cases was to announce that their plane had been flying over international waters. But, of course, they had no way of proving their claim, and we had concrete proof that the opposite was true. Some of the crew members had been killed, but one or two were captured alive. We returned the corpses to the US immediately, but the survivors we held.[3]

Other than that case, the US has ceased to violate our airspace. Naturally, while they're always looking for an opportunity to spy on others, the Americans will never allow anyone to fly over their own

3. An American RB-47 jet reconnaissance bomber was shot down by a Soviet interceptor in July, 1960, over the Barents Sea. Two of the six crewmen survived and were captured.

territory. As for the Soviet Union — which has a legitimate interest in reconnaissance and intelligence — it would have been difficult for us to send our planes over America, since we're too far away. The United States was not threatened by us. The exact opposite was true. After all, it was our country, not the United States, which was surrounded by military bases in Europe, Asia, and Africa. The US was practically out of range for our airplanes, and we had only a few missiles that could reach the US. So the U-2 affair was a unilateral, unprovoked demonstration of their supposed superiority and outrageous treachery. The Americans were showing that they didn't give a damn about anyone else, that they would pursue only their own selfish goals. They wanted to dictate to us their conditions from a position of power.

I'm convinced that we handled the matter in the best way. For one thing, despite Eisenhower's bragging about how the US had a right to continue spy flights in the future, violations ceased after we shot down Powers's plane. The Americans now knew that we were both willing and able to fire on any plane that flew over our territory. We had no use for the policy of the Gospels: if someone slaps you, just turn the other cheek. We had shown that anyone who slapped us on our cheek would get his head kicked off. The Americans had been taught a lesson. They had learned the limit of our tolerance. They now knew that American imperialism would not go unpunished if it overstepped this limit. We showed the whole world that while all other Western powers might crawl on their bellies in front of America's mighty financial and industrial capital, we wouldn't bow down — not for one second. Our goal was peace and friendship, but we wouldn't let ourselves be abused and degraded.

The U-2 affair was a landmark event in our struggle against the American imperialists who were waging the Cold War. My visit to the United States the preceding fall had seemed to herald a promising shift in US policy toward our country, but now — thanks to the U-2 — the honeymoon was over.

The Paris Summit

OUR hopes for reaching an agreement in the upcoming four-power negotiations in Paris had suffered a terrible setback because of the

U-2 affair. However, the date for the conference had already been set. The leaders of the four powers were all planning to come. World public opinion was overwhelmingly in favor of our going ahead with the meeting as scheduled. We didn't want to be responsible for the failure of the meeting, nor did we want to be blamed for the disappointment a failure would cause. So, while we continued to condemn the United States for its policy of spying on us, we decided not to cancel the Paris meeting on our own initiative.

The time came to prepare for the trip and to select members of our delegation. It had already been arranged that each delegation would be led by the head of government or head of state. Therefore my own name was immediately approved by the leadership. Another representative would be the Minister of Foreign Affairs, Comrade Gromyko. But then we found out that the Americans were going to bring their Defense Minister.[4] In response I suggested we include Comrade Malinovsky in our delegation. If the Americans wanted to place this particular significance on their participation in the meeting, then we should counteract by bringing our own Defense Minister.

Before leaving, we prepared the necessary documents. These were devoted to advancing the goal of peaceful coexistence and finding a solution to the controversial issues, above all the German question and disarmament. I was particularly concerned about disarmament. Recently a great deal of dangerously flammable material had accumulated. If an explosion were touched off by a spark, a terrible war would break out.

The day came to leave for Paris. We selected our Il-18 for the flight. Both in appearance and in technical qualities, it's a perfectly good plane. We were feeling much more self-confident before this summit than before our earlier participation at another four-power meeting in Geneva, when we were embarrassed to land in a two-engine plane while all the other leaders arrived in four-engine ones.[5]

After we were already in the air flying toward Paris, Andrei Andreyevich Gromyko, Comrade Malinovsky, and I began to think over the situation. We felt our responsibility — and the tension that went with it — more acutely than ever before. We were haunted by the

4. Thomas S. Gates, Jr., the US Secretary of Defense, was included in the delegation in the capacity of Eisenhower's "principal military advisor."

5. Khrushchev has confessed his embarrassment over arriving in Geneva for the 1955 summit meeting aboard "a modest two-engine" Ilyushin-14 (*KR*, I, 395).

fact that just prior to this meeting the United States had dared to send its U-2 reconnaissance plane against us. It was as though the Americans had deliberately tried to place a time bomb under the meeting, set to go off just as we were about to sit down with them at the negotiating table. What else could we expect from such a country? Could we really expect it to come to a reasonable agreement with us? No! So the conference was doomed before it began. These doubts kept nagging at my brain. I became more and more convinced that our pride and dignity would be damaged if we went ahead with the meeting as though nothing had happened. Our prestige would suffer, especially in the third world. After all, we were the injured party. If anybody had a right to bring the matter of the U-2 up, it was our side. Naturally, some countries would blame us for the failure of the meeting. Let them. We simply could not go to Paris pretending everything was fine.

The idea came to me that we should make some basic alterations in the declaration we had prepared for presentation at the outset of the negotiations. Our reputation depended on our making some sort of protest: we owed it to world public opinion, particularly public opinion in Communist countries and those countries fighting for their independence. How could they count on us to give them a helping hand if we allowed ourselves to be spat upon without so much as a murmur of protest? Therefore we would have to change our opening declaration so that it would make clear that we were standing up to defend our honor. I saw that the only way out was to present the United States with an ultimatum: the Americans would have to apologize officially for sending their spy plane into the USSR, and the President of the United States would have to retract what he said about America's "right" to conduct reconnaissance over our territory.

I expressed these thoughts to Andrei Andreyevich Gromyko aboard the plane. He agreed. Then I talked it over with Malinovsky. He, too, said he felt I was absolutely right. I dictated my ideas for a new declaration to the stenographers we had with us, and Andrei Andreyevich instructed his staff to sit down and draft a new declaration. The document had to be turned around 180 degrees. Since we hadn't discussed the new declaration with the collective leadership, we immediately transmitted the draft to Moscow for examination by the other comrades. That was possible because we had stenographers, as well as communications staff and facilities, with us on board. We received an answer from Moscow right away; the comrades in the leadership gave their complete approval to our new position. Thus we had left Moscow with a set of documents pointing in one direction, and we landed in Paris with documents pointing in the opposite direction.

When we arrived, I thought to myself, "Well, here we are, ready to demand an apology from the President. But what if he refuses to apologize? What if he doesn't call off reconnaissance flights against us?" I remembered that when we were Eisenhower's guests in Washington, we had given him an invitation to pay a return visit to the Soviet Union. He had accepted our invitation with thanks. But under the conditions that had developed, with our relations falling to pieces, we couldn't possibly offer our hospitality to someone who had already, so to speak, made a mess at his host's table. To receive Eisenhower without first hearing him apologize would be an intolerable insult to the leadership of our country. That's why the thought crossed my mind that in our declaration we should threaten to withdraw our invitation to Eisenhower unless he gave us his assurances that the U-2 flights would be canceled. The other members of the delegation agreed. We quickly dispatched this new position to Moscow and immediately received approval from the leadership.

And so we were ready to begin the four-power meeting. We were charged up with explosive ideas. Our delegation was like a powerful magnet which repels foreign bodies of opposite charge. Anything could happen.

In accordance with the rules of diplomatic courtesy, I paid a visit on de Gaulle soon after our arrival. As for Macmillan, I had already expressed to him my displeasure at the conduct of the United States. I told both de Gaulle and Macmillan that I wouldn't be satisfied until I had both Eisenhower's apology for what he had already done and his assurances that it wouldn't happen again. De Gaulle and Macmillan tried to restrain me in my anger and determination, saying the four-power meeting would fail if I insisted on such a statement from Eisenhower. They said the United States was a great country that couldn't possibly make the sort of statement I was demanding. I replied that we weren't a second-rate country ourselves, that in terms of population and territory we were bigger than the United States, and that, besides, we didn't accept the idea that big countries like the US should get away with abusing small countries — to say nothing of the Soviet Union, which is the biggest country of all. My anger was building up inside me like an electric force which could be discharged in a great flash at any moment.

The time came for the meeting to begin. We wanted our own stenographic report of the meeting, so we told our stenographer from the Council of Ministers, Nadezhda Petrovna, to get ready. She was an extremely intelligent woman. I respected her then, and I still respect her. Whenever I gave a speech, either Nadezhda Petrovna or her colleague from the Central Committee, Nina Ivanovna, would take it down in shorthand. Since, for the most part, I worked out of the Council of Ministers, I used Nadezhda Petrovna more often than not. Just before the meeting the French, who were organizing everything, told us that a measure had been adopted to conduct the meeting with no stenographers present. We were flabbergasted. I told Malinovsky we should make Nadezhda Petrovna a member of our delegation with the rank of secretary. This was a bit tricky because stenographers were women while secretaries were usually men, but there was no law which said you couldn't have a woman with rank of secretary.

"Well, well," I laughed, when informing Nadezhda Petrovna of our decision, "you've just been promoted; you've just been given diplomatic rank." She gave a brief, thin smile, then went back to looking her usual, serious self. She was a taciturn, austere woman; she didn't have much of a weakness for joking around. But she was a good-looking woman, a brunette with a dark complexion and black eyes. People on my staff who knew her better than I did used to tell me she was half gypsy. Her mother was Ukrainian, but her father was a gypsy, and she had inherited his handsome features. She wore a black dress like Carmen. She looked like a queen. After we promoted her from stenographer to a member of our delegation, we joked that no other country in the world could boast such a representative.

We also had a superb interpreter, Comrade Sukhodrev. People used to say, "Khrushchev has an interpreter who really knows English." I had great respect for him and have nothing but the fondest memories of him. He had a typically Ukrainian name, but there wasn't a trace of Ukrainian accent in his speech. He spoke like a typical Russian. Our English-language specialists and foreign newsmen used to tell me that Comrade Sukhodrev was a brilliant interpreter. I think he's still serving at his post.[6]

We went into the conference hall to begin the meeting. The other delegations entered and took their places. The English were the first to arrive. Macmillan and I shook hands. At just that moment the members of the US delegation came in and went right to their places. We greeted them, but very cautiously, as though simply to acknowledge their presence. "Okay," we were saying, "we see you." From the other side of the table they returned the signal: "We see you, too, but we're not going to shake hands with you because there's a conflict between us — you could even say psychological warfare. In short, we don't nurture any respect for each other."

Before the meeting was formally called to order, we addressed ourselves to de Gaulle, as the head of the host country, asking him to allow us to make a statement. We wanted to see what the reaction would be on the part of the President of the United States. De Gaulle already knew the content of our statement. He gave me the floor, and I started to read. In a situation like this I knew I couldn't speak off the top of my head. Every word had to be exact, and every sentence had to be constructed in just the right way. We knew perfectly well that every word was being taken down. We were sure that the other delegations also had aides who doubled as stenographers and were making a shorthand transcript of what was being said. Therefore we wanted our statement to be exactly worded, leaving no room for any misinterpretation that might be used to the advantage of our adversaries.

I demanded an apology from President Eisenhower, as well as assurances that no more American reconnaissance planes would be permitted to fly over Soviet territory. My interpreter, Comrade Sukhodrev, told me he noticed, while reading the English translation of my statement, that Eisenhower turned to his Secretary of State, Mr. Herter, and said, "Well, why not? Why don't we go ahead and make a statement of apology?" Herter said no — and he said it in such a way, with such a grimace on his face, that he left no room for argument on the issue. As a result, Eisenhower refused to apologize. Thus, once again, Eisenhower showed himself to be under the strong influence of his Secretary of State. At the earlier four-power

6. V. M. Sukhodrev was also official interpreter for Brezhnev during his visit to the US in June, 1973.

meeting in Geneva, Eisenhower took all his cues from the late Dulles. Now he was following instructions from Herter. To me, this incident meant that if Eisenhower had followed his own good instincts and used his own considerable intelligence, he would have done the right thing and given in to our demand; he knew it was possible for him to give us the apology and assurances we were asking for. But unfortunately, Eisenhower wasn't the one who determined foreign policy for the US. He let himself be pushed around by his Secretaries of State, first Dulles and now Herter.[7]

I finished reading my statement and sat down. Frankly, I was all worked up, feeling combative and exhilarated. As my kind of simple folk would say, I was spoiling for a fight. I had caused quite a commotion, especially with the passage in which we warned we would rescind our invitation to Eisenhower if we didn't receive satisfaction from the American side. There was a long awkward moment when nobody knew what to do. I think it was Eisenhower himself who gave the signal: he stood up and his delegation followed his lead. Then we all left. We had set off an explosion that scattered the four delegations into their separate chambers. The conference table, which was to have united us, had crumbled into dust.

Later de Gaulle informed us through his Foreign Minister that we would meet again after the other three delegations — the US, Britain, and France — met to discuss our statement and determine their attitude toward it. This was to be expected. Eisenhower would have to meet with his own people and then with his French and British allies in order to work out a general line. We had no hope or expectation that de Gaulle would make a public statement in our favor, but we felt our position was bound to appeal to his instincts. He always unswervingly guarded the honor of France and the French people, so we suspected that, secretly at least, he was sympathetic to our

7. In Moscow, just before coming to Paris, Khrushchev spoke to foreign journalists, angrily denouncing Secretary of State Christian Herter's justification of the U-2 flight: "Mr. Herter's declaration has raised doubt here concerning the accuracy of our earlier opinion that the President did not know about these flights." That same day Eisenhower held a press conference in Washington confirming that he believed high-altitude espionage was "distasteful" but "a vital necessity." Three days later, on May 14, Khrushchev and Malinovsky arrived in Paris. Khrushchev was the opening speaker at the meeting of the four heads of government. He called upon Eisenhower to repudiate spy flights and punish those responsible for the U-2 affair. He also suggested that the summit be postponed for six or eight months, until after the US elections. Eisenhower replied that "these flights were suspended after the recent incident and are not to be resumed."

defense of our own honor. As for the Americans, we knew they couldn't possibly swallow the bitter pill we were trying to force down their throats; they couldn't publicly acknowledge their wrongdoing. This meant that the four-power negotiations were over before they began. But, nevertheless, we would have to wait for the outcome of the meeting between the US, British, and French delegations.

While we waited, we had a free day on our hands that we hadn't anticipated. What should we do? Where should we go? Of course we could always go sightseeing around Paris, but Comrade Malinovsky had a better idea. In World War I, he'd been a machine gunner with a detachment of Russian troops sent to France as part of the Russian Expeditionary Force. During the defense of Paris he'd been stationed in a village out in the country. So he suggested, "Let's go visit the place where our unit was quartered during World War I. The old peasant whose house we lived in is probably dead, but his wife was a young woman. Maybe she's still alive."

"Well, Rodion Yakovlevich," I said, "do you know the road well enough to get us there without a guide?"

"Yes. I know the way and I know some of the people we'll meet when we get there."

I wanted to go very much. Not only would it be a personal pleasure for Rodion Yakovlevich and me to visit the village, but it might have some political benefits as well. He was a Russian soldier who had lived in France and had shed his blood to defend Paris against the Germans. The German question was one of the problems we had now come to Paris to discuss, so I thought it would be a good idea for our Minister of Defense, a marshal of the Soviet Union, to return to the French village where he had fought the Germans over forty years ago. We hoped this gesture would arouse some sympathy among the French people for our position on how to liquidate the consequences of German aggression in World War II.

Only Rodion Yakovlevich and myself, along with our bodyguards, went to the village. No one else had any reason to go. Gromyko stayed behind in Paris to take care of any matters that might come up. We were expecting some cables from Moscow and wanted to keep in touch with the other delegations in case they wanted us to clarify our position on some matter.

So Rodion Yakovlevich and I got in our car and drove out of Paris

along one of those beautiful French country roads lined on both
sides with full, shady linden trees. It was a warm, sunny day, but
evidently there had recently been a bad storm, because at one point
the road was blocked by a fallen linden tree. Along came a road
repair crew with axes and saws to clear the tree off the road. I took an
ax from one of the workers and began to chop away furiously, so that
the chips were flying. The French people gathered around pointing
and laughing: here was the Russian Prime Minister wielding an ax
like a woodcutter! Actually I'd never been a woodcutter, but since
childhood I'd been used to doing hard physical labor, first in the
mines and later in the factory. The photographers and movie camera
men were recording this whole scene on film. I knew it wouldn't do
our delegation's image any harm for people to see that our government is made up of workers and that the head of our government,
despite his age, could still do strenuous work with his hands. When
we finished cutting the tree in half, we dragged the pieces to the side
of the road, got back in our car and drove on.

Rodion Yakovlevich Malinovsky turned out to be an excellent
guide. He led us straight to the village.[8] We went to a house where
he'd been billeted with another soldier so many years before. The
owner came out to meet us as we got out of the car. He was a man of
about forty or forty-five. We introduced ourselves, and Malinovsky
explained, "We've come to say hello to you and your mother if she's
still alive. Surely she'll remember me — a friend of mine and I used
to live out behind your house in your woodshed."

He received us graciously and invited us into the house. His
mother — Malinovsky's former landlady — appeared, and I shook
hands with her. Rodion Yakovlevich asked her whether her husband
was still alive. "No," she said, "my old man died a long time ago.
Now, as you see, my son is grown up and has children of his own."

Malinovsky explained to me that her husband had been a lot older
than she was. She had been young and beautiful. Malinovsky's
comrade, who lived with him in the woodshed, had courted this
woman, and she in turn had been in love with him. Malinovsky used
to collect some interest off the romance himself because she used to
treat him to milk, sour cream, and all sorts of wonderful bits of
French cooking. It was hard to imagine this woman as a fresh, young

8. Pleurs-sur-Marne, seventy miles from Paris. The account of their visit which
follows appears, in shorter form, in *KR*, I, 200, 202.

girl. Now her face was wrinkled and pinched like a hag's; she looked as though she had suffered a lot.

The owner of the house, her son, hurried off somewhere and came back with a few bottles of wine. Then he brought out some cheese, which the French traditionally serve with wine. But the important thing was the kindness of their souls and the warmth with which they received us.

We sat down to the table and began to drink. The old woman joined us. Malinovsky started right in telling stories about the old days when he had lived there. I got the impression that the old woman didn't want to indulge in those memories: she kept an expression of indifference on her face.

After a while we went out onto the street, where the villagers were gathering around. I don't know why, but they were mostly middle-aged and older people — no youngsters. A village is a village, and there must have been some children around, but we didn't see any. Maybe the younger people simply weren't interested in us, but I doubt it. Malinovsky found a fellow about our age whom he recognized from the old days and asked him in French, "Heh! You used to have a little tavern here. Is it still around? Do you still go there?"

The peasant smiled and said, "Yes, the tavern still exists. You still remember it, eh?"

"Of course, I remember it very well."

"Then you probably remember that beautiful girl who worked there and used to serve us wine."

"Yes," said Malinovsky, smiling, "I certainly do."

They all laughed. "He remembers! She was the village beauty! But she's not around any more. For all we know she may be dead."

"Yes, indeed," said Malinovsky, "she was really something, all right."

The girl had obviously left a mark on his memory. If she were still alive, she would no longer be young and probably no longer beautiful. The years pass and take their toll. I remember that during World War II Malinovsky used to tell stories about this unbelievably beautiful girl. The owner of the tavern hired her as a waitress to attract soldiers and young people to buy his wine. But there was no foolishness on the part of this woman or on the part of the soldiers toward her. Of course, in such cases all sorts of frivolous things are possible, but Malinovsky told me nothing of that nature. I believe the men in the village simply enjoyed looking at her for her beauty. She made an impression on Malinovsky that lasted for years after. What more do you want? If this woman had allowed herself to do certain things, I'm sure that as a former soldier and as a marshal he wouldn't have deprived himself of the pleasure of sharing such reminiscences with me. Malinovsky was a man who loved women, especially beautiful women. He used to tell me so himself, particularly when recalling his experiences in Spain during the struggle against Franco. "I've loved some beautiful girls in my time," he said.

Before long other Frenchmen started arriving. The word spread quickly among the villagers that the visitor was the Soviet Minister of Defense who had been a soldier in a Russian unit stationed in this village more than forty years before.

"Of course we remember you!" they all said. "You had a Russian bear in your unit, didn't you?" Malinovsky laughed and explained to me that he and his comrades had picked up a bear cub on the way to France and taken it with them.

That evening, when we drove back to Paris from the village, Comrade Gromyko was waiting for us with some news: the four-power conference had been canceled. I think it was Eisenhower who made the decision, and the other two delegations — the British and French — did nothing to pressure him into making concessions to us.[9]

After the decision to cancel the conference was made, Macmillan came to see me. During our conversation he took a neutral position on the U-2 issue, which had generated the conflict between us and the Americans. As a reasonable man he obviously had no desire to defend the American position, but he couldn't speak out against his ally either. He argued only that we had demanded too much, that we should have been more flexible, and that we made a mistake in rescinding our invitation to Eisenhower. I could tell from the expression on his face that, basically, Macmillan understood our position, but that he was saying all this as a formality in order to register his general solidarity with the United States. He admitted as much when he said, "Mr. Khrushchev, England is no longer able to take an in-

---

9. On May 19, three days after the abortive summit meeting, Khrushchev held a press conference at which he threw a tantrum, making it very clear that he was not satisfied by Eisenhower's statement and that de Gaulle and Macmillan's efforts at mediation had failed.

dependent stand on issues of international politics. It used to be that Great Britain was the ruler of the seas and could determine policy toward Europe and the whole world. But that era has passed. Now the two mightiest states in the world are the United States and yourselves, the Soviet Union. Therefore many things depend on you now." I listened with pleasure and pride. He was absolutely right. We said good-bye to each other cordially. That was my last meeting with him.

Afterwards I paid a call on General de Gaulle. He took a position more or less similar to Macmillan's, although I sensed that de Gaulle was more bitterly disappointed than Macmillan with the collapse of the conference. It could be that he had had greater hopes and expectations. I can't be sure. I'm basing this opinion only on the impression I got from my reading of the expressions on their faces. I said farewell to President de Gaulle and went back to my embassy, where we were staying.

Later, Comrade Thorez and his wife came to see us. Unlike Macmillan and de Gaulle, he smiled and expressed complete approval of our handling of the situation. We had a fraternal exchange of opinions. His only worry was that the French people might not correctly understand what had happened. We knew enough to expect that the West would try to blame everything on us. Someone unsophisticated in politics, a layman, might find it difficult to see why the conference had fallen apart. I asked Comrade Thorez what he thought would happen.

"Of course the imperialists will try to take advantage of your statement," he said, "but our Party and the public will take your side, because your position is based on the principle of mutual respect among nations."

Shortly afterwards I was told that Canon Kir from the city of Dijon wanted an appointment with me. On my previous official visit to France, I had passed through Dijon, but he had been unable to see me. The priest came to see me in Paris; we had an interesting and congenial talk over a glass of coffee in the courtyard of our embassy. He told me how sorry he was that he hadn't been able to see me when I was in France as President de Gaulle's guest, and he voiced his full approval of the position we had taken over the U-2. When the time came for Canon Kir to leave, I asked, "What sort of transportation do you have?" He replied that, naturally, he didn't own a car. I suggested he take mine; my driver would take him wherever he wished. He gratefully accepted my offer. This pleased me, especially because we were in a tense time. The French radio was already making noises to stir up antagonism among the French public against the Soviet Union and its policies. The bourgeois press was heaping abuse on me, personally, blaming me for the failure of the conference. Canon Kir's visit came at just the right time for me, for our embassy, and for our policy. He couldn't be considered a Communist, although he was a man of leftist convictions. Anyway, he showed great level-headedness by taking advantage of my offer that he use my car.

The situation had reached the point where it was inadvisable for me to stay any longer. The bourgeois propaganda machine was working at full throttle to antagonize everybody against the Soviet Union. We drove to the airport. As I recall, we went in a convertible. I specifically asked to be driven in a convertible. Some of the people along the side of the road waved at me in a friendly greeting, while others shook their fists at me. There was nothing unusual or unnatural about that. It wasn't just the bourgeois elements who shook their fists at me — it might also have been common people, workers who followed the Social Democrats and didn't understand our policy.[10]

Many years have passed since then, but I'm still convinced that we handled the matter correctly. Moreover I'm proud that we gave a sharp but fully justified rebuff to the world's mightiest state, that we put the Americans in their place when they violated our sovereignty. There's an old Russian saying: once you let your foot get caught in a quagmire, your whole body will get sucked in. In other words, if we hadn't stood up to the Americans, they would have continued to send spies into our country. Eisenhower said that the Americans had a right to fly over the territory of any society which is "closed." Well, if a "closed society" is one which controls its borders, then perhaps that's what we are. We are prepared to receive hospitably any guests whom we invite — but any uninvited guests will get what they deserve. The Soviet Union is still a new state, a socialist state founded by Vladimir Ilyich Lenin, but we had taken our rightful place in the world. Despite the aggressive actions of the United States, we were determined to continue our general line based on the policy of peaceful coexistence as originally formulated by Lenin.

10. Throughout his memoirs, Khrushchev refers to Western socialists and members of other "bourgeois liberal" parties as Social Democrats.

19

The United Nations

LATER in 1960 the leadership had to decide who to send to the session of the United Nations General Assembly in New York that fall.[1] Usually it's the Minister of Foreign Affairs who leads a governmental delegation to the General Assembly, but that year, because there were some important questions the UN should deal with, we decided to make an exception and have me, as Chairman of the Council of Ministers head the delegation. We wanted to draw the attention of the whole world to the cause of liberating the peoples still living under colonial oppression. I suggested that we should go to the UN and propose establishing a date by which all colonialist countries would have to grant independence to their colonies. We felt this plan would be a milestone in the struggle for peace, so we wanted to work out our proposal carefully in advance and yet not give our adversaries a chance to prepare their opposition. We made sure our intentions didn't leak out into the press while the Foreign Ministry and other government bodies were working out the details of our plan.

By suddenly announcing that the Soviet delegation would be headed by Prime Minister Khrushchev, we poured oil on the fire which had been started by the U-2 affair. A few voices called for common sense, but on the whole the anti-Soviet elements which control the American press reacted violently and started cursing the policy of the Soviet Union at the top of their lungs.

When the announcement was made that I would lead our country's representatives to New York, other socialist countries in Europe also decided to send delegations headed by either their Chairman of the

1. The Fifteenth General Assembly of the United Nations in September, 1960.

Council of Ministers or Secretary of the Central Committee. Then a number of nonsocialist countries decided to send their heads of government: Nehru would come from India, Tito from Yugoslavia, Macmillan from Great Britain.

When the time came to plan our departure for New York, there was something wrong with our Tu-114, which was the only airplane which could take us nonstop from Moscow to New York. We had a choice of flying by way of London in another plane or traveling by ship. (I remember Molotov used to go to America by flying to London and then boarding a British vessel bound for New York.) In the end we settled on making the trip in one of our own Soviet ships. It was a small but comfortable passenger liner. As I recall, it had been made in Holland before the war.[2]

We arranged for representatives of the other Warsaw Pact governments to join us on the voyage. The crossing was supposed to take ten days. I would have plenty of time to prepare the speech I was going to make to the General Assembly, and we would have a chance to hold meetings and discuss matters with our allies, so that we'd be sure to present a unified position toward the various questions on the agenda of the General Assembly.

Our naval experts advised us that the best route was to cross the Baltic Sea from Kaliningrad. Once all the delegations were assembled on board, we said good-bye to our friends who had come to see us off. Our ship blew its whistle and set off. It was evening, but the sky was still light, so we were able to watch the shore of our Motherland as we headed out to sea.

The worry had come up about whether NATO might try some sort of diversionary action against our ship. There was certainly ample opportunity. The Atlantic Ocean is an enormous space, with plenty of room to sink a ship without anyone's ever being the wiser. With all the witnesses dead, NATO could always say that the ship had accidentally hit a mine left over from World War II. There had been such instances in the past, so we couldn't exclude the possibility, but there wasn't very much we could do about it. Our navy suggested that we be escorted by two minesweepers, one in front and one

2. The *Baltika* was indeed Dutch-made. She was built in Amsterdam in 1940 and was used by the Germans until she was captured by the Russians and put into service with the Soviet fleet. The ship had been called the *Vyacheslav Molotov* until 1957, when the crusty Kremlin veteran fell from power in a head-on collision with Khrushchev.

behind; but the minesweepers could accompany us only through the English Channel. Once we left French and British waters, they had to turn back. So the Minister of Merchant Marine arranged for all the Soviet shipping then in the North Atlantic to keep an eye on us and come to our rescue in case of trouble.

The second day out the Baltic turned unfriendly. Thick fog set in, and we could hear buoys and sirens all around us. There was practically no visibility, so the captain had to navigate from buoy to buoy, as in a relay race. Finally the fog lifted, and we could make out the coast of Denmark. Newsmen in airplanes and helicopters began flying out from the shore, diving down and swooping dangerously low so that they could take pictures of us. They circled over our heads, nearly touching the mast. We must have caused quite a sensation for the Western journalists. I guess they were just responding to the demands of their readers for pictures of our voyage to New York. We regularly tuned in news reports about ourselves on the ship's radio, and our interpreters would translate them for us.

Once we passed through the straits and into the open sea, I was overcome by a new and rare feeling. This was the first time in my life that I'd been surrounded by water as far as the eye could see. A man can't help but experience a special sensation. It was very pleasant.

After a while the rocking and rolling of the ship began to have an effect on us. For me, it caused only a slight uncertainty when I tried to walk. But for others it was more serious. The barometer by which we measured the effect was attendance at the dinner table. When mealtime came, we were often told that Comrade So-and-so would not be joining us and we shouldn't wait for him. It became so bad that only a few of us were showing up to eat. One comrade who was especially prone to seasickness was Dr. Vladimir Grigoryevich. I'd known him for many years and had the highest respect for him as a man and a doctor, but he was always the first to head for his bunk when the ocean turned rough. As for our security guards, well, they had to be guarded themselves to keep them from falling down: they got so seasick they could hardly stand up.

My own constitution turned out to be pretty sturdy, and I didn't succumb to seasickness. I found my sea legs quickly and slept normally. In fact, my sleep was all the deeper when the sea was rough. While most of the others — that is, those who could still walk — were moving around with a strange color and a sad expression on their faces, I would take brisk strolls in the fresh air on the deck. I never missed breakfast or lunch or dinner. Sometimes there would be only one other person at the table, a member of another fraternal socialist delegation. We would crack jokes about our comrades who were sick. (I don't think seasick passengers appreciated these jokes too much.) There were those who, on the basis of an old naval tradition, demanded that dinner be accompanied by a glass of vodka, but as fewer and fewer people showed up for meals, vodka ceased to be in much demand.

Whenever the weather turned nice and the sun came out, we would pass the time playing various shipboard games. I remember one game involved sliding a large puck across the deck with a stick and trying to make the puck come to rest in a grid, divided into numbered squares, each representing a different number of points. We couldn't get enough of this game. Those who weren't actually playing would gather round, rooting and expressing the sorts of feelings experienced by fans at any other sporting event. I also participated in this game, though I'd never heard of it or seen it before.

We also had some more serious pastimes. We did a lot of reading and held meetings to prepare for the Assembly session, and we were regularly informed about developing political situations in various parts of the world. I remember we followed particularly closely the struggle then going on in the Congo between the colonialists and the revolutionary forces fighting for independence. That was a period of great tension, not only for Africa, but in the Soviet Union's relations with the United States. Not long before, the summit meeting in Paris had failed because the US sent a U-2 reconnaissance plane over our territory.

Suddenly, one day at sea, I was informed that a submarine had been sighted on the surface so close to our ship that I could see it clearly through my binoculars. It was huge, and the waves were rolling over it. The submarine was not flying a flag, but there was no doubt to whom it belonged: the United States. Here we were, going about our own business. So why did this submarine have to come to the surface and keep us company? It was undoubtedly a military demonstration of some sort, an unfriendly show of force. I think the Americans wanted to splash cold water in our faces. The submarine tailed us for a while; then, after it had made its presence felt, it submerged. That's all there was to it. But the point had been made.

As we approached New York, we were briefed on a regular basis about what the American press was saying and what sort of a reception was waiting for us. The Americans were seeing to it that we'd be serenaded, as our people say, by a bunch of howling tomcats. We were informed, for instance, that reactionary forces were planning a demonstration against our ship as soon as we entered New York Harbor. Sure enough, no sooner did we catch sight of New York's skyscrapers and come into the mouth of the Hudson River than we saw a boat full of demonstrators coming out toward us.[3] They were all dressed up in strange costumes, waving posters in our direction, holding up scarecrows of some kind, and chanting slogans at us through megaphones. Our people were translating the slogans. The demonstrators were hurling abuses at us, degrading our country and its representatives. We all came out onto the deck, pointing and laughing. As far as we were concerned, the demonstration was a masquerade staged by the aggressive forces of the United States. Between our ship and theirs were police launches making sure that the demonstrators could get within earshot of us without actually getting in the way of our ship.

When we came in to dock, I was infuriated at the condition of the pier. It was in terrible condition — a real eyesore, practically falling to pieces. I'm sure some Americans made fun of the Russians for arriving at such a decrepit pier. But I didn't go looking for a scapegoat. I had only myself to blame. When preparing for our trip, our ambassador to the United States, Comrade Menshikov, had warned us that if we wanted to rent a decent pier for our ship, it would cost a lot of money. In America everything is measured in dollars. So I'd said, "Why the hell should we waste our money on a pier? What difference does it make where our ship is moored? Tell our ambassador to bargain for the cheapest place there is!" Well, we got the cheapest, all right.

Once we came ashore we found that the only people there to greet us were a few of our own diplomats and socialist comrades, as well as a lot of newsmen. There were no demonstrators. The police weren't allowing anyone near us. We were whisked away to the residence we own in New York. That's where most of our diplomatic

---

3. These demonstrators were members of the International Longshoremen's Union (whose president, Harry Bridges, Khrushchev had found so hospitable in San Francisco the year before). The protesters chartered boats to picket the *Baltika* as it entered New York Harbor and approached its pier.

corps accredited to the United Nations lives, and during my stay in New York it was to be the temporary residence of the head of the Soviet Union.

Shortly after our arrival I was informed about what seamen in our country call a "full-scale emergency": one of our sailors had jumped ship. He went to a police station and asked for asylum. The people telling me about this were terribly agitated. I tried to calm them down, saying, "Don't make it sound so important. So he's left. Let him taste the capitalist bread. He'll find out soon enough how much it costs and what it tastes like in New York."

Journalists were constantly following me around, and I knew I'd better be ready to give them some sort of explanation about the sailor who had jumped ship. As I expected, at the first opportunity a reporter asked, "Mr. Khrushchev, what do you think about the Russian sailor who asked for asylum in the US?"

"I know of the incident," I replied. "I regret it very much. I'm sorry for the young man involved. He has no experience, no profession. I think it will be hard for him to adapt to the conditions in America. He acted foolishly and impetuously. If he'd only told me he wanted to stay in the United States, I would have been glad to help him, just so he could see what it's like."

The tension in the air disappeared at once. The journalist had expected a very different sort of reaction from me. They thought I would start condemning the sailor or heaping abuse on him. But I fooled them: I expressed my regret rather than my indignation. As a result, the journalists failed to make any capital out of the incident. There was no way the bourgeois press, which has such a weakness for sensation, could blow the affair out of proportion.

At that time the American press was full of pieces about how Khrushchev ought to be met, what sort of demonstrations should be organized, what limitations should be placed on us. For instance, there was an order issued to the effect that the delegation of the Soviet Union could not leave the district in New York where the United Nations was located.[4] I don't know whether the federal government or Governor Rockefeller was responsible for the order, but we didn't let it bother us. On the contrary, we felt that all these re-

4. The US government restricted Khrushchev to the island of Manhattan in order to "guarantee his security." Ambassador Menshikov protested that the curb was an "unfriendly act."

strictions revealed America in its true light. We came to New York determined to show that American imperialism isn't all-powerful and that we knew our rights, despite the anti-Soviet howling and growling that was stirred up against us.

I should mention that in my opinion it was a mistake to have made New York the headquarters for the United Nations in the first place. Frankly, it was our own mistake. Stalin had the key vote when the decision was made on where to locate the UN. The choice was between the United States and Great Britain — that is, between Roosevelt and Churchill. Stalin was the third party who could tip the scales in favor of one or the other. I don't really blame Stalin for deciding in favor of Roosevelt. At that time, just after the war, Stalin felt that the United States had a higher degree of bourgeois democratic freedom than other capitalist countries, and I agreed with him. Besides, the US, unlike Great Britain, did not have any overseas colonies. Furthermore, there was a feeling after the war that the US was less likely to interfere in the affairs of the European continent. All things considered, New York seemed like the best choice at the time.

But history has taken a different course. America is now conducting the policies of an international gendarme, so its role isn't exactly compatible with the United Nations. I now think it would have been better if the UN had been based in an old, established capitalist country, such as Great Britain. At one point, in the heat of argument over the German question, we suggested moving the UN headquarters to West Berlin. But our partners refused to recognize the validity of our proposal, and I don't think they will ever give in. Who knows if the time will come when people will acknowledge the necessity of transferring the UN headquarters to a country where conditions are better. It's especially important to move the UN somewhere more acceptable now that most African nations are liberating themselves from colonial oppression. It's scandalous for representatives of these African nations to come to a country where black people are not even considered human beings, where there is discrimination, where they aren't allowed in restaurants or hotels, where there are signs saying "whites only," where people are suppressed just because they have black skin — this is simply unacceptable. Sometimes African delegates to the UN are subjected to such abuse.

Our own diplomats in New York didn't live too badly. I remember the accommodations set aside for me were perfectly satisfactory, although not what you'd call luxurious. Our residence was in the center of New York, right in the midst of a thickly populated part of the city. Wherever you looked all you could see was glass, concrete, rooftops, and great stone slabs of buildings so high that only a few patches of sky were ever visible. I was not overly impressed by the majesty of this colossal city; after all, I'd already been there on my previous visit to the US.

While I wasn't particularly struck by the sights of the city, I was unpleasantly surprised by the noise. There was an enormous number of automobiles in New York, all making a terrible racket and choking the air with gasoline fumes. On top of this I had to listen to the nerve-wracking, unceasing roar of the motorcycles. These belonged to the policemen who were protecting me. They kept changing shifts all through the night. You can't imagine what a racket they made. After a few hours, the motorcycles that had been parked outside were cold and had to be revved up when they were started. It would first sound like people clapping, then like gunfire, then like artillery shells exploding — and all right under my window. It was impossible to sleep. No matter how tired I was, I'd lie there awake, either listening to one shift leaving or waiting for another shift to arrive.

This state of affairs, too, I blame on the U-2 affair. Ever since the failure of the summit meeting in Paris, the US press had been whipping up hostility toward our country and our leadership. The Americans couldn't reconcile themselves to the fact that we had slapped them in the face by forcing President Eisenhower to take back what he had said about Gary Powers. While everywhere else in the world, thinking people condemned the United States, there in New York the atmosphere around our delegation and around me personally was tense. You can imagine the opportunities this tension created for all kinds of trashy elements in American society. It was a perfect chance to speak out with as much arrogance as they could muster. As a result, the American government was forced to take measures to protect us from aggressive acts. That's why all those policemen were roaring up and down on their motorcycles round the clock outside my window.

The motorcycle police were not my only constant companions: there were also the newsmen who kept a permanent vigil at the building where I was living. A few dozen correspondents used to stay there all night. Some had ordinary cameras, others had movie cameras, and they would record every step I took. But under the conditions I've described, it was difficult for me to walk around much. In fact, it was impossible for me to go out for a stroll. So the only way I could get a breath of fresh air — if the air in New York can be called fresh — was to go out on the balcony outside my apartment. Several times a day I would go out and watch the commotion on the streets down below.

One day I received a note from one of the newsmen assigned to cover my stay. The note went something like this: "Mr. Khrushchev, you often go out onto your balcony. As a journalist, I welcome this because it gives me a chance to see you and even talk to you. But for your own good, I would like to warn you about the danger here. Perhaps you are not aware of the peculiarities of New York. Anything is possible in this city. Who knows what may have been planned against you. Someone could shoot at you from a passing car or from the windows on the other side of the street. As someone who wishes you well, I would like to ask you not to walk out onto your balcony, thus exposing yourself to dangers which could be very real in your case."

After reading this note, I went walking on the balcony even more than before. Nothing untoward happened. But I must say, I was touched by the humanity of this newsman. I don't remember whether he was the correspondent of a proletarian or a bourgeois newspaper. That's beside the point. He treated me as one human being treats another.

Shortly after we got settled in New York, the General Assembly session began. I had visited the UN during my previous trip to America, so I had some idea of what to expect. The first item on the agenda was electing a president of the session. Our candidate was from Poland or one of the other socialist countries, while the West's was from Ireland.[5] We knew we didn't have much hope of our socialist candidate being elected, since the United States could — and would — veto him, but we had a moral right to nominate our own candidate. The vote was taken, and the Irishman received an absolute majority. As it turned out, he was an able and objective administrator. We had nothing against him personally. In fact, our sympathies had always been with the Irish when they were fighting the

5. The Soviet bloc candidate was Jiri Nosek of Czechoslovakia, who was defeated for the Presidency of the Assembly by Frederick H. Boland of Ireland.

British after World War I. Andrei Andreyevich [Gromyko] encouraged me to get to know the new speaker of the General Assembly and to exchange opinions with him. As I recall, he was a representative of the Irish intelligentsia, some sort of professor. He made a good impression on me.

Formal debates and votes were conducted to determine the agenda and the composition of committees and subcommittees. On each body, seats were set aside for socialist countries, Western countries, and newly created states that had recently received their independence from colonialist overlords. This was all very new for me. I'm an old man, a pre-Revolutionary man. I can still remember from my early youth reading newspaper articles about the State Duma back in the days of Rodzyanko.[6] But I'd never actually participated in governmental or municipal democratic organizations. So my visit to the UN as the head of the Soviet delegation was my first exposure to a parliament representing different classes and different political systems.

Tempers sometimes reached the boiling point. One delegation would make a point of showing its displeasure with certain speakers from other delegations. Our delegation stood for the defense of democratic principles and supported those proposals, especially economic ones, which were to the advantage of socialist and so-called nonaligned countries. Everyone would get very agitated during the speeches, and the Western representatives would often resort to the methods of bourgeois politics to register their disapproval of some speeches. They would stage all sorts of obstructions, banging on their desks and making noise. We began to pay them back in kind. After all, it was the first time I'd ever been at such a session. We, too, could stage an obstruction. We would raise havoc, pound our feet, and so forth.

As the head of our delegation, I used to speak out on certain issues in reply to speeches made by other delegates. All sorts of interesting situations arose. I remember once the representative of the Philippines was addressing the Assembly. It's hard to say how old a man he was. He was of the yellow race, and it's hard for us Europeans to figure out the age of such men. (I always had this problem when meeting Chinese.) Anyway, the Filipino made a speech in support of

6. M. V. Rodzyanko, a leader of the Duma, or tsarist parliament, before the Revolution.

the policies being conducted by the United States. He was acting like a sycophant of American capitalism and imperialism. I spoke out violently against him. I used the following expression, which is perfectly common among our people: "You'd better watch out, or we'll show you Kuzma's mother." [7] When I said "we," I was speaking from the standpoint of the socialist countries, and I wasn't threatening him in a military sense but warning him in an economic sense. I was referring to the development of culture and other benefits of the way of life enjoyed under our social and political system. But the Filipino apparently was startled by my remark. When he next took the floor, he said, "Mr. Khrushchev has said something about 'Kuzma's mother,' and our interpreter can't find it in any dictionary."

Our delegation burst into laughter. This wasn't the first time we'd encountered someone who couldn't understand a simple Russian expression. I used to meet Americans who asked what was all this about Kuzma's mother. Later, the Filipino came up to me in the lobby during a recess and offered me his hand. He was somewhat apologetic about his speech and said he hadn't meant any harm to the Soviet Union.

A more serious conflict arose over the question of Spain. When seats were assigned at the opening of the Assembly, it was our bad luck to be put right behind the Spanish delegation. The chief delegate was getting along in years and had a big bald spot on the top of his head.[8] He had a thin, wrinkled face and a long nose. He was a perfectly nice man, and if our relations with Spain had been normal, I would even have said he was a respectable man. But our relations weren't normal. We could show nothing but disgust for the Spanish delegation and its leader. Just before leaving Moscow to come to New York, Comrade Dolores Ibarruri asked me a favor. She asked me to look for an opportunity to hold the Franco regime up to shame. Ever since arriving in New York, I'd been thinking about how to do this and yet not be rude at the same time. Of course, a certain amount of rudeness was unavoidable; but I wanted to act according to parliamentary procedure.

So here I found myself sitting right behind the Spanish represen-

7. The colloquialism "We'll show you Kuzma's mother" means, "You'll see where you end up." The Filipino delegate, Francisco A. Delgado, referred in his pro-American speech to Soviet suppression of the Hungarian revolt and forced annexation of the Baltic states.
8. Spanish Foreign Minister Fernando María Castiella.

tative. In my thoughts I was pecking away at the bald spot on his head with my nose, and I imagined the face of my friend Dolores Ibarruri beaming with pleasure. As the debate proceeded, I suddenly saw an opportunity to speak out against Spain. Colonialism was being discussed, and I asked for the floor. I denounced Franco's "reactionary, bloody regime," and used other expressions well known to Communists and others who fight against dictatorships like Franco's. Thus I'd fulfilled the task given me by Comrade Dolores Ibarruri.

Well, the Spanish representative demanded the floor to make a reply. At one point, our own delegation, myself included — and the other socialist delegations, too — began making noise, shouting and yelling. Actually, I even took off my shoe and pounded on the desk. Needless to say, this caused quite a reaction among the journalists, the cameramen, and others. Our friends used to joke about it whenever we met, although some people did not seem to understand this unparliamentary method. Nehru, for instance, said that I shouldn't have used such a method. This was highly characteristic of Nehru, and I understood him perfectly well. Nehru was a neutralist. He occupied an intermediary position between the capitalist and socialist countries. He wanted to play the role of a bridge, and to maintain peaceful coexistence in the world.

When the Spaniard came back to his seat, we exchanged some harsh words. Even though we didn't understand each other's language, it was perfectly clear from our gestures and the expressions on our faces what we were saying to each other. Suddenly a policeman came up to us. He wasn't an American policeman, but one who was responsible to the Secretary General of the United Nations. A big man, probably an American by nationality, he came up to us and stood like a statue between the Spaniard and myself. He was making it plain that if a fistfight broke out, he was there to break it up. Actually, there were cases when delegates attacked each other and started throwing punches.

Our relations with the American delegation were distant, to say the least. In fact, we had no regular contacts with the US delegates. I remember only that among them were a number of black people. One in particular stood out: a big, heavy-set, pleasant-looking Negro woman. These black people were included as part of an effort to show that in the United States people of all colors enjoy equal rights.

The Chinese were another delegation that we had no direct contact with. When I say "the Chinese," I mean the representatives from Taiwan. We, of course, were devoted heart and soul to the People's Republic of China, so naturally we used every means at our disposal to show our disdain whenever the Taiwanese spoke at the Assembly. We staged obstructions, pounded our feet, and so on, and the other socialist countries joined us in these protests. We did everything we could to deprive Taiwan of its seat and transfer the mandate to the government in Peking, which in fact represents all China. I honestly hoped that with so many former colonies joining the United Nations, the balance of power would shift in favor of our proposal to seat the People's Republic of China. But unfortunately, many of these newly formed states had received their independence in theory but remained under the heel of the colonialists in fact, and they voted along with the United States and the imperialist nations.

So much for our dealings with the delegations from the capitalist and developing nations. I should say something about the other socialist delegations. In a word, our relations were close and harmonious. Our position on various questions was united. The representatives of the other socialist countries had plenty of opportunity to express their own opinions, and rarely did their viewpoint differ from our own.

However, already at this time, there was one little cloud forming on the horizon and beginning to cast a shadow over the relations among socialist countries. The problem was with the Rumanian delegation.[9] I had nothing against them personally: they were intelligent, sophisticated fellows with a good grasp of international politics. I certainly liked and respected their Foreign Minister. But unlike the representatives from the other socialist countries, the Rumanians had a way of failing to notify their fraternal allies in advance about what they were going to do or say during the Assembly session. The Rumanians were always trying to demonstrate Rumania's complete independence in promoting its own initiatives at this international forum. As a result they were sometimes catching the other socialist delegations by surprise. I wasn't particularly bothered by this — I thought it was just the Rumanians' way of doing things; but some other comrades were offended, and they began to object. They felt

9. The Rumanian delegation was headed by Party chief Gheorghe Gheorghiu-Dej; the Foreign Minister was Avram Bunaciu.

Meeting de Gaulle in Paris at the time of the 1960 summit meeting

Announcing the U-2 incident in Moscow . . .

and, in Paris, denouncing the US for the overflights

Shuffleboard on the decks of the *Baltika*

At the United Nations

PHOTOS BY ALFRED EISENSTADT AND AL FENN, *Life*

With Dag Hammarskjöld in the USSR

With Kennedy in Vienna

A bear hug for Castro at the UN

Castro (*left*); Alekseyev, the Soviet ambassador to Cuba;
Brezhnev; and Khrushchev during Castro's visit to Russia

En route to Scandinavia

Khrushchev's grave in Novodevichy Cemetery in Moscow

the Rumanians were too impatient, always trying to get ahead of the others. I was perfectly willing to treat the whole matter calmly, as long as they didn't step out of bounds when it came to the basic issue of socialist unity. As far as I could tell, they simply wanted to emphasize the independence of the Rumanian position. Later it became clear that this behavior was not just peculiar to these delegates, and that it was dictated by a general policy being developed among the Rumanian comrades.

No such problems clouded our relations with the fraternal republics of the Ukraine and Belorussia. I took a special interest in their contribution to the proceedings; and when the time came for the Ukrainian and Belorussian representatives to address the Assembly, I attached great importance to their speeches. I asked the heads of the two delegations to make their speeches in their native languages, Ukrainian and Belorussian.[10] First, as a matter of principle, I felt it was important that each people in the Soviet community of nations should speak with its own voice. But more important, I counted on these speeches having a political effect in the United States and Canada by striking a sympathetic chord among the hundreds of thousands of Ukrainians and tens of thousands of Belorussians who live in North America. I was sure that the statements by our Ukrainian and Belorussian representatives would be broadcast over the radio, and that many Americans and Canadians of Ukrainian and Belorussian descent would listen in.

As it turned out, the Ukrainian delegate gave his speech in his own language, but the Belorussian did not. I was very upset. "No," said the Belorussian, "we can't prepare our statement in our language; we don't even have a typewriter with a Belorussian keyboard. We have no choice but to prepare it in Russian."

"Well," I replied, "I guess you don't have any choice, but this will be most detrimental to our policy on nationalities. The enemies of the Soviet system will try to say that the republics of the USSR aren't true republics at all, that their native languages are suppressed, that the Ukrainians are allowed to speak Ukrainian only for consumption abroad, and that even in an international forum like the General Assembly the Belorussian delegate has to speak in Russian."

In the end, both statements, the Ukrainian's and the Belorussian's

10. Ukrainian Premier N. V. Podgorny, who went on to become Chairman of the Presidium of the Supreme Soviet, and Belorussian Premier K. T. Mazurov.

were well received. Of course, it's always difficult to say whether a speech is well received in an organization like the United Nations. Unlike our meetings at home, where policy statements are always greeted positively, you get all sorts of different reactions at the UN. Some members of the audience applaud wildly, others just listen tolerantly, while still others react in a hostile way. This is characteristic of every bourgeois parliament.

Before taking our proposals and positions to the floor of the General Assembly, we would often have internal meetings among ourselves. First, we'd hold a conference that was restricted to the USSR delegation and the delegations of the Ukraine and Belorussia. After that, we'd meet with the other socialist countries. There was one complication: we could never be sure that we weren't being overheard. We didn't want our strategy to become known to our enemies — that is, to American intelligence, which was our major adversary. Therefore, when we wanted to exchange opinions among ourselves, we would either do it while going for walks outdoors or we would take special precautions to jam any eavesdropping devices.

It was possible for us to take walks outdoors only on Sundays, when the Assembly was not in session and we had our day off. We went to the country, where our UN mission had a wonderful mansion.[11] In Russia, it's what we would call a dacha.

There was a problem. The weekend place belonging to our mission was beyond the limit which the government imposed on our freedom of movement. Our diplomatic representatives assured me that, if we asked, we would be given special permission to leave the city. At first I was reluctant to beg for any favors. It was a point of honor. But there really wasn't any choice: either we could let ourselves be cooped up in our apartment in the city all the time or we could apply formally for permission to go to the country. I realized we'd just have to abide by the regulations of our hosts, no matter how unfair they might be. So we applied for and received permission, and we went to the country.

Well, "going to the country" wasn't quite as simple as it sounds. There was more to it than just getting in a car and driving out of town. We had to have an American police escort, with signals flash-

11. The Soviet retreat is a mansion in Glen Cove, New York, on the north shore of Long Island.

ing and sirens wailing, rerouting traffic along our route. Naturally, these trips attracted a lot of attention. I suspect the police used to announce them in advance because all along the way there would be small crowds of people expressing their opinion about our delegation. The larger share of these expressions were unfriendly. People would stick their tongues out at us and wave posters with slogans against the Soviet Union and to me as a representative of the Soviet Union.

Even when we got to our residence in the country, it was still hard to find peace and quiet. The house was surrounded by a park with lovely green lawns, where we would go for walks. It was all very rich and luxurious, even by American standards. But it wasn't very peaceful. The police who escorted us from the city would sit around and wait while we took a walk, and there was always the sound of people hooting and whistling and passing cars honking their horns. Comrade Menshikov told me that people were expressing their rage against our presence in America. All this was a consequence of the conflict that occurred when we shot down the American U-2 plane. Despite the fact that the United States had committed an act of aggression against the Soviet Union, the American man in the street reacted as though it were the other way around. But that's hardly surprising: the average American had long since been conditioned to think whatever he was told to think.

Ours was not the only delegation that received unfriendly treatment at the hands of the Americans. There were also the Cubans. The Americans committed a hostile act against the delegation headed by Fidel Castro. The Cubans had rented rooms in some hotel, but they were thrown out. Of course, the US government pretended it was a private affair between the Cubans and the hotel proprietor and refused to interfere. I was told that Fidel Castro was furious and that, as a former guerrilla, he was threatening to pitch a tent in a square near the UN building. Then, out of the blue, he received an invitation from the proprietor of a hotel in Harlem, so Castro decided to establish himself there.

When we learned about this outrage which had been committed against the Cuban delegation, we were indignant. We decided that I should go to the hotel in Harlem and shake Castro's hand as a gesture of sympathy and respect. Not that Castro needed anyone to feel sorry for him. He is a man of strong will. He understood perfectly well that he was being harassed as part of the reaction of American monopolies to the policies which his government had been conducting in Cuba since he seized power. I asked one of our people to telephone Castro right away and, if he wasn't at the hotel, to leave word that Khrushchev would like to visit him as soon as possible. The word came back that Castro thanked me for calling and offered to come to us instead. I took this to mean that he thought because the Soviet Union is a great country and his was a young revolutionary government representing a small country, it would be proper for him to pay a visit to me first, then later I could make a return call on him.

I felt it would be better for me to make the first visit, thereby emphasizing our solidarity with Cuba, especially in light of the indignation and discrimination they were being subjected to. There was another reason for my going to see him at his headquarters. The Cuban delegation was in Harlem and the owner of the hotel was a Negro. By going to a Negro hotel in a Negro district, we would be making a double demonstration: against the discriminatory policies of the United States of America toward Negroes as well as toward Cuba.

"Call Castro and tell him I'm on my way," I ordered. I told my bodyguard that we were going to drive to Harlem. My security people immediately called up the American head of my police escort. (I knew him already from my previous trip to the US.) He said that I might encounter some unpleasantness in Harlem and tried to persuade me not to go there. This made me all the more determined. I didn't want the newspapers writing that Khrushchev was afraid of Negroes, afraid of being physically abused in Harlem. So I got into a car and went straight to Castro's hotel.

Naturally, the journalists got there first. They know everything. I don't know where they found out. Maybe from the police, maybe from our own people. I couldn't get away from them. In addition to the newsmen and photographers and movie cameramen, an enormous number of Negroes had gathered around.

Castro was waiting for us at the entrance. This was my first meeting with him. He made a deep impression on me. He was a very tall man with a beard, and his face was both pleasant and tough at the same time. His eyes sparkled with kindness toward his friends. We greeted each other by embracing. When I say "embrace," I'm using the word in a rather specialized way. You have to take into consideration my height as opposed to Castro's. He bent down and enveloped me with his whole body. While I'm fairly broad abeam, he wasn't so thin either, especially for his age.

We went to his suite. As we made our way through the hotel, I could see right away that, except for Negroes, no one would live in a place like this. It was old and poor, and the air was thick and heavy. The rooms hadn't been cleaned. The linen on the beds obviously wasn't fresh, and there was a certain odor you find in overcrowded places with bad ventilation.

Castro expressed his pleasure at my visit, and I repeated my sentiments of solidarity and approval of his policy. The meeting was very brief; we exchanged only a few sentences. We said good-bye, and I went back to my residence.

You can imagine the uproar this episode caused in the American press and elsewhere as well.

The next day we arrived at the General Assembly building before the session began. A few minutes later Castro's delegation appeared. I suggested that we go greet the Cubans, and my comrades agreed. We made our way from one end of the hall to the other, and Castro and I embraced demonstrably. We wanted everyone to know that fraternal relations were forming between our country and Cuba. The democratic press welcomed this development, while the bourgeois press reflected the interests of aggressive circles in capitalist countries by picking Fidel and me to pieces. But this was as it should be. I always say, if our friends praise us and our enemies heap abuse on us, it means we are conducting policy along correct class lines.

As the General Assembly session dragged on, I found the debates less and less interesting. The issue on which I was scheduled to speak, independence and colonialism, was near the end of the agenda and therefore still a long way off. But while my days were sometimes boring, the evenings were always busy. It was traditional for delegations to the UN to give receptions in each other's honor, and almost every evening we were either giving a reception ourselves or attending one given by someone else. These occasions provided additional grounds for establishing contacts. Making an official visit to some country is always a complicated operation, but in 1960 virtually everyone was concentrated in New York for the General Assembly.

For example, Hassan, Crown Prince of Morocco, asked to be introduced to me there in New York. We laid the foundation for improved relations between our countries. (Later, when his father died and Hassan became king, it was useful that he and I had already been on good terms with each other.) At another dinner given for us by the Indian delegation, I remember I had a long discussion with Prime Minister Nehru. One particularly memorable banquet was given by Mr. Balewa, Prime Minister of Nigeria. (His life was to end tragically during the coup d'etat carried out by the military in Nigeria.) [12] Balewa was obese and very tall. Naturally he was black, but the color of his face was different from the color of the Senegalese and other Africans. I was used to seeing black people with an almost bluish tint to them, but Balewa had traces of white in his skin. Perhaps he's not pure Negro. Of course, he possessed all the manners of a European. The reception he gave was no different from any of the others I was invited to during the Assembly session. Mr. Balewa seated me across from himself; this is supposed to be the most honored seat. Also at our table was the representative of Great Britain, whom I'd never met before.[13]

At that time we were most interested in Nigeria. We wanted to have diplomatic relations with this mightiest and richest African state. We knew that the former capitalists wouldn't let Nigeria out of their clutches if they could possibly help it. They wanted to keep Nigeria an economic prisoner and exploit its rich natural resources. They certainly didn't want the Nigerians to start building socialism. Prime Minister Balewa, according to our information, was playing right into the capitalists' hands. He was comfortably well-off himself, a member of the bourgeoisie. Granted he was building a new, independent state, but he was doing so under capitalist conditions. Regardless of his people's suffering and impoverishment at the hands of the British, Balewa went out of his way to be accommodating to Great Britain. To put it bluntly, he was turning Nigeria into a satellite of British capital.

Our attitude was to wait and see what happened. We regarded men like Balewa as temporary people, who had been brought to power by the colonialists. After all, some of those countries even had

12. Alhaji Abubakar Tafawa Balewa was Prime Minister of Nigeria until 1966, when he was overthrown and killed in an army mutiny.

13. Great Britain was represented by Foreign Secretary Sir Alec Douglas-Home, but Prime Minister Macmillan was also in attendance and had private talks with Khrushchev.

English officers in their armies. Nevertheless, we were pleased that Balewa invited Comrade Gromyko and me to his dinner. We took it to mean that Balewa had been pressured by his own people into openly establishing contact with a representative of the Soviet Union — and that our policies were slowly but surely being recog-nized in Nigeria.

First and foremost, we had come to New York with the intention of championing the cause of those countries that were straining to free themselves of colonial status. The subject of my scheduled speech to the General Assembly was to be the question of granting indepen-dence to all the nations of the world. But the session just kept drag-ging on, and I was beginning to lose interest. I knew, however, that I couldn't leave without making my speech. It would have looked as though we didn't attach much importance to the colonial issue.

I remember when my turn to speak came. My address lasted about two hours. I think it made quite an impression, especially on the former colonial peoples. Here we were, the representatives of the Soviet Union, expounding Lenin's policy of national and social liber-ation, opposing the oppression of one man by another, proclaiming a man's right to dignity and freedom from enslavement. We were speaking for the country of Lenin, the country of soviets, and I think our reputation among the former colonial peoples was enhanced greatly.

The discussion touched off by my speech was substantive and agi-tated. Naturally some people reacted with enthusiasm, others with hostility, just as you'd expect in a bourgeois parliamentary forum. Then came the time to formulate a resolution. We had already worked out a resolution in advance.[14] In matters like this we had a real craftsman in Andrei Andreyevich [Gromyko]. He'd been with the UN since its inception. He really knew his way around the kitchen, so to speak, and he was very useful to us when we had to cook something up of our own. When it came time to lobby for our resolution among the other delegations, the United States didn't quite accept it. Not that the Americans rejected our resolution out-right, but they tried to soften some of the points in it and smooth some of the sharp corners. This was just what we expected from the US. We'd maneuvered America into a ticklish position. On the one

14. Khrushchev's two-and-a-half-hour address was an attack on the organizational structure and leadership of the UN as well as a call for the abolition of colonialism.

hand, the US's allies — England, France, Portugal, Spain, Holland — were all colonialists or former colonialists. So for America to support us would mean going against the interests of her colonialist allies. On the other hand, the Americans didn't want to come out directly against our resolution because they knew they still had to deal with the former colonies themselves, especially on the enormous African continent. So we had placed the US in a real dilemma. We felt it was important for the United Nations to exert some kind of moral pressure on the US and other governments to speed up the process of liberating colonial peoples.

After a number of behind-the-scenes exchanges, Andrei Andreyevich told us that Portugal and Spain would oppose our resolution, but the United States, England, and France would support it. This, of course, was a great victory. Great Britain was a colonial power, yet they voted for our resolution. The United States, while technically not a colonial country, is an imperialist state; it uses its capital and credits and military interference to keep an oppressive grip on the throats of small countries. Yet we forced the US to vote for our resolution.

We had attained our goal. The Soviet Union, which had always conducted a policy of equal rights for all the nationalities who inhabit our great Motherland, was now fighting for this same policy on an international scale. The absolute majority of the delegations voted to accept our resolution. As a result we derived great recognition and political satisfaction.

One developing country whose rights we tried to support in those days was the Congo, where a sharp political struggle was under way between Lumumba, leader of the revolutionary forces of the left, and Tshombe, who was an agent of the Belgian monopolists, colonialists, and other reactionary forces.[15] All the way across the Atlantic on our way to New York we had kept in close touch with our Foreign Ministry about the situation in the Congo, sending and receiving coded messages between our ship and Moscow.

It was over the issue of the Congo that serious tensions cropped up in our relations with Hammarskjöld, the Secretary-General of the United Nations. Originally we had thought highly of him and sup-

15. Congolese Premier Patrice Lumumba was in conflict with Moise Tshombe, a secessionist provincial leader who declared Katanga independent of Leopoldville in 1960, shortly after the Congo itself achieved independence from Belgium.

ported his candidacy when he was nominated to the post of Secretary-General. Like his predecessor, Trygve Lie, Hammerskjöld was from Scandinavia. During my own visit to Scandinavia I heard nothing but the best about these men; I think they were both members of bourgeois liberal parties.[16]

However, when the question of the Congo arose, we had a head-on clash with Hammarskjöld. We felt he insufficiently supported the progressive forces which were locked in battle with the colonialist government of Belgium. During my presence at the General Assembly a major scandal flared up between Hammarskjöld and me — not just over the Congo, but over other issues as well. For instance, we came up with the idea that the United Nations would be better served if, instead of having one Secretary-General, the UN apparatus should be headed by three officers, one representative for each of three groups of countries with similar social and political systems: the capitalists, the socialists, and the nations in between which had liberated themselves from the colonialists but were still nonaligned or neutral while they determined their course of development.

Some people who thought they were pretty smart kept trying to convince me that my idea wasn't possible, and even some who were friendly toward us insisted that having three heads of the UN would paralyze the organization. But I was convinced I was right and promoted the idea enthusiastically. After all, why should three leaders "paralyze" the UN? Look at the Security Council: it has fifteen members, including five permanent ones with veto power. Why shouldn't the Secretariat be administered in the same way, headed by a troika which would take into account the interests of all three sides, rather than just one side? No doubt, it would sometimes take a bit longer to act on certain matters, but perhaps in some cases that would be just as well. Sometimes it would be better not to have a question solved at all than to have it solved by one man who is under the influence of the capitalist countries. To look at it realistically, we had no hope of having a Secretary-General who was a Communist — or even a non-Communist promoted by our socialist camp. The capitalist countries would never have stood for it. So why shouldn't we at least have one representative among three to guard our interests in the Secretariat?

Unfortunately, we were never able to get very far with this pro-

16. Dag Hammarskjöld and his predecessor Trygve Lie were affiliated with the Labor parties of their native Sweden and Norway respectively.

posal because the capitalist countries were against it and made the
nonaligned countries come over to their side. So the idea failed to
win support on the testing ground of the General Assembly. We had
a real fight with Hammarskjöld, and our relations with him went
down the drain. We decided to block his candidacy when he came
up for reelection to the Security Council. But, as it turned out, it
never came to that. Hammarskjöld went to the Congo on an inspection trip to gain firsthand information about the situation there, and
his plane crashed while landing. At the time our intelligence people
informed me that, in fact, the plane didn't crash accidentally; it was
shot down by Lumumba's forces.[17] Whatever happened, Hammarskjöld was dead, and the post of Secretary-General was vacant.

The candidacy of U Thant was introduced. He represented Burma,
a country with which we had good relations. We knew we could
count on him to be more flexible than Hammarskjöld; U Thant
wouldn't allow the UN to do anything detrimental to the interests of
the Soviet Union, the socialist countries, and those countries that
were unaligned to military blocs. I remember that at first, when Andrei Andreyevich was working out our position, we decided to vote
for U Thant as a provisional, temporary Secretary-General. Then I
thought better of it and suggested, "Let's not impose any conditions
on him; let him be a full Secretary-General like the others before
him." Andrei Andreyevich disagreed. I explained to him that we
wouldn't find a better candidate than U Thant. So we gave him our
support with no strings attached, so to speak.

U Thant was, of course, glad to have our vote and our recognition.
During his first term he showed himself to be a man of principle,
someone who didn't let himself be led around on a leash by the
United States. Naturally, from a strictly proletarian, Communist point
of view, he failed to satisfy all our demands. But if you take into account the nature of this international organization — which, you
might say, consists of seven pairs of clean creatures and seven pairs
of unclean creatures, plus all sorts which are neither clean nor unclean [18] — then you'll see that the UN needs someone who can sat-

17. Hammarskjöld was killed in September, 1961, when his chartered airliner
crashed en route to a meeting with Tshombe, with whom he was trying to end the
fighting. Lumumba himself was dead by then.
18. This is a very approximate paraphrase of a passage in the Bible about Noah's
Ark: "Of every clean beast thou shalt take to thee by sevens, the male and his female:
and of beasts that are not clean by twos, the male and his female. Of fowls also of the
air by sevens, the male and the female." Gen. 7:2–3.

isfy as many members of the collective as possible while maintaining some basic positions of principle. U Thant has been a successful Secretary-General and, all in all, I think the United Nations has been a useful organization.

You could say that the UN had a predecessor — the League of Nations, an organization which died without fulfilling its task because it failed to halt the outbreak of World War II. The United States refused to join the League, and Germany pulled out when it felt strong enough to start a war it could win. Then we, too, were forced by events to quit. But for all its failures, even the League of Nations in its own time was a step in the right direction. It was formed back in the days when the Soviet Union was a lone island of socialism surrounded by enemies, and the capitalist system was the most powerful in the world, controlling the strings of war and peace. The USSR wasn't taken into account — we were just "a colossus on feet of clay," as Churchill and others used to say. But that's all ancient history now. Churchill's successor Macmillan acknowledged to me personally that Britain no longer ruled the waves and the Soviet Union was one of the two great powers. The League of Nations' successor, the UN, has come a long way, too.

Of course, there have been times when questions were decided at the UN in a way completely unsatisfactory to us — sometimes in direct contradiction to our wishes and interests. I'm thinking about the question of seating the People's Republic of China and the question of when to send troops into a country in order to maintain existing conditions. But on the whole, the UN has helped us avoid a major war. To me, the organization is like a cold, cleansing shower: once people go through it, they tend to be a bit more tolerant and a bit more realistic about the prevailing conditions in international affairs. The UN has a way of restraining some people in their zeal so that a third world war is less likely to break out. I'm not saying that the world has been rolling along smoothly on well-greased rails ever since the end of World War II. On the contrary, there's been a lot of friction, many conflicts, even military confrontations. In the years since the end of the war we haven't had a single prolonged breathing space when the guns weren't silent and sabers weren't rattling and bombs weren't falling. But these outbreaks have been limited to localized conflicts.

The time will come when the world will be a single organic unity.

The peoples of the world will have a social system based on Marxism-Leninism, and in no country will there be either exploiters or exploited. Capitalist relations between people will be liquidated, and socialist relations will become firmly established. I also look forward to the day when China will take a more reasonable position than it has occupied up to now. In the meantime, during the transitional period, the most reasonable thing to do is abolish military alliances, remove all troops from foreign territories, and ultimately abolish all armies so that countries will have only police forces for internal purposes. When I say "transitional period" I mean the period of transition from a capitalist society to socialism and then to Communism. During this period the United Nations has great positive significance. Partly thanks to the UN, our class enemies, the enemies of the new system of the future, are forced to reconcile themselves to the existence of socialist countries. They realize that the only choice is between peaceful coexistence and a hopeless, blood-letting war that no one would win. The international policies of all countries are like streams which flow into the enormous basin of the United Nations.

And so, my visit to the General Assembly had come to an end. We had traveled to New York by boat, but now that we were ready to return home, we were told that our plane, the Tu-114, was once again ready to make the trip. Since we were in a hurry to get back, we decided to fly. It had taken us ten days to cross the ocean by ship, yet it took us only ten hours to fly home.

20

John F. Kennedy

The Vienna Summit

I F I had to compare the two American Presidents with whom I dealt — Eisenhower and Kennedy — the comparison would not be in favor of Eisenhower. Our people whose job it was to study Eisenhower closely have told me that they considered him a weak President. I have to agree. He was a good man, but he wasn't tough. There was something soft about his character. As I discovered in Geneva and Paris, he was much too dependent on his advisors. It was always obvious to me that being President of the United States was a great burden for him. I remember that as the time for the presidential elections drew near, he told me, "My service in the White House is coming to an end."

"Mr. President," I said, "don't you think it would be possible to get Congress to permit you to run for a third term?"

"No, I've had it up to here with being President. I don't want the job any more, and I don't think I should even try." I believe he was being perfectly sincere. His authority and prestige were so great in the US that he would have had no trouble getting elected for a third term, and, of course, there was the precedent of Roosevelt. But, as Eisenhower explained, "Roosevelt served for more than two terms because of the war, and now there are no such special conditions. I have one wish and one wish only: to bring my political career to an end."

Eisenhower's choice for his successor was Vice-President Nixon. The Democratic party had to choose between Kennedy and Stevenson. Stevenson was making his third try for the Presidency, and he had wide support. For the Soviet Union and from the standpoint of the class struggle, there wasn't much difference in the three candidates. Each of them held a capitalist position, and each could be expected to conduct American policy more or less as it had been conducted under Eisenhower. But there was substantial difference in the shading of their political characters.

Let's take Nixon, for example. He belonged to the same party as Eisenhower, but he was different. Eisenhower was more acceptable to us than Nixon. I hadn't forgotten how, the year before, Nixon had made statements aimed against the Soviet Union almost from the moment I arrived in the United States as a guest of President Eisenhower. I remember having told the President, "This is, to say the least, a rather tactless way for your Vice-President to treat a guest." [1]

Stevenson we knew from his visit to the Soviet Union and from my warm meeting with him at Garst's farm during my own trip to the US. We knew him to have a tolerant — I'd even say friendly and trustworthy — attitude toward the Soviet Union.

We had little knowledge of John Kennedy. He was a young man, very promising and very rich — a millionaire. We knew from the press that he was distinguished by his intelligence, his education, and his political skill. I'd met him once, during my visit to Washington, when the Committee on Foreign Relations gave a reception in my honor. Fulbright, who was the chairman, introduced me to all the members of the committee, including Kennedy. "I've heard a lot about you," I said. "People say you have a great future before you." [2]

However, we knew Stevenson better, and we had confidence in his intention to improve relations between our two countries, so his would have been the most acceptable candidacy as far as we were concerned. But the Democratic Party did not nominate him. Stevenson had already been nominated for President twice and defeated twice; the Democrats didn't want to risk a third time. They decided to bet on Kennedy instead.

The battle between the two parties began. The Americans are very

1. During his visit to the US in September of 1959, Khrushchev criticized Vice-President Nixon for having made "unfriendly statements" in an address to the American Dental Association.

2. Senator J. William Fulbright, Chairman of the Senate Foreign Relations Committee, had invited Khrushchev to meet with twenty-five senators, including Kennedy, during the trip.

good at making you think a huge struggle over major issues is under way, a struggle which will determine whether the United States will continue to exist or not. But in essence the battle between the Democrats and Republicans is like a circus wrestling match. The wrestlers arrange in advance who will be the winner and who will be the loser — before they even enter the arena. Of course, I'm not saying that the outcome of an American election is actually prearranged by the two candidates, but they're both representatives of the capitalist circles which nominated them; and everyone knows that the foundation of capitalism will not be shaken, regardless of which candidate is elected. The President is elected by working people, but as we see it, he conducts a policy which is incompatible with working-class interests. The President supports the bourgeoisie and big monopolistic capital. That would have been true of Stevenson, as well as Kennedy and Nixon.

Still, once the Republicans had nominated Nixon and the Democrats had nominated Kennedy, we had to make a choice in our own minds. We thought we would have more hope of improving Soviet-American relations if John Kennedy were in the White House. We knew we couldn't count on Nixon in this regard: his aggressive attitude toward the Soviet Union, his anti-Communism, his connection with McCarthyism (he owed his career to that devil of darkness McCarthy) — all this was well known to us. In short, we had no reason to welcome the prospect of Nixon as President. Therefore we took it very seriously when Eisenhower came out in favor of Nixon, giving speeches in support of his candidacy. Eisenhower, after all, had great influence on American public opinion.

Nixon's vice-presidential running mate was Cabot Lodge, who had accompanied me around the US. I'd always had good relations with Mr. Lodge. Before the election he came to Moscow — not on any sort of official invitation from the Soviet government but, as we say, as a free cossack.[3] He asked for an appointment with me, and I received him. We met as old friends. In our talks he tried to convince me that relations between our countries wouldn't suffer if Nixon were in the White House. He didn't say they'd get better, just that they wouldn't get worse. He said Nixon was not really the sort of man he deliberately appeared to be at election rallies. "Mr. Khrushchev," said Lodge, "don't pay any attention to the campaign speeches. Remem-

3. Lodge conferred with Khrushchev in Moscow in February, 1960.

ber, they're just political statements. Once Mr. Nixon is in the White House I'm sure — I'm absolutely *certain* — he'll take a position of preserving and perhaps even improving our relations."

I had the feeling that Cabot Lodge's remarks to me were worked out in advance by Nixon and Eisenhower. They'd sent him to talk to me so that our press would neither attack nor praise him. As he put it, "We don't need your endorsement of Mr. Nixon." We knew perfectly well that any endorsement from us would be a disadvantage for a candidate. Lodge was asking us to maintain a position of complete neutrality. This was correct and reasonable, and we tried to stick to it. Nonetheless, in our hearts, we still felt that Kennedy's candidacy was more in our interests than Nixon's.

In the heat of the campaign, just before election day, the United States addressed itself to us, officially asking for the release of Powers and the pilots shot down in the Arctic. Powers by that time had already been convicted and sentenced. (I remember his father and his wife came to the trial.) [4] The Americans asked us to grant clemency to him and let him go. We had nothing against doing this; there was no need for us to keep Powers in prison. But the question was, when? The timing of Powers's release had great political significance. At that time voices in the press were saying that whichever candidate could show himself more able to improve Soviet-American relations stood a better chance in the election. In fact, they weren't just talking about America's relations with the Soviet Union, but with me, personally — by name. That's typical of the bourgeois press: it always plays up the individual leader.

I expressed my opinion to the leadership: "The United States government has asked us to release Powers. Now is *not* the time to do it because the two presidential candidates are both trying to cash in on an improvement in relations. If we release Powers now it will be to Nixon's advantage. Judging from the press, I think the two candidates are at a stalemate. If we give the slightest boost to Nixon it will be interpreted as an expression of our willingness to see him in the White House. This would be a mistake. If Nixon becomes President, I don't believe he will contribute to an improvement in relations between our countries. Therefore, let's hold off on taking the final step of releasing Powers. As soon as the elections are over we'll hand him over."

4. Powers's wife, mother, and father attended his trial in August, 1960; he was convicted and sentenced to ten years' confinement.

My comrades agreed, and we did not release Powers. As it turned out, we'd done the right thing. Kennedy won the election by a majority of only two hundred thousand or so votes, a negligible margin if you consider the huge population of the United States. The slightest nudge either way would have been decisive.[5]

So Eisenhower left the White House and Kennedy became President. Later, when I met him again, I found Kennedy a pleasant and reasonable man, and I felt I could joke with him about the election: "You know, Mr. Kennedy, we voted for you."

He looked at me closely and smiled. "How?"

"By waiting until after the election to return the pilots."

He laughed and said, "You're right. I admit you played a role in the election and cast your vote for me."

Of course, it was a joke, but it reflected the reality of the situation, and I must say I had no cause for regret once Kennedy became President. It quickly became clear he understood better than Eisenhower that an improvement in relations was the only rational course. Eisenhower had fully appreciated the danger of the Cold War leading to a hot war; he'd told me more than once, "I'm afraid of war, Mr. Khrushchev."

Kennedy feared war too. He never told me in so many words, but he seemed determined to do something, to take concrete steps. He knew that war brings impoverishment to a country and disaster to a people, and that a war with the Soviet Union wouldn't be a stroll in the woods — it would be a horrible, bloody war. For the first time the United States would have to fight on its own territory rather than send its soldiers over to fight in Europe. In a war fought with nuclear missiles, the American monopolists, who had profited from wars in the past, would see the economic might of the United States destroyed. Kennedy understood all this very well and wasn't afraid to call things by their own names. Therefore from the beginning, he tried to establish closer contacts with the Soviet Union with an eye to reaching an agreement on disarmament and to avoiding any accidents which might set off a military conflict.

In America the press is very influential, but Kennedy had great influence, too. He was a flexible President and, unlike Eisenhower, he was his own boss in foreign policy. He hired bright, young, well-educated advisors who were equally flexible. Therefore Kennedy

---

5. Kennedy's margin of victory was 115,000 votes. Powers was not released until February, 1962, in exchange for convicted Soviet spy Rudolf I. Abel.

was able to bring the press around in favor of a summit meeting. He let us know he would like to meet with representatives of the Soviet Union. As I've already mentioned, the bourgeois press likes to play up personalities, so American newspapers would always cast it in terms of Kennedy wanting to meet with me personally, with Mr. Khrushchev, the head of our government.

We, too, wanted to establish contacts with Kennedy because we shared his fear of war. I certainly was afraid of war. Who but a fool isn't? I've got no qualms about coming right out and saying we were afraid of war. That doesn't mean I think we should pay any price to avoid war. Certainly we shouldn't back down at the expense of our self-respect, our authority, and our prestige in the world. On many occasions while I was head of the government we were confronted with the jealousy and aggressiveness of others toward our position, and we had to counterattack these forces. By counterattacking when we did, we won a number of significant moral victories. But these were victories in the Cold War. We managed to avoid a hot war. Kennedy seemed committed to the same goal.

Once we decided the time was ripe for a Kennedy-Khrushchev meeting, we received a proposal that it be held at some mutually agreeable place on neutral territory — not in the USSR, the US, nor in Paris, where the recent four-power conference had collapsed. Helsinki, Geneva, and Vienna were all considered, as far as I remember. Kennedy was in favor of Vienna, while we wanted to meet in Helsinki since we felt that the Finns had a better understanding of our policy than the Austrians. However, the Austrians at that time were adhering to their promise to conduct a policy of neutrality, so we agreed on Vienna as an appropriate place for the meeting.

The composition of the delegations was announced. Kennedy was to bring his Secretary of State, Mr. Rusk, and we brought our Minister of Foreign Affairs as well as some officials from other ministries to help us analyze points raised during the meetings on various diplomatic, economic, and military matters confronting our two nations.[6]

We were confidentially informed that Kennedy's mother and his wife would be accompanying him to Vienna. As a result, my comrades urged me to take my own wife too, so that the women

6. The US side consisted of Kennedy, Secretary of State Dean Rusk, Ambassador Llewellyn Thompson, Charles Bohlen, and Foy Kohler, Assistant Secretary of State for European Affairs. The Soviet side: Khrushchev, Gromyko, Menshikov, and A. F. Dobrynin, the US desk officer at the Soviet Foreign Ministry and future ambassador to Washington.

would be able to chat with each other at receptions and during the day while we were tied up in meetings. At first I resisted the idea. Ever since the time of Stalin, a sort of asceticism was the rule in the leadership; women were kept away from receptions and out of discussions. The only exception Stalin used to make was for Molotov's wife.[7] Very, very rarely Voroshilov's wife would appear at the theater. The government box was usually occupied exclusively by men. Other than that, the women were kept out of sight, and I was reluctant to take Nina Petrovna with me to Vienna. However, my comrades — most of all Anastas Ivanovich Mikoyan — were insistent. Of all of us, Anastas Ivanovich was the most knowledgeable on etiquette and protocol. He said it would create a good impression if I took Nina Petrovna with me, so finally I gave in.

We arrived in Vienna and were well received.[8] There were no demonstrations against us — only expressions of courtesy and respect in keeping with our rank. The Viennese waved their greetings, and their faces expressed their pleasure that their city had been chosen as the site for this meeting. The Austrians were well disposed toward us because after Stalin's death we signed a peace treaty with them and withdrew our troops, which had been stationed on their territory for a long time. The Austrians gave me credit for having played a leading role in the decision to pull out of Austria, and they were quite right. They didn't have any idea what sort of internal struggle had taken place before we signed the peace treaty, and I don't deny it was on my initiative that the correct decision was finally made.

For my part, I was very satisfied with the Austrian government. I thanked the Prime Minister and the President for doing everything they could to see that our meeting came off without a hitch. The Austrian government fulfilled the obligations it had undertaken when it signed the treaty with the USSR; that is, it followed a policy of neutrality. We'd been fully prepared to encounter unfriendly manifestations in Vienna, but none occurred.

The President of Austria, who was then a Social Democrat, made

7. P. S. Zhemchuzhina. See *KR*, I, 259–261.
8. Khrushchev and Kennedy arrived separately at the beginning of June, 1961: Kennedy flew in from Paris, where he had met with de Gaulle; Khrushchev came by train from Czechoslovakia and was welcomed at the station by, among others, Molotov, who was serving as Soviet representative to the International Atomic Energy Commission. The two political foes had reportedly not seen each other since the Anti-Party Group affair of 1957.

sure that no complications or unpleasantnesses clouded our visit. The Prime Minister did the same.

Who did I know in the Austrian leadership? I was personally acquainted with the Foreign Minister, Mr. Kreisky. I'd also known Raab, with whom we'd actually concluded the treaty. His successor followed the same policies.[9] He was a small-time capitalist. He even said as much. "Mr. Khrushchev, I'm just a small-time capitalist — *ein kleiner Kapitalist.*" Small-time, big-time, what really mattered was that he was a capitalist, and capitalists are all alike, no matter how much capital they own. He was like our own Social Democrats in that he held a bourgeois position. Even a small-time capitalist has a big appetite for amassing more than he has, and greed determines his attitude toward the working class. But Raab understood the necessity of having friendly relations with our country. We respected him for signing the peace treaty with us and for conducting a policy of neutrality ever since. He was considered a liberal by reactionaries in Austria. He and his government also deserved credit for ensuring that my meeting with Kennedy would be held in the best possible conditions.

The talks with Kennedy started. Our agenda included the same issues on which President Eisenhower and I had been unable to reach an agreement: the German question, the Berlin question, disarmament, mutually profitable economic contacts, the old problem of Lend-Lease, and the normalization of relations between our countries.

The most pressing and thorny issue facing us was the German problem, on which John Kennedy took the same position Eisenhower had held before him. Eisenhower was a Republican, while Kennedy was a Democrat, but as far as the German question was concerned, it was just six of one, half a dozen of the other. Both parties had the same policy, which was to defend the aggressive interests of monopolistic capital and the leading position of the United States in the world, without taking anyone else's interests into account. On Germany and Berlin, Kennedy's position was barely dis-

9. Julius Raab, the leader of the People's Party, who had visited the USSR in 1958, resigned as Chancellor (a post Khrushchev calls Prime Minister) because of ill health in April, 1961, two months before the Kennedy-Khrushchev summit meeting. Raab was succeeded by Alfons Gorbach, also of the People's Party. Gorbach and President Schärf were the official hosts of the summit. Bruno Kreisky of the Socialist Party, the current Chancellor, was then Foreign Minister.

tinguishable from Eisenhower's. However, he seemed to have a better grasp of the idea of peaceful coexistence than Eisenhower did. I hadn't forgotten how Eisenhower's finance advisor Dillon had to ask me what peaceful coexistence *was*. I didn't hear any such stupid questions from Kennedy. He'd already come out in favor of peaceful coexistence in public statements. This was a step in the right direction and could become the basis for resolving a whole complex of problems.

Kennedy recognized the need to avoid military conflict. He felt we should sign a formal agreement to the effect that we would adhere to the principles of peaceful coexistence. But what he meant by peaceful coexistence was freezing existing conditions in all countries insofar as their social and political systems were concerned. Well, this concept was completely unacceptable to me, and I told him so.

"Mr. President, we, too, would like to come to an agreement with you on the principles of peaceful coexistence, but for us, that means agreeing not to use force in solving disputes and not to interfere in the internal affairs of other countries — it does not mean freezing the conditions which prevail in those countries today. The question of a country's sociopolitical system should be decided by that country itself. Some countries are still determining what sort of system is best for them, and we have no business 'freezing' them into one form or another."

"I don't agree," he replied. "We must freeze their systems. Otherwise all sorts of undercover agents can undermine a country's government." [10]

Kennedy wanted to maintain the status quo in the world. I was also in favor of the status quo, and still am, but we differed in our understanding of what this term meant. For us, "maintaining the status quo" meant agreeing not to violate the borders that came into existence after World War II — and especially not to violate them by means of war. Kennedy, however, had in mind the inviolability of borders *plus the enforced preservation of a country's internal social and political system*. In other words, he wanted countries with capitalist systems to remain capitalist, and he wanted us to agree to a guarantee to that effect.

This was absolutely unacceptable. At that time many people still

10. The "status quo" argument came up because Kennedy mentioned a speech Khrushchev had given in January pledging to support wars of national liberation.

lived under colonialism. Did he really expect us to help the colonialists continue their oppression of their colonies? I tried to make him see that his was a reactionary position and that not only did we disagree with him, but we sympathized with those forces which were trying to change the existing system in some parts of the world, particularly in developing countries.

"Mr. President, your proposal smells of the olden days. Let's make a brief excursion into history. There was a time when the United States was a British colony. You had your revolt, achieved victory, and became an independent state. You decided on your political system by yourselves. Now take us for example: we, too, rose up in revolution and chose the system under which we now live. According to your proposal, other countries would have had a right to interfere and prop up British rule in the American colonies and tsarism in Russia. In fact, England and France — not to mention some other countries — did wage a war of intervention against the young Soviet State, and you know your history well enough to remember how that ended.

"Furthermore, Mr. President, history has seen holy alliances before and can show us what became of them. Nicholas I of Russia played a leading role in the Holy Alliance, which helped the Austrian monarchy suppress a revolt in Hungary — a disgraceful interference in a country's internal affairs. It was a case of one emperor helping another to maintain reactionary regimes in Europe. History demonstrated the weakness of that policy when the alliance fell apart. The time has passed for treaties among monarchs trying to guarantee the stability of their thrones against forces which would like to change the conditions in their country. There is no point for us to talk now about forming a holy alliance. We cannot do it and we will not do it. Not only will we not support your proposal, but we will fight against it with all the means at our disposal.

"You see, Mr. President, we can't agree with you on freezing the status quo because that would mean depriving people of opportunities to decide their destinies for themselves. We stand for socialism, and you stand for capitalism. Let the other people of the world decide for themselves under what social and political system they will live."

Had John Kennedy realized the implications of the proposal he was making, I don't think he would have suggested freezing internal political systems. He was a highly intelligent President, but here he was defending his class and defending capitalist tradition — and he wanted us to be party to such a thing! Frankly, I was somewhat surprised at him. Therefore I couldn't help using a little irony to mock what he was suggesting. I think even today the Americans still haven't given up the point of view Kennedy set forth to me. My belief is confirmed by the war which the United States has been waging in Vietnam, Laos, and Cambodia. Indeed, that war represents nothing but the desire of the United States to preserve capitalism and the landlord system in those countries. The peoples of Vietnam, Laos, and Cambodia are fighting to establish better conditions for working people. We Communists, of course, believe that the best conditions are to be found under the Communist system, under socialism.

What positive conclusions could be drawn from my talks with Kennedy on peaceful coexistence? Most important, he understood that the first stage of peaceful coexistence was the prevention of war — particularly war between the United States and the Soviet Union. But he wasn't willing to go much beyond the basic point.

We also discussed the problem of Lend-Lease. I repeated to him what I had told Eisenhower: "We are grateful to you for the help you gave us during the war. Your help was essential in our struggle against our common enemy. You gave us material aid, and it was very valuable. But we gave our blood, and blood is more expensive than the materials we received from you. Therefore we feel that we have long ago repaid you with interest for your Lend-Lease shipments." But capitalists are all the same. They say, "The blood was your own. We supplied you with things for which we expect to be paid in cash."

I'd like to say a few words about the way Kennedy conducted his side of the talks. We were sitting in a room with only our interpreters, Rusk, and Gromyko. I don't remember Kennedy making any inquiries of Rusk, nor do I remember Rusk giving Kennedy any advice. To my mind this meant Kennedy had a good grasp of international issues and was well prepared for the talks. It was quite a difference from Eisenhower's behavior in Geneva and Washington, when first Dulles and then Herter were always prompting him. John Kennedy and I met man to man, as the two principal representatives of our countries. He felt perfectly confident to answer questions and make

points on his own. This was to his credit, and he rose in my estimation at once. He was, so to speak, both my partner and my adversary.
Insofar as we held different positions, he was my adversary; but insofar as we were negotiating with each other and exchanging views,
he was my partner whom I treated with great respect. It was my
judgment that if the President understood the policy of peaceful
coexistence, he would conduct a policy of peaceful coexistence —
and he wouldn't make any hasty decisions which might lead to military conflict. A man like this I could respect.

I think he respected me, too. With every passing year our economic and military might was growing. Each year we made more
progress in the exploration of space and in the development of our
missiles and nuclear weapons. We had conducted many tests, and
our nuclear bombs were more and more versatile; we had a wider variety of both tactical and strategic weapons. The strengthening of our
armed forces gave added weight to the voice of our country's leadership, although we deliberately restrained ourselves from getting embroiled in power politics, the politics of Allen Dulles.

By the time Kennedy came to the White House and we had our
meeting in Vienna, there had already been a shift in the balance of
power. It was harder for the US to pressure us than it had been in the
days of Dulles and Truman. It was for this reason that Kennedy had
felt obliged to seek an opportunity to reach some kind of agreement.
As it turned out, though, there was still no realistic basis for an agreement acceptable both to the United States and to the Soviet Union.

Kennedy and I held our conversations during the day. Then, in the
evenings, the Austrian government would arrange lavish receptions
in our honor. We were invited to the theater and also, I think, to the
opera. Once we were shown a circus act with horses. Of course,
there are performing horses in all circuses, but this was something
different: first, there was a huge quantity of horses, and second, the
riders put their mounts through the most complicated theatrical
paces.[11] It was a beautiful show, one of the most interesting sights to
be seen in Vienna — and Vienna has many spectacles to be proud of.

At one reception Kennedy introduced me to his wife and to his
mother. Jacqueline, Kennedy's wife, was a young woman whom the
journalists were always describing as a great beauty. She didn't
impress me as having that special, brilliant beauty which can haunt

11. The exhibition by the Lippizan horses at the Spanish Riding School.

men, but she was youthful, energetic, and pleasant, and I liked her very much. She knew how to make jokes and was, as our people say, quick with her tongue. In other words, she had no trouble finding the right word to cut you short if you weren't careful with her. My own conversation with her consisted of nothing more than small talk, the sort you'd expect at receptions or during intermissions at the theater. But even in small talk she demonstrated her intelligence.

That's about all there is to my impression of Kennedy's wife. As the head of the Soviet delegation, I couldn't care less what sort of wife he had. If he liked her, that was his business — and good luck to them both. The same was the case with his mother. We knew she was a millionaire, and consequently we had to keep in mind whom we were dealing with at all times. We could smile courteously and shake hands with her, but that didn't change the fact that we were at opposite poles.

It was at one of these receptions or evenings at the theater that I had my last meeting with Kennedy. I remember he looked not only anxious, but deeply upset. I recall vividly the expression on his face. Looking at him, I couldn't help feeling a bit sorry and somewhat upset myself. I hadn't meant to upset him. I would have liked very much for us to part in a different mood. But there was nothing I could do to help him. The difference in our class positions had prevented us from coming to an agreement — despite all possible efforts on my part. Politics is a merciless business, but that realization didn't keep me from feeling sorry for Kennedy. As one human being toward another, I felt bad about his disappointment.

I knew his enemies, especially aggressive politicians, would take advantage of him and tease him, saying, "See? You wanted to show off your abilities by meeting Khrushchev and sweet-talking him into an agreement. We've always said the Bolsheviks don't understand the soft language of negotiations; they understand only power politics. They tricked you; they gave your nose a good pull. You got a going-over from them, and now you've come back empty-handed and disgraced." That's what I imagined the President expected to hear when he got home.

I felt doubly sorry because what had happened did not create favorable conditions for improving relations. On the contrary, it aggravated the Cold War. This worried me. If we were thrown back into the Cold War, we would be the ones who would have to pay for it.

The Americans would start spending more money on weapons, forcing us to do the same thing, and a new, accelerated arms race would impoverish our budget, reduce our economic potential, and lower the standard of living of our people. We knew the pattern only too well from our past experience.

So my meeting with Kennedy came to an end and we said goodbye to each other with our positions basically unchanged and the tensions between our countries somewhat increased. Yet despite our worries and disappointments, it was still worth something that we had met and exchanged opinions.

I think that Kennedy was more intelligent than any of the Presidents before him. I'd like my Communist brothers to understand me correctly when I pay such compliments to the late President of the United States. To give a man credit when credit is due doesn't entail any whitewashing of the social and political system that man represents. Kennedy was a capitalist and a representative of the capitalists; he was faithful to the capitalist class right up to the last day of his life. But he understood that the socialist camp had gained such economic and cultural might — and was in possession of so much scientific and technical knowledge, including the means of war — that the United States and its allies could no longer seriously consider going to war against us. I'll always respect him for that.

The time came for Kennedy to leave Vienna. I didn't see him off. I wouldn't have been expected to. Kennedy was escorted to the airport by Austrian officials, including Kreisky, the Secretary of State who is now Chancellor. Afterwards Kreisky asked for an appointment with me and I received him. He had a reputation as the most elastic of the Social Democrats. Personally I knew him to be a flexible politician who favored improving relations with socialist countries. I also knew him to be in close touch with Willy Brandt, who was then Burgomaster, or Mayor, of West Berlin and is now the Chancellor of West Germany. Brandt and Kreisky were friends; both had emigrated to Sweden during the war and both were Social Democrats.[12]

My talk with Kreisky was useful for both of us. He told me the impressions he had while seeing Kennedy off: "The President was very gloomy at the airport. He seemed upset, and his face had changed. Obviously the meeting did not go well for him."

12. Willy Brandt of the West German Social Democratic Party, Mayor of West Berlin, had met with Kennedy in Washington shortly before the Vienna summit. He became Chancellor in 1969.

"Yes," I replied, "I saw the mood he was in. But that's because the President still doesn't quite understand the times in which we live. He doesn't yet fully understand the realignment of forces, and he still lives by the policies of his predecessors — especially as far as the German question is concerned. He's not yet ready to lift the threat of world war which hangs over Berlin. Our talks were helpful in that they gave us a chance to sound each other out and get to know each other. But that's all, and it's not enough."

To tell the truth, I recounted for Kreisky everything I'd told Kennedy. I knew that what I said would get back to Kennedy — and it would also be passed on to Willy Brandt. I hoped that by underscoring our determination not to abandon our intentions we might succeed in encouraging these leaders toward rational discussions and ultimately a reasonable agreement — all, hopefully, without raising temperatures to the boiling point.

After Kennedy had left, the Austrian government arranged a reception or dinner in my honor. Then the time came for us to leave, too. Our departure was accompanied by all the appropriate ceremonies and traditional honors. Soon I was back in Moscow.

The Berlin Crisis

To put it crudely, the American foot in Europe had a sore blister on it. That was West Berlin.[13] Anytime we wanted to step on the Americans' foot and make them feel the pain, all we had to do was obstruct Western communications with the city across the territory of the German Democratic Republic. Stalin had tried to take advantage of the West Berlin issue, but he suffered a defeat.[14]

After Stalin's death, we continued to insist that West Berlin was not, as our former allies argued, part of the Federal Republic of Germany. Every time the Western countries violated the sovereignty of the GDR — every time they treated West Berlin as though it were part of West Germany — they added heat to a highly flammable, potentially explosive situation.

As a solution, we proposed a peace treaty which, among its provi-

13. This section supplements and amplifies Khrushchev's recollections of the 1961 Berlin crisis as presented in *KR*, I, 452–460.
14. The reference here is to the Berlin blockade and airlift.

sions, would make West Berlin a free city. We were prepared to make that concession only on the condition that there would be two internationally recognized German states, both of which would be members of the United Nations.

As I've already related, I discussed the German question in some depth with President de Gaulle during my visit to France. He said that he had been in favor of a divided Germany ever since the war and that he had urged Stalin to support the idea of more than two independent Germanys.

"Mr. Khrushchev," he said, "you probably know the position France took during the Potsdam discussions. We were in favor of more radical means; but Mr. Stalin didn't back us up, and our proposal wasn't accepted."

"Yes, Mr. President," I said, "I remember your position during the Potsdam talks, and I think I understand Stalin's reasons for not supporting you. At the time we had somewhat different ideas about the status and development of postwar Germany."

I believe de Gaulle understood the danger of German revanchism, and I appreciated his willingness to accept the fact that, according to the Potsdam Agreement, West Berlin was a separate entity and shouldn't be considered part of West Germany. I also appreciated de Gaulle's assurance that France would never join arms with Germany to fight against the Soviet Union.

Where I parted company with de Gaulle was on the question of West Germany's role in NATO and the necessity of a peace treaty. De Gaulle felt that we should agree to leave well enough alone and that we shouldn't disturb the military, social, and political balance which had developed between the Warsaw Pact and NATO alliances. As for the peace treaty, he tried to argue that we had nothing to gain from such a treaty and that we should be content with what we already had. We couldn't accept such reasoning. Our Communist worldview obliged us to insist upon a peace treaty as the only way to normalize relations among all countries, including the two Germanys, and as the only way to guarantee full sovereignty for our ally, the German Democratic Republic.

De Gaulle couldn't understand that, or at least he pretended not to understand it. His attitude was: "East Germany is yours, so keep it. You're the rulers there. Don't bother us and don't try to weaken our position by trying to force all these changes." But we were insistent. We wanted our comrades in the GDR to be genuinely independent — to be able to build their own diplomatic, cultural, and economic relations with socialist and capitalist countries alike, according to their own interests and needs.

Then came my talks in Vienna with Kennedy. Once again, the most acute problem facing us was the German question. All other matters, notably disarmament, depended upon our finding a solution in Germany — and the German question in turn depended on the issue of West Berlin. Since my talks the year before with de Gaulle, the West Berlin issue had been growing like a tumor on an otherwise healthy body. It was more important than ever that we remove the tumor.

I told Kennedy that if he didn't agree to sign an agreement on Germany, resolving once and for all the status of Berlin, we would be forced to sign a unilateral agreement with the German Democratic Republic.[15] Once that happened, the GDR would no longer be covered by the terms of the Potsdam Agreement; it would be covered instead by the new treaty, which would be signed by us and any other countries willing to sign it. In practice, of course, only the socialist countries would have signed such a unilateral treaty.

In concrete terms, the signing of a unilateral treaty would mean that the GDR received from us the authority to conduct its own policies with regard to Western countries wishing to use the territory of the GDR for access to West Berlin. As a sovereign state, the GDR would have been entitled to be less flexible in these matters than we had been.

What I said might have sounded like a threat to Kennedy. He understood what I was saying, and he didn't like it. Nor did he like our proposal to turn West Berlin into a free city. He was afraid that once West Berlin became a free city, we would move in and occupy it — although, of course, we had no such intention.

In response to our position, Kennedy argued that according to the Potsdam Agreement there was only one Germany and therefore no peace treaty could be signed by anyone until there was a single government in Germany. This was the same line the Americans had been giving us all along. Our talks with Kennedy in Vienna were a repeat of the talks we'd had with Eisenhower.[16]

The hands of the clock were turning. But the passage of time was in our favor; it was running out for the Americans. I think Kennedy

15. Such an agreement would have excluded the Western Allies.
16. His talks with Eisenhower at Camp David in 1959.

understood clearly that he'd be in an uncomfortable position if we solved the Berlin question unilaterally, but he wasn't psychologically prepared for a bilateral solution. He was under great pressure, both from his military and from American public opinion, which wasn't yet ready to accept our proposal.

Thus, in the final analysis, while my talks with President Kennedy in Vienna were satisfactory for neither of us, they represented a defeat for him. We intended to exercise our rights [over the German question], and there was nothing he could do — short of military action — to stop us. Kennedy was intelligent enough to know that a military clash would be senseless. Therefore the United States and its Western allies had no choice but to swallow a bitter pill as we began to take certain unilateral steps.

We decided the time had come to lance the blister of West Berlin. It was no longer possible to avoid using the surgeon's knife, but we wanted to conduct the surgical operation under anesthesia. Even though we were going to resort to the use of sharp instruments, now that diplomatic means had failed, we wanted to make sure that the patient felt as little pain as possible. We also wanted to avoid postoperative complications.

Shortly after the meeting in Vienna, we publicized our intention of signing a peace treaty with the GDR.[17] We made it clear that as East Germany's allies we would stand up to anyone who tried to violate the border between the GDR and the FRG.

We then learned that Kennedy had sent to Berlin a general who had commanded the American troops in Germany at the end of World War II.[18] We took that as a signal that the Americans interpreted our intention to sign a peace treaty with the GDR as a threat and were posing a counterthreat of their own. Well, we had our own response to that.

The American general's opposite number at the end of World War II was Marshal Konev. After an exchange of opinions about what to do, I suggested to the leadership that we appoint Konev commander in chief of our own troops in Germany. To use the language of chess,

17. In June, 1961, a matter of days after his summit meeting with Kennedy, Khrushchev announced a December 31 deadline for a four-power settlement on Berlin. The "or else" was a separate Soviet–East German peace treaty and a new blockade of West Berlin — a threat he never carried out.

18. General Lucius D. Clay, US military governor in postwar Germany. He had been largely responsible for the Berlin airlift.

the Americans had advanced a pawn, so we protected our position by moving a knight.[19] In effect, the Americans had said to us, "If you're going to sign a treaty with the GDR, you'll have to deal with one of our generals who is well known to you. You know what that means: it means we're ready for armed conflict." We replied, "If you insist on holding up the shield of war against us and thwarting us in our intentions, then we're ready to meet you on your own terms."

Konev went to Berlin and took over as commander in chief from General Yakubovsky, who became Konev's deputy.[20] However, we stressed to Marshal Konev that his appointment was temporary and symbolic, and that as soon as the situation returned to normal he would return to Moscow. Naturally, our announcement in the press that Konev was going to Berlin did nothing to relieve the tensions that were building up. On the contrary, it aggravated them. Nevertheless, we recommended that Konev pay the customary courtesy call on his American opposite number. "Try to establish contacts with the US general," I told Konev before he left to go to Berlin.

Meanwhile, the GDR had been tightening its border control. We'd long since decided that free passage in and out of Berlin was nothing more than a loophole for capitalist intelligence services, allowing them to collect information on the location of our troops. The only way to close the loopholes was to close the border. At our instigation, Comrade Ulbricht instituted a system of visas for passage in and out of East Germany. There were also special passes for people entering and leaving Berlin. In other words, we helped the GDR to establish the same procedures governing immigration and border security which exist in other sovereign states.

At one point I asked our ambassador in the GDR, Pervukhin, to send me a map of West Berlin.[21] We deliberated on our tactics and set a certain date and hour when the border control would go into effect.[22] We decided to erect antitank barriers and barricades. We also

19. Khrushchev is making a pun here: in Russian a chess knight is called in Russian *kon'* ("horse"), which is also the root of Konev's surname. Konev was recalled to temporary service from retirement on August 10, while Clay did not resume command in West Germany until August 18.
20. Marshal I. I. Yakubovsky, subsequently commander in chief of the Warsaw Pact.
21. M. G. Pervukhin, Soviet ambassador to the GDR, was a former Presidium member who had been demoted for allegedly supporting the Molotov-Malenkov-Kaganovich Anti-Party Group.
22. By "border control," Khrushchev means the erection of the Berlin Wall, a euphemism he uses throughout his account of the crisis.

planned to use our own troops to guard the border, although the front line would consist of German soldiers. Our own men would be a few meters behind them, so that the West could easily see that Soviet troops were backing up the German troops. We wanted to give the impression that the whole operation was being carried out by the [East] Germans in cooperation with their Soviet allies.

The date for the beginning of border control was to be August 13, 1961. We kidded among ourselves that in the West the thirteenth is supposed to be an unlucky day. I joked that for us and for the whole socialist camp it would be a very lucky day indeed.

We kept our plans secret until the last minute. When the day and hour arrived, our troops occupied the border positions. There was immediately a terrific uproar, but we had successfully and unilaterally helped the GDR to exercise those functions of a sovereign state which the GDR would have enjoyed as a result of a peace treaty.

I took a personal concern in these developments. Since our military had the right to go in and out of West Berlin, I decided to take advantage of this right. Together with the commandant of Berlin, who happened to be one of our officers, I visited the city incognito; I never got out of the car, but I made a full tour and saw what the city was like.

The establishment of border control straightened things out at once. Discipline in East Germany increased. Plants began working better. So did collective farms. Comrade Ulbricht informed us that there were immediate improvements in the economy of the GDR. The population of West Berlin had been shopping for food in East Berlin, taking advantage of lower prices there. Thus, the West Berliners had been devaluing the East German mark, placing a heavy burden on the shoulders of the GDR's peasants and workers, and therefore extracting political as well as economic gains from the situation. Once we established border control, we put an end to that business.

I should mention that it was a difficult task to divide the city of Berlin because everything is intertwined. The border goes along a street, so one side of the street is in East Berlin while the other is in West Berlin. But what could we do? History had created this inconvenience, and we had to live with it.

We began to receive information that certain forces were preparing to destroy "the Wall," as it was called in the West. They were planning forcibly to restore unrestricted passage in and out of the city. The situation came to a head when the Twenty-second Party Congress was in session.[23] Konev was attending the Congress as a delegate. He reported that the Americans were getting ready to move in and destroy the border installations with infantry and bulldozers. We told Konev to station our tanks out of sight in the side streets and move them out to confront the Americans when they crossed the border. Konev did as we instructed. He reported that as soon as the American jeeps, trucks, personnel carriers, and bulldozers crossed the border, they found themselves looking down the barrels of our tanks. Both sides stopped in their tracks and squared off against each other for a whole night.

The next morning the Party Congress carried on with its work. Konev reported that the situation at the border in Berlin was unchanged. No one was moving, except for those moments when the tank operators on both sides would climb out and walk around to warm up.

"Comrade Konev," I said, "I think you'd better order our tanks to turn around and pull back from the border. Don't have them go very far. Just get them out of sight in the side streets again. I'm sure that within twenty minutes or however long it takes them to get their instructions, the American tanks will pull back, too. They can't turn their tanks around and pull them back as long as our guns are pointing at them. They've gotten themselves into a difficult situation, and they don't know how to get out of it. They're looking for a way out, I'm sure. So let's give them one. We'll remove our tanks, and they'll follow our example."

Konev did exactly as I told him and reported that the American tanks had turned around and disappeared in about twenty minutes — just as I predicted. That was the end of it. The West had been forced to recognize the establishment of border control and the separation of capitalist West Berlin from socialist East Berlin, the capital of the German Democratic Republic.

I would say that we didn't quite achieve the same sort of moral victory that a peace treaty would have represented, but on the other hand we probably received more material gains *without* a peace

23. At the Twenty-second Party Congress, Khrushchev openly attacked Albania and China.

treaty. If the West had agreed to sign a treaty, it would have meant concessions on our part, particularly with regard to the movement of people across the border. Subsequently there were occasional violations of the border. A certain number — in fact quite a few — people tried to get out of East Berlin. I heard about one case in which a group rammed the barricade with a truck and escaped into West Berlin. We told [the GDR authorities] that measures would have to be taken to prevent such incidents from being repeated. We didn't want intelligence agents operating in East Berlin to be able to avoid arrest by running away to West Berlin.

We had our doubts about the ability of the [East] Germans to control their own borders. The guards were equipped with firearms, but it's not so easy for a soldier to shoot a fellow German. We expressed this concern to our German comrades, and they answered, "Russians fought Russians for several years in your Civil War, didn't they? And they used firearms, didn't they? So why do you think a German's hand would tremble if he were performing his class duty? Why should he shirk from shooting another German in defense of his socialist republic?" That was a good point. Even though incidents continued to occur from time to time, the border troops in the GDR were well grounded in the teachings of Marxism-Leninism. They understood their class obligations as well as their military duty. They did what they had to do to protect their socialist fatherland.

As time went by, the West began to put out feelers through confidential and unofficial channels, as well as through the press. The capitalists realized that control had been firmly established in Berlin and the Russians wouldn't back down. Word reached us that the West acknowledged our rights but hoped we wouldn't aggravate the situation any further. The Americans recalled their commander, and we immediately summoned Marshal Konev back to Moscow. We also pulled back the troops which had been mobilized during the crisis. Thus we had achieved our purpose of controlling the border of the GDR in the absence of a peace treaty. We had secured for the GDR its sovereign rights. That was reward enough for our efforts, and it made us pleased and proud. I was more pleased than anyone, because I had been the one who thought up the solution to the problem which faced us as a consequence of our unsatisfactory negotiations with Kennedy in Vienna.

I still remember Kennedy telling me in Vienna that according to the Potsdam Agreement, there existed only one Germany and therefore if a peace treaty were signed, it would have to create a government for a united Germany. He kept arguing that point, despite my refusal to interfere in the internal affairs of the GDR. Well, whom has time borne out? Haven't things worked out differently from what Kennedy said? Now Brandt himself has found it necessary to recognize the GDR. As premier of one Germany, he has met with the premier of the other Germany. That may not constitute *de jure* recognition of the existence of two Germanys, but it is certainly *de facto* recognition. We set the stage for this development [in 1961] when we took advantage of our rights and prevented serious incidents before they happened. In so doing, we forced Kennedy and the Western Allies to swallow a bitter pill.

The Cuban Missile Crisis

THE Caribbean crisis was an important test for us.[24] It was a test of our abilities at a time when we might have had to resort to the use of nuclear weapons. I have already made statements about the episode both in public and in my memoirs, but I wish to add some thoughts here.

Fidel Castro was our friend, and revolutionary Cuba was threatened by the saber-rattling militarists of the Pentagon. Reactionary circles in the United States treated Cuba as a festering sore on their country's own body. The intelligence agency of the American army organized an invasion force consisting of Cuban counterrevolutionaries. The Americans miscalculated. They did not plan well. They overestimated the strength of the counterrevolutionaries. They thought that the invasion would trigger an uprising in support of the counterrevolution. But that was wishful thinking. Castro handled the situation brilliantly. It took him, I think, only three days or a little more to smash the invaders to pieces.

However, we knew that the Americans wouldn't let the matter rest there. We knew they couldn't reconcile themselves to the rout of the counterrevolutionaries. We knew the US would never swallow such

24. This chapter supplements and amplifies Khrushchev's recollections of the October, 1962, Cuban missile crisis as presented in *KR*, I, 488–505.

a bitter pill. Even after the abortive invasion, the Americans were determined to liquidate Cuba's independent social and political system and establish in its place a puppet regime headed by a new Batista.[25]

We had information — which, by the way, was later confirmed — that the American government had pledged itself to organize a better-trained and better-equipped landing force.[26] This time the invasion was to be supported by American forces. We knew that the United States was very experienced in such operations. The US would simply take the flag of another republic, pledge to support some hard-core reactionaries who would allegedly have landed on their own territory, and justify the whole thing as an "internal struggle" within that country. In fact, of course, the US would simply throw mercenaries or regular troops into the fighting in order to do the job.

In one respect, the American attitude was only natural. The US couldn't accept the idea of a socialist Cuba, right off the coast of the United States, serving as a revolutionary example to the rest of Latin America. Likewise, we prefer to have socialist countries for neighbors because that is expedient for us. However, we treat this problem with understanding. It's our position that such problems are solved not by war, but by internal forces — specifically, by the people and the working class.

The United States, on the other end, was bent on directly interfering in the internal affairs of Cuba. The Americans wanted to force Cuba away from the path of socialism and make it drag behind American policy, just as it had before the victory of the Cuban revolution, when puppet presidents made it easy for the US to exploit Cuba.

For our part, we wanted Cuba to remain revolutionary and socialist, and we knew Cuba needed help in order to do so. Cuba is a small island in both population and territory. It doesn't have much in-

25. Fulgencio Batista was the dictator toppled by Fidel Castro and forced into exile in 1959.

26. According to Tad Szulc, writing in the February, 1974, issue of *Esquire,* "The Central Intelligence Agency, presumably acting with President Lyndon Johnson's authority . . . , set in motion in late 1964 and 1965 a new secret plan to combine Castro's assassination with a second invasion of the island by Cuban exiles from bases located this time in Costa Rica and Nicaragua. . . . It was an incredibly wild scheme because the resolution of the 1962 Cuban missile crisis, which brought the U.S. and the Soviet Union to the brink of nuclear confrontation, was based in part on Washington's commitment to let Castro be. . . . Actually, the whole assassination-invasion plan had to be canceled when a rebellion unexpectedly erupted in the Dominican Republic in April, 1965."

dustry of its own, and its army is equipped with weapons bought from other countries. When I say "weapons," I mean real weapons — not just field weapons. They probably manufacture their own rifles, but they don't produce their own heavy stuff. It was up to us to supply it.

We had no other way of helping them meet the American threat except to install our missiles on the island, so as to confront the aggressive forces of the United States with a dilemma: if you invade Cuba, you'll have to face a nuclear missile attack against your own cities. Our intention was to install the missiles not to wage war against the US, but to prevent the US from invading Cuba and thus starting a war. All we wanted was to give the new progressive system created in Cuba by Fidel Castro a chance to work.

Without our missiles on Cuba, the island would have been in the position of a weak man threatened by a strong man. I'm not saying we had any documentary proof that the Americans were preparing a second invasion; we didn't need documentary proof. We knew the class affiliation, the class blindness, of the United States, and that was enough to make us expect the worst.

When Castro and I talked about the problem, we argued and argued. Our argument was very heated. But, in the end, Fidel agreed with me. Later on, he began to supply me with certain data that had come to his attention. "Apparently what you told me was right," he said. That in itself justified what we then did.[27]

We stationed our armed forces on Cuban soil for one purpose only: to maintain the independence of the Cuban people and to prevent the invasion by a mercenary expeditionary force which the United States was then preparing to launch. We had no intention of starting a war ourselves. We've always considered war to be against our own interests. We've never thought in terms of any other than defensive war. Anyone with an ounce of sense can see I'm telling the truth. It would have been preposterous for us to unleash a war against the United States from Cuba. Cuba was 11,000 kilometers from the Soviet Union. Our sea and air communications with Cuba were so precarious that an attack against the US was unthinkable.

As tensions rose to the point where war might break out, our countries resorted to secret diplomacy. We maintained contact with Presi-

27. An interruption occurs here, but from the text it is apparent that Castro at first resisted Khrushchev's proposal to install missiles in Cuba as a deterrent to further American intervention.

dent Kennedy through his brother Robert. He came to our embassy and expressed, on behalf of the President, a desire to reach an agreement. He also consented to transmit our demands to the President.

Our position was this: we would withdraw our missiles from Cuba on the condition that the United States would make a public statement, pledging not to invade Cuba and promising to restrain its allies from doing so.

President Kennedy said that in exchange for the withdrawal of our missiles, he would remove American missiles from Turkey and Italy. We knew perfectly well that this pledge was of a symbolic nature: the American rockets in Turkey and Italy were already obsolete, and the Americans would promptly replace them with more modern ones. Besides, the US was already equipping its navy with Polaris missiles. Nevertheless, by agreeing even to symbolic measures, Kennedy was creating the impression of mutual concessions.[28]

The resolution of the Caribbean crisis came as a historic landmark. For the first time in history, the Americans pledged publicly not to invade one of their neighbors and not to interfere in its internal affairs. This was a bitter pill for the US to swallow. It was worse than that: the American imperialist beast was forced to swallow a hedgehog, quills and all. And that hedgehog is still in its stomach, undigested. No surgical operation to remove the hedgehog is possible as long as the Soviet-American agreement on Cuba is in effect.

We behaved with dignity and forced the US to demobilize and to recognize Cuba — not *de jure*, but *de facto*. Cuba still exists today as a result of the correct policy conducted by the Soviet Union when it rebuffed the United States. I'm proud of what we did. Looking back on the episode, I feel pride in my people, in the policies we conducted, and in the victories we won on the diplomatic front.

The experience of the Caribbean crisis also convinced us that we were right to concentrate on the manufacture of nuclear missiles rather than on the expansion of our surface navy, as Kuznetsov had recommended and which he admitted would have cost billions and taken at least ten years.[29] Just having atomic bombs and long-range bombers would not have been enough because in those categories

28. In his own memoir of the crisis, *Thirteen Days*, Robert Kennedy relates his version of discussions with Ambassador Dobrynin on the removal of US Jupiter missiles from Turkey and Italy. Also according to Robert Kennedy, the meeting Khrushchev refers to here was held at the Justice Department, not at the Soviet embassy.

29. See Chapter 2 for Khrushchev's review of the controversy with Kuznetsov over the surface fleet.

we lagged behind the US. But when we created missiles which America and the whole world knew could deliver a crushing blow anywhere on the globe — that represented a triumph in the battle of wits over how best to expend the resources of our people in defending the security of our homeland.

What can I say about the other leaders who played a role in the affair? As for Fidel Castro, all I can say is that I wish him and his people success in the building of socialism.

During the crisis, I never had an opportunity to find out what President de Gaulle's attitude was. The American press claimed that de Gaulle sent word of French support to Kennedy at the most critical moment. That's possible, but it's also possible that de Gaulle did the opposite.[30]

I'd like to say a few words about John Kennedy. You can find people who will tell you that Kennedy was to blame for the tensions which might have resulted in war. Well, this is my answer to those clever people who like to ask clever questions: You have to keep in mind the era in which we live. This is a transitional period in history. The question of who will prevail over whom is being resolved on a worldwide scale. The dying capitalist system is grasping at straws to maintain, and if possible to strengthen, its position. It was in that context that the Caribbean crisis arose. We found ourselves in a serious confrontation with the President of the United States. In such situations, one cannot be afraid of conflict, but at the same time one must keep one's wits and not allow the conflict to turn into war. In other words, one must have an intelligent, sober-minded counterpart with whom to deal. At that point in my political career, my partner was Kennedy, the head of the mightiest capitalist country in the world. I believe he was a man who understood the situation correctly and who genuinely did not want war. He realized that the time had passed when such disputes could be decided by force. He was realistic enough to see that now the might of the socialist world equaled that of the capitalist world.

Kennedy was also someone we could trust. When he gave us public assurances that the US would not organize an invasion of Cuba,

30. According to Robert Kennedy, former Secretary of State Dean Acheson used US air reconnaissance photographs of the Soviet installations on Cuba "to quickly convince French President Charles de Gaulles of the correctness of our response and later to reassure Chancellor Adenauer. Macmillan made it clear the US would have his country's support."

either on its own or through its allies, we trusted him. We accepted the concession he was making and made a concession of our own by withdrawing our nuclear weapons from Cuba.

What kind of man was Kennedy? As regards our backgrounds, he and I were poles apart. I was a miner, a metal fitter, who — by the will of the Party and the people — rose to be the Prime Minister of my country. Kennedy was a millionaire and the son of a millionaire. He pursued the goal of strengthening capitalism, while I sought to destroy capitalism and create a new social system based on the teachings of Marx, Engels, and Lenin. As our meeting in Vienna demonstrated, we held diametrically opposing views on many important questions.

Despite the irreconcilability of our class antagonism, however, Kennedy and I found common ground and a common language when it came to preventing a military conflict. For example, we agreed to establish a direct line of communication between us, bypassing diplomatic channels, to be used in case of emergency. Some people may say, "Who needs it?" I say it may come in handy some day.[31]

I would like to pay my respects to Kennedy, my former opposite number in the serious conflict which arose between our countries. He showed great flexibility and, together, we avoided disaster. When he was assassinated, I felt sincere regret. I went straight to the [US] embassy and expressed my condolences.

31. The Washington-Moscow "hotline" agreement was signed in June, 1963.

21

Visit to Scandinavia

W E received a joint invitation from Denmark, Norway, and Sweden to visit those three countries, but the Scandinavian press
stirred up a real witches' sabbath; it went on such a rampage of
abuse against our Soviet delegation, our policies, and our state that
we had to postpone the trip. Then, after our official visits to the
United States and France [in 1959 and 1960], the Scandinavian governments renewed their invitation. At first, we were embarrassed by
it, having already refused to go once, but everything was smoothed
over through diplomatic channels.[1]

Our first stop was Copenhagen, the capital of Denmark. We were
taken on a tour of the city and shown the embankment and the
famous mermaid, which is known the world over. As I recall, some
villain had sawed off the mermaid's head just before our arrival. The
public was outraged, and the press was writing about little else. The
mermaid had a special significance for every Dane. By the time we
saw her, the mermaid's head had been replaced so skillfully you
couldn't find a trace of what had happened.

Nina Petrovna was with me. The Danes honored her by asking that
she break the traditional bottle of champagne against the prow of a
ship that was being launched.

The Danes are marvelous shipbuilders. Their products are modern
and highly maneuverable, with excellent steering mechanisms. In
the past, we'd done a lot of business with Danish shipyards. Then,
after Stalin's death, we got into a very unpleasant exchange with the
Danes. One day, out of the blue, they suddenly refused to accept an

1. Khrushchev's real reason for postponing his Scandinavian trip in 1959 was his
desire to visit the US instead. He finally went to Scandinavia in June, 1964.

order we'd placed for a twelve-thousand-ton oil tanker. They explained that the aggressive NATO alliance, of which they were a member, had decided to limit the capacity of our shipping industry by passing a regulation which prohibited any NATO country from selling the USSR vessels of more than three to five thousand tons. Of course, the United States was the instigator of that policy. The incident led to some heated arguments between the Danes and us, some of which spilled over into the press. Later, the discriminatory rule was rescinded, and the Danes began accepting our orders again; but we didn't forget the episode.

During my stay in Copenhagen and my talks with the Danish leaders, we discussed general questions relating to the Warsaw Pact and NATO, but we realized Denmark didn't play a significant role in NATO and therefore made no effort to persuade the Danes to alter their foreign policy.

Our hosts arranged a tour so that we could familiarize ourselves with Danish agriculture, particularly the dairy industry. As I recall, the arrangements were made both by the government and the opposition. The leader of the opposition, who had formerly been Prime Minister, took us to his farm.[2]

I simply don't have the words to express my pleasure at seeing Danish agriculture up close. Of course, I'd read about their dairy farms and heard about them from our own agronomists; but now I was able to see them with my own eyes. If I felt any disappointment, it was because there was no way I could claim to the Danes that our agriculture was on the same level as theirs. We felt a twinge of bitterness that a capitalist enterprise should achieve such incredible success. Danish farmers are real miracle workers. Of course, what is miraculous for us is run-of-the-mill for other countries. It's all a question of level of advancement, of knowing the right agricultural techniques and skills, and of being able to make the most of the latest scientific achievements.

I remember when visiting one dairy farm, I was taken into a cow shed in which every stall had a label on it showing the percentage of fat in the milk produced by each cow. The numbers were as high as 5, 6, and 7 percent. Imagine that! Seven percent fat! It was a dream. In our country we don't dare use the percentage of fat in our milk as the productivity gauge. We measure a cow's output in liters. The average fat content in our country is 2.5 percent, while in Denmark

2. Eric Ericsen, Liberal Party Prime Minister from 1950 to 1953.

it's 5 percent. In other words, two liters of our milk are worth one of theirs.

The dairy farmer — I think it was the opposition leader — gave me two prize cows and a bull at a cattle exhibition. When I got home, I ordered our Ministry of Agriculture to turn these cattle over to a research institute so that we could study them and try to improve our native breed of dairy cattle.

I have nothing but the best memories of my talks with the leaders of the Danish Communist Party. We had a friendly exchange of views on various international issues and general questions facing the Communist movement. My counterpart in these talks was Jespersen, the Secretary of the Danish Party.

As I recall, the Danish Party was then experiencing certain difficulties stemming from a split which had occurred many years' before. Immediately after World War II the Party had been headed by Larsen, a Party member of long standing and a leader of some stature in the international Communist movement.[3] He used to come to the Soviet Union and drop by at the Central Committee for talks with me. He impressed me as a straightforward, pleasant, and trustworthy man. I remember once in Moscow he raised a matter which slightly surprised me.

"Comrade Khrushchev," he said, "I don't understand why you print such big bank notes. Paper is expensive, and you're wasting money. Besides, your bank notes are too big to fit conveniently into a wallet." He pulled out his billfold and showed me some of their [Danish] paper money.

"All I can tell you, Comrade Larsen, is that big bills are just a tradition in Russia. I don't think there's any other reason. I very much appreciate your thoughtful, practical advice. Next time we print new currency, we'll take what you say into account."

Our State Bank and Ministry of Finance also proposed that we print smaller notes. Shortly afterwards we took Larsen's advice and saved a great deal of money as a result.

In short, my relations with Larsen had been perfectly congenial.

3. Aksel Larsen was ousted from the Communist Party leadership and replaced by Knud Jespersen in 1958 because he attended that year's conference of the Yugoslav League of Communists, thus defying a boycott imposed on the Yugoslav Party by the Soviet camp. By attending, Larsen made it clear that he intended to pursue a course independent of Moscow. In 1959 he was suspended from the Communist Party, and in that same year he founded the Socialist People's Party. Jespersen's pro-Moscow Danish Communist Party has been the only Scandinavian Party to remain unflinchingly loyal to the Soviet line.

Later, however, we became enemies. He attended some international conference at which he took a position which was at variance from the general line of the other Parties. If I remember correctly, he was pro-Yugoslav. As a result, he came under fire and was censured or even expelled by his comrades. He then broke off from the Communists and formed his own party, the Socialists, which started off with a small following but ended up with considerable influence among the Danish voters.

Naturally, we supported the Communist Party and Comrade Jespersen, even though Larsen still called himself a Marxist-Leninist and even though his Socialist candidates sometimes did better than those supported by the Communist Party in the parliamentary elections.

During my visit to Denmark we ran into Larsen at a meeting between our delegation and various parliamentary leaders. We didn't even say hello or shake hands. We just bowed slightly. He asked a few barbed questions, and in reply I think we mocked his political position rather than take it seriously. The Danish press, which opposed the Communist movement, made use of this encounter between Larsen and me. It was the one dark spot on our visit to Denmark.

I got along very well with the Prime Minister of Denmark, a Social Democrat. He and his wife took Nina Petrovna and me to their apartment outside of Copenhagen.[4] It was in a small, undistinguished town which looked like a working-class suburb. The houses were mostly two-storied cooperatives with nice lawns and small gardens. You could see into the neighbors' yards, and they could see into yours. In short, the Prime Minister lived comfortably but not luxuriously.

His wife was a sociable woman — an actress — somewhat younger than her husband. She took Nina Petrovna on a tour of their rooms, while the Prime Minister and I sat at a table in the garden and had a talk over tea and coffee.

The Danish government arranged for us to be received by the royal family at its country residence. We were warned that the King

4. Premier Jens Otto Krag and his wife, Helle Virkner, had married in 1959, when he was Foreign Minister. She continued her career as an actress throughout the 1960's and into the '70's. Soviet Prime Minister Kosygin reportedly has said he found her the most charming of all his counterparts' wives.

was a passionate hunter, so we weren't too surprised when we arrived at the palace and learned that he hadn't yet returned from the hunt. We were greeted by the Queen, who entertained us with some conversation until the King appeared. The Queen was simply dressed. She looked like a well-to-do woman but didn't wear any regal finery.[5]

The King, too, when he arrived, made an unexpected impression on us. He didn't look different from anyone else. He wasn't wearing what you'd expect a king to wear — no uniform, no robes, no regalia. He had on just an ordinary business suit. His skin didn't look particularly pale and pampered the way kings and queens are usually depicted in paintings. He could easily have been mistaken for an average man of just about any profession.

Since we knew he loved hunting, we gave him a Tula shotgun with over-and-under barrels. The King tried to assemble it the moment he got his hands on it. He had difficulty and became impatient. I tried to help him but got confused myself, since I'm not used to over-and-unders. I'm much more familiar with classical side-by-side shotguns. In the end we asked our security chief, Comrade Litovchenko, to show the King how to put his new gun together. Even though he demonstrated his complete ignorance about how to assemble his gift, the King was obviously delighted.

For us, over-and-under barrels were still a novelty, but the Europeans had been making them for years. I had a couple, one from Belgium and the other from Germany. Of course, in the hands of a good marksman, our Tulas can stand up against any Western shotgun.

Later I was introduced to the King's daughters, the princesses.[6] The youngest daughter was still just a girl, and she had a very nice appearance. I'd even say she was beautiful, although, of course, you can always find varying opinions about a woman's looks. This girl made an immediate impression on our delegation. She looked like a fresh flower. We were told she was already engaged to the King of Greece. When I heard this, I could barely restrain myself from expressing my sympathies to her. Kings are out of fashion these days,

5. King Frederik IX and Queen Ingrid received Khrushchev for lunch at their summer palace in Fredensborg.
6. Princesses Margrethe, Benedikte, and Anne-Marie, who was then seventeen years old.

and the Greek throne was especially shaky. Therefore I couldn't help feeling compassion for this little girl who no doubt would have to experience quite a bit of unpleasantness as the queen of Greece.

Now there are some people who might say, "Here's Khrushchev, a former worker, feeling sorry for royalty!" Yes, I felt sorry for her, but not as royalty — I felt sorry for her as a human being. I would have been pleased to hear she was engaged, if only her bridegroom weren't a king. I knew this lovely little princess had some disagreeable surprises in store for her. And I was right. Some years later, the Greek colonels staged a coup d'etat and the royal couple had to flee to Italy.[7]

Later we traveled to Norway, which also has a monarchy. Naturally, I paid my respects to the Norwegian King.[8]

I'd been told that his late father believed so much in democracy that he used to ride a streetcar to the place where he liked to fish, and the other passengers sometimes took him for an average citizen. Whether he really behaved so democratically I can't say for certain, but there was such a story about him.

I had to be prepared for my reception with the King of Norway because he had a rather strange physical defect. My advisors warned me that he might burst into loud laughter for no reason at all. He didn't laugh at something funny. He just had this handicap or sickness. Therefore, if he started laughing in my presence, I was supposed to pretend that nothing had happened and that I hadn't noticed anything.

We were taken to a palace which didn't look like a palace at all. There was nothing regal about it. It couldn't be compared to our tsars' palaces I'd visited in Leningrad and Peterhof, especially Catherine's palace or Paul's at Tsarskoe Selo. The Norwegian palace looked just like any other big capitalist's house. We were met at the door by a man wearing a khaki-colored military uniform of some sort. He showed me into a study, offered me a chair, and we both sat down. I suddenly realized this was the King. He could easily have been mistaken for the gardener.

---

7. Princess Anne-Marie married King Constantine II of Greece in September, 1964. The Greek royal couple went into exile in Rome in 1967 after an abortive countercoup against the ruling military regime. Constantine was formally deposed and the monarchy abolished in 1973. For another example of Khrushchev's attitude toward royalty — namely Queen Elizabeth II of England — see *KR*, I, 407.

8. Olav V, son of Haakon VII.

Our talk was formal and brief. We didn't touch on any matters of substance. After all, what's there to talk about with the King of Norway? As in other Scandinavian countries, the King doesn't determine government policy — his ministers do.

The Prime Minister was Gerhardsen, the leader of the Social Democrats.[9] He was a former construction worker who had been a bricklayer during the German occupation of Norway. During the war the Hitlerites arrested him, and it wasn't until our armies drove the Germans out of northern Norway that he was liberated from a concentration camp. He and I paid homage to the Soviet and Norwegian soldiers who gave their lives in the fight against the Nazi occupiers and the Gestapo.

The policies of the Gerhardsen government were for the most part liberal, although we felt that Norway still didn't make a sufficient effort to withdraw from NATO. Norway is our next-door neighbor, and its membership in the NATO alliance has represented a threat to our borders. Even now NATO conducts military maneuvers both at sea and in the mountains close to our territory. However, considering the alternative posed by the reactionary politicians in the Norwegian parliament, we certainly favored Gerhardsen.

His wife was also a Social Democrat.[10] She had once visited our country as the head of a youth organization. She served as Nina Petrovna's guide on a tour of various schools and social organizations.

The Prime Minister's wife played an active role in the political life of Norway. She belonged to the left wing of the Social Democratic party and therefore was closer to the Communists than her husband. The Norwegian Communists all called her by her first name. I remember hearing that when the Norwegian working class went out into the streets, she joined the Communists and left-wing Social Democrats who were building barricades. Of course, there was no fighting. These barricades were only symbolic. But nonetheless it was significant that the Prime Minister's wife would participate in such a demonstration on behalf of the proletariat's struggle against its class enemy, the bourgeoisie.

We met the leaders of the Norwegian Communist Party at an outdoor reception given by our ambassador in Oslo. They were good, in-

9. Einar Gerhardsen, of the Labor Party.
10. Werna Gerhardsen met her husband in the Labor movement and continued to be politically active, with a reputation for being to the left of him. She accompanied Gerhardsen on state visits to the USSR in 1955 and 1965.

telligent comrades (although later — after I'd already retired — some of them clashed with us on the Chinese issue). Even though they were in opposition to their government in power, our Norwegian comrades spoke highly of Prime Minister Gerhardsen.

They explained that the ruling Social Democrats had only the slimmest majority over the highly influential bourgeois oppositionists in the parliament. At a critical moment, if Gerhardsen were in danger of being toppled from the premiership, the Communists would throw their support to him rather than allow the bourgeois party to form a government.

During my stay in Oslo, Gerhardsen asked to have a talk with me, just man to man. I agreed, although I think in the end Gromyko was present, too. Sometimes Gerhardsen and I called each other Mister, sometimes Comrade. I believe he was the first to use a proletarian form of address with me.

"Comrade Khrushchev," he said, "it doesn't look like we're going to win the next parliamentary elections. I'm afraid the bourgeois party will come to power, and we'll become the opposition. We've been constantly losing votes. Now we have only a one-seat majority in the parliament, and that seat doesn't even belong to us — it belongs to another party, which occupies an intermediary position between our party and the bourgeois party.[11] Now it looks like we're going to lose that seat in the next elections."

"Why is this happening?" I asked him. "Your constituency is made up mostly of workers. Why should they vote for the candidates nominated by the bourgeois party? Why should the working class vote against its own interests? Maybe you should rethink your platform and come out with a new, more radical program to attract those elements in the working intelligentsia and peasantry who might otherwise vote for bourgeois candidates."

I could see a faint smile on Gerhardsen's lips and a touch of irony in his eyes as he answered: "You know, Comrade Khrushchev, we can't possibly have a more radical program than the one we have now."

"Why not? If you don't, you'll end up alienating your working-class constituency, and they'll vote against you."

He looked at me for a moment and decided to be more sincere: "You know, Mr. Khrushchev, we do have one other party in this

11. The Socialists were the Labor Party's coalition partners.

country which has a more radical platform but gets much fewer votes in the elections than we do. Therefore I don't think more radicalism is the answer to our problems."

It wasn't hard for me to figure out what "other" party he was talking about. I knew perfectly well he was referring to the Communist Party, which had only five or six deputies in the parliament.

I decided to put the question more concretely and directly: "Then tell me, Mr. Gerhardsen, what do you think is the real reason the workers won't vote for you?"

"I'll tell you why," he said. He looked very sad. "It's because many of our workers now have their own houses, their own boats and yachts — in short, private property. We've put forward legislation that levels a tax on all property above a certain price. Our workers have to pay this tax, so now they're voting for the bourgeois party which is promising them all sorts of tax privileges."

Even though he knew his government had only a few months left in office, Prime Minister Gerhardsen still didn't dare take the decisive step of pulling out of NATO. This makes me think his Social Democrats were still somewhat afraid of the Soviet Union and were fundamentally committed to bourgeois policies. Nevertheless, I felt sorry for him. Later he did indeed lose so many votes among the workers that his party fell from power. I believe that to this day the Social Democrats are still in the opposition.

I remember that before every parliamentary election, the Norwegian Social Democrats would always ask us to come to their rescue by buying Norway's surplus herring.[12] We were always glad to oblige because their herring was well prepared and cheap, and there was a great demand for it in our country. From a strictly commercial point of view it was a favorable deal for us because, as our Ministry of Finance told me, our fishery and cannery costs were much higher than the Norwegians'. Therefore we could buy herring from the Norwegians and sell it in our stores at the usual price and make a nice profit. The only limiting factor was our insufficient reserves of gold and hard currency to pay for it.

The Norwegians — like the Danes — also sold us ships. That trade, too, was mutually beneficial. The Norwegian capitalists made money and therefore created more jobs for the Norwegian working class. We were treated very courteously by the Norwegian ship-

12. Thus giving an election-eve boost to the economy.

builders and other industrialists. Obviously they were pleased to have our orders and were looking forward to more contracts in the future. Just as she had in Denmark, Nina Petrovna helped launch a ship in Norway.

It's no wonder the Norwegians are such excellent shipbuilders and seafarers. They're descended from the Vikings who, historians now tell us, voyaged all the way to North America, where they founded their own settlements. There's even an aria in some opera in which a Viking sings: "We were born at sea and we'll die at sea." [13]

I remember we traveled by ship to Stockholm. It takes some time to wend your way up the long, winding bay. You feel as if you're sailing up a wide river rather than an inlet of the ocean. I stayed on deck throughout the whole journey. I couldn't take my eyes off the beautiful scenery. I wanted to take in everything there was to see. I could see the shore of the mainland on both sides, many yachts, and countless islands. All along the way we passed marinas, vacation resorts, and small towns. Sailors, bathers, and villagers waved their greetings to us, and we waved back.

Sweden is a truly beautiful country with a high standard of living. The Swedes impressed me with their good, healthy looks, their tasteful, modest clothes, and their advanced, practical technology.

As in Denmark and Norway, we visited a shipyard in Sweden, and Nina Petrovna once again launched a ship. By now she was, you might say, acquiring a certain skill, and we joked with her about what a good job she was doing.

I was taken to visit a farm outside of Stockholm. When we arrived, the farmer was at the wheel of a combine harvester which mowed alfalfa and then mechanically squeezed the stems so the plant dried evenly. I'd never seen such equipment before. I have to admit I didn't even know it existed. The farmer also showed me a special amphibious tractor which could either mow hay in a field or clear the weeds out of a pond for cattle feed. I told our specialists to buy some of these machines and to study the feasibility of manufacturing them on our own.

According to protocol, we had to pay a visit to the King of Sweden. I remember him as a tall, distinguished-looking old man with gray hair and ramrod-straight posture. He had the bearing of a guardsman.

13. N. A. Rimsky-Korsakov's *Sadko*.

I believe he had been a soldier in his youth — though you can be sure that, as a prince, he was no ordinary guardsman. He was a scholar or scientist of some kind, and before I left on my trip, our own scientists had given me a collection of books which they thought might be of interest to the King in his research. I presented it to him as a gift either for his own library or for the Swedish Academy.[14]

We had a number of useful talks with the King's Prime Minister, Erlander.[15] Usually these talks were conducted in the presence of Comrade Gromyko.

One day Erlander suggested we go out into the country, where the government had what we would call a dacha. Erlander took us to a beautiful lake and suggested that we go rowboating. First we went out together, but later in the afternoon I took a boat out by myself and rowed rather far into the middle of the lake. In the evening we had a semiofficial dinner at which we exchanged opinions on international issues.

Like his counterparts in Denmark and Norway, Erlander was a Social Democrat. In our talks he threw in a few leftist phrases, and some considered him a leftist — but, of course, that was only from the standpoint of the West. However, he did speak out in favor of disarmament more vigorously than other Social Democrats.

More important, Sweden — *un*like Denmark and Norway — maintained a neutralist policy. Sweden felt free to criticize both NATO and the Warsaw Pact, although the Swedes were more disposed toward the NATO countries than they were toward us. That's only natural because Sweden is a capitalist country — regardless of whether it has a so-called "workers' government" headed by Social Democrats.

I used to joke about Sweden's neutrality with Mr. Sohlman, who for many years was the Swedish ambassador to the Soviet Union and the senior representative of the other ambassadors.[16]

"Well, Mr. Sohlman," I used to say, "relations between our countries are all right now, but we haven't forgotten our history. We have to keep an eye on you, lest you make another march on Poltava."

14. Gustavus VI (Gustavus Adolphus) was a highly regarded archaeologist.
15. Tage Erlander, of the Social Democratic Party.
16. Rolf Sohlman, Swedish ambassador to Moscow from 1947 to 1964 and dean of the diplomatic corps from the mid-1950's. His wife, Zinaida, was Russian by birth.

"You know, Mr. Khrushchev," Sohlman would answer, "after the lesson your Peter I taught our Charles XII at the Battle of Poltava, not only have we never again waged war against Russia — we've never waged war at all. We've been neutral ever since." [17]

Peter I and Charles XII were long since dead, so I had no qualms against making jokes about them — though I must say, the events we were kidding about had been fairly bloody.

Sohlman had a Russian wife and a teen-aged son who spoke Russian like a native. Sometimes Russians in the company of foreigners will make a point of demonstrating their hostility toward their own country, but Mrs. Sohlman was always very civil. No doubt, like her husband, she was a bourgeois capitalist, but she was always respectful toward the Soviet government and Soviet State. Sohlman himself was a loyal Swede and certainly no Communist. But he never gave us grounds for complaining that he was misinforming his government about our policies.

Among the other Swedish officials I met, I should mention a woman who was the Minister of Culture.[18] I think her ministry was also supposed to take care of church affairs. She came up to me at a reception and was very cheerful: I think she was a bit in her cups.

"Mr. Khrushchev," she said, "I'd like to ask your advice about something. Pretty soon we're going to be awarding the Nobel Prize for literature. There are two candidates in the Soviet Union." She named them. "What do you think? I'm inclined to support this one" — and she named her favorite.

"Why are you asking me? I can't influence your decision."

"I'd still like to hear your opinion."

"Well, in that case," I said, "both writers certainly deserve the prize, but neither of them enjoys very wide support in my country. We have more acceptable candidates. I think our public would be much more satisfied if the prize were awarded to a third writer."

"And who would that be?"

"Mikhail Aleksandrovich Sholokhov. If you took a poll in our country, I think the majority would vote for Sholokhov. I know our

17. At the Battle of Poltava in 1709, Tsar Peter I dealt a crushing blow to King Charles XII of Sweden.

18. There was no Minister of Culture in the Swedish cabinet. The only woman in the cabinet at that time was Ulla Lindstrom, minister without portfolio, who did play an active part in cultural matters.

intelligentsia and our literary community would certainly be pleased if he won the prize."

She let the matter drop there, and I decided not to say anything more about it myself. After all, the Nobel Prize is an internal question for the Swedish government. Besides, for us to beg for the prize would be beneath our dignity — it would be degrading. We have our own prizes. The Nobel Prize, for instance, can't be compared to the Lenin Prize.

A year or so later, after I'd already retired, I learned that the Swedes had awarded the prize to Sholokhov. I think the Swedish government must have taken into consideration my remarks to the Minister of Culture.

There is only one other incident from my Scandinavian trip I'd like to mention — one I remember with particular pleasure and gratitude. The Social Democratic mayor of Goteborg gave me an excellent camera which takes wonderful pictures. I've made good use of it since I've had to face the idleness of retirement. After all the stormy political activity I used to engage in, the emptiness of a pensioner's life has often been very depressing. Sometimes I don't know what to do with myself. I don't know what to do with my time. This idleness has been dragging on for quite some time, and I don't know when it will end. My camera helps me fill the vacuum of my life. I'm especially grateful for this camera and for my happy memories about the city of Goteborg and its kind mayor.

Epilogue

IN this time of scientific and cultural enlightenment, while the human mind soars to heights it has never reached before, man simultaneously expends more energy than ever before on perfecting the means of his own destruction. The world is divided into camps, each preparing to annihilate the other. In addition to the struggle going on between the opposing classes within individual societies, the world is rent by conflicts between states with different political systems.

Some people thought that World War II would be the war to end all wars because mankind would agree never to let such massive destruction happen again. But we've now reached the point where some people are talking about a World War III. You can't just brush such a suggestion aside by saying, "No, that's impossible now that there are nuclear weapons." World War III *is* possible. There are more than enough crazy people around who would like to start one.

I know that *our* government doesn't want war; and when I was in the leadership, I did everything I could to avoid war. But anything is possible.

To those people who claim that the development of nuclear weapons precludes war, I say that the development of nuclear weapons precludes *limited* war — that is, it precludes war fought with conventional weapons. Now there is the ever-present danger that big states will be drawn into a military conflict between smaller states; and once that happens — no matter what guarantees, assurances, and agreements may exist — it's hard to believe that a drowning man won't clutch at straws.

In other words, now that the big countries have thermonuclear weapons at their disposal, they are sure to resort to those weapons if they begin to lose a war fought with conventional means. If it ever comes down to a question of whether or not to face defeat, there is sure to be someone who will be in favor of pushing the button, and the missiles will begin to fly. Once one side, in desperation, starts using atomic and hydrogen bombs, a global disaster will be upon us. I once expressed this idea in a speech — and I recently heard a bourgeois journalist refer to my speech over the radio.

The United States has been our potential enemy; certainly it has been our most powerful and our most dangerous adversary. If we had given the West a chance, war would have been declared while Dulles was still alive.

But we were the first to launch rockets into space, and we exploded the most powerful nuclear devices. We performed those feats first, ahead of the United States, England, and France — which are the principal performers in the orchestra of international politics, with the Americans calling the tune for their allies. Our scientific accomplishments and our obvious military might had a sobering effect on aggressive forces in the US, Britain, France, and, of course, in the Bonn government. They soon realized that they had lost their chance to strike at us with impunity.

It's no small thing that we have lived to see the day when the Soviet Union is considered, in terms of its economic and military might, one of the two most powerful countries in the world. As I've already related, Macmillan and de Gaulle, two sober-minded men, both readily acknowledged our importance in the world arena and admitted that we had surpassed Britain and France. "Well, Mr. Khrushchev," de Gaulle said, "France doesn't have the stature and influence she once had; today the United States and the Soviet Union are the two great powers." [1]

Eisenhower, too, was not an unintelligent man, and I think he was speaking honestly — that is, I don't think he was trying to deceive me — when he told me he was frightened of a big war. He'd been commander in chief of our allies' armed forces during World War II, and he could concretely imagine what a war fought with missiles and nuclear weapons would be like. Even though the time wasn't ripe for a [disarmament and inspection] agreement, I think Eisenhower was

1. This paragraph also appears in *KR*, I, 506–507. Khrushchev is referring to his conversations with the two leaders in Paris after the collapse of the 1960 summit meeting.

sincere — and I don't care if some people sneer at me for praising the President.[2]

I remember President Kennedy once stated in a speech or at a press conference that the United States had the nuclear missile capacity to wipe out the Soviet Union two times over, while the Soviet Union had enough atomic weapons to wipe out the US only once. He added, "The United States is nonetheless obliged to respect the Soviet Union and to avoid conflicts." When journalists asked me to comment on Kennedy's statement, I said jokingly, "Yes, I know what Kennedy claims, and he's quite right. But I'm not complaining — as long as the President understands that even though he may be able to destroy us twice, we're still capable of wiping out the US, even if it's only once. I'm grateful to the President for recognizing that much. We're satisfied to be able to finish off the US the first time around. Once is quite enough. What good does it do to annihilate a country twice? We're not a bloodthirsty people."

These remarks of mine drew some smiles from the newsmen.

I can't express the same confidence about subsequent American Presidents — especially Nixon. To my way of thinking, he's unpredictable, I'd even say unbalanced. I don't know what motivates him, other than his obvious ideological hatred for Communism and everything progressive.

The main issue now is for all the leaders of the world to recognize that war *must* be prevented because, if it breaks out in this day and age, it will bring disaster to the whole planet. Mao Tse-tung believes that a new war would weaken the capitalist countries and therefore lead to further revolutionary gains for the proletariat. That's ridiculous. War would do as much harm to the socialist countries as it would to anyone else.

Despite what Mao says, social reform is an internal question, to be decided by the people of each country on their own. I'm speaking now about the class struggle, a long and difficult process which can't be resolved at the conference table. The capitalists and the working class can't be reconciled in friendly meetings.

The struggle will end only when Marxism-Leninism triumphs everywhere and when the class enemy vanishes from the face of the earth. Both history and the future are on the side of the proletariat's ultimate victory. Gradually in some cases, suddenly in others, the political conditions in capitalist countries will change for the better; the

2. Khrushchev is referring to his talks with Eisnhower at Camp David in 1959.

people will have the final say, and the existing relationship between exploiters and exploited will dissolve.

We Communists must hasten this process by any means at our disposal, *excluding war*. We must remember that while the capitalist powers are unlikely to risk a world war, they will never miss an opportunity to conduct subversive ideological policies against us. I consider that normal and legitimate. The capitalists use their ideological propaganda, and we use ours. We must never forget that our enemies are always working against us, always looking for a chance to exploit some oversight on our part.

There's a battle going on in the world to decide who will prevail over whom: will the working class prevail, or the bourgeoisie? The working class is convinced that the bourgeoisie has exhausted itself and that its days are numbered, while the bourgeoisie believes it can rule forever.

Every right-thinking person can see clearly that the basic questions of ideology can be resolved only when one doctrine defeats the other. As long as the capitalists refuse to give an inch, as long as they swear to fight to the bitter end, how can we Communists, we Marxists-Leninists, even consider compromises in the ideological field?

There's no way. To speak of ideological compromise would be to betray our Party's first principles — and to betray the heritage left us by Marx, Engels, and Lenin.

It was with this conviction in mind that I allowed myself at one point to use the expression "We will bury the enemies of the Revolution." I was referring, of course, to America. Enemy propagandists picked up this phrase and blew it all out of proportion: "Khrushchev says the Soviet people want to bury the people of the United States of America!" I said no such thing. Our enemies were purposely distorting a few words I'd just let drop.

Later at press conferences I elaborated and clarified what I'd meant. We, the Soviet Union, weren't going to bury anyone; the proletariat of the United States would bury its enemy, the bourgeoisie of the United States. My statement referred to an internal question which every country will have to decide for itself: namely, by what course and by what methods will the working class of a given country achieve its victory over the capitalists? [3]

The struggle, then, is a struggle going on within each country be-

3. This passage also appears in *KR*, I, 512–513.

tween its own proletariat and its own bourgeoisie. As I've said many times at press conferences and in speeches during the years when the direction of our policies depended largely on me, there can be no such thing as peaceful coexistence in the sphere of ideology and the class struggle, but there can and must be peaceful coexistence in the sphere of relations among states with differing political systems.

Peaceful coexistence has been the most reasonable strategy during the period of transition from capitalism to socialism — in other words, the period in which we now live. Peaceful coexistence serves the interests of socialists and capitalists alike — as well as the so-called intermediary peoples who recently freed themselves from colonial oppression. I continually made speeches propagating the idea that we must live in cooperation and harmony with the capitalist world.

For one thing, we still have a lot to learn from the capitalists. There are many things we still don't do as well as they do. It's been more than fifty years since the working class of the Soviet Union carried out its Revolution under the leadership of the Great Lenin, yet, to my great disappointment and irritation, we still haven't been able to catch up with the capitalists. Sometimes we jokingly say that capitalism is rotten to the core. Yet those "rotten" capitalists keep coming up with things which make our jaws drop in surprise. I would dearly love to surprise *them* with our achievements as often. Particularly in the field of technology and organization, "rotten" capitalism has borne some fruits which we would do well to transplant into our own socialist soil.

Vladimir Ilyich Lenin himself established the doctrine of peaceful coexistence among states. Wasn't it Lenin who said that there should be mutual contacts and mutual exchanges of opinions between the Soviet Union and the capitalist countries? Wasn't it Lenin who said that revolution is not for export? Therefore, just as we oppose the export of *counter*revolution, we also oppose the export of revolution. We should adhere to Lenin's guidance and leave the business of overthrowing capitalism to the people of each country. We should make noninterference obligatory.

If the big powers interfere in the affairs of smaller countries, the possibility of all-out war — hence the danger of total destruction — will be many times increased. We've been peacefully coexisting with the big capitalist countries ever since 1945. Numerous local conflicts have broken out around the world but have not spread into global war because the major powers have stayed out — with the exception, I hasten to add, of the American militarists who have behaved like gangsters disguised as gendarmes in Vietnam.

Now, rather than talking about war, we should be talking about disarmament.

Our military objectives have always been defensive. That was true even under Stalin. I never once heard Stalin say anything about preparing to commit aggression against another country. His biggest concern was putting up antiaircraft installations around Moscow in case our country came under attack from the West.

We've long since replaced these antiaircraft guns with more sophisticated weapons. Thanks to the work of our scientists, such as our brilliant designer Sergei Pavlovich Korolyov, we have developed ICBM's that represent an effective deterrent against any aggressive moves our enemies might be tempted to make.

What if our foes did launch a missile strike against us? In addition to being able to strike back, would we also be able to shoot down their missiles before they landed on us? Theoretically, of course, science provides us with the means to do so. I used to say sometimes in my speeches that we had developed an antimissile missile that could hit a fly, but of course that was just rhetoric to make our adversaries think twice. In fact, it's impossible to intercept incoming ICBM's with pinpoint accuracy and total reliability; even if you knock down most of them, a few are bound to get through.

President Johnson restrained himself from trying to develop an ABM system; but when Nixon came into the White House, he announced that the US was going to build up its ABMs. That, of course, encouraged the Soviet Union to speed up its own program, lest our country fall behind the US. The step-up in our program has in turn goaded the Americans into stepping up theirs. And so it goes. It's a vicious circle. There's no end in sight.

The case of the ABMs is a perfect example of how idiotic the arms race is. The spiraling competition is an unending waste of human intellectual and material resources, and it increases the chances of a military catastrophe — a World War III. Once again, I can't help comparing Nixon to Eisenhower, with whom I exchanged experiences about the way our military men were always putting pressure on the government to give them money for new weapons. Naturally, the updating of defenses is necessary, but it can go to absurd extremes.

We must keep in mind that military competition is profitable for the circles of monopolistic capital in the West, while it's economically damaging for the socialist world. We must never forget the true character of all imperialists, monopolists, and militarists, who are interested in making money out of the political tension between nations. If we try to compete with the West in any but the most crucial areas of military preparedness, we will be further enriching wealthy circles in the United States who use our military buildups as a pretext for overloading their own country's arms budget.

The reactionary forces in the West know it's expedient for them to force us to exhaust our economic resources in a huge military budget, thus diverting funds which could otherwise be spent on the cultural and material needs of our peoples. We must not let ourselves be caught in that trap. We must remember that the defense industry is a nonproductive sector of our economy. It doesn't satisfy the needs of our people. Military expenditures are a bottomless pit, into which the imperialist camp would like to see us pour our economic potential. We must not give in to the provocations which our enemies will commit against us; we must not let ourselves be provoked into producing unnecessary weapons.

Even though I haven't been able to name them all, I hope I've made clear how much I appreciate the work which our scientists and designers have done to enhance the technological prestige of our country in the field of defense. However, we must remember that the advancement of science and technology can be like a whip, cracking over our heads, encouraging us to spend more and more money on national security. We can always build better rockets or better bombs tomorrow than the ones we have today. But the goal of accumulating the very latest weapons in sufficient quantity to be completely safe, once and for all — that goal is an illusion, a dream.

We should be realistic and see that, at the instigation of Churchill even in his retirement, the Western powers forced the arms race on us during the Cold War. The arms race has been part of a calculated plan to hinder the development of our economy, impede the growth of our standard of living, sow the seeds of disarray and dissatisfaction — and, if possible, bring about the collapse of socialism and a restoration of capitalism in our country.

After the war we had a rationing system. The means of production were turned over largely to the production of weapons. The memory of the war we had just won against the Hitlerite occupiers made our people willing to tighten their belts and endure hardship. They did so out of patriotism and out of fear for the lives of their loved ones. Almost any sacrifice was justified if it gave us the military potential to deter our adversaries from attacking the Soviet Union.

When I was the leader of the Party and the government, I, too, realized that we had to economize drastically on the building of homes, the construction of communal services, and even the development of agriculture in order to build up our defenses. I went so far as to suspend the construction of subways in Kiev, Baku, and Tblisi so that we could redirect those funds into strengthening our defense and counterattack forces. We also built fewer athletic stadiums, swimming pools, and cultural facilities.

I think, at the time at least, I was right to concentrate on military spending, even at the expense of all but the most essential investments in other areas. If I hadn't put such a high priority on our military needs, we couldn't have survived. I devoted all my strength to the rearmament of the Soviet Union. It was a challenging and important stage of our lives.

Now that I'm living with my memories and little else, I think back often to that period when in a creative surge, we rearmed our Soviet army. I'm proud that the honor of supervising the transition to the most up-to-date weaponry fell on me as the Chairman of the Council of Ministers and the First Secretary of the Central Committee. While I was in office our people and our army became invincible.[4]

However, we were taking a risk by allocating so much of our resources to the military sector. Once we reached the point where we had what it took to defend ourselves and deter our enemy, we readjusted our economy. We recognized that if our people didn't have potatoes we couldn't expect them to shout "hooray" all the time — and if they did shout "hooray," it would be in a rather weak voice. We began to economize on our military expenditures.

Now that I'm no longer active, I can't help noticing from my position as a pensioner that the economizing trend we started seems to have been reversed, that now money is being wasted on unnecessary items and categories, and that this new trend of military overspend-

4. This paragraph is also in *KR*, I, 516.

ing is putting a pinch on some of the more important, but still under-financed, areas of our country's life. However, I'm isolated from the world, and I should speak only about what I know. I know that the capitalists were the first to form a military alliance after the war and that we were the first to propose the dissolution of the two opposing alliances, NATO and the Warsaw Pact. We should continue to press toward that goal.

Meanwhile, we should keep in mind that it's the size of our nuclear missile arsenal, and not the size of our army, that counts. The infantry has become, so to speak, not the muscle but the fat of the armed forces. Therefore the manpower of the army should be reduced to an absolute minimum. The fewer people we have in the army, the more people we will have available for other, more productive kinds of work. This realization would be a good common point of departure for the progressive forces of the world in their struggle for peaceful coexistence.

We must also press for arms control. We were able to persuade the imperialists that it was in their interests, as well as in ours, to limit the arms race. During my political career we reached a partial agreement on nuclear testing. We agreed to ban tests in three spheres: the air, the land, and underwater. The treaty was signed in Moscow on August 5, 1963. It was a good beginning, but the United States refused to include underground tests in the ban.

However, I must also say that the Americans proposed certain arms control measures to which we could not agree. I'm thinking now about their insistence that a treaty include a provision for on-site inspection anywhere in our country. In general, the idea of arms control was acceptable to us. Zhukov, who was the Defense Minister at the time, and I agreed in principle to on-site inspection of the border regions and to airborne reconnaissance of our territory up to a certain distance inside our borders, but we couldn't allow the US and its allies to send their inspectors criss-crossing around the Soviet Union. They would have discovered that we were in a relatively weak position, and that realization might have encouraged them to attack us.

However, all that has changed. While it might still be true that the United States has a quantitative advantage over us — and that NATO has a quantitative advantage over the Warsaw Pact — in terms of total accumulated means of destruction, we no longer lag behind to any significant degree. In my last years as head of the government, our military theoreticians calculated that we had the nuclear capacity to blast our enemies into dust. We stockpiled enough weapons to destroy the principal cities of the United States, to say nothing of our potential enemies in Europe.

Therefore, I think there is no longer any reason for us to resist the idea of international control. If I had any influence on the policy of the Soviet Union, I would urge that we sign a mutual agreement providing for more extensive inspection than was possible when Zhukov and I deliberated. More specifically, I would favor on-site inspection in designated parts of the country around our frontiers. (When I talk about our frontiers, I'm talking about our western borders. I'm putting aside the problem of our eastern borders because we have a special situation there with China. The pathological hatred of the Chinese for the Soviet Union and our ideological line makes an understanding with them impossible for me to imagine.)

Sticking to the matter of our relations with the West, I'd also favor on-site inspection at all military bases, especially airfields. It's essential that airfields be open to inspection, so that neither side could concentrate troop transports for a sneak attack. We're afraid of a surprise attack by our enemies just as much as they're afraid of such an attack by us. We need a system of inspection as much as they do.

In short, I would like to see us sign a mutual treaty of nonaggression and inspection. I emphasize "mutual." The treaty would have to be genuinely reciprocal; neither side should try to deceive or cheat the other. It would be a grave mistake if one party to the treaty assumed the other party to be a fool. As long as the treaty was truly mutual in its provisions and implemented in good faith by both sides, I can see nothing standing in the way of our signing it.

"But what about espionage?" people might ask. "Wouldn't we be inviting NATO to send spies into our country masquerading as control commission inspectors?" My answer to that is: we'll learn as much about the other side's military technology as it will learn about ours. In other words, we will have the same opportunities as our potential enemies to engage in military intelligence. After all, what is military intelligence but an attempt to find out what your adversary is doing? And isn't that basically the same thing as arms control inspection? Both sides are engaged in military intelligence, just as both are engaged in counterintelligence. As long as there are two opposing social systems in the world, those whose profession is espionage won't be out of a job.

Besides, I was never too impressed by our ability to keep secrets from the enemy. The size and composition of our army was supposedly top secret, but the Americans and British knew that information anyway. I once asked Comrade Malinovsky why the latest data about our army and weaponry was always turning up in the foreign press.

"What's going on here?" I said. "Is there a spy in our General Staff, or what?"

He shrugged his shoulders and replied, "I can't say for sure, but I think the enemy must keep track of what we're doing through standard intelligence-gathering means."

Naturally, we don't want to undress all the way and stand before NATO inspectors as naked as Adam. Perhaps in the first stage of an arms control agreement, we could extend inspection to all our defense plants but allow the inspectors to see only the final products as they come off the line, without letting them subject our hardware to technological analysis. That way, we could keep secret the design of certain weapons. Such an arrangement would necessarily be temporary, but it might give us time to work out other, more far-reaching agreements to prevent World War III.

Up until now, I've hesitated to mention my thoughts on extending arms control over rocket technology and the deployment of warheads. You could say I've been saving the subject for dessert. Missiles, of course, are the most destructive means of all — and, I don't care whether you call them offensive or defensive. I believe that until we have established mutual trust with our current adversaries, our ICBM's must be kept in readiness as our major deterrent. It is to be hoped that someday missiles, too, can be included in a disarmament agreement; but for the time being, our ICBM's are necessary to maintain the balance of fear. (By the way, I think the author of this phrase, "balance of fear," was that faithful dog of capitalism Dulles.)

What if the capitalists drag their feet in agreeing to disarmament? I certainly know from my own experience how difficult it is to get them to agree on anything. I believe that even if a Soviet-American agreement on bilateral reduction in military spending were impossible, we should go ahead and sharply reduce our own expenditures — unilaterally.

If our enemies want to go on inflating their military budgets, spending their money right and left on all kinds of senseless things, then they'll be sure to lower the living standards of their own people. By so doing, they will be unwittingly strengthening the position of the Communist and progressive forces in their own midst, enabling them to cry out in a still louder voice against the reactionary forces of monopolistic capital.

If we were unilaterally to curtail the accumulation of military means, we would be demonstrating that in socialist countries the interests of the people and the government are one and the same, while in capitalist countries the government represents only the interests of those who produce the means of destruction. Our good example will be noticed by the working class in capitalist countries, and it will give fighters for peace a chance to conduct mass propaganda in their countries.

By taking the initiative in scaling down the arms race, we will also appeal to the intelligentsia in the West and all over the world. Of course, I know we're not going to appeal to Goldwater. I'm operating on the assumption that the United States isn't made up solely of Goldwaters. Even among capitalists there are honest intellectuals, people of different religions, different social strata, and different levels of wealth, all united in the struggle to maintain peace among the nations.

I've already talked about that wonderful Frenchman, the late Canon Kir, a man who was devoted to promoting peaceful coexistence right up to the last day of his life.

Cyrus Eaton is another highly reasonable, well-intentioned man, despite the fact that he's a capitalist.[5] He's committed to peaceful coexistence among the US, the Soviet Union, and other countries; and there's no point in alienating him just because he's a capitalist. He and others like him exert pressure on their governments to resist the aggressive forces which keep the world teetering on the brink of the Cold War, in danger of plunging any moment into a hot war.

The forces of peace are considerably more numerous than the forces of war. If we can encourage the peace movement by submitting to mutual arms control and even — should it be necessary —

5. The contrast is between Barry Goldwater, the conservative Republican senator from Arizona, and Cyrus Eaton, a Cleveland industrialist and millionaire of left-wing political persuasion who entertained Khrushchev on his visits to the US. For Khrushchev's views on Canon Kir of Dijon, see Chapter 17.

unilaterally reducing our own armed forces, we should do so. Our ultimate goal should be to reach an agreement with other countries to destroy all weapons, to disarm completely, and to dismantle military alliances.

Any leadership which conducts a policy of arms control and disarmament must be courageous and wise. The members of that leadership must be able to exercise their own independent judgment and not let others intimidate them.

Who, in our own country, are the "others" who can intimidate the leadership? They are the military. I don't reproach the military for that — they're only doing their job. The military is made up of men who are ready to sacrifice their lives for the sake of their Motherland. However, leaders must be careful not to look at the world through the eyeglasses of the military. Otherwise, the picture will appear terribly gloomy; the government will start spending all its money and the best energies of its people on armaments — with the result that pretty soon the country will have lost its pants in the arms race.

I've said quite a bit about the internal forces in the West, the militarists and representatives of big monopolistic capital, who have a stake in producing the means of destruction and who put pressure on the government to increase military expenditures. In our country, of course, since we have no private capitalist ownership and no big industrialists, we have no militaristic class as such. But our military puts similar pressure on our government. I'm not saying there's any comparison between our military in the socialist countries and capitalist generals, but soldiers will be soldiers. They always want a bigger and stronger army. They always insist on having the very latest weapons and on attaining quantitative as well as qualitative superiority over the enemy.

Once again, let me say: I'm not denying that our military men have a huge responsibility, and I'm not impugning their moral qualities. But the fact remains that the living standard of the country suffers when the budget is overloaded with allocations to unproductive branches of consumption. And today, as yesterday, the most unproductive expenditures of all are those made on the armed forces.

That's why I think that the military can't be reminded too often that it is the *government* that must allocate funds; it is the government that must decide how much the armed forces can spend, and it is the government that must set policy on the nature of our relations with other countries, including the obligations our country undertakes with regard to arms control and disarmament.

We should be careful not to idolize the military. Among the military in the socialist countries, you can find people who tend to regard the defense establishment as a higher caste. It is important to keep such people in check, to make sure they don't exercise too much influence.

The military is prone to temptations; it is prone to indulge in irresponsible daydreaming and bragging. Given a chance, some elements within the military might try to force a militarist policy on the government. Therefore the government must always keep a bit between the teeth of the military.

When I say "the government," I mean the collective leadership, and I stress the word *collective*. There must, of course, be an outlet for individuality. Individual initiative must be able to express itself. But the decisions which guide and influence our Soviet State ought to be made collectively.

When I was the head of the government and also held the highest post in the Central Committee, I never made a decision on my own, without consulting and securing the approval of my comrades in the leadership. The conditions were such that it was impossible for one man to dictate his will to the others; I was in favor of those conditions, and I did my best to reinforce them.

I also did my best to resist the counsel of those who can't stop shouting, "We'll destroy our enemies! We'll wipe them out!" It requires considerable inner maturity and a well-developed understanding of the world not only to grasp the narrow bureaucratic aspects of defense policy, but also to see things in the broader perspective.

A government leader should keep in mind exactly what sort of destruction we're capable of today. He should be aware of the losses his own country will suffer if, God willing, he were able to destroy his enemies. There are those who don't seem able to get it into their heads that in the next war, the victor will be barely distinguishable from the vanquished. A war between the Soviet Union and the United States would almost certainly end in mutual defeat.

Can you picture what would be left after a few hydrogen bombs fell on Moscow? Forget about "a few" — imagine just one. Or Washington? Or New York? Or Bonn? It staggers the mind. All the mathematical calculations made during war games, all our computers, are worthless in trying to comprehend the magnitude of the destruction we would face.

It's infinitely better to prevent a war than to try to survive one. I know all about bomb shelters and command posts and emergency communications and so on. But listen here: in a single thermonuclear flash, a bunker can be turned into a burial vault for a country's leaders and military commanders.

All right, I know people will say, "Khrushchev is in a panic over the possibility of war."

I am not. I've always been against war, but at the same time I've always realized full well that fear of nuclear war on the part of a country's leader can paralyze that country's defenses. And if a country's defenses are paralyzed, then war really is inevitable: the enemy is sure to sense your fright and try to take advantage of it. I've always operated on the principle that I should be clearly against war but never frightened of it. Sometimes retreat is necessary, but retreat can also be the beginning of the end of your resistance. When the enemy is watching your every move, even death is a thing to be faced bravely.

Besides, what kind of panic would you expect from a man my age? I'm nearly seventy-seven years old. As they say, I'm no longer on my way to the fair — I started my journey home a long time ago. Who knows how many years my ticker has left to run. Everything I've said in my memoirs, I say as a Communist who wants a more enlightened Communist society — not for myself, because my time has already come and gone, but for my friends and for my people in the future.

Appendix

Sample Pages of the Khrushchev Transcripts

NIKITA KHRUSHCHEV'S memoirs are based on approximately 180 hours of oral dictation, which were tape-recorded, transcribed, translated into English, and edited for publication in two volumes, *Khrushchev Remembers* (1970) and the present book, *Khrushchev Remembers: The Last Testament* (1974). The transcript, or "original," for the first volume was prepared in the Soviet Union; it has been verified against the tape recordings, which in turn have been authenticated by spectrographic analysis. The transcript for the second volume was prepared in the United States; the tapes from which it was made have likewise been authenticated. In this appendix are facsimiles of thirty-six sample pages from the transcripts of both volumes.

First Volume

Second Volume

сигналом для других партийных организаций и те тоже начинали проводить собрания и принимать резолюции в таком же духе в поддержку Центрального Комитета.

Надежда Сергеевна Аллилуева училась у нас на текстильном факультете химиком по искусственному волокну. Там она была избрана группоргом. Когда проходили собрания, она, как и другие группорги, всегда приходила ко мне, как к секретарю партийной организации согласовывать характер резолюции, формулировки.

Я себе представлял, какая задача возлагалась на меня. Я должен был дать установку и я ее давал, но я всегда оглядывался: я даю установку, но ведь она же пойдет домой и расскажет Сталину. А Сталин? Как он оценит? Правильна ли она? Соответствует ли Генеральной линии партии? Поэтому всегда это был для меня сложный момент. У Винченко есть рассказ "Пиня". Так я чувствовал себя, как герой этого рассказа Пиня. А Пиня был выбран в камере тюрьмы старостой и раз Пиня был старостой, он принимал решение.

Я, как секретарь партийной организации Промышленной академии, давал свои установки. Все это потом сказалось в мою пользу. Эти установки по тому времени были правильными, они соответствовали духу и времени Генеральной линии партии. Поэтому я никогда не встречал поправок.

Нужно казать о Надежде Сергеевне Аллилуевой. Я с исключительно большим уважением к ней относился и уважал ее за ее умение вести себя. Она была женой Сталина, но многие не знали, что она та Аллилуева. У нас еще был Аллилуев, он был членом бюро ячейки. Сам - шахтер дальневосточный! Поэтому Аллилуева не производила впечатления. Да и ее отец - старый большевик, Аллилуев, тогда не был известен. Она приезжала в Промышленную академию всегда на трамвае - за ней машина никогда не приходила. Она уходила вместе со всеми и приезжала вместе со всеми и поэтому не было приметно, что она является женой человека, который занимает такое положение и пользуется таким уважением у абсолютного большинства в партии и в стране.

Так началась моя партийная деятельность в Москве. В январе 1931 г. была партийная конференция. Тогда районные партийные конференции проводились или через 6 месяцев или через год. На этой конференции в январе я был избран секретарем районного партийного комитета Бауманского района, а Коротченко был избран Председателем районного совета. Заворгом стал тов. Трейвас - очень хороший товарищ. Агитмассовым отделом заведовал, по-моему, тов. Розов, тоже очень хороший деятельный человек. Потом у Шурова кончилась карьера - не помню, или его арестовали, или он покончил жизнь самоубийством в Сибири в 1937 году.

Фамилия Трейваса в 1920 годы была широко известна, как комсомольского деятеля. Это был дружок Саши Безыменского. Они вместе были активными деятелями Московской организации. Это был очень дельный, хороший, умный человек. Но меня тогда Каганович предупредил, что мол у него имеется политический изъян — он в свое время, когда шла острая борьба с троцкистами, в числе так называемых 93-х комсомольцев, подписал декларацию в поддержку Троцкого. Безымянский ее тоже подписал.

— Поэтому, — сказал Каганович, — требуется настороженность, хотя сейчас Трейвас полностью стоит на партийных позициях, не вызывает никаких сомнений и он рекомендуется Центральным Комитетом заоргом.

Сейчас, когда прошло столько лет я должен сказать, что Трейвас очень хорошо работал, преданно, активно. Это был умный человек и я им был очень доволен. Я с ним работал только полгода, а потом меня избрали секретарем Краснопресненского райкома. По партийной лестнице это было повышение, потому что Красная Пресня занимала более высокие политические позиции, чем Бауманский район, ввиду ее исторического прошлого: восстания 1905 года. Она была ведущей партийной районной организацией в Москве. Трейвас остался в Бауманском районе.

После меня секретарем Бауманского райкома избрали, по-моему, Марголина.

Трейвас трагично кончил свою жизнь. Он был избран секретарем Калужского Горкома партии и хорошо работал там. Гремел, если так можно сказать, Калужский горком, но когда началась эта мясорубка 1987 года, то он не избежал ее. Я уже встретился с Трейвасом, когда он сидел в тюрьме. Тогда Сталин выдвинул идею, что секретари обкомов должны ходить в тюрьму и проверять правильность действий чекистских органов. Поэтому я тоже ходил.

Помню тогда Реденс был начальником управления ОГПУ Московской области. Эта тоже интересная фамилия. Она интересна тем, что он, бедняга, тоже кончил трагически. Он был арестован и расстрелян и, несмотря на то, что он был женат на сестре Надежды Сергеевны — Анне Сергеевне. Они были со Сталиным свояки. Я много раз встречал Реденса на квартире у Сталина на семейных обедах, на которые я тоже приглашался.

Сталин шутил по нашему адресу:

— Ну, отцы города.

Он приглашал меня, как секретаря Московского городского партийного комитета и Булганина, как Председателя Моссовета.

Одним словом, много было сказано в пользу того, чтобы я ориентировался на партийную работу и, не закончив свою учебу, уже не возвращался бы к этому. Таким образом из Бауманского района я через полгода стал работать секретарем райкома в Красной Пресне. Еще через полгода на городской партийной конференции я уже был избран вторым секретарем городского партийного комитета. Я очень болезненно пошел на это. Я еще не покончил с своими надеждами закончить высшее образование, окончить Промышленную

В 1935 году москвичи отпраздновали окончание первой очереди строительства метрополитена. Многие получили Правительственные награды. Я был удостоен Ордена Ленина - это мой первый орден. Булганин получил Орден Красной Звезды. Это мотивировалось тем, что он уже награждался ранее Орденом Ленина за успешное руководство работой электрозавода, директором которого он был. Помнится, Булганин имел Орден Ленина за десятым номером. Это тогда очень подчеркивалось. У меня был орден Ленина с номером около 110. Мы пышно отпраздновали завершение строительства. Метрополитен был назван именем Кагановича. Тогда было модно среди Членов Политбюро, да, и не только Членов Политбюро "приобретать" для себя заводы, фабрики, колхозы, районы, области и пр. целое соревнование. Эта нехорошая тенденция родилась при Сталине.

В 1935 году Каганович был выдвинут Наркомом Путей Сообщений и освобожден от обязанностей Секретаря Московского Комитета Партии. Меня

выдвинули на Пост Первого Секретаря Московского Областного комитета партии и Первого Секретаря Московского Городского комитета партии. На ближайшем Пленуме ЦК я был избран кандидатом в Члены Политбюро.

Мне было приятно и лестно, но больше было страха перед такой огромной ответственностью. Помню до этого времени я еще возил и хранил свой личный инструмент. Как у всякого слесаря были там кронциркуль, литромер, метр, керн, чертилка, угольнички всякие. Я тогда еще не порвал мысленно связи со своей профессией. Считал, что партийная работа - выборная, и в любое время я могу быть неизбранным и вернусь к своей основной деятельности.слесаря, рабочего. Но я превращался уже в профессионального общественного партийного работника.

столом. Ну, нас Посольство информировало тогда, что жена Идена — это племянница Черчиля и что она, видимо, унаследовала некоторые качества от Черчиля в питейных делах, что она изрядно выпивает, ну, я бы не сказал, чтобы мы заметили, что она ~~умеет~~ злоупотребляла этим качеством, значит, ну, выпивали все и она в том числе в компании тоже не отказывалась и выпивала. Я помню, значит, она подняла такой вопрос, потому что мы когда приехали, вели беседы и мы в это время основательно опирались на нашу силу, мы уже к этому времени имели бомбардировочную авиацию послевоенную, у нас были бомбардировщики ТУ-16, я уже не говорю, что у нас в большом количестве, как они назывались, это ИЛ-27 что-ли, это первые наши реактивные бомбардировщики, очень хороший бомбардировщик, фронтового действия, вообщем вооружение было мы считали хорошее, у нас пополнился флот, мы построили несколько крейсеров, эсминцев и строили подводные лодки, но все это по сравнению с Западом недостаточное количество было, за исключением ракет, ракет было что-то, межконтинентальных ракет, по-моему, вообще не было или были считанные единицы, но ракеты на 5000 км у нас было достаточное количество и поэтому Англию-то мы могли припугнуть, мы ее доставали, она была на таком расстоянии, досягаемом нашими ракетами и мы собственно давали понять, что располагаем средствами, которые могут нанести большой урон противнику, если вздумает на нас напасть, а это значит не только на Великобританию эти ракеты могли полететь, уже не говоря о Западной Германии и Франции или другие страны, которые входили в НАТО: Дания, Голландия, Норвегия, Бельгия, таким образом, это уже их, видимо, беспокоило. Я это рассказываю к тому, что за обедом нас, к нам обратилась с вопросом жена Идена. Какие у вас ракеты, далеко они могут летать? Я говорю:"Да, они могут далеко. Наши ракеты не только могут доставать наши острова, Британские острова, но и дальше значит, большая дальность у них". Она так это прикусила язык, это было немного несколько грубовато такое и это могло послужить, могла быть расценена какая-то угроза, но во всяком случае мы и преследовали такую цель, значит, мы угрожать не собирались, но хотели показать, что мы не просители и что мы сильная сторона и, следовательно, с нами надо договариваться, но нам ультиматум предъявлять нельзя, потому что это невозможно с нами разговаривать сейчас языком ультиматума. Но когда нас пригласил Иден, мы условились, он нам посоветовал, что раньше утречком мы должны поехать в учебные заведения их под Лондоном, а оттуда уже приехать в Чеккерс. С нами в учебные заведения поедет Ллойд. Ну, так Ллойд заехал за нами, мы с Булганиным сели, по-моему, Курчатов не был с нами, мы были вдвоем и, по-моему, был, конечно, Громыко, безусловно был, даже сейчас я и этого не помню, видимо, был. Мы поехали, по дороге когда мы ехали с этим Ллойдом, Ллойд очень вел себя любезно и шутил, мы сидели как раз втроем в машине, он обращается ко мне и говорит, что мне пошептала на ухо, подлетела и на ухо пошептала, что ̃ы продаете вооружение Йемену, я говорю: "Так разные птички летают и они разное шепчут. Мне тоже вот птичка подлетела и пошептала, что Вы оружие продаете Египту, вы продаете Ираку,(а тогда Ирак это было самое реакцион-ое правительство) вы продаете Ирану оружие, вы всем продаете оружие, кто только хочет купить у вас, а если даже не хочет, так птичка говорит, что вы навязываете. Так что птички разные бывают". Да, ну, все это было в виде шутки. Он говорит:"Верно, разные, и нам шепчут, видимо, и вам шепчут". Я говорю:"Вот пусть шепчут, пусть бы птички шепатпли чтобы мы взаимное взяли обязательство, чтобы никому не продавать оружия, это было бы выгодно и для дела мира". Когда мы приехали в учебное заведение, а это учебное заведение я забыл сейчас инак оно называется. Это избранные, видимо, состоятельные, когда проректор нас водил и показывал нам аудитории этого учебного заведения и двор показывал, я не помню зашли мы в дверь какую-то и мы увидели какую-то шутку сделали над пртретом этого проректора или даже скульптура этого проректора была там. Он глянул и довольно спокойно+"Вот это наши студенты, они обязательно любят посмеяться над нашим братом" и довольно спокойно прошел, стал рассказывать о проделках студенческих, которые они позволяют себе и ничего не сделаешь, молодежь, так молодежь, от них все можно ожидать

Студенты к нам интерес проявили, но я бы сказал вяло, потому что это публика была не пролетарская, она воспитывала людей для правительства, для правительственных ведомств и консервативного склада и поэтому на какое-то понимание и сочувствие к нам, мы и не могли рассчитывать, да этого и быть не могло. После этого учебного заведения мы приехали в Чеккерс, я уже говорил,как мы провели обед и прогулку перед обедом. Иден нас пригласил остаться ночевать, мы ночевали в Чеккерсе, все другие, по-моему, уехали, кроме Идена. Постройка, внутреннее расположение комнат в этой даче были, она, по-моему, была в два этажа и консолями, поэтому на втором этаже,.. внизу была бильярдная, столовая и другие службы, а наверху там были спальни и разместили, показали, где Булгани будет размещаться, показали, где я буду размещаться и таким образом нас разместили по углам этого дома с Булганиным, ну, я плохо сориентировался и наутро я рано поднялся, дом еще спал, значит, дело было нечего, я оделся, захотел пойти к Булганину, пошел к Булганину, и я видимо, не видимо, я спутал расположение и я к двери подошел, думал, что это дверь Булганина и стал стучать, и страх и удивление раздался женский голос, я буквально убежал и тогда определил, что мне немножко надо было

Мы прилетели в Бухарест с Маленковым,
там уже были представители Чехословацкой партии во главе с Новотным,
болгарские товарищи были во главе с Живковым и румынские товарищи на
месте, они участвовали тов. Деж и не помню кто еще входил в состав делегации компартии Румынии. Когда мы изложили положение дел и как мы
его понимаем, которое сложилось в Будапеште, многое нам · доказывать
не приходилось, потому что все товарищи, которые прибыли, они также
были осведомлены, как и мы, потому что их послы там были и довольно
хорошо были информированы, информировались Правительства и Компартии.

Кроме того, значит, некоторые пограничные районы Венгрии, они
стали искать контакта с награничными районами Чехословакии, Румынии
с тем, чтобы, значит, опираться на них и даже некоторые районы просили
оружие у соседних с тем, чтобы вооружаться против Будапешта, то есть
против руководства контрреволюции, которое уже возглавляет Надь Имре.
Поэтому все единодушно без всяких колебаний: надо и надо немедленно.
В Бухаресте был поставлен вопрос и румынами главным образом и болгара-
ми, что они тоже хотели бы своими воинскими частями участвовать в ока-
зании помощи революционным рабочим Венгрии в борьбе против Венгреской
контрреволюции, которую возглавляет Надь Имре. Ну, мы зан мали позицию
что никто не должен участвовать, кроме войск советских, которые нахо-
дятся сейчас в Венгрии по Потсдамскому соглашению и поэтому войск этих
достаточно и участия других не требуется. Ну, в шутку, шутили с румын-
скими товарищами, да, тем более румыны рвутся сейчас в бой против нкнх
контрреволюции и румынам этот поход знакомый, в свое время они участвовали в разгроме революции, которая возглавлялась Бела Куном в 1919 г
Пошутили, позлословили на этот счет и договорились, что надо это дело
делать и пожелали нам успехов и нем медлить.

Ну, мы как условились, я не знаю, да, в этот же вечером, уже было
темно, мы вылетели в Югославию, как договорились с югославами. Летели
мы на ИЛ12 или не знаю, погода была отвратительная, летели мы через
горы ночью, в горах был какой-то ураган, грозовые тучи, молнии сверка-
ли, одним словом, я не спал и сидел у окна самолета, я много летал,
всю войну самолетом пользовался и после войны, но в таких тяжелых пе-
реплетах перелета я еще никогда не был. Самолетом управлял очень опыт-
ный летчик генерал Цыбин и он тоже доложил, что условия очень тяжелые.
Впереди нас шел наш разведывательный самолет, точно такой же как и наш
но он должен был в какой-то степени освещать, идя впереди нашего самолета, и говорить какая обстановка. Мы связь потеряли с этим самолетом, таким образом, мы должны были сами ориентироваться но местности,
а тогда и оборудования на аэродроме, на котором мы должны были при-
землиться, а мы летели на Брионские острова в Югославии, оборудования

никакого не было, это примитивный такого военного времени аэродром без всякого оборудования, да и наш самолет не был вооружен, как теперь самолеты вооружены радиолокационным оборудованием. Но здесь уже мастерство тов. Цыбина, дало ему возможность и он благополучно приземлился. Мы приземлились, мы спросили пришел ли сюда наш самолет, который впереди шел, мы думали, что может быть связь потерял, может быть рация вышла из строя, но он сел, ответили, что нашего самолета не было и мы ничего не знаем об этом самолете. Это еще больше обеспокоило нас за судьбу экипажа. Тут же нас ожидал автомобиль, мы пересели из самолета в автомобиль и поехали к пристани с тем, чтобы на катере приехать на остров Риони, где находился тов. Тито. Когда мы летели в такой качке, Маленков, совершенно, ну, превратился в какой-то труп, его очень укачивает и даже при поездке на автомобиле, даже на ровной дороге, значит, а здесь мы летели, большая качка была, а потом мы приехали на катер, очень сильная волна была на море, маленький катер, мы пересели на катер, Маленков лег и глаза закрыл, я очень уж беспокоился, как мы прибудем на остров Бриони и в каком состоянии будет Маленков, но выбора у нас не было, ждать мы не могли хорошей погоды, сидеть у моря и ждать погоды, как говорит русская поговорка. Мы прибыли на остров Риони. *Бриони* Там нас уже ожидал Тито, он нас радушно принял, обнялись мы, расцеловались, хотя у нас до этого были натянуты отношения и они натягивались по мере развертывания событий в Венгрии, на Венгерской основе, потому что у нас были разные позиции по этому вопросу. Приехали мы Риони, где размещался Тито и доложили ему, зачем мы приехали и поставили перед ним вопрос, как мы его понимали и как мы хотели этот вопрос решать и мнение Тито. Как быть? Я ожидал, что нам придется более сложную выдержать атаку со стороны Тито и более сложную в сравнении с тем, как мы эти вопросы обсуждали с польскими товарищами. И тут мы неожиданно были приятно поражены, Тито сказал абсолютно правильно и надо немедленно пустить в дело войска, оказать помощь Венгрии и разгромить контрреволюцию, начал горячо начал доказывать необходимость этого мероприятия. Следовательно, весь наш заряд, который мы говорили, ожидая, что будет какое-то сопротивление и поэтому надо будет нам доказывать, а может быть еще сложится и так, что мы уедем, еще не договорившись до единого понимания, это еще больше бы осложнило наше положение и вдруг мы получили такое полное признание и поддержку и даже я бы сказал такое подталкивание на быстрые действия или решительные действия в этом вопросе.

Во время одной из бесед Хо Ши Мин достал из портфеля советский журнал, кажется, "СССР на стройке" и попросил Сталина расписаться. Во Франции гоняются за автографами и Хо Ши Мин тоже не был свободен от этого. Да и ему было соблазнительно приехать во Вьетнам и показать автограф Сталина.

Как-то уже после своего отъезда Хо Ши Мин письменно обратился к нам с просьбой. Наряду с другим он просил, чтобы ему прислали хинин, потому что народ очень страдает от малярии. У нас было организовано его производство в промышленных масштабах.

Сталин расщедрился и говорит:

- Послать ему полтонны.

Я много раз встречался с товарищем Хо Ши Мином.

Говоря о товарище Хо Ши Мине, я хотел бы вспомнить нашу работу в период подготовки проведения Женевского Совещания. В этот период у нас были самые лучшие отношения с Вьетнамом и такие же хорошие отношения с Коммунистической партией Китая. На подготовительном совещании в Москве Китай был представлен Чжоу Энь Лаем, а Вьетнам - Президентом Хо Ши Мином и Премьер-Министром Фан Ван Донггом. Мы отрабатывали нашу позицию на Женевском Совещании, разбирались в обстановке, которая сложилась во Вьетнаме. Положение было очень тяжелым. Движение находилось на грани краха. Партизаны очень нуждались в соглашении, чтобы сохранить те завоевания, которых добился вьетнамский народ в борьбе против оккупантов.

Ханой был в руках французов и мы на него не претендовали. Другие города и провинции, занятые французами, тоже сохранялись за ними. Если взять карту, на которой были отражены наши требования номер I, то она пестрела островами внутри Северного Вьетнама, в которых находились французские оккупанты.

После одного из Совещаний, которое проводилось в Екатерининском Зале в Кремле, подошел ко мне Чжоу Энь Лай, взял меня за пуговицу, отвел в угол и говорит:

- Тов. Хо Ши Мин мне сказал, что положение у них безнадежное и если они не добьются прекращения огня в ближайшее время, то видно они не смогут противостоять французским войскам. Поэтому они решили отходить к китайской границе с тем, чтобы Китай, значит, двинул свои войска, как он сделал в Северной Корее и помог вьетнамскому народу выбить французов из Вьетнама.

Чжоу Энь Лай сказал, что они не смогут этого сделать, так как они потеряли в Корее много людей и эта война дорого им стоила. Поэтому сейчас ввязаться в новую войну, они не в состоянии и согласиться с просьбой Хо Ши Мина не могут.

Я обратился с просьбой к тов. Чжоу Энь Лаю:

— Борьба идет очень жестокая и вьетнамцы хорошо дерутся. Французы несут большие потери. Поэтому не надо говорить Хо Ши Мину, что Вы не окажете им помощи, если они будут отходить под ударами французов к Вашей границе. Пусть это будет ~~святой ложью~~. Пусть вьетнамцы верят, что им помогут и это будет каким-то дополнительным источником ~~сопротивления~~ вьетнамских партизан французским оккупантам.

Чжоу Энь Лай согласился не говорить товарищу Хо Ши Мину, что Китай не вступит в войну с французами на вьетнамской территории.

Однако тогда свершилось буквально чудо. Когда делегации приехали в Женеву, Вьетнамские партизаны одержали крупнейшую победу и заняли крепость Дьен Бьен Фу. На первом заседании Мендес Франс, который тогда возглавлял французское правительство и предложил разграничить силы Франции и Вьетнама по 17-й параллели. Признаться, когда нам сообщили эту новость из Женевы, мы от удовольствия ахнули. Мы такого не ожидали. Это был максимум, на который мы претендовали. Мы дали указания нашим представителям в Женеве потребовать перенести демаркационную линию южнее, на 15-ю параллель. Но мы предупредили, что это для торга, а принять надо предложение Мендес Франса и, таким образом, закрепить завоевания коммунистов Вьетнама. Договор был подписан.

Нужно отдать должное Мендес Франсу. Он трезво и правильно оценил ситуацию, которая сложилась. У партизан ихих во Вьетнаме были трудности, но не меньше трудностей было и у французской армии. Это был разумный шаг и он положил конец войне французов во Вьетнаме. Франция вышла из войны и эвакуировала свои войска.

Все было бы хорошо, если бы выполнялись Женевские Соглашения. Через два года должны были пройти всеобщие выборы и мы не сомневались, что Хо Ши Мин, то есть коммунисты и прогрессивные силы Вьетнами на них одержат победу. Но тут появился зловещий Даллес и Соединенные Штаты навязали Вьетнаму кровопролитную войну, которая продолжается до сих пор. Об этом я не буду сейчас говорить, потому что все и в печати освещается и политическим деятелям хорошо известна эта история. Однако в связи с тяжелым для меня сообщением смерти подлинного коммуниста, видного деятеля международного коммунистического движения товарища Хо Ши Мина хотел бы еще рассказать о сложном положении Вьетнама в связи с конфликтом с Китаем.

Я помню когда проходило Совещание коммунистических рабочих партий в 1960 году, Китай был представлен Лю Шао Ци. Китайцы выступили против нас. Особенно оголтело вел себя агент Мао Цзе Дуна Энвер Ходжа. После его выступления выступала товарищ Ибаррури. Она с возмущением говорила, что Энвер Ходжа можно сравнить с собакой, которой дают хлеб, а она кусает эту руку. Так и он выступил против Коммунистической партии Советского свои силы. А потом будет видно.

Я думаю, что заявление, что тогда будет видно, предопределяло, что мы, видимо, не будем нейтральными до истечения этой войны, а на каком-то этапе все равно включимся в эту войну. Ну, это рассуждения сейчас о понимании будущего с позиции того времени.

(Когда я приезжал из Киева, то редко имел возможность располагать своим временем. Чаще всего мне звонил Сталин, чтобы я приезжал к нему. Я приезжал и другой раз я заставал Сталина одного. Тогда было легче обмениваться мнениями и особенно предлагать свои взгляды и высказывать свои нужды, которые я всегда привозил с Украины. Чаще же когда я приезжал то у Сталина обязательно были Молотов, Ворошилов, Каганович, Жданов не всегда бывал: он в то время работал Секретарем Ленинградского Обкома и бывал редко. Берия бывал, Каганович чаще бывал. Ну кто еще? Микоян, конечно, всегда бывал. Вот этот круг людей.)

Однажды, когда я приехал в Москву, это, по-моему, уже была поздняя осень 1989 года, Сталин меня пригласил к себе на квартиру:"Приезжайте ко мне, покушаем. Будет Молотов и Куусинен".

Куусинен тогда работал в Коминтерне.

Я приехал в Кремль, на квартиру к Сталину. Начался разговор и по ходу разговора я почувствовал, что это продолжение предыдущего разговора, собственно уже реализация принятого решения о том, чтобы предъявить ультиматум Финляндии,значит. Уже договорились с Куусиненом, что он возглавит Правительство,создающейся Карело-Финской ССР (Карелия до этого была автономной республикой, входившей в состав Российской Федерации. А тогда решался вопрос о том, что она будет союзной республикой.

Было такое настроение, что Финляндии будут предъявлены ультимативные требования территориального характера, которые она отвергла при переговорах и, если она не согласится, то начать военные действия. Такое мнение было у Сталина. Я, конечно, тогда не возражал Сталину. Я тоже считал, что это правильно, что достаточно громко сказать, а если на слово не поверят, то выстрелить из пушки и финны поднимут руки, согласятся с теми требованиями, которые были выставлены нашим государством.

Я опять повторяю, какие конкретно территориальные претензии были выдвинуты, какие политические требования, какие взаимоотношения должны были сложиться, я сейчас не помню, но видимо какие-то условия были выдвинуты с тем, чтобы Финляндия стала дружеской страной. Эта цель преследовалась, но как это выражалось, как формулировалось, я этого не знаю. Я даже эти документы и не читал и не видел.

Тогда Сталин говорил: "Ну, вот сегодня будет начато дело".

Мы сидели довольно долго, потому что был уже назначен час. После истечения этого времени был послан Кулик — Маршал Артиллерии — он должен был практически организовать артиллерийский обстрел границы Финляндии.

Ожидали и Сталин был уверен и мы тоже верили, что не будет войны, что финны примут наши предложения и тем самым мы своей цели достигнем без войны. Цель — это обезопасить нас с Севера.

Финляндия — ее территория и ее естественные ресурсы мало дополняли наши необъятные территориальные возможности и наши богатства. Финляндия богата лесом, но не может же она равняться с нами. Не эта сторона нас привлекала. На первом плане тут были вопросы безопасности, потому что Ленинград находился под угрозой. Я вот уже несколько это раз повторяю. Я хотел бы, чтобы правильно поняли обстановку того времени, то как я понимал Сталина и в чем я был полностью согласен со Сталиным.

Вдруг позвонили, что произвели выстрел. Финны ответили ответным артиллерийским гнем. Фактически началась война. Я говорю это, потому что существует другая трактовка: финны первыми выстрелили и поэтому мол мы вынуждены были ответить. Но это всегда, когда войну начинают, говорят о том, что ты же первый выстрелил или же ты мне первый пощечину дал, а я уже тебе отвечаю.

Раньше говорят был порядок: это в операх хорошо показывают бросали перчатку, поднимали перчатку, а потом выходили на дуэль. Но то прошлые времена, а уже в наши времена войны, к сожалению, начинали вот так.

Вопрос о том, имели ли мы право юридическое и моральное на такие действия? А юридического права, конечно, мы не имели. С моральной точки зрения, желание обезопасить себя, дговориться с соседом, как это сделать оправдывало нас в собственных галзах.

Война началась, значит. Я уехал через несколько дней на Украину. Мы были уверены, что если финны приняли наш вызов и развязалась война, то так как величины несоизмеримые, этот вопрос будет решен и решен быстро с небольшими потерями для нас. Так понимали, так хотели, но история этой войны показала совсем другое.

Война стала довольно упорной. Финны показали большую воинственность, большие военные способности. У них была хорошо организована оборона и наши попытки пробиться к Карельскому перешейку (это самый удобный с точки зрения войны путь) ни к чему не привели. Он оказался нам не по зубам. Обнаружились хорошие железобетонные укрепления, хорошо расположенная артиллерия. Мы наткнулись на действительно созданную неприступную крепость для наших войск.

справлялась с задачей, которая была поставлена но прикрытии городов
и электростанций. Она не допускала бомбежки и сбивала американцев.
В основном тогда наша авиация была вооружена истребителями МИГ-15.
Это был новый наш истребитель с реактивным двигателем. Очень маневренный и очень хороший истребитель. Американцы в ходе войны перевооружили свою авиацию, ввели новый истребитель, который был более быстроходен и более мощен. Против этих истребителей наш истребитель МИГ-15 был слаб и мы стали терпеть поражения. Американцы прорывались и бомбили безнаказанно. Мы уже не обеспечивали прикрытие и утеряли свое господство в воздухе.

Когда создалось такое трагическое положение для Северной Кореи и мы сочувствовали Ким Ир-Сену и народу Северокорейской республики, вдруг прибыл Чжоу Энь-Лай. Я не присутствовал при его встрече со Сталиным. Сталин был тогда на юге и Чжоу Энь-Лай прямо полетел туда. Об этих переговорах узнал уже позже, когда Чжоу Энь-Лай улетел.

Сталин, когда вернулся в Москву, рассказывал, что Чжоу-Энь-Лай прилетел по поручению Мао Цзэ-Дуна посоветоваться как быть. Он спрашивал Сталина выдвигать ли на территорию Северной Кореи китайские войска, чтобы (у корейцев уже не было войск) преградить путь на север южнокорейцам и американцам или же не стоит.

Сперва, поговорив со Сталиным, они вроде пришли к такому выводу, что не стоит Китаю вмешиваться. Потом, когда Чжоу Энь-Лай готовился улететь, кто-то проявил инициативу - то ли Чжоу Энь-Лай по поручению Мао Цзэ-Дуна или же Сталин и они опять вернулись к обсуждению этих вопросов. Тогда согласились с тем, что Китай выступит в поддержку Северной Кореи. Китайские войска уже были подготовлены и находились на самой границе. Считали, что эти войска вполне справятся, разобьют американские и южно-корейские войска и, таким образом, восстановят положение.

Чжоу Энь-Лай улетел. Я его не видел и не слышал и говорю только то, что узнал потом по рассказам самого Сталина. Там никого не было, по-моему, кроме Сталина.

Я сейчас точно не помню, что это был Чжоу Энь-Лай, а кажется Чжоу Энь-Лай был, я даже сейчас не твердо могу помнить, но, видимо, это был он потому что тогда главным и умным посыльным Мао-Цзэ-Дуна был Чжоу Энь-Лай. Сталин к нему с уважением относился и мы тоже очень уважали Чжоу Энь-Лая, считали его умным, гибким и современным человеком, с которым можно говорить и можно друг друга понимать.

Так был решен вопрос о том, что Китай вступает в войну добро-

вольцами. Он: не объявлял войну, а послал добровольцев и этими добро-
вольцами командовал Пын Де-Хуэй. Мао Цзэ-Дун дал очень высокую оцен-
ку Пын Де-Хуэю. Он говорил, что это лучшая, самая яркая звезда на ки-
тайском военном небосклоне.

Начались бои. Нужно сказать, что китайцы действительно останови-
ли продвижение южнокорейцев и северо-американцев. Или упорные бои.

Сохранились все документы, в которых Пын Де-Хуэй докладывал обстановку Мао Цзэ-Дуну. Он составлял очень обширные телеграммы, в которых излагал планы военных действий против американцев. Там намечались рубежи, намечались сроки и силы, которые нужны. Он категорично
заявлял, что они будут разбиты, будут окружены, что будут решающие
фланговые удары. Одним словом, несколько раз в этих планах, которые
сообщались Мао Цзэ-Дуну, а Мао приписывал их Сталину, громились войска
США и война кончалась.

К сожалению война не кончалась. Китайцы терпели очень большие
поражения. Мы получили сообщение, что при налете на командный пункт,
был убит китайский генерал - сын Мао Цзэ-Дуна. Мао Цзэ-Дун потерял
сына в Северной Корее.

Война продолжалась и война была очень упорной и кровавой. Китай
очень нес большие потери, потому что его техника, вооружение значи-
тельно уступала США. Тактика была построена, главным образом, на ис-
пользовании живой силы - и оборона и наступление.

Война принимала затяжной характер. Уже стабилизировались фронты
и с той и с другой стороны. С той и с другой стороны проявлялось упор-
ство, но северо-корейцы вместе с китайскими стали вытеснять южнокорейцев и американские войска опять заняли Пхеньян и отогнали их на границу, которая была установлена договором о капитуляции Японии.

В это время Сталин умер. Война продолжалась. Я эту войну сейчас
представляю в своих записях, конечно, схематично, потому что я по памяти все говорю, а документов например, в которых решались вопросы по
оказанию военно-технической помощи северо-корейцам, я вообще не видел.
Их никто не видел, кроме Сталина. Но в основу нашей политики я знал.
Документы, которые мы получали от нашего посла, я все их читал. В это
время я уже получил право гражданства и стал почту читать. Сталин сказал, чтобы мне рассылали документы, а то раньше я почты не получал.

Когда я работал на Украине я никакой почты Политбюро не получал,
кроме тех вопросов, которые непосредственно относились к Украине или
ко мне лично. Тут я уже получал донесения, полученные от Пын Де-Хуэя,
которые Мао пересылал Сталину, Сталин их рассылал, и я таким образом

лучше знал положение дел, которое сложилось в Северной Корее.

Вот собственно Корейский вопрос. Об окончании войны в Корее я расскажу позже.

Дело врачей.

Я хотел бы сейчас рассказать о так называемом деле врачей.

Однажды Сталин пригласил нас к себе в Кремль и зачитал письмо врача. Какая-то Томашук - женщина, врач писала, что она работает в лаборатории врачом и была на Валдае, когда умер Жданов. Она описывала в своем письме, что Жданов умер потому, что его лечили врачи неправильно, ему назначали такие процедуры, которые должны были привести к смерти. Она писала, что все это делалось преднамеренно.

Естественно, если бы так было на самом деле, то каждый бы возмутился такому злодейству. Тем более врачи. Это же совершенно противоестественно. Врач должен лечить, оберегать здоровье, а не убивать жизнь, не убивать человека.

Если бы Сталин был бы нормальным человеком, то он по-другому бы реагировал на это письмо. Мало ли таких писем поступает от людей с ненормальной психикой или люди, которые с сложных позиций подходят к оценке того или другого события или действий того или другого лица. Сталин был очень восприимчив к подобной литературе. Я считаю, что этот врач тоже был продуктом сталинской политики. Он внедрил в сознание всех, что мы окружены врагами, что в каждом человеке нужно видеть неразоблаченного врага. Сталин призывал к бдительности и говорил, что даже если в доносе есть 10% правды, то это уже положительный факт. Но это 50%! А поддаются ли вообще учету проценты правды в таких письмах, как подсчитать эти проценты?

Призвать к такому подходу к людям, с которыми ты работаешь, это знаете ли-создать дом сумасшедших, где каждый будет выискивать не существующие факты о своем приятеле. А именно так было, это поощрялось. Натравляли сына против отца, отца против сына. Это называлось классовым подходом.

Я понимаю, что классовая борьба делит семьи и делит очень жестоко, ни перед чем не останавливается. Классовая борьба определяет позиции того или другого члена семьи. Я приветствую это и это нормально, потому что вопрос борьбы за лучшее будущее, за построение социализма, это не парадное шествие, а кровавая, мучительная борьба. Я это знаю. Я сам участник этой борьбы.

Сталин подошел к радиоле и начал ставить пластинки. Слушали музыку, русские песни, грузинские.

Потом он поставил танцевальную музыку и начали танцевать. У нас единственный в это время признанный танцор – Анастас Иванович Микоян. Все его танцы походили один на другой – и русские, и кавказские, все они начало свое брали с лезгинки. Он танцевал, потом Ворошилов танцевал. Танцевали все. Я никогда ног не передвигал, из меня танцор "как корова на льду", но я тоже танцевал. Каганович танцевал. Он тоже танцор не более высокого класса, чем я. Маленков тоже такой. Булганин когда-то танцевал, видимо, в молодости. Он русское что-то вытаптывал в такт. Сталин тоже танцевал – что-то ногами передвигал и руки расставлял. Тот, видимо, человек никогда не танцевал. Я бы сказал, что настроение было хорошее. Я не хотел танцевать не потому что чем-то был связан, а просто я никогда не танцевал и не умел танцевать Если бы умел я бы тоже Микояну компанию составил.

Молотова в это время с нами уже не было. У нас Молотов был танцором городским. Он воспитывался в интеллигентной семье, потом студентом был. На вечеринках он бывал студенческих и знал танцы. Он музыку любил и сам он на скрипке играл. Вообще он был музыкальный человек. Я не знаток и плохой ценитель, но в моих глазах он был танцором первого класса.

Пели, подпевали пластинкам, которые заводил Сталин.

Потом появилась Светланка. Я не знаю, вызвали ли ее по телефону, или она сама приехала. Она приехала и попала в стаю людей немолодых, мягко говоря. Приехала трезвая молодая женщина и Сталин ее сейчас же заставил танцевать. Она уже устала, я видел, что она еле-еле танцует. Отец требует, а она уже не может танцевать. Она встала, к стенке плечом прислонилась и стояла около радиолы. К ней подошел Сталин и я тоже подошел к Светланке. Стояли мы вместе. Сталин пошатывался.

Он говорит:"Ну, Светланка, танцуй. Хозяйка, танцуй."

Она говорит:"Я уже танцевала, папа. Я устала".

Он ее взял пятерней за волосы, за чуб и подтянул. Я смотрю, у нее уже и краска на лице выступила и слезы появились на глазах. Мне так было жалко смотреть, так жалко было Светланку. А он потянул ее и дернул.

Это было проявление любезности отца к дочери. Безусловно, потому что Сталин очень любил Светланку. Васю он тоже любил, но Васю он и критиковал за пьянство и за недисциплинированность. А Светланка училась хорошо и поведение ее, как девушки было хорошее. Я ничего

Я уже не помню какого числа в октябре выступил Президент Кеннеди с заявлением, что русские ставят на Кубе ракеты с ядерными зарядами и угрожают Америке, в связи с чем они принимают меры.

И они начали принимать меры. Они сосредоточили вокруг Кубы огромное количество, массу кораблей, прямо окружили остров. Сосредоточили авиацию на своих ближайших аэродромах. Подготовили десантные средства, пехоту. Одним словом, они мобилизовали огромные силы. Все завертелось.

Мы тогда считали, что американцы видят наши ракеты и они пугают нас, а сами они не меньше, чем мы, боятся атомной войны. Когда американцы обнаружили наши ракеты, мы еще не успели все туда завезти и наши корабли шли на Кубу через эту армаду американского флота. Американцы их не трогали и не проверяли. Мы в октябре почти завершили перевозку.

Мы поставили ракеты. Этой силы достаточно, чтобы разрушить Нью-Йорк, Чикаго и другие промышленные города, а о Вашингтоне и говорить нечего. Маленькая деревня. Америка, пожалуй, никогда не имела такой реальной угрозы быть разрушенной, как в этот момент.

Началась переписка. Нам писали, мы им написали. С нашей стороны вел переписку, диктовал послания я. Мы уже чувствовали, что военные силы Америки могут выйти из-под контроля Президента. Позже об этом и сам Президент нам сказал. В своих письмах Кеннеди ультимативно потребовал, чтобы мы вывезли оттуда ракеты и бомбардировщики ИЛ-28. Они знали, что они там. Когда бомбардировщики прибывали, они летали, конечно, а в полете их все "собаки" знают. Это первый наш реактивный бомбардировщик. Хороший бомбардировщик, но он был сделан в 1949 году. Тогда он был богом, ну, а к тому времени мы его сняли с производства, но на вооружении он еще состоял.

Я сейчас уже не помню всех наших телеграмм, но был такой момент, когда одну ночь я не спал дома, я ночевал в Совете Министров, потому что нависла реальная возможность начала войны.

Мы демонстрировали свое спокойствие, ходили в Большой Театр. Мы хотели показать своему народу, своей стране, что мы в театре, оперу слушаем, значит, все спокойно. За границей за нами тоже пристально следили, каждый шаг наш анализировался.

Прошло пять или шесть дней и нам сообщает посол, что к нему пришел брат Президента Кеннеди - Роберт. Он оказал, что уже шесть дней и ночей не был дома. Глаза красные, видно, что человек не спал.

Он сказал:

- Мы обращаемся с просьбой к тов. Хрущеву, пусть он нам поможет ликвидировать конфликт. Если дальше так будет продолжаться, то Прези-

дент не уверен, что его не могут сбросить военные и захватить власть.
Армия может выйти из-под контроля.

Я не отрицал такой возможности, тем более Кеннеди — молодой Президент, а угроза безопасности Америки.

- Вам будет, - сказал он, - передано послание от Президента. Мы просим, чтобы был положительный ответ. Мы с Президентом просим, чтобы Хрущев поддержал нас.

В этом документе они настойчиво требовали вывезти ракеты и ИЛ-28. Мы получили это послание и по его тону почувствовали, что действительно накал очень большой. Мы написали ответ, где говорилось, что ракеты мы установили в целях обороны и не преследовали никаких других целей, кроме предотвращения вторжения на Кубу, чтобы Куба развивалась так, как хотят кубинцы, а не так, как хотела бы третья сторона?

Поэтому мы вели переписку и по официальным каналам, а наиболее доверительные письма передавали через брата Президента. Он оставил послу свой телефон и просил звонить в любое время. Когда он говорил с послом, он чуть не плакал:

- Я. - говорит, - детей не видел (у него было шесть душ детей) и Президент тоже. Мы сидим в Белом доме не спим, - и глаза красные-красные.

Мы должны были быстро перестроиться.

Я тогда сказал

- Товарищи, надо искать по возможности достойный выход из этого конфликта, но с обязательным сохранением Кубы.

Тогда мы и написали, что согласны вывести ракеты и бомбардировщики при условии, что Президент даст заверение о том, что на Кубу не будет вторжения ни американских, ни чьих-то других сил.

Тут мы начали нажимать и Кеннеди согласился сделать такое заявление.

Мы устраивали обструкцию, мы ногами топали, и не только наша делегация
но и социалистические страны. И другие формы использовали выражения
протеста. Но все-таки в таком огромном здании с таким количеством
заседавших, наш протес, конечно, должного эффекта, который мы бы хотели получить, не имел. Поэтому и сейчас еще Китай еще не является,
не признан и не имеет своего представителя в ООН, несмотря на то,
что мы на всех заседаниях выступали в предложением о том, чтобы
ек лешить мандата представителя Тайваня, что он не является представи-
те ем Китая. И что мандат должен получить народное правительство
Китая в Пекине. Большинства, к сожалению, мы еще не собирали.
Это было для нас большое разочарование, потому что америка проводила
и проводит агрессивную политику в отношении Китая и других соц стран,
но много стран уже многих родилось,, которые были колониями, они по
лучили независимость, они имели своих представителей в ООН. Я,
признаться кжк питал надежду, что это изменит расстановку сил при
голосовании и создадутся реальные возможности принять решение
лишить мандата Тайвань и это мандат вручить правительству, которое
действительно представляет весь Китай -- Народный Китай, но, к сожален
независмоть-то получили юридическу, но фактическое подчинение
колонизаторам оставалось. Ивопросы, которые стояли, они иногда голосовали вместе, а они были для них на положении рабов или рабами. Вот
такой процесс еще и сейчас не получил своего разрешения и к сожалению
голосование по многим вопросам проходит под влиянием США, а они навы-
зывают решения, которые выгодны империалистическим державам, США,
которые являются лидерами такой политики.

Во время пребывания моего на ассамблее ОН у нас разгорелся большо
скандал, столкновение в с Хаммаршельдом, секретарем ОН, по национал-
ности швед, Мы его знали и к нему относились неплохо одно время.
Мы поддерживали его кандидатуру, когда выдвинута она была на пост

секретаря ОН. До этого был норвежец, социал-д мократ. Не знаю по какому вопросу, но у нас очень обострились отношения с этим секретарем, это -- во времена Сталина. Хотя, когда я был в Норвегии, то мне его хвалили. Не знаю, познакомили ли меня с ним, но вообще хвалили, что он относится к СССР хорошо, даже сейчас. Так сложились условия, и вообще, этот пост секретаря ОН трудный, тогда кандидатуры была выдвинута Хаммаршельда. Я не знаю, какой он партии принадлежал, видимо каким-то либералам бурж партий. Когда возник вопрос в Конго, когда обострились там столкновения, то мы считали, что он недостаточно поддерживает те страны, которые ведут борьбу с колониальным правитель-ством Бельгии в отношении прогрессивных сил в Конго, нну ну и по другим вопросам, конечно у нас были тогда. Но наибольшее обострение, кажется, было у нас по этому вопросу. Тогда у нас возникла такая идея, с тем, чтобы ОН в равной степени ÷÷÷÷÷÷÷÷÷÷÷÷ обслуживали три стороны по составу стран по своему соц пол положению: кап страны, соц страны, и промежуточные страны, которые получили независимость, но которые еще не определились, и проводят позицию неприсоединения к блокам. Мы тогда выдвинули такую идею: не секретарь в единоличном лице должен возглавлять аппарат ОН, а три представителл. Один, чтобы представлял страны капиталистического мира, другой -- соц, а третий представлял страны, освободившиеся от колонийаторов, и равные права у них, и они должны были решать все только тройкой. Это была наша идея, я её выдвинул, я её горячо поддерживал. Мне тогда доказы-вали некоторые умники, что это невозможно, и даже люди, которые неплохо относились к нашей политикеи и нашему сов государству, что это невозможно, что это заморозит дела и нельзя будет продвинуть никакого вопроса. Но я рассуждал так и все мои товарищи по руководству /мы обсуждали/ со мною согласились, что значит заморозить? Что значит

тройка? Ведь существует нечто подобной в ОН -- Совет безопасности.

Ведь в СБ там пятнадцать человек, но пять стран являются неизменными,

они не переизбераются и вопрос о мире решаются этими пятью странами,

и, если одна из этих пяти сrран будет голосвать по тому или иному вопросу

против, то этот вопоc считается непринятым, но такое же могло

быть положение и по текущим вопросам, а текущие вопросы имели большое

значение и в это время уже секретариат управлял уже войсками ОН,

которые были в некоторых странах и в том числе они уже были в Конго.

Поэтому в зависимости от того, какая избераеется директива, какие

люди выбираются на командные посты войсками ОН, такая и будет проводится

политика этими войсками, которые посылаются. Поэтому мы

считали, что надо было бы иметь тройку, которая бы этим делом

руководили, чтобы три политические стороны, которые в этом деле заинтересованы,

чтобы они имели представителей своих и чтобы эти пред

ставители решали с учетом интересов каждой стороны, котоую каждй из

них представляет. Если говорить, вопросы могли бы медленей решаться,

но это даже другой раз хорошо, когда медленно решается, даже в интересах

стран, чтобы вопросы совсем не рашались, т.е. не решались

бы так, как хотел бы решить один, единолично, который больше

зависел от кап стран своими выборами. Поэтому он, естественно,

в своей деятельности оглядывался. Кроме того, у нас не было надежды,

чтобы мы могли выдвинуть на пост секретаря коммуниста из социалистических

ческих стран даже, не коммуниста даже, но который был бы выдвинут

из наших социалистических стран. Это не допустили бы. Значит

они приследуют определенную политическую цель, когда выбирается и

выдвигается кандидатура на этот политический пост, так почему бы нам

не противопоставить свою политику и выдвинуть своего представителя,

чтобы без согласия нашего представителя не могло быть принято решение, направленное против социалистических стран, или против интересов
неприсоединившихся стран и против капиталистических стран. Там был бы
их представитель, который бы стоял на страже их интересов. На этот
счет была очень бальшая перепалка и мы с Хаммаршельдом испортили
отношения до конца, до предела. И я не знаю, когда я был, я по-моему
не встречался с Хаммаршельдом. Но это не исключено, может быть
встречался, потому что в вопросах встреч между государствами это не
считается, что, если они встречаются, то они дружат, это бывает дип-
ломатическая необходимость иногда вынуждает к такой встрече, хотя
Хаммаршельд нас в свое время удовлетворял и мы его поддерживали.
Вот такое обострение мы имели на этой ассамблее, но, к сожалению,
когда мы зондировали почву, мы не смогла продвинуть такое решение
потому что эти капиталистические державы были против этого, и они
увлекли за собой эти страны, которые принимали политику неприсоединения к блокам. Поэтому наше предложение оно бы не нашло поддержки,
не только не нашло бы, но оно и ушей бы не нашло. Мы тогда решили
переориентироваться и, когда выбирался секретарь, а на этой ассамблее,
по-моему ассамблее выбирался. Но не помню, может быть, наследующий
год. Но, когда выбирали надо было избрать или переизбрать Хаммаршельда, мывыступили против него. И этого было достаточно, что он
не пройдет. Видимо, совет безопасности рекомендовал ОН. Наш голос
был решающим, если мы голосовали против, то эта кандидатура не выстав-
лялась.

Тогда возникла кандидатура У Тана, который и сейчас является
секретарем. Я с У Таном, по-моему, знаком был до этого времени. Но
не твердо говорю. Во-первых он -- представитель Бирмы. С Бирмой
у нас были хорошие отношения, я считаю, что у нас и сейчас очень хорошие.

Поэтому мы считали, что Бирма, т.е пред Бирмы У Тан будет политику п
проводить более эластичную, во всяком случае, не будет допускать такой
политики, которая бы нанесет ущерб Сов Союзу и соц странами и неприсо-
единившимся странам к военным блокам.

И мы не ошиблись в поддержании кандидатуры, но, т.к произошла
большая острота, обостренность при выборах, то договорились на
этом вопосе, что это -- временно, на первый срок, временно. На первый
срок или даже на более короткий временный срок его избрать с тем,
чтобы потом вернуться к этому вопросу. Когда он отбыл этот свой
временный срок, У Тан, и показал,что он человек принципиальный и
что он не идет на поводу США и проводит политику с учетом интересов
соц стран и неприсоед стран. Тогда мы изменили свою политику.
Я даже помню сперва, когда зарзрабатывалась наша директива, то
Андрей Андреич даже разработал, что мы тоже будем голосовать за него,
но как за временногосекретаря. Я предложил: давайте мы будем сейчас
голосовать за него без оговорки, а выдвинуть его как секретаря, как
и другие до него изберались. Но Андрей Андреич посмотрел. А я ему
об'яснил, что мы лучшего кандита сейчас чем У Тан не будем иметь, а
наша идея, видимо, будет провалена. Поэтому нам не следует сейчас
её выдвигать, давайте мы сойдёмся на У Тане. И мы проголосовали
за У Тана. УТан, конечно, был очень доволен, что он нашел наше приз-
знание, а это было признание правильности его политики. И он и сейчас
продолжает возглавлять этот пост. Я думаю, что в мое время, когда
я возглавлял Советское правительство, он вел и мы не имели к нему
никаких претензий и сейчас, по-моему, продолжает он такую политику.
Претензии, что такое претензии с нашей стороны? Конечно, если бы
мы подходили к вопросам с чисто классовых, пролетарских пкоммунисти-
ческих позиций к его деятельности, то конечно, он бы не удовлетворял

наши запросы, но, принимая во внимания характер этого учреждения международного, когда в этом учреждении состоят семьпар чистых и семь пар нечистых, как говорится, и есть еще промежуточные -- ненечистые и нечистые, то этот человек должен проводить политику, чтобы удовлетворить состав этого об'единения, чтобы каждого участника, то это невозможно, вообще невозможно, поэтому нужна была большая гибкость и очень проницательный ум. с тем, чтобы можно было не усложнять вопрос который решается, не обострять отношения, а уметь сглаживать, но придерживаясь определенной позиции, чтобы это сглажевание было с нашей точки зрения не переходило бы предела. Я думаю, что У Тан очень хорошо справился с своей задачей. Он не раз конфликтовал с США и продолжает сейчас занимать этот пост. И я думаю, что это лучшее из всего того, что было.

Да Хаммаршельд, я теперь помню, как решился вопрос о Хаммаршельде. Он выехал в Конго, когда там велись бои между войсками, которые поддерживали политику Лумумбы. Лумумба тогда -- я сейчас не помню -- или уже был тогда арестован или уже убит. А с другой стороны был Чомбе. Это -- представитель был монополистических кругов Бельгии, реакционная личность была. И Хаммаршельд поехал от ОН как секретарь проинспектировать или ознакомиться на месте /это тоже инспекция/ и при посадке самолет разбился. Тогда мне докладывала наша разведка, что, собственно, он не разбился, а его сбили войска Лумумбы. Но так или иначе он погиб, хаммаршельд. Таким образом, место освободилось и была выдвинута кандидатура У Тана, -- я не буду повторять -- и он и сейчас занимает этот пост.

Об учреждении ОН. Мое отношение к этому учреждению. Я оцениваю деятельность этого учреждения положительно, хотя деятельнсоть этого учреждения, как история свидетельствует, очень много решается вопросов, которые нас абсолютно не удовлетворяют и даже противоречат нашим инте-

создать условия для работы в какой-либо другой стране. Но я считаю,
что политически это не оправдывалось. Но это не столь острый вопрос
сегодня и будет ли он решен в будущем -- трудно мне сказать, да я,
в общем и не хочу гадать. История покажет. Если это будет целесообразно,
то это будет сделано. На этом можно было бы поставить, как говориться,
точку при диктовки моих воспоминаний о поездке в ОН и о роли этих ОН
с моей точки зрения.

Хочу продолжить диктовку своих воспоминаний о пребывании на
ассамблее. Когда корабль прибыл в Н Й, мне сообщили о чрезвычайном
происшествии на корабле, как моряки говорят, ЧП. ЧП заключалось в
том, что один из матросов корабля покинул корабль и не вернулся на
него и явился в полицию и попросил убежище. Мне сообщили это с
большим волнением люди, которые это сообщали, я их успокоил. Не при-
давайте большого значения -- ушел и ушел. Пусть попробует капиталистических хлебов, он узнает, почем хлеб в Н Й и какой он на вкус.
Но я уже знал, что меня встретят журналисты, которые сопровождали неот-
ступно, и надо подготовится дать им объяснение. На первой же встрече
они задали мне вопрос: г-н Хрущев, как вы смотрите, что матрос из
вашего корабля не вернулся на корабль и попросил убежища в США?
Я это слышал, мне рассказывали об этом. Я очень сожалею -- молодой человек, неопытный и не имеет никакой квалификации и я сочувствую ему.
Повидимому, ему придется очень тяжело приспосабливаться к условиям
американцев, ничего у него нет. Глупо он поступил, необдуманно. Если
бы он сказал мне, что он хочет остаться, я бы ему даже оказал помощь
на первых парах, когда он будет приспосабливаться к местным условиям.
А так я сочувствую ему, что ему будет очень тяжело приспособиться.
Весь накал, который был у журналистов, сразу исчез. Они ожидали совсем другой реакции от меня. Они считали, что я буду чернить его, осуждат

его или что другое, но чтоугодно, только не то, что они слышали,
что я кроме сочувствия, никаких негодований невыражал в его адрес.
и таким образом пропала сенсация, они не могли заработать на этом деле.
это было очень показательно и таким образом этот инцедент не мог быть
раздут, до таких размеров, на которые всегда падка буржуазная печать.
и был памятный такой случай для меня -- несколько меня даже тронуло.
Около резиденции, где я размещался, а это на большой улице, наш был
угловой дом. не знаю, сколько там корреспондентов было -- наверное
несколько десятков, -- но некоторые там так и ночевали, не отхо-
дили. там были фотокорреспонденты и корреспонденты и с кинокамерами,
ну буквально они регистрировали каждый мог шаг. но в условиях н Й я
гулять не имел возможности, это было просто невозможно. поэтому я
выходил на свежий воздух, если можно так назвать воздух н Й, но другого
не было, поэтому я разминку делал, прохаживаясь по комнатам и выходил
на балкон. С балкона я все-таки наблюдал движение в городе и было
какое-то разнообразие впечатлений и поэтому я получал какую-то передышку.
и пользовался этим почти каждый день и не однажды, иногда несколько
раз в день я выходил на балкон: шумно, улицы все время проходили машины. большое насыщение транспорта на улицах н Й. Я однажды получил
записку от журналиста, я не помню сейчас фамилию, он подписался. Он написал такое: г-н Хрущев, вы выходите на балкон и
мне, как журналисту это приятно, мы сможем с вами встречаться и брать
у вас интервью, но я хотел бы вас предупредить, что вы, видимо, плохо
учитываете особенности НЙ. Н Й на все способен и поэтому выходить
для вас на балкон, -- это не безопасно. Здесь всякая всячина может
быть организована против вас. Могут с машины быть выстрелы, могут с
окон быть выстрелы, которые расположены против вашего дома. А я, как
ваш доброжелатель, это бы учли и не показывались бы на и тем самым не

подвергались бы опасности, которая может вам грозить. Я прочел эту
записку — я продолжал выходить, чем более раз получил я эту записку.
Тем более всё обошлось благополучно. Но я, когда сейчас вспоминаю,
что меня очень тронула человечность этого корреспондента, этого
человека. Я не знаю, кто он по своим политическим убеждениям, являея
ли он корреспондентом какой-нибудь пролетарской газеты или это буржуаз-
ный корреспондент, но человечность, которая была проявлена, меня это
тронуло, поэтому я и сейчас вспоминаю об этом человеке, как о человеч-
ном человеке. Я не продиктова, как мы возвращались обратно из НЙ в
Москву, да и путь обратный морской был очень долгий и не хотелось тра-
тить столько времени. Я сейчас вспомнил, что мы были вынуждены избрать морской транспорт потому, что какие-то дефекты были выявлены на
самолетах ТУ 114, а это-единственный самолеты, которые мог нас доста-
вить без посадки — Москва НЙ. Кроме того, видимо, у нас и был тогда
только один такой самолет, один экземпляр, поэтому, когда были выявлены какие-то дефекты, то мы другого самолета не имели и у нас был
или же лететь в Нью Лондон, а с Лондона воспользоваться международной
трассой других стран самолетами или кораблем. И мы тогда решили,
при ть на своем собственном советском корабле. Обратно, когда надо
было возвращаться, мне сообщили, что самолет уже исправлен, выправлен и
Андрей Николаевич Туполев не сомневается в надежности и мы решили
обратно использовать наш самолет ТУ 114. Еще был такой инцедент, но
уже такого, провокационного характера. Я только не помню было ли это,
когда я вылетал из Н Й, или это было, когда я вылетал из Вашингтона,
когда я был гостем президента США. Когда все уже погрузились и мы
ожидали минуты для вылета, вдруг мне начальник охраны сообщил, что
позвонил кто-то неизвестный, вызвал его к телефону и предупредил, что
на самолете Хрущева заложена бомба. И на этом разговор оборвался. Он

было много хороших день и арбузов, а в Польше этот продукт не выращи-
вается. Договорились, что это будет хорошо расценено. Посчитали,
сколько можно, сколько нужно и доставили в Люблин один или два самолета.
Мы условились, что каждому крестьянину мы дадим по арбузу и дыне.
Когда привезли -- поляки, видимо,между собой совещались -- то Виттов
поставил вопрос, что представителям правительства не давать, а все отдать
крестьянам. Что же это, говорю, г-н Витас, вы лишаете удовольствия и себя
ии нас лишаете удовольствия угостить вас, чтобы вы попробовали, какие
прекрасные продукты выращивают украинские колхозники. Вы вот попробуйте
у нас замечательный сорт дыни есть -- "колхозница". Он говорит: "колхозница"? Потом, когда мы уже обедали, мы опять вернулись к этому разго-
вору. Он говорит: это "колхозница"? Я говорю: да. А он: а почему она
не красная? Это он шутил так, если колхозница, то обязательно должна
быть красная по цвету. Я говорю: она не красная, цвет у нее желтоватый,
а по вкусу она вкусная, ароматная, сладкая. Но это говорило о том, что
человек этот в польском коммитете занимал особую позицию по отношению к
сов союзу. И несмотря на его сдежанность, она в мелочах, но просказовала,
в виде колкости, направленной против Украины и вообще против советов.
Я узнал, что недалеко от Люблина немцы построили печи и там были бараки
заключенных и они там уничтожались. Привозили не только из Польши
заключенных, но там было, говорят, и западных стран много. Как раз в это
время там были раскопки могил и работала, видимомо, какая-то комиссия,
которая все это свидетельствовала и актировала. Мы с Булганиным решили
поехать Я, видимо, ему предложил :: поедем, говорю, посмотрим, я хотел
бы посмотреть и сам бы убедится в зверствах немцев еще раз. Я уже
видел зверства немцев и очень много, но печи, где они сжигали, специально
сделанные, я не видел. И мы поехали с Булганиным. Это было лето, было

тепло, даже жарко. Раскопки были могил: вынимали трупы, а некоторые просто вырывали, а трупы уже не вынимали, потому что уже сгнили. Ходить там было очень тяжело. Булганин просто сбежал. Удушающий трупный запах. Я силу воли имел неплохую. Я ходил и все осмотрел и не подал виду потому что там работали врачи, люди, которые раскопки вели и поэтому было неудобно показать, что мы такие белоручки и не выносим трупного запаха. Я потом посмотрел эти газовые камеры -- мы с Булганиным прошли -- все это было по-немецки продумно. Камеры имели внешний вид как временные бани. С оконцем стеклянным, как тюремный глазок, а это было для наблюдения, что уже загнанные в эти камеры, под видом того, что они идут туда принимать душ, мыться, что они уже мертвы. Потом оттуда брали и -- в крематорий и сжигали в печах. Золы много было. и я еще видел, что некоторые кости не до тла сгоревшие. Потом пошли мы в барак. Бараки склады были. ~~Потом~~ В одном бараке я видел огромное количество обуви, мужской и дамской. Это мне руководитель, который там комендант был, он мне сказал, что это все немцы отбирали, сортировали и увозили потом в Германию. Потом отделение, в котором огромное количество было женских волос, косы. Одним словом, немцы, как хозяева, как на скотобойне, они все сортировали: копыты к копытам, рога к рогам, а волосы тоже все шерсть, так и человеческие остатки, предметы туалета, все это было рассортировано: там были очки, там были гребешки, и другие предметы человеческого быта и туалета -- все это было рассортировано и по полочкам разложено. Это производило ужасное впечатление и это невообразимо, что это делали люди, культурные люди. Мы высокого мнения были о высокой культуре. И вот эта немецкая культура под руководством Гитлера. Это было её конкретное проявление. Потом мы с Ник Мих Булганиным поехали в город Холм. Холм -- это был губернский город при

царской России до первой мировой войны. И уже к этому времени уже были
об'явлены коррективы к договору, подписанному Молотовым м Рибентропом,
что этот гоород и другие районы отходят к Польше. Мы проехали по городу
посмотрели: город не большой. Он не сохранил в моей памяти никаких
особых особенностей. Но особой положение занимал там православный
собор. Мы решили поехать туда и посмотреть. Нам открыл священно-
служитель этого собора, старый человек, седой, как русские попы, православные попы. И он нам показывал этот собор и рассказывал о его
исторической ценности. Мне запомнилос, что он назвал какое-то число и
год, когда был построен этот собор, и что собор этот строили православные,
православная церковь, но, говорит, в истории этого собора были
времена, когда поляки превращалиего в костел, а потом православные
превращали его в православную церковь. И он говорил с такой
грустью, что вот мы сейчас узнали, что правительство советское Холмх
отдают Польше и теперь придут ксендзы и опять будет господствовать като-
лицизм. Явно он оперировал к нам. Мы были в военной форме, в генеральской
и думал, что мы можем оказать какое-то влияние на изменение положения дел,
с тем, чтобы этот город остался в соотиве сов. союза с тем, чтобы он
стал собором православия. но это я так дикутю мимоходом, как реагировали
разные слои населения на отход этих территорий в состав полтского
государства. Ну, мы ничего не сказали, кроме того, что эта территория
отходит к польскому государству, а уж вопрос о церквях -- это нас не каса-
ется, какяя религия будет им пользоваться: католическая или православная.
Это -- косвенное дело для русских, потому что в сов союз отделена церковь
от государства, и мы, государсртво, не вмешива:мся во внутренние дела
церквей. Мы вернулись в Люблин.

Люблин в моей памяти остался как хороший городок, небольшой.

67

Я не знаю, какая там была промышленность и вообще была ли, кроме кустарных и мелких предприятий, но не знаю совершенно, какая направленность была в этой прсмышленности и что она вырабатывала. Я несколько раз бывал в Люблине и ввстречался там с руководством зародившегося нового правительства.

Когда все вопросы были решены, надобность отпала для контактов: уже были созданы у нас постоянные представительства украины и болоруссии. И с польской стороны уже были выделены лица, которые приехали к нам в Киев. И они занимались теми же вопросами, которыми занималось наше в ~~храниткикетия~~ представительство: регистрация населения польской национальности, которое пожелало бы выехать в Польшу и содействовало им в переезде. Это считалось нармализацией наших добрососедских отношений и решения взаимных вопросов,которые касались наших двух государств: Советской украины и Польши, а также Сов Белоруссии и Польши.

Надобности у меня уже не было выезжать в Люблин, но я частенько встречался в Москве -- другой раз вызывал Сталин в Москву, видимо специально, когда приезжали польвкие товарищи -- с тем чтобы я видел их, когда нужно было Сталину, чтобы притенции, которые польские товарищи пред'являли на те или другие населенные пункты или другие вопросы. Тогда Сталин не хотел сам отказывать, и он вызывал меня, чтобы меня противопоставить: вот мол решай те с Хрущевым. Вы его знаете и он вас знает решайте: договоритесь, а это и будет договоренность. Но Сталин, когда отдавал, он не спрашивал меня, он сам отдавал и изменил границу, которая была и изменил в пользу польского государства. Болезненно на это реагировали украинская общественность. А, когда нужно было не дать, не удовлетворять потребности, которые пред'являлись со стороны польских товарищей, он тогда эту функцию мне подбрасывал, чтобы я отказывал.

ливается у нас. И я с большим удовольствием, мы с Ниной Петровной принимаем её. И нам это напоминает о хороших временах, когда был жив её отеци наш друг и руководитель польского государства, тов Берут.

Я потом много много раз встречался у Сталина с польскими товарищами. Видимо, Сталин все-таки меня приглашал в те времена, когда приезжали польские товарищи в Москву. Поэтому, многие вопросы, которые обсуждались, я был свидетелем. Я говорю "свидетелем", потому что все вопоосы решал Сталин. Он спросить мог, но не советоваться. Он мог спросить ввиде справки о том или другом человеке или другие вопросы, которые возникали у него. А решал он все сам.

Гомулка окреп и определилфсь, что он занял одно из ведущих мест — все-таки главное лицо, которое было доверенным у Сталина и на которое опирался Сталин, — это был Берут. Берута признавали, и, я думаю, что даже Гомулка признавал Берута за руководителя в то время, но, по-моему, все-таки он это доверие выражал по-особоиу. А другие руководители, которые были, признавали по существу за руководителя тов Берута. Он завоевал ведущее место в руководстве и Сталин поддерживал это. И я считаю, что Берут заслуживал этого и он пользовался доверием и уважением.

Война шла к концу. Я уж не помню, было ли это, когда война продолжалась, или, когда уж была принята капитуляция Германии, встал вопрос, что приезжает, возвратился в Польшу Миколайчик из Лондона и, следовательно, должна создаться какая-то коалиция.по руководству польским государством. Я даже думаю, что, наверное, война продолжалась и Сталин вынужден был ситаться с союзниками — а Черчилль особенно нажимал на Сталина о том, чтобы Миколайчик приехал, что, мол, Микалайчик является другом Сов Союза, что он, по-моему, писал такие письма к Сталину: он с уважением относится и к Сталину и к нашему государству и что на него вполне можно положиться

как на главу польского государства потому, что то, что Черчилль его
выдвигал, а он уже выполнял эту роль главы польского правительства в изг-
нании, которое находилось в Лондоне. Он только должен был переехать в
Варшаву и занять как бы свой кабинет и свое место как премьер-министр
Польши.

Он вернулся в Варшаву, но, по-моему, он и временно не занимал такого
поста. Я не помню уж, какой это орган был, в который влился Миколайчик
и в каом качестве -- тоже не помню -- и другие, которые с Миколайчиком
были. Видимо Сталин тогда отписал Черчиллю в переписке, что будут выборы
и тогда вопрос будет решен.

И действительно после разгрома немцев пришло время, когда надо
было выборы проводить. Выборы эти прошли. Миколайчик был выставлен,
другие буржуазные деятели Польши были выставлены кандидатами в сейм.
Таким образом, были организованы выборы, был произведен опрос населения
персонально, кому они доверяют и выдвигают в руководство. Влияние
Миколайчика в деревне было довольно высоко, да и не только, видимо, в
деревну, а и в городах, потому что Польша тогда еще имела следы пилсуд-
ского руководства, ППС-овского, руководства, в больше было большое количество людей, которые были восстановлены против сов союза и подписания
договора с Гитлером, подписанного Рибентропом и Молотовым. Это тоже
оставило нехороший след и какая-то часть населения польского не могла
понять и смириться, что мол, советский союз с Гитлером решили начало войны,
которая первым делом обрушилась на Польшу, на Варшаву, на польское госу-
дарство, на польский народ. Поэтому, выборы эти были довольно сложные,
но по условиям международным -- видимо, это было обусловлено как-то
между лидерами сов государства и Великобритании и США на каком-то периоде -
и надо было, чтобы было выражено было народом свое мнение. Следовательно,

Миколайчик вернулся и были организованы эти выборы.

Я помню, Ванда Львовна Василевская уже не принимала участияв
эти выборах -- отказалась от руководства. Я не знаю, после выборов,
но она свою кандидатуру не выставляла на этих выборах, потому что было
определено... . - ` ` ` `

.... с плеча такие крупные политические вопросы. И она отказалась. Я
думаю, что Ванда Львовна и по политическим соображениям и довольно сугубо
личным вопросам потому, что она так была привязана к Корнечуку, что это
у нее последняя надежда была женская найти опору и эту опору она нашла в
лице Корнейчука. Поэтому, вопрос стоял: или Корнейчук или Польша. И она
для себя выбор оставляла, что Корнейчук и, поэтому, она отказалась
приезжать. А я ей прямо говорю: вот вы наверное, уедите -- война-то
кончилась. А она: Нет, я не уеду. Я уеду только тогда -- она так резко
говорила -- когда Польша будет социалистической Польшей, а в буржуазную
Польшу я не поеду. Вы что, хотите меня выживать из Киева, не хотите, чтобы
я здесь была". Но это она уже шутила, она знала мое отношение и мое
уважение к ней и, таким образом, она выразила свое отношение и отказалась
вернуться в Польшу. Хотя отношения к ней были тоже там неровные. Я считаю, что Берут относился к ней с большим уважением и симпатией, но такого
отношения -- у меня сложилось впечатление -- я не чувствовал со стороны
тов Гомулки. К ней очень хорошо относился Берман, к ней очень хорошо относился председатель Госплана в Польше Минц и другие товарищи. Но она
относилась к руководству критически и эта критическая её струнка отражалась
в какой-то недомолвке с Гомулкой.

Я её об этом не расспрашивал, это ко мне не относилось и я не хотел
прокладывать какой-то борозды и уже в своем уме фиксировать какой-то раскол,
недоверие к кому-нибудь из руководителей польского государства. Но у меня

тогда сложилось такое чувство. Видимо, она в чем-то и выражала эти чувства.

Когда проходили выборы и когда закончились выборы Ванда Львовна частенько все-таки ездила в Варшаву, потому что там осталась пристарелым человеком её мать, которую она очень любила ~~и с большой теплотой она рассказывала о ней и она, поэтому, ездила в Варшаву~~ проведать свою мать. И она, как политический деятель, писательница, встречалась со своими друзьями писателями, политическими деятелями и привозила свои настроения и свои впечатления о новой Польше, как она строится.

Она рассказывала шутку: поляки очень остро могут шутить по текущим политическим моментам. Вот как проходили выборы: На выборах получили абсолютное большинство кандидаты, выставленные от Об'единенной рабочей партии Польши и крестьянской партии /я не помню, как она называлас Но как проходил и по какому списку проходил Миколайчик, я уже не помню. Но, видимо, Миколайчик организовал уже свою партию и он был лидером этой партии. В этом смысл заключался политики, которую проводил Черчилль, чтобы продвинуть Миколайчика, чтобы на выборах он получил большинство и, таким образом, он определял бы и внутреннюю и внешнюю политику польско го государства. Он хотел, чтобы направленность политическая была бы созвучна капиталистическим странам и чтобы Польша была союзником кап стран. В этом была основа политики Черчилля, человека, который ненавидел советсткую систему и ненавидел коммунистические партии, которые были организатором и оплотом и создателем социалистичкеских государств.

И когда были эти выборы и Миколайчик получил абсолютное меньшинство, а другие партии -- ПОРП и другие партие, которые шли под руководством партии на выборы -- они получили большинство. Тогда поляки очень остро выдумали такую поговорку: Когда об'явили результаты выборов, поляки так говорили: "Цо то есть за шкатулка" /т.е. урна избирательная/. цо то

есть за шкатулка? Опущали Миколайчика в эту шкатулку, а вытаскиваешь

Гомулку. Тут и рифма получилась и остро политическое такое.

Следовательно поляки тогда, среди польской интеллигенции --

а я считаю она сочиняла эти острые такие поговорки -- что они не верили,

что выборы были об'ективные, что они были подтасованы коммунистами, что

большинство голосовало за Миколайчика, а при подсчете голосов получилось,

большинство получил Гомулку. Поэтому: что это за шкатулка, в которую опус-

каешь бюллетень Миколайчика, а вытаскиваешь Гомулку.

Но, одним словом, как бы не расценивала какая-то часть населения.

А запад конечно, был на стороне такого пониания, что тут были выборы

такие, что не дали об'ективно провести эти выборы, а особенно подсчитать

результаты этих выборов, таким образом, Миколайчик получил меньшинство.

581

Но мы все-таки отдали распоряжение маршалу Коневу, чтобы он подтягнул наши войска поближе к Варшаве. Они были на Западе, и, по-моему, одна или две дивизии были сняты со своего расположения и маршем двинулись на Варшаву, не на Варшаву, а к Варшаве вернее. Ну, все пути были контролируемы министерством внутренних дел, в котором министр сидел вместе с Гомулкой, и, поэтому, человек он был, который стоял вместе с Гомулкой. Ну, Гомулка узнал и подошел ко мне и очень нервно -- а он человек искренний и выражал, когда был недоволен, более прямо выражал свое неудовольствие и я его за это уважал, потому что я ему верил как коммунисту и поэтому я после первого знакомства -- я об этом уже диктовал, я Сталину о нем написал в записке. Эта записка имеется сейчас в архивах нашего ЦК.

"Тов Хрущев, я имею свидения, что движутся войска к Варшаве. Я вас прошу, я требую приказать, чтобы они перестали двигаться, чтобы они вернулись в казармы, что это будет непоправимое". Все это он так нервно говорил и нервно встал, подошел ко мне, потом сел на место, потом опять и у него уже пена на губах появилась. Глаза у него выражали не враждебность, а взволнованность необыкновенную. Я его в таком виде никогда больше не видел.

Я, конечно, уклонулся от прямого ответа. Я говорю: это вы получаете информацию неверную. Он через несколько минут опять ко мне подошел: "Нет, подтверждения дали, что войска движутся". Он опять стал и кричать просить и требовать, чтобы остановить войска. И начал высказывать: "Да вы что думаете, что Польша добивается.................

..........................класса, интересами социализма и его развития и завоевания коммунистического общества. Этого можно достичь, только обединившись силами пролетариами и, а в данной ситуации...........

Index

Abakumov, G. T., 190
Abel, Rudolf I., 491n.5
ABMS, 533. *See also* missiles and rocketry
Abramovich (engineer), 94
Academy of Sciences, 40n.12, 61, 62
Acheson, Dean, 356, 378, 513n.30
Adams, John Quincy, 354n.11
Adenauer, Konrad, 161n.31, 356–362
administration, 135, 138. *See also* bureaucracy
Adzhubei, A. I., 76n.10, 317n.7, 371n.15, 390n.25, 420n.6
Adzhubei, Mrs. A. I. *See* Khrushcheva, Rada
Afghanistan, 298–300, 301, 318
Afonov, I. I., 121
Africa, 334–340, 465, 468, 482. *See also* individual states
agriculture, 36, 141, 535; Khrushchev's interest in and responsibility for, 93, 106–138; productivity in, 112–122, 124–125, 127, 128, 130–131, 134–135, 143; plenum sessions on, 112, 119–122, 136n.30, 137, 138; and tax on private produce, 113, 120; mechanization of, 118, 122, 125–126, 129, 215; and corn campaign, 131–135; Polish, 182, 210–211, 213; Bulgarian, 187–188, 277; Rumanian, 214, 233; Chinese, 273, 274; US, 391, 396–400; French, 434–435; Scandinavian, 516–517, 524. *See also* collective farms; food; state farms; Virgin Lands campaign
Ahmad, Saif al-Islam, 341n.18
Aidit, Dipa Nusantara, 323, 326, 328–329
aircraft, Soviet. *See* aviation, Soviet
aircraft, US. *See* United States
aircraft carriers, 20, 31, 34
Air Force, Soviet. *See* aviation, Soviet

Air Force, US. *See* United States
Akhtyrsky (Civil War hero), 236–237
al-Badr. *See* Badr, Saif al-Islam Mohammed, al-
Albania: Soviet relations and Comecon, 194–195, 211n.22, 219, 231, 266–268; Labor (Communist) Party of, 194, 267–268; and China, 266, 280; Khrushchev denounces, 507n.23
Algeria, 342–343, 418, 421, 422, 439
All-Union government, 124; Party Congress, 236n.6
Allied Control Commission, 185n.3, 192n.22, 289n.86
Allies, World War II, 19, 171, 220, 348, 352; and Berlin blockade, 191–192
Alliluyeva, Svetlana, 129n.25, 132n.27
America. *See* United States
American National Exhibition (Moscow), 364–366
An series (aircraft). *See* aviation, Soviet
Anders, Wladyslaw, 153n.19
Anne-Marie, queen of Greece, 520n.7
Antarctic mission, 66n.12
antiballistic missiles, 533. *See also* missiles and rocketry
Anti-Party Group, 14, 18n.13, 74n.4, 126n.22, 493n.8, 505n.21
anti-Semitism, 78, 79n.16, 178–179, 180–181. *See also* Jews
Antonescu, Ion, 184
Antonov, O. K., 36
Apollo 11, 56n.32
Arab-Israeli War, 343–346
architecture, 91–93, 94, 97–98, 104. *See also* housing
Arctic Circle, 448, 490
Armenia, 295, 296
arms control and arms race, 14, 68–71, 500,

STROBE TALBOTT, who translated and edited both volumes of *Khrushchev Remembers*, has written about Communist affairs from Moscow and Belgrade. He studied Russian literature at Hotchkiss, Yale, and Oxford, where he was a Rhodes Scholar. From 1971 to 1973 he was East European correspondent for *Time*. His wife, Brooke Shearer, is also a journalist.

JERROLD L. SCHECTER, who was instrumental in the acquisition of the Khrushchev archive, is diplomatic editor of *Time*. He began his studies on the Soviet Union at the University of Wisconsin and continued them at Harvard as a Nieman Fellow. He was a *Time* correspondent in Hong Kong and bureau chief in Tokyo. The author of *The New Face of Buddha: Buddhism and Politics in Asia*, he is currently working with his wife and five children on a book about their experiences in Moscow, where he was head of the Time-Life Bureau from 1968 to 1970.

EDWARD CRANKSHAW, who provided introductions for both volumes of *Khrushchev Remembers*, has been closely identified with Russian affairs for the past thirty years. He has visited Russia and East Europe frequently, until 1968 principally as correspondent for *The Observer*. In addition to a biography of Khrushchev, published in 1966, he is the author of *Cracks in the Kremlin Wall, Russia Without Stalin*, and *Khrushchev's Russia*. He is now working on a study of nineteenth-century Russia.